THE
NEW BOOK
OF
KNOWLEDGE

THE
NEW BOOK
OF
KNOWLEDGE

Grolier Incorporated, Danbury, Connecticut

VOLUME 10

J-K

ISBN 0-7172-0531-2 (set)

GROLIER **COPYRIGHT © 2000 BY GROLIER INCORPORATED**

J, the tenth letter in the English alphabet, is the youngest of the 26 letters. It is a descendant of the letter I and was not generally considered a separate letter until the 17th century. The early history of the letter J is the same as the history of the letter I.

I is a descendant of the ancient Phoenician and Hebrew letter *yod* and the Greek letter *iota*. The word *yod* probably meant "hand." *Yod* was written like this: ૧

The Greek alphabet was based on that of the Phoenicians. In the classical Greek alphabet the I occupied ninth place and had only the vowel sound. The Romans used the Greek alphabet but made some changes in it. In their speech the letter I stood for both sounds—the I vowel sound and the Y semiconsonant sound. The Y sound of the letter eventually passed into a "dy" sound and later into the J sound (as in *juggle*) that the English letter has today.

Between the 11th and the 17th centuries the written letter, too, underwent some changes. Medieval scribes, and later the printers, began to add a tail to the letter. They added the tail to the second I when two I's were together, and to any I at the beginning of a word. Since a beginning I almost always has a consonant sound, the long form, J , came to be used generally for the consonant sound of the letter. Eventually the tail became a curve and developed into our modern J. The old form of the letter, I , was kept for the vowel sound.

In English we pronounce the letter J by placing the middle of the tongue against the roof of the mouth and forcing the breath out with the vocal chords vibrating. The main sound of the letter in English is that heard in the word *January*. Sometimes, however, the J is pronounced like a Y, as in *hallelujah*.

The letter J is found in some abbreviations, such as J.P. for Justice of the Peace or jet propulsion, Jr. for Junior, and J.C.S. for Joint Chiefs of Staff.

Reviewed by Mario Pei
Author, *The Story of Language*

See also Alphabet.

SOME WAYS TO REPRESENT J:

The **manuscript** or printed forms of the letter (left) are highly readable. The **cursive** letters (right) are formed from slanted flowing strokes joining one letter to the next.

The **Manual Alphabet** (left) enables a deaf person to communicate by forming letters with the fingers of one hand. **Braille** (right) is a system by which a blind person can use fingertips to "read" raised dots that stand for letters.

The **International Code of Signals** is a special group of flags used to send and receive messages at sea. Each letter is represented by a different flag.

International Morse Code is used to send messages by radio signals. Each letter is expressed as a combination of dots (•) and dashes (––).

The game of jacks is played with six-pointed metal or plastic pieces and a ball. The object is to collect the jacks between bounces of the ball.

JACKS

The game of jacks originated many hundreds of years ago. No one knows exactly where it was first played. In Europe and South America, it was originally played with stones or tiny animal bones. In China it was called Jop Jee and was played with stones, pieces of broken roof tiles, or tiny pillows filled with sand. In the United States and many other countries today, it is played with six-pointed metal or plastic pieces called jacks.

Many different games can be played with jacks. But in all games the object is to collect the jacks between bounces or tosses of a small rubber ball. Jacks can be played by one person or by many. When more than one person plays, each player throws a jack toward a line, usually drawn in the dirt. The player whose jack is closest to the line goes first.

▶BASIC JACKS

In the basic game of jacks, the player begins by scattering six jacks with one throw. Then the player bounces the ball and, with the same hand, quickly picks up a jack and catches the ball again. This jack is set aside. And the steps are repeated until all the jacks are picked up. Then the player scatters the jacks and picks them up two at a time, then three at a time,

and so on. In the last step of the game, all six jacks are collected in one sweep of the hand.

If the player picks up the wrong number of jacks or misses the ball, a miss is called and the next player takes a turn. Points are scored only when a player completes all the steps of the game. Then the player puts the six jacks on the back of one hand, tosses them in the air, and tries to catch them with the same hand. One point is scored for each jack caught. The player with the most points when the game ends is the winner.

Different rules can make jacks an easier or a more difficult game. In games called "easies," players can touch other jacks while picking up the required number. This makes it simple to separate "kissies" (two jacks touching) and "haystacks" (jacks nested one inside the other). In "strictsies," no touching is allowed. This makes the game much more difficult. Some players have a rule that permits them to shout "garbage" or "overs" if they do not like the lay of their jacks. Then they can scatter them again.

▶VARIATIONS

In a version of jacks called "Pigs in the Pen," the jacks are not picked up. Instead they are whisked into a pen made by cupping the hand on the ground. The free hand is used to bounce the ball, push jacks into the pen, and catch the ball again. The play follows the same steps as in basic jacks. A variation of this game is called "Pigs over the Fence." In this game the player makes a fence by resting the side of one hand on the ground. The jacks are tossed over the fence as they are collected.

Another version of the basic game is called "Reverse." In this game, players first progress from picking up jacks one at a time to six at a time. Then they reverse the order and go from six at a time down to one at a time.

"Fancy" is a game for experts. In this variation the ball is thrown high enough to bounce three times before it is caught. To make the game more difficult, the jacks are sometimes set up in a straight line. They must be picked up in succession (one after another)—which can be difficult when you are trying to collect five or six at a time.

FRED FERRETTI
Author, *The Great American Book of Sidewalk, Stoop, Dirt, Curb, and Alley Games*

JACKSON. See MISSISSIPPI (Cities).

ANDREW JACKSON (1767-1845)

7th President of the United States

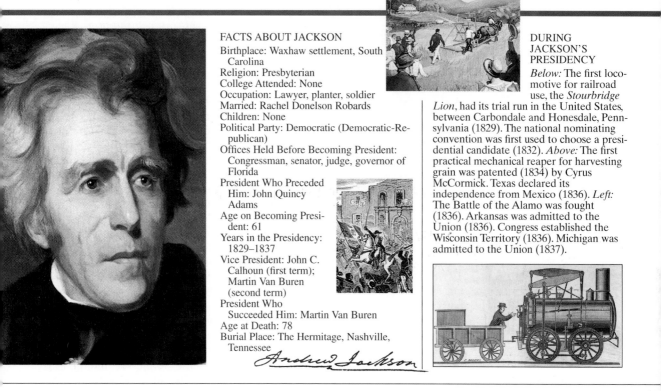

FACTS ABOUT JACKSON

Birthplace: Waxhaw settlement, South Carolina
Religion: Presbyterian
College Attended: None
Occupation: Lawyer, planter, soldier
Married: Rachel Donelson Robards
Children: None
Political Party: Democratic (Democratic-Republican)
Offices Held Before Becoming President: Congressman, senator, judge, governor of Florida
President Who Preceded Him: John Quincy Adams
Age on Becoming President: 61
Years in the Presidency: 1829–1837
Vice President: John C. Calhoun (first term); Martin Van Buren (second term)
President Who Succeeded Him: Martin Van Buren
Age at Death: 78
Burial Place: The Hermitage, Nashville, Tennessee

DURING JACKSON'S PRESIDENCY

Below: The first locomotive for railroad use, the *Stourbridge Lion,* had its trial run in the United States, between Carbondale and Honesdale, Pennsylvania (1829). The national nominating convention was first used to choose a presidential candidate (1832). *Above:* The first practical mechanical reaper for harvesting grain was patented (1834) by Cyrus McCormick. Texas declared its independence from Mexico (1836). *Left:* The Battle of the Alamo was fought (1836). Arkansas was admitted to the Union (1836). Congress established the Wisconsin Territory (1836). Michigan was admitted to the Union (1837).

JACKSON, ANDREW. Andrew Jackson made such a lasting impression upon his times that the period when he was president is usually called the Age of Jackson or the Era of Jacksonian Democracy. As the victor in the battle of New Orleans, during the War of 1812, he was one of the nation's most famous military heroes. As president he stood for equality of opportunity and for the right of ordinary Americans to better themselves. The average American responded by taking a far more active interest in politics than ever before. When Jackson was first inaugurated, in 1829, one admirer wrote, "It was a proud day for the people—General Jackson is *their own* president!"

Jackson's hardiness when marching with his troops and his unwavering devotion to their welfare led them to nickname him Old Hickory. The name stuck and well fitted Jackson's vigor and determination as president. A visitor to the White House in 1832 wrote of him, "In person he was tall, slim and straight. … His head was long, but narrow, and covered with thick grey hair that stood erect, as though impregnated with his defiant spirit; his brow was deeply furrowed, and his eye … was one to 'threaten and command.' … His whole being conveyed an impression of energy and daring."

▶ EARLY YEARS

Andrew Jackson was born on March 15, 1767, in the Waxhaw settlement on what was then the frontier of South Carolina. His parents, Andrew and Elizabeth (Hutchinson) Jackson, were immigrants from Northern Ireland. Young Jackson's father had died a few days before his birth, and he was raised, with two older brothers, by his widowed mother, who lived with relatives. He acquired some schooling and grew up a tall, lanky boy with reddish sandy hair and a quick temper.

During the Revolutionary War, Jackson, at the age of 14, fought with the patriots against

Taken prisoner by the British during the Revolutionary War, the 14-year-old Jackson was slashed with a sword by an officer whose boots he refused to clean.

the British at the Battle of Hanging Rock. Taken prisoner, he was slashed with a sword by a British officer whose boots he had refused to clean, receiving a scar he bore for the rest of his life. He was soon released but saddened by the death of his surviving brother and his mother.

At 16, Jackson occupied himself in Charlestown, South Carolina, spending a substantial legacy from his grandfather. He returned to the frontier with a horse and no money. He tried schoolteaching and then studied law.

▶ LAW, MARRIAGE, AND POLITICS

In 1787, Jackson passed his bar examination, enabling him to practice law. The next year he moved westward with the first group of pioneers to travel the Cumberland Trail to Nashville, which was then a cluster of log cabins within a stockade on the Cumberland River. There his fortunes flourished with those of the town and the territory, which in 1796 became the state of Tennessee.

In 1791, Jackson married Rachel Donelson Robards. Both he and Rachel believed that she was legally divorced at the time. But the divorce decree was not granted until two years later, and they were remarried early in 1794. Jackson was devoted to his wife and furiously re-

Rachel Donelson Robards married Andrew Jackson in 1791. She died shortly after his election as president in 1828.

sented any gossip about the marriage. In 1806 an insulting comment about Rachel led to a duel between Jackson and a fellow attorney, Charles Dickinson, in which Jackson was wounded and Dickinson was killed. Jackson's hot temper would involve him in many such duels.

Jackson improved his fortunes by speculating in land, or buying and then selling the property. In 1795 he obtained a tract of land where he raised cotton and built his handsome and graceful home, the Hermitage, completed in 1819. While his personal fortunes were improving, he was advancing equally well as a lawyer-politician. Whatever Jackson may have lacked in legal knowledge, he made up for with forthright common sense. He served as a prosecuting attorney, and when Tennessee became a state in 1796, he was elected its first representative in Congress. He resigned in 1797 to seek, and win, a seat in the U.S. Senate.

Business problems forced Jackson to resign from the Senate in 1798 and return to Nashville. He was appointed to the state superior court, where he was regarded as a fair and energetic judge. In 1802 he was elected major general of the Tennessee militia. Returning to private life in 1804, although he kept his militia command, he devoted himself to developing his property and to breeding and racing Thoroughbred horses.

▶ MILITARY HERO

Outbreak of War.   The outbreak of the War of 1812 with Britain opened a new chapter in Jackson's life and set him on the path to fame. In 1813, in command of his militia forces, he was sent to subdue Creek Indians who had massacred settlers in what was then the Mississippi Territory. At the subsequent Battle of Horseshoe Bend, in 1814, he routed the Creeks and gained his first military reputation. Commissioned a major general in the regular army, he was given responsibility for the defense of New Orleans, the port city that was the key to the Mississippi River.

Battle of New Orleans.   The main British attack against the city came on January 8, 1815. Jackson's forces included U.S. troops reinforced by militia from

Jackson (on white horse) became a national hero after leading American forces to victory against the British at the Battle of New Orleans in 1815.

Tennessee and Kentucky, some civilians, and a band of pirates led by Jean Laffite. Concealed behind hastily built fortifications, they concentrated a deadly fire upon the advancing columns of British infantry. Three times the British attacked, and three times they were driven back, suffering more than 2,000 casualties, including the death of their commander, before breaking off the battle. American casualties totaled less than 100.

Actually, the Treaty of Ghent ending the war had already been signed, although the news had not yet reached New Orleans. But had the British taken the city, they would have been in a position to make new demands rather than ratifying the treaty. In any event, in a war that had seen few American successes, Jackson became a national hero.

See the article on the War of 1812 in Volume W-X-Y-Z. An article on Jean Laffite appears in Volume L.

Florida Campaign. Jackson returned home but was recalled to service in late 1817 to deal with attacks by Seminole Indians near the Florida border. He provoked an international incident in 1818 by pursuing the retreating Seminoles into what was then Spanish Florida, capturing two towns and executing two British subjects suspected of hostile actions. The United States purchased the territory the following year, and Jackson briefly served as its governor in 1821.

▶ **THE ROAD TO THE WHITE HOUSE**

After he returned to the Hermitage, Jackson's old political friends began to promote him for the presidency. The first step was to have him regain his seat in the U.S. Senate, which was accomplished in 1823. The next was to launch him nationally as a candidate in the presidential election of 1824, to succeed the retiring James Monroe.

Election of 1824. Jackson's rivals were John Quincy Adams, secretary of state under Monroe; Representative (and later Senator) Henry Clay of Kentucky; and William H. Crawford, Monroe's secretary of the treasury. Jackson won 99 electoral votes, as well as a plurality of the popular vote, to 84 for Adams, 41 for Crawford, and 37 for Clay.

Since none of the candidates had received a majority, the election, as provided for in the Constitution, had to be decided by the U.S. House of Representatives. Clay gave his support to Adams, who was elected president. When Adams later appointed Clay secretary of state, Jackson's followers raised the cry of "bargain and corruption." Four years later, however, Jackson was to even the score.

Election of 1828. The 1828 election was marked by an enormous increase in the number of voters, with three times as many people going to the polls as had in 1824. The campaign itself revolved more around personalities than issues. Enthusiastic voters, although lacking any clear-cut idea of his views, turned overwhelmingly to Jackson, giving him 56 percent of the popular vote. He carried 15 of the then 24 states, winning 178 electoral votes to 83 for Adams.

Jackson's pleasure in his election was overshadowed by the death of Rachel, in December 1828. Her niece, Emily Donelson, would serve as White House hostess for much of his presidency.

▶ PRESIDENT

Jacksonian Democracy. Great crowds hailed Jackson's inauguration and jammed the White House to shake his hand. One observer, however, lamented, "The reign of King 'Mob' seemed triumphant." The small but powerful group of men who held federal offices also shuddered, for the ambitious politicians who had promoted Jackson's candidacy hoped to obtain positions for themselves and their lieutenants. Senator William L. Marcy of New York asserted, "To the victor belong the spoils."

Jackson agreed to some political concessions to his followers. In so doing, he made officeholding somewhat more democratic. He informed Congress that official duties could be made "so plain and simple that men of in-

Jackson's opponents depicted him as King Andrew the First trampling on the Constitution in this political cartoon of the period.

telligence may readily qualify themselves for their performance." Jackson adopted the principle of rotating offices among deserving candidates. Although his opponents charged him with introducing a "spoils system," most of the people he appointed were not any less qualified than their predecessors.

During Jackson's administration, another device of democratic politics came into existence, the national nominating convention. Originated by the Anti-Masonic Party, a short-lived third party, it was also used by the Democrats—as the Jacksonians now called themselves—in 1832.

Indian Removal. Jackson's interest in western settlement and his feelings as a former Indian fighter led to his policy of moving all eastern Indian tribes to lands beyond the Mississippi River, under the Indian Removal Act of 1830. Although the U.S. Supreme Court tried to prevent the state of Georgia from expelling the Cherokees in 1832, Jackson would not enforce the court's decision. The removal policy was popular with white settlers who acquired the valuable land, but it proved tragic for thousands of Indians.

Internal Improvements. Another of Jackson's policies was less popular—his refusal to allow federal money to be spent on internal improvements unless they were interstate, or between states, in nature. In 1830 he vetoed as unconstitutional the Maysville Road Bill, which would have provided a federal subsidy to help build a turnpike in Kentucky. However, Jackson did sign bills providing far more government funds than earlier presidents had for the building of interstate roads and for improvement of rivers and harbors.

The Clash with Calhoun. On the question of states' rights versus supremacy of the federal government, Jackson clashed sharply with his vice president, John C. Calhoun of South Carolina. Calhoun had earlier proposed a theory of nullification, under which a state could refuse to obey acts of Congress it considered unconstitutional. Congress then

---

IMPORTANT DATES IN THE LIFE OF ANDREW JACKSON

1767	Born at the Waxhaw settlement, South Carolina, March 15.
1784–87	Studied law and was admitted to the bar.
1788	Moved to Nashville, later capital of Tennessee.
1791	Married Rachel Donelson Robards.
1796–97	Served in the U.S. House of Representatives.
1797–98	Served in the U.S. Senate.
1802	Elected major general of the Tennessee militia.
1814	Defeated Creek Indians at the Battle of Horseshoe Bend during War of 1812; promoted to major general, U.S. Army.
1815	Defeated British at the Battle of New Orleans, January 8.
1821	Appointed governor of the Florida Territory.
1823	Returned to the U.S. Senate.
1824	Defeated for the presidency; election decided by the U.S. House of Representatives.
1829–37	Served as seventh president of the United States.
1845	Died at the Hermitage in Nashville, Tennessee, June 8.

would either have to drop the disputed act or obtain its approval through a constitutional amendment. Calhoun hoped to win the president to this states'-rights view. But Jackson revealed his strong feelings on the issue at a banquet in 1830, when, looking directly at Calhoun, he offered the toast, "Our Federal Union—It must be preserved."

Jackson completed the Hermitage, near Nashville, Tennessee, in 1819, and it remained his home for the rest of his life. He and his wife, Rachel, are buried in its garden.

The Eaton Affair: Cabinet Breakup. At the same time, Jackson was engaged in a troublesome personal dispute with Calhoun and his followers over their refusal to treat with respect the wife of Secretary of War John H. Eaton. Scandalous rumors were circulating concerning Mrs. Eaton. Jackson furiously defended her, for he had suffered much from rumors concerning his own wife, and he believed they had been a factor in her death. The combination of political and personal complications led in 1831 to the breakup of Jackson's cabinet. As a result, Calhoun's followers were eliminated from the cabinet. Martin Van Buren, the secretary of state, who had loyally backed Jackson, replaced Calhoun as the president's "heir."

The Nullification Crisis. This issue came to a head the next year, when South Carolina adopted an ordinance of nullification declaring that the high protective tariffs, or taxes on imports, of 1828 and 1832 were invalid within its borders. Privately, Jackson threatened to hang Calhoun. Publicly, he prepared to use military force against South Carolina. In a proclamation he denounced nullification as treason: "I consider the power to annul a law of the United States, assumed by one State, incompatible with the existence of the Union, contradicted expressly by the letter of the Constitution, unauthorized by its spirit, inconsistent with every principle on which it is founded, and destructive of the great object for which it was formed."

In the Senate, meanwhile, Henry Clay arranged a compromise that gradually lowered the tariff. The crisis ended, and the doctrine of nullification was dead. See the article on Henry Clay in Volume C.

The Bank of the United States. With equal force, Jackson moved during these same years against the second Bank of the United States. The bank, which had received a 20-year charter in 1816, was three-fourths privately owned and was privately managed, but it was the depository of government funds. Because of its size and through its branches in several states, it operated as a large and profitable monopoly and was able to dominate banking throughout the United States. In 1832, Jackson vetoed a bill to recharter the bank, denouncing it as unconstitutional and dangerous.

▶ **SECOND TERM**

Jackson was re-elected overwhelmingly in 1832, winning 219 electoral votes to 49 for his opponent, his old political enemy Henry Clay. His popular vote totaled more than 56 percent. Martin Van Buren became vice president, Calhoun having resigned to enter the U.S. Senate. See the article on John C. Calhoun in Volume C.

The Bank War Renewed. During his second term, Jackson continued his war against the Bank of the United States, whose original charter still had three years to run. He removed federal deposits from it and placed them in state banks, or so-called pet banks. Jackson's destruction of the bank led to a vast increase of "cheaper" paper money in circulation, a growth in land speculation, and inflation. To combat this, in 1836, he issued the Specie Circular, which required payment in gold or silver (specie) for public land, but this policy contributed to an economic depression in 1837, after he left office.

Foreign Affairs. In foreign affairs, Jackson was successful in ending disputes with Britain and France. He formally recognized Texas' independence from Mexico in 1837, in the closing days of his administration, although he rejected calls for its joining the United States, because of the inevitable controversy over slavery that would ensue.

▶ **RETIREMENT**

With the inauguration of Martin Van Buren as president in 1837, Jackson left the White House, his popularity undiminished. He lived on for some eight more years in the Hermitage, still erect in his 70's and still interested in national politics. Illness gradually weakened him, and his last years were troubled by financial problems. When he died on June 8, 1845, one of his admirers declared, "He was the embodiment of the true spirit of the nation." He was buried in the Hermitage garden, next to Rachel.

FRANK FREIDEL
Harvard University

JACKSON, JESSE (1941–   )

Jesse Jackson is a Baptist minister, civil rights leader, and two-time candidate for the Democratic nomination to the presidency of the United States. Since the mid-1960's, he has worked to improve the social and economic conditions of African Americans and other minority groups.

Jesse Louis Jackson was born on October 8, 1941. He was raised in Greenville, South Carolina, by his mother, Helen Burns Jackson, and his adoptive father, Charles Henry Jackson. He attended North Carolina Agricultural and Technical University, where he met his future wife, Jacqueline Davis, with whom he had five children. Jackson earned a bachelor of arts degree in sociology in 1963. He later attended the Chicago Theological Seminary. In 1968, he was ordained a Baptist minister.

Civil Rights Leader. While in school, Jackson became involved in the civil rights movement and closely associated with Dr. Martin Luther King, Jr. He became a field director for the Congress of Racial Equality (CORE). In 1966 he helped found Operation Breadbasket, an organization associated with the Southern Christian Leadership

Jesse Jackson has been an active civil rights leader since the 1960's. He gained national political recognition in 1984 and 1988 as a candidate for the Democratic nomination for the U.S. presidency.

Conference (SCLC). His goal was to improve economic opportunities for African Americans. In 1971, Jackson founded a self-help human rights organization called Operation PUSH (People United to Serve Humanity). As national president from 1971 to 1983, he promoted economic development, housing development, health care programs, and academic excellence.

Presidential Candidate. In the early 1980's, Jackson began speaking out on foreign-policy issues. In 1983, he became a national political figure when he declared himself a candidate for the 1984 Democratic presidential nomination. He was the first African American presidential candidate to win significant support. He formed the National Rainbow Coalition, Inc., a political organization, and spoke out for social and economic justice, peace, and environmental reforms.

In 1987, Jackson made a bid for the 1988 Democratic presidential nomination, attracting twice as many popular votes and three times the number of delegates that had pledged to support him in 1984. He won 13 state primaries and caucuses to place second in the race.

In 1990, Jackson was elected to one of the two "shadow" seats in the U.S. Senate from the District of Columbia, to lobby for statehood for the district. He remains influential in politics and an important voice on civil rights, both at home and abroad.

ANNA KOSOF
Author, *Jesse Jackson*

JACKSON, LILLY MAY. See MARYLAND (Famous People).

JACKSON, THOMAS JONATHAN ("STONEWALL") (1824–1863)

Thomas Jonathan Jackson was one of the great Confederate generals in the U.S. Civil War, who earned the nickname "Stonewall" for his cool steadfastness in battle. He was born in Clarksburg, Virginia (now in West Virginia), on January 21, 1824. Orphaned at the age of 6, he lived much of his early life with his uncle, Cummins E. Jackson. The family was poor, and an appointment to the U.S. Military Academy at West Point, in 1842, gave him his only opportunity to obtain a higher education.

Early Career and Marriage. On graduating from West Point in 1846, Jackson was commissioned a second lieutenant of artillery and served in the Mexican War (1846–48), where he was promoted to first lieutenant and made a brevet major (an honorary rank) for gallantry in action. After further service in the Seminole campaign in Florida, he resigned from the army in 1851 and accepted a teaching post at the Virginia Military Institute (VMI) in Lexington.

In 1853 he married Elinor Junkin, who helped him overcome an almost crippling shyness and provided the first happy home he had known. Her death in childbirth a year later left him in despair for months. In 1857 he married Mary Anna Morrison. For the next four years he devoted himself to his work at VMI and to the Presbyterian Church. Religion was to be a great influence and comfort in his life.

Outbreak of Civil War. Jackson had been loyal to the United States. But when Virginia seceded from the Union and joined the Confederacy in April 1861, he followed his state and was commissioned a brigadier general in the Confederate Army. At the First Battle of Bull Run (Manassas), the first major battle of the Civil War, he held a hill against heavy Union attack. He received his famous nickname when a fellow Confederate general, who was trying to rally his own men, pointed to Jackson's troops and cried, "There is Jackson standing like a stone wall. Let us determine to die here, and we will conquer!"

Shenandoah and Later Campaigns. Jackson went on to even greater exploits. In 1862, in the Shenandoah Valley of Virginia, he led a force of about 18,000 men against three

Union armies totaling about 60,000 troops. In a lightning campaign up and down the narrow valley, Jackson fooled the Union generals and beat them one by one, using tactics that are still studied as models of courage, speed, and surprise.

Called to Richmond, Virginia, by General Robert E. Lee to help defend the Confederate capital, Jackson became Lee's ideal partner. In command of a wing of Lee's army, he played an important role in the Confederate victory at the Second Battle of Bull Run. At Antietam (Sharpsburg), where he rushed to Lee's aid, he again stood like a stone wall and helped save Lee's Army of Northern Virginia. He was promoted to lieutenant general and given command of a corps.

Death. Jackson met his death at the Battle of Chancellorsville in 1863. After one of the great flank marches in military history, he attacked the Union forces and drove them into Lee's waiting trap. During a lull in the fighting, Jackson and his staff rode ahead of the Confederate lines looking for the enemy. On his way back, after dark, Confederate soldiers mistook Jackson and his men for Union cavalry and fired on them. Jackson was wounded and had to have his arm amputated. Pneumonia set in as a result of his wounds, and on May 10, 1863, he died. The Confederacy fought on for two more years, but after Jackson's death, its victories were few.

FRANK E. VANDIVER
Author, *Mighty Stonewall*

JACKSONVILLE

Many cities have a nickname, but Jacksonville has had several. In the early 1900's, Jacksonville was known as the "gateway to Florida" because trains and ships from the North passed through this busy Atlantic Ocean port, carrying tourists and goods across the state. Jacksonville became the "bold new city" following its merger in 1968 with surrounding Duval County to form the largest city in Florida. People have also called Jacksonville "river city," because the majestic St. Johns River flows through the city on its way to the Atlantic. Another nickname, "Florida's first coast," refers to that northeast region of the state, of which Jacksonville is the heart, that was first settled by the French and Spanish in the 1500's.

Today Jacksonville is a Sun Belt city of more than 670,000 people. The metropolitan area has a population of over 900,000. About one fourth of the city's residents are of African-American heritage. Unlike some other parts of Florida, in which there are large numbers of retired people, Jacksonville has a balance of young, working-age, and retired people.

Jacksonville has a diversified economy, with important contributions coming from its banking and insurance establishments, busy port, railways, and regional distribution facilities. Manufacturing, construction, real estate, and retail sales also contribute to the city's economy. During World War II, the United States Navy built bases in Jacksonville, and these bases subsequently became major military installations.

Places of historical interest include Fort Caroline National Monument, which commemorates the French Huguenot Settlement of 1564, and the Kingsley Plantation State Historical Memorial. Culturally, the Jacksonville Symphony Orchestra and the Florida Ballet have achieved regional prominence. Museums include the Jacksonville Art Museum, the Jacksonville Museum of Arts and Sciences, and the Cummer Gallery of Art.

For sports fans, the city is known for the Gator Bowl, an annual college football game held in a sports stadium of the same name, and the Tournament Players Championship in golf. Tourists and residents alike enjoy the annual jazz festival, the Jacksonville Zoo, and the city's beaches along the Atlantic.

The city has four accredited colleges and universities: Edward Waters College, Florida Junior College, Jacksonville University, and the University of North Florida.

The original inhabitants of the Jacksonville area were the Timucuan Indians. French, Spanish, and English explorers and colonists came to the region beginning in the 16th century. The United States acquired Florida in 1821, and the next year the city was founded and named for Andrew Jackson, the first military commander of the territory.

During the U.S. Civil War, Union troops occupied Jacksonville four times. Following a devastating fire in 1901, the city was quickly rebuilt. The second half of the 20th century has seen the growth of suburbs, expressways, shopping centers, and office parks, which, combined with the climate and life-style, make Jacksonville an attractive and increasingly popular city in which to live.

JAMES B. CROOKS
University of North Florida

After Jacksonville merged with Duval County, the city became one of the nation's largest cities in area, covering some 760 square miles (1,970 square kilometers).

JADE

Jade is a gemstone that almost glows. People have prized it for thousands of years. The Chinese language uses the same word to mean both "jade" and "precious stone." Jade also is known in China as the Jewel of Heaven. The English word "jade" comes from the Spanish *piedra de ijada*. This means "colic stone." The Spanish called it this because they believed jade cured stomach pains.

Because jade is a tough and hard stone, early people used it to make axes, hammers, knives, and other useful tools. Later, people used it for bowls, decorative carvings, jewelry, and amulets (charms to protect their wearers from evil or to bring them luck).

Jade can be either of two separate minerals, **jadeite** or **nephrite.** These look so much alike that only an expert can tell them apart. Jadeite is slightly harder. It also has a translucent glow and comes in more colors. Nephrite is less translucent, and is far more common.

Jade is found in a wide variety of colors. It is white in its pure state, but enough mineral impurities are usually present to make jade bright yellow, red, or one of the many shades of green. It may even be found, although rarely, in shades of blue or mauve. Some jade may be the translucent white of melting snow or the opaque yellow-white of mutton fat. Most jade is mottled (spotted) and streaked. Black jade, which is actually a very dark green, is known to exist in only a few carvings. The most desired shade of jade is an emerald-green, or "Imperial," jade. This color may be almost transparent.

Jade is so tough that it is very difficult to carve. Steel chisels will not work. Instead, gritty materials are rubbed over the surface until it wears away.

China is the country where jade has been of greatest importance. For 3,000 years the Chinese have been making lovely jade carvings. They have always collected jade and used it for personal decoration. The earliest designs of 11th century B.C., were often decorated with stylized geometric patterns. Many centuries later the geometric designs changed to less formal and more graceful designs. Then many symbols were carved in jade. The symbols reflected ideas in Taoism and Buddhism, the important religions of China. Practically every creature—from the dragon (one of the most popular symbols) to the butterfly—has been carved in jade by the Chinese.

The Chinese admire jade so much that those who can afford it always carry small pieces with them. They believe that when jade is fingered, some of its secret virtue rubs off.

Jade is found in Burma, New Zealand, Mexico, Guatemala, Siberia, China, and the United States. It is mined from medium-size boulders on hillsides and in stream beds. The quality of the jade is judged from polished panels that are cut in the stone.

Morton R. Sarett
President, Jewelry Industry Council

See also Gemstones; Jewelry.

Jade is ideal for intricate carving. The delicate branches of the trees in this 19th-century Chinese landscape might have fractured in a stone less tough.

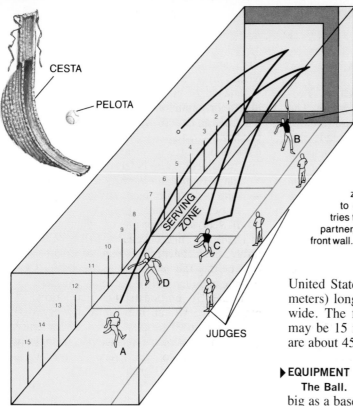

CESTA

PELOTA

FOUL

1
2
3
4
5
6
7
8
9
10
11
12
13
14
15

SERVING ZONE

B

C

D

A

JUDGES

The server (A) must stand behind line number 11. The serve goes to the front wall and must then land in the serving zone — between lines 4 and 7. But it is legal to catch the serve before it lands. Player B tries to catch A's serve in the air, but misses. B's partner, C, takes it on a bounce and returns it to the front wall. A's partner, D, prepares to return C's throw.

JAI ALAI

Jai alai (pronounced ''high lie'') is known as one of the world's fastest and most exciting sports. It is something like handball, except that a long, narrow basket, strapped to the arm, is used to throw the ball against a wall. The rock-hard ball often travels at 150 miles (240 kilometers) an hour.

For hundreds of years, jai alai has been a popular sport in Spain. It began in the Basque region. In the Basque tongue, *jai alai* means ''merry festival.''

▶ THE COURT

Jai alai is played in a theaterlike building called a *fronton*. The court, or *cancha*, has high walls on three sides. Spectators sit behind a protecting screen on the fourth side. The front wall has a border of wood at the bottom and at the side near the spectators. A ball bouncing on the wood counts as a foul. The remainder of this wall is made of granite thick enough to withstand the terrific striking force of the balls. The other two walls and the rest of the playing surface are concrete. Court sizes vary, but a typical jai alai court in the United States measures about 176 feet (53.6 meters) long and about 35 feet (10.7 meters) wide. The foul area at the side of the court may be 15 feet (4.6 meters) wide. The walls are about 45 feet (13.7 meters) high.

▶ EQUIPMENT

The Ball. The ball, or *pelota*, is almost as big as a baseball. It has a core of hand-wound rubber, covered lightly with linen and two layers of hardened goatskin. It is as lively as a golf ball but much harder and heavier.

The Basket. The curved wicker basket, or *cesta*, is about 2 feet (60 centimeters) long. It has finger sockets on the back and is strapped to the wrist. It is made of reeds woven over a thin frame of wood. The *cesta* used by front-court players is smaller than that used by back-court players.

Clothing. The players wear helmets, sneakers, white pants with a red or blue sash, and white or colored shirts bearing numbers.

▶ HOW TO PLAY

The object of jai alai is to throw the ball to the front wall so that when it returns, it will be difficult for an opposing player to catch the ball in the basket and return it to the front wall. The ball may touch the sidewall, the back wall, or the floor. For example, a ball can be taken in the air after it has hit the front wall, or it can be taken off the back wall before it strikes the floor a second time. This is called the *rebote* shot.

The ball can be thrown with the forearm, from either side of the body. But the throw that is most used and most powerful is the one up and overhead, in an action similar to that used by a discus thrower. The two-hand grip, with the right forearm in front and the left hand behind the right one to support and push it, is used mostly to catch and throw the ball when it is close to the sidewall. It is also used to make the back-wall return. Even if players are left-handed, they must wear the *cesta* on the right hand.

▶ NUMBER OF PLAYERS AND SCORING

Single matches (two opposing players) or doubles matches (two players on each side) are played. The number of points required to win is settled before the game begins. Six, seven, or eight players or teams of two players each may participate. Each player or team of players is given a numbered position, from 1 to whatever number of players or teams there may be. Scoring is one point less than the number of players or teams playing. Thus, in a doubles match with eight teams (16 players), a score of 7 would be required to win.

The game is played on a drop-out system. The player or team losing a point must go to the end of the line to await a turn again on the court. The player or team winning the point continues on the court until losing a point or winning the game. If at that time another player or team has the next highest number of points and a third player or team has the third highest number of points—and there are no ties for second place or third place—the second and third positions will be awarded immediately, and the game is over.

If there is to be a play-off of a tie for second or third after the winner has been declared, the players or teams play off in the order in which they were defeated. This is the order in which they are seated on the waiting bench.

▶ GROWTH OF JAI ALAI

There are jai alai *frontons* in Egypt, Cuba, Italy, France, Mexico, China, Spain, the Philippines, the United States, and most South American countries.

In the United States the first game was played in 1904 at the Louisiana Purchase Exposition in St. Louis, Missouri. Thereafter jai alai had success for a short time in New Orleans, Chicago, and New York. About 1926 it was played for the first time in Miami, Florida, and it became extremely popular in that state. Immense and beautiful *frontons* have been built in several cities in Florida, as well as in Connecticut.

José Cruz Salsamendi
Former Players' Manager
Dania (Florida) Jai Alai Palace

JAIL. See Prisons.

JAKARTA

Jakarta is the capital and largest city of Indonesia and the most populous city in Southeast Asia. It is the economic and cultural center of the country, as well as the seat of the government. The city's metropolitan area, Jakarta Raya, has the status of a special capital region.

Jakarta is built on the northwestern tip of the island of Java, at the mouth of the Liwung River, looking out to the Java Sea. Tandjung Priok, its busy seaport nearby, is visited by ships from all over the world. Freighters bring in coal, iron, machinery, and automobiles and carry away cargoes of rubber, tin ore, clothing, shoes, electrical and electronic equipment, hides, tea, copra, citronella oil and fiber, and other exports.

People come from all over Indonesia to work and set up business in Jakarta. Today the city has more than 8 million inhabitants. The

population has increased so rapidly since the 1940's that Jakarta has a severe housing shortage and problems of water supply, health, and sanitation. New buildings are constantly going up, but there are never enough. The city's streets are crowded with automobiles, bicycles, and pedestrians.

Jakarta is the center of Indonesian life. The main industries, the government offices,

Canals, or *kalis*, built long ago by Dutch settlers, cut through many parts of the city.

New luxury hotels line many of the wide avenues in Jakarta.

the presidential palace, the embassies and consulates, and the centers of culture and education are found here. Trains from all over the island of Java converge on the huge white stone railroad terminal near the center of the city. Jets from major cities all over the world land at the modern international airport at nearby Kemajoran. They fly in over rice paddies that have been planted and harvested by hand for 1,000 years.

Jakarta has wide streets bordered with tall palm trees. It has narrow, congested alleys, and it has its canals, or *kalis*. These waterways date back to the days of the Dutch settlers. Along some of the smaller canals are narrow, quaint buildings that they put up centuries ago. A main canal, Tjiliwung, cuts through one section of the city. In the morning, people wash their clothes in the canal. During the heat of the day they bathe in the cool water.

Jakarta has many hotels, shops, theaters, and movie houses. The largest museum, Gedung Artja, was established in 1862. It houses an extensive library and one of the best collections of Asian art in Southeast Asia. Other places of interest are the aquarium at Paser Ikan, which is the fish market, and the Raden Saleh Zoo. The main campus of the University of Indonesia, in Jakarta, attracts students from all over Southeast Asia.

▶ HISTORY

The city was founded in 1527 and called Sunda Kelapa. It became the capital of the Hindu-Sundanese kingdom of Padjadjaran. When it was captured by the Sultan of Bantam, the name was changed to Djajakarta. After a while it became known as Djakarta.

The Dutch who came to the area in the early 1600's rebuilt the town in 1619 and gave it a new name—Batavia. It grew in importance and became the hub of trade for the Dutch East India Company in Southeast Asia. In the closing years of the 18th century the Dutch government took control of the Dutch East India Company. Batavia became the capital of the Netherlands (Dutch) East Indies. The city remained under Dutch rule until World War II, when it was seized and occupied by the Japanese.

In 1945, at the war's end, the Indonesian people declared their independence from the Netherlands. Djakarta became the capital when the independence of the Republic of Indonesia was officially recognized in 1949. The spelling of the city's name was changed to Jakarta in 1972. The area of the city has expanded greatly from its historic center to meet the needs of the growing population.

Reviewed by INDONESIAN CONSULATE GENERAL

JAMAICA

Jamaica is an island nation in the Caribbean Sea. Its name comes from an Indian word meaning "land of wood and water." The name is fitting, for Jamaica has forested mountains and many swift-flowing streams and waterfalls. Jamaica's fertile soil and warm climate have combined to make the island a treasure house of tropical crops. Its magnificent scenery attracts many tourists, who are vital to the country's economy.

▶THE PEOPLE

Jamaica has many different peoples and cultures. At one time the island was inhabited by Arawak Indians, but they died out after European colonists arrived. The first colonists were Spanish. The British came soon after and ruled the island for almost 300 years. Large numbers of Africans were brought to Jamaica as slaves to work on sugarcane plantations. When slavery was abolished, Chinese and East Indians came to Jamaica as laborers. Lebanese and Syrians also settled there as traders.

Today about 90 percent of Jamaicans are of African or mixed African and European ancestry. However, many different racial patterns can be found on the island. It is possible to meet Jamaicans who are a mixture of all four major ethnic groups—African, East Indian, white, and Chinese.

Each group has made its special contribution to Jamaica. The East Indians brought their methods of rice cultivation. The African influence is apparent in art, music, and folk dancing. The Spanish introduced sugarcane and citrus fruits to the island. Chinese, Lebanese, and Syrians have been active in Jamaican business. Many favorite sports, such as cricket, polo, soccer, and horse racing, are British. The government, commerce, and schools are modeled on the British system, and English is the official language.

Most Jamaicans are Christians. They belong to various Protestant denominations, the largest being the Church of England, and to the Roman Catholic Church. There are also a number of Hindus and Muslims. One small sect, the Rastafarians, look to Ethiopia as their spiritual home.

Many of the people are farmers. Some till their own small farms, while others work on sugarcane, banana, or coffee plantations. Many other Jamaicans now work in tourism

Although they are mainly of black African descent, Jamaica's people came from many lands. Former prime minister Edward P. G. Seaga (*center*) is of British and Asian ancestry.

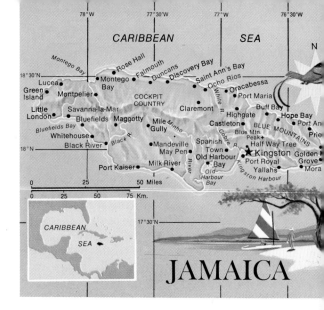

JAMAICA

and other service industries, for the government, and in manufacturing and mining.

Jamaica has a large population for a country of its small size. Overpopulation has long been a problem. Many Jamaicans have gone to the United Kingdom, the United States, and other countries in search of jobs. This emigration has helped to relieve some of the population pressure.

▶ THE LAND

Jamaica lies about 500 miles (800 kilometers) southeast of the United States. In area it is the third largest island in the Caribbean, after Cuba and Hispaniola (Haiti and the Dominican Republic). These three islands, together with Puerto Rico, form the group known as the Greater Antilles. Jamaica is a mountainous island; about half the land rises more than 1,000 feet (300 meters) above sea level. Mountains stretch from west to east across the island, rising in the east to the towering Blue Mountain range. Blue Mountain Peak, the highest point in Jamaica, is 7,402 feet (2,256 meters) above sea level. The mountains are rugged, with many narrow ravines and sharp, knifelike ridges.

A limestone plateau surrounds the Blue Mountains and covers more than three fourths of the island. In some places the plateau extends to the sea, forming cliffs that rise far

above the water. Parts of the plateau are honeycombed with caverns and caves and pitted with sinkholes. One section in the northwest is known as the Cockpit Country because it contains a great number of deep circular basins. The soil in some of the larger basins is excellent for farming.

Very little of Jamaica is flat. The coastal plains are low and level, but they are narrow and interrupted by cliffs. One of the largest lowland areas is on the southern coast in the vicinity of Kingston, the capital. This is a densely populated and highly productive farming area.

Climate. Jamaica has a tropical climate, and there is no cold winter season. It is slightly cooler in winter than in summer, with winter temperatures averaging 75°F (24°C). The amount of rainfall varies from one place to another. It is heaviest on the northern slopes of the Blue Mountains, which lie in the path of the northeast trade winds. This area can receive as much as 150 inches (3,800 millimeters) of rain a year. Jamaica is occasionally subject to destructive hurricanes. The worst in the island's history, Hurricane Gilbert, struck in 1988. It made tens of thousands of people homeless and destroyed much of Jamaica's farmland and crops.

Natural Resources. Fertile soil and extensive deposits of bauxite (aluminum ore) are

"Land of wood and water" is the name its earliest known inhabitants gave to Jamaica. Lush woods cover much of the mountainous island, and rivers and streams flow swiftly across the land.

Tourism plays an important part in Jamaica's economy. Tourists are attracted by the island's scenic beauty, sunny climate, white beaches, and clear waters.

Jamaica's most important natural resources. The island's climate and scenic beauty, which led to the development of the tourist industry, might also be considered important natural resources. In addition there are large deposits of gypsum (used in making plaster and plasterboard) and limestone, and small amounts of manganese, iron ore, and copper.

▶ THE ECONOMY

Jamaica's economy is based on the mining and processing of bauxite and on agriculture and tourism. Jamaica is one of the world's leading producers of bauxite, which traditionally has been its most valuable export and chief source of income. This income, however, is dependent on world market demands. When demand for bauxite declines, prices fall, and Jamaica's economy suffers.

Sugarcane is the most important commercial crop. Sugar and by-products of sugarcane, such as rum and molasses, are leading exports. Bananas, citrus fruits, spices, coffee, cacao (from which cocoa and chocolate are

made), and copra (dried coconut meat) are other important exports. Jamaica's banana, coffee, and coconut crops were among those that were especially hard hit by Hurricane Gilbert in 1988.

Tourism is one of the island's most important industries, ranking with the export of bauxite as a major source of income.

Jamaica's manufacturing industries include sugar refining, rum distilling, and the production of cigarettes and cigars, textiles, clothing, and building materials.

▶ CITIES

Kingston, the capital of Jamaica, is the only major city on the island. Kingston was founded in 1692, after an earthquake had destroyed nearby Port Royal. It became a busy seaport, as well as the center of Jamaica's commerce and culture. Kingston replaced Spanish Town as the capital in 1872.

In addition to the impressive government buildings, Kingston has art galleries, museums, and the Hope Botanical Gardens. The island's racetracks, polo fields, and sports stadiums are near Kingston. A short distance outside the city is the main campus of the University of the West Indies.

Montego Bay, with its beautiful harbor and famous Doctor's Cave beach, is Jamaica's most popular resort. It lies at the edge of the Cockpit Country. Montego Bay was once an

---

FACTS AND FIGURES

JAMAICA is the official name of the country.

THE PEOPLE are known as Jamaicans.

LOCATION: Caribbean Sea.

AREA: 4,243 sq mi (10,990 km²).

POPULATION: 2,500,000 (estimate).

CAPITAL AND LARGEST CITY: Kingston.

MAJOR LANGUAGE: English (official).

MAJOR RELIGION: Christian (Protestant, Roman Catholic).

GOVERNMENT: Constitutional monarchy. **Head of state**—British monarch. **Head of government**—prime minister. **Legislature**—Parliament (consisting of a House of Representatives and a Senate).

CHIEF PRODUCTS: Agricultural—sugarcane, bananas, spices, coffee, cacao, copra, rice, tobacco, corn. **Manufactured**—refined sugar, rum, cigars and cigarettes, textiles, clothing, building materials. **Mineral**—bauxite, gypsum, limestone.

MONETARY UNIT: Jamaican dollar (1 dollar = 100 cents).

NATIONAL ANTHEM: "Eternal Father, bless our land."

Founded in 1692, Kingston has grown into a modern city with a metropolitan population of about 500,000. The building in the foreground is the ministry of foreign affairs.

Arawak Indian village. Today it is the island's second most important commercial center. The town is surrounded by sugar and banana plantations and cattle ranches. There are many ruins and landmarks dating back to the days when both slavery and pirates flourished in Jamaica.

Spanish Town was at one time the colonial capital of Jamaica. It was probably laid out by Christopher Columbus' son Diego in the early 1520's and remained the capital until 1872. Mandeville is an important industrial center. Port Antonio is a busy port and seaside resort. Ocho Ríos, another popular seaside resort, is the commercial center of an important agricultural region. It is also the shipping point for nearby bauxite mines.

▶HISTORY AND GOVERNMENT

Christopher Columbus landed in Jamaica in 1494, on his second voyage to America. Spanish settlers arrived in the early 1500's. The Spanish used the Arawak Indians as laborers, and when the Arawaks died out, they imported slaves from Africa. The British invaded Jamaica in 1655. British control of the island was formally recognized by Spain in 1670 in the Treaty of Madrid. When the Spanish departed, some of the slaves, known as Maroons, escaped to the mountains, where they lived as free people in their own territory.

Jamaica prospered because of its sugarcane. After slavery was abolished in 1833, most of the freed slaves became farmers on their own land. The island's economy suffered from a lack of plantation workers, so East Indians and Chinese were brought to Jamaica as contract workers. After an uprising by poor blacks in 1865, the local white government was dissolved. Jamaica became a crown colony in 1866, ruled directly by Britain. It was granted its own constitution and a large degree of self-government in 1944 and won complete independence on August 6, 1962.

Jamaica recognizes the British monarch, represented by a governor-general, as its head of state. The powers of the monarch and governor-general are largely ceremonial. Political power rests with the Parliament, which is composed of an elected house of representatives and an appointed senate. The leader of the majority party in the house of representatives serves as prime minister, or head of government.

Since independence, Jamaica has been governed by its two main political parties, the People's National Party (PNP) and the Jamaican Labour Party (JLP). Labour leader Sir Alexander Bustamante (1884–1977), the nation's first prime minister, served until 1967.

In 1972, Michael Norman Manley (1924–97), the leader of the PNP, became prime minister. Manley followed a policy of "democratic socialism." He nationalized industry and established close relations with Cuba. During the 1970's, Jamaica suffered severe economic problems, especially a high rate of unemployment and inflation and a decline in exports. Political violence led to a sharp drop in tourism and foreign investment. In elections held in 1980, the JLP, led by Edward P. G. Seaga, came to power. Prime Minister Seaga adopted a policy of free enterprise in an effort to restore Jamaica's economy. Seaga and the JLP were returned to office in the 1983 elections, but in 1989, Manley and the PNP regained control of the government. Manley retired in 1992 and was succeeded as party leader by Percival Patterson, whose PNP won re-election in 1993 and 1997.

JOHN F. LOUNSBURY
Arizona State University

JAMES

James is a version of the biblical name Jacob. Seven Scottish kings from the House of Stuart reigned (r.) under this name. The last two also ruled England and Ireland.

James I, the first Stuart ruler of England, was the only child of Mary, Queen of Scots. An unpopular and stubborn monarch, he often quarreled with Parliament, particularly over financial matters. To many he was known as the Wisest Fool in Christendom.

▶ KINGS OF SCOTLAND

James I (1394–1437) (r.1406–37), son of Robert III, spent his youth in captivity at the English court. Allowed to return home in 1424, he was determined to enforce law and order. But his firmness and taxation of the nobles led to his brutal assassination.

James II (1430–60) (r.1437–60), son of James I, used artillery force against his barons in order to maintain power. He was killed during the Wars of the Roses.

James III (1452–88) (r.1460–88), son of James II, was highly cultured, but his alleged greed and fondness for low-born friends infuriated the nobles. Defeated by them at Sauchieburn, he was mysteriously murdered in flight from the battlefield.

James IV (1473–1513) (r.1488–1513), son of James III, developed a Scottish navy. His alliance with France prompted an unwise invasion of England, where he was killed at the Battle of Flodden.

James V (1512–42) (r.1513–42), son of James IV, was plagued by disputes between pro-English (Protestant) and pro-French (Catholic) factions. He died shortly after his defeat by the English at Solway Moss.

▶ KINGS OF ENGLAND, IRELAND, AND SCOTLAND

James I (1566–1625) of England and Ireland (r.1603–25) was also **James VI** of Scotland (r.1567–1625). The only child of Mary, Queen of Scots, his youth was dominated by strife between Protestants and Catholics. Not until 1595 was he able to bring Scotland under his firm control. In 1603 he inherited (through his great-grandmother Margaret Tudor) the throne of England, succeeding the childless Elizabeth I. The King James Bible was commissioned by him, and Jamestown, the first English colony in America, was named after him.

James II (1633–1701) of England and Ireland (r.1685–88) was also **James VII** of Scotland (r.1685–88). The second son of Charles I, James spent most of his youth in exile following his father's execution (1649). He returned to England in 1660 as Duke of York under his brother, King Charles II. The American colony of New York was named after him. As king, James tried to make England a Catholic country, which led to his removal from the throne in the Glorious Revolution of 1688. He was succeeded by his Protestant daughter, Mary II, and her husband, William III. He died in exile.

CHARLES KIGHTLY
Contributor, *The Illustrated Dictionary
of British History*

JAMES, HENRY (1843–1916)

The American writer Henry James was an influential force in the development of the modern novel. He was born in New York City on April 15, 1843. His wealthy parents had four other children, including William James, who became a well-known philosopher and psychologist. Henry's father, a brilliant and eccentric philosopher, counted leading writers and thinkers among his friends. The five James children grew up in a scholarly atmosphere and were expected to think for themselves. They were educated chiefly by private tutors and governesses, and they traveled extensively in Europe.

At the age of 21, James published his first works—a short story and a book review. His first novel appeared in the literary magazine *Atlantic Monthly* in 1870. He continued to travel in Europe and finally decided to live there permanently. In 1875 he went to Paris, meeting such leading French writers as Émile Zola and Gustave Flaubert. He settled in London the following year.

The subject that most interested James was the contrast between the cultures of the Old World and the New. Many of his 22 novels and more than 100 short stories set Americans and their values in conflict with their European counterparts. James's work can be divided into three periods. His early novels and stories, written from the early 1870's to the early 1880's, are simpler and more readable than those works written during the middle and late periods.

Early Writings. James's second novel, *Roderick Hudson* (1875), was the first in what he considered his official body of work. Both it and his next novel, *The American* (1877), are about American men who are changed by their exposure to European society. James gained fame with his short novel *Daisy Miller* (1878), the story of an unsophisticated American girl traveling in Europe who innocently defies traditional European social customs. Other novels from this early period are *The Europeans* (1878), *Washington Square* (1881), and *The Portrait of a Lady* (1881).

Middle Period. Between 1882 and 1895, James published several stories and novels, including *The Bostonians* (1886). He also attempted to succeed as a dramatist, but his plays were not well received. In 1897, James

Henry James was one of America's most influential modern novelists. His unique style and detailed character studies won him international fame.

purchased Lamb House in Rye, Sussex, where he lived for the rest of his life. The first work he completed there was *The Turn of the Screw* (1898); a compelling horror story about a governess and two children, it can also be read as a psychological study. In this novel, as well as in *The Spoils of Poynton* (1897) and *The Awkward Age* (1899), James experimented with unusual points of view.

Later Life. James's final creative phase saw the publication of three brilliant novels—*The Wings of the Dove* (1902), *The Ambassadors* (1903), and *The Golden Bowl* (1904). These works are difficult to read, for by this time James had perfected a style that was complex and wordy. He himself considered *The Ambassadors* to be the best of his works.

James described his philosophy of writing in his notebooks and in the critical prefaces he wrote for a 24-volume edition of his work published in 1907–17. His criticism and his travel writings are also masterful prose works.

In 1915, moved by patriotism for his adopted country and impatience with America's refusal to come to Britain's aid in World War I, James became a naturalized British citizen. He died in London on February 28, 1916.

DORIS L. EDER
Yale University

JAMES, JESSE (1847–1882)

Jesse James was one of the most notorious outlaws in the history of the American West. He was the leader of a ruthless gang that stole thousands of dollars in a series of daring robberies. James became a legend, and his deeds, some real and some invented, are part of the folklore of America. During his lifetime, James helped create the myth that he was a soft-spoken gentleman bandit who stole from the rich to give to the poor. These stories gained James sympathy with law-abiding citizens. But legend cannot change the fact that he was a thief and a killer.

Jesse Woodson James was born in Centerville (now Kearney), Missouri, on September 5, 1847. His father, a Baptist minister, died when Jesse was a boy. His mother later married Dr. Reuben Samuel. When the U.S. Civil War broke out in 1861, Missouri remained in the Union. But the Samuels sympathized with the South. When Jesse was 16 he and his older brother Frank joined a band of Confederate raiders who attacked Union forces.

After the war ended in 1865, Jesse James led a gang of bandits in daring crimes that shocked the country. The gang, which included his brother Frank, robbed banks, trains, and stagecoaches. Though a number of his men were either captured or killed, Jesse James managed to escape the law.

In 1881, James bought a house in St. Joseph, Missouri. To disguise himself he grew a beard and changed his name to Tom Howard. For a while he lived quietly with his family, which included his wife and two children. James was joined by two members of his gang, Bob and Charley Ford. Bob Ford was secretly planning to kill James for a $10,000 reward. On April 3, 1882, he was able to carry out his plan. When James removed his gun and holster and stood on a chair to dust a picture, Ford shot him in the back of the head.

Many people mourned the death of the legendary Jesse James. They sang a song about "that dirty little coward that shot Mr. Howard and laid poor Jesse in his grave."

Reviewed by DAVID ALLEN CLARK
Author, *Jesse James*

JAMES, WILLIAM (1842–1910)

William James, the great American psychologist and philosopher, was born in New York City on January 11, 1842. His father was a philosopher whose friends included Ralph Waldo Emerson and Henry David Thoreau. William's younger brother, Henry, became a famous American novelist.

William was a lively boy, full of fun and willing to try his hand at anything. Because the James family traveled a lot, William was educated partly in private schools, partly by his father, and partly by tutors in England, France, Switzerland, and Germany. For a while he hoped to become an artist, but by the time he was 19, he had decided that his real talent was not for art but for science.

James entered Harvard in 1861 to study chemistry and medicine. He was a bright and eager student. In 1865 he was chosen by his professor, the great Louis Agassiz, to go on a scientific expedition to Brazil.

James graduated from Harvard as a doctor of medicine in 1869. He returned there in a few years to teach physiology and, later, psychology. He became more and more interested in how the human mind works.

James was a great teacher and a hearty, fun-loving man. He married in 1878 and had a happy family life. His first book, *The Principles of Psychology* (1890), was a brilliant success. Then came *The Varieties of Religious Experience* (1902), which explores the ways religious experience affects human behavior.

James's philosophy is called pragmatism. The best known of his many books on the subject is *Pragmatism: A New Name for Some Old Ways of Thinking* (1907). In it, James did not try to find final answers to the stubborn problems that have troubled thinkers since the ancient Greeks. Instead he urged people to choose beliefs that would help them to lead active, successful lives. If a belief in God made people happy, James argued, it was not important whether or not God existed.

James died in his home in Chocorua, New Hampshire, on August 26, 1910.

Reviewed by HOWARD OZMON
Author, *Twelve Great Philosophers*

English colonists braved a difficult voyage in three small ships to settle Jamestown, Virginia, in 1607. Copies of the original ships can be seen in Jamestown today.

JAMESTOWN

In April, 1607, the ships *Susan Constant* (also known as the *Sarah Constant*), *Godspeed,* and *Discovery* arrived off the coast of what is now Virginia. During the stormy four-month voyage from England, several of the 120 men on board had died. The survivors searched for a safe anchorage, and on May 14 they founded Jamestown, the first successful English settlement in the New World. They had been sent by the Virginia Company of London (called the London Company). This trading company had been granted a charter by King James I. Almost half of the ship's passengers were "gentlemen," who had never worked with their hands. They were coming to search for gold and to establish a colony in Virginia, as all the land in North America then claimed by England was called. This vast area stretched from Maine to North Carolina.

The Early Years Were Difficult

The Englishmen chose to settle on a point of land up a wide river, which they promptly named the James in honor of their king. There they began to build a fort. It faced the river and was in the form of a triangle, with guns mounted at each corner. It was named James Fort. Soon houses were built around it, and the name became James Towne. In June the ships sailed back to England, leaving the settlers behind. They set to work digging for gold in the sandy soil. But there was no gold. In August, famine and disease struck. By winter's end, all but 38 or 40 of the small group were dead.

The following year Captain John Smith, one of the original settlers, took charge. He persuaded Powhatan, an important Indian chief, to give corn and meat to the desperate colonists. Smith claimed that his life had been spared from Powhatan's anger on one occasion by the chief's daughter, Pocahontas. Most important, however, Smith made the "gentlemen" stop looking for gold and begin raising crops for food. But they did not have any experience as farmers, and harvests were poor. The settlers were starving when they should have had plenty. Ships brought supplies, but never enough. And they brought more mouths to feed. Under Smith's leadership, glassworks and 20 houses were built. Settlers learned to fish, hunt, and grow corn. Then disaster struck.

Smith was wounded in a gunpowder explosion and returned to England, leaving the colony without a strong leader. Indians attacked. Disease and starvation almost wiped out Jamestown. Only about 60 settlers survived the dreadful winter of 1609–10 that came to be known as "the starving time." In May, 1610, the first governor, Sir Thomas Gates, arrived. It was decided to return to England with all Jamestown survivors, giving up the colony as a failure. They had proceeded about 14 miles (23 kilometers) down the James River when Lord De La Warr arrived with supplies and new colonists. The settlers turned back, determined to try again. Under the rough military discipline of Sir Thomas Dale, who became governor in 1611, the colonists built a bridge, dug a well, and planted gardens and field crops. Dale was a tyrant, but strong discipline was needed to keep the colony going.

A Cash Crop Saved the Colony

In 1612 a Jamestown settler, John Rolfe, began growing the West Indian weed, tobacco. His experiments were successful. At last the colony had a cash crop that would begin returning profits to the investors in England who had paid the expenses of settlement. Tobacco, not gold, was the real wealth of Virginia. Rolfe further guaranteed the colony's security by marrying Pocahontas in 1614, thus creating an alliance with the Powhatan Indians. In 1619 the first representative assembly in the New World, the House of Burgesses, met at Jamestown. New settlements sprang up along the James River. Eventually Jamestown was abandoned for healthier locations and more fertile land. But the Jamestown "gentlemen" had planted England in America, and the American wilderness had made farmers out of them.

Today part of the original Jamestown site is under the control of the Association for the Preservation of Virginia Antiquities. The rest belongs to Colonial National Historical Park, administered by the National Park Service. A short distance from the original site is Jamestown Festival Park. Features of the park include a reconstruction of James Fort, full-scale models of the ships that brought the first settlers from England, and demonstrations of Early American crafts.

MARY LEE SETTLE
Author, *O Beulah Land*

See also THIRTEEN AMERICAN COLONIES; SMITH, JOHN.

Jamestown colonist John Rolfe married Pocahontas, the daughter of an Indian chief, in 1614. The couple traveled to England, where Pocahontas died in 1617.

January

January is named after the old Roman god Janus. He was a two-faced god, with one face looking toward the past and the other toward the future.

Place in year: 1st month.
Number of days: 31.
Flower: Snowdrop.
Birthstone: Garnet.
Zodiac signs: Capricorn, the Goat (December 22–January 19), and Aquarius, the Water Bearer (January 20–February 18).

1
- **Paul Revere** born 1735
- **Betsy Ross** born 1752
- Abraham Lincoln issued the Emancipation Proclamation, 1863
- *New Year's Day*
- Independence Day in Haiti
- Independence Day in Sudan
- Founding of Republic of China in Taiwan

2
- **Pope Gregory XIII** born 1502
- Georgia ratified the Constitution, 1788

3
- **J.R.R. Tolkien** born 1892
- Alaska became the 49th state, 1959

4
- **Jacob Grimm** born 1785
- First American presidential election, 1789
- Utah became the 45th state, 1896
- Independence Day in Burma

5
- Nellie Tayloe Ross became first woman governor in U.S., Wyoming, 1925
- *George Washington Carver Day*

6
- **Saint Joan of Arc** born 1412
- **Carl Sandburg** born 1878
- New Mexico became the 47th state, 1912
- *Epiphany*

7
- **Millard Fillmore** born 1800
- Transatlantic telephone service between New York and London first began, 1927

8
- Eleventh Amendment to U.S. Constitution, modifying the Supreme Court's power, ratified, 1798
- Andrew Jackson defeated British at Battle of New Orleans, 1815
- President Wilson stated his Fourteen Points to Congress, 1918

9 • **Richard M. Nixon** born 1913

10 • Thomas Paine published *Common Sense,* 1776
• First great oil discovery in Texas, 1901
• First United Nations General Assembly met in London, 1946

11 • **Alexander Hamilton** born 1755
• **Sir John Macdonald** born 1815
• **William James** born 1842
• Independence Day in Chad

12 • Hattie Caraway of Arkansas became first woman elected to U.S. Senate, 1932

14 • **Benedict Arnold** born 1741
• **Albert Schweitzer** born 1875

15 • **Molière** born 1622
• **Gamal Abdel Nasser** born 1918
• **Martin Luther King, Jr.,** born 1929

16 • Eighteenth Amendment to U.S. Constitution, outlawing sale of alcoholic beverages, ratified, 1919

17 • **Benjamin Franklin** born 1706
• **Anne Brontë** born 1820
• **Anton Chekhov** born 1860

18 • **Daniel Webster** born 1782
• **A. A. Milne** born 1882
• Versailles Peace Conference opened, 1919

19 • **James Watt** born 1736
• **Robert E. Lee** born 1807
• **Edgar Allan Poe** born 1809
• **Sir Henry Bessemer** born 1813
• **Paul Cézanne** born 1839
• *Robert E. Lee's Birthday* (celebrated in 12 Southern states)

20 • First basketball game played, Springfield, Massachusetts, 1892
• *Inauguration Day* (every four years)

21 • **John Charles Frémont** born 1813
• **Stonewall Jackson** born 1824
• *Nautilus,* first atomic submarine, launched, 1954

22 • **Francis Bacon** born 1561
• **Lord George Gordon Byron** born 1788
• **U Thant** born 1909

23 • **John Hancock** born 1737
• **Édouard Manet** born 1832
• National holiday in Liechtenstein

24 • **Frederick the Great** born 1712
• **Edith Wharton** born 1862
• Gold discovered in California, 1848

25 • **Robert Boyle** born 1627
• **Robert Burns** born 1759
• Transcontinental telephone service established in U.S., 1915

26 • **Douglas MacArthur** born 1880
• Michigan became the 26th state, 1837
• Australia Day in Australia
• Republic Day in India

27 • **Wolfgang Amadeus Mozart** born 1756

• **Lewis Carroll** born 1832
• **Samuel Gompers** born 1850
• Canadian Great Western Railway opened, 1854
• Thomas Edison granted first patent for his incandescent light, 1880
• U.S. astronauts Grissom, White, and Chaffee killed by fire in Apollo spaceship, Cape Kennedy, Florida, 1967

28 • **Auguste Piccard** born 1884
• **Jackson Pollock** born 1912
• First commercial telephone service, New Haven, Connecticut, 1878
• Vietnam War cease-fire signed, 1973

29 • **Thomas Paine** born 1737
• **William McKinley** born 1843
• Kansas became the 34th state, 1861
• Baseball's American League formed, 1900

30 • **Franklin D. Roosevelt** born 1882
• Congress bought Thomas Jefferson's library as the basis for Library of Congress, 1815
• Adolf Hitler became Chancellor of Germany, 1933

31 • **Franz Schubert** born 1797
• **Irving Langmuir** born 1881
• **Jackie Robinson** born 1919
• First U.S. earth satellite, Explorer I, launched, 1958

Third Monday in January:
Martin Luther King's Birthday.

The calendar listing identifies people who were born on the indicated day in boldface type, **like this.** You will find a biography of each of these birthday people in *The New Book of Knowledge.* In addition to citing some historical events and historical firsts, the calendar also lists the holidays and some of the festivals celebrated in the United States. These holidays are printed in italic type, *like this.* See the article HOLIDAYS for more information.

Many holidays and festivals of nations around the world are included in the calendar as well. When the term "national holiday" is used, it means that the nation celebrates an important patriotic event on that day—in most cases the winning of independence. Consult *The New Book of Knowledge* article on the individual nation for further information on its national holiday.

JAPAN

Japan is an island nation of East Asia. It is composed of four large islands and many smaller ones, which extend in a narrow arc, northeast to southwest, for a distance of about 1,500 miles (2,400 kilometers) off the eastern coast of Asia. The four main islands are Honshu (the largest and most populous), Hokkaido, Kyushu, and Shikoku.

Japan's culture is a blend of traditional Japanese values and modern Western ideas. Japan is the world's oldest monarchy. Its emperors traced their descent from Jimmu, who, according to mythical tradition, unified Japan and became its first emperor more than 2,500 years ago. Modern Japan, however, is a constitutional monarchy. The emperor is the symbol of the nation, with little political power.

Until slightly more than a century ago, Japan, by its own choice, was almost completely isolated from the rest of the world. Reluctantly opening itself to Western countries in the mid-19th century, it adopted modern technology and quickly became an industrial and military power. Following the destruction of World War II, Japan rebuilt its economy and now ranks among the world's leading industrialized nations.

▶THE PEOPLE

The islands of Japan were probably settled by peoples migrating from the mainland of Asia. Over a period of many centuries they developed into a distinctive people, the Japanese. The Ainu, a people quite different from the Japanese, are the descendants of the earliest settlers of the islands. Only a few thousand have survived. Most Ainu now live on the northern island of Hokkaido.

Japan is largely a nation of city dwellers. The Ginza (*below*) is one of the main shopping and entertainment districts of Tokyo, Japan's capital and largest city.

The Great Buddha at Kamakura (*left*) dates from the 13th century. A Shinto priest (*right*) prepares to dedicate a shrine. Shinto and Buddhism are Japan's major religions.

Japan is one of the world's most densely populated countries. It has about half the population of the United States, but in area it is smaller than the state of California. More than 80 percent of the Japanese are city dwellers, and the number is increasing.

Religion

Shinto and Buddhism are the major religions of Japan. A very small minority of Japanese are Christians.

Shinto, meaning "the way of the gods," is a native Japanese religion. Its followers worship the forces of nature and emphasize cleanliness. Its gods, like those of ancient Greece, often personify the forces of nature. Shinto came under the influence of Buddhism, which was introduced from China. Buddhism brought a new faith and a new philosophy to Japan. Today, most Japanese see no contradiction in participating in both Shinto and Buddhist ceremonies. In fact, the typical Japanese marriage ceremony is performed according to Shinto rites, while the funeral service is Buddhist.

FACTS and figures

JAPAN is the official name of the country. Its people call it Nippon or Nihon, meaning "base of the sun."

LOCATION: Islands off the eastern coast of Asia.

AREA: 145,834 sq mi (377,708 km²).

POPULATION: 123,500,000 (estimate).

CAPITAL AND LARGEST CITY: Tokyo.

MAJOR LANGUAGE: Japanese.

MAJOR RELIGIONS: Shinto, Buddhism.

GOVERNMENT: Constitutional monarchy. **Head of state**—emperor. **Head of government**—prime minister. **Legislature**—National Diet (consisting of the House of Councillors and the House of Representatives).

CHIEF PRODUCTS: Agricultural—rice, potatoes, wheat, barley, sweet potatoes, soybeans, tangerines and other fruits, tea, raw silk, livestock. **Manufactured**—iron and steel, motor vehicles, electrical machinery, ships, chemicals, textiles, electronic equipment, high-technology products (including computers and microchips), medicines. **Mineral**—coal, copper, lead.

MONETARY UNIT: Yen.

A Japanese rock garden (*left*) gives a feeling of tranquillity. Bedding, called *futon* (*top*), is laid out at night on a *tatami*-covered floor. A traditional Japanese meal (*above*) includes a variety of dishes, which are artistically arranged to enhance the food.

Way of Life

Dwellings. A traditional Japanese house is small; it is made of wood and has a tiled roof. Most houses are surrounded by a bamboo fence or hedge. Because Japan is such a densely populated country and space is limited, Japanese gardens are small. They usually contain some shrubbery and perhaps a group of carefully arranged rocks, all designed to give a feeling of peace and quiet.

On entering a Japanese house one takes off one's shoes. The floors in the inner rooms are covered with *tatami,* or rush matting. Sliding doors made of wood and paper enclose the rooms. Ideally, the Japanese house is sparsely furnished, but because of limited space, the average house tends to be cluttered. To one side of the main room is the *tokonoma,* an alcove (a small separate area) decorated with a hanging scroll—usually a painting or a poem beautifully written with a brush. Next to the scroll is a flower arrangement of simple beauty and perhaps one or two art objects. A low, wide table is used for eating and writing. Japanese traditionally sit on *zabuton,* or cushions, instead of chairs. Bedding, called *futon,* is laid out at night on the *tatami* and put away in closets during the day.

This traditional style of living is rapidly changing, particularly in the cities. Apartment houses are replacing the small homes. Western-style furniture, electrical appliances, and modern kitchen equipment are now common in Japanese homes.

Few homes have central heating, however, even in the cities. Portable kerosene stoves provide the main source of heat. Many houses also contain a *kotatsu,* a sunken area heated by an electric coil under a table. The *kotatsu* is usually located in the main room, and when a quilt is placed over the table, family members can tuck their feet into the sunken area and sit in comfort or eat a meal, even in the cold of winter.

The Traditional Bath. Although many new homes and apartments have Western-style baths and showers, the majority of Japanese still prefer the traditional Japanese bath. The bathtub is made of wood. It is quite deep and large enough to accommodate several people. The custom is to wash oneself thoroughly with soap and water before getting into the tub to soak. For this reason, the floors of the bathrooms are built to allow water to drain. One takes a bath to relax in the hot water, not just to get clean.

Marriage. The once-usual custom of arranged marriages is rapidly changing. But even when a man and woman have independently chosen each other, they still favor a traditional marriage ceremony. A Japanese bride wears an ancient hairstyle, now usually a wig rented for the occasion. A white band is tied around the top of her hair to hide the "horns of jealousy" that every woman is believed to possess. The bride's ceremonial kimono, or robe, is black or white, with a colorful design at the hem. Her *obi* (a sash used to fasten the kimono) is tied at the back in a butterfly knot—the symbol of a young, unmarried woman. If she wears traditional dress after she is married, she will tie the *obi* in a drum knot. It is fashionable for the groom to wear Western-style attire, rather than the formal men's kimono with a pleated overskirt called *hakama*.

Dining and Etiquette. An invitation for dinner to a Japanese home is considered a great honor. Japanese etiquette, or prescribed behavior, is quite different from that of Western countries. At a family-style dinner, the dishes are placed in the center of the table and everyone reaches for the food with chopsticks. For more formal dinners, the guests are provided with individual serving trays. The plates and bowls are often purposely unmatched and are chosen to enhance the food, which is artistically arranged. A typical dinner might consist of steamed rice, pickled vegetables, and a main dish of *tempura*—fish or vegetables dipped in batter and fried in deep oil. Or the main dish might be *sukiyaki*—a combination of sliced beef or chicken with an assortment of vegetables, which is cooked at the table.

The Japanese language has many polite phrases appropriate for different social situations. It would be considered rude if a guest, or even members of the family, started to eat without first bowing and saying, "*Ita-daki-masu* [I gratefully receive this food]." After the meal is over, one bows again and says, "*Gochiso-sama* [Thank you for the delicious meal]." Formal bows are once again exchanged when the guest is ready to leave. The guest says, "*Arigato gozaimasu* [Thank you]" and "*Sayonara* [Good-bye]," and the host tells the guest repeatedly, "*Mata dozo* [Please come again]."

The Tea Ceremony. Tea is the favorite beverage of the Japanese and an ever-present part of daily life. A cup of tea is always offered to a guest. The formal tea ceremony, during which the tea is brewed and served, requires quiet concentration and the strict observance of rules. The ceremony is filled with spiritual meaning, and its correct performance was once considered one of the necessary social graces of Japanese women.

The tea ceremony (*top, right*) and the art of flower arranging, or *ikebana* (*right*), are distinctively Japanese cultural traditions. Both are centuries old and originally had religious significance.

Business Practices. The business world of Japan has become completely Westernized, although some traditional customs remain. Checks and documents are stamped with the seal of a person's name or of a company, instead of being signed. People in business exchange name cards when they first meet. Japanese surnames, or last names, come before the given name. For instance, Yukio (given name) Ogawa (surname) is addressed as Ogawa Yukio-san. (*San* is used for Mr., Mrs., and Miss.)

One's rank is strictly observed in business. At New Year's and mid-summer, gifts are sent to clients and superiors. In small offices and shops, the *soroban,* or abacus (an ancient but rapid calculating device), is used. However, most business establishments in Japan, as in the United States or Europe, have the latest electronic equipment.

Language

The Japanese language is thought to be related to Korean, Manchurian, and Mongolian, and more distantly to Finnish and Hungarian. But these connections lie in the remote past. Until the 5th or 6th century A.D., when Chinese characters were introduced, the Japanese had no writing system. Thereafter, a system was developed for writing Japanese using Chinese characters (*kanji*). Using *kanji* as a base, the Japanese devised two syllabic alphabets—*hiragana* and *katakana*. Each represents the same 47 syllables, and the alphabets are used together with *kanji* in writing modern Japanese. Children first learn *hiragana* and *katakana* and are gradually introduced to *kanji*. There are more than 60,000 *kanji,* but most people have a general knowledge of from 3,000 to 4,000 *kanji*. To simplify matters, most books and newspapers use only 1,850 *kanji*—the same number high school graduates are expected to master. There is also a method of writing Japanese—called *romaji*—using the Roman alphabet.

Japanese is traditionally written from top to bottom, beginning at the right-hand side of the page. In modern books, especially those dealing with scientific subjects, the text appears in Western style—straight across from left to right. Children do their homework with a pen or pencil. But, because the art of beautiful writing, or calligraphy, is much esteemed, they also learn to write Japanese using a brush and black ink.

Education

The Japanese place a high value on education. Modern schools began in Japan more than a century ago. After World War II, Japanese schools adopted a system similar to that of the United States. Nine years of schooling (six of primary school and three of middle school) are compulsory for Japanese children, and nearly all continue on to high school for three additional years. Higher education also resembles the four-year college system of the United States. There are more than 450 colleges and universities in Japan, as well as many specialized schools and junior colleges.

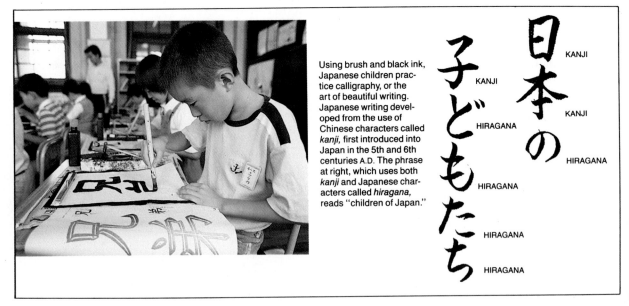

Using brush and black ink, Japanese children practice calligraphy, or the art of beautiful writing. Japanese writing developed from the use of Chinese characters called *kanji,* first introduced into Japan in the 5th and 6th centuries A.D. The phrase at right, which uses both *kanji* and Japanese characters called *hiragana,* reads "children of Japan."

日本の子どもたち

KANJI
KANJI
KANJI
HIRAGANA
HIRAGANA
HIRAGANA
HIRAGANA
HIRAGANA

Holidays and Festivals

The four seasons bring welcome changes to the nature-loving Japanese. Numerous holidays and festivals are celebrated throughout the year, honoring nature, children, and the Shinto and Buddhist religions.

New Year. By far the most important holiday is New Year's Day. At year's end people rush about paying debts and preparing for the festivities, which last a week. At midnight on December 31, the temple bells announce the passing of the old year and the arrival of the new. It is customary to eat long noodles called *soba* as the last meal of the year. Decorations of bamboo and pine, which stand for strength, devotion, and faithfulness, are placed at the front gate of each house.

On New Year's Day itself, everyone eats *mochi,* or little dumplings made of pounded boiled rice. Temples and shrines are filled with people, many dressed in colorful kimonos. New Year's Day is also one of the two occasions in the year when the gates of the emperor's palace grounds are open to the people. The emperor and empress appear on the palace balcony and greet the throngs of people who have come to wish them ''*Banzai.*'' This means ''ten thousand years'' and is their way of saying ''Long may you live.'' At home, boys fly kites, while girls play a game much like badminton.

Girls' Day. March 3 is celebrated as Girls' Day, also known as the Festival of Dolls. Because it is the time that peach blossoms are in full bloom, it is also called the Peach Festival. Young girls wear their best kimonos and visit each other to admire their dolls.

Cherry Blossom Viewing. By early April the cherry blossoms are at their peak. Although there is no formal festival as such, it is customary for families to go on picnics at this time to enjoy the flower most loved by the Japanese.

Iris Festival. Traditionally, May 5 was observed as Boys' Day or the Iris Festival. The long, bladelike leaves of the Japanese iris were placed in a boy's bath to give him a martial, or fighting, spirit. The festival is now celebrated by all children, but the symbols of courage and strength honor boys especially. Brightly colored paper or cloth carp—a fish known for its courage—are flown from tall bamboo poles that are set up in front of every home where there is a boy.

New Year's Day is Japan's most important holiday. Decorations for the holiday, which lasts a week, are purchased at a Shinto shrine (*top*) and at a shop (*above*) that specializes in "good luck" arrows. Cherry blossoms, much loved by the Japanese, are eagerly viewed (*below*) at their blooming in early April.

Kabuki actors are elaborately made up to show the characters they play. Originating in the 17th century, the Kabuki theater was more realistic and livelier than the earlier Nō drama.

Star Festival. Held on July 7, the Star Festival commemorates a romantic legend about the Princess Weaver Star, who falls in love with a cowherd star on the banks of the Heavenly River (the Milky Way) but is fated to meet him only once a year.

Feast of the Lanterns. The Buddhist Feast of the Lanterns, or *Obon,* is held on July 15 in some areas and on August 15 in others. It honors the spirits of one's ancestors, who are believed to return once a year to visit their families. During the day families visit the graves of their ancestors. In the evening the streets are decorated with brightly colored lanterns to light the way for the visiting spirits. A communal dance, the *bon odori,* is performed energetically. After the celebration the spirits are escorted to a river or lake if there is one nearby and sent off in miniature straw boats filled with food and incense.

Harvest Thanksgiving Festival. This festival is celebrated in October. Farmers express their gratitude to the Shinto gods of the harvest by offering them the first fruits of the field.

Shichi-Go-San. November 15 is a day of much excitement for girls of 7, boys of 5, and all children of 3. This festival is called Shichi-Go-San (''7–5–3''). It is a day when the children receive presents and visit shrines with their parents to pray to the Shinto gods for health and happiness.

Apart from these traditional holidays, in recent years Christmas has become popular in Japan, even though Christians are only a tiny minority. It is not unusual for young Japanese to exchange presents or to visit a department store to see a huge Christmas tree or Santa Claus on display. However, New Year's remains the customary time for Japanese families to gather for a reunion.

Entertainment and Sports

Nō and Kabuki. Entertainment in Japan is rich and varied, ranging from ancient stage dramas to the types of modern drama performed in Western countries.

In the classical theaters of Nō and Kabuki, the actors are all men, who play the roles of beautiful women, villains, and heroes. The older Nō plays are slow moving and simple in plot. Actors wear masks and move with studied gestures, which have deep symbolic meaning. In the more lively Kabuki plays there are many thrilling moments. When a popular actor makes his entrance on the ''flower walk,'' a narrow platform leading from the back of the theater to the stage, devoted fans shout words of praise and applaud him as he walks by. Kabuki actors do not wear masks. Instead, their faces are elaborately painted to show the characters they play.

Bunraku. Another ancient and popular theatrical art is *Bunraku,* a puppet play. The puppets are much larger than Western ones and are themselves works of art. Each puppet is guided by three puppet players, who are

▲ Sumo, an ancient form of wrestling, is a traditional Japanese sport. Big and heavy, a sumo wrestler depends on strength and agility to force an opponent off his feet or out of the ring.

Although an adopted sport, baseball is as popular in Japan as it is in the United States. The many professional teams include the Tokyo Giants and the Nagoya Dragons, playing here in a Tokyo stadium. ▼

dressed entirely in black so as to remain unseen by the audience. The master player controls the head and right hand; a senior assistant, the left hand; and a junior assistant, the body and legs. As the puppets dance, laugh, cry, and do battle, they look almost human.

Geishas. Geishas provide yet another form of entertainment, mainly for men. A geisha is a female entertainer who has been trained from her youth to move and speak with grace. She also learns to sing, dance, and play musical instruments—all of the traditional kind—and to become expert in the art of flower arrangement and the tea ceremony. Geishas are expected to dress with taste and elegance. Hiring geishas for an evening's entertainment can be very expensive and is usually reserved for business affairs.

Movies. Movies and television are the chief sources of popular entertainment today. Japanese have won awards at international film festivals for pictures such as *Rashomon* and *Gate of Hell*. Other acclaimed Japanese films are *The Seven Samurai* and *Ran*. Young Japanese are also fond of American movies, jazz, and rock music.

Sports. Japan is a sports-minded nation. Baseball, tennis, golf, and skiing are all popular. Indeed, baseball is almost the national sport, and professional and amateur teams are followed with wild enthusiasm. One traditional Japanese sport is sumo, an ancient form

of wrestling. Sumo wrestlers are generally very big and heavy. A wrestler's hair is tied up in a coiled knot on top of his head. He wears a type of loincloth so that the audience can see every muscle in his body. The match is lost by the wrestler who first steps outside the ring or touches the ground with anything but the soles of his feet. Two other traditional sports are karate and judo, which are also useful for self-defense. In karate, one uses the hand, either open or closed; the elbows; and the feet. In judo, the student is trained to use the movements of an opponent to achieve the momentum needed for a throw.

Mount Fuji, Japan's highest mountain, is located on Honshu. An inactive volcano, its graceful and perfectly shaped form has long inspired Japanese poets and artists.

▶THE LAND

About two hundred million years ago the continental shelf of the Asian mainland rose up to form a long crest of islands, of which Japan is a part. The islands are actually the peaks of submerged mountain ranges. Like all the lands along the rim of the Pacific Ocean, Japan has many active volcanoes and frequent earthquakes. Most earthquakes are minor and cause little or no damage, but some have been violently destructive. The worst earthquake in Japan's history struck the area around Tokyo, the capital, in 1923, resulting in the deaths of thousands of people.

The major bodies of water surrounding Japan are the Pacific Ocean in the east, the Philippine and East China seas in the south, and the Sea of Japan in the west. Japan faces three nations on the Asian mainland: China, Korea, and the Russian Federation.

Mountains and Forests. Almost 75 percent of Japan's land is mountainous, and about two thirds of it is forested. Japan's most famous mountain and the highest in elevation, Mount Fuji, rises to 12,388 feet (3,776 meters). Located on the island of Honshu, Fuji is a dormant (inactive) volcano, which the Japanese regard as sacred. Its graceful, snowcapped form has long inspired poets and artists.

Rivers. Japan has no long rivers. The largest river, the Shinano, has a length of only about 230 miles (370 kilometers). Most of the others are too short and swift-flowing to be suitable for transportation. They are, however, important as sources of hydroelectric power.

The Inland Sea. The Inland Sea, a picturesque waterway dotted with about 700 islets, is partly enclosed by the islands of Honshu, Shikoku, and Kiyushu. Ships and fishing boats travel between its coastal ports. The beauty of the sea has been depicted in traditional Japanese paintings.

Climate. The country's climate is affected by two ocean currents. The warm Japan Current flows northward from the Philippines along Japan's eastern, or Pacific, coast. This area, as a result, has a milder climate than the western, or Sea of Japan, coast. The cold Oyashio Current originates in the Bering Sea off the coast of Siberia. It flows southward along the eastern coast of Hokkaido, producing a much cooler climate in this region.

Japan has abundant rainfall, ranging from about 40 to 100 inches (1,000 to 2,500 millimeters) annually. Because of this, much of Japan is covered with green foliage. The year falls into four distinct seasons—pleasant springs; generally hot and humid summers; clear, bright autumns; and cool to cold winters, with frequent snowfall in some areas.

Mineral Resources. Japan does not have an abundance of mineral resources. It has many kinds of minerals, but except for some coal, copper, and lead, none exist in any quantity.

The Main Islands

Although Japan comprises thousands of islands, most of them are quite small. The four main islands make up almost all of Japan's land area and are home to virtually all of its people.

Honshu. This largest and most populous of the four main islands has about 60 percent of Japan's total land area. It contains many of the largest cities and has about 80 percent of the country's population. The Kanto Plain, situated in the eastern part of the island, is a major agricultural and industrial region and the site of the capital, Tokyo. Other chief cities of Honshu are Yokohama, Osaka, Nagoya, and Kyoto. Lake Biwa, Japan's largest lake, is located near Kyoto.

Hokkaido. The northernmost island, Hokkaido is second largest in area but only third in population. It is a rugged land, without the quiet beauty of the other islands. Because of its climate—cold and bleak for much of the year with heavy snowfall—Hokkaido was, until about a century ago, regarded as an outpost. It now has large cities and flourishing industries. It is a popular resort area for winter sports. The chief city is Sapporo.

Kyushu. The most southerly of the main islands, Kyushu is second in population after Honshu and third in area after Hokkaido. Because of its relatively small size, it is the most densely populated of the islands. Its major cities include Fukuoka, Kitakyushu, and Nagasaki.

Shikoku. Shikoku is the smallest of the main islands, both in area and population. Until the recent completion of a bridge linking it to Hiroshima on the island of Honshu, Shikoku was fairly isolated from the rest of the country. Its largest city is Matsuyama.

Other islands of importance are the Ryukyus and Bonins. The Ryukyus are a chain of more than 100 mountainous islands situated south of Kyushu. Okinawa is the largest and most important of the Ryukyus. The lightly populated Bonins lie about 600 miles (970 kilometers) southeast of the main islands.

Hokkaido is Japan's northernmost island and the second largest in area. A rugged land, its climate is cold and snowy for much of the year. The heavy snowfall makes Hokkaido a popular area for winter sports.

Rice fields on Honshu are terraced in order to cultivate as much of the land as possible. Honshu is the largest and most heavily populated of Japan's islands, with about 60 percent of its total area.

Once a small village called Edo, Tokyo is now one of the world's largest cities. The building housing the National Diet, or legislature, is in the foreground.

▶MAJOR CITIES

The Japanese are chiefly a nation of city dwellers. Cities are scattered throughout the islands, although most of the largest are on Honshu. Eleven Japanese cities have populations of 1,000,000 or more, and several others are approaching this figure.

Tokyo. Tokyo, the capital, is one of the world's largest cities. Formerly called Edo, it was renamed when it became the imperial capital in 1868. It was given the name Tokyo (''eastern capital'') to distinguish it from the former capital, Kyoto, in western Honshu. Tokyo is not only the center of government, but of industry, commerce, finance, and education as well. The city is described in greater detail in the article TOKYO in Volume T.

Yokohama. Located just south of Tokyo, Yokohama is Japan's second largest city and its largest port. It is a center of heavy industry, including steelmaking, shipbuilding, and the manufacture of trucks and other motor vehicles. Originally a small fishing village, Yokohama grew rapidly after it was opened to foreign trade in 1858. The city was heavily damaged by bombing in World War II but has been rebuilt with wide boulevards and modern buildings.

Osaka. Situated on Osaka Bay, the eastern arm of the Inland Sea, Osaka is one of Japan's leading seaports, along with Yokohama and Kobe. Often likened to the U.S. city of Chicago, Osaka is one of Japan's most industrialized cities. It is the subject of a separate article in Volume O.

Kyoto. Kyoto was the capital of Japan for more than 1,000 years, until the seat of government was moved to Tokyo in 1868. The city is still the center of religion and of traditional Japanese arts. Kyoto and its places of interest are described further in Volume J-K.

Nagoya. Nagoya is situated almost in the center of Honshu. Located on Ise Bay, it has an excellent harbor. It is the heart of Japan's automobile industry and is also noted for its fine pottery, porcelain, and enamelware.

Sapporo. The capital of Hokkaido, Sapporo is a rapidly growing city. Its major industries include food processing, machinery repair, printing, construction, and mining. It was host to the 1972 Winter Olympic Games.

Kobe. Located in western Honshu on Osaka Bay, across from the city of Osaka, Kobe is Japan's second most important seaport. It is an industrial city as well, producing ships, iron and steel, and textiles.

Other cities with populations of at least 1,000,000 are Kitakyushu, an urban-industrial complex created in 1963 from the merger of five cities; and Fukuoka (both on Kyushu); and Kawasaki and Hiroshima (both on Honshu). Hiroshima is perhaps best known internationally because of its devastation by an atomic bomb in 1945, during World War II.

▶ THE ECONOMY

In the middle of the 19th century, Japan was still a predominantly agricultural country. Within two generations, the Japanese, by a combination of government leadership and private enterprise, created an industrial and commercial power of international importance. Despite the enormous destruction of World War II, Japan quickly rebuilt its economy. Although the country remained in a prolonged recession that began in the late 1980's, by the turn of the century its productive capacity was still exceeded by only one other nation in the world, the United States.

Agriculture

Because so much of Japan is mountainous and forested, only about 15 percent of its total land area can be used for farming. Every bit of usable land is valuable, and Japanese farmers grow crops on plots of land that often seem too small or too steep to be cultivated. Even

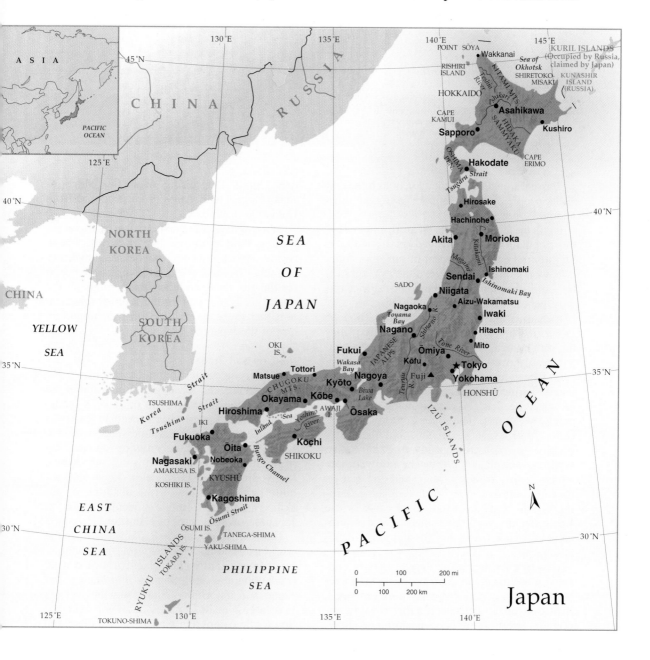

Much of the work of rice farming is now done by machine, but the planting and transplanting (*above*) must still be done by hand. Japanese fleets harvest fish (*right*) in home waters and around the world.

so, Japan is unable to produce enough to feed all its people and must import large quantities of some foods.

Until the end of World War II, about half the population was engaged in agriculture. Slightly more than 5 percent of the labor force now works on the land. Nevertheless, agriculture still plays an important role in the economy, especially the cultivation of rice.

Rice Farming. Rice is the staple food of Japan. In fact, the term for "boiled rice" has the same meaning as "meal." Small, neat patches of green rice paddies dot the countryside. The rice paddies are built on different levels. Farmers use dikes to control the flow of water needed for rice growing from one paddy to another. The highest paddy collects water from a nearby stream, and the water trickles downhill from paddy to paddy. Rice seedlings are planted during the rainy season, which begins in early June, and the rice is harvested in September. Although some farming is still done by hand, most farmers use small tractors and other mechanized equipment especially designed for the small Japanese farms.

Livestock Raising. The Japanese now consume more meat and dairy products than ever before, and as eating habits have changed, livestock raising has become increasingly important. Shortage of good pastureland, how-

ever, limits the raising of cattle. Much of Japan's meat and dairy products come from Hokkaido or abroad.

Other Agricultural Products. After rice, the leading food crops include potatoes, wheat, barley, sweet potatoes, soybeans, tangerines and other fruits, and tea. Silkworms are raised for the silk they produce. Japan grows all the rice it needs, but among the foods it must import are soybeans, which form an important part of the Japanese diet.

Industry and Trade

Industry accounts for much of Japan's national income and for a large proportion of the country's jobs. The growth of Japan's industry, and manufacturing in particular, has been a key element in its economic success. Today Japan's industries face growing competition from other countries such as South Korea. Many products once made in Japan that require large quantities of raw materials or unskilled workers are now being made in Japanese-owned factories elsewhere in Asia.

Manufacturing. Japan remains among the world leaders in several categories of manufactured goods. Shipbuilding and iron and steel production are declining in importance, but Japan and the United States are the world's two largest manufacturers of motor vehicles. Some other important Japanese manufactured

Industry is the mainstay of the Japanese economy. Among its leading manufactures are steel (*left*) and a wide variety of high-technology products, including integrated circuit chips.

products include electrical machinery, chemicals, textiles, television sets, cameras, and videocassette recorders. Japan is a major manufacturer of such high-technology products as computers, microchips, and electron microscopes. It is also moving rapidly to leadership in the field of biotechnology, which involves the design and manufacture of artificial body parts and the creation, in the laboratory, of new genetic materials and methods of fighting disease.

Fishing.   Japan is one of the world's foremost fishing nations. Fish and shellfish are a basic food of the Japanese, and one of the first impressions a newcomer has of the country is the smell of fish in marketplaces, at small fish stalls, and even in the food sections of modern department stores. The waters surrounding Japan are rich in a variety of fish, including sardines, mackerel, and yellowfin tuna. Octopus, cuttlefish, and eels are other delicacies. Seaweed is also harvested for food. Japanese fishing fleets also regularly travel the waters of the world, with factory ships equipped to process the catch at sea.

Cultured Pearls.   The cultured-pearl industry is distinctive to Japan. In the late 19th century the Japanese Mikimoto Kokichi created the modern cultured-pearl industry when he devised a practical method of producing pearls artificially by injecting an irritant into the oyster. Some of the largest pearl farms are located at Pearl Island in Ago Bay, where the water temperature and other conditions are ideal for the oysters.

Foreign Trade.   Japan is by necessity a trading nation. In addition to much of its food, it must import almost all the raw materials needed for industry because it has so few mineral resources of its own. In return, Japan exports manufactured products around the world. Its chief exports, by category, are machinery, transportation equipment, chemicals, scientific and optical equipment, metals and metal products, and textiles.

Japan exports many more manufactured goods than it imports, a fact that has often been criticized by such trading partners as the United States. Its recent economic problems contributed to the recession that engulfed much of Asia in the late 1990's.

Energy

The country's major energy sources are water power, imported petroleum and natural gas, and nuclear energy. Production of coal has declined steadily, and many Japanese mines have been closed. Traditionally, wood charcoal was an important item of everyday life, but gas and kerosene are now commonly used as fuel in homes. Nuclear energy now supplies about 12 percent of Japan's electric power.

▶GOVERNMENT

Japan is governed under a constitution that went into effect in 1947. The lawmaking body is the National Diet, which is composed of two houses, the House of Representatives and the House of Councillors. The House of Representatives, made up of 500 members, is elected for a term of four years. The House of Councillors, made up of 252 members, is elected for six years, with one half of its membership elected every three years.

The head of government is the prime minister, who is chosen by the Diet. The prime minister, in turn, appoints the other ministers of the cabinet, all of whom are responsible to the Diet. The Liberal-Democratic Party (LDP), a conservative political party, governed Japan from its founding in 1955 until 1993, when it fell from power after a series of scandals and charges of corruption. Three prime ministers (including Japan's first Socialist leader since 1946) successively led opposition coalition governments before the LDP regained the prime ministership in 1996.

The emperor, who formerly held great power, now serves as the symbolic head of state under the present constitution. He now has only ceremonial duties.

The judicial branch of the government consists of the various courts, headed by the Supreme Court, which has a chief justice and 14 other justices.

Japan is divided into 47 prefectures, each of which is administered by an elected governor.

▶HISTORY

Japan's geographical location has played an important role in its history. Japan lies close enough to the mainland of Asia to have been strongly influenced by China. At the same time, the waters surrounding the Japanese islands long served as a barrier against invasion. After the first migrations of peoples from the mainland in the far distant past, Japan successfully resisted attempts at invasion until its defeat in World War II. This water barrier also encouraged the isolation that marks periods of Japanese history.

Legend of the Sun Goddess. The Japanese call their country Nippon or Nihon. It means "base of the sun," suggesting that Japan, the easternmost country of Asia, is the land where the sun rises. The national flag depicts the sun —a red ball—against a white background.

The Japanese emperors traced their ancestry to a sun goddess, who in turn was descended from the god Izanagi. A myth tells how the Japanese islands were created:

One day long, long ago the heavenly being Izanagi dipped his jeweled spear into the deep waters, and the shining crystal drops that scattered formed the islands of Japan. Izanagi had made the sun goddess, Amaterasu, the ruler of the heavenly kingdom. She loved the beautiful islands that sparkled in the blue waters below and proclaimed that they should always be ruled by her descendants. "You, my grandson," she told Prince Ninigi, "go, and govern these islands, and may the prosperity of the imperial house be as everlasting as that of heaven and earth." The prince descended over the floating bridge of heaven to the Japanese islands.

For many hundreds of years the legend of the Sun Goddess was accepted as history by the Japanese. The goddess is worshiped at the Grand Shrine of Ise, in western Honshu. It is the most important Shinto shrine in Japan and is also the family shrine of the emperor.

According to the 8th-century *Kojiki* ("Record of Ancient Matters"), which is Japan's earliest written history, Jimmu, the great-grandson of Prince Ninigi, became Japan's first emperor in 660 B.C. This document also stated that all succeeding emperors were to be regarded as sons of heaven—an idea that originated in China. The mythical origins of the imperial family have since been rejected by the Japanese, and the emperor is no longer looked upon as divine. However, the emperor and his family are still regarded with affection and respect by most Japanese, especially those of the older generation.

Early Settlers. The earliest settlers of Japan about whom much is known were the Jomon people, who came from the Asian mainland. They fashioned pottery, used tools and weapons made of stone, and lived by hunting, fishing, and gathering nuts and fruits. They lived in Japan from about 8000 B.C. to 300 B.C.

They were followed by waves of new settlers, who migrated to Japan from northeastern Asia by way of the Korean peninsula. They landed in Kyushu and pushed northward. It is these new settlers, in the main, who are considered the ancestors of the Japanese. Some of the Jomon people were killed. Some mingled with the new immigrants, while others fled to the northernmost island. It is thought that the

Ainu are in part the descendants of the Jomon people.

Ainu Customs. The customs of the Ainu were quite different from those of the Japanese. Their chief deity (a god or goddess) was the goddess of fire. The bear held an important place in Ainu customs. A cub was raised, sacrificed, and eaten with great ceremony in a religious ritual. This feast of thanksgiving, called the Bear Festival, was held to bid farewell to the god of the mountains, who was said to visit the earth in bearskins and bring gifts of bear meat for the people.

The Yamato State: Chinese Influence. The new settlers in Japan were organized in clans, or large social groups related through a common ancestor. Gradually, regional states were formed. One of these, known as the Yamato state, unified Japan politically sometime in the 4th or 5th century A.D. Its leader became the emperor, and its gods became the gods of Japan.

Japan first came under the influence of China in the 3rd or 4th century A.D. The development of the Yamato state would have been very different without the influence of this powerful, highly civilized neighbor. China at the time had a written language, a sophisticated tradition of philosophy and literature, the Buddhist religion, and an advanced system of bureaucratic government. Between the 6th and 7th centuries these Chinese elements began to enter Japan in increasing volume. The Japanese adopted the Chinese writing system. They learned Chinese arts and crafts, including how to cast bronze and make fine pottery and porcelain, and how to grow tea, raise silkworms, and weave silk. Buddhism, too, was adopted by the Japanese, and while it did not replace Shinto, it soon became the major religion. The first capital, built in 710 at Nara on Honshu, was designed in the Chinese style.

Fujiwara Rule. From the end of the 8th until the 12th century, Japan was governed by the imperial and other aristocratic clans. Only those born within these clans could hold offices at the emperor's court. The most important clan was the Fujiwara, who held the highest offices. Fujiwara daughters became the wives of emperors. The emperors themselves often ruled only as ceremonial figureheads, while the Fujiwara held real power.

During the centuries of Fujiwara rule, life in the countryside was backward. The people were poor and heavily taxed. In contrast, Kyoto, which had become the new capital in 794, was filled with magnificent palaces and temples. Masterpieces of painting, sculpture, and literature were created by the Kyoto nobility. The noblemen wrote in Chinese. However, it was the women, writing in Japanese, who created the classics that are still read today. One, *The Tale of Genji,* is the story of the life and loves of Genji, the "shining prince." Another, *The Pillow Book,* is filled with descriptions, often amusing, of the court.

For more information on Japanese art, architecture, and literature, see the separate articles following this article.

Samurai. While aristocratic life flourished in Kyoto, new forces were emerging in more distant regions of Japan. To maintain law and order and to protect their rice fields, a new class of mounted warriors arose. They were called *samurai,* which means "those who serve." The samurai fought with bows and arrows and with swords. They were very much like the European knights of the Middle Ages. At first these warriors held only local power in the countryside, where they co-operated with governors sent out from the imperial court. But eventually the samurai became

The Ainu are believed to be descended from the earliest known inhabitants of Japan. Now few in number, they live on the northern island of Hokkaido.

Minamoto Yoritomo (*above*) founded the first shogunate, or military government, in Japan at Kamakura in the late 12th century. A *samurai* (*left*) was a mounted warrior similar to a European knight of the Middle Ages.

more powerful, and from the 12th to the 19th century, they were the rulers of Japan.

Kamakura Rulers: The First Shoguns. The first military government was established in Kamakura in eastern Honshu in 1185. Its founder took the title of ''Barbarian-Conquering-General''—whose shortened form in Japanese is *shogun*. He claimed to be merely the military ruler, while the emperor ruled over the civil government in Kyoto. But, in fact, he gradually gathered all power into his own hands and those of his samurai followers, leaving the emperor more powerless than ever.

The ''Divine Wind.'' During the 13th century, the Mongol emperor of China, Kublai Khan, sent emissaries to Japan with the demand that it submit to his rule. The shogun in Kamakura ignored the demand and beheaded the emissaries. Kublai Khan was so angered that he sent thousands of ships to invade Japan. The first attack was inconclusive, but during the second, a great storm appeared that destroyed many of the enemy ships. The rest of the ships were forced to retreat. The Japanese

called this storm *kamikaze*, or ''divine wind,'' in the belief that it had saved them from foreign invasion.

Kyoto Shogunate: The Ashikaga. The second period of military rule began in the early 14th century. The samurai had become so numerous and so overly ambitious that the rulers in Kamakura could no longer control them. After rebellions broke out, a new military government took power, headed by the Ashikaga clan. The new shogun settled in Kyoto, where he built himself a magnificent palace. Although the emperor still resided in Kyoto, a separate civil government no longer existed, except on paper.

The Ashikaga shoguns built great temples and gardens, which still can be seen today. Several, like the Silver Pavilion, are national treasures. It was the great age of Zen Buddhism. The Ashikaga were patrons of monasteries and of painters, poets, and writers.

The Dark Age. As Ashikaga rule began to decline in the middle of the 15th century, Japan was plunged into a dark age of constant warfare, which was to last for nearly a century. Feudal lords, called *daimyo,* each with his fortified castle and army of samurai, arose in every part of Japan. Hundreds of such daimyo competed for power, drafting foot soldiers from among the peasants to enlarge their armies.

The First Europeans. Just at this time the first Europeans arrived in Japan. In 1543 three Portuguese traders who had been sailing along the China coast were blown out to sea and eventually landed on an island south of Kyushu. They were treated hospitably. Their firearms, in particular, aroused much excitement among the samurai, who quickly copied them and used them to advantage in their wars.

News of the coming of the foreigners and of their unusual possessions spread throughout the country. The Portuguese themselves, on hearing of the discovery of Japan, at once fitted out expeditions to trade in this new market. Within a few years the traders were followed by missionaries. Other foreign expeditions also made their way to the Japanese islands. During the short but successful mission of the Spanish Jesuit Saint Francis Xavier, the first Christian church was built in Japan, and hundreds of Japanese were converted to the Roman Catholic religion.

Three Leaders of the 16th Century. Three men—Oda Nobunaga, Toyotomi Hideyoshi, and Tokugawa Ieyasu—were destined to play important roles in the history of 16th-century Japan. A well-known story compares the characters of the three.

Nobunaga says: "Nightingale, if you do not sing, I shall kill you."
Hideyoshi says: "Nightingale, if you do not sing, I shall make you."
Ieyasu says: "Nightingale, if you do not sing now, I shall wait until you do."

Oda Nobunaga was the first to gain power. After ousting the weakened Ashikaga shogun from Kyoto, he eliminated all of his rivals, successfully using the new firearms in a decisive battle. But the ruthless Nobunaga was not popular. In 1582, after a brief rule of nine years, he was killed by one of his own men. He was succeeded by Hideyoshi.

Many stories are told about Hideyoshi. Beginning as a common soldier, who could neither read nor write, he became Japan's greatest warrior. He was an ugly man—his nickname

as a child had been *Kozaru,* or "Little Monkey." After several years at a monastery, to which his despairing parents had sent him, he entered the service of a daimyo. He then joined Nobunaga's army, where he quickly rose to become his chief general.

By 1590, Hideyoshi had brought all of Japan under his control. But the arrogant and boastful warrior had an even greater ambition: He dreamed of conquering China. The armies he sent to the mainland, however, suffered severe losses in Korea, and they were withdrawn soon after Hideyoshi's death in 1598.

Tokugawa Ieyasu was a clever politician as well as a brilliant general. He was known for his patience and his sense of justice. After defeating all of his opponents in battle in 1600, he established a military government that lasted until the middle of the 19th century. Under the Tokugawa shoguns, Japan enjoyed two and a half centuries of peace.

The Tokugawa Shogunate. Following the example of the first Kamakura shogun, Tokugawa Ieyasu established his shogunate, or military government, in eastern Japan, at Edo (the future Tokyo). Originally a small village, within a century it was to grow into a city of a million inhabitants.

Ieyasu took direct control of one third of Japan, settling his own soldiers in Edo. The rest of the land he distributed to other lords, especially favoring those who had proved their loyalty to him in battle. Those he trusted most were settled, along with their thousands of

Ieyasu, founder of the Tokugawa shogunate, established his government at Edo (the future Tokyo) in 1600. The Tokugawa shoguns ruled Japan until 1868.

The arrival in Japan in 1853 of four U.S. warships under Commodore Matthew C. Perry led to the opening of Japan to trade with Western nations.

samurai, on lands bordering his own. Those he least trusted were sent to distant regions in Kyushu or Shikoku. Ieyasu also formed a council of the most trustworthy lords as his advisers. When later shoguns were too young or too weak to rule effectively, the council took over and governed Japan.

Some Important Events Under the Tokugawa. In the 1630's, under the third shogun, Christianity was banned in Japan. Fearing that the Japanese lords who had converted to Christianity would not remain loyal to his government, the shogun ordered all foreigners to leave Japan and all Christian converts to give up their new religion. Anyone who refused to obey the order was sentenced to death. Many Japanese did renounce Christianity, but others died for their faith.

Beginning in the mid-17th century, not only were foreigners forbidden to enter Japan, the Japanese themselves were forbidden to travel outside the country. Any who did so were liable to execution on returning. The reason for this harsh law, like the one banning Christianity, was to ensure the security of Japan. The one exception to the order against foreigners was in the port city of Nagasaki on Kyushu, far from the capital at Edo, where a handful of Dutch, Chinese, and Korean merchants were permitted to trade. For two centuries, Nagasaki remained Japan's only outlet to the rest of the world, through which a few books on Western science entered.

Commerce grew within Japan as peace and a more stable society brought economic expansion. Art, literature, and drama reached new heights of expression. The Kabuki play —more realistic than the earlier Nō drama— became popular among the emerging middle classes in the cities. While some literature was serious and dealt with heroes and military virtue, most city people preferred romances and comic sketches of ordinary folk.

The function of the samurai changed. After many years of peace, they became a class of hereditary government officials rather than warriors. Although they still wore swords and trained in the military arts, education and learning had now become more important.

Arrival of Perry: Fall of the Tokugawa. In 1853, Commodore Matthew C. Perry of the United States Navy arrived in Japan with four warships. He carried a letter from U.S. President Millard C. Fillmore, requesting Japan to open its ports to trade and to give better treatment to American sailors shipwrecked on Japanese shores. Perry returned the following year with additional ships. The Tokugawa government, aware that China had been defeated by the British in the Opium War of 1841 and fearful of the guns of Perry's warships, agreed to his demands for a treaty. The Treaty of Kanagawa granted the United States trading rights at two ports and permitted an American diplomat to reside in the country. A more extensive commercial treaty was signed in 1858. Japan signed similar treaties with other Western nations. These outside contacts upset the political balance within Japan. In 1868 the Tokugawa shogunate was overthrown and a new government took its place.

Modernization of Japan: Meiji Period. In theory the new government was a return to power by the emperor, who left Kyoto and settled in Edo, which was renamed Tokyo. The period in Japanese history that followed is known as the Meiji Period, after the Emperor Mutsuhito (1852–1912), who took the name Meiji, meaning ''Enlightened Rule.'' In practice,

During the reign of the Emperor Meiji (1852–1912), Japan became a modern, industrialized nation. Japan's virtual destruction of a Russian fleet at the Battle of Tsushima Strait (*below*) in the Russo-Japanese War (1904–05) made the nation a military power as well.

however, the new government was controlled by a very capable and tough-minded group of young samurai, who were determined to make Japan a strong, modern nation, on the model of Western nations.

They built railroads, factories, and dockyards, laid telegraph lines, and established banks—all that was necessary, in fact, to the economy of a modern nation of the time. They also created a new army and navy, equipped with the latest weapons and powerful warships. With these Japan defeated China in the Sino-Japanese War (1894–95) and Russia in the Russo-Japanese War (1904–05), thus establishing itself in the eyes of the world as a power to be taken seriously.

More important, Japan's leaders created a new school system and modern universities. By about 1900, nearly all Japanese, rich and poor, could read and write. Young people were also sent abroad to study, and foreigners were invited to Japan to advise the government. In 1889 a constitution was proclaimed. It was not fully democratic, but it did provide for elections. Political parties were gradually formed, and the people began to have a voice in the government.

Imperial Expansion. As a result of its victories over China and Russia, Japan acquired Taiwan, southern Sakhalin Island, and the Liaotung Peninsula on the Chinese mainland. It gained a foothold in China's northern region

IMPORTANT DATES
IN JAPANESE HISTORY

538?	Buddhism was introduced to Japan from China.
607	First Japanese envoy was sent to China.
645	Taika reform: Japan adopted the legal codes and administrative structure of China.
710	The first permanent capital, modeled after the capital of China, was founded at Nara.
712	The first written history of Japan, the *Kojiki*, was set down.
794	The imperial capital was moved to Kyoto.
857–1160	The Fujiwara family, first of the powerful clans, ruled Japan. A refined culture flourished in the capital city of Kyoto.
1008	*The Tale of Genji*, one of Japan's greatest literary works, was written by Lady Murasaki.
1156	A military clan first entered Kyoto.
1185	Another clan set up a military government in Kamakura more powerful than the Kyoto court.
1274	Japan fought off Kublai Khan's first invasion.
1281	A storm at sea (*kamikaze*, or ''divine wind'') saved Japan from Kublai Khan's second attempt at invasion.
1338	The Ashikaga clan began its rule of Japan—a golden age of arts and letters developed.
1469–1568	Era of constant wars.
1543	Japan had its first contact with the West when Portuguese traders landed on an island off Kyushu. They introduced firearms to Japan.
1549	Saint Francis Xavier introduced Christianity.
1590	Toyotomi Hideyoshi unified Japan.
1603	Tokugawa Ieyasu made Edo (now Tokyo) his military capital, establishing the Tokugawa shogunate.
1630's	Most foreigners were ordered to leave Japan; Christianity was banned.
1853	Commodore Matthew C. Perry arrived in Japan with four warships and a letter from U.S. President Millard Fillmore.
1854	Perry returned with a larger fleet. The Treaty of Kanagawa was signed.
1858	Japan signed commercial treaties with the United States, Britain, Russia, the Netherlands, and France.
1868	Meiji Restoration: the Tokugawa shogunate surrendered its powers to Emperor Meiji.
1881	Japan's first political party was organized.
1895	Japan acquired Taiwan and other Chinese territories in the first Sino-Japanese War.
1905	Japan defeated Russia in the Russo-Japanese War and gained recognition as a world power.
1910	Japan annexed Korea.
1914–1918	Japan sided with the Allies in World War I.
1923	A severe earthquake struck Tokyo and Yokohama, killing some 140,000 people.
1931–1932	Japan occupied Manchuria, which became the puppet state of Manchukuo.
1937	Japan invaded North China.
1940	Japan allied itself with Germany and Italy.
1941	Japan attacked Pearl Harbor, Hawaii, bringing the United States into World War II.
1945	The United States dropped atomic bombs on Hiroshima and Nagasaki. Japan surrendered.
1956	Japan was admitted to the United Nations.
1964	Summer Olympic Games were held in Tokyo.
1971	United States and Japan signed a treaty restoring Japanese sovereignty to Okinawa.
1988	First trains passed through the Seikan Tunnel, the longest tunnel in the world.
1989	Emperor Hirohito died; Crown Prince Akihito ascended the throne.
1993	The Liberal-Democratic Party, which had governed Japan since 1955, fell from power.
1995	The most destructive earthquake since the 1923 Tokyo disaster destroyed parts of Kobe and killed more than 5,000 people.
1996	The Liberal-Democratic Party regained power.
1998	The Akashi Kaikyo bridge, the world's longest suspension bridge, opened.

of Manchuria and control of Korea, which it formally annexed in 1910. Like the Western powers on which it had modeled itself, Japan had become not only a highly industrialized nation, but one with imperialist ambitions and colonies of its own.

During World War I (1914–18), Japan sided with the Allied Powers, which included Britain, France, and, from 1917, the United States. Although Japan saw little fighting, it won additional territory in China as well as island colonies in the Pacific. These had formerly belonged to Germany, the defeated leader of the Central Powers.

Rise of the Militarists. The decade following the end of the war was a period of prosperity and relative political freedom for Japan. In the late 1920's and early 1930's, however, a time of growing worldwide economic depression, military extremists began to exert growing pressure on the government. In 1931, Japanese military officers in Manchuria used the pretext of a bombing by Chinese of a Japanese-owned railroad (the Mukden Incident) to occupy all of Manchuria, which became a puppet state of Japan. Soon after, the civilian government of Japan was replaced by one dominated by military leaders. In 1937, following a clash between Chinese and Japanese troops at the Marco Polo Bridge near Peking, Japan began a full-scale invasion of China. By 1938, Japanese forces had gained control of the eastern part of the country.

World War II. World War II began in Europe with Germany's invasion of Poland in 1939. In 1940, Japan formed an alliance with Germany and Italy as one of the Axis Powers.

Japan's policy of expansion in Asia led to increasing tension with the United States. When Japanese troops moved into French Indochina (now Vietnam, Laos, and Cambodia) in 1940–41, the United States cut off all trade with Japan. On December 7, 1941, the Japanese navy launched a surprise attack against the U.S. naval and military bases at Pearl Harbor in Hawaii. The attack brought the United States into the war against Japan and Germany on the side of the Allies. In the early stages of the war in Asia, the Japanese won dramatic victories, quickly occupying Malaya (now Malaysia), Singapore, the Netherlands East Indies (now Indonesia), Burma (Myanmar), the Philippines, and many of the islands in the Pacific.

Defeat of Japan. Eventually the superior economic strength of the United States and its increasing military and naval power began to tell. The Japanese forces were slowly pushed back from their initial territorial gains, until, by 1945, they were fighting for the survival of their own home islands. Japan had suffered millions of battlefield casualties, the collapse of its economy, and the devastation of many of its cities by bombing. When Japan's leaders ignored calls for surrender, U.S. President Harry S. Truman reluctantly ordered the dropping of the newly developed atomic bomb. The bomb, dropped on Hiroshima on August 6, 1945, killed or injured more than half the city's population. Two days later, the Soviet Union declared war on Japan and sent its troops into Manchuria. A second atomic bomb was dropped on Nagasaki on August 9.

On August 14, 1945, the Emperor Hirohito announced the surrender of Japan. The official surrender document was signed on board the battleship USS *Missouri,* anchored in Tokyo Bay, on September 2, 1945.

For more information on World War II, including the origins of the war, see the article WORLD WAR II in Volume W-X-Y-Z.

Postwar Period: A Changing Society. An Allied army, under U.S. General Douglas MacArthur and composed mainly of American forces, remained in Japan until 1952. Under MacArthur's administration, political, social, and economic reforms were introduced that greatly changed Japanese society.

A new, democratic constitution was adopted, ensuring political equality. Women were permitted to vote and to own property for the first time. Japan renounced war forever. The large industrial complexes, controlled by a few wealthy families, called *zaibatsu,* who had contributed to Japan's military expansion, were broken up. Land was distributed among the farmers who worked it. Schools were reorganized and textbooks were rewritten to give more accurate accounts of Japan's historical beginnings. Hirohito himself, in a nationwide broadcast, told the Japanese people that he was not divine. An American was invited to Japan as a teacher for the crown prince, Akihito, the heir to the throne. Akihito later broke an ancient tradition by marrying a commoner —one not belonging to a noble family. He succeeded his father, Hirohito, as emperor in 1989.

Emperor Akihito and Empress Michiko have ruled Japan since the death of his father, Hirohito, in 1989. Japan is the world's oldest surviving monarchy.

Japan Today. Young Japanese are growing up in a Japan far different from the one their parents and grandparents knew. Because schools are co-educational, young men and women now have a more relaxed attitude toward each other. Parents and children talk to each other more frankly, and there is more respect for individual rights. A higher standard of living and a more varied diet have increased the average Japanese life span to 81 years, one of the highest in the world.

Throughout their history the Japanese have shown a remarkable ability to absorb new ideas and influences and adapt them to their own needs. This ability accounts in part for the great strides the Japanese have made in science, industry, and technology. At the same time, Japan remains a nation with distinctive cultural traditions. Although Japan's recent economic problems are challenging its traditional ways of doing business, the country remains a powerhouse in the world economy.

RACHEL E. CARR
Author, *The Picture Story of Japan*
Reviewed and updated by ALBERT M. CRAIG
Harvard University
Editor, *Japan: A Comparative Perspective*

This statue of the Buddha Amida is the masterpiece of the 11th-century Japanese sculptor Jocho. It is carved of wood and covered with a layer of gold leaf.

JAPANESE ART AND ARCHITECTURE

In traditional Japan, no distinction was made between the fine arts of painting and sculpture and the decorative arts—ceramics, lacquer, textiles, and the like. All were thought to be equally valid forms of artistic expression. Even an everyday object, if finely designed and crafted, was considered a work of art.

Today, this emphasis on design and craftsmanship continues. And, although many Japanese artists have adopted styles and techniques popular in Europe and the United States, traditional art forms such as those discussed in this article remain important. Exceptionally talented artists working within these traditions are honored as ''Living National Treasures.'' They are encouraged to teach their skills to a new generation of artists.

▶SCULPTURE

Most sculptures made before the mid-19th century were objects of worship displayed in temples and shrines. Statues of the gods of Buddhism (a religion of Indian origin introduced to Japan from China and Korea) and of the native Shinto religion were most common. But likenesses of famous monks and powerful rulers appeared after the 13th century.

The earliest sculptures were made of clay. Small clay figurines resembling humans and animals have been found in Neolithic sites (dating from 10,000–3,000 B.C.) throughout the country. During the 4th–6th centuries A.D., large clay figures of men, women, animals, and even boats and houses were placed around the great mounded tombs of powerful rulers.

The introduction of Buddhism to Japan in the 6th century influenced sculpture techniques, styles, and subjects. During the 6th–8th centuries, known as the classical era of Buddhist sculpture, temple sculptures of the Buddha and other gods were often made of gilt (gold-covered) bronze because of its value and awe-inspiring appearance. One of the most impressive gilt bronze statues from this period is a 52-foot (16-meter) seated Buddha in the Todaiji, a temple in the city of Nara. It was made in a lifelike style typical of the arts of the 8th century.

Most statues of the 9th century were carved of wood, a material that could be readily obtained throughout Japan. At first, statues were carved from solid blocks of wood, but they were heavy and tended to crack over time. Gradually, sculptors developed a better method. Many small pieces of wood were joined together like a jigsaw puzzle and then covered with thin layers of lacquer, gold leaf, and paint. The 11th-century sculptor Jocho is thought to have perfected this technique. His masterpiece, a graceful figure of the Buddha Amida, is the main object of worship in the Byodoin, a temple near Kyoto. The joined wood block technique developed by Jocho continued to be used by sculptors until the 19th century.

▶PAINTING

Japanese paintings have often had religious themes. Hanging scrolls depicting the Buddha and other gods were displayed in temples and shrines. Most of these works were painted on paper or silk using ink, colors, and gold leaf. Other, less formal paintings of gods were

The paintings in handscrolls were made to illustrate an accompanying text. This scene is from a famous 13th-century scroll about the conflict between two great warrior clans.

common in temples of the Zen school of Buddhism. They were painted with loose, flowing brushstrokes using black ink only. Paintings using both ink and colors were usually produced in temple workshops by specially trained monk artists. But those painted in black ink alone were created by amateurs as well as professional artists.

Beginning in the 10th century, paintings with nonreligious themes were increasingly collected by wealthy aristocrats. Especially popular were **handscrolls,** long narrative scrolls that contained both text and paintings. Sections of text, written in calligraphy (beautiful writing), were alternated with pictures illustrating the story. Handscrolls were about 12 inches (30 centimeters) high and up to 50 feet (15 meters) long. They were held horizontally in the hands and unrolled to reveal the story little by little. The subject matter of handscrolls ranged from moving romantic tales to historical battle stories.

Screen painting is often thought of as one of the most characteristic forms of Japanese art. Painted screens were a feature of Japanese residential architecture as early as the 8th century. Traditional Japanese houses do not have fixed walls. Instead they have sliding doors that may be opened or closed depending on whether a large or small space is needed. Folding screens, made up of several panels each, serve as additional, portable room dividers. Both sliding doors and folding screens are used as painting surfaces.

The subject and style of a screen painting reflect its owner's taste and the function of the room for which it was designed. For the sliding door panels of a formal audience hall, military rulers favored such subjects as muscular lions and tigers and colossal, ancient trees, often placed against a dazzling gold foil background. The intended effect was to impress the viewer with the owner's power. Screens used in private chambers had gentler images. Landscapes softly painted in black ink, alone or with touches of color; close-up views of flowers and trees; and scenes of seasonal pastimes were popular subjects.

The 16th and 17th centuries are considered the great age of screen painting. The Kano, a hereditary school of painters, and another group of artists known as the Rimpa school are especially famous for their work in this medium. Although the most acclaimed painters of the Edo period (1615–1868) were screen painters, they were often skilled in other art forms as well. For example, the Rimpa school artist Korin is renowned for his bold and colorful screen designs. He is equally famous for the robes he painted for the wives of wealthy merchants and for the ceramics he painted for his brother, the potter Kenzan.

▶WOODBLOCK PRINTS

Woodblocks were first used in Japan to reproduce religious texts and images. By the 17th century they were widely used to print inexpensive pictures and illustrated books that were eagerly collected by members of all social classes. Costly scroll and screen paintings were owned by the rich, but anyone could afford to buy woodblock prints. The variety of subjects found in prints reflects the wide-ranging interests and experiences of this new audience.

Prints showing famous actors in their favorite roles and beautiful women dressed in luxurious kimonos (robes) were much in demand. Some printmakers, such as those of the Torii

and Kaigetsudo schools, specialized in these two categories. The artists Hokusai and Hiroshige are acknowledged as the greatest masters of the landscape print. Their works generally feature views of scenic national landmarks such as Mount Fuji.

Prints by these and other artists active in the 18th and early 19th centuries were among the first Japanese pictures collected in the West. French impressionist painters, intrigued by the prints' distinctive design and bold use of color, adapted some of the Japanese techniques in their own work.

▶LACQUER

Lacquer is another distinctive Japanese art form that is as much appreciated in the West as in Japan. The Chinese originated the technique of coating objects made of wood, leather, or other materials with the sap of the lac tree (a relative of poison ivy). But Japanese craftsmen brought the art to new heights. They combined lacquer with gold leaf cut into various shapes and sizes to create elaborate designs.

When dry, lacquer forms a hard, waterproof surface that makes it ideal for coating anything from cups and bowls to furniture and saddles. However, high-quality lacquerware requires the application of at least 30 layers of lacquer.

Right: This wine container of about 1600 is a notable example of Japanese lacquerware, which was often decorated with gold leaf.
Below left: One of the earliest types of Japanese ceramic ware is Jomon, or cord-marked, pottery. This earthenware food vessel dates from about 3000–2000 B.C. *Below right:* A woodblock print (1831–33) by Hokusai shows the effects of a gust of wind on travelers passing through a rice field. Mount Fuji rises in the background.

Painted sliding door panels (*The Old Plum*, painted about 1650) form a temporary wall in a traditional Japanese room. Other traditional features are an alcove for displaying paintings and straw floor mats, called *tatami*, which are used for seating. Small, low tables, folding screens, and other furnishings are removed when not in use.

Because of this time-consuming procedure and the cost of the materials needed, fine lacquerware is a luxury item.

▶CERAMICS

Japan has one of the oldest ceramic traditions in the world. Earthenware vessels called Jomon, or "cord-marked," after their distinctive surface decoration, are believed to have been made as early as 10,000 B.C. Until the 17th century A.D., all Japanese ceramics were either earthenware, a reddish, nonwaterproof ware that is fired at low temperatures; or stoneware, a harder ware that is fired at a high temperature and often glazed (given a glossy finish for beauty and resistance to water).

The rise during the 16th century of a tea-drinking ritual known as the tea ceremony stimulated the growth of ceramic production. A wide range of shapes, sizes, and glazes developed in response to the requirements of the tea ceremony. The centerpiece of the tea ceremony is a beautiful teabowl, from which guests take turns sipping a special green tea. Other ceramic wares are used for preparing the tea and serving the accompanying meal.

The technique of making porcelain was introduced to Japan in the 17th century by Korean potters who settled on Japan's southernmost island of Kyushu. Porcelain is an extremely hard, white ceramic that is fired at very high temperatures. Highly decorated and often designed with the Western market in mind, porcelain wares were eagerly collected by Europeans.

▶ARCHITECTURE

The earliest forms of public architecture in Japan were Buddhist temples and multi-storied pagodas built on stone platforms and crowned with gracefully curved and overhanging tile roofs. These basic two models were established in the 8th century. They were largely inspired by Chinese architecture.

Residential architecture reflecting native Japanese tastes developed in the Heian period (792–1185). From that time on, the homes of wealthy people typically were rambling structures consisting of many single-storied, shingled buildings linked by covered corridors. Homes were surrounded by spacious gardens with flowers, trees, artificial ponds, and hills.

Although sliding doors and screens were used in the Heian period, many other distinctly Japanese architectural features did not come into widespread use until several centuries later. These include covering floors with straw mats called *tatami* and providing rooms with built-in bookshelves and alcoves for displaying paintings. Today most Japanese homes have at least one room furnished in this traditional manner.

CHRISTINE M. E. GUTH
Art Historian

JAPANESE LITERATURE

The Japanese, who were greatly influenced by China from ancient times, used Chinese as their written language for many centuries. Not until the 9th century did the Japanese develop a writing system of their own. This system is one of the most complicated in the world. It is based on a combination of Chinese characters (adapted to Japanese words) and *kana*, which are symbols used to represent the basic sounds (syllables) of the Japanese language.

The Japanese language is structurally very different from Chinese. But it has borrowed so many Chinese words that an educated Japanese person can understand Chinese well enough to get an idea of what is being said, even with no formal instruction in Chinese. For more information on the Japanese language, see the article JAPAN in this volume.

The Japanese developed literary forms and traditions that were different from those of China. However, they were influenced by Chinese literature until the modern age, usually thought of as beginning in 1868 with the period known as the Meiji Restoration.

▶**POETRY**

The history of Japanese literature begins with poetry put into writing in the 8th century, when the Emperor's court was located in the city of Nara. The Japanese preference for short poems was evident even from this early period. Japan's first poetry collection, the *Man'yoshu* (Ten Thousand Leaves), was compiled about the mid-8th century. Most of its 4,500 poems are written in the *tanka*, or "short poem," form. A *tanka* has only five lines and a total of 31 syllables. (The structure of Japanese poetry is based on syllable count rather than on accent or rhyme.)

The classical tradition of court poetry, centered on the *tanka*, reached its high point during the Heian period (794–1185), when the royal court was located at Heian (present-day Kyoto). Court poets used the *tanka* mainly to express their feelings about love and the beauty of nature. Because of the brief length of the *tanka*, poets relied on the power of suggestion and tried to achieve many layers of meaning in their verses.

From the late 12th century to the late 16th century, when the samurai, or warrior, class ruled Japan, "linked verse" gradually replaced the *tanka* as the main form of poetry. Linked verse was created by dividing the five lines of the *tanka* into two units, or "links," of three lines and two lines. Without preparing in advance, poets joined in groups of three or more to compose. Each, in turn, composed a link of poetry, alternating three-line and two-line links. Each link had to be related in some way to the one just before it. These jointly written poems often extended to 100 or even 1,000 links. Linked verse was greatly influenced by the traditions of earlier court poetry. But it also dealt with more earthy, everyday subjects and was composed by people from all classes of society, not just court poets.

The last major form of poetry that developed in pre-modern Japan was the *haiku*. *Haiku* was a product of the merchant culture that flourished in the cities during the peaceful and prosperous Tokugawa period (1600–1867), when Japan was ruled by the military government of the Tokugawa family. *Haiku* is probably the shortest form of poetry ever used for serious purposes. It consists of only three lines and a total of 17 syllables—the same structure as the first three lines of the *tanka* and the first link of linked verse. Like the *tanka* poets, writers of *haiku* often use the form to express their feelings about nature, and they try to suggest more than can be said in three brief lines. Unlike *tanka* and linked verse, *haiku* remains enormously popular among the Japanese.

▶**PROSE**

Prose literature first evolved in Japan during the 9th and 10th centuries. From the beginning it was closely linked to poetry. In fact, the oldest examples of Japanese prose writing are explanatory introductions to poems.

The masterpiece of Japanese prose literature is *The Tale of Genji*, a lengthy novel written in the early 11th century by Lady Murasaki, a

---

The Japanese verse form called *haiku* is well known all over the world. A *haiku* has 17 syllables, usually in three lines of 5, 7, and 5 syllables. The following is a *haiku*, with a translation, by Matsuo Bashō (1644–94), a master of the *haiku* form:

furuike ya	The ancient pond
kawazu tobikomu	A frog leaps in
mizu no oto	The sound of the water

Left: Lady Murasaki is shown writing her masterpiece, *The Tale of Genji*, in this 19th-century painting. **Above:** In the *Nō* theater, which combines words, music, and dance, the principal players wear masks.

lady-in-waiting at the royal court. In recounting the adventures of its hero, Genji, the novel brings to life Japanese court society in Kyoto during its most brilliant period. *The Tale of Genji* has had a powerful influence on the thinking and taste of later Japanese writers.

Despite the example of *The Tale of Genji,* the Japanese of pre-modern times much preferred briefer forms of prose, such as diaries and collections of stories, essays, and the like. Even long works of prose tend to have very loosely constructed plots. One famous example is *The Tale of the Heike,* a "war tale" that tells of the fighting between two great warrior clans in the 12th century. The same is true of later works, such as the writings of Ihara Saikaku, who recorded the way of life of the merchant class of the late 17th century. Although Saikaku's books are sometimes called novels, they are more like series of loosely connected stories, with little of the character development found in *Genji* or in modern novels.

In modern times (after 1868), the most important form of literature in Japan has been the novel. In developing the novel, Japanese writers of the late 19th and 20th centuries were greatly influenced by the literature of Western countries, including France, England, Russia, Germany, and the United States. Today, Japanese novels have been translated into many languages and are widely admired. The modern Japanese novel gained special recognition in 1968, when Kawabata Yasunari won the Nobel Prize for literature.

▶ **THEATER**

The first major form of Japanese theater was the *Nō,* or "ability," theater. It was created in the late 14th and early 15th centuries, largely by Kan'ami and his son Zeami, actors and playwrights who were supported by the warrior rulers of that age. Centered on dancing, the *Nō* is extremely slow-moving and symbolic. The most popular *Nō* plays deal with events and legends from the past and are often concerned with the quest for Buddhist salvation or enlightenment. The richest literary passages of a *Nō* play are written in the language of classical court poetry.

The second major form of theater in Japanese history is *Bunraku,* or puppet theater. Like *haiku* poetry and the prose of Ihara Saikaku, *Bunraku* was a product of the merchant culture of the Tokugawa period. The puppet theater's greatest playwright was Chikamatsu Monzaemon, who flourished in the early 18th century. Perhaps best known among Chikamatsu's plays are those that deal with the double suicide of lovers torn between their human feelings and the rigid demands of society.

The *Kabuki* theater was also created during the Tokugawa period. In *Kabuki,* however, scripts merely provide guidelines for actors and do not have the same literary value as the scripts of the puppet theater.

PAUL VARLEY
Author, *Japanese Culture*

JARVIS, ANNA. See WEST VIRGINIA (Famous People).
JASON. See GREEK MYTHOLOGY.

JASPER NATIONAL PARK

Jasper National Park, in the province of Alberta, is one of the largest of Canada's national parks. It is also one of the most scenic.

Located high in the Rocky Mountains in the western part of the province, the park covers an area of about 4,200 square miles (10,878 square kilometers). It borders Banff National Park on the south and Mount Robson Provincial Park on the northwest. On a clear day Mount Robson, the highest peak in the Canadian Rockies, can be seen some distance away.

The Columbia Icefield can be reached via the Icefields Parkway, which connects Jasper National Park with Banff National Park. One of the most beautiful highways in the world, it reaches elevations of 7,000 feet (2,134 meters) in some places and gives the traveler breathtaking views of majestic snowcapped mountains, forest-clad valleys, and shimmering lakes and rivers.

The park contains a huge wildlife preserve where moose, elk, grizzly bears, bighorn sheep, mountain goats, and many other animals live in their natural surroundings. It is also home to a great variety of birds, including golden eagles, and supports a diversity of plant species.

Jasper National Park was established in 1907. It was named for American-born Jasper Hawes, who came to the area in 1803 and worked for the North West Company. The park could not be easily visited by the public, however, until 1912. That year the Grand Trunk Pacific Railway line (now the Canadian National) was extended from Edmonton, across the park, and through the Yellowhead Pass to the Pacific coast.

Maligne Lake shimmers beneath majestic mountain peaks in Jasper National Park. Located high in the Rocky Mountains in western Alberta, Jasper is one of Canada's largest national parks.

Several other mountains in the park are noted for their height. The highest is Mount Columbia at 12,294 feet (3,747 meters). The Twins is almost as high. Next is Mount Edith Cavell, named for the heroic British nurse who was executed by the Germans in World War I (1914–18). The Athabasca River rises in the park, at the foot of the Athabasca Glacier in the Columbia Icefield.

Today Jasper National Park is dotted with hotels and campsites that serve millions of people. Every year visitors enjoy the activities—hiking, swimming, horseback riding, fishing, golf, and downhill and cross-country skiing—for which the park is famous. Many other visitors come just to relax and view such beautiful spots as Maligne Lake and Miette Hot Springs.

The only town in the park is Jasper, which has hotels, restaurants, and other facilities. The town is also the setting for two annual winter carnivals, in January and early March.

JOHN S. MOIR
University of Toronto

JAVA. See INDONESIA.

JAY, JOHN
(1745–1829)

John Jay was a patriot and one of the most accomplished diplomats of the Revolutionary War period. Considered a founder of the United States, Jay is best remembered for *The Federalist* essays, written to promote the adoption of the U.S. Constitution, and for helping negotiate the 1783 treaty that guaranteed America's independence from Great Britain. He also served as the first chief justice of the U.S. Supreme Court (1789–95) and as governor of New York (1795–1801).

Jay was born in New York City on December 12, 1745. His father, Peter, was a leading merchant in the New York colony. At the age of 15, John entered King's College (now Columbia University). After graduation he studied law and received his license to practice in 1768.

In 1774, Jay married Sarah Van Brugh Livingston. That same year he became active in colonial politics and went to Philadelphia to serve as a New York delegate to the First Continental Congress. Opposed to radical change, Jay supported early efforts to negotiate with Great Britain, fearful that a revolution would lead to mob rule. But by the time the Declaration of Independence was issued in 1776, Jay had become a firm supporter of the revolutionary cause.

During the war years, Jay helped write a constitution for New York and served as its chief justice. In December 1778, he was elected president of the Second Continental Congress, which then served as the central government of the united colonies. Jay served in this post until September 1779, when he was appointed minister to Spain.

In 1782, a year after the British Army surrendered to the Americans at Yorktown, Jay was called to Paris, France, to help Benjamin Franklin and John Adams negotiate a peace treaty with Great Britain. In the Treaty of Paris, signed in 1783, the British recognized the independence of the United States.

Jay returned home in 1784 to find that Congress had appointed him U.S. secretary of foreign affairs. In this new post he tried to persuade Spain and Great Britain—both of which still had land holdings surrounding the United States—to respect American territory. But he met with little success, mainly because the fledgling American government, which at that time was operating inadequately under the Articles of Confederation, did not yet have any influence or credibility.

To strengthen the national government, Jay, Alexander Hamilton, James Madison, and others urged the ratification of a new constitution that would give the federal government more authority. To promote their cause, they wrote a series of essays called *The Federalist* and had them printed in newspapers. These essays (five were written by Jay) did much to persuade Americans to accept the present Constitution and the new form of government it established. In 1789, after the Constitution had been adopted, newly elected president George Washington appointed Jay the first chief justice of the United States Supreme Court.

In 1794, Washington sent Jay to Great Britain to settle disputes that threatened to lead to another war. Americans wanted the British to vacate the forts they still occupied in American territory around the Great Lakes. Americans also objected to the British seizing American ships and seamen bound for France, then at war with Great Britain. The resulting agreement, known as **Jay's Treaty**, settled the first issue in the Americans' favor, but not the second. Still, overall, it kept peace between the two nations and assured free commerce between them.

When Jay returned from London in 1795, he discovered he had been elected governor of New York. He served for six years, then retired to his estate at Bedford, New York. He died on May 17, 1829.

BERNARD EISENBERG
Hunter College

Jazz, a form of music that developed in the United States, is now played and enjoyed around the world. Characterized by its use of syncopated rhythms, blue notes, and improvisation, jazz can be played by large bands, small combos, and solo performers. *Clockwise from left:* the Count Basie Orchestra, pianist Chick Corea, the Modern Jazz Quartet.

JAZZ

"Jazz" is a word that has come to describe a variety of contemporary musical styles. But it was originally the name given to a music first played by African Americans in the early years of the 20th century. This early jazz was a type of folk music; that is, it was performed by people in a community simply for their own enjoyment. Since then, jazz has evolved into both a means of artistic expression and a form of commercial entertainment. It is now performed by people of all races and nationalities and enjoyed by audiences around the world. It has influenced almost every other kind of music in the United States and Europe, and it has produced many of the world's most distinguished instrumentalists, composers, and singers.

Early jazz was a blending of musical elements from Europe and Africa. The first jazz musicians borrowed their ideas of melody and harmony, as well as the instruments they used, from European musical traditions. What made jazz sound different from any other kind of music played in the United States in the early 1900's were certain elements assumed to be African in origin. Foremost among these was **rhythm**. All music makes use of rhythm; one way to think of it is as the element that moves a piece of music along from one note to the next. But jazz rhythm was more pronounced—it made people want to clap their hands or tap their feet.

What was African about this new approach to rhythm was **syncopation**. It means playing a game of sorts with the rhythmic pattern, stressing beats that normally would not be acccented. In other words, instead of ONE-two-THREE-four, the beat might be one-TWO-three-FOUR. Syncopation can be found in all kinds of music, but jazz syncopation had more in common with that found in some African music. In jazz, there was almost a beat between the beats: AH one-AND A two-AND A three-AND A four.

Another African element in jazz had to do with **pitch**—the relative highness or lowness of a musical tone. In jazz, as in the traditional music of Africa and that of many other non-European countries, the musician often seems to be "bending" certain notes as they are played or sung. That is, the note produced seems to fall in between two notes of a scale. These notes eventually came to be referred to as **blue notes**. They are a key element in jazz and in the many kinds of music that have been influenced by jazz.

The final new element in jazz that was perhaps more African than European in origin was the use of **improvisation**. To improvise means to make something up on the spot. Jazz improvisations may be based on the melody of the music being played, or they may be based on the chords to that melody. A chord is the tone produced when two or more notes are played at the same time. Chords are the sounds beneath a melody—what a friend would play on the piano as you sang the melody to a song. Jazz musicians, as they improvise, often ignore the melody and invent new melodies from those piano chords on the spur of the moment.

▶ **EARLY HISTORY**

Most of what we know about the origins of jazz is based on recordings. But jazz was not recorded until 1917, and by that time it had already existed for a decade or more. Another way to learn about the origins of jazz is

---

OUTSTANDING JAZZ RECORDINGS

A basic jazz collection should start with the following CD's:

- The Smithsonian Collection of Classic Jazz (Smithsonian Collection of Recordings SMI-CD-033)
- Louis Armstrong, *Portrait of the Artist as a Young Man* (Columbia/Legacy C4K-57176)
- *Jelly Roll Morton & His Red Hot Peppers* (Bluebird 6588-2)
- *The Fletcher Henderson Story: A Study in Frustration* (Columbia/Legacy C3K-57596)
- Bix Beiderbecke, *Volume 1, Singin' the Blues* (Columbia Jazz Masterpieces CK-46175)
- Duke Ellington, *The Blanton-Webster Band* (Bluebird 5859—2-RB); *The Far East Suite* (Bluebird 07863—66551-2)
- *The Essence of Billie Holiday* (Columbia/Legacy CK-47917)
- Count Basie, *The Complete Decca Recordings* (Decca/GRP GRD-3-611)
- Charlie Parker, *The Complete Dial Sessions* (Stash ST-CD567-70); *The Charlie Parker Story* (Savoy Jazz SVY-0105)
- Thelonious Monk, *Brilliant Corners* (Fantasy/Original Jazz Classics OJCCD-026)
- Miles Davis, *Birth of the Cool* (Capitol C21Y-92862); *Kind of Blue* (Columbia/Legacy CK-40579)
- John Coltrane, *Giant Steps* (Atlantic 1311-2); *A Love Supreme* (Impulse GRD-155)
- Ornette Coleman, *The Shape of Jazz to Come* (Atlantic 1317-2).
- World Saxophone Quartet, *Revue* (Black Saint 120056)

---

to examine two earlier forms of African American music: ragtime and the blues.

Ragtime took shape in St. Louis, Missouri, and other midwestern American cities in the late 1800's. A typical ragtime piece had several different melodies. Each would be played one after the other, with some repeats. More significantly, ragtime featured a high degree of rhythmic syncopation, thus anticipating jazz. An important difference between ragtime and jazz, however, is that ragtime allowed for very little improvisation.

Ragtime was usually played on piano, although there were also ragtime banjo players, and quite a few ragtime pieces were written for full orchestra. Its leading composer was Scott Joplin, who won fame for his piece "The Maple Leaf Rag" (1899). Ragtime caught on very quickly, becoming the 20th century's first popular music craze. The most famous popular song to use ragtime's synco-

ragtime

the blues

Profiles of notable jazz musicians appear along this time line. Consult the Index to find more information about the following artists mentioned in this article: Louis Armstrong, John Coltrane, Miles Davis, Ella Fitzgerald, Benny Goodman, W. C. Handy, Scott Joplin, Charlie Parker, and Bessie Smith.

Bessie Smith

pated rhythms was "Alexander's Ragtime Band" (1911), by Irving Berlin.

The Blues. The origins of the blues are even more mysterious than those of jazz. In 1912, W. C. Handy copyrighted a song called "Memphis Blues." Two years later, another of Handy's songs, called "St. Louis Blues," became such a big hit that it was soon followed by many other songs with the word "blues" in their titles. Yet even the people of that day knew that the blues was much older—it is a form of music that sounds as old as time. Some people say that the blues can be traced back to slavery. Others believe that it is something African slaves brought with them to America, but this seems very unlikely.

Like the earliest jazz, the earliest blues blended musical elements from different cultures. It was African in sound, but it borrowed its narrative structure—the way it told a story—from Anglo-Scots ballads. A song is not necessarily a blues just because it is slow and sad or because the singer complains about having the blues. The blues is a strict musical form, twelve measures in length. It is also a form of poetry. In a typical blues lyric, the opening line is sung twice, then followed by a third line that rhymes with it. Each line takes up four measures of music, for a total of twelve measures.

The blues probably originated in the Mississippi Delta in the early 20th century, about the same time that jazz was taking shape elsewhere. Like jazz, it uses blue notes. A blues performer who both sings and plays guitar often sounds as though he or she is

carrying on both ends of a conversation, singing a line and then bending the strings of the guitar in such a way that the guitar seems to be singing, too. This is sometimes referred to as **call and response**, and it is a common feature in traditional African music. Just as blues guitarists often seem to be "talking" on their instruments, so do jazz horn players. It suggests that jazz and the blues sprang from the same roots.

The earliest blues performers tended not to be professional entertainers. Most of them were men, but by the 1920's, a number of popular women entertainers had incorporated the blues into their acts. It was these women who popularized the blues, singing both blues songs and their own versions of popular songs with jazz accompaniment. The greatest of these women singers was Bessie Smith, who influenced many jazz instrumentalists as well as many other blues singers.

▶ NEW ORLEANS JAZZ

Jazz was initially associated with New Orleans, the Louisiana city that many people still believe was the music's birthplace. In the early 1900's, New Orleans was perhaps the most multicultural city in the United States, a trade port with a mix of French, Spanish, and African American influences. Perhaps as a result of this, early New Orleans jazz was a mix of different cultural elements. It combined the deep emotion of the blues and African American spirituals with Spanish and Caribbean rhythms, along with elements of ragtime and European folk music.

The New Orleans style of jazz—nicknamed **Dixieland**, but not until much later—introduced a new style of improvisation. In addition to piano, banjo, drums, and bass or tuba, a typical New Orleans ensemble of the early 1920's included trumpet (or cornet), trom-

Louis Armstrong

Ferdinand "Jelly Roll" Morton (1885–1941), born in Gulfport, Louisiana, was one of the first great New Orleans jazz artists. He began his career as a ragtime pianist and later worked as a musician in several cities. He began recording in 1923, as a solo pianist and with his band, the Red Hot Peppers. Many of his compositions have become jazz standards.

bone, and clarinet. These three horns would often improvise on the melody all at once, with the trumpet or cornet player taking the lead and the trombonist and clarinetist weaving their improvisations around that.

However, the most important feature of New Orleans jazz may have been its new approach to rhythm. New Orleans rhythm was complex, but it was also very relaxed.

The most important musicians produced by New Orleans in the early days of jazz were trumpeter, cornetist, and singer Louis Armstrong and pianist and composer Ferdinand "Jelly Roll" Morton.

Armstrong first demonstrated his brilliance as a member of a New Orleans band led by cornetist Joseph "King" Oliver. Eventually he surpassed Oliver to become the first great jazz improviser. Armstrong moved away from the group improvisations of earlier New Orleans jazz. Instead, he favored improvisations by one player at a time, accompanied only by the rhythm section (usually piano, bass, and drums). Armstrong's most famous solos in-

clude those on "West End Blues," "Struttin' with Some Barbeque," and "Sweethearts on Parade." His fresh approach to melody and rhythm influenced other jazz musicians of the 1920's and 1930's and extended into popular music.

Jelly Roll Morton can be said to have practically invented the notion of jazz composi-

new orleans jazz

Jelly Roll Morton with the Red Hot Peppers

tion, by blending improvisation with written music. In this, he set an example for later jazz composers. His most important pieces were "King Porter Stomp," "Dead Man Blues," and "Black Bottom Stomp."

There were other important jazz musicians from New Orleans during this period, notably clarinetist and soprano saxophonist Sidney Bechet.

At a time when the music of African Americans was not being recorded, the first jazz recordings were made in 1917 by a white group from New Orleans who called themselves the Original Dixieland Jazz Band. It was this band's recordings that popularized the word "jazz" and started a craze for this kind of music. The commercial success of this band's recordings was the first sign that jazz could no longer be thought of as a folk music of significance only to one group of people. Jazz would soon be heard all over the world, and it would be played by white musicians as well as by African Americans.

JAZZ SINGERS

Jazz instrumentalists and singers have always influenced one another. Early jazz horn players often sounded as though they were talking or singing through their horns. As time went on, jazz singers began to attempt to improvise as though they were playing horns. Even when they were singing words, they wanted to be able to take as many liberties with a melody as a jazz instrumentalist might take. Many jazz singers **scat**. Scat singing is a form of vocal improvisation in which a singer departs from a song's words, offering instead his or her own version of the sounds a jazz horn player might make.

However, there are as many possible approaches to jazz singing as there are approaches to instrumental jazz improvisation. Billie Holiday (*pictured*), whom many people consider to have been the greatest jazz singer of them all, never scatted. She simply sang the melody, often completely reshaping it as she went along.

An early kind of New York jazz was Harlem "stride" piano, so named because the pianist's left hand often sounded like someone walking, or taking giant strides. Harlem stride owed much to ragtime but allowed for a much higher degree of improvisation.

New York was also the birthplace of the big-band style of jazz. Big bands included a greater number of instrumentalists than did New Orleans ensembles. Then, as now, a big band usually included three different instrumental sections: brass (trumpets and trombones), reeds (saxophones and clarinets), and rhythm (piano, guitar, bass, and drums).

The most influential of the early big bands was Fletcher Henderson's. In Henderson's band, as in others of the period, there was some improvisation, but a good deal of the music was arranged, that is, written down beforehand. Henderson and Don Redman, the band's chief arrangers, devised a way to pit one section of the

big bands

Duke Ellington with his band

▶ THE RISE OF BIG BANDS

Historians used to say that jazz came up the Mississippi River from New Orleans, landing first in Chicago, Illinois, and then in New York City. There is some truth to this theory, if only because that was the route traveled by Louis Armstrong, who joined a band led by Fletcher Henderson after arriving in New York in 1924. But jazz was being played in New York long before Armstrong got there.

band against another, using the same principle of call and response used in the blues. For example, the brass section might state a phrase and the saxophones would answer. This is still a characteristic big-band sound.

The Henderson orchestra also produced many of the most important soloists of the late 1920's and 1930's. In addition to Louis Armstrong, at various times its members included trumpeter Roy Eldridge, alto saxophonist Benny Carter, and tenor saxophonist Coleman Hawkins.

The Henderson band's white counterpart, at a time when jazz performance remained rigidly segregated, was the Paul Whiteman Orchestra. This was the band that introduced George Gershwin's *Rhapsody in Blue*, in 1924. Its outstanding soloists included trumpeter Leon "Bix" Beiderbecke, trombonist Jack Teagarden, guitarist Eddie Lang, and violinist Joe Venuti. Beiderbecke was especially important, bringing a quieter and more reflective sound to jazz improvisation.

Big bands caught on with the public in the late 1930's, and their popularity lasted through World War II (1939–45). People who danced to the big bands during that period are likely to remember it as the big-band era, but jazz historians tend to call these same years the **swing era**. Swing was the name given to a carefree style of jazz of the 1930's

one of his country's greatest composers, writing over 1,000 jazz and non-jazz works.

With the help of his band members, Ellington combined composition and improvisation in especially imaginative ways. Instead of pitting the brass instruments against the reeds, as earlier big-band orchestrators had done, he grouped instruments together in unexpected and highly effective new ways. His best-known numbers are popular melodies like "Sophisticated Lady" and "Mood Indigo." But the works that best demonstrate his genius as a composer and arranger are instrumental pieces, such as "Ko-Ko" and "Concerto for Cootie."

▶ MODERN JAZZ

After big-band swing, the next significant development in jazz was bebop. Bebop and the styles that have followed it, including

swing

Edward Kennedy "Duke" Ellington (1899–1974) born in Washington, D.C., was a pianist, bandleader, and one of the most important composers in jazz history. Ellington moved to New York in 1923; he and his orchestra were stars of Harlem's famous Cotton Club. Radio broadcasts from the club made him a national celebrity, while films, recordings, and European tours brought international fame.

Jean Baptiste "Django" Reinhardt (1910–53) a guitarist born in Liverchies, Belgium, was the first important European jazz musician. Reinhardt, a Gypsy, lost the use of two fingers of his left hand in a caravan fire and as a result developed an unusual two-fingered playing technique. In 1934 he founded, with violinist Stephane Grappelli, the Quintet of the Hot Club de France.

Dizzy Gillespie

Django Reinhardt
with Stephane Grappelli

and 1940's, but it also refers to the almost indefinable sense of forward motion heard in practically all good jazz.

Some of the most popular big bands of the 1930's and 1940's were those led by Benny Goodman, Artie Shaw, Glenn Miller, Jimmy and Tommy Dorsey, Woody Herman, Jimmie Lunceford, Chick Webb, and Andy Kirk. Perhaps the greatest big band of all was the one led by pianist and composer Edward Kennedy "Duke" Ellington. Ellington was

"cool" and "hard bop," are sometimes referred to as modern jazz.

Bebop, a very adventurous form of music, has come to be associated with small groups rather than with big bands. A typical bebop ensemble includes trumpet, one or two saxophones, piano, bass, and drums.

However, the big bands—in particular, the one led by William "Count" Basie—prepared the way for what is usually called modern jazz. In tenor saxophonist Lester Young, the band had the most original and daring jazz improviser since Louis Armstrong. With Basie himself on piano, the band also featured a rhythm section that accompanied the soloists with a flowing feeling completely new to jazz.

The musicians who originated the style that was eventually named bebop did so, for the most part, at informal gatherings called **jam sessions**. Bebop was more harmonically complex than earlier styles of jazz had been. Bebop musicians improvised not so much on the melody of a tune, but on the tune's underlying chords. Even more important was bebop's rhythmic complexity.

bebop

Bebop quickly became associated with New York City, but its roots were in the southwestern United States, specifically Kansas City, Missouri. The Basie band had been formed there, and alto saxophonist Charlie Parker, the greatest of the bebop musicians, grew up there. Just as Louis Armstrong had twenty years earlier, Parker reshaped jazz in his own image. He improvised with a quickness and logic that astonished both audiences and his fellow musicians.

Thelonious Monk

Thelonious Monk (1917–82) was born in Rocky Mount, North Carolina, and raised in New York City. A gifted youth, he began playing piano professionally in 1935. As a composer and performer, playing in bands led by Coleman Hawkins and Dizzy Gillespie, he had a key role in the development of bebop. But Monk did not win widespread fame until he was in his 40's, when his compositions such as "Round Midnight," "Misterioso," and "Brilliant Corners" were recognized as masterpieces.

COMPOSITION IN JAZZ

A defining feature of jazz is its extensive use of improvisation, and an important job of the jazz composer is to present musicians with strong material on which to improvise. A jazz score might be as detailed as a classical music score, but it might also be just an outline. Jazz composers tend to be instrumentalists, and much of what qualifies as composition in jazz takes place in performance, with the composer as a full participant. In other words, the score is not completed until it has been performed. And the next time it is performed, it may sound very different.

Major jazz composers include pianists Jelly Roll Morton, Duke Ellington, and Thelonious Monk; bassist Charles Mingus (*pictured*); and, more recently, pianists Tadd Dameron, Carla Bley, and Toshiko Akiyoshi.

In addition to Parker, bebop's leading figures included trumpeter John Birks "Dizzy" Gillespie, trombonist J. J. Johnson, pianist Earl "Bud" Powell, vibraphonist Milt Jackson, bassist Ray Brown, and drummers Kenny Clarke and Max Roach. Pianist and composer Thelonious Monk was among the most important of the early bebop musicians, but his full significance did not become apparent until the 1950's.

Cool and Hard Bop. In the 1950's, bebop itself evolved into two different schools, one called cool and the other called hard bop. The trumpeter Miles Davis, who had started his career in Parker's band, helped set the rules for both styles. Cool introduced airy new textures to jazz. Along with Davis, its leading figures included trumpeter Chet Baker, tenor saxophonist Stan Getz, baritone saxophonist Gerry Mulligan, pianist Lennie Tristano, and arranger Gil Evans. Hard bop returned to jazz some of the fervor of the blues and of black church music. In addition to Davis, its leading figures included trumpeter Clifford Brown, tenor saxophonist Theodore "Sonny" Rollins, pianist Horace Silver, and drummers Art Blakey and Max Roach.

How can we tell if a performance is an example of bebop, cool, or hard bop? Often we cannot, because the three styles can be very similar.

▶ LATER DEVELOPMENTS

Some people felt that jazz had reached a form of perfection with bebop and that there was no place else to go. But some jazz musicians began to look for other ways to improvise, and this search has continued to the present day.

Modal Jazz. Beginning in the late 1950's, some jazz musicians attempted to simplify jazz improvisation by improvising on scales rather than chords. (A scale is a series of ascending or descending notes.) In particular, they investigated **modes**, types of scales used in much of the world's music, including that of Africa and Asia. The album that first showed musicians the endless possi-

cool and hard bop

Charlie Parker

John Coltrane

free jazz

Ornette Coleman

Ornette Coleman (1930–   ), born in Fort Worth, Texas, is a saxophonist and composer who developed a highly individual approach to harmony and improvisation. Largely self-taught, Coleman began playing alto sax in his early teens. His album *Free Jazz* (1960) influenced many jazz artists of the 1960's. His later work reflects his explorations of other musical styles, including rock and the music of Morocco.

One musician, Miles Davis, was closely associated with each.

Davis led the most influential band of the 1950's. It combined elements of bebop, hard bop, and cool. But it also pointed to future developments in jazz. Its members included tenor saxophonist John Coltrane, who quickly emerged as the most influential figure in jazz since Charlie Parker. Davis led another influential band in the 1960's. It included tenor saxophonist Wayne Shorter and pianist Herbie Hancock, two other musicians who had a great impact on jazz in the decades that followed.

bilities of modal improvisation was Miles Davis' *Kind of Blue* (1959).

One of the musicians on that album was John Coltrane, who went on to record a number of influential modal pieces of his own. But Coltrane never completely gave up improvising on chords. He took this more traditional approach to an even greater complexity on "Giant Steps," perhaps his most famous recorded performance. He often combined both approaches, as on *A Love Supreme* (1964).

Free Jazz. Before his death in 1967, Coltrane also became a leading figure in what

Wynton Marsalis

Miles Davis

fusion

Wynton Marsalis (1961–   ), a trumpeter, was born in New Orleans, Louisiana. The son of a jazz pianist and teacher, he studied both jazz and classical music from an early age. In 1980, while still a student at New York's Juilliard School, he joined Art Blakey's Jazz Messengers. He quickly won acclaim for his brilliant technique and improvisational skills. In 1984 he became the first musician to receive Grammy Awards for both classical and jazz recordings.

is sometimes called free jazz. This style takes a number of different approaches to improvisation but is generally characterized by its free approach to rhythm. The traditional rhythm or accompanying instruments—including bass and drums—take a leading part in a performance, along with the horns.

But the key figure in free jazz was alto saxophonist Ornette Coleman, who is also the man who coined the phrase "free jazz." Coleman's approach to jazz was so original that when he first appeared on the scene in 1959, some other musicians accused him of not knowing how to play his horn. But Coleman's music communicates its own sort of beauty. His most famous performances include "Lonely Woman," "Ramblin'," and "Beauty Is a Rare Thing."

Fusion. Another trend in jazz since the late 1960's has been the attempt to combine elements of jazz with elements of rock and roll. This kind of jazz involves the use of amplified instruments. It is sometimes called fusion. Again, a key figure in this movement was Miles Davis. Some others include pianist Chick Corea, guitarist John McLaughlin, and the members of the group Weather Report.

▶ **JAZZ TODAY**

Since the 1960's, the most creative jazz musicians have begun to question the basic assumptions of jazz and to answer these questions in their own way. They have looked for new ways to combine improvisation and composition, and they have introduced new instruments into jazz ensembles. Among these musicians are pianist Anthony Davis, soprano saxophonist Steve Lacy, alto saxophonists Anthony Braxton, Julius Hemphill, and Henry Threadgill, tenor saxophonist David Murray, and the members of Air, the Art Ensemble of Chicago, and the World Saxophone Quartet.

It is important to remember that one style of jazz never simply replaces the style that came before it. Almost every kind of jazz is still being played somewhere. Perhaps the most famous living jazz musician is trumpeter Wynton Marsalis, who was still in his teens when he began to make a name for himself in the early 1980's. Marsalis has demonstrated that not all the possibilities of earlier forms of jazz have been exhausted. He has helped bring younger audiences to jazz.

Today jazz is heard in the world's leading concert halls, as well as in dark, smoky nightclubs. The audience for jazz is international. Many of the world's leading jazz festivals take place in Europe or Japan. The first important foreign-born jazz musician was the guitarist Django Reinhardt, a Belgian Gypsy who was one of the most inventive soloists of the early 1940's. Current important foreign-born musicians include French violinist Stephane Grappelli, German trombonist Albert Mangelsdorff, South African pianist Abdullah Ibrahim, Belgian pianist Martial Solal, Dutch pianist Misha Mengelberg, and British bassist Dave Holland.

FRANCIS DAVIS
Contributing editor, *The Atlantic Monthly*

THOMAS JEFFERSON (1743-1826)

3rd President of the United States

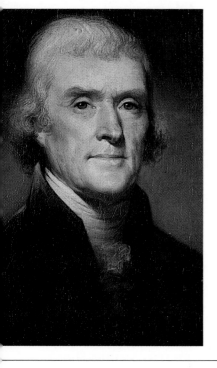

FACTS ABOUT JEFFERSON

Birthplace: Shadwell, Albemarle County, Virginia
Religion: Christian (no specific denomination)
College Attended: College of William and Mary, Williamsburg, Virginia
Occupation: Lawyer, planter
Married: Martha Wayles Skelton
Children: Martha, Mary (the only children to live to maturity)
Political Party: Republican (also known as Democratic-Republican).
Office Held Before Becoming President: Vice President
President Who Preceded Him: John Adams
Age on Becoming President: 57
Years in the Presidency: 1801–1809
Vice President: Aaron Burr (1st term); George Clinton (2nd term)
President Who Succeeded Him: James Madison
Age at Death: 83
Burial Place: Monticello, near Charlottesville, Virginia

DURING JEFFERSON'S PRESIDENCY

Left: Tripoli, one of the Barbary States of North Africa, declared war on the United States, setting off the Tripolitan War (1801–05), which was fought mainly at sea. The United States Military Academy was opened (1802). Ohio was admitted to the Union (1803). The Louisiana Territory was purchased from France (1803), doubling the size of the United States. The Twelfth Amendment to the Constitution, clarifying presidential elections, was ratified (1804). The expedition of Meriwether Lewis and William Clark reached the Pacific Ocean (1805). *Below:* The first practical steamboat, Robert Fulton's *Clermont*, traveled up the Hudson River from New York City to Albany (1807).

JEFFERSON, THOMAS. Thomas Jefferson is best known as the author of the Declaration of Independence and as third president of the United States. But he was also a diplomat, an architect, a musician, a scientist and inventor, a strong supporter of religious freedom, and an early advocate of public education. He was the founder of the University of Virginia and the greatest patron of learning and the arts in his generation. Although he lived 83 years, he never ceased to be young in spirit. He was always learning something new, always trying to contribute to human progress. In his range of interests, perhaps no other American except Benjamin Franklin ever matched him.

▶ EARLY LIFE

Although renowned as a champion of democracy and friend of the common people, Jefferson was a member of a favored class by birth and training. He was born on April 13, 1743, at Shadwell, his father's home in Albemarle County, Virginia, then on the edge of western settlement. His father, Peter Jefferson, was a successful landholder as well as a noted explorer. He provided his son with excellent opportunities for education and left him a considerable estate. His mother, Jane Randolph, belonged to one of the leading Virginia families.

Jefferson was educated privately during his youth. He studied Latin and Greek before going to the College of William and Mary in Williamsburg at the age of 17. He learned French early and later acquired a knowledge of Italian and Spanish. At college he developed an interest in science and mathematics, and in the colonial capital of Williamsburg, he got to see government in operation. He would later be a part of that government.

In appearance, Jefferson was tall and lean, sandy-haired, and inclined to freckle. Although somewhat awkward, he was physically strong and a fine horseman. A friendly man,

A Declaration by the Representatives of the UNITED STATES OF AMERICA, in General Congress assembled.

When in the course of human events it becomes necessary for one people to dissolve the political bands which have connected them with another, and to assume among the powers of the earth the separate and equal station to which the laws of nature & of nature's god entitle them, a decent respect ... that they should declare the causes

Jefferson (seated at rear) was chosen to write the Declaration of Independence, adopted in 1776. At the top is a draft of the document in Jefferson's hand.

posed to slavery, but his proposals to abolish it in Virginia failed. He himself was an especially kind master. On a small hilltop he built a house, later extensively remodeled, which he named Monticello—meaning "little mountain" in Italian. He was his own architect and builder.

Because of his position as a leading planter, Jefferson was expected to take part in the colonial government. In 1769, at the age of 25, he was elected to the House of Burgesses, the Virginia legislature, where he would serve until the outbreak of the American Revolution. He disliked speaking in public, partly because his voice was not strong, but he excelled on committees and soon showed his skill as a writer. From the beginning he belonged to the group that most strongly upheld the rights of the American colonies against the British government, which then ruled them. It was afterward said of Jefferson that he was the pen of the American Revolution, as George Washington was the sword.

▶ **REVOLUTIONARY PATRIOT**

Jefferson said many times that he never liked public life, and he might have remained quietly at home in Virginia if the conflict between the American colonies and Britain had not become critical. One of the sparks that helped ignite American feeling against the British government was the severe measures it imposed against the colony of Massachusetts after the so-called Boston Tea Party in 1773. As a protest against taxes and other grievances, the colonists had dumped a cargo of British tea into Boston Harbor.

The issue, as Jefferson saw it, was between freedom and tyranny. When he became a

although he could be stiff at first meeting, he made and kept many friends.

▶ **LAWYER, PLANTER, AND BURGESS**

Jefferson studied law under George Wythe, the most famous law teacher in Virginia, and at 24 was admitted to the bar. Legal fees provided only part of his earnings, however, and he was supported mainly by the income from his lands. These were doubled by the inheritance of his wife, Martha Wayles Skelton, whom he married in 1772. But his wife's estate was burdened with a heavy debt from which he never escaped.

Jefferson owned about 10,000 acres (4,000 hectares) of land, much of it forested, and from 100 to 200 slaves. He was always op-

member of the Second Continental Congress in Philadelphia in 1775, after the outbreak of the Revolution, he was already known as an ardent patriot. Because of his writing ability and because, as a Virginian, he was a representative of the largest colony, he was chosen to write the Declaration of Independence. This document, adopted in 1776, proclaimed to the world that the 13 American colonies were now independent of Britain. Seven more years of war were to follow, however, before Britain accepted the idea of American independence.

See the article on the Declaration of Independence in Volume D. For a complete account of the American Revolution and the events leading up to it, see the article REVOLUTIONARY WAR in Volume Q-R.

▶ **LEGISLATOR AND GOVERNOR**

Jefferson returned to Virginia in 1776. He served in the House of Delegates, part of the new Virginia legislature, until 1779, when he was elected governor. To Jefferson, his service in the Virginia legislature during this period was of particular importance. Believing that the American Revolution was not only a struggle against foreign rule but also a fight for the rights of the individual, he set out to reform the laws of Virginia. His aim was to replace the artificial aristocracy of birth and wealth, to which he himself belonged, with a natural aristocracy of talent and virtue.

Jefferson set the highest value on his Bill for Establishing Religious Freedom, which he introduced in 1779 but which was not passed until seven years later. It called for the complete separation of church and state and for the freedom of people to think and worship as they liked. A second measure, the Bill for the More General Diffusion of Knowledge, which would have created a system of public schools in Virginia, failed to pass. Jefferson was ahead of his time in this, but his ideas on education had great influence on others.

Jefferson's years as governor of Virginia, from 1779 to 1781, were unhappy ones. He had little power under the existing state constitution, and, to make matters worse, in his last year, the British invaded Virginia. The legislature fled, and for a time the state had no governor. Jefferson was blamed, although there was little he could have done. An inquiry into his conduct cleared him of all charges, but the criticism so distressed him that he determined never to return to public

IMPORTANT DATES IN THE LIFE OF THOMAS JEFFERSON

1743	Born at Shadwell in Albemarle County, Virginia, April 13.
1762	Graduated from the College of William and Mary.
1767	Admitted to the bar; began practicing law.
1769–75	Served in the Virginia House of Burgesses.
1772	Married Martha Wayles Skelton.
1775	Elected delegate to the Second Continental Congress.
1776	Appointed to the committee to draw up a proclamation of independence; drafted the Declaration of Independence.
1776–79	Served in the Virginia legislature (House of Delegates).
1779–81	Served as governor of Virginia.
1783–84	Served as a delegate to Congress from Virginia.
1785	Published *Notes on the State of Virginia*.
1785	Appointed minister to France.
1790–93	Served as secretary of state.
1797–1801	Served as vice president.
1801–09	Served as third president of the United States.
1819	University of Virginia chartered.
1826	Died at Monticello, July 4.

Monticello was Jefferson's hilltop home in Virginia for much of his life. He designed the building himself. Its name means "little mountain."

Jefferson as he looked in the early 1790's. He was tall and lean, with red hair, and inclined to freckle.

life. During his retirement he began his *Notes on the State of Virginia*. Originally an account of the natural resources, government, and society of his own state, it grew to be continental in scope.

▶ **CONGRESSMAN**

Jefferson probably would have remained in Monticello if his wife had not died in 1782, leaving him lonely and desolate. Of the six children born to them, only three girls had survived. He sent his two youngest children, Mary and Lucy, to live with an aunt (where Lucy later died). But he kept his eldest daughter, Martha, with him. Yielding to the wishes of friends, he accepted election to Congress in 1783. Although he served only briefly, he was its most useful and industrious member. He recommended adoption of the dollar as the American monetary unit and the decimal system for its coinage. His report on the government of the western territory anticipated the Northwest Ordinance of 1787, which formed the basis for the creation of new states from western lands. It was the system under which the United States as it exists today was gradually developed. He also drafted a report on the 1783 peace treaty with Britain that ended the Revolutionary War.

▶ **MINISTER TO FRANCE**

Jefferson now had to turn his eyes eastward, for in 1784 he was sent to Paris to help negotiate treaties of commerce between the new United States and the countries of Europe. The American mission had only limited success, but the next year Jefferson was appointed minister to France, succeeding the popular Benjamin Franklin.

Jefferson's five years in Paris were among the most interesting of his entire life. He took his daughter Martha with him, and after a time he sent for his other daughter, Mary. He enjoyed to the fullest the architecture, art, and music of the Old World, bought books by the dozen, and made friends of scholars and scientists. He learned many of the secrets of French cooking and became an authority on French wines. Jefferson also traveled widely and kept careful records of the things he saw. He wrote to American friends about them and sent home samples of European animals and plants. His drawings of a Roman temple in France served as a model for the capitol building in Richmond (which had succeeded Williamsburg as Virginia's state capital). It also spurred the classic revival in American architecture.

Jefferson formed a low opinion of European kings. He especially disliked the French monarchy. But France had shown friendship to the United States and had helped it financially and militarily during the American Revolution, and Jefferson was determined to strengthen this tie at a time when the young republic had hardly any other friends.

Jefferson saw the outbreak of the French Revolution in 1789, his last year in Paris. He feared that it would get out of hand, as it did later, but he approved of this revolt against what he considered royal tyranny.

▶ **SECRETARY OF STATE**

Jefferson returned home that same year. Rather reluctantly he accepted the invitation of President George Washington to become the first secretary of state (then called secretary of foreign affairs) under the new Constitution. He took office in 1790 and served until the end of 1793.

During this time occurred his historic conflict with Alexander Hamilton, the young and brilliant secretary of the treasury. In foreign affairs Jefferson, who believed that Britain was still an enemy, tried to keep the United States friendly to France and the cause of liberty it now represented. Hamilton favored the British and preferred the rule of a monarch to that of the French revolutionaries. But when war broke out between France and Britain in 1793, both men agreed that the United States should stay out of it.

Jefferson's daughter Martha Randolph often served as his White House hostess. Jefferson's wife had died in 1782.

Jefferson objected to certain of Hamilton's policies as favoring merchants and financiers rather than farmers. Most of the people in the United States were then farmers, and Jefferson always thought of himself as one. He believed in individual liberty more than Hamilton did and trusted the people more. He thought that Hamilton was trying to increase the power of the national government beyond what was permitted by the Constitution. Jefferson favored the strict interpretation of the Constitution, believing that this would prevent tyranny.

For additional information on Alexander Hamilton and his ideas, see the article on him in Volume H.

▶ VICE PRESIDENT

In the presidential election of 1796, John Adams, who was Washington's vice president, was the candidate of the Federalists, who supported a strong national, or federal, government. Jefferson was the choice of the Republicans (also known as Democratic-Republicans), who opposed the policies of the Federalists. Adams won election by a majority of three electoral votes. According to the electoral system then in effect, Jefferson became the vice president. There has never been another situation quite like this in U.S. history, in which the president was also the recognized leader of the party opposed to the government.

This was the time of what Adams called the "half-war" with France. Diplomatic relations between the United States and France were broken, and there was fighting between their two navies. Jefferson was charged with favoring the French in the dispute, although in fact he did not do so. The wartime mood also led to the passage in 1798, by a Federalist-controlled Congress, of the Alien and Sedition Acts. Under their provisions, foreigners could be deported from the country if they were thought dangerous, and journalists and others who criticized the government could be sent to jail.

For more information on the Alien and Sedition Acts and other events of this period in U.S. history, see the article on John Adams in Volume A.

▶ THE ELECTION OF 1800

The presidential election of 1800 was also marked by confusion. Jefferson and Adams were again the candidates of their parties. Adams, whose popularity, along with that of the Federalists, had fallen drastically, lost his bid for re-election. But the election resulted in a tie between Jefferson and his own vice-presidential candidate, Aaron Burr. For months it was uncertain who would be president. The outcome was finally determined when the House of Representatives elected Jefferson, as the majority of the voters had intended. (The manner in which presidents were elected was clarified by the Twelfth Amendment to the Constitution, ratified in 1804.)

▶ PRESIDENT

His Presidency: An Overview. Jefferson's inauguration as president in 1801 was the first transfer of power in the United States from one political group to another. That it was accomplished peacefully made it especially noteworthy. Jefferson served two terms in office, winning re-election in 1804 by a wide margin. He reduced taxes, abolished offices that he thought unnecessary, and generally governed in a spirit of toleration and humanity. The hated Alien and Sedition Acts were repealed or allowed to expire. He also worked well with Congress, respecting the constitutional separation of powers between the executive and legislative branches of the government.

But he also had to endure personal attacks on his character by his enemies, perhaps more than any other president. Among the false accusations was that Jefferson was an atheist (that he did not believe in God) and that he was immoral. In spite of this, for nearly all of his administration, he enjoyed enormous popularity among the American people.

The New Capital. Jefferson was nearly 58 when he became president. He was the first chief executive to be inaugurated in Washington, D.C., which had become the seat of government during the last year of the Adams administration. Although it was called a city, Washington was then really just a village in the wilderness. Only one wing of the original Capitol had been built, and the president's residence (it officially became known as the White House much later) looked like a big bare box. The columns that now adorn the entrance were not yet in place.

Nevertheless, Jefferson had the place furnished handsomely and gave delicious dinners there. He did not like formality or ceremony, however, preferring the relaxed atmosphere he was used to at Monticello. The duties of hostess were occasionally shared by his daughters, Martha and Mary, now married and with their own families. Mary's death in 1804 would be a severe blow to Jefferson.

Louisiana Purchase. The most notable achievement of Jefferson's presidency was his purchase from France in 1803 of the Louisiana Territory. The acquisition of this vast territory, lying between the Mississippi River and the Rocky Mountains, doubled the area of the United States at a stroke. Jefferson had already prepared the Lewis and Clark expedition, which explored the virtually unknown region and eventually reached

Vice President Aaron Burr (firing) became notorious after killing Alexander Hamilton in a duel in 1804. Burr was later charged with treason but acquitted.

A political cartoon of the period shows Jefferson's dilemma over the Embargo of 1807. His pocket is being picked at the same time by Britain's King George III (left) and the French emperor Napoleon.

the Pacific Ocean. The purchase aroused alarm among New Englanders, who feared that their small states would become unimportant, but it delighted most Americans. Actually, Jefferson himself had wondered if the purchase was constitutional but was persuaded of its legality. See the articles on the Lewis and Clark Expedition and the Louisiana Purchase in Volume L.

The Federalist Judges. Less successful was the outcome of his dispute with the Federalist judges, particularly the many appointed in the waning days of the Adams presidency. Considering the judges biased against his administration, Jefferson rejected many of the late appointments and sought to impeach an associate justice of the Supreme Court. But he was rebuffed by U.S. Chief Justice John Marshall, a Federalist. The dispute, although of little importance now, resulted in one of the Supreme Court's most important decisions, *Marbury* v. *Madison* (1803). In it, Marshall established the right of judicial review, under which the Court could declare a law unconstitutional.

An article on John Marshall appears in Volume M.

The Tripolitan War. In 1801 war broke out between the United States and Tripoli, one of the Barbary States situated along the coast of North Africa. The Barbary States lived by piracy, and the United States and other countries paid them tribute, in the form of yearly sums of money, to allow their merchant ships to cross the Mediterranean Sea unmolested. The immediate cause of the conflict was the demand by Tripoli for additional tribute, which the United States refused. Fought mainly at sea, the war ended in 1805 with the capture of the Tripolitan fortress of Derna by U.S. land and sea forces.

The Burr Conspiracy. Soon after his inauguration for a second term in 1805, Jefferson was caught up in the strange events involving his former vice president, Aaron Burr. (George Clinton had succeeded Burr in that office.) Already notorious for having killed Alexander Hamilton in a duel in 1804, Burr was suspected of conspiring to set up an independent empire in the Southwest. He was tried for treason but acquitted by a court presided over by Chief Justice John Marshall. See the separate article on Aaron Burr in Volume B.

The Embargo. Jefferson's most vexing problems as president grew out of the war between Britain and France, which had resumed and involved much of Europe. Both sides ignored the neutral rights of the United States, but since Britain commanded the seas, its actions most offended Americans. Particularly objectionable was the practice of impressment, in which British warships stopped American vessels and impressed, or forced, American seamen into British service. Not wanting either to submit or be forced into war, Jefferson, in 1807, gained passage in Congress of the Embargo Act, which halted exports to both Britain and France.

Measures of this sort had been used successfully by the colonists against the British before the Revolution. However, the embargo was bitterly opposed by shippers, especially in New England, who claimed that it did more harm than good, and that the government was tyrannical in enforcing it. The

A larger-than-life-size statue of Thomas Jefferson stands in the Jefferson Memorial in Washington, D.C. The memorial was dedicated in 1943, two centuries after his birth.

embargo's failure was painful to Jefferson, and it was repealed at the very end of his presidency.

▶ **LAST RETIREMENT**

After his friend James Madison, who had served as his secretary of state, succeeded to the presidency in 1809, Jefferson returned to Monticello. There he spent the last 17 years of his life. He was often surrounded by his grandchildren, whom he adored, but he had so many other visitors as well that he fled for part of each year to another place of his, Poplar Forest, near Lynchburg, Virginia. He spent much of his time writing letters. Many of them were to his old opponent John Adams, with whom he discussed books, government, religion, and almost everything else. Jefferson was in financial difficulties during his last years and was practically bankrupt at his death.

Jefferson's last great public service was the founding of the University of Virginia in 1819. It was the only accomplishment that he valued as much as his authorship of the Declaration of Independence and the Virginia Bill for Religious Freedom. He designed the university's buildings himself and selected the first professors.

Jefferson died on July 4, 1826, the 50th anniversary of the Declaration of Independence; John Adams died the same day. He was buried at Monticello, beside his wife. Two centuries after his birth, in 1943, a memorial to Jefferson was dedicated in Washington, D.C., establishing his place alongside George Washington and Abraham Lincoln among great Americans.

DUMAS MALONE
University of Virginia
Author, *Jefferson and His Time*

JEFFERSON CITY. See MISSOURI (Cities).

JELLYFISH
AND OTHER COELENTERATES

If you live near the sea, you have probably seen some of the oldest forms of life on Earth. Their traces have been found in rocks nearly 7 million years old. These soft-bodied creatures called coelenterates, or cnidarians, lived in the ancient seas long before the first fish. They include jellyfish, hydras, corals, sea wasps, and sea anemones.

There are about 9,500 species, or kinds, of living coelenterates. All of them are found in water, and most of them are found in salt-water environments of oceans and bays and brackish water (a mixture of fresh and salt water) environments of estuaries. Many coelenterates of today resemble those early relatives that existed millions of years ago.

▶ CHARACTERISTICS OF COELENTERATES

Jellyfish and their relatives are not true fish. All fish are vertebrates, or animals with backbones. Coelenterates are invertebrates. Unlike most fish and other water animals, they do not have fins, legs, or tails. Nor do they have scales or shells to protect them.

Giant Jellyfish

Body Structure

The coelenterate's body is little more than a hollow jellylike bag. One layer of cells forms the outside of the bag. Another layer lines the inside. Soft, watery jelly separates the two layers of cells. The body has one opening, or mouth. The coelenterate takes in food, such as the larvae of crustaceans, mollusks, and worms, through its mouth. Some species even take in small fish. Once inside the body cavity, the food is digested by the inside layer of cells. Any undigested food is thrown out through the same opening.

Tentacles, or feelers, that look like hanging threads surround the mouth. The tentacles of some species have stinging cells called **nematocysts**. Each stinging cell contains a capsule in which a long, hollow thread is coiled. The barbed tip of the thread sticks out of the cell and acts like a trigger. The stinging cells can be stimulated by chemicals given off by potential prey and predators, by physical touch, or by increased water pressure from the slightest of movements. When the cells are stimulated, their coiled threads spring out. The barbed tips pierce the body of the victim,

injecting it with poison fluid. (Coelenterates' bodies produce new stinging cells to replace the used ones.) The tentacles capture the food and draw it into the opening.

In some coelenterates, the poison is so powerful that it can paralyze large creatures, even human beings. Anyone who has ever brushed against a jellyfish knows that the sting can be quite painful. Even when the animal is washed up on shore, the stinging cells keep their power for some time.

A coelenterate that does not have stinging cells can grasp small animals that swim into its tentacles and carry them in through its mouth.

Along with the stinging cells and the body plan, coelenterates have other features in common. Coelenterates have no blood or central nervous system. However, they do have nerve cells scattered in the jelly between the cell layers. They also have cells that respond to light, touch, and the pull of gravity. These sensory and nerve cells send information to the muscle cells that make the animals move.

The Body of a Coelenterate

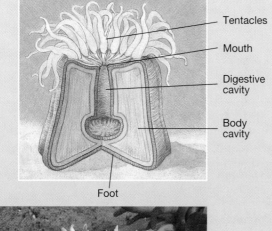

Tentacles

Mouth

Digestive cavity

Body cavity

Foot

Found within the world's seas is a group of simple creatures known as coelenterates. Although the various species differ greatly from each other in appearance, all of them share the same basic body structure (*diagram, left*). The soft body of the coelenterate contains a digestive cavity that opens to the outside through the mouth. A ring of tentacles, with stinging cells called nematocysts (*diagram, below*), typically surrounds the mouth.

Sea Pen

Sea Anemone

Nematocysts

Undischarged (filament coiled)

Discharged (filament uncoiled)

Basic Body Forms

Coelenterates are an interesting group of animals because they are found in two basic body forms: the **polyp** and the **medusa**. Some kinds of coelenterates have both forms at different stages of their lives. Others exist in only one form all their lives. Though they appear different, both body forms have the same basic structures.

A polyp has a body shaped like a hollow cylinder. One end typically remains fixed to rocks and shells or to the ocean floor by a footlike disk. At the other end, the tentacle-ringed mouth faces upward. Sea anemones, hydras, and adult corals grow as polyps.

Although they are attached to something, these animals can make motions. They can move their tentacles and stretch or shrink their bodies. For example, when a sea anemone is feeding, its body and petal-like tentacles extend upward, ready for a tiny animal to swim or drift against one of them. But when danger threatens, such as low tide, the animal draws in its tentacles and looks like a brown, lumpy knob.

Also, a polyp does not always remain fixed to one spot. It may glide along slowly on its sticky base. It may also use its tentacles as arms, somersaulting base over tentacles. But some part of the body is always touching another surface. A few hydras can produce a gas bubble in their base. Then they float up to the surface of the water.

Some polyps—corals, for example—usually live in groups, or colonies. The individual polyps may be close together or joined in various ways. Most of these colonies remain in one place, their tentacles capturing prey that swim within their reach.

A medusa has a body shaped like an umbrella or a bell. The mouth points down in this form, and the tentacles float outward. Medusae (plural of medusa) are able to swim about freely. However, they are relatively poor swimmers and usually go wherever currents and winds push them. They do have some movement control. By contracting their umbrella-shaped bodies, they are able to change their direction and depth in the water. Adult jellyfish and sea wasps are medusae.

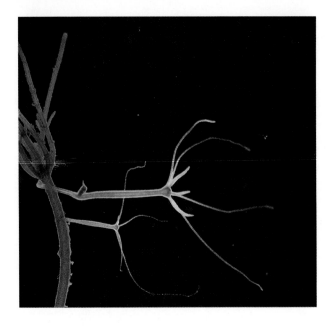

With its first offspring anchored below it on a plant stem, a hydra once again begins budding. The new bud can be seen forming from the stalklike body of the parent hydra.

drops off from the parent and takes up life on its own. In time it produces its own buds.

▶ KINDS OF COELENTERATES

Different kinds of coelenterates vary in size, color, and even shape. Coelenterates are separated into four classes, or large groups. They are Hydrozoa, Scyphozoa, Anthozoa, and Cubozoa.

Hydrozoa

Hydrozoans include freshwater hydras and hydroids, or hydralike animals, which usually live in saltwater environments.

Freshwater Hydras. Freshwater hydras are small solitary polyps that live in ponds, lakes, and streams. They are usually found on the underside of the leaves of water plants and lily pads. They are some of the few coelenterates found in fresh water. Many kinds are no bigger than a pencil point. Others may grow $\frac{1}{2}$ inch (1 centimeter) tall. Hydras can be green, pink, yellowish, or brownish in color. They look like frayed bits of string.

Unlike most hydrozoans, freshwater hydras have no medusa stage. Along with the typical methods of reproduction, the tiny freshwater

Reproduction

Almost every kind of coelenterate can produce offspring, or make copies of themselves, by means of both sexual reproduction and asexual reproduction.

During sexual reproduction, male reproductive cells (sperm) and female reproductive cells (eggs) are produced. Fertilization takes place when the sperm and egg unite. From the fertilized egg, a new creature is formed.

During the process of **budding**, an asexual form of reproduction, a budlike lump forms on the coelenterate's body. In a few days the bud has tentacles and a mouth. Eventually it

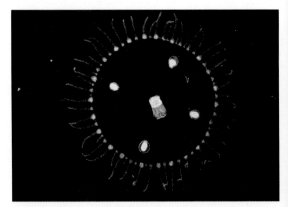

Even though an *Obelia* colony (*right*) remains fixed in one place, its medusa offspring (*above*) can swim freely and shed its eggs far from the parent colony. As a result, *Obelia* and other hydroid colonies like it are spread over a wide area.

WONDER QUESTION

WONDER QUESTION

What is a reef community?

All the living things that inhabit a reef—the stony structure formed by some colonial corals—make up a reef community. Within the reef community, there is a diversity of life rivaling that found in a tropical rain forest. One of the most productive reef communities is the Great Barrier Reef (*left*), off the coast of Queensland, Australia. Among other life-forms, there are more than 350 species of corals and 1,500 species of fish in this community!

hydra can regrow lost parts through **regeneration**. If a hydra is cut into many pieces, almost every piece will grow into a new hydra. It is its ability to regenerate that has given the hydra its name: Hydra was a many-headed monster of Greek mythology that could grow two heads for each one cut off.

Hydroid Colonies. The hydroids, or hydralike animals, usually live in colonies in saltwater environments. There are two basic kinds of colonies: fixed and floating.

Obelia is an example of a **fixed colony**. It stays attached to the sea bottom. An entire colony forms from one polyp. Each member of the colony is so small that it can hardly be seen by the unaided eye. Yet each has a job to do for the colony. Some members are food-gathering polyps. Their tentacles capture food for the entire colony. Other members are reproductive polyps.

Medusa buds develop in the reproductive polyps. In time, the young medusae swim out of the mouths of the parent polyps. When the tiny bell-shaped creatures become adults, the females produce eggs and the males produce sperm. The fertilized medusa eggs develop into polyps. From each polyp a new *Obelia* colony may begin.

Most hydrozoan colonies, like the *Obelia*, stay fixed to the sea bottom. But there are some floating colonies. The most familiar example of a **floating colony** is probably the one formed by the Portuguese man-of-war.

Many people think of the Portuguese man-of-war as a single medusa. But it is really a large colony of medusae and polyps. The balloon is a medusa that is filled with gas. The colony drifts with the ocean currents and is blown by the wind. The balloon, which is usually 6 to 8 inches (15 to 20 centimeters) across, acts like a sail. When the balloon empties, the colony sinks below the surface.

Under the balloon hang long tentacles, as much as 40 feet (12 meters) long. These are made up of many small polyps, which serve the colony in different ways. The reproduc-

Generations of medusae and polyps form the long, potent tentacles of the Portuguese man-of-war. As the tentacles trail through the water, they easily trap and kill prey.

tive polyps produce little medusae, which swim away and start new colonies.

Stinger polyps, working together, can capture a large fish and deliver it to the feeding polyps. The stinger polyps can be dangerous or even fatal to a human swimmer. When a colony is blown ashore, the stingers remain poisonous for a long time.

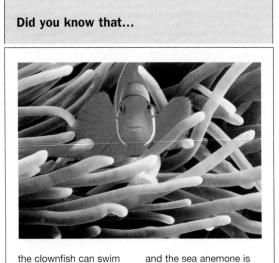

the clownfish can swim and rest among the sea anemone's deadly tentacles without getting stung? Scientists are not sure exactly how the clownfish escapes the sting of the sea anemone. But they do know that the clownfish starts the relationship with caution. It begins by spending short periods of time among the poisonous tentacles. Gradually the clownfish increases the time until it can rest safely in the anemone's tentacles for long periods.

The unusual relationship between the clownfish and the sea anemone is beneficial to both. Inside an anemone's mass of stinging tentacles, the clownfish is safe from its predators. Any predator that tries to get at the clownfish risks fatal stings. The clownfish can also dine on any leftovers that result when the anemone captures food and on the anemone's waste products. In return, the clownfish removes parasites and waste products from the anemone. The clownfish, which aggressively guards its territory, may also drive away the anemone's predators.

Scyphozoa

The coelenterates called scyphozoans include most of the larger jellyfish. Some jellyfish are shaped like cups or bells. Others look more like umbrellas or saucers. Some are col-

ored a soft pink or purple. Others, such as the lion's manes and sun jellies, are bright yellow and gold. Still others have striped patterns on their upper sides.

Some jellyfish, such as the bright blue-and-orange sea blubbers, are among the largest animals without backbones. They may measure about 12 feet (3.5 meters) in diameter. Their tentacles may extend more than 100 feet (30 meters) beneath them. Moon jellyfish may grow to 10 inches (25 centimeters) in diameter and sometimes even to 2 feet (0.5 meter). Other jellyfish are colorless and the size of a fingertip.

The moon jellyfish is a typical scyphozoan. It swims or floats freely in the water. On the upper side of a fully grown moon jellyfish, you may see a pink or orange pattern like a four-leaf clover. The four "leaves" are the reproductive organs. In male jellyfish they produce sperm cells, which are released through the animal's mouth into the water. In female jellyfish the reproductive organs produce eggs, which remain inside the body until they are fertilized.

The eggs develop in four long, trailing mouth folds. These folds hang down from the mouth and, like the tentacles, bear stinging cells. When the eggs hatch, the young settle on the bottom of the ocean. They develop into a shape very different from the parent animal. They become polyps.

Like the parent jellyfish, the young polyp has stinging cells and catches food with its tentacles. It grows for several months. Gradually the polyp comes to look like a stack of fringed saucers. One by one the saucers pinch off from the polyp and swim away. Each becomes a separate little medusa. In most jelly-

It is the external skeletons of hard corals, such as the lettuce coral (*below*), that serve as the foundation for the world's tropical reefs. Soft corals, such as the branching coral (*left*), have internal skeletons. Their delicate forms and brilliant hues help create the undersea gardens decorating coral reefs.

fish, the medusae go on to produce polyps, and the cycle begins again.

Anthozoa

The anthozoans, which are sometimes called flower animals, are polyps with a flowerlike appearance. Included in this group are the sea anemones, corals, sea fans, sea pens, and tube anemones. They are found all over the world in both deep and shallow saltwater environments. These coelenterates, which have no medusa stage, vary greatly in size and may be solitary or colonial.

The sea anemone is an example of a solitary anthozoan. It is a giant polyp, compared to a hydra. It may be as large as 3 feet (1 meter) in diameter and 3 inches (8 centimeters) tall.

They reproduce in several ways. Sometimes new sea anemones are produced by budding. At other times one sea anemone simply divides into two parts, and each part becomes a new individual. Sea anemones also reproduce sexually. They produce reproductive cells that are thrown out through the animal's mouth. The sperm cells join the egg cells in the water, and the fertilized eggs develop into young animals.

Young sea anemones, which lack tentacles, swim about in search of food. They feed on fish and any other live animal they can manage to snare. Finally they settle on the bottom, attaching themselves to underwater objects with a footlike disk or burrowing in the bottom mud or sand. In time, their tentacles grow.

Corals are the anthozoans that usually form colonies. Although corals appear in a wide variety of forms, hard (or stony), thorny, or soft, they are all tiny polyps. Like other animals in this group, corals reproduce without a medusa stage.

As coelenterates, some corals are unique. They produce a hard outside skeleton made mostly of limestone. Because of this characteristic, some colonial corals are able to form huge structures called reefs. The coral reefs are made up of live corals living atop the limestone skeletons of their ancestors.

Anthozoans form some interesting relationships with other sea organisms. Many corals, as well as anemones, house microscopic single-celled algae on and in their tissues. The algae help the corals by providing

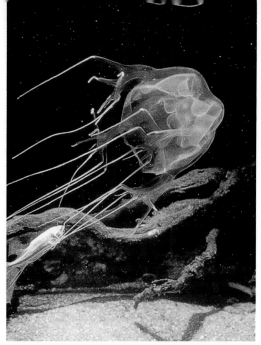

The beautiful but deadly sea wasp is found off the coasts of northern Australia and southeastern Asia. Its venomous sting can lead to death in a matter of minutes.

some of the raw materials they need to grow and build tissue. In turn, the corals give off waste products that the algae use for their life processes. Another mutually helpful relationship exists between some anemones and hermit crabs. The hermit crab places an anemone on the snail shell in which the crab lives. With its ready sting, the anemone helps protect the crab from predators. For its services, the anemone receives particles of food dropped by the crab.

Cubozoa

The body of the cubozoan is shaped like a cube or square. A tentacle or group of tentacles is found at each corner of the square. Cubozoans are strong swimmers and aggressive predators, feeding mostly on fish.

Several coelenterates in this class are considered dangerous because of their stings, but one is feared above all others. The cubozoan known as the sea wasp, or box jellyfish, can produce welts on anyone who comes in contact with its tentacles. Its stings are dangerous, and if a person is badly stung, they can even be fatal.

Reviewed by CLYDE L. MacKENZIE, Jr.
Research Fishery Biologist
National Marine Fisheries Service

See also ANIMALS; CORALS.

A young boy was the first person to be vaccinated against smallpox by Edward Jenner, who discovered the vaccine.

JENNER, EDWARD (1749–1823)

Edward Jenner was an English doctor who discovered a way to prevent people from getting the deadly disease called smallpox.

Jenner was born on May 17, 1749, in the town of Berkeley, Gloucestershire, where his father was a minister. When Edward was 5 years old, his father died. The oldest son in the family, Stephen, helped bring up the five younger children. He saw to it that each one had a proper education.

Edward started school when he was 8 years old. After finishing grammar school he was apprenticed to Daniel Ludlow, a surgeon in a nearby town. Edward wanted to learn to be a surgeon himself.

When he was 21, Jenner went off to London to study under Dr. John Hunter, one of the most famous surgeons of all time. For a large fee, Hunter took young students into his home as "resident pupils." Besides learning to be a surgeon, Edward met many scientists. He became interested in science as well as medicine.

In 1773 Jenner began to practice medicine in his native town of Berkeley. Besides being a doctor and a surgeon, Jenner collected fossils, observed plants and birds, and showed an interest in natural history. He was not a very good observer, and none of his scientific work was important. But he kept up his contacts with scientists and doctors he had known in London.

▶ **JENNER'S DISCOVERY OF SMALLPOX VACCINATION**

Smallpox is a highly contagious disease that often occurs in epidemics. Those who recover from it are usually left with pitted scars all over the skin. The scars are caused by pocks, or little blisters, produced by the disease. The only protection known in Jenner's day was to take some liquid from a pock on a smallpox victim's skin and put it in the arm of a healthy person. This was called inoculation. It would usually give the healthy person a mild case of smallpox, and then he could not get smallpox again.

But sometimes a person who was inoculated developed a serious case of smallpox. Thus, people who allowed themselves to be inoculated took a very big chance that they might be harmed instead of protected.

Jenner heard people in the country say that dairymaids who had had cowpox did not catch smallpox. Cowpox is a cattle disease that can be caught by people who milk cows having the disease. It is a very mild disease, although it does produce blisters. Jenner believed that by inoculating healthy people with cowpox he could keep them from getting smallpox.

The scientists and doctors who studied Jenner's evidence found it hard to believe. For example, many people who once had cowpox later got smallpox. Jenner answered that they had not had "true" cowpox. Since a person who has had smallpox cannot get it again, Jenner argued that cowpox and smallpox were the same disease. He even renamed cowpox "smallpox of the cow," although they seemed to be different diseases.

In spite of these differences Jenner devoted the rest of his life to trying to convince people that they would be safe from smallpox if they were inoculated with cowpox. This method came to be called vaccination after the Latin word for "cow." Jenner was given large sums of money by the British Government to help him in his program of vaccination and in appreciation of his contribution to humanity. Slowly people began to see that vaccination was successful. Today epidemics of smallpox have become rare because of the excellent protection given by vaccination.

Jenner died on January 26, 1823.

DUANE H. D. ROLLER
University of Oklahoma

JEREMIAH

Jeremiah, the Old Testament prophet, was born about the middle of the 600's B.C. He came from a priestly family who lived in the village of Anathoth near Jerusalem. His story is in the colorfully written book of Jeremiah in the Bible. Some of it was told by Jeremiah himself.

The story in the Bible tells that when Jeremiah was still a young man, God told him he had been chosen to be a prophet. Jeremiah protested at first. He said he was too young for the task. But God touched Jeremiah's mouth and said, "Behold, I have put my words in thy mouth."

Jeremiah grew up at a time when his homeland, Judah, was controlled by the Assyrians. In 609 B.C. the Assyrian Empire fell to the Babylonians. Jeremiah warned his fellow Judeans to accept Babylonian rule. If they did not, he said, the Babylonians would destroy them or make them slaves.

Jeremiah's warning was read to the people on the steps of the great temple in Jerusalem. It was also read to the king. But the king had been put on the throne by the Egyptians, allies of the Assyrians. He burned Jeremiah's warning in anger.

Jeremiah was threatened and called a traitor, and he was imprisoned for a time. Yet he continued to warn the Judeans to accept Babylonian rule, which he said was a punishment from God. Jeremiah believed that God had turned against the Judeans because they had stopped being religious. But Jeremiah felt deep sympathy for them, expressed in his beautiful laments in the book of Jeremiah.

Many things that Jeremiah predicted came true. Jerusalem fell and was almost entirely destroyed by the Babylonians in 586 B.C. The Judeans were afraid of being enslaved by the Babylonians. Many fled to Egypt, and Jeremiah went with them reluctantly.

In Egypt, Jeremiah continued to be a strict judge of his people. He condemned them bitterly for worshiping false gods. Very little is known about the last part of his life. According to legend, he was stoned to death by some of his own people.

LLOYD R. BAILEY
Duke University

JEROME, SAINT (331?–420)

Saint Jerome, a great Bible scholar and a father of the early Catholic Church, was born about 331 in the town of Stridon in what is now Croatia. His full name was Sophronius Eusebius Hieronymus.

Jerome, whose parents were Christian, spent his youth in Rome, where he was educated and baptized. In about 368 he went to Gaul, and while there, he decided to devote himself entirely to the religious life. He went to Aquileia in northern Italy, where he joined a monastic community. In 373 he left Italy for the East and lived for several years as a hermit in the Syrian desert. There he fasted, prayed, and studied Hebrew.

In 382, Jerome returned to Rome and became secretary to Pope Damasus. During this time, Jerome bitterly attacked the worldly life of some of the clergy. After Damasus' death in 384, Jerome returned to the East and founded a monastery at Bethlehem.

Between 390 and 405, Jerome translated the Old Testament from Hebrew into Latin. He continued to revise the Old Latin version of the New Testament, a task he had begun earlier. Jerome's edition of the Bible, known as the Vulgate, was a brilliant achievement. It established him as one of the leading scholars of his day. Most Bibles used today by Catholics are based on his version. He also wrote many books on church and Bible history.

In 415, Jerome published a series of commentaries against the Pelagians, followers of the British monk Pelagius (360?–420). The Pelagians challenged many basic ideas of the church. As a result of his attacks, the Pelagians threatened Saint Jerome's life. He was forced to leave his monastery and go into hiding until 418. Two years later, Jerome died at his monastery in Bethlehem.

September 30, the day of Saint Jerome's death, is his feast day. On that day, Catholics throughout the world honor him.

Reviewed by ROWAN A. GREER
Yale Divinity School

JERSEY CITY. See NEW JERSEY (Cities).

A view of Jerusalem from the Mount of Olives.

JERUSALEM

Jerusalem! Does any other city in the world mean so much to so many people? Jerusalem is sacred to three great faiths—Judaism, Christianity, and Islam. To Jews, Jerusalem represents the heritage of their ancient nation and the promise of their new state, Israel. To Christians, Jerusalem is the city where the Crucifixion and Resurrection of Jesus Christ took place. To Muslims, Jerusalem is the site from which Mohammed rose to heaven to receive the blessing of Allah. For centuries, it has been the Holy City for millions of people.

Many believe that Jerusalem's name comes from the ancient Hebrew word *Yerushalaim,* which means "City of Peace." But peace is something Jerusalem has seldom known during its long history. Jews, Christians, and Muslims have fought and died for the privilege of ruling Jerusalem's stones. The city has paid a terrible price for its sacred status.

▶ HISTORY

No one knows how or when Jerusalem was founded. Perhaps its location made it a natural camping site for the caravans of ancient times. Or perhaps the abundance of water in natural springs drew wandering tribes to its oases. In any event, Jerusalem was listed in a census compiled in the 19th century B.C. by scribes of Egyptian kings.

About 1000 B.C., the Hebrew ruler King David captured Jerusalem and made it the capital of the kingdom of Israel. David made a natural but fateful choice. Jerusalem perches high on the Judean hills, not far east of the Mediterranean Sea and just west of the Jordan River Valley and the Dead Sea. This location, astride the natural caravan routes that linked Asia Minor and Africa, gave Jerusalem special importance. It stirred the attention and the jealousies of its neighbors.

Several years after David's death, King Solomon built his famous Temple of gold and cedar. The Temple was destroyed by the Babylonians in 587 B.C., and the Jews were carried off to exile in what is now Iraq. About 50 years later, the Jews returned to Jerusalem and painstakingly rebuilt their Temple. They were attacked repeatedly by their neighbors. But they ruled Jerusalem until 333 B.C., when the city fell to the Greeks. It was ruled by a series of non-Jewish peoples until 167 B.C. Then Jews, under leaders called Maccabees, revolted and regained their capital and their independence.

The next 100 years represented a high point of Jewish civilization. That glorious era ended when Palestine became a Roman protectorate under King Herod I. It was during the time of Roman rule that Jesus Christ was born in nearby Bethlehem and was crucified in Jerusalem.

Once again, in A.D. 66, the Jews revolted against foreign rule. This time, after four years

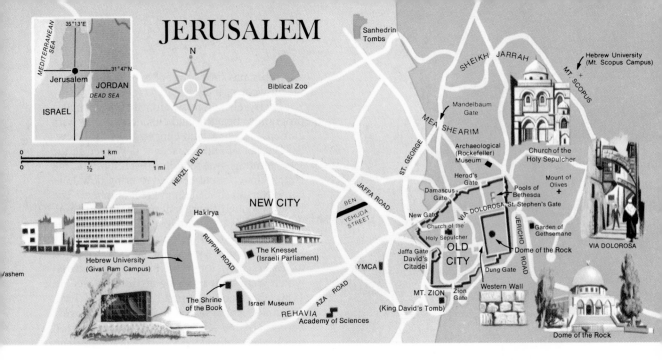

JERUSALEM

Dome of the Rock

of fighting, the Romans leveled the Jewish Temple and destroyed Jerusalem. The Jews were banished from the land—carried off as slaves or scattered in what was later known as the Diaspora, or dispersal.

In 638, the tribal warriors of another faith, Islam, stormed out of the deserts of the Arabian Peninsula to claim the city. Jerusalem's Muslim rulers were far more tolerant than earlier conquerors had been. There was no slaughter or great destruction, and there was a general acceptance of the Christian and Jewish faiths.

Jerusalem's next conquerors, Christian Crusaders from Europe, were not so kind to the city. But the kingdom they established in 1099 lasted only until 1187, when the brilliant Kurdish general Saladin won the city back for Islam. After that, Muslims continued to rule Jerusalem. It became part of the Ottoman Empire after 1500.

In the closing stages of World War I, in 1917, the British defeated the Ottoman Turks in a battle outside the city. The mayor, carrying a white flag made from a hospital bedsheet, surrendered to the British general Sir Edmund H. H. Allenby. General Allenby refused to enter the city on horseback. He said he would not ride a horse over the stones on which Christ had carried his cross.

After World War I, the League of Nations gave Britain a mandate, or charter, to govern Palestine, with Jerusalem as its administrative capital. Jewish immigration to both Palestine and Jerusalem increased greatly between 1920 and 1945. By the end of World War II, 100,000 of the 160,000 people of Jerusalem were Jews. The pressure to create a Jewish state in Palestine became very great when the extent of the Nazi slaughter of the Jews became known. But the Arabs of Palestine strongly opposed this idea.

The British despaired of finding a solution to the Palestine problem that was acceptable to both Jews and Arabs. They turned the problem over to the United Nations. In November, 1947, the U.N. General Assembly voted to divide Palestine into two separate states, one Jewish and one Arab. Jerusalem was to be made an international city under U.N. administration.

The Jewish Agency, which represented the Jewish people, reluctantly accepted the plan. But the Arabs rejected it. When the British left in May, 1948, fighting between the two peoples broke out. Arab forces soon gained control of the Old City, and the only road to Jerusalem was in Arab hands. For several weeks, the Jews of Jerusalem were under siege. Finally, the Israelis carved an emergency route across the Judean hills. At night, volunteers from Tel Aviv carried food to the Jews of Jerusalem and kept the Arabs from occupying the entire city.

An armistice between Israel and its Arab neighbors in 1949 ended the fighting. It left Jerusalem a divided city. The Old City was in

The Western Wall (Wailing Wall) is Judaism's most sacred shrine.

Jordanian hands, and most of the New City was controlled by Israel. The Israeli parliament, the Knesset, proclaimed the Jewish half of Jerusalem the capital of Israel. But the United States and most other countries of the world refused to recognize this action. They set up their embassies in Tel Aviv instead.

Jerusalem remained a divided city until the outbreak of the Arab-Israeli War in June, 1967. Barbed wire marked the dividing line. Pilgrims could pass from one side of the city to the other at only one place. This was an armed checkpoint called the Mandelbaum Gate.

The 1967 war lasted only six days. On June 7, Israeli forces crashed into the Old City through St. Stephen's Gate and quickly subdued its Jordanian defenders. Three weeks later—in violation of the terms of the 1949 armistice—the Knesset declared Jerusalem a reunited city under Jewish rule. The barbed wire

and other physical reminders of the city's division were torn away.

The Israeli administration then launched a program to beautify and enhance the city with gardens, theaters, and concert halls. The Jewish Quarter of Old Jerusalem, destroyed in the 1948 fighting, was rebuilt. Most important, the Israeli Government decided to bring new Jewish settlers to Jerusalem in great numbers. The Israelis wanted to prevent the city from being divided into Arab and Jewish sections again. Jews settled in Old Jerusalem, where only Arabs had lived. Many Arab lands were seized to make way for new Israeli settlements, which were built in a ring around the city. In 1980, the Knesset formally proclaimed Jerusalem the capital of Israel. These actions were opposed by the Arabs. Many other nations felt that Israel's refusal to recognize that Jerusalem was also important to the Arabs would make it more difficult to achieve a lasting peace in the area.

▶ THE OLD CITY

Jerusalem's heart is its old, walled city. Inside the walls are the three sacred sites that for centuries have been Jerusalem's glory and the cause of so many of its agonies—the Wailing Wall, the Church of the Holy Sepulcher, and the Dome of the Rock.

To step inside these walls, built by the Ottoman ruler Suleiman the Magnificent in the 1500's, is like stepping back in time into the days of the Biblical Middle East. Here are the very places where the Prophets spoke, where Jesus of Nazareth uttered his parables and carried his cross, where Mohammed meditated.

The Old City is a puzzle of vaulted alleyways and hidden passages, of cobbled steps and streets so narrow that four people cannot walk side by side. Only a few of these streets are wide enough for cars. Instead, donkeys do the work. They deliver the city's food as they might have in the time of Christ. Their spindly legs sway under loads of oranges, carrots, radishes, and tomatoes from the surrounding countryside. Tiny shops line many alleys. Their owners shout at passersby in half a dozen languages, and their windows are full of souvenirs. Everywhere, the alleys smell of roasting coffee, lamb grilling on open spits, and exotic spices. Tourists from all over the world mix with Arabs in flowing robes and turbans, Franciscan monks in dark brown robes, and young Israeli farmers in shorts and T-shirts.

The most famous of these alleys is a series of zigzags called the Via Dolorosa, or Way of Sorrow. From a point just inside St. Stephen's Gate, it traces the path over which Jesus Christ carried his cross on his way to Calvary. There are 14 stations, or stops, along the narrow cobbled route. Each one commemorates an event of that terrible ordeal. Every Friday, pilgrims and tourists, led by chanting Franciscan monks, thread their way along the Via Dolorosa. Their destination is the Church of the Holy Sepulcher, believed to be built over the site of Christ's Crucifixion and burial. The church is a tangle of chapels, dark passageways, and domes.

Just a short distance away is a high wall of huge limestone blocks. Two thousand years ago, these massive boulders formed the Western Wall of the courtyard that surrounded the Temple. This wall has long been known as the Wailing Wall. Jewish people all over the world turned toward it during their long exile, to mourn for their Promised Land and to pray for the rebirth of their nation. At any time of day or night you will find Jews praying here. Many of them kiss the stones or simply stare in awe at the boulders that long have meant much to their people.

Not more than a five-minute walk away is the Dome of the Rock, known to Muslims as the *Haram as Sharif* (Noble Sanctuary). It is

On Good Friday, thousands of Christian pilgrims retrace Christ's path to Calvary along the Via Dolorosa.

The Dome of the Rock, built in A.D. 691 and restored many times, is one of Islam's holiest sites.

the third holiest site in Islam, after Mecca and Medina in Saudi Arabia. The golden dome sparkles above its eight-sided base of blue and green tile. It is set in a broad white marble courtyard on the southwest corner of the Old City, below the Mount of Olives and the Garden of Gethsemane. The ceiling of the huge dome is covered with inscriptions to Allah. Below it is a massive gray stone that is believed to be the one on which Abraham was preparing to sacrifice his son Isaac when God stayed his hand. Muslims also believe that it bears the handprint of the Angel Gabriel, who held the rock firmly to earth when Mohammed ascended from it to heaven.

Jerusalem contains many other shrines. King David, the city's founder, is believed to be buried on Mount Zion overlooking the southern flank of the Old City. The same hilltop also shelters the room in which, according

A colorful street market in the Arab quarter of the Old City.

to Christian tradition, Christ gathered his Apostles for the Last Supper. That evening he was taken prisoner in the Garden of Gethsemane, where he had gone to pray. At the Pool of Bethesda (Bethsaida), Christ is said to have healed a man who had been ill for 38 years. Just outside the city is Ein Kerem, where John the Baptist was born.

▶ **THE NEW CITY**

Modern Jerusalem is a lively, bustling city of almost 400,000 people. Thousands of visitors flock there every year, and the leading industry is tourism. Jerusalem is also an important center of the diamond trade. And small factories turn out a wide variety of consumer goods, such as shoes, leather products, clothing, electrical appliances, and plastics.

Because the city is high above sea level, the air is clear and dry. Especially at sunset or early in the morning, a rosy, golden light seems to glow from Jerusalem's soft yellow limestone buildings. Spring and fall are lovely seasons. Sometimes there is snow in winter. During the summer, when the desert wind called the khamsin blows, the city can become uncomfortably hot.

Downtown, the New City is crowded with stores, hotels, offices, and coffee houses. Its main street, Ben Yehuda Street, has been converted into a pedestrian mall. Jerusalem's residential communities reflect the different backgrounds of the people. There is Rehavia, settled by well-to-do Israelis, where you will still hear German spoken in the streets. Very orthodox Jews live in Mea Shearim. The police close the streets in Mea Shearim to cars on Saturday. The people living there believe that driving a car on the Sabbath violates religious law, and they will throw stones at you if you do. Across a little valley is Sheikh Jarrah, where many wealthy Arabs live.

Jerusalem has several fine museums. Among the most famous are the Israel Museum and the Archaeological (Rockefeller) Museum. The Israel Museum complex includes an art museum, an archeological museum, a sculpture garden, and the Shrine of the Book, which houses the Dead Sea Scrolls. The Biblical Zoo is popular with almost all visitors. It has a large collection of animals mentioned in the Bible, with an appropriate Biblical quotation over each animal's cage. The people are justly proud of the modern campus of Hebrew University and of the Hadassah-Hebrew University Medical Center. The building housing the Knesset is built on a hillside west of the city. Nearby are massive buildings that house most of the government offices.

One of the most awe-inspiring sights in modern Jerusalem is the Yad Vashem, the memorial to the 6,000,000 Jews who perished in the Holocaust (Hitler's attempt to destroy the Jewish people).

▶ **THE FUTURE**

The question of who should rule Jerusalem is a major obstacle to a lasting peace in the Middle East. Almost all the nations of the world refuse to recognize Israel's claim to sovereignty over Jerusalem. And the Arab nations bitterly resent Israeli attempts to claim one of the holiest cities in Islam as their own. "Pray for the peace of Jerusalem" is a line from a psalm written for King David. It is as appropriate today as it was when it was first sung centuries ago.

LARRY COLLINS
Co-author, *O Jerusalem*

See also ISRAEL; PALESTINE.

Jesus was born in a stable in Bethlehem. In the background, an angel tells shepherds the news of his birth. (*The Nativity*, 1423, by Gentile da Fabriano.)

JESUS CHRIST

Jesus Christ was a Jewish prophet and teacher who founded the Christian religion. He preached and taught in Palestine almost 2,000 years ago.

To Christians, Jesus is the Son of God, and to most of them he is divine. Christians believe that God sent him to earth to save humankind. Many non-Christians have thought Jesus a great teacher. Muslims, for example, have regarded him as an important prophet.

▶THE STORY OF JESUS

Most of what we know about Jesus is based entirely on the New Testament of the Bible. His story is told in four books called the Gospels ("gospel" means "good news"). These books are Matthew, Mark, Luke, and John. They are named for the men who are thought to have written them. Matthew and John were disciples (or apostles) of Jesus. That is, they followed him, learned from him, and later spread his teachings. Many scholars think Mark and Luke knew other apostles of Jesus.

The Gospels are four different interpretations of Jesus' story. They sometimes differ from one another in details. For example, John's Gospel tells that Jesus drove money changers from the Temple in Jerusalem at the start of his ministry (when he began to teach). The other Gospels place this event at the end of his ministry. All of the writers agree, however, on the importance of Jesus. They consider him the Son of God.

Most scholars agree on an outline of Jesus' life. He was born shortly before the death of King Herod the Great in 4 B.C. (Herod was a ruler appointed by the Romans, who then controlled Palestine.) He grew up in Nazareth with Mary, his mother, and Joseph, her husband. When he was about 30 years old, Jesus began his ministry. His words and deeds won him followers, but they also made enemies. About A.D. 30, he was arrested in Jerusalem and condemned as a rebel against the Roman Empire. He was executed by crucifixion (being nailed to a cross), then a penalty for common criminals. After his death, some of his followers said he had appeared to them. They believed that God had raised him from the dead.

This outline is expanded and interpreted in the Gospels, which also tell what Jesus taught. Following is a summary of Jesus' story as it appears in the Gospels.

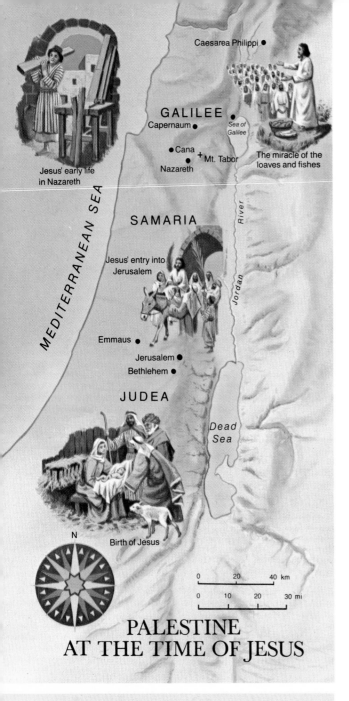

Caesarea Philippi •

GALILEE
Capernaum •
Sea of Galilee
• Cana
Nazareth + Mt. Tabor
The miracle of the loaves and fishes

Jesus' early life in Nazareth

MEDITERRANEAN SEA

SAMARIA

Jesus' entry into Jerusalem

Jordan River

Emmaus •

Jerusalem •
Bethlehem •

JUDEA

Dead Sea

N

Birth of Jesus

0   20   40 km
0   10   20   30 mi

PALESTINE AT THE TIME OF JESUS

What does the name "Jesus Christ" mean?

The name "Jesus" is the Greek version of a common Hebrew name, Joshua. It means "savior." "Christ" is actually a title. It comes from a Greek word that means "anointed one." ("Messiah," which comes from the Hebrew language, has the same meaning.) In the Old Testament, priests and kings were anointed with oil on taking office. This was a mark of great honor. A belief grew up that, one day, God would send an "anointed one" to restore the fortunes of the Jewish people. Because Jesus' followers believed that he was this savior, they called him Messiah, or Christ.

Birth and Early Years. The Gospels tell that Jesus was born miraculously, without a human father. An angel appeared to Mary and told her that she would bear a son, who would be the Son of God and the Messiah.

Shortly before Jesus was born, Mary and Joseph traveled to Bethlehem to be counted in a census. Because the town was crowded, they were forced to find shelter in a stable, and Jesus was born there. His cradle was a manger. Angels appeared to shepherds in nearby fields and proclaimed the birth of the Messiah. And wise men in the East heard of Jesus' birth. These men, called the Magi, followed a star to Bethlehem to find the "king of the Jews," and they brought gifts of gold and rare fragrances.

King Herod heard of Jesus' birth through the Magi, and he feared a rival. An angel appeared to Joseph in a dream and warned him that Herod intended to harm the child. Joseph and Mary fled with Jesus to Egypt. Herod, angered, ordered the killing of all the boys in Bethlehem two years old and younger.

After Herod's death, Jesus, Mary, and Joseph returned to live in Nazareth. Jesus probably grew up learning Joseph's trade, which according to Matthew's Gospel was carpentry. When he was 12, he went to Jerusalem with Mary and Joseph to celebrate the Jewish holiday of Passover. He became separated from them, and they found him in the Temple talking with the teachers, who were amazed at his understanding of religious questions.

Ministry. Jesus' public life began with his baptism by John the Baptist, a prophet who appeared in the wilderness of Judea preaching repentance. (Baptism is a ceremony in which water is used to symbolize the washing away of sin and the entrance into a new way of life.) The Gospels tell that when Jesus was baptized, the Spirit of God, in the form of a dove, rested on him, and a heavenly voice proclaimed him God's Son. After this, Jesus went into the desert for 40 days to prepare for his ministry. There he was tempted by Satan, who urged him to use his powers as the Son of God for his own benefit. Jesus refused.

Jesus then began teaching in Galilee. He chose twelve disciples to help in his work. The first disciples were Simon (renamed Peter), Andrew, James the Elder, and John. Later, Jesus was joined by Philip, Bartholomew,

Matthew, Thomas, James the Younger, Thaddeus, Simon, and Judas Iscariot.

The Gospels collect many of Jesus' teachings into long speeches. The Sermon on the Mount is the most familiar of these. Jesus also taught through parables—brief stories or comparisons that illustrate moral or religious principles. Jesus' miracles were also part of his ministry. The Gospels tell that he walked on the waters of the Sea of Galilee and stilled a storm. He changed water into wine at a wedding feast in Cana. And he fed thousands of people from a few fish and loaves of bread. But most of his miracles were miracles of healing. He cured lepers, restored sight to the blind, healed the lame, and cast out demons. He raised three people from the dead.

Each of the Gospels weaves Jesus' words and deeds into a story. In three of the books, the turning point comes when Peter acknowledges Jesus as the Messiah. Jesus then predicts his own death and resurrection. Soon after, Peter, James, and John see Jesus in glory. A light shines on him from heaven, and a voice proclaims him the Son of God. This event is called the transfiguration. It looks ahead to the resurrection.

Arrest and Crucifixion. Jesus and his disciples went to Jerusalem to celebrate the Passover. Jesus entered the city in triumph, riding a donkey, an animal that is a symbol of meekness. People spread palm branches before him and welcomed him.

Three of the Gospels state that Jesus next went to the Temple and drove out people who were changing money and buying and selling. He said that the Temple should be a place of prayer, not a marketplace. This angered the Jewish religious leaders, and they began to plot his death.

On the night of his arrest, Jesus shared a Passover feast with his disciples. At this meal, known as the Last Supper, he predicted that he would be betrayed and put to death. He

A miracle fills the nets of the disciples with fish from the Sea of Galilee. (*The Miraculous Draught of Fishes*, tapestry from a drawing by Raphael.)

Jesus dies on the cross. The inscription above his head reads, "This is Jesus of Nazareth, King of the Jews." (*The Crucifixion,* mid-1300's, by Taddeo Gaddi.)

gave bread to the disciples, saying, "This is my body." And he gave them wine, saying, "This is my blood." Christians remember the Last Supper in their sacrament of communion.

After the supper, Jesus and his disciples went to the Garden of Gethsemane. There, in exchange for 30 pieces of silver, Judas Iscariot pointed out his master to the Temple police. Jesus was taken to the Sanhedrin, the council that oversaw Jewish affairs. After condemning him for blasphemy, the Sanhedrin turned him over to Pontius Pilate, the Roman governor. Pilate attempted to free Jesus. It was the custom to free one prisoner during Passover, and Pilate offered to release Jesus. But the crowd that had gathered outside his palace demanded Jesus' death. Pilate then ordered him executed for claiming to be king of the Jews.

The next day, a Friday, Jesus was crucified along with two thieves on Mount Calvary, outside the city walls. He was forced to wear a crown of thorns and to carry his own cross to the site.

Resurrection. On the Sunday following Jesus' death, women went to his tomb and found it empty. An angel announced to them that Jesus had been raised from the dead. The Gospels tell stories of how Jesus appeared to the disciples—in Jerusalem, in Galilee, and on the road to Emmaus. He asked the disciples to go out into the world, to tell his story and teach what he had taught. According to tradition, he left the earth and ascended to heaven after 40 days.

Each of the Gospels has its own way of explaining the empty tomb and the appearances of Jesus. But they agree about the central importance of the resurrection. For the New Testament writers, the resurrection proved that Jesus was the Son of God.

▶ **WHAT JESUS TAUGHT**

Jesus' message concerned the Kingdom of God. He preached that God would soon be king in the sense that He would triumph over every evil. The world of sin and evil would end, and God's followers would live forever.

Many Jewish prophets predicted the end of the world and God's triumph. But Jesus went further. He said that the future Kingdom of God was present on earth—in his own person and ministry. It could be seen in his miracles of healing.

Part of Jesus' message had to do with the promise offered by the Kingdom of God. For example, in the new age the injustices of this world would be righted. The meek, the merciful, the pure in heart, the peacemakers, the poor, and the persecuted would be rewarded. Jesus sometimes used parables to describe the promise of the Kingdom. The parable of the mustard seed, for instance, tells how a tiny seed grows to become a tree. In the same way, the tiny "seed" of Jesus' ministry could be compared to the future Kingdom of God.

Jesus described entry into the Kingdom as a challenge as well as a promise. People who accepted the promise were challenged to lead a new kind of life. They were expected to live in complete obedience to God's will. Jesus' teaching differed from Old Testament law because it considered not only people's actions but also their thoughts. For example, Jesus

condemned the hatred that leads to murder as well as murder itself. The challenge of the Kingdom was also taught in parables, such as the parables of the prodigal son and the good Samaritan. Some of Jesus' teachings were unacceptable to other Jews because they seemed to contradict standard practices, such as strict observance of the Sabbath.

The most striking part of Jesus' teachings is found in his command to love one's enemies. He insisted that people should not repay evil with evil. In Chapter 12 of Mark's Gospel, Jesus says:

> And thou shalt love the Lord thy God with all thy heart, and with all thy soul, and with all thy mind, and with all thy strength: This is the first commandment. And the second is like, namely this, Thou shalt love thy neighbor as thyself.

ROWAN A. GREER
Divinity School, Yale University
Reviewed by REV. NEIL J. MCELENEY, C.S.P.
Catholic University of America

See also APOSTLES, THE; BIBLE (New Testament); BIBLE STORIES; CHRISTIANITY, HISTORY OF; JOHN THE BAPTIST; MARY, VIRGIN.

An angel announces the resurrection of Jesus. (*Three Marys at the Sepulcher*, early 1300's, by Duccio di Buoninsegna.)

JET LAG. See BIOLOGICAL CLOCK.

JET PROPULSION

Jet engines power today's fastest airplanes and missiles. They can move an airplane faster than any other type of engine because of the principle on which they work.

▶ THE JET PRINCIPLE

Jet engines were an important development in aviation, and they have been widely used since they were first developed. But the principle on which they work has been known for hundreds of years. It can be stated this way: For every force in one direction, there is an equal force in the opposite direction. This is known as the reaction principle. A rotating lawn sprinkler, which shoots streams of water from its nozzles, shows how this principle works. The stream of water shooting out exerts a force in one direction. According to the principle, there is also an equal force in the opposite direction, so the sprinkler rotates in that direction. The same kind of reaction force pushes an aircraft forward when the exhaust shoots out of the rear of a jet engine. The forward motion of the plane is not provided by the force of the jet exhaust against the air in the rear. It is provided by the reaction force inside the engine.

Structure of the Jet Engine

Aircraft jet engines are usually shaped like long, hollow tubes. The engine has four basic parts. They are the compressor, the burner (or combustor), the turbine, and the jet, or exhaust, nozzle.

The compressor is a fan or pump that operates at high speed. It raises the pressure of air entering the front of the engine. The compressed air goes into the burner, where it is sprayed with fuel. The fuel-air mixture is ignited by a hot electric spark from ignition plugs in the burner. The burning gases start to expand. The engine is built so that the burning gases can escape only toward the rear, and the high pressure produced in the burner drives them in that direction with tremendous force.

According to the reaction principle, the escaping gases push the engine forward with an equal force. The burning gases also supply the energy that runs the compressor. As the gases flow outward, they pass through the blades of the turbine rotor, causing it to rotate. The rotor drives the compressor, which is connected to it by a driveshaft. After the gases leave the turbine, they

A mechanic works on a jet engine. Because of the principle of jet propulsion, jet-powered aircraft can fly at extremely high speeds.

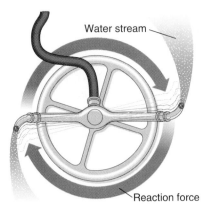

A rotating lawn sprinkler illustrates the principle on which jet engines work: Every action has an equal and opposite reaction. The shooting stream of water exerts a force in one direction, causing the sprinkler to rotate in the opposite direction.

Water stream

Reaction force

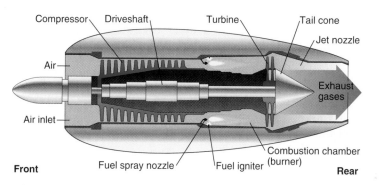

Compressor Driveshaft Turbine Tail cone Jet nozzle

Air

Air inlet

Exhaust gases

Front

Fuel spray nozzle Fuel igniter Combustion chamber (burner) Rear

In a turbojet engine, the aircraft is driven forward by hot exhaust gases, produced by burning fuel with compressed air. The burning gases also power the turbine that drives the compressor.

A turboprop engine operates on the same principle as a turbojet, but the turbine also powers a propeller, which provides most of the force that drives the aircraft forward.

pass out of the jet nozzle at the rear at high speed, again exerting enormous force toward the rear. Consistent with the reaction principle, the force exerted in the opposite direction is just as strong. This force drives the aircraft forward.

The amount of reaction force created by the engine depends on the speed and weight of the gases coming out of the jet nozzle. The speed of the aircraft may be changed by increasing or decreasing the amount of fuel that is sprayed into the burner.

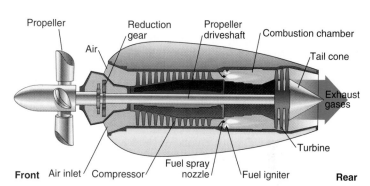

Propeller Reduction gear Propeller driveshaft Combustion chamber Air Tail cone

Exhaust gases

Turbine

Front Air inlet Compressor Fuel spray nozzle Fuel igniter Rear

Types of Jet Engines

Several different types of jet engines are used in aircraft. The engine described above, which has a compressor, burner, turbine, and jet nozzle, is called a **turbojet**. This type of engine powered early jet aircraft.

A **turboprop** engine is similar to a turbojet, but the turbine also turns a shaft that drives a propeller in front. Turboprop engines are used on some planes that require a great range of speeds but do not need to fly as fast as military fighter planes or commercial airliners. Some turboprop engines have two turbines—one for the compressor and one for the propeller.

Turbofan engines have a second turbine, which drives a fan near the front of the engine. The fan acts something like a propeller, creating relatively low-speed air that passes around the outside of the engine,

which helps produce the force that drives the aircraft forward. The rest of the air enters the engine. Turbofan engines are widely used in commercial airliners because they burn fuel more efficiently. They are also quieter than the turbojet engines that were used in earlier airliners. And turbofans perform better over a wide range of aircraft speeds.

The simplest type of jet engine is the **ramjet**, which has been used in high-speed missiles. The ramjet is little more than a pipe open at both ends. It has only a burner and a jet nozzle. No compressor is used. As the engine moves along, air is rammed in at great

In a turbofan engine, a second turbine runs a fan, which draws most of the incoming air around the engine, providing additional force to drive the aircraft. The rest of the air enters the engine.

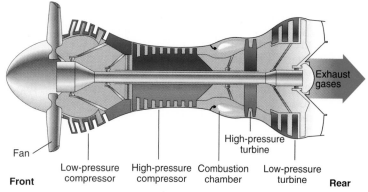

Exhaust gases

Fan Low-pressure compressor High-pressure compressor Combustion chamber High-pressure turbine Low-pressure turbine

Front Rear

speed. This is enough to compress the air, so no mechanical compressor is needed. There is no turbine in the ramjet because none is needed to run the compressor.

Air must be rushing into the ramjet very fast before the engine can operate, and the ramjet must be propelled by another kind of engine until it is moving fast enough to start operating. Generally, ramjets are unable to operate at aircraft speeds below about three times the speed of sound.

All the jet engines described so far need oxygen from the atmosphere in order to run. Another type of jet engine, the **rocket**, carries its own oxygen, so it can fly outside the Earth's atmosphere, where there is no oxygen. This is why rockets are used to power spaceships. But rockets are very inefficient.

To overcome the inefficiencies of rockets, researchers have begun to investigate the supersonic combustion ramjet, or **scramjet**, engine. Air enters this engine at speeds of up to 25 times the speed of sound, mixes with fuel, and burns. Scramjets hold the promise of operating from takeoff all the way to orbit, using oxygen available in the atmosphere. One problem in the development of scramjets has been getting the high-speed air entering the engine to mix properly with the engine's fuel and burn.

▶ HISTORY OF JET ENGINES

A British pilot, Frank Whittle, came up with the idea of a jet engine in 1929. He was granted a patent in 1931 and five years later began to develop a working engine. At about the same time, German physics student Hans von Ohain also began developing a model for a jet engine. With World War II looming, the two inventors knew nothing of each other's work, and each operated under the strictest secrecy.

Von Ohain's engine was ready first, and on August 27, 1939, a German Heinkel He-178 aircraft made the first turbojet engine flight. England's first jet aircraft flight followed in May 1941, when a Gloster E.28/39 aircraft was flown with a Whittle-designed jet engine. Today Whittle and Von Ohain are generally recognized as independent co-inventors of the jet engine.

The United States was late to enter the jet engine field. The first American jet aircraft, the Bell XP-59A Airacomet fighter, was tested in October 1942. Although the engine performed well, the plane was heavy and slow and was never produced in large quantities. The first mass-produced jet aircraft in the United States was the Lockheed P-80 Shooting Star, a fighter plane that first flew in January 1944. Shooting Stars took part in the first all-jet dogfights in history, during the Korean War. Their foes were Soviet-built MIG-15 jet fighters.

In the years that followed, jets became the most important type of aircraft, greatly increasing the reliability and safety of modern air transportation. Most commercial and military aircraft are now jet-propelled.

▶ JET AND PISTON ENGINES

The jet engine has several advantages over the piston engine. The jet is lighter in weight and delivers more power for each unit of engine weight. The jet works better at high speeds and high altitudes. It also has far fewer moving parts and so requires much less maintenance. Commercial jet engines can typically fly 12,000 hours or more before they have to be removed from an aircraft for maintenance.

On the other hand, the piston engine works better than the jet engine at speeds below 400 miles (about 645 kilometers) per hour and at low altitudes. It also uses fuel more efficiently and is quieter than the jet engine at these low speeds. The designs of both types of engines have been modified to lessen exhaust gas pollution, and great strides have been made in reducing the noise produced by jet engines.

Engine designers have had no trouble getting high speeds and power from jet engines. The main problem in jet development has been finding strong enough materials for the engines. The intense heat inside a jet engine would melt most materials. This problem is especially troublesome with turbine blades. They must withstand extreme heat, as well as rapid whirling, when the engine is running at top speed. Researchers are constantly looking for tougher metals and alloys that can withstand greater heat and thereby increase the fuel efficiency of the jet engine.

Reviewed by Stanley W. Kandebo
Aviation Week and Space Technology

See also AVIATION; ENGINES; INTERNAL-COMBUSTION ENGINES; TURBINES.

JET STREAMS

Jet streams are huge bands of air that flow around the Earth at high altitudes. Wind speeds in jet streams often reach a hurricane force of 74 miles (119 kilometers) per hour and can even exceed 250 miles (402 kilometers) per hour. Such wind speeds would be very destructive if they occurred at ground level. But jet streams never reach the ground although some flow as low as the tops of mountains.

Jet streams were first identified by pilots during World War II (1939–1945). When the pilots flew their planes west, very fast winds slowed the planes' speeds, but when they flew east, these winds helped them move faster. Meteorologists called these winds the jet stream. We now know that there is more than one.

Jet streams, like all winds, are produced by differences in air pressure from one place to another. Winds develop when regions of high pressure near regions of low pressure cause air to flow from the high pressure area to the low pressure area. Large wind systems like the jet stream are also affected by the Earth's rotation, which causes them to blow to the right in the Northern Hemisphere and to the left in the Southern Hemisphere.

There are several different jet streams in the Earth's atmosphere in the area known as the troposphere. Most occur between 5 and 10 miles (8 and 16 kilometers) above sea level. But there are also low-level jets that form 1 mile (1.6 kilometers) or less above the ground. The high-level jets are larger, and they last longer. They are typically thousands of miles long but only about 300 miles (483 kilometers) wide and 2 to 3 miles (3 to 5 kilometers) deep. They can blow for months on end, but their speed and location sometimes change. Low-level jets usually last only a few days or even a few hours.

There are two main high-level jet streams: the subtropical jet and the polar front jet. Both blow from west to east. The subtropical jet is found between about 20° and 35° latitude almost 10 miles (16 kilometers) above sea level. It is stronger and steadier than the polar front jet in the winter, but it almost dis-

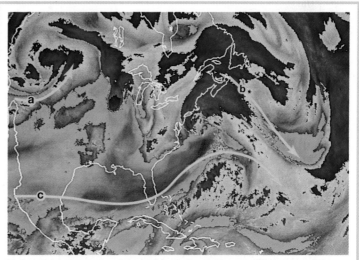

To locate jet streams, meteorologists study weather satellite images of the atmosphere, identifying boundaries where regions of cloudiness and dry air meet. By comparing the shapes of these boundaries to models based on years of observation, they can pinpoint those boundaries where jet streams flow. Here, computer-generated colors show areas of clouds (grays, greens, reds) and dry air (oranges). Arrows a, b, and c mark the central positions of three jet streams.

appears in the summer. The polar front jet blows all year long in a meandering pattern that changes from day to day. In the winter, it is often found between 30° and 50° latitude. In the summer, it moves toward the poles and is usually found north of 45° latitude. The polar front jet often marks the boundary between warm tropical air and cold polar air.

Two other high-level jet streams are the polar night jet and the easterly jet, which form in the area of the Earth's atmosphere known as the stratosphere. The polar night jet forms over the poles in winter. The easterly jet, blowing from east to west, forms in the summer over India just south of the Himalayas and reaches to the west coast of Africa.

Low-level jet streams often form when winds are channeled by mountain ranges. On many clear spring and summer nights in the midwest, a low-level jet blows from south to north about 2,000 feet (610 meters) above the Great Plains just east of the Rocky Mountains. This jet may help in the formation of nighttime thunderstorms there. In the summer, another low-level jet forms east of Somalia in Africa and blows toward India. Known as the Somali jet, it helps bring rain to India during the summer monsoon.

STANLEY DAVID GEDZELMAN
Professor of Meteorology
City College, City University of New York

See also WEATHER; WINDS.

JEWELRY

Jewelry is made in a great variety of types and from many different kinds of materials. Precious jewelry is made of the rarest and most beautiful metals and gemstones. Non-precious jewelry is made of materials that are easier to find and less expensive.

Early men adorned themselves with pebbles, shells, berries, and feathers. They made necklaces of pieces of stone, horn, or the teeth of animals. Indians of early America wore necklaces of wampum (beads of polished shells), bone, and metal. Primitive peoples in many parts of the world still wear similar decorations.

▶ MATERIALS USED IN JEWELRY

Gold. Gold is the oldest precious metal used in jewelry. The use of it dates back to the earliest Egyptians. It is easily worked and strongly colored. It was the most valuable metal until recently, when platinum came into use. But gold is still preferred by many people.

Pure gold is much too soft for most jewelry. Therefore it is usually mixed (or **alloyed**) with silver, copper, or zinc. The purity of gold

---

What is a carat?

The carat is the standard unit of weight for a gemstone. By international agreement 1 carat equals 200 milligrams, or about $\frac{1}{142}$ ounce.

The word "carat" comes from the Greek word for locust or carob tree. The locust tree, which is common in the Mediterranean area, produces seeds that all have almost exactly the same weight. For centuries locust seeds were used to weigh gems.

But it was difficult to trade gems when a gem might have a slightly different standard weight at each weighing. So in 1907 the 200-milligram standard weight was proposed. By the end of 1913 this weight was an accepted legal standard in all the chief gem-trading centers.

The word "karat" (spelled with a K) is used in the United States for the unit measure of the purity of gold. Gold that is pure (without any other metal or impurity in it) is 24-karat. But solid gold is too soft for use. So other metals must be mixed with it to strengthen it. Metals used in this way are called alloys. Alloyed gold is always less than 24 karats. A common accepted standard gold has 14 parts of gold to 10 parts of another metal and is called 14-karat (14K) gold. Eighteen parts of gold to six parts of another metal makes 18-karat (18K) gold.

---

is measured in units called **karats**. Pure gold is 24-karat. A mixture of 18 parts of pure gold to 6 parts of alloy is called 18-karat gold. Fourteen-karat gold contains 14 parts of gold to 10 parts of alloy. Gold may be stamped 18K, 14K, or 10K after alloying. By varying the amount and kind of the alloy, the color of the gold may be made red, yellow, green, or white.

Costume jewelry that appears to be gold is often made of a base, or foundation, metal like bronze or tin. The base metal is given a gold wash to make it look like gold. Or sometimes it is covered with gold leaf, which is a thin sheeting of gold. One popular substitute for gold is a combination of copper and zinc called pinchbeck gold.

The word "pinchbeck" comes from the name of the inventor of the combination, Christopher Pinchbeck (1670–1732). When Pinchbeck's substitute was first sold, it was not offered as real gold. However, as time has passed the word "pinchbeck" has come to mean cheap falseness.

Platinum. Platinum has been used for jewelry only in recent years. It is the only metal that is more valuable than gold. Like gold, platinum is too soft to use by itself in most jewelry. It is usually mixed with the metal iridium. This glistening, grayish-white combination of metals makes an especially attractive setting for diamonds.

Palladium. Palladium is a rare metal very similar to platinum. But it is lighter, cheaper, and easier to work with. It has a shimmering pearl-gray color. Palladium is sometimes used in engagement and wedding rings.

Silver. Silver is the most popular of the four precious metals used in jewelry. It is the least expensive, and it is long-lasting. Like the other precious metals, it is easily made into jewelry by craftsmen.

Sterling silver, according to law in the United States, may not contain less than 92.5 percent silver. The rest of it is copper. There is no legal limitation on the amount of silver in a silver-plated article. Silver plate is made by coating a base, or foundation, metal or alloy with a layer of pure silver. By using only a very thin coating of silver, craftsmen can make very cheap silver-colored costume jewelry.

Jewelry Enamel. Enamel is made by melting finely ground glass. It melts at a lower temperature than the metal it is applied to, which is usually bronze or gold. After the enamel paste has been applied, it is fired, or heated, until it melts. It is this firing that turns it into a hard, glassy surface.

Enamel is often used in jewelry to add glowing color. It may be used with gemstones, or it may be used alone. In early days the only way for a goldsmith to add color to his jewelry was to use brightly colored gemstones. To fit into the design of the pieces of jewelry, these stones had to be ground to size. The grinding was a long, painstaking process. By using enamel instead of gemstones, the goldsmith was able to create the same effect more easily.

Cameos. A cameo is a gemstone that has been carved so that ornaments or figures stand out against a flat background. In a cameo the carved part that stands out is a different color from that of the background. Many cameos are cut so skillfully that small faces on them are easily recognized.

Cameos are usually sculptured on stones such as onyx, sardonyx, or agate. To be used for a cameo, the stone must have layers of different colors. One of these layers is carved. The next layer is not carved. It provides a background for the sculptured layer. Many cameos are cut on a white layer with either a black or brown layer in the background.

Gemstones. Natural pearls, coral, and rare, colorful stones from the earth are called gemstones. Imagine the awe of a caveman when he picked from the mud a stone of a sharp, bright color. Perhaps the color changed as he moved his hand. Perhaps a ray of sun caused a flash of light. No wonder gemstones have been believed to have special powers. No wonder so many legends have grown up about them. Every month of the year has a gemstone traditionally connected with it. The list of birthstones appears with the article GEMSTONES.

The **precious** gems are diamonds, natural pearls, sapphires, emeralds, and rubies. These are the rarest and, in the opinion of many, the most beautiful stones. They are measured by weight. One **carat**, the standard of measure, equals about 1/142 ounce. These precious gems are used in the most expensive jewelry. They are the ones used for crowns and jewels of state.

Among the gemstones called **semiprecious** are garnet, amethyst, topaz, opal, aquamarine, jade, and turquoise. Many of these stones are exceptionally lovely, and they are often combined in settings with the precious stones.

Most gemstones are minerals, but four gemstones used for jewelry are not. These are pearls, coral, amber, and jet. Coral, amber, and jet are semiprecious gemstones. Natural pearls are precious and highly prized. They are especially flattering to a woman's complexion.

Natural pearls are found in the pearl oyster. They are formed by the oyster's coating a small irritating object in its shell with mother-of-pearl. Cultured pearls are just as lovely but not as valuable. They are formed in the same way, but the irritating object is put into the oyster's shell by man. Simulated pearls—glass beads coated or filled with a paste of silvery fish scales—are used for inexpensive costume jewelry.

Synthetic Stones. Jewelry is often set with glittering imitation or synthetic stones. Imitation stones are made of glass or some other material that looks like a natural stone. Synthetic stones are made in the laboratory out of the same materials and by the same processes as natural stones. Many of the man-made stones are beautiful, but they do not compare in value with those produced by nature.

Plastics. Plastics are becoming increasingly popular in jewelry. They are made in beautiful colors. They shape easily into unusual designs and are light enough to be used in large, elaborate pieces of jewelry.

▶ **IMPORTANT JEWELRY STYLES IN HISTORY**

Ancient Jewelry Styles. Beautiful jewelry was being made 4,000 years ago. Gold and silver, enamel, artificial glass gems, and turquoise and other gemstones were all used by the Egyptians. They wore rings, earrings, and brooches, just as we do now. They also wore heavy jeweled collars, breastplates, and headdresses. The styles were rich and ornate.

To the ancient Greeks the beauty of a piece of jewelry was as important as the value of the materials used to make it. Fine threads of gold were shaped to look like butterflies or grasshoppers. The Greeks also liked cameos. Jasper, amber, and coral were among their favorite gemstones.

The most beautifully made jewelry in history was made by the Etruscans, who lived in northern Italy. They designed jewelry in intricate patterns and made it with great skill. Instead of a shiny surface, their gold jewelry had a grainy surface, as if fine gold powder had been evenly sprinkled on it.

The Romans wore very elaborate jewelry, designed to show off their wealth. Both men and women wore large gemstones. They especially liked emeralds and pearls. Sapphires, amethysts, garnets, opals, and moonstones were also popular. The Romans loaded their fingers, sometimes *all* their fingers, with rings.

In A.D. 395 the Roman Empire split in two. The eastern portion, called the Byzantine Empire, became the most powerful state of the whole Mediterranean area. The Byzantine capital, Constantinople, took Rome's place as the center of art and style. The jewelry styles of Constantinople influenced the whole Western world. Byzantine designs featured symbols and formal patterns. Gold pieces were enameled in bright reds and blues. Ropes of pearls and emeralds were worn by the very few wealthy people. Their clothing was so encrusted with jewels that it was sometimes difficult for them to move.

Jewelry of the Middle Ages. During the Middle Ages most of the jewelry craftsmen were monks. The monks devoted their energy to making religious decorations for the churches. Most of the precious gems used were part of the loot that Crusaders brought back from their trips to the Holy Land. Many of the pieces of jewelry brought back from the Holy Land had pictures of pagan or mythological gods on them. They were, however, used as religious decorations by the Christians—apparently without much question.

Guilds began sometime after the 9th century. By 1327, goldsmiths were recognized as working in a major craft and formed their own association in London. This guild of the Worshipful Company of Goldsmiths of London was proud of its reputation. It insisted that its members do work of good quality.

An unusual type of jewelry made during the Middle Ages was the pomander, an openwork metal ball that held perfume. It was a very useful article to have in the cities of those days because city smells were so unpleasant.

Renaissance Jewelry. The Renaissance, the time of new interest in art and knowledge, began around 1300. People became interested in jewelry along with other beautiful things. New methods of making it were developed. In the 15th century gem-cutters learned to cut a diamond to give it brilliant, sparkling lights. Without this brilliance a diamond looks no prettier than a piece of dull glass.

Jewelry of the Renaissance period was very colorful. One jewel might be made up of many different stones and enamels. In addition, pearls might be hung from it. The English wore the greatest quantities of jewelry. King Henry VIII (1491–1547) kept his hands loaded with rings. He is said to have owned 234 rings and 324 brooches. Many rich people wore as many as three rings per finger.

Before the 16th century men wore as much jewelry as women did and sometimes even more. They used jewelry as a symbol of their wealth or rank in society. When, in the 16th century, women began to wear more jewelry than men, new types of designs were made. Jewelry was designed in the form of butterflies, frogs, bugs, flowers, trumpets, and even mousetraps.

The delicately made pendant was the most popular form of jewelry. Such a pendant was often decorated with a religious or mythological scene. Also popular with women was a girdle (a flexible belt worn over outer clothing) on which small jewelry pieces were hung.

Jewelry of the 17th, 18th, and 19th Centuries. After the reign of Queen Elizabeth I of England (1533–1603) women began to cut back on the great quantities of jewelry they had worn. But men still wore quantities of flashing gems, especially on their hats. More delicate jewelry came into style. All over Europe historic pieces of jewelry were melted down and remodeled.

Around 1799, when Napoleon I (1769–1821) became ruler of France, the styles of ancient Greece and Rome became popular again. Men wore less jewelry than women. Women wore jeweled rings on their toes. Cameos became popular because the Empress Josephine (1763–1814) was fond of them.

Greek styles did not last long. In 1837,

Above: French crown used for the coronation of Louis XV in 1722. Left: Indian necklace from the Mogul Empire in the 18th century: emeralds, rubies, sapphires, and pearls. The back of the necklace is beautifully enameled gold.

when Victoria (1819–1901) became queen of England, styles began to change. Victorian jewelry was often decorated with tiny figures of knights in armor and elegant ladies. Pieces of jewelry were often worn for sentimental reasons instead of for their real beauty.

Late in the 19th century French designers began to make pieces of outstanding beauty and delicacy. René Lalique (1860–1945), a jeweler and glassmaker, was the greatest of all these designers. Lalique used stones for their beauty instead of for the money they represented. He became well-known for the lovely and unusual styles in which he combined precious and semiprecious stones. He made glassware in unusual colors and designs.

Peter Carl Fabergé (1846–1920) was another important French designer. He is most often remembered for the decorated egg-shaped boxes he made while designer for the Russian court.

Oriental Jewelry. The jewelry of the Orient is unlike jewelry made anywhere else in the world. The delicate designs have changed little through the centuries. Craftsmen today make fragile pendant earrings in the same way they were made 300 years ago.

There has always been a wide variety of

gems in India. It is an important market for precious stones, especially rubies and sapphires. The Chinese are famous for their jade. Tibetans and Mongolians use coral and turquoise set in silver and gold.

▶RINGS

Finger rings are the most common form of jewelry. There are engagement rings, wedding rings, birthstone rings, signet rings, school rings, coronation rings, religious rings, and mourning rings—to name a few. Rings have also had a part in the great events of history.

Bridal Rings. No one knows just when bridal rings were first used. Some historians say that when a caveman captured a woman, he tied rings of rope around parts of her body to keep her soul from escaping. When he was certain she would stay under his control, he bound her finger with a ring of the same rope. For centuries a ring symbolized the obedience of the ring wearer to her master. As time went on, instead of grass or rope rings women were given leather, amber, or ivory rings. Then even longer-lasting materials like iron, bronze, copper, silver, and gold were used.

Bridal rings are still used by most people. At one time the English Puritans tried to stop the use of rings at weddings, because they thought ring wearing was a pagan custom. But people kept wearing rings anyway. Originally the bride received only one ring. It was presented to her at the betrothal, or time of engagement. It was not until a few hundred years ago that a bride received two rings. Now a woman often receives a decorative ring at the time of her engagement. She receives a plainer ring, usually just a band, at her wedding.

In the two-ring wedding service both the bride and the groom receive a ring. This service was once popular only in Europe or among people with a European background. During World War II, American couples began using a double-ring ceremony. At the present time this is still the practice.

Signet Rings. In the Middle Ages, when many people could not read or write, signet rings were very useful. A signet ring was engraved with an emblem or portrait of its owner. The emblem could be stamped on a piece of softened wax on an envelope, to identify the owner. Merchants, especially, found signet rings useful for marking goods. Some people today still enjoy wearing signet rings, even though they have lost their original practical value.

Mourning Rings. Rings have often been given to guests at important ceremonies. It once was the practice to give gold rings to

Above: Contemporary jeweled animal pins from Van Cleef & Arpels. Right: Contemporary jewelry from Cartier: diamonds, emeralds, rubies, and sapphires.

wedding guests. But this practice never became as popular as that of giving funeral rings. As far back as the Middle Ages a will might set aside a certain sum of money for funeral rings. In the 17th century, funeral rings were often engraved inside with the name and the date of death. The outside of the ring might be decorated with a gold skeleton or a container with a lock of the dead person's hair.

In America, just after George Washington died in 1799, many people wore mourning rings, as well as mourning lockets and brooches. Each of these had a tiny painting of an unhappy young woman (representing grief) mourning over Washington's tomb. This custom of wearing mourning rings is no longer practiced.

▶ OTHER ARTICLES OF JEWELRY

Jewelry for the Hair. Women have been wearing jeweled ornaments in their hair for thousands of years. A large number of different decorative ornaments have been worn: coronets or tiaras, bands, jeweled caps, combs, and hairpins. When long hair for women is stylish, hair jewelry is more important than when hair is worn short.

Earrings. Earrings can be flattering, exciting, and very elegant. The women of early Greece were so fond of earrings that their jewelers designed larger and larger ones for them. Finally the earrings became too heavy for the ears to hold. Then they were hung from decorations on top of the head. Early Phoenician women pierced their ears along the rim, as well as at the lobe. In this way they could wear many small dangling earrings at one time. When they turned their heads, the earrings tinkled like little bells. Hindu women wear nose rings in addition to earrings.

Necklaces. Necklaces are worn by primitive peoples as one of their chief forms of jewelry. During some periods of history men as well as women have worn necklaces. Some ancient Greek and Roman soldiers wore heavy gold collars. King Henry VIII, who ruled England from 1509 to 1547, wore beautiful collars of precious gems.

Where women wear clothing that leaves the neck and shoulders bare, necklaces are especially popular. Chains, beads, and chokers are all worn. Chain necklaces sometimes have pendants, lockets, or other such decorations attached to them.

Brooches, Clips, and Pins. A brooch was originally an ornamental pin used to hold garments together. Early people wore simple ring brooches to fasten their tunics at the neck. When pins with catches were invented, brooches became more decorative. Very delicate brooches were used on lace. The Scottish brooch, worn to hold heavy tartans on the shoulder, is a very heavy type of pin. Some of them are more than 11 centimeters (4½ inches) wide.

The clip is a form of brooch that pinches or grips the material instead of piercing it with a pin. Lapel pins are a form of brooch used only for decoration.

Bracelets. Bracelets have been worn by both men and women. Although most of them are worn around the wrist, many have been designed to be worn close to the elbow.

Until the time of wristwatches, bracelets were only ornamental. Now both men and women wear wristwatches, sometimes set in ornamental bracelets. Men and women may also wear identification bracelets and strictly decorative bracelets.

One type of bracelet that has been popular with women is a chain with small charms attached to it. Each charm may represent some special event or person to the wearer.

Jewelry for Men. In the 1800's and early 1900's, men wore little jewelry. They did wear rings, cuff links, tie clips, wristwatches, and identification bracelets. At special times they also wore stickpins, shirt studs, and perhaps watch chains. But today men wear jewelry of all kinds.

▶ FAMOUS PIECES OF JEWELRY

The Ring of the Fisherman. The most famous of all religious rings is the Ring of the Fisherman, the gold seal ring of the pope. The ring shows St. Peter in a boat, fishing. The name of the reigning pope is around this. At the pope's death the ring is either broken in half or buried with him. A new one is made for each new pope.

Scandal over a Necklace. One of the most famous necklaces of all time was the diamond necklace that became one of the causes of the French Revolution. Louis XV (1710–74) had ordered a fabulously expensive necklace of beautiful diamonds for his mistress Madame du Barry (1746–93). Before the jewelers finished making it, Louis XV died of smallpox. The jewelers tried to sell the necklace to the new king, Louis XVI (1754–93), to give to Marie Antoinette (1755–93). But he could not afford it, and she never saw it. The necklace itself disappeared. However, it became a symbol of the royal family's extravagance at a time when many of their subjects were starving.

An Opal Ring. There is a story about a Roman senator named Nonius, who had a large and exceptionally beautiful opal. Mark Antony (83?–30 B.C.), a famous Roman ruler, saw the opal and wanted it to give to Cleopatra (69–30 B.C.). He knew Nonius would not want to leave Rome. So he gave Nonius the choice of handing the opal over to him or being banished from Rome. Nonius accepted the bitter fate of leaving Rome—with his opal.

A Gift Egg. A famous Fabergé egg was made in 1906 for Czar Nicholas II (1868–1918) of Russia to give to his wife, Alexandra Feodorovna (1872–1918). For many years it had been the Russian custom to present decorated eggs at Easter time. This egg is one of the loveliest ever given. The outer shell of the egg is made of pale-purple enamel decorated with diamond ribbons and bows. A large diamond is set on the pointed end. Inside the egg are gold water lilies and a swan on a blue aquamarine lake. The swan moves automatically.

▶**HOW JEWELRY IS MADE**

In early days all jewelry was made by hand. The first machines were used in 1869. Gradually more and more machine processes were developed. At first they were used only to make cheap jewelry. As methods improved, mass production was also used by manufacturers of better-quality jewelry.

Fine Jewelry. The method used to make a number of identical pieces of fine jewelry is called **casting**. A master model is made, generally of metal. Then a rubber impression, or mold, is made of the master model. Molten wax is cast in the rubber mold to make a wax model. This wax model is used to form a second mold, made of plaster of paris. This plaster mold is placed in an oven, and the wax is melted out. A hole left in the plaster lets the wax escape and the precious metal enter. The plaster mold can be used only once. The first, or rubber, mold may be used hundreds of times.

The casting process is much faster than working each piece separately. But it is far from an automatic process. Each step must be done by hand. Great care and a high degree of skill are necessary.

Not all fine jewelry begins as a casting. Much of it starts as a flat piece of precious metal, which is turned into an original design. When a jeweler works this way, he uses many different hand tools, such as files, punches, saws, mallets, and pliers. He also uses a blowtorch to solder the parts of an article together.

Jewelry is also made by **stamping**. In this process the metal is pressed between two shaped steel surfaces called dies. Dies are expensive to make, so stamping is used only to

---

HOW TO MAKE YOUR OWN JEWELRY

It is fun to wear jewelry you have made yourself. Nicely made gifts of jewelry are pleasing to give. There are many different kinds of jewelry that are not difficult to make. An easy one for a beginner is a bracelet of twisted wire.

Copper wire is a good material to work with. It has an attractive color. It is soft enough to be twisted easily with simple tools.

You will need large pliers or a vise, small pliers, wire cutters, a file, and sandpaper. These tools are likely to be in a family's toolbox.

Take a few short pieces of wire at first, to practice twisting. This twisting will give you an idea of how easily you can shape your jewelry. As you work with it you may get some ideas of how you want your finished piece to look.

To twist the wire, one end is held firmly in the vise or heavy pliers. The other end is held in the small pliers, so that you can twist it. First twist just one wire alone. See the effect created by twisting it loosely and also by twisting it firmly. Then twist two wires of the same size together. Twist two wires of different sizes together.

When you have created a twisted wire pattern you like, make three strands of it. Braid them together for a bracelet band about 6 inches long.

Use nippers to cut the ends neatly. File and sand the ends smooth. This must be done carefully, so that the bracelet is comfortable to wear. Slowly bend the bracelet to shape.

If you want the surface of your bracelet to stay shiny, brush it with a clear lacquer, such as clear fingernail polish.

make large quantities of jewelry of the same pattern. Stamping usually makes the article in two halves, which then have to be joined together.

Costume Jewelry. Costume jewelry is made of nonprecious stones and inexpensive metals. Mass-production methods are used. Costume jewelry is very popular because it is low in price and therefore may be discarded when it is no longer fashionable. The designs for costume jewelry once were copied from the designs of precious jewelry. Now costume jewelry is made in many different original designs. Some of the designs become so popular that they are copied in precious jewelry.

The cheaper kind of costume jewelry is simply stamped out of a base metal, usually brass, by punch presses. The better costume jewelry is made by the casting process, which gives greater variation in design.

In either case the parts are then electroplated, assembled, and polished. Some of the cheap jewelry and novelty items are lightly dipped in melted silver or gold, or colored. They may simply be lacquered to give a polished effect. Alloys of tin are used instead of precious metals. Rhinestones take the place of diamonds. Simulated pearls are used instead of real ones, and colored "stones" are glass.

▶**THE JEWELRY INDUSTRY**

New York City is a world center for gems and jewelry design. Its beautiful creations find their way to markets all over the world. Fashion influences in clothing usually start in Europe, but jewelry designs often start in New York.

Early History of the Jewelry Industry

The jewelry business has been active during every period of history when jewelry was in demand. In early Egypt, in India, in Renaissance Europe, in colonial America—in all corners of the earth there have been people who were talented goldsmiths and silversmiths.

The old-time jewelers learned their trade thoroughly. A good craftsperson could shape a ring, repair a clock or watch, or fix a pair of spectacles and do all of these jobs well.

Jewelry shops were small, with at most five or ten employees in each one, and the tools were rather simple. A person had to learn every part of the business, from melting the metal to finishing and packing the pieces made. The worker melted the ore, bars, or coins of precious metal in a blacksmith's forge, then pounded the metal thin on an anvil, using hand tools. Each article was then cut with shears, neatly soldered, trimmed, and filed by hand.

People used jewelry as a way to save money. Money could not be saved in banks, for until the 1800's there were few banks available. But money that was turned into articles of gold and silver could be easily identified if these articles were specially designed and marked. Being easy to identify, they were not as likely to be stolen as a pile of coins might be.

Coins of past times, unlike present coins, were almost pure silver or gold. The customer gave the jeweler the coins needed to make the jewelry article the person wanted. Then these coins were melted down to make the article. Therefore, the jeweler had to be someone whom people could trust as they would trust a banker. A dishonest jeweler could cheat the customer by keeping some of the precious metal and mixing another metal with it.

The Jewelry Industry Today

The jewelry industry today, as always, involves more than just the making of pieces of personal adornment. It is actually a family of many industries that make and sell products through jewelers and jewelry stores. The industry also includes suppliers of silverware, gemstones, watches and clocks, and fine china and glassware.

For a long time the name "jeweler" was given only to a craftsperson who made jewelry. Today those who sell jewelry, as well as those who make or repair it, are called jewelers. The persons hired by a manufacturer or a retailer to design new pieces of jewelry are also called jewelers. Generally retail jewelers know a great deal about gems and jewelry and they can give their customers good advice as well as information about the products they sell.

MORTON R. SARETT
President, Jewelry Institute Council

See also GEMSTONES; JADE, PEARLS.

JEWETT, SARAH ORNE. See MAINE (Famous People).

Moses, pictured here receiving the Tablets of the Law (the Ten Commandments) from God, led the Hebrews out of slavery in Egypt and made them a single nation.

JEWS

Who are the Jews? Most are followers of the religious faith called Judaism, but some who are called Jews follow no religion. The Jews are not a distinct race, and they live in many countries of the world. But wherever the Jews have scattered around the world, they have kept their own identity—they are the descendants of the traditions, culture, and beliefs that began with the biblical patriarch Abraham and have come down through Moses and David and Solomon and the biblical ''Children of Israel'' to the modern age.

The history of the Jews is long and complex and worked into the fabric of almost all the countries of the world. The Jews are responsible for the Old Testament Scriptures and their deep influence on the Western world. In addition to Judaism, the Jews launched two great world religions—Christianity and Islam. The Jewish mark is also on the literature, ethics, social structure, economic development, and science of the West. Names that stretch from Jesus and Paul through Spinoza and right into the modern world of Freud and Einstein indicate that the influence of the Jews went beyond their own heritage. For nearly 3,000 years the history of the Jews has also

been profoundly tragic. Few peoples have been so bitterly attacked, few histories so saddened by discrimination, persecution, and mass annihilation. Yet the Jews have survived and outlived their persecutors throughout history.

There is no simple answer to the Jewish capacity for survival. However, faith in a special destiny was taught by early leaders and cherished through dark centuries. The Jews have held to the belief that they were chosen by God for a purpose, selected to fulfill a mission, to teach and carry out principles of social justice and peace. The mission is expressed by the Hebrew salutation for greeting and for departure: *Shalom*—''Peace!''

▶BIBLICAL ORIGINS

The Bible tells the stories of Adam and Eve —whom God created as the first man and woman—and of their descendants, who became the founders of the races of humankind. The stories are set in the Tigris-Euphrates Valley in present-day Iraq. There lived a group of nomadic (wandering) tribes and their forefather, Abraham. The saga of his descendants and their families became the first religious teaching of Jews and Christians through the centuries. There was the long period of slavery in Egypt. There was the triumphant revolt and the flight called the Exodus, in the 13th century B.C., under an inspired leader, Moses. Moses is the real father of the Hebrew people, the forebears of the Jews. He united the loose, nomadic tribes into a people. The Bible also ascribes to Moses the role of Lawgiver. His genius established a moral code built around the Ten Commandments. The lessons of his leadership became the foundation of the Hebraic (Jewish) faith. Jews have always remembered the Egyptian bondage and the Exodus. The holiday of Passover directs all descendants of Moses to remember that once they were slaves in Egypt.

How did these wandering desert people ever get to the land of Canaan, known in later history as Palestine? All evidence indicates that there was a slow filtering in of tribes, a piecemeal acquisition of territory, family by family, clan by clan, with the continuous conflict that makes up such a large part of the Book of Judges. This is the period of local heroes and heroines, of Barak and Deborah and their courage, of Gideon and his clever military strategy, of Samson and his great physical strength.

David was the hero king of Judah and Israel and the successor of Saul. He completed the conquest of the Philistines begun by Saul and made Jerusalem his capital. This statue, by the 17th-century Italian sculptor Bernini, depicts David as a young shepherd about to slay the Philistine giant Goliath with his slingshot.

The article JEWS discusses the history of the Jewish people, from biblical times to the creation of the state of Israel in the 20th century. The article JUDAISM discusses the beliefs and practices of the Jewish religion. Numerous other articles in this encyclopedia, such as those on individual prophets or Jewish holidays, contain more information on these subjects. Please consult the index under "Jews" and under "Judaism."

The Hebrew Kingdoms

The Philistines, who were a great power in the region, posed a serious threat to the early Hebrews. They forced the loosely joined Hebrew tribes to unite under a single leader, Saul, who won victories against them. Reigning near the end of the 11th century B.C., Saul usually is regarded as the first Hebrew king.

Saul was followed by King David, one of the Bible's most attractive characters. David was a hero from boyhood, when he slew the Philistine giant Goliath with his slingshot. David consolidated the military gains of Saul. He cleared the frontiers and made Jerusalem the capital. He brought the Ark of the Covenant to Jerusalem. The sacred Ark, an oblong chest, contained two stone tablets on which the Ten Commandments were written. Thus the capital city also became a religious shrine.

After David came his son Solomon, who further consolidated the little state. Folklore attributes extraordinary wisdom to him. He is called the author of the Book of Proverbs and of other "wisdom" literature of the Bible. Solomon was a master diplomat, a man of great vision. He built roads, fortresses, and a royal palace. He built the Temple that was to become the center of the religion and sacred practices of the Hebrews until the extinction of their national life.

Civil War and Secession

After Solomon's reign (which ended in the late 10th century B.C.), the political life of the Hebrew kingdom differed little from the pettiness and dreariness of other kingdoms of the times. Deep resentment over mounting taxes resulted in revolution and a split in the kingdom. The north seceded, carrying with it the largest part of the population and territory. It became the kingdom of Israel. The smaller southern portion became the kingdom of Judah.

The kingdom of Israel survived for about two centuries. It was torn by internal quarrels and was caught in the rivalries of empires surrounding it. About 734 B.C. the Assyrians invaded Israel. They killed many Israelites and exiled thousands more, scattering them throughout the Assyrian empire.

The Kingdom of Judah

Judah (also called Judea) in the south had less intrigue and violence than Israel. But the giant empires on all sides were strong and greedy. In 586 B.C., Jerusalem fell to the conquering Babylonians. The Temple built by Solomon was destroyed, and the Judean survivors were exiled. But the Judeans in exile, unlike the Israelites, refused to forget their homeland. Those who had been resettled in Babylonia retained their religious identity. They came together in gatherings that became the forerunner of the synagogue (a place of coming together). They listened reverently and affectionately to their leaders and prophets, notably Ezekiel. He gave them hope that one day the dry bones of the valley of Judah would have the breath of life again and there would be a restoration. The prophecies were miraculously fulfilled. When Cyrus of Persia took control of the Palestinian lands in 538 B.C., he permitted the exiles to return to their homes and even to rebuild the Temple. A vigorous remnant of the Judeans joyously accepted the challenge, and for 600 years there was another Jewish state.

One of the towering figures in the Old Testament, the prophet Jeremiah denounced his people and their leaders when they strayed from the word of God.

The Prophets and Their Role

The otherwise meaningless history of Israel and Judah attained immortality because of the emergence of those extraordinary personalities, the Hebrew prophets. These were men who had the ability to sway whole masses of people. They set forth new standards of morality far ahead of their times. They scolded, berated, and threatened their people, but always with love and deep devotion. Their sermons were angry because the Hebrews were not living up to their highest promise. Earlier prophets even dared to attack royalty. Nathan denounced David when he took another man's wife. But the great tradition of prophecy came to its climax with the spiritual geniuses who vastly broadened the meaning of Judaism: Amos, Hosea, Isaiah, and Micah, all of whom lived in the 8th century B.C., and Jeremiah, who lived in the 7th and 6th centuries B.C.

Amos and Hosea. Amos, a simple herdsman, ridiculed those who brought sacrifices to the Temple but did not come with pure hearts. Hosea condemned the callousness and cruelty that he found wherever he turned. Hebrew life had become so unbalanced, with a pious surface and a corrupt inner core, that he likened it to "a cake unturned, burnt on one side, the heart raw and sour."

Isaiah. Amos and Hosea were simple men who rose out of the corrupt society of the kingdom of Israel. Isaiah was an aristocrat of the kingdom of Judah. He lashed out against those who assumed that Hebrews could sin without fear of punishment because they were God's Chosen. He said there could be no favoritism in moral life. Indeed, exactly because the Hebrews knew God earlier and knew him better, more was expected of them. Not only special privileges but also special responsibilities had been conferred by God on the Hebrews.

Micah. After Isaiah came Micah to summarize all the teachings of the prophets. Micah, too, was of the poor and wretched, and he understood them. He concentrated on the essence of the Hebrew faith, rather than on form. Micah said, "What doth the Lord require of thee, but to do justly, to love mercy, and to walk humbly with thy God?" This was the true heart of the Hebrew religion.

Jeremiah. But the tower of them all was Jeremiah. Jeremiah was obliged to denounce the people he loved and to prophesy their doom. In the midst of war, he was a pacifist.

In the midst of national danger, he denounced the character and motives of the leaders. The masses cursed him. The rulers imprisoned him. Jeremiah would not be stilled. He brought to his suffering and reluctant people a conception of God that was personal. Jeremiah made the Hebrew people see that God was not far off in space but in every person's heart. God was within reach. When there was honesty, compassion, and true brotherhood, God was near. Jeremiah did not live to see the redemption of his people, but his message of a personal God close to everyone, needing no intermediaries, no special rites or sacrifices—other than the love of a pure heart—remained as an eternal blessing.

Destruction and Dispersion

The Jewish state was re-established when the exiles returned from Babylonia in 538 B.C. They joined up with those who still lived in the land to begin the slow process of reconstruction. It was not easy. There were problems of mere physical survival in the midst of devastation. Little states were pawns in the power politics of the empires of the day.

Religious crises also threatened the Jews. In the early years after the return from Babylonia, the determination to protect all that had been saved during exile bred a fierce religious zeal. Pious practice became a test of personal loyalty. The religions of non-Jews were scorned. A new group of prophets had to remind the people that God was not the property of the Jews alone, but that he lived among all people. This is the meaning of the Book of Ruth and the Book of Jonah, which resist the bigotry and hatred of the times.

In the 4th century B.C. the country fell again, this time to Alexander the Great. The Greek conquest under Alexander brought in pagan customs and rites that attracted great numbers of young Jews. Some youths even abandoned Jewish traditions and values—a severe threat to a people trying to survive.

A century and a half after Alexander, the Greek ruler, Antiochus Epiphanes (King of Syria), compelled pagan worship within the sacred Temple, and he persecuted Jews who held to the traditional ways. But this only united the stubborn folk. Under Judah Maccabee and his brothers a revolt flared. A Jewish victory came in 165 B.C. The Jewish state was independent once again. Judah Maccabee's

The Western Wall (sometimes called the Wailing Wall) in Jerusalem is all that remains of the Temple, destroyed by the Romans in A.D. 70. It is the holiest shrine for Jews.

triumph is celebrated in the Festival of Hanukkah, or the Festival of Lights. He established the Hasmonean dynasty, and in the uneasy century that followed, the basic principles of Judaism as it is known today were established.

In the first century B.C. the Jewish state came under the power of the Roman Empire. Rome's rule was tyrannical, and a Jewish revolt began in Jerusalem in A.D. 66. After a long and fierce Jewish resistance, the Roman legions conquered Jerusalem in A.D. 70. They executed the Jewish leaders and exiled the whole people. The Romans destroyed the ancient Temple—only the western wall was left standing. This became known as the Wailing Wall and has remained the holiest place of prayer for Jews to this day. Three years later, in A.D. 73, the Roman legions captured Masada, the last stronghold of Jewish resistance. The Jewish state was completely destroyed. But the Jewish people survived—in exile.

▶ THE COMMUNITIES OF EXILE

Even before the total destruction of the Jewish state, the destiny of the Jews had become highly fragmented. Its pieces formed mosaics in the history of many parts of the world.

Egypt. One important community settled in Egypt. By the 1st century A.D. the Jewish community living in Egypt numbered perhaps 250,000 people. They lived with security and a high degree of material and cultural success. The Jews of Egypt spoke Greek. This was the period of the Septuagint (the translation of the Old Testament into Greek). This had an enormous influence on the pagan world and later on the early Christian world as both learned about Judaism through translation. This was also the time of Philo Judaeus, one of the outstanding Jewish philosophers. Philo tried to bridge the world of the Greeks and that of the Jews by skillfully fitting Jewish ideas into Greek forms.

Babylonia. Babylonia remained a major Jewish settlement even after many Jews returned to Palestine from exile there. The Jewish community in Babylonia grew steadily through the centuries, especially after the Roman conquest of the Jewish homeland. Jews moved into the center of Babylonian life as politicians, merchants, artisans, farmers, and cattle breeders. In this period the Talmud was created. The Talmud is a major commentary on the Bible and on Jewish law, ethics, and religious practice. The glory of Babylonia lasted nearly 1,000 years, until A.D. 1040. In that year the Turks took control of the region. Soon after, the lights of Babylonia went out forever.

Yemen and the Arabian Peninsula. Flourishing Jewish communities existed in the Arabian Peninsula for centuries, especially in the oases of the south and of the northwest. In Yemen in the 5th century A.D. a pagan prince, Dhu Nuwas, became a convert to Judaism and carried his whole province with him. For some decades the established religion of Yemen was Judaism. Jews found a good home in other parts of the Arabian Peninsula. Their language was Arabic. They were artisans, merchants, and goldsmiths, often prospering above most other natives. Here, in the 7th century, Mohammed developed the basis for Islam, a faith that was to spread from the plateaus of central Spain to the subcontinent of India and beyond. Mohammed was sharply repudiated by the pagan priests. In despair he appealed to the Jewish community for help, offering to accept a large part of Judaism and to include Jewish festivals and heroes in his own religion. All he wanted in return was financial support and to be recognized as part of the succession of Jewish prophets. To the Jews, however, he was an uneducated man, unable to read or write, and they rejected his appeal. Mohammed never forgot the refusal of recognition or the insults. Having failed to gain their support, he turned against the Jews and drove them from their settlements. The Sura of the Cow in the Koran —the Islamic, or Muslim, holy book—summarizes Mohammed's passionate resentment of the Jews.

Spain—The Golden Years Before the Dark. In the long horror that was to be European life for the Jewish people, one place and one period offered a stretch of sunshine and prosperity. The Jews lived in Spain from the 7th century until their expulsion in 1492, a span of more than 750 years. An early period of persecution ended in 711, when the Muslim conquest of the Iberian (Spanish) Peninsula began. The legacy of hatred had already begun to soften. Muslim Spain offered the Jews their greatest opportunities. Spain became a refuge for those persecuted and expelled elsewhere, attracting Jews from as far away as the now-fallen Babylonia. Jews rose to leading positions in many parts of Spain. The great mass of the Jewish population lived in comfort and security. Cultural and religious activities blossomed. Poets like Solomon Ibn Gabirol (1021?–58?) and Judah Halevi (1080–1141) and the physician-philosopher Moses Maimonides (1135–1204) are revered in Jewish history. In this area Jewish learning formed a bridge between Arab and Christian learning. Jewish scholars interpreted and translated, serving as intermediaries between two creative cultures.

But the 14th century brought a change. Christian princes strove to drive out the Muslims. As Christian victories reclaimed the land, the lives of Muslim and Jew became desperate. In 1391, terrifying riots took place in Seville, a citadel of culture. It was clear that a golden age was coming to an end. Thousands of Jews were slaughtered as the riots spread to other parts of the Spanish peninsula. At first many sought to escape by conversion to Christianity. Those who did were known as Marranos (the Spanish word for "swine"). Some Marranos, no longer identified with the Jewish community, moved into high positions, even in the church. However, it was obvious that the conversions were often forced and that the old faith of Judaism was practiced secretly. Resentment against the Marranos blazed fiercely. Decade upon decade was filled with tragic stories of betrayals of the Marranos. They suffered torture, loss of their property, and death by fire in the public square.

In 1483, Torquemada, whose name became synonymous with fanatic cruelty, was appointed chief inquisitor, responsible for the purity of Christianity in Spain. Torquemada was determined to destroy the Marranos who still secretly practiced Judaism. And in time, he sought to expel from Spain all Jews who had never converted to Christianity. Torquemada asked King Ferdinand and Queen Isabella to sign edicts of expulsion. In 1492 the entire Jewish community of Spain, people whose ancestors had been part of the country for more than seven centuries, was expelled. Lands, estates, treasures, simple possessions —all were confiscated by the state. Perhaps 150,000 refugees, or more, fled abroad on the roads of Europe and North Africa.

▶THE NIGHTMARE OF EUROPE IN THE MIDDLE AGES

By this time all of Europe had become a hell for Jews. They existed without dignity and without security, ever subject to the whim of those in power. Attacks against the Jews increased with the Crusades, a movement of the Christians who had vowed to wrest the Holy Land from the Muslim Turks. There were many noble Christians who, especially in the beginning, took part in these Crusades. But there were criminal elements who joined simply for the loot. What better prey than the Jews and their possessions? From 1096, when the Crusades began, and for a century after, their trail across Europe was disgraced with looting, arson, torture, massacre, and expulsion of the Jews.

Pope Innocent III in 1215 initiated the practice of forcing Jews to wear a special badge, a special color, or some clothing that would degrade, ridicule, or set them apart. In 1239, Pope Gregory IX attacked the Talmud as if it were a great evil. He claimed the Talmud included insulting references to Jesus and Chris-

tianity and ordered all sets seized and burned. For decades thereafter, synagogues and homes were raided periodically. There were public trials of the Talmud, followed by wholesale burning of books in the public squares. Learning that had been preserved for centuries was turned to ashes. In every country the Jews were confined by law to special areas—the ghettos—always in the vilest part of town. Jews were compelled to stay within the restricted quarter, permitted outside only at special hours, identified by special dress, and controlled by curfews.

Expulsion of the Jews now became common. England expelled its Jews in 1290, though from time to time a family like the Montagues would be allowed to return as a

Even though they had lived in the country for more than 750 years, the Jews were expelled from Spain by King Ferdinand and Queen Isabella in 1492.

special favor. France expelled its Jews in 1306. The rule was not strictly enforced, and some thousands drifted back. A new expulsion order was issued in 1322, and then again in 1394. The principalities and dukedoms of Germany went through epidemics of expulsion. This is why, through the centuries when the Jews had no homeland and no security, they turned to writing and studying, depending more on God's mercy than human kindness. They became the People of the Book, since they could not be a people close to hearth and home or to friendship and comradeship.

A few bright spots shone the more brightly because of the almost universal darkness. When Spain expelled its Jews, refuge was offered in Turkey. Jewish settlement in Turkish territory grew until by the end of the 16th century Constantinople had one of the largest Jewish communities in the world. Doors were also opened in Poland. In this period Poland consisted of a loose federation of local independent principalities. The middle-class talents of the Jews were needed, and therefore Poland welcomed them. There were perhaps 50,000 Jews in Poland at the beginning of the 16th century; 150 years later the Jewish population had grown to more than 1,500,000. This was the largest concentration of Jews in Europe.

Meantime, smaller groups worked themselves into Italian life. During the Renaissance the governments of Italy's city-states were more tolerant than those elsewhere. In the middle of the 16th century many thousands of Jews found a haven in the little Dutch republic, which had thrown off the yoke of Spain. In 1657, Oliver Cromwell permitted Jews to return to England. But safety, security, and acceptance were almost always elusive. In the brutal mid-17th-century wars between Poland and the Cossacks of Russia, the Jews became victims of both sides. Poland was finally divided among the major European powers, and it disappeared from the map in 1795. Russia swallowed the largest part, with smaller portions going to Prussia and Austria. Russia therefore inherited the largest number of Jews. Poland did not reappear as a nation until the end of World War I.

In summary, on the eve of the French Revolution in 1789 the Jewish situation was, as it had been so often, bitter and uncertain.

▶EMERGENCE INTO A MODERN WORLD

The French Revolution, at the end of the 18th century, changed the history of Europe and affected the status of the Jews. France became the first country in Europe to establish complete citizenship for them. From the rubble and strife of the French Revolution rose an extraordinary man, Napoleon Bonaparte. Wherever his legions were victorious, Napoleon's modern ideas went, too. Everywhere he rooted out medieval practice, introducing reform. Napoleon's attitude toward Jews was not one of personal affection, but he would not tolerate medieval bigotry. Proclamations of emancipation were announced in every land he annexed for his empire. The Jews would now be full citizens. This meant that Jews were no longer a separate nationality but a religious group. Jewish national life would have to be absorbed into the political life of the states in which they lived.

After Napoleon's defeat at Waterloo, however, many European nations went through a strong reaction. Attempts were made to return to ancient and discredited practices. Restrictions were renewed in Germany, Austria, and Prussia. In Italy, Jews were forced every year to attend a sermon in which Judaism was denounced. In the late 19th century, anti-Semitism (hatred of the Jews) convulsed France in the Dreyfus case, when a Jewish army officer was falsely accused of selling military secrets to Germany. Years went by before he could be vindicated and freed from prison.

But clocks can never be turned all the way back. The liberal movement, once begun, gathered strength. There was growing confidence in the future. Educational opportunities were improved for all. Standards of living were rising. The lot of Jews, as of other people, was improved. In England, Lionel Rothschild, a Jew, took his seat in Parliament in 1858. Many German states lifted the more depressing restrictions. In Austria after 1867, Jews were permitted to live everywhere as full citizens. In 1870, Jews in Italy were released from galling humiliations.

To be sure, anti-Semitism did not disappear from the political and social life of each country. But in most cases it became simply the expression of dislike. Basic freedoms remained unchallenged. Jews took on the responsibilities of citizenship, educated their children, and entered most occupations.

Unfortunately, the vast political, social, and economic changes of the Industrial and French revolutions did not penetrate Russia and eastern Europe. From the days when Catherine the Great ruled Russia (1762–96) until World War I, eastern Jews suffered repression and degradation. In 1791, Catherine established the Pale of Settlement. This limited Jews to a very narrow sector of territory along the western frontier, driving them off the land into ghetto towns and villages. The terrible practice of conscripting Jews for military service at the age of 12 began under Czar Nicholas I. These draftees had to remain in service for 30 years, their lives so ordered that all relationship with family and with their Jewish faith was lost.

The last of the Russian czars was Nicholas II. He was superstitious and weak. The country was in a state of angry revolutionary activity, which Nicholas repaid with the cruelest repression. One of the worst years in Russian history was 1905, filled with executions and exile. For the Jews it was a climax to decades of despair. Thousands of homes were destroyed, and hundreds of men, women, and children were massacred.

▶ THE HOLOCAUST

The horrible genius of the 20th century was Adolf Hitler, a man of surpassing evil whose very name has become a curse. He fed on the German need for vengeance after Germany's defeat in World War I, and in the Nazi Party built a powerful instrument for destruction. He came to power in 1933 and used the following six years to re-arm the Germans and to threaten the democracies. Concession after concession was made to keep Hitler from erupting. But in 1939, Hitler felt that the time was ripe to carry out his plans. The Nazis invaded Poland, and World War II began.

For the Jews, Hitler had a deceptively simple plan—total destruction. He began the annihilation as soon as he came to power. Jews were removed from all positions in German government, education, and commerce. Terrifying anti-Jewish laws were passed. When war came, Hitler ordered wholesale butchery. Gas chambers and crematories were added to the already brutal concentration camps. Approximately 6,000,000 men, women, and children were executed in the most horrifying massacres in history, which have since become known as the Holocaust. In 1945, Germany was defeated. Hitler committed suicide. Nazi leaders were captured and executed. The Nazi apparatus was destroyed.

But for the Jews there was no comfort. Tattered remnants of Jewish communities that once flourished in Germany, Austria, Czechoslovakia, Hungary, Romania, and Poland were all that survived. Most of the Jews were displaced and stateless persons on a hopeless march back and forth across Europe. The European era in Jewish history lay buried in the mass graves of concentration camps— Bergen-Belsen, Buchenwald, Dachau, Auschwitz. For more information on the Holocaust, see the article HOLOCAUST in Volume H.

▶ THE FORMER SOVIET UNION, ISRAEL, AND THE UNITED STATES

In our own day, three centers of Jewish life emerged. In the former Soviet Union, some 1,800,000 Jews living under Communism shared the burdens of totalitarian life. More than 3,500,000 Jews living in Israel have gloried in the dignity of independence. The United States, the largest center of all, became a home for more than 5,800,000 Jews, the most powerful and influential community of all Jewish history.

Russia and Ukraine

The Communist revolution in Russia transformed the life of every inhabitant. Although Jews survived, they did not survive as Jews. All forms of religion and cultural identification with the past were forbidden by the atheist government. Assimilation, quick absorption into the Soviet Union, with its godless pattern of life and thought, was encouraged. Soviet youth learned to look on religion as superstition. Jewish or Christian, they broke with the faiths of their families.

The overthrow of Communism and the breakup of the Soviet Union at the end of 1991 has greatly affected Jews along with other former Soviet citizens. Most Jews now find themselves living in the independent nations of Russia and Ukraine, with smaller numbers in other countries that were former Soviet republics. Increasing numbers have emigrated, chiefly to Israel and the United States. What life will be like, under their new governments, for those who stay behind remains to be seen.

A modern city in an ancient land, Tel Aviv was founded by Jews in 1909. It was later joined with the much older city of Jaffa and now makes up Israel's largest metropolis.

Israel—The Homeland Regained

Few dreams last 2,000 years, but that of a homeland in Israel (Palestine) was never abandoned. Even after the Jewish state was destroyed by the Romans, small groups of Jews remained or kept returning, bribing their way, if only to weep at the Wailing Wall in Jerusalem for the Temple and lost glories. The few Jews who continued to live in Palestine thus became trustees for the whole Jewish people. For Jews dispersed throughout the world, the prayer was always "Next year in Jerusalem." But for long centuries this was merely a sentimental dream. The ancient land passed from one set of rulers to another: Roman, Crusader, Arab, Turk. Only a miracle could fulfill the dream of a scattered people who possessed neither political nor diplomatic power.

In the mid-19th century, nationalism surged throughout the Western world. Eastern European Jews, who lived where persecution was most fierce, were urged to migrate to Palestine. If enough Jews settled the land, concessions for independent life might be gained from the ruling Turks. These hopes and dreams were encouraged by Theodor Herzl (1860–1904), the founder of modern Zionism. Zionism was a political movement to restore the Jewish homeland in Palestine. At the end of the 19th century, European anti-Semitism was especially ugly in the events surrounding the Dreyfus case. Herzl felt that there could never be respect or dignity for Jews unless they had their own homeland. Herzl awakened little interest among more comfortably placed Jews, especially in Western Europe. But his vision excited the imagination of the eastern communities of Jews and the small groups in the poorer sections of the West. The Zionist movement grew slowly during Herzl's lifetime. Then, amid the violent changes of World War I, the miracle came as the Turkish empire collapsed.

The instrument was the skillful diplomacy of Dr. Chaim Weizmann (1874–1952), a Polish Jew who became a naturalized British subject. His scientific achievements helped enormously in the British war effort. Because of Dr. Weizmann, England issued the Balfour Declaration. This document stated that one of the Allied war aims would be the re-establishment of a Jewish homeland in Palestine. After the Allied victory of 1918 the promise was fulfilled, and Palestine was placed under British mandate as a Jewish homeland. But serious problems developed almost at once because of bitter opposition from the Arab population of Palestine and surrounding states.

Riots, terror raids, guerrilla attacks, and almost full-scale war followed. The British began to regret their pledge and to whittle down the meaning of the Balfour Declaration. Yet immigration continued. Settlements grew. The arid soil began to flower. Schools were established and Hebrew again became a living language.

Fleeing Hitler, many thousands of Jews sought entry to Palestine. The British, fearful of further angering the Arabs, placed obstacles in the way of new immigration. But desperate people found a way, and the settlements in Palestine continued to multiply. During World War II the Jews of Palestine loyally supported the Allied side. The Arabs as vigorously supported the Nazis. Acknowledging the Jewish choice, the British promised that valor and loyalty would not be forgotten. British postwar politics, however, decreed otherwise, for Britain needed Arab co-operation in the Middle East. Britain reversed its position, cut off Jewish immigration, and forbade further sale of land. Between 1945 and 1948 the Jews waged a double battle against the Arabs and the British. At last British patience was exhausted, and Britain surrendered the dispute and the mandate to the United Nations. After a historic debate the United Nations partitioned the country, giving part to the Arabs and part to the Jews, each with sovereignty in their own area. Jews now wrote their declaration of independence and declared the birth of the state of Israel in 1948.

Israel, newborn and reborn, pitted itself against six Arab states: less than 1,000,000 Israelis against 40,000,000 Arabs. With rare military ingenuity and courage, the Israelis won. Israel was recognized by most nations of the world, except the Arab nations, and was admitted to the United Nations in 1951. Israel grew in strength and vitality. Immigrants poured in. Compounded by a healthy birthrate, the population rose to more than 4,000,000, of which some 85 percent were Jews, by the mid-1980's. Desert was reclaimed and converted into green pastures and gardens. Industry supplemented agriculture, and the standard of living rose steadily. Schools and universities flourished. But Israel's serious conflicts with its Arab neighbors persisted. For a further discussion of the history of the state of Israel, see the article ISRAEL in Volume I.

The United States

Jews had migrated to the New World from the earliest explorations. There were Marranos in the voyages of Columbus. Jews arrived in America during the Revolutionary War and during the periods of westward expansion. Their numbers increased whenever persecution drove them from Europe. When the democratic hopes of the mid-19th century failed in Europe, there were new tides from Germany, Poland, and Russia. The mightiest migrations, this time of whole villages and towns, began after the 1882 May Laws of Russia. By the outbreak of World War I there were more than 2,500,000 Jews in the United States. All those who yearned for freedom were welcomed to a land where there was desperate need for workers to develop its industrial and commercial life.

Jews contributed greatly to the economic development of the country. They influenced its manufacture and retail trades, its entertainment industries, music, and the arts and sciences. By the mid-20th century there were more than 5,000,000 Jews in the United States. This was the largest, most secure, most influential settlement in all Jewish history. Jewish Americans sat on the bench of the United States Supreme Court, in the Senate, and in the House of Representatives. Some were governors, mayors, and special advisers to presidents.

A vigorous Jewish community life developed in the United States. This movement was supported by welfare fund organizations with a wide variety of religious, cultural, and philanthropic activities. A new leadership was taking over, born and bred in the United States. In 1924 the Johnson Immigration Law set severe limits to all immigration, especially from the areas of eastern and southern Europe. American Jewish life could no longer be enriched by people from the old centers of culture and learning. It had to be developed from within. The flourishing institutions of the American Jewish community—synagogues, temples, community centers, schools, and publication societies—rose to the challenge. Two strong sources of inspiration—the new American Judaism and the state of Israel—exist to ensure a future that will be worthy of the legacy from the past.

ABRAM L. SACHAR
Chancellor, Brandeis University

JOAN OF ARC, SAINT (1412–1431)

Saint Joan of Arc is honored by the people of France as one of their greatest heroines. The daughter of a farmer, she was born on January 6, 1412, in Domrémy, a village in northeastern France. During her childhood much of France was ruled by the Burgundians, a powerful group of nobles who had joined with the English to gain control of the country. The French king, Charles VI, died in 1422, and the heir to the throne, the Dauphin Charles, had taken refuge in southern France.

The villagers of Domrémy longed for the day when the English would be driven from the land and the Dauphin Charles raised to the throne. Despite the constant warfare, Joan's childhood was not unusual. She did not attend school, but she learned to spin and sew from her mother. She helped with chores around the family farm and was regarded by her neighbors as a devout child.

When she was about 13 years old, Joan's life was dramatically changed. She began to hear "voices," which she later identified as those of saints Catherine and Margaret, and of Michael the Archangel. During the next few years the saints appeared to her and told her that she must bring peace to France by having the Dauphin crowned king. Joan asked how she, a young girl, could help her country, but the voices simply said it was God's command.

At first Joan sought aid from the military commander of a nearby town, who was loyal to Dauphin. He dismissed her as foolish and sent her home. But on her second trip, Joan succeeded in persuading him to help her. He gave her some soldiers for protection and sent her to Chinon, where the Dauphin was staying.

According to some accounts, the Dauphin was warned of Joan's coming and decided to test her to see if she was in earnest. He arranged for one of his friends to pose as the Dauphin, but Joan was not misled by this move. In a room filled with people she picked out the real Dauphin. She convinced him that her mission was genuine by telling him a secret her voices had revealed to her.

Charles agreed to let her lead his troops to Orléans, an important city that the English were trying to capture. During the battle Joan was wounded, but she refused to leave. The French soldiers were impressed by her courage and fought with great spirit. The English, believing that Joan was a witch, fled in fear. Spurred on by the victory, the French won more battles. On July 16, 1429, Joan led the French triumphantly into the city of Reims. On the next day she stood nearby as the Dauphin was crowned Charles VII. The Maid of Orléans, as Joan came to be called, had carried out the first part of her voices' command.

Anxious to complete her mission of freeing France, Joan urged the King to continue the fight against the enemy. Charles, however, was content with his crown and wished to hear no more of war. Also, many of his counselors were jealous of Joan's success and tried to turn Charles against her. Without the full support of the King, the French troops began to suffer losses. Eventually Joan was captured by the Burgundians during an attack on Compiègne.

Charles made no attempt to gain her release, but the English eagerly bought her from the Burgundians. She was then brought to Rouen on charges of witchcraft. Her judges were French clergymen who supported the Burgundians and English. Throughout her trial Joan defended herself with great bravery and simplicity. However, she was found guilty and sentenced to death. Under the harsh treatment of her captors, Joan signed a confession. Instead of being freed as she had hoped, Joan was sentenced to life imprisonment. She then rejected her confession as false, and the court again sentenced her to death.

Joan, then only 19 years old, was burned at the stake in Rouen on May 30, 1431. Her ashes were thrown into the river Seine. But many French people firmly believed that the Maid was innocent and that her voices had not been the work of the devil. The English were finally driven from France, and Charles began an examination of Joan's trial. Pope Calixtus III established a new court in 1455, which judged that Joan had been wrongly executed. The Catholic Church declared Joan a saint in 1920 and celebrates her feast on the anniversary of her death, May 30.

KATHLEEN McGOWAN
Catholic Youth Encyclopedia

JOGGING AND RUNNING

You see them everywhere, it seems—on indoor tracks and outdoor tracks, on city streets and country roads, along the sides of asphalt highways, on paths in parks. Who are they? They are joggers and runners—men and women, girls and boys, of all ages, sizes, and shapes.

There are about 20,000,000 joggers and runners in the United States alone. Why are so many people running? They run because running is good exercise—and it is fun.

▶ JOGGING AND HEALTH

In the 1950's and 1960's, many people became concerned about the increase in heart disease. Dr. Paul Dudley White, a well-known cardiologist (heart doctor), began telling people that strenuous exercise is good for the heart. The heart is a muscular pump, and strenuous exercise makes muscles strong. In 1968, Dr. Kenneth Cooper wrote a book called *Aerobics,* in which he encouraged people to jog or run regularly. He had found that of all the strenuous sports—soccer, cycling, swimming, and so on—jogging and running are the most beneficial.

Jogging does more than strengthen the heart. It builds lung capacity, so that more oxygen is delivered to the blood. It strengthens the circulatory system, so that more blood reaches body cells. It uses up calories and improves muscle tone, so that you can do more work without tiring. For many people, it reduces emotional tension. In short, jogging makes you feel healthier and happier.

The main difference between jogging and running is speed—running is faster. But there is no clear line between the two. Because both are natural activities for young people, many schools have started jogging and running programs in their gym classes. And hundreds of thousands of young people are jogging and running on their own.

▶ STARTING A JOGGING PROGRAM

Everyone, young and old alike, should have a medical checkup before starting to jog or run. In general, children should not run fast for long distances. Their muscles are not yet properly developed for speed running. But many children can easily cover long distances at a slow jog. In adolescence, when your body is changing, you may need to adjust your program. Jog only when you feel up to it.

It is a good idea to start out slowly. Some people walk for several weeks until they build up the stamina to jog. But plan to jog regularly—at least three times a week, 15 minutes each time. Before each jog, warm up with sit-ups and stretching and bending exercises. (A number of such exercises are described in the article PHYSICAL EDUCATION in Volume P.) Many people walk briskly before jogging.

When you jog, hold your arms slightly away from your body, with the lower arms parallel to the ground. Keep your back straight, and remember to breathe deeply, with your mouth open. Do not take long strides. The way your foot hits the ground is important. Some experts suggest a flat-footed landing. But most joggers let the heel strike the ground first.

After each run, cool down. A good way to do this is to walk until perspiration slows and breathing becomes normal. Do not sit down if your heart is still beating heavily.

As a beginner, you may think about taking part someday in track events at school or in group runs, called "fun runs," that have been organized in many communities. You may even become interested in the greatest of all events—the marathon. Give yourself time to think about activities such as these.

▶ EQUIPMENT AND SAFETY

The only equipment a runner needs is a good pair of running shoes. These should have cushioned heels and padding to absorb shock. Clothing should suit the weather. Wear bright colors and attach reflectorized tape to your clothing to make it visible.

It is best to jog on a school track or on a level stretch of dirt, grass, or gravel. But you can jog almost anywhere if you watch out for dangerous conditions. Avoid ground with obstacles such as exposed tree roots, rocks, and overhanging branches. Along roads, always run facing oncoming traffic. In cities, use the sidewalks and watch for traffic at intersections. Never jog at dusk or at night, when drivers might not see you.

Finally, know when to stop. If you become too tired or develop muscle cramps, you have been jogging too long. And remember that jogging is not racing. Jogging is slow running that, with patience, builds health and endurance.

RICHARD BENYO
Managing Editor, *Runner's World*

JOHN XXIII, POPE (1881–1963)

Pope John XXIII was born Angelo Giuseppe Roncalli on November 25, 1881. His birthplace was Sotto-il-Monte, a tiny village near Bergamo in northern Italy. The eldest son of a large peasant family, young Roncalli received his early education in nearby village schools. When he was 11, he enrolled in the seminary at Bergamo. He completed his seminary studies in Rome and was ordained a priest in 1904.

The following year Father Roncalli became secretary to the bishop of Bergamo. During World War I, he served with the medical corps and the chaplain corps of the Italian Army. In 1921 he was called to Rome to help direct missionary activities. While performing these duties, he was made a monsignor.

In 1925, Monsignor Roncalli was made an archbishop and appointed to the papal diplomatic corps. He was sent to Bulgaria and then to Turkey and Greece. In 1944 he was transferred to France. He proved himself a skillful diplomat as well as a humanitarian. In Turkey he had interceded with the Nazis to prevent deportation of Jews from eastern Europe.

In 1953, Roncalli was made a cardinal and Patriarch of Venice. Five years later he was elected pope.

Pope John devoted his reign to the promotion of peace and understanding among people of all faiths around the world. Two of his most famous encyclicals (letters written by the pope and addressed to the world) were *Pacem in Terris* ("Peace on Earth") and *Mater et Magistra* ("Mother and Teacher"). For his accomplishments he won the Balzan Peace prize in 1963.

Perhaps the foremost accomplishment of Pope John's brief reign was the calling of an ecumenical council at the Vatican in 1962. It was the first time in almost 100 years that such a council had been called. He hoped it would help bring unity to all Christians.

Pope John died in Rome on June 3, 1963, at the age of 81. His death was mourned by people throughout the world.

KATHLEEN McGOWAN
Catholic Youth Encyclopedia

JOHN PAUL II, POPE (1920–)

When Karol Cardinal Wojtyla was elected pope on October 16, 1978, he became the first Polish pope in history and the first non-Italian pope since Adrian VI (pope 1522–23), who was Dutch. And at 58 he was the youngest person to be elected pope since Pius IX, who was 54 when he was elected in 1846.

Karol Wojtyla was born on May 18, 1920, in the town of Wadowice, southwest of the former Polish capital city of Cracow. His mother died when he was young, and his father supported the family for the most part on a military pension. After high school he attended classes at the Jagiellonian University in Cracow. But the Nazis invaded Poland in 1939 and closed the university.

Wojtyla worked in a quarry and later in a chemical plant, and he began to study for the priesthood through classes that were held in secret by members of the university's theology faculty. He was also active in an anti-Nazi theater group and other underground activities. After World War II, he finished his seminary studies and was ordained a priest on November 1, 1946. He then studied at the Angelicum University in Rome and the Catholic University of Lublin in Poland.

Wojtyla first served as a curate in a small Polish village. He then was chaplain to the students at Lublin, where he became a faculty member. He wrote books and articles on ethics. He was made auxiliary bishop of Cracow in 1958 and Archbishop of Cracow in 1964. He attended all sessions of Vatican Council II. In 1967 he became a cardinal. Although the practice of religion was difficult in Communist Poland, Wojtyla encouraged his people by word and example. He even confronted government officials on their behalf.

As pope, John Paul II has supported human rights, social justice, family values, and world peace. In 1981 he was shot in St. Peter's Square in Vatican City. Although badly wounded, he recovered. The reason for the attack remains unclear. His extensive travels have formed his image as a "people's" pope. His trips include visits to Africa, Brazil, and the United States.

Reviewed by THADDEUS HORGAN, S.A.
Director, Graymoor Christian Unity Center

JOHN THE BAPTIST

The New Testament tells us that Saint John the Baptist was the son of Zacharias. John's mother, Elizabeth, was related to Mary, the mother of Jesus. John is called the Baptist because he baptized people, washing away their sins with the waters of the Jordan River.

The story of John's birth is told in the Gospel of Saint Luke. Elizabeth and Zacharias, married many years, were childless. One day an angel appeared to Zacharias and told him Elizabeth would give birth to a son who was to be called John. Zacharias asked the angel for a sign so that he might believe him. Punishing Zacharias for his disbelief, the angel struck the old man dumb. As the angel predicted, Elizabeth had a son. Zacharias, asked to name the child, wrote "John" on a tablet and immediately regained his power of speech.

At an early age, John left his parents and went to live and pray in the desert. He wore the hides of animals and ate locusts and wild honey. When he was about 27 years old, he came out of the desert and began to preach to other Jews. John told them that the kingdom of God was near. Many of John's followers thought he was the Messiah, sent by God to establish His kingdom. But John said that he was preparing the way for the Messiah. Many came to John to be baptized, Jesus among them. John identified Jesus as the Messiah and sent some of his disciples to follow him. Later, John was imprisoned because he criticized the ruler of the Jews, Herod Antipas, for marrying his own brother's wife.

The sixth chapter of the Gospel of Saint Mark tells the story of John's death. On Herod's birthday his stepdaughter, best known as Salome, danced in his honor. Herod asked how he might reward her. She demanded the head of John, which was brought to her on a plate.

The Catholic Church calendar has two feast days in honor of Saint John the Baptist—June 24 and August 29.

KATHLEEN MCGOWAN
Catholic Youth Encyclopedia

ANDREW JOHNSON (1808–1875)

17th President of the United States

FACTS ABOUT ANDREW JOHNSON

Birthplace: Raleigh, North Carolina
Religion: Christian (no denomination)
College Attended: None
Occupation: Tailor
Married: Eliza McCardle
Children: Martha, Charles, Mary,
  Robert, Andrew
Political Party: Democratic; Republican
  (National Union) during Civil War
Office Held Before Becoming President:
  Vice President
President Who Preceded Him:
  Abraham Lincoln
Age on Becoming President: 56
Years in the Presidency: 1865–1869
(succeeded Abraham Lincoln, April 15, 1865,
  after Lincoln's assassination)
Vice President: None
President Who Succeeded Him: Ulysses
  S. Grant
  Age at
  Death: 66
  Burial Place:
  Greeneville,
  Tennessee

DURING ANDREW JOHNSON'S PRESIDENCY

The 13th Amendment to the Constitution, abolishing slavery, was ratified (1865). Nebraska was admitted to the Union as the 37th state (1867). *Left:* Alaska was purchased from Russia (1867) for $7.2 million. Dynamite was invented by Alfred Nobel of Sweden (1867). The Dominion of Canada was established (1867). *Below left:* The first practical typewriter was developed (1867) by Christopher Sholes. *Below:* The U.S. House of Representatives voted to impeach the president, who was subsequently acquitted by the U.S. Senate (1868).

JOHNSON, ANDREW. When President Abraham Lincoln died on April 15, 1865, from an assassin's bullet, just as the Civil War was ending, the man who had to fill his place and take up his unfinished work was Vice President Andrew Johnson of Tennessee. Without preparation or warning, the new president was suddenly called upon to handle the most complicated problem the federal government had ever faced. This was the problem of how to deal with the defeated South and how to reunite a country that had been torn apart by four years of war.

Johnson made great efforts to carry out this task. But he was unable to reduce the bitterness between North and South and bring the country's affairs back to normal. He was a man of courage and good intentions, but he did not know how to take advice or how to work with people. His disagreements with Congress led to his impeachment—a formal charge of misconduct or crime. He was the only U.S. president to be impeached and he barely avoided being removed from office.

▶EARLY YEARS

No American president ever began his life in greater poverty than Andrew Johnson. He was born on December 29, 1808, in Raleigh, North Carolina, the younger of two surviving children of Jacob and Mary McDonough Johnson. Jacob Johnson was employed as a porter and handyman. One winter day in 1811, he rescued two men from drowning in an icy river, but he himself died soon afterward from exhaustion and cold. Andrew was thus left fatherless at the age of 3. The penniless widow supported herself and her two young sons, Andrew and his brother, William, by weaving cloth, but on more than one night, the family went to bed hungry.

At the age of 14, Andrew was apprenticed to a tailor. The boy learned quickly, and before long, he ran away to work for himself. In 1826, when he was 18, the Johnson family moved to Greeneville, Tennessee, where Andrew started his own tailor shop.

Johnson never went to school, but he had learned a little reading at the tailor's house in Raleigh. In Greeneville he married Eliza McCardle, who taught him to write. Five children were born to them, three boys and two girls. His tailoring business did well and he bought property in the town. He became a leader of the young men of the neighborhood, who would often meet at the A. Johnson Tailor Shop to discuss politics and hold debates on public affairs.

▶ HE ENTERS POLITICS

Johnson was elected to his first political office, town alderman, in 1829. Thereafter, his rise in politics was rapid. He served as mayor of Greeneville and in both houses of the state legislature. In 1843, he was elected to the first of five terms in the U.S. House of Representatives. He was elected governor of Tennessee in 1853 and a U.S. senator in 1857. He was serving in the Senate at the outbreak of the Civil War in 1861.

Johnson thought of himself as a man of the common people, and he was a popular speaker among the simple mountain folk of eastern Tennessee. In a voice that could be heard for great distances, he would address them on the benefits of democracy and honest labor and on the evils of high taxes and government spending. Johnson often spoke of his own humble beginnings. He pointed to himself as an example of how a poor boy might rise to wealth and prominence through ambition and hard work.

▶ SECESSION AND CIVIL WAR

The secession crisis of 1860–61 opened an entirely new chapter in Johnson's life. When Lincoln was elected president in 1860, the Southern states, including Johnson's own state

Eliza McCardle married Andrew Johnson in 1827 and played an important role in his life. A schoolteacher, she taught him to read and encouraged his political career.

of Tennessee, prepared to secede, or break away, from the Union. One of the main disputes between North and South was over slavery. Johnson, like nearly all Southerners, was loyal to the institution of slavery. But unlike most Southerners, he was even more loyal to the United States. He was ready to sacrifice everything to keep it from breaking apart.

During 1861, Johnson traveled all over his home state, trying to persuade the people not to take Tennessee out of the Union. Time after time he risked his life as he faced crowds of people who had once been his friends but were now his enemies, telling them that secession was treason. In self-defense he had to carry a loaded pistol everywhere, and on more than one occasion, he was forced to use it. Johnson did not give up until the last hope of saving his state was gone, Tennessee eventually seceding in June 1861.

Although Johnson was now a man without a state, he stayed on in Washington, D.C., as the loyal senator from a disloyal state. Previously a lifelong Democrat, as a Unionist he now allied himself with the Republicans, the party of Lincoln.

IMPORTANT DATES IN THE LIFE OF ANDREW JOHNSON

1808	Born in Raleigh, North Carolina, December 29.
1826	Settled in Greeneville, Tennessee.
1827	Married Eliza McCardle.
1829	Elected mayor of Greeneville.
1835	Elected to the first of several terms in Tennessee legislature.
1843–1853	Served in the U.S. House of Representatives.
1853	Elected governor of Tennessee.
1857–1862	Served as U.S. senator from Tennessee.
1862	Appointed military governor of Tennessee.
1865	Inaugurated as vice president of the United States, March 4; took office as president on death of Abraham Lincoln, April 15.
1865–1869	17th president of the United States.
1874	Elected to the U.S. Senate from Tennessee.
1875	Died near Carter Station, Tennessee, July 31.

Andrew Johnson's tailor shop still stands in Greeneville, Tennessee. Here, as a young man, he first made his mark in business and in politics.

Andrew Johnson was Abraham Lincoln's vice-presidential running mate in the 1864 election campaign. After Lincoln was assassinated in 1865, Johnson became president.

▶ MILITARY GOVERNOR TO VICE PRESIDENT

After the Union Army recaptured parts of Tennessee in early 1862, Lincoln, deeply impressed with Johnson's courage, asked him to return as the state's military governor. Johnson instantly agreed. He remained at his post until nearly the end of the war, although there was hardly a week during that entire period when his life was not in danger. His loyalty had its reward. When Lincoln ran successfully for re-election in 1864, he chose Johnson as his vice president.

▶ PRESIDENT

At their inauguration in 1865, an incident took place that gave the public an unfavorable first impression of the new vice president. Johnson had been suffering from typhoid fever, and his friends suggested that he take a little whiskey, then considered a remedy for many ailments. He took too much, however, and his inaugural speech was confused. Six weeks later, Lincoln was dead and Andrew Johnson was president.

The Reconstruction Question. With the war finally ended in 1865, a majority of Northerners wanted to ensure that the South's loyalty to the Union would never again be in danger. In addition to the preservation of the Union, the victory had resulted in the destruction of slavery. The North now felt that the South should give the newly freed blacks the same protection and the same rights as other citizens. Most Republicans in Congress, however, felt that the Southern states would not take such steps without a certain amount of outside pressure. They believed that laws would have to be passed to "reconstruct" the South.

Johnson's Stance. Johnson's failure to understand Northern feelings on this question of reconstruction led to the failure of his entire presidency. A strong believer in states' rights, he felt that the South should be allowed to deal with blacks in its own way, without interference from the federal government. Johnson believed that he, and not Congress, should decide when the Southern states were ready for readmission to the Union. In his opinion they should be readmitted immediately. He insisted that Congress had no right to pass laws for the South when Southern representatives were not present to vote on them.

The Dispute with Congress. However, Congress was unwilling to readmit the Southern representatives until a full study could be made of conditions in the South. These differences of opinion led to the bitterest quarrel that has ever occurred between a president and Congress. Matters were made worse when several Southern legislatures late in 1865 and early in 1866 passed state laws, known as Black Codes, which discriminated severely against blacks.

Early in 1866, Congress passed the Freedmen's Bureau bill and the Civil Rights bill, which gave some federal protection to Southern blacks. Johnson vetoed (rejected) them both, although the Civil Rights bill was repassed over his veto. Later in the year another Freedmen's Bureau bill was successfully enacted. In the spring, Congress approved the 14th Amendment to the Constitution, which defined citizenship to include blacks and entitled them to the equal protection of the laws. It also stated that certain leaders of the former Confederate government could not hold public office until further notice. Johnson advised the Southern states not to ratify, or approve, the amendment. (It was ratified in 1868.)

All of this led Congress to pass the Reconstruction Acts in March 1867. They were vetoed by Johnson but were repassed over his veto. The acts put the South under full military occupation, set up new state governments, and

This ticket of admission to Johnson's Senate impeachment trial dates from 1868. Johnson was found not guilty by the margin of a single vote.

gave blacks the right to vote and hold public office. Many former Confederate leaders were forbidden either to vote or to hold office.

Impeachment. The dispute came to a head in 1868. Earlier, in 1867, Congress had enacted the Tenure of Office Act, which forbade the president from removing certain office-holders without the approval of the Senate. Johnson had wanted to get rid of Secretary of War Edwin M. Stanton, because he thought Stanton was too friendly with leaders in Congress. Early in 1868 he dismissed Stanton. The House of Representatives thereupon impeached the president; that is, it officially accused him of breaking the law. In his trial by the Senate, which followed, Johnson was judged not guilty by the bare margin of one vote. It was found that the Tenure of Office Act did not apply to cabinet members who were held over from a previous term, and Stanton had been appointed by Lincoln.

Foreign Affairs. The Johnson administration was involved in two important events abroad. In 1866, Secretary of State William H. Seward, who had served in the post under Lincoln, forced France to withdraw its troops from Mexico, where it had earlier attempted to create an empire under Maximilian of Austria. Seward also negotiated the purchase of Alaska from Russia in 1867, although the price, $7.2 million, was thought much too high.

▶**LATER YEARS**

After his acquittal by the Senate, Johnson served out the rest of his term of office without further disturbance. He sought but failed to win the Democratic nomination for president, and with the end of his term in 1869, he returned to Tennessee. For several years thereafter, he tried, without success, to return to public office. Finally, in 1874, he was once more elected to the Senate from his home state, taking his seat in March 1875. Johnson was able to attend only the one session, however. He suffered a stroke and died on July 31, 1875.

ERIC MCKITRICK
Columbia University
Author, *Andrew Johnson and Reconstruction*
See also IMPEACHMENT; RECONSTRUCTION PERIOD.

JOHNSON, JAMES WELDON (1871–1938)

James Weldon Johnson was a poet, teacher, diplomat, and civil rights leader. He was also one of the intellectual leaders of the African American movement of the 1920's known as the Harlem Renaissance.

Johnson was born in Jacksonville, Florida, on June 17, 1871. His mother was the first African American woman to teach in a Florida public school. James did well in school. He read a great deal and also wrote poems and stories. After graduating from Atlanta University, he became principal of his old elementary school in Jacksonville. At the same time, he began a newspaper and studied law. He was the first African American to pass the bar examination in Florida. Later he moved to New York City, where he and his brother, John Rosamond, wrote popular songs together.

In 1904, Johnson gained recognition while working on President Theodore Roosevelt's election campaign. He was later appointed consul in Venezuela and in Nicaragua. He held those posts from 1906 until 1912, when he resigned from consular service to publish what became his best-known novel, *The Autobiography of an Ex-Colored Man*. His first book of poetry, *Fifty Years and Other Poems*, followed in 1917. He edited the first anthology of black poetry as well as collections of spirituals. His work, *God's Trombones: Seven Negro Sermons in Verse* (1927) was adapted for the stage, and his autobiography, *Along This Way*, appeared in 1933.

Johnson was also a leading civil rights figure. In 1920 he became the first black executive secretary of the National Association for the Advancement of Colored People (NAACP). Johnson resigned from the NAACP in 1930 to teach at Fisk University in Nashville, Tennessee. After 1934 he was also a visiting professor of literature at New York University. He died on June 26, 1938, following an automobile accident.

DANIEL S. DAVIS
Author, *Struggle for Freedom: The History of
Black Americans*

JOHNSON, JOHN HAROLD. See ARKANSAS (Famous People).

LYNDON BAINES JOHNSON (1908–1973)

36th President of the United States

FACTS ABOUT LYNDON B. JOHNSON

Birthplace: Near Stonewall, Texas
Religion: Disciples of Christ
College Attended: Southwest
    Texas State Teachers College
Occupation: Teacher, rancher
Married: Claudia Alta
    (Lady Bird) Taylor
Children: Lynda Bird, Luci Baines
Political Party: Democratic
Office Held Before Becoming
    President: Vice President
President Who Preceded Him: John F. Kennedy
Age on Becoming President: 55
Years in the Presidency: 1963–1969
(succeeded John F. Kennedy, November 22,
    1963, after Kennedy's assassination)
Vice President:
Hubert H.
Humphrey
President Who
Succeeded Him:
Richard M. Nixon
Age at Death: 64
Burial Place:
Johnson City,
Texas

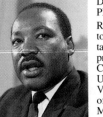

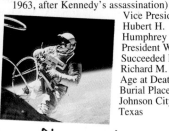

DURING LYNDON B. JOHNSON'S PRESIDENCY

Ratification of the 24th Amendment to the Constitution (1964) banned poll taxes in federal elections. The president proposed his Great Society program to Congress (1965). *Below:* The first U.S. combat troops arrived in South Vietnam (1965), enlarging the scope of the Vietnam conflict. *Below left:* Major Edward H. White became the first U.S. astronaut to walk in space (1965). Congress established the Department of Housing and Urban Development (1965). The Department of Transportation was created (1966). The 25th Amendment to the Constitution, dealing with presidential disability, was ratified (1967). Assassinations claimed the lives of civil rights leader Dr. Martin Luther King, Jr. (*above*) in Memphis, Tennessee (1968), and Senator Robert F. Kennedy in Los Angeles, California (1968).

JOHNSON, LYNDON BAINES. On November 22, 1963, ninety-nine minutes after the assassination of President John F. Kennedy in Dallas, Texas, had stunned the nation, Vice President Lyndon Baines Johnson took the oath of office as president of the United States and was flown immediately to Washington, D.C., to assume his new duties. Of all the vice presidents who have succeeded to the presidency, Johnson was perhaps the most thoroughly trained in politics. Most of his adult life had been spent in public service, and he had built a notable record of accomplishment, both as vice president and in Congress, where he had served as majority leader of the Senate.

Johnson won election as president in his own right by a wide margin in 1964. His major achievement was a series of domestic reforms known as the Great Society program. But his administration was also marked by controversy over the Vietnam War, which eventually led to his decision not to seek re-election to a second term in 1968.

▶ EARLY YEARS

Lyndon Johnson was born on August 27, 1908, on a farm near Stonewall, Texas. He was the eldest of the five children of Samuel Ealy Johnson and Rebekah Baines Johnson. The early years of his life were spent on the farm and in the neighboring town of Johnson City. The town had been named for Lyndon's paternal grandfather, Sam Ealy Johnson, Sr., and his brother (Lyndon's great-uncle), Tom Johnson. The brothers had settled in the area before the Civil War to raise cattle, which they then drove over the trails to Kansas.

Young Lyndon was brought up neither in poverty nor in luxury. The Johnson family was not terribly poor, but it certainly was not rich. There was always enough food on the table, decent clothing, and at least one pair of shoes for each member of the family. Lyndon had a pony to ride to school—but ponies were commonplace in that area. There were few extras, however, and money was never plentiful. Lyndon earned his own spending money by delivering newspapers and shining shoes. His grades were generally good at school in Johnson City, and his mother was determined that he should receive an adequate education.

When Johnson graduated from high school, however, he resisted the idea of going to college. With several of his friends he decided to go to California to make his own way. He soon found that this was not easy, although he worked at any job he could get. He washed dishes, waited on tables, ran an elevator, and did farm work whenever he could find it. Finally, homesick, he worked and hitchhiked his way back to Texas, where he got a job with a road construction crew.

After a few months of this, he told his parents that he was going to try to learn to work with his head instead of his hands. He borrowed $75 for his tuition and entered Southwest Texas State Teachers College in San Marcos, Texas, majoring in history. To help pay his expenses, Johnson worked as a janitor. Later he obtained a better paying job as a secretary in the college president's office. An energetic student, he led the debating team, edited the college newspaper, and was a member of the literary society. In 1930 he graduated with a bachelor of science degree.

▶ POLITICS, MARRIAGE, AND WAR

After his graduation, Johnson became a teacher in the public school system of Houston, Texas, but not for long. Political activity was a tradition in the families of both his parents, his father having served five terms in the Texas legislature, and Lyndon Johnson was fascinated by politics. In 1931 he left his teaching post to become secretary to a newly elected congressman, Richard M. Kleberg, a family friend.

The young Lyndon Johnson grew up on his father's farm near Stonewall, Texas, and in the nearby town of Johnson City, named for his grandfather.

In 1934, Johnson married Claudia Alta Taylor, of Marshall, Texas, who was known by her childhood nickname of Lady Bird. They had two daughters, Lynda Bird and Luci Baines.

In Washington, Johnson benefited from his family's friendship with Congressman Sam Rayburn. Rayburn was rising to a position of great power in Washington, eventually becoming Speaker of the U.S. House of Representatives. He was responsible for Johnson's appointment in 1935 as Texas state director of the National Youth Administration.

Johnson served in the NYA for two years, resigning in 1937 to become a candidate for the House of Representatives. Campaigning on a firm pledge of support for President Franklin D. Roosevelt and his New Deal, he received almost twice as many votes as his nearest opponent. He was re-elected for five successive terms.

Roosevelt showed a personal interest in the young Texan from the time he entered Congress. He was immediately named to the Naval Affairs Committee, an assign-

Johnson is seen here with President Franklin Roosevelt in 1937, the year he won election to Congress, where he strongly supported Roosevelt's New Deal program.

IMPORTANT DATES IN THE LIFE OF LYNDON BAINES JOHNSON

1908	Born near Stonewall, Texas, August 27.
1930	Graduated from Southwest Texas State Teachers College.
1934	Married Claudia Alta (Lady Bird) Taylor.
1935	Appointed Texas state director of National Youth Administration.
1937	Elected to the U.S. House of Representatives.
1941– 1942	Served in the U.S. Navy, December—July.
1948	Elected to the U.S. Senate; became Democratic majority leader, 1954.
1961	Inaugurated vice president, January 20.
1963	Took office as 36th president after the assassination of President John F. Kennedy, November 22.
1965– 1969	Served a full term as president.
1973	Died at Johnson City, Texas, January 22.

After the assassination of President John F. Kennedy in Dallas, Texas, on November 22, 1963, Vice President Lyndon B. Johnson was sworn in as the new president on the plane that would take him back to Washington, D.C. Jacqueline Kennedy, the president's widow, is at right; Lady Bird Johnson is at left.

ment of unusual importance for a freshman congressman. In 1941, Johnson ran for the U.S. Senate in a special election, but he was defeated.

When the United States entered World War II on December 8, 1941, Johnson, a member of the Naval Reserve, asked to be called up for active duty. The first member of the House of Representatives to go into uniform, he served a little more than seven months before Roosevelt ordered all members of Congress in military service to return to Washington. During most of his naval service, Johnson was assigned to the Pacific Theater of Operations. He held the rank of lieutenant commander and was awarded the Silver Star medal.

▶ U.S. SENATOR

In 1948, Johnson again ran for the Senate and won. He was assigned to the Armed Services Committee, and in 1950, when the Korean War broke out, he helped establish the Preparedness Investigating Subcommittee. He became its chairman and conducted a series of investigations of defense costs and efficiency. These investigations brought him national attention. They also earned him the respect of senior members of the Senate.

Johnson quickly advanced to a position of leadership. In 1953, he was chosen minority leader, the youngest man ever named to the post by either major political party. He won re-election to the Senate in 1954. Since the

Democrats had gained control of the Senate, Johnson became majority leader. His duties were to schedule legislation and to help pass measures favored by the Democrats.

▶ VICE PRESIDENT

Johnson's success as Senate majority leader led to his being widely mentioned as a possible Democratic presidential candidate. He was Texas' "favorite son" candidate at the party's national convention in 1956. It was not until 1960, however, that he made a serious bid for the nomination. He received 409 votes on the first and only ballot at the Los Angeles convention, but the nomination went to Senator John F. Kennedy of Massachusetts. Johnson was then nominated for vice president, having been personally chosen by Kennedy as his running mate. The Kennedy-Johnson ticket won the 1960 election, but received an extremely close margin of the popular vote.

An active vice president, Johnson traveled across the country on speech-making tours to present the administration's viewpoint and journeyed to many foreign countries. He attended meetings of the National Security Council as well as cabinet sessions and served as chairman of the National Aeronautics and Space Council and the President's Committee on Equal Employment Opportunity.

▶ PRESIDENT

Johnson was in Dallas on a political trip with President Kennedy in 1963, when Kennedy was shot and killed by a sniper's rifle fire. He was sworn in as the 36th president of the United States on the plane carrying him back to Washington. Johnson's first efforts were devoted to calming the nation's fears. In an address before a joint session of Congress, a few days after assuming the presidency, he called for passage of Kennedy's legislative program. To investigate the assassination, he created a presidential commission headed by Chief Justice Earl Warren. An article on the Warren Report appears in Volume W-X-Y-Z.

In his first State of the Union message in January 1964, Johnson presented a broad program of legislation to Congress. Most of his major proposals were enacted during the long session of Congress that followed. Among them were a substantial reduction in taxes, a far-reaching civil rights bill, and an antipoverty program.

The Election of 1964. Johnson easily won the Democratic nomination for president in 1964. For his vice president, he chose Senator Hubert H. Humphrey of Minnesota. The Republican candidates were Senator Barry Goldwater of Arizona for president and Representative William E. Miller of New York for vice president. Johnson received 61 percent of the popular votes cast and 486 electoral votes to Goldwater's 52. It was the most one-sided presidential election since 1936.

The Great Society. Acting on Johnson's program, which he hoped would help build what he called a "great society," Congress passed much legislation in 1965. Federal aid to education, funds for the depressed Appalachia region, creation of a new Department of Housing and Urban Development, hospitalization insurance for the elderly (Medicare), and changes in the immigration laws were some of the measures provided. Congress also approved the Voting Rights Act of 1965, designed to protect the voting rights of blacks.

In 1966, at the president's urging, another new cabinet-level department was created—the Department of Transportation. Legislation passed by Congress in 1967 included a 13-percent increase in Social Security benefits and a federal air-pollution control bill.

In 1968 a civil rights bill with strong open housing provisions was passed by Congress.

Foreign Affairs. In foreign affairs, events in Panama, the Dominican Republic, the Middle East, and Vietnam caused the administration particular concern. In Panama, dissatisfaction with the existing Panama Canal treaty led to rioting in 1964 and the temporary breaking of diplomatic relations with the United States. Relations with Panama were improved by Johnson's agreement to begin negotiations on a new treaty. Reports of Communist influence in a rebel movement in the Dominican Republic prompted the president to send troops to that country in 1965. The troops were withdrawn after a peaceful election the following year. In the Middle East the situation remained tense following the 1967 Arab-Israeli war.

Johnson's most controversial decision was to increase the number of U.S. troops in South Vietnam and to bomb sites in North Vietnam. The Vietnam War became the most crucial issue facing the president in 1967 and 1968. Johnson frequently found himself attacked by

Johnson's expansion of the Vietnam conflict provoked enormous controversy. The growing division within the United States over the war eventually led to his decision not to seek renomination as president in 1968.

The Johnson family in the White House: Lady Bird Johnson is seated, with daughters Lynda Bird (left) and Luci Baines (right) standing on either side of the president.

both "doves," who were opposed to the war, and by "hawks," who supported the war but criticized his handling of it.

▶ **WITHDRAWAL FROM POLITICS**

In March 1968, in an address to the nation, Johnson announced a halt in the bombing of North Vietnam. More startling was his announcement that he would not seek renomination for the presidency, citing the growing division within the country over the war. The Democratic nomination went, instead, to Vice President Hubert Humphrey, who was defeated in the 1968 election by Richard M. Nixon. After departing from the White House in 1969, Johnson retired to his ranch in Johnson City, Texas, where as president he had often entertained visiting dignitaries. Suffering from an earlier heart ailment, he died suddenly on January 22, 1973, at the age of 64.

BOOTH MOONEY
Author, *The Lyndon Johnson Story*

JOHNSON, PHILIP (1906–   )

The American architect Philip Cortelyou Johnson was born in Cleveland, Ohio, on July 8, 1906. He attended Harvard University, where he studied Greek and philosophy. After graduating in 1927, he became increasingly interested in architecture and architectural history. But it was not until 1939 that he returned to Harvard to pursue a career in architecture.

Johnson's special interest as an architect is in linking interior and exterior spaces and in accenting the approach to a building. His first major construction was his own home, called the Glass House, built in New Canaan, Connecticut, in 1949. A technical triumph, the building consists of a single room with all-glass walls suspended from a slender steel frame. Its simple geometric lines and use of glass and steel materials reveal the influence of Ludwig Mies van der Rohe, a leader of the style of modern architecture called the **international style**.

Johnson worked with Mies on the design of New York City's Seagram Building, completed in 1958. Mies's influence is evident in the steel beams and glass of the exterior. The building's elegant interior, however, is Johnson's own design. Among Johnson's later works is the New York State Theater at Lincoln Center, which was finished in 1964. This magnificent building includes an auditorium that seats more than 2,700 people.

In the 1970's, Johnson moved away from the utter simplicity of the international style and began to add traditional architectural elements to his designs. Perhaps the best-known example is his American Telephone and Telegraph Company Building in New York City, which was completed in 1984. It is often called the Chippendale Building because its rooftop resembles the broken triangle motif that is characteristic of Chippendale furniture. This building design helped to define the architectural movement that came to be called **postmodernism**.

HOWARD E. WOODEN
Director Emeritus
The Wichita Art Museum

JOHNSON, RICHARD M.   See VICE PRESIDENCY OF THE UNITED STATES.

JOHNSON, SAMUEL (1709–1784)

Samuel Johnson, the English writer and lexicographer (dictionary maker), was born in Lichfield, Staffordshire, on September 18, 1709. The son of a country bookseller, Sam attended Pembroke College, Oxford. But he had to leave for lack of money, and he educated himself mainly through books in his father's shop. Large and awkward, he also suffered from ill health all his life.

In 1735, Johnson married Elizabeth (Tetty) Porter, a widow with several children. He opened a school where he taught Greek and Latin, but when the school failed, he went to London to become a writer. His first poem, a satire called *London*, was published in 1738. This was followed by *The Vanity of Human Wishes* (1749), which reflects a gloomy outlook that contrasts with, but is balanced by, Johnson's zest for life.

In 1746 a group of publishers commissioned Johnson to put together a dictionary of English. He worked on it for nine years with very little help and in 1755 produced *A Dictionary of the English Language*. Johnson's dictionary contains sometimes humorous definitions of 40,000 words then in use among educated people. During the 1750's, Johnson also wrote satirical essays for *The Rambler* and *The Idler*. In 1762, King George III freed him from poverty with a pension.

Johnson's *History of Rasselas, Prince of Abissinia*, a moral tale in a colorful setting, appeared in 1759. His edition of Shakespeare was published in 1765. His last major work was *The Lives of the English Poets* (1779–1781). Johnson was also a shrewd critic.

But Johnson is remembered most as a brilliant talker, with a sense of humor and an attractive if contradictory personality. This side of Johnson was made famous by James Boswell in his *Life of Samuel Johnson* (1791), one of the great biographies of all time. Boswell met Johnson in 1763 and for years recorded his remarks, habits, and travels.

Johnson died in London on December 13, 1784, and was buried in Westminster Abbey.

DORIS L. EDER
Yale University

JOHNSON, WALTER. See IDAHO (Famous People).

JOHNSON SPACE CENTER. See SPACE AGENCIES AND CENTERS.

JOHNSTON, ALBERT SIDNEY. See KENTUCKY (Famous People).

JOHNSTON, JOSEPH EGGLESTON. See CIVIL WAR, UNITED STATES (Profiles: Confederate).

JOINT CHIEFS OF STAFF. See UNITED STATES, ARMED FORCES OF THE.

JOKES AND RIDDLES

Jokes are as old as the spoken word. In every age in history, people have told funny stories to make one another laugh. In the Middle Ages in Europe, the court jesters, or fools, amused rulers and their courts with jokes and tricks. At first, court jesters ·sang of brave deeds, or gestes. But as time went by, they became tellers of jokes and funny stories.

During the later Middle Ages and the Renaissance, the jokes told by jesters began to appear in collections, or jestbooks. One of the best-known English jestbooks was *Tarlton's Jests*, which appeared about 1611. Richard Tarlton was the favorite jester of Queen Elizabeth I. While she was queen, jesters were at the height of popularity. After she died, official court jesters disappeared, but joke-telling and joke books continued.

The most famous name in the history of jokes and joke books is that of Joe Miller, an English actor who lived from 1684 to 1738. After he died, John Mottley, an English playwright, published *Joe Miller's Jests*.

While we no longer have court jesters, we still have people whose job it is to make us laugh—the clown in the circus, the comedian on television, the ventriloquist with a dummy. We still laugh at many of the same things that made people laugh long ago: jokes that have surprise endings, tall tales, and stories of foolish people. Here are some examples.

Linda's mother called up the stairs to her, "Linda, did you put out the light?"
Linda said, "How should I know? It's too dark in here to see."

Kevin to Teacher: Would you be mad at me for something I didn't do?
Teacher: Of course not, Kevin.
Kevin: That's good, because I didn't do my homework.

A salesman approached Jimmy, sitting on the steps of a house. "Sonny," he asked, "is your Mommy home?"

"Yes," replied Jimmy.

The salesman began to ring the bell. He rang and rang and rang, but there was no answer. Finally he turned back to Jimmy and said angrily, "I thought you said that your Mommy was home."

"I did," replied Jimmy, "but this isn't my house."

Fern: That's a strange pair of socks you have on—one is red and the other is green.

Elaine: Yes, and the funny thing about it is that I have another pair at home exactly like this one.

Teacher: If we breathe oxygen in the daytime, what do we breathe at night?

Sally: That's easy. Nitrogen, of course.

"Joey's been walking since he was 8 months old," his mother told a friend.

"Good heavens!" the friend exclaimed. "Isn't he tired?"

A puzzling statement or question, sometimes in the form of a rhyme, is a riddle. Asking riddles is the world's oldest quiz game. Riddles are also called conundrums. Sometimes a riddle is based on a pun, or play on words—like this one, which you've surely heard: "When is a door not a door?" "When it's ajar (a jar)." Others point out an unexpected likeness between two very different things. Here is one example: "Why is a pencil like a funny story?" "They both have a point."

We ask one another riddles today as a form of amusement, but people long ago took riddles very seriously. Ancient oracles often answered questions and gave advice in the form of riddles, and rulers used riddles to send secret messages to one another. These serious riddles were also called enigmas.

Greeks and Romans held riddle contests at their feasts and gave laurel wreaths to the winners. According to some ancient legends, people's lives sometimes depended on their giving the correct answer to riddles. In one famous Greek myth, Oedipus, the hero, solved a riddle asked by the Sphinx. "What goes on four legs in the morning, on two at noon, and on three in the evening?" The answer was, "People, who crawl as children, walk erect as adults, and use a cane in old age."

If you stop to think about it, you realize that several well-known nursery rhymes are really riddles. Humpty Dumpty, of course, is the riddle of a broken egg. People in countries all over the world have their riddles. Some of the following riddles are from the folklore of English-speaking countries.

How does a hippopotamus get down from a tree?
It sits on a leaf and waits for fall.

What do you have that is easiest to part with?
Your comb.

What has four wheels and flies?
A garbage truck.

What goes up every time the rain comes down?
An umbrella.

What word is pronounced wrong by the best of scholars? Wrong.

There is something lighter than a feather that you can't hold even 10 minutes. What is it?
Your breath.

If two's company and three's a crowd, what are four and five?
Nine.

What coat is always wet when you put it on?
A coat of paint.

What happens when a duck flies upside down?
It quacks up.

What is the difference between here and there?
The letter *t.*

Why do bees hum?
Because they don't know the words.

Why do birds fly south?
Because it's too far to walk.

How long should your legs be?
Long enough to reach the ground.

What's the best way to catch a squirrel?
Climb a tree and act like a nut.

What time is it when an elephant sits on a fence?
Time to get a new fence.

What did one strawberry say to another?
If you weren't so sweet, we wouldn't be in this jam.

Reviewed by DAVID ALLEN CLARK
Author, *Jokes, Puns, and Riddles*

JOLLIET, LOUIS (1645–1700), AND JACQUES MARQUETTE (1637–1675)

Louis Jolliet and Father Jacques Marquette are often credited with being the first white persons to view the waters of the upper Mississippi River. They were surely the first to travel down the river for any distance. Their discoveries added greatly to knowledge of the Mississippi Valley and Great Lakes region.

Louis Jolliet was born in Quebec City in New France (now Canada) in 1645. He studied at a Jesuit seminary but decided not to become a priest. In 1667 he went to Europe to study science. He returned home with the idea of becoming a fur trader and an explorer. In 1669 he explored the Lake Superior area.

Jacques Marquette was born at Laon, France, in 1637 and was educated as a Jesuit missionary. In 1666 he went to New France. He learned the difficult Indian languages and worked among the Ottawa and Huron Indians. In 1671 he founded the mission of St. Ignace in the Mackinac region.

Indian tales of a "great river" to the west had reached Governor Frontenac of New France. In 1672 he asked Jolliet to explore the rumored river and find out where it ran into the sea. Perhaps this was the long-sought westward passage through the continent. Jolliet turned to Father Marquette for help.

All winter the two men prepared for their trip. In May 1673, they and five companions set out in two canoes. They crossed Green Bay and reached the Wisconsin River, which carried them to the Mississippi. They went down the Mississippi as far as the Arkansas. There Indians convinced them that the Mississippi continued south instead of west to the Pacific Ocean. The explorers turned homeward. Marquette's poor health forced him to remain at Lake Michigan for the winter. While there he wrote a journal of his discoveries.

Marquette returned to the Mississippi the following year to start a mission among the Kaskaskia Indians. He died in Michigan in 1675 beside a river that now bears his name.

Jolliet continued to work as an explorer, investigating the Labrador coast and the area between the Saguenay River and Hudson Bay. Before his death in 1700, he was given the island of Anticosti in the St. Lawrence River as a reward for his work.

JOHN MOIR
Carleton University (Ottawa)

JONAH.   See BIBLE STORIES.

JONES, CASEY.   See RAILROADS (Profiles).

JONES, JOHN PAUL (1747–1792)

John Paul Jones was the foremost officer in the American Navy during the Revolutionary War.

John Paul (his real name) was born in Kirkcudbrightshire, Scotland, on July 6, 1747. After an apprenticeship to a shipowner, Jones twice served on ships transporting slaves. But he found it an "abominable trade" and quit after a few years.

Jones was returning to Scotland in 1768 as a passenger in the brig *John* when both the master and the mate died. Jones took over command. The owners, impressed, made him master of his own ship, although he was only 21. Jones was disliked by his crews because of his exacting demands and severe discipline. Twice, charges were brought against him for murder. He was cleared of the first charge, and the second "murder" was actually a case of self-defense. But fearing that action would be taken against him, he fled to Virginia and called himself John Paul Jones.

At the outbreak of the revolution, Jones was commissioned lieutenant in the new Continental Navy. In 1776 he was given temporary command of the *Alfred,* the first naval ship commissioned by Congress.

Jones was promoted to captain and, in June 1777, was given command of the *Ranger,* which was ordered to France. The following April, he captured the British sloop of war *Drake* in the Irish Sea.

Soon after, Jones succeeded in getting a larger command, a rotted French East Indiaman, or merchant ship, of 40 guns. He named the ship *Bonhomme Richard* in honor of Benjamin Franklin. In August 1779, a squadron under Jones's command sailed for another raid on British shipping and coast towns. His ships took 17 prizes (captured ships).

John Paul Jones's dramatic victory over the *Serapis* made him a hero of the Revolutionary War. He became known as the founder of the United States Navy.

On September 23, 1779, off Flamborough Head near Hull, England, Jones fought the battle that gave him his place in history. With three ships, he engaged the 50-gun *Serapis* and the 22-gun *Countess of Scarborough*, two British ships of war. At sundown the *Bonhomme Richard* bore down on the *Serapis*. The fight, again in full view of the shore, raged 3½ hours into a moonlit night. The heavier-gunned *Serapis* made a wreck of the *Richard,* but this did not break Jones's will to victory. Shortly before the mainmast fell, the *Serapis* surrendered and was boarded by Jones and his crew. From there they watched the *Richard* sink.

After the victory the squadron with its prizes sought safety in Holland. On December 27, 1779, forced out by the Dutch, Jones slipped through the British blockade. In 1781 he was formally thanked by Congress.

In 1783, Jones went to Paris. Some years later he accepted a rear admiral's commission in the Russian Navy. But he fell into disfavor with his superior, Prince Potemkin, and he returned to Paris. He died there alone on July 18, 1792. His remains were returned to the United States in 1905 and now lie in a crypt beneath the Naval Academy chapel.

Jones was greatly admired, but he had few friends because of his colossal egotism. He was a keen student of naval strategy and an excellent ship handler. But what gave John Paul Jones his lasting place in the history of his adopted country was his unconquerable fighting spirit, as expressed in his reply to a demand for surrender during the *Serapis* battle: "I have not yet begun to fight."

JOHN D. HAYES
Rear Admiral, U.S. Navy (Ret.)

JONES, ROBERT TYRE (BOBBY), JR. (1902–1971)

Bobby Jones became a legend in sports history by achieving what was called golf's grand slam. In one year, 1930, he won all four of the world's major championships—the British Amateur, the United States Amateur, the British Open, and the United States Open. No one else has ever accomplished this feat.

Robert Tyre Jones, Jr., was born in Atlanta, Georgia, on March 17, 1902. He began playing golf when he was 5 years old. At the age of 14, he won the Georgia state title. Jones became known for his smooth swing and for his precise putting with an old club named "Calamity Jane." In 1923, at the age of 21, he won his first U.S. Open championship.

In 1922, Jones earned a degree in mechanical engineering from the Georgia Institute of Technology. He received a B.S. degree from Harvard University in 1924. After his marriage in June of that year, Jones studied law at Emory University. He was admitted to the Georgia bar in 1928.

From 1923 through 1930, Bobby Jones won 13 major tournaments, including 4 U.S. Opens, 3 British Opens, and 5 U.S. Amateurs. He was also a member of 5 victorious Walker Cup teams, serving twice as captain. He made his grand slam at the age of 28. He then retired from tournament golf to practice law.

In 1951, Jones was chosen by U.S. sportswriters and broadcasters as the outstanding golfer of the first half of the 1900's. He was the founder and lifetime president of the Augusta National Golf Club in Georgia, home of one of golf's most competitive events, the Masters Tournament. Bobby Jones, golf's greatest amateur, died on December 18, 1971.

GENE WARD
Sports Columnist, *New York Daily News*

JOPLIN, SCOTT. See ARKANSAS (Famous People).

JORDAN

Jordan is an Arab kingdom in the Middle East. Its official name is the Hashemite Kingdom of Jordan. The name comes from the country's location along the Jordan River in Southwest Asia and from the family of its rulers, the Hashemites. Jordan is a fairly young nation, although its people have lived in the region for many centuries. Once part of the Ottoman Turkish Empire, which was broken up after World War I (1914–18), it was established as a self-governing emirate (a territory ruled by an emir, or prince) by the British in 1923. It gained complete independence in 1946 as the Hashemite Kingdom of Transjordan. The name Transjordan (meaning across or beyond the Jordan) was later changed to Jordan.

▶THE PEOPLE

Nearly all Jordanians are Arabs. There are small communities of Circassians, Armenians, and Kurds. The Circassians are descendants of people who migrated from their homeland in the Caucasus mountain region of southern Russia in the mid-19th century. The Kurds are a non-Arab people of the Middle East. A large part of the population is made up of Palestinian Arab refugees who fled to Jordan during the Arab-Israeli wars of 1948–49 and 1967. Some of the Palestinians have settled in cities and towns. But many still live in camps built by the United Nations.

Some Jordanians are farmers. Others work in trade, commerce, government, and industry in the cities. There are also nomadic people of the desert who herd sheep, goats, and camels.

Religion and Language. The vast majority of the people are Muslims, including the Circassians and Kurds. There is a small Christian minority. The largest Christian group belongs to the Greek Orthodox Church. Arabic is the official language, but many people also speak English.

Education. The Jordanian Government has been making an effort to improve the educational system by training more teachers and building more schools. Many of the Palestinian refugee children attend schools supervised by a United Nations agency. The main institution of higher learning is the University of Jordan in Amman, the capital. Yarmouk University, in the city of Irbid, was founded in 1975.

A large part of Jordan's population is made up of Palestinian Arabs who became refugees during the Arab-Israeli wars. Many live in camps built by the United Nations.

Way of Life. More than 60 percent of Jordan's people live in cities or large towns. The rest live in villages in the countryside. The nomads traditionally traveled between settled areas and the desert each season, seeking pasture and water for their livestock. Nomads once made up a considerable part of the population, but only a small percentage of the people still follow this way of life.

The basic foods are vegetables, fruits, rice, and meat, eaten with a flat, round bread. Country people often wear traditional Arab dress, including a white or checkered head covering and a cloak or robe for men, and long skirts and shawls for women. City people generally wear European-style clothes or a combination of traditional and modern dress.

▶ **THE LAND**

Jordan's borders have varied since it became an independent nation in 1946. Originally situated east of the Jordan River, it annexed the territory west of the Jordan—known as the West Bank—in 1950. The West Bank has been under the control of Israel since 1967. Jordan maintained some economic and political relations with the Arabs of the West Bank until 1988, when it officially severed all ties to the region.

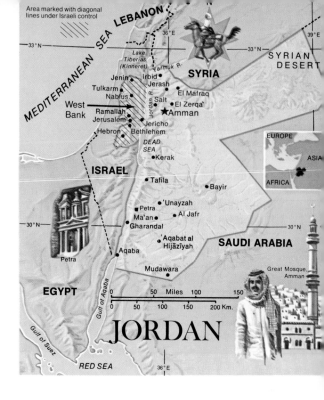

FACTS and figures

HASHEMITE KINGDOM OF JORDAN is the official name of the country.

LOCATION: Southwest Asia.

AREA: 35,475 sq mi (91,880 km²).

POPULATION: 4,200,000 (estimate).

CAPITAL AND LARGEST CITY: Amman.

MAJOR LANGUAGE: Arabic (official).

MAJOR RELIGIOUS GROUP: Muslim.

GOVERNMENT: Constitutional monarchy. **Head of state**—king. **Head of government**—prime minister appointed by the king. **Legislature**—National Assembly (consisting of the House of Notables and the House of Representatives).

CHIEF PRODUCTS: Agricultural—wheat, barley, citrus fruits, tomatoes and other vegetables, olives, watermelons, grapes, livestock. **Manufactured**—refined petroleum products, chemicals, fertilizers, cement, processed foods, leather products, textiles. **Mineral**—phosphates, potash.

MONETARY UNIT: Jordanian dinar (1 dinar = 1,000 fils).

The land consists of three main regions: the eastern desert; a high plateau in the west; and the Jordan River valley. The eastern desert makes up most of Jordan's territory. But the plateau is the most heavily populated region and the site of the major cities. The plateau drops sharply to the Jordan River valley, most of which lies below sea level.

The Jordan and its main tributary (branch), the Yarmuk, are the only important rivers. The Jordan flows into the Dead Sea, which is a salt lake. The shoreline of the Dead Sea averages about 1,296 feet (395 meters) below sea level, making it the lowest point on the surface of the Earth.

Climate and Natural Resources. Jordan's climate is generally hot and dry. In summer, temperatures may reach 120°F (49°C). In spring and early summer, a hot, dry wind called the khamsin blows in from the eastern desert. Rainfall is sparse, averaging less than 15 inches (380 millimeters) a year.

Jordan has few natural resources. Only about 10 percent of its land is suitable for farming, and much of that has limited use because of a lack of water. Forests cover less than 1 percent of the land. Unlike some of its oil-rich neighbors, Jordan has no petroleum deposits. Its most valuable minerals are phosphates and potash, which are used chiefly in making fertilizers.

THE ECONOMY

Agriculture. Less than 10 percent of the work force is now engaged in agriculture. The chief crops are wheat, barley, oranges and other citrus fruits, tomatoes and other vegetables, olives, watermelons, and grapes. Sheep and goats, along with smaller numbers of cattle and camels, are raised as livestock.

Industry and Trade. Jordan's most important industries are the mining of phosphates and potash, and the refining of crude oil shipped by pipeline from Saudi Arabia. The leading manufactured goods include refined petroleum products, chemicals, fertilizers, cement, processed foods, leather products, and textiles.

Jordan is one of the world's leading exporters of phosphates. It also exports chemicals, fertilizers, fruits and vegetables, and livestock products. An additional source of income is the money sent home by Jordanians working abroad, mainly in other Arab countries of the Middle East.

MAJOR CITIES

Amman is Jordan's capital and largest city, with about one third of the country's population. Located in the north, about 50 miles (80 kilometers) east of the Jordan River, it is also the center of Jordan's commerce and industry. The city is an ancient one. In biblical times it was known as Rabbah Ammon. It later was ruled by the Greeks and then the Romans. A large outdoor theater dating from Roman times still stands. Amman was a small town under the Ottoman Turks, but it grew rapidly as the capital of Transjordan. The city's population swelled with the arrival of Palestinians fleeing the Arab-Israeli wars.

El Zerqa (or Zarqa), the second largest city, lies just north of Amman. It is the center of Jordan's oil-refining industry. Other major cities include Irbid, in the northwest; and Aqaba, Jordan's only port, located on the Gulf of Aqaba in the south.

The ruins of the ancient city of Petra are one of Jordan's most important historical

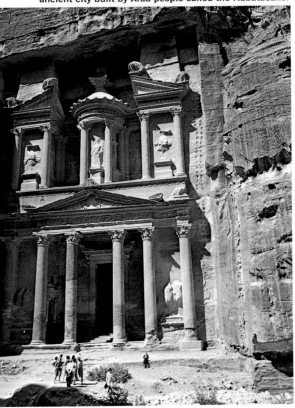
One of many monuments cut into the cliffs at Petra, an ancient city built by Arab people called the Nabataeans.

Amman, the capital of Jordan, is the largest city and chief industrial center of the nation.

sites. Identified with the fortress of Sela in the Bible, Petra was the capital of the Nabataeans, an Arab people, from the 300's B.C. until its conquest by the Romans in A.D. 106.

▶ GOVERNMENT

Jordan is a constitutional monarchy. The king is head of state and also exercises wide powers in the government. He appoints the prime minister, who heads the Council of Ministers. The king approves laws passed by the legislature, commands the armed forces, appoints judges, and has the power to declare war. The legislature is the National Assembly. It consists of the Senate, whose members are appointed by the king, and the House of Representatives, which is elected by the people.

▶ HISTORY

Settlements existed in the Jordan region over 6,000 years before the birth of Christ. The biblical kingdoms of Ammon, Edom, Gilead, and Moab once covered most of the area of modern Jordan. Later, part of the Jordan region was incorporated into the Hebrew kingdom of Judah. Because it stood along a major trade route to the Mediterranean Sea, Jordan attracted many invaders. The Greeks conquered the region in the 4th century B.C. They were followed by the Romans (who ruled the area from the 1st to the 4th century A.D.) and later by the Arabs (in the 7th century A.D.), who converted the people to Islam. From 1516 to 1918, Jordan was part of the Ottoman (Turkish) Empire.

After the defeat of Turkey at the end of World War I, the League of Nations gave what was then called Transjordan (the region east of the Jordan River) as a mandate to Great Britain. Abdullah ibn Hussein, an ally of Britain, became the emir, or prince, of Transjordan. When Transjordan became independent in 1946, Abdullah became king of the new Hashemite Kingdom of Transjordan.

Transjordan and other Arab nations opposed the creation of Israel from part of the British mandate of Palestine. During the 1948–49 Arab-Israeli War, Transjordan occupied the West Bank of the Jordan River. In 1950 it adopted its present name—the Hashemite Kingdom of Jordan. King Abdullah was assassinated in 1951. He was succeeded briefly by his son Talal, and in 1952 by his grandson Hussein, who assumed power officially in 1953.

Jordan, a largely Muslim country, has many mosques. The mosque tower is a minaret, from which Muslims are called to prayer.

Recent History. Jordan lost the West Bank to Israel in the 1967 Arab-Israeli War. Many Palestinian Arabs fled across the Jordan River. Some joined the Palestine Liberation Organization (PLO), which became a powerful force and a challenge to Hussein's authority. A war between the PLO and Jordan in 1970–71 ended in a PLO defeat. But in 1974, Hussein acknowledged the PLO as the sole representative of the Palestinians.

In 1988, Hussein formally gave up his claims to the West Bank. In 1993, Israel and the PLO signed an accord giving Palestinians limited self-rule in the West Bank city of Jericho and in the Gaza Strip. Jordan followed, in 1994, with an agreement to end its state of war with Israel. Later Hussein played a key role in mediating peace talks between the Israelis and Palestinians.

Shortly before King Hussein died in February 1999, he named his eldest son, Abdullah II, heir to the throne.

ALEXANDER MELAMID
New York University

See also PALESTINE.

JORDAN, BARBARA. See TEXAS (Famous People).

JORDAN, MICHAEL. See BASKETBALL (Great Players); CHICAGO (Famous People).

JORDAN, VERNON E., JR. See CIVIL RIGHTS MOVEMENT (Profiles).

JOSEPH

Joseph is one of the most colorful characters in the Bible. His father was the patriarch Jacob. His mother was Rachel. Joseph's story is told in the book of Genesis.

Jacob had twelve sons, but Joseph was his favorite. As an expression of his love, Jacob gave Joseph a beautiful "coat of many colors" that he had made himself. The gift made Joseph's brothers jealous.

Joseph had dreams of greatness. Twice he dreamed that he would rule over his brothers. In one dream he and his eleven brothers were binding sheaves of wheat, and his brothers' sheaves bowed down to his. In the other dream, the sun and moon and eleven stars bowed down to him.

Joseph told his brothers about the dreams. The dreams made them so angry that they wanted to kill him. So they cast him into a pit, hoping he would die. But a caravan of merchants on their way to Egypt saved Joseph in order to sell him as a slave. In Egypt they sold him to Potiphar, captain of Pharaoh's guard.

Joseph was then about 28 years old and a handsome young man. Potiphar's wife fell in love with him. When Joseph did not accept her love, she made false charges against him to her husband. Potiphar had Joseph arrested and put in prison.

In prison Joseph's talent for interpreting dreams was discovered. On one occasion he explained the dreams of two officers of Pharaoh's court, the chief butler and the chief baker. What he told them came true.

One night Pharaoh was troubled by dreams. The next day he sent for all the wise men and all the magicians in Egypt. None of them could explain the dreams. Finally Joseph was called. Pharaoh told Joseph about seven thin cows that ate up seven fat cows and seven thin ears of corn that swallowed seven plump ears. Joseph said that both dreams meant the same thing. Seven years of plenty were coming and, after them, seven years of famine. Joseph also suggested putting aside large quantities of food to provide for the time of famine.

Pharaoh was so grateful to Joseph that he made him viceroy, or governor, of Egypt. He also gave him an Egyptian girl, Asenath, for his wife. She was the daughter of a priest in the city of On. Asenath and Joseph had two sons—Manasseh and Ephraim.

In time all happened as Joseph had said. After 7 years of plenty, famine came. Eventually it spread to the land of Canaan, where Joseph's family lived. Joseph's father sent all his sons except the youngest, Benjamin, to Egypt, where there was grain to be bought.

As governor, Joseph was in charge of selling the grain. Joseph saw his brothers and recognized them at once, although they did not recognize him. He also noticed that the youngest brother, Benjamin, had not come. He asked them to fetch him. When they had done this, Joseph tested them. He had his servant place one of his own silver cups in a sack that belonged to Benjamin. Then he accused Benjamin of stealing the cup. One of the other brothers, Judah, pleaded with Joseph to spare the boy. He even offered himself as a substitute if Joseph insisted that someone had to pay for the crime with his life. Since Judah spoke for all the brothers, Joseph was satisfied that they had changed their cruel ways, and he revealed who he was. When Joseph's father heard that his favorite was still alive, he was overjoyed.

Joseph told Pharaoh about his father and brothers. The Pharaoh gave them land in the fertile valley of Egypt called Goshen. The family settled there and prospered.

After living in Egypt about 17 years, Joseph's father died. Joseph and his brothers took his body to Canaan and buried him with their ancestors in the Cave of Machpelah.

When Joseph returned to Egypt his brothers feared that, with their father dead, Joseph would now take revenge upon them. But Joseph told them, "Fear not," for vengeance was in God's hands, not his. He said that their evil had turned into good, for he had been able to save many lives.

Joseph lived to an old age and died in Egypt. Before he died he made his family promise that they would one day bury him in Canaan. When Moses led the Jews out of Egypt to Canaan, the promise was fulfilled. The Bible says, "Moses took the bones of Joseph with him."

MORTIMER J. COHEN
Author, *Pathways Through the Bible*

JOSEPH, CHIEF. See INDIANS, AMERICAN (Profiles).

JOSÉPHINE, EMPRESS (1763–1814)

Marie-Josèphe-Rose Tascher de la Pagerie, who became the wife of Napoleon I and empress of the French, was born on the island of Martinique in the French West Indies on June 23, 1763. Her father was a sugar planter.

Rose, as she was called by her family, attended a convent school. When she was 16 she went to Paris. There she married a young army officer, Vicomte Alexandre de Beauharnais. Two children were born to them: Eugène, who was to become viceroy of Italy, and Hortense, who would later marry Louis Bonaparte and become queen of Holland.

During the Reign of Terror that followed the French Revolution, the couple was imprisoned. The Vicomte was guillotined in 1793, and his wife narrowly escaped the same fate. At the end of the Terror she was freed.

Her charm and wit soon won her a place in Parisian society. When she was 32 years old she met Napoleon Bonaparte, then a young army officer of 26. He called her Joséphine, the name by which she became known.

On March 9, 1796, Joséphine and Napoleon were married. Her political influence contributed greatly to Napoleon's being given his first major command, of the Army of Italy, which led to his first great victories. In 1804, Napoleon was proclaimed emperor. During the coronation in Notre Dame Cathedral, the Emperor removed his crown and placed it gently on his wife's head.

The Empress was not to enjoy this position long. Government officials demanded the divorce of Napoleon and Joséphine if she did not bear an heir, and in 1809 the Emperor finally agreed. Joséphine retired to her estate at Malmaison, near Paris. Napoleon, now married to Marie Louise of Austria, remained Joséphine's friend and often traveled to Malmaison to see her.

Joséphine begged to go into exile with Napoleon after his defeat in 1814, but she was refused permission. When Napoleon heard of her death on May 29, 1814, he was overcome with grief.

Reviewed by ALBERT DE VIDAS
Fairfield University

JOSHUA

Joshua, one of the greatest military leaders in the Old Testament, lived in the late 13th century B.C. His father was Nun. Joshua was Moses' loyal friend and aide. He went with Moses to Mount Sinai and waited at the foot of the mountain while Moses received the Ten Commandments. When Moses died, Joshua became the leader of the Israelites.

The book of Joshua in the Bible tells how the Israelites conquered and distributed the land of Canaan under Joshua's leadership. Joshua and his soldiers captured many cities and towns in Canaan and defeated 31 kings. The Israelites never conquered all of Canaan, but Joshua's victories helped them spread their power throughout the land.

One of the best-known stories in the book of Joshua is about the fall of the city of Jericho. The Bible says that the Lord commanded Joshua to tell his people to march around the wall of Jericho once a day for six days. Priests were to carry the ark, the chest containing the sacred writings of the Israelites. Seven priests should march in front of the ark and blow on seven ram's-horn trumpets. On the seventh day the people should march around the city seven times. When the priests blew their trumpets, the people should shout, and the wall would fall.

Joshua told the people the Lord's commands, and they followed them. On the seventh day they marched around the city seven times. Then the priests blew their trumpets. "The people shouted with a great shout," and the wall of Jericho fell down. The Israelites rushed into the city and captured it.

Joshua also helped to bring peace to the land. By dividing the land among the tribes, he prevented many quarrels over land ownership. It was an important step toward creating a peaceful Israelite nation. After Joshua distributed the land, he gathered all the tribes together at Shechem and told them to serve the Lord "in sincerity and in truth."

According to the Bible, Joshua died at the age of 110.

LLOYD R. BAILEY
Duke University

A youthful sports reporter interviews a winning team for her local television station. Journalists—who include television and radio reporters and photographers and camera operators as well as writers and editors— collect, communicate, and comment on the news.

JOURNALISM

The function of journalism is to collect, communicate, and comment on the news—the day-to-day events of public interest that take place in our lives. The news can be communicated in many ways. It may be printed in newspapers, newsletters, and magazines, for use at a time and place of the reader's choice. It may be read or told by reporters over radio and television broadcasts. It may be transmitted over news wires and computer networks. Sometimes the news is conveyed by means of images such as photographs and cartoons.

The professionals who take part in collecting, writing, editing, and reporting news in the media are known as journalists. They include reporters, writers, photographers and camera operators, editors, commentators, analysts, graphic artists, and designers.

The word "journal" comes from the Latin word *diurnus*, meaning "belonging to a day," and refers to a written daily record of noteworthy events, transactions, or experiences. Throughout history, people have kept written accounts of important daily events, as well as information of ongoing interest, such as birth and death notices, reports of crimes, records of battles and wars, and descriptions of laws passed and repealed. A journalist, then, is a person who keeps the journal, or record, of public transactions and events.

Journalism in action is actually the process of telling as many people as possible, "Guess what happened today!" Many journalists are in a constant race to keep track of what is going on in their towns, their states, their countries, and the world. "Breaking news" is the term used for stories about things that are happening fast—things that people look to journalists to tell them about.

▶ KINDS OF JOURNALISM

Modern news stories usually break, or appear first, on the **broadcast media**, that is, radio and television. These media present the news with maximum speed. Most radio stations broadcast the news every hour or half hour and can interrupt a program with a news bulletin if an important story occurs. However, a newscast usually contains only a few important details about each story.

The combination of sound and pictures on a television newscast can have a great impact on the viewer. Most television networks and stations have regularly scheduled news programs several times a day and, like radio stations, can interrupt other programs at any time. Important events can be covered in depth through special reports, documentaries, and panel discussions.

See the articles RADIO and TELEVISION to learn more about the history and technology of radio and television broadcasting.

News stories can be analyzed in greater depth in the **print media**, that is, newspapers and magazines. The main emphasis of a daily newspaper is on day-to-day events of general

A newsstand displays the wide range of newspapers and magazines available to readers. Once the only source of news, the print media retain a key role in journalism.

interest. Most papers offer a combination of international, national, and local news. They also provide background information, in-depth analyses, and editorials.

Most magazines are published weekly or monthly. Because they have more time to gather information, they often provide more explanatory information than newspapers do. Some magazines cover current general issues; others specialize in a particular field.

See the articles MAGAZINES and NEWSPAPERS for more information.

Both the print and broadcast media use a process called networking to transmit news quickly and efficiently. For the print media, this is done by distribution through **news groups**, which are corporations that own several publications, or through **wire services**, such as the Associated Press (AP), United Press International (UPI), and Reuter's. Wire services are organizations that collect and write news stories and sell them to subscribing newspapers and magazines. In the broadcast media, networking takes place through broadcast networks, such as the American Broadcasting Corporation (ABC) and National Public Radio (NPR). The networks distribute programming to local affiliated stations via microwave relay or communications satellites.

▶ THE ROLE OF JOURNALISM

In a democracy, journalism performs a very important role: to inform the public of events that affect their lives. Journalists are often referred to as the eyes and ears of citizens who cannot attend every meeting of a legislative body or corporate board. To vote responsibly, people must rely on credible journalists to provide accurate and timely information regarding public issues.

Besides informing the public by reporting the news, journalists also interpret the news, usually through background articles and editorials. At times journalists suggest what actions the public should take; they may also give their opinions of the likely results of a particular policy or event.

Journalism plays a key role in social reform. Journalists called investigative reporters probe into the activities of government and business and expose wrongdoing. This "watchdog" role is very important in protecting the interests of the public.

A fourth function of journalism is to entertain. In addition to serious news topics, journalists also present human-interest stories, humorous commentaries, and information on popular culture. They bring us lively and interesting information about the world around us.

Most democratic governments recognize the right of journalists to express themselves freely. They believe that a free press is necessary in maintaining a free society. In the United States, freedom of speech and of the press is guaranteed by the First Amendment to the Constitution.

With freedom comes responsibility. If journalists have the right to speak freely, they also have a duty to present information as accurately and objectively as possible. They try to keep free from pressures and restrictions that might affect their coverage of the news.

Journalism's interest in the pressing issues of the day means that there will often be controversy about what journalists write. Controversy can be beneficial, sparking interest in an important issue. But journalists have sometimes been accused of overemphasizing scandalous or sensational stories simply to increase profits, in the process invading the privacy of their subjects and even distorting the truth. These concerns have prompted some supporters of truthful news coverage to propose that journalism be regulated. Other people, however, believe that the control of news has more harmful effects than does the need to use judgment in assessing news reports.

Another important journalistic issue is protecting the identity of news sources. If the person who is the source of a controversial story is unwilling to speak for publication, the journalist may offer him or her anonymity, which is a promise that that person's name will not be used in the story. (A good journalist will make certain that several other people are willing to say the story is true.) Protecting the anonymity of sources is regarded by journalists as a right and a duty. In certain court cases, reporters have been called as witnesses and ordered to identify the source of their information. Some reporters have gone to jail rather than reveal their sources.

There have been many court decisions upholding the right of the press to be present at trials and to cover court cases. But judges will sometimes limit news coverage if they believe that reporting on the case will affect the ability of the defendant to get a fair trial. Reporters and photographers have also been barred from some courtrooms. Whether photographers and television cameras can be present in U.S. courtrooms is still an open question. In some states and at some court levels, cameras are allowed and entire trials are televised. In other courts, including the U.S. Supreme Court, cameras are never allowed.

A relatively new issue concerns the effects of modern technology on journalistic practices. Television and high-speed telecommunications enable journalists to reach into almost every home in the United States almost immediately. This immediacy often brings the nation together, but it can also cause problems. For example, television news has been criticized for reporting the first results from elections before the voting booths are closed. Does this influence the people who come to vote during the final hours of an election?

Reporters crowd around an interview subject. Most print and broadcast journalists are in a constant race to keep track of breaking news. The public relies on journalists to provide accurate and timely information on important issues.

In addition to reporting the news of the day, most television networks also provide in-depth coverage through special reports, panel discussions, and interviews with figures in the news. Television news is presented with great immediacy and can have a strong impact on the viewer.

Profiles
(in historical sequence)

Joseph Pulitzer (1847–1911), a powerful newspaper editor and publisher, was born in Mako, Hungary, and immigrated to the United States at age 17. He began his journalism career as a reporter in St. Louis, Mo. In 1878 he bought and merged two St. Louis newspapers to create the *Post-Dispatch.* He later purchased the *New York World* and built it to a large circulation. An impassioned believer in the role of the press in a democracy, Pulitzer was known for thorough news coverage and crusading editorials but also used sensationalism to boost circulation. Pulitzer established the most prestigious award in American print journalism, the Pulitzer Prizes. See the article PULITZER PRIZES in Volume P.

William Randolph Hearst (1863–1951), born in San Francisco, Calif., was a publisher and industrialist who built one of the largest publishing empires in the United States. Born into wealth, Hearst made a name as a publisher by buying and building newspapers, and later magazines, news services, radio stations, and motion picture companies. Beginning with the *San Francisco Examiner,* Hearst combined sensationalism and reform to successfully compete with the newspapers of his rival, Joseph Pulitzer. Other Hearst papers included the *New York Journal-American, Los Angeles Examiner,* and *Chicago Herald-Examiner.*

Walter Lippmann (1889–1974) was an editor and news analyst known for his knowledge of public affairs. Born in New York City and educated at Harvard University, he became a staff member of the *New Republic* in 1913 and an editor of the *New York World* in 1922. Lippmann attained world fame as a syndicated col-

umnist between 1931 and 1971. His columns ran in hundreds of newspapers worldwide, and he published scores of articles and books on world politics, U.S. foreign policy, and issues of freedom and public service. He won many awards and honors, including two Pulitzer Prizes and the Presidential Medal of Freedom.

Henry Robinson Luce (1898–1967) was the editor, publisher, cofounder, and creator of some of America's most influential and popular magazines. Born in Tengchow (now Penglai), China, and educated at Yale University, he became a reporter for the *Baltimore News* in 1922. He cofounded the weekly newsmagazine *Time* in 1923, created the business magazine *Fortune* in 1930, and developed photojournalism with the creation of *Life* in 1936. He also published *Sports Illustrated, Architectural Forum,* and *House and Home.* His highly successful magazines formed the publishing organization known as Time, Inc. Luce received many awards and honorary degrees during his lifetime.

Ernie Pyle (1900–45) was a well known and widely read columnist during World War II. He was born in Dana, Ind., and educated at Indiana University. Pyle held numerous positions as a news reporter, but it was as a war correspondent and columnist for Scripps - Howard newspapers that Pyle made his reputation. He wrote the story of the ordinary soldier from the trenches, exposing himself to enemy fire in the process. His daily columns told about the dangers and fears, the

heroism and the humor of life at the front lines. Pyle covered the war in Europe and Africa before moving to the Pacific war theater in 1944. He was killed while observing the advance of U.S. troops near Okinawa. He received a Pulitzer Prize for his reporting in 1944.

Edward R. Murrow (1908–65), born in Greensboro, N.C., was a longtime radio and television broadcast journalist. He earned a degree in speech from Washington State College in 1930. He joined CBS in 1935. As a CBS correspondent from England during World War II, he became famous for his accurate and dramatic reporting. Murrow returned to the United States in 1946 and produced a CBS weekly radio program called *Hear It Now,* which moved to television in 1951 as *See It Now.* One of the most important contributions to television journalism was his exposé of the tactics of U.S. senator Joseph McCarthy in his anti-Communist campaign. Murrow was appointed director of the U.S. Information Agency in 1961.

Chet Huntley (1911–74) was best known as a co-anchorman with David Brinkley for NBC television. Together, the two produced the Huntley-Brinkley Report, a popular evening TV news program that

Henry Robinson Luce

Edward R. Murrow

▶ CAREERS IN JOURNALISM

Journalism can be an exciting career. Journalists meet and interview government leaders and other notable people. They may travel around the world in the course of covering a story. They receive public recognition for their work and may even become famous in their own right.

The field of journalism offers a wide range of career opportunities for young people, not only in writing and editing, but in photography, television reporting and producing, cinematography, and graphic arts and design.

Most successful reporters and editors became involved in journalistic writing at an early age. School newspapers provide an opportunity for budding journalists to have their work published and can have a vital impact on school communities.

While on-the-job experience has always been important in the field of journalism, modern newspapers, magazines, and radio and television networks and broadcast stations usually require that their professional personnel be college graduates. Students can work toward college degrees in departments of journalism and mass communication. Modern journalism and communication courses span all media, including printed formats, radio, and television. Internship programs offer students an opportunity to work at a news outlet at least once during their college years.

---

lasted for fifteen years. Born in Cardwell, Mont., Huntley spent his boyhood years on his grandfather's sheep ranch. He began his journalism career while he was a student at the University of Washington, at radio station KPCB. In a short time he became involved in every aspect of station operations. After college he held a number of jobs before moving to NBC in 1955. There he found himself teamed with David Brinkley for the 1956 political conventions, a combination that worked well. Huntley won numerous awards, including seven Emmys.

Walter Cronkite (1916–), longtime anchorman of the CBS evening news, was often called the most trusted journalist in the United States. Born in St. Joseph, Mo., he attended the University of Texas and worked as a reporter for the *Houston Post* before joining the United Press (UP) wire service in 1939. During World War II, he was sent to London as a war correspondent. After the war, he stayed in Europe as UP's Moscow bureau chief. He joined CBS in 1950. As news anchorman from 1962 to 1981, Cronkite covered some of the most important events of the time for CBS, including the Kennedy assassination, the *Apollo II* moon landing, the Vietnam War, and Watergate.

Helen Thomas (1920–), a veteran wire service reporter, was born in Winchester, Ky., the daughter of Lebanese immigrants. She graduated from Wayne State University in Detroit in 1942. A year later she joined United Press International (UPI) as a radio newswriter, becoming a member of UPI's national staff in 1956. Her coverage of President-elect John F. Kennedy and his family in 1960 led to a post at UPI's White House Bureau. In 1974 she was promoted to bureau chief, becoming the first woman to head a wire service's White House staff. Thomas was also the first woman to serve as president of the White House Correspondents' Association.

Allen Neuharth (1924–), born in Eureka, S. Dak., is a journalist and publisher who created the first national general-interest daily newspaper, *USA Today*. Neuharth began his lifelong association with the newspaper business at age 11, when he started work as a newspaper carrier. After graduating from the University of South Dakota, he worked as a reporter and editor. In 1963 he joined the Gannett newspaper organization, becoming president in 1970 and chairman in 1979. Under Neuharth's management, Gannett became the largest and most profitable publicly owned U.S. newspaper chain. With the 1982 launch of *USA Today*, Neuharth became a pioneer in the use of color illustrations in newspapers.

Carl Rowan (1925–) is a noted print and broadcast journalist. Born into poverty in McMinnville, Tenn., he excelled as a student, receiving degrees from Oberlin College and the University of Minnesota. In 1948, he joined the *Minneapolis Tribune*, becoming its first African American reporter. Rowan wrote a series on the effects of discrimination laws on blacks, which brought him national recognition. Under President John F. Kennedy, he served as deputy assistant secretary of state for public relations and as ambassador to Finland. He was head of the U.S. Information Agency in 1964 and 1965. Rowan returned to full-time journalism as a columnist for the *Chicago Daily News* and, later, the *Chicago Sun-Times*. He also appeared regularly as a television and radio news commentator.

Barbara Walters (1931–) is a newscaster and television host known for her interviews. Walters was born in Boston and educated at Sarah Lawrence College. She worked as a writer and reporter for NBC's *Today* show, becoming a full-time newscaster in 1964. In 1974, she was made co-anchor of *Today*, and in 1976 she hosted the first *Barbara Walters Special* on prime-time television. In 1976, she joined ABC, becoming the first woman to co-anchor the evening news. In 1977 she arranged the first joint interview of Egypt's President Anwar Sadat and Israel's Prime Minister Menahem Begin. She became co-host of the ABC news magazine show *20/20* in 1984. Walters has won four Emmy Awards.

Walter Cronkite

Carl Rowan

Barbara Walters

► HISTORY

Until the 1920's, journalists worked exclusively in the print media—newsletters, newspapers, and magazines. Newsletters and newspapers evolved first, many centuries ago, initially as handbills following in the tradition of proclamations by a town crier and posted handwritten public notices. The development of the printing press during the 1400's allowed such notices to be printed in quantity, and the spread of literacy encouraged their use.

The early newsletters contained information mainly about commerce and business. Gradually, the publications also came to include opinions and commentaries on news and issues of broad interest. Newspapers continued to grow in number and coverage, and journalism had begun to emerge as a distinct profession by the mid-1700's.

Development of U.S. Journalism. The first regularly published American newspaper, the *Boston News-Letter*, appeared in Boston in 1704. It was not long before daily newspapers appeared in major cities across America.

The first true American newspapers were largely political in coverage, supporting or criticizing the views and records of politicians. Their relatively high price of six cents per copy put them out of reach of most people.

The first issue of *Time* magazine

About 1830, some papers began to publish the news in smaller sheet sizes that working people could afford. Soon there were many small-sheet newspapers competing for the mass market. Called penny papers because many sold for one cent per copy, they emphasized news over politics and featured human-interest stories as well as editorial commentary.

By the late 1800's, a number of large daily newspapers exerted considerable influence on their readers in the United States. Publishers began to feel their power. Some made a conscious effort to serve the public interest and, sometimes, to sway public opinion. They acquired many newspapers, creating nationwide chains of ownership. Aggressive competition and an interest in controversial news stories set the tone for modern journalism.

At about the same period, national wire services came into being. The first in the United States was the Associated Press, started in 1848. These services provided breaking news to newspapers all over the world, first by telegraph and later by teletype.

Magazines became popular in the mid-1800's but at first focused on fields of special interest rather than on general news. At the turn of the century, some magazine journalists attacked corruption in business and government. These reformers were called **muckrakers**, because they unearthed information usually hidden from the general public.

Time, the first weekly newsmagazine, was founded in 1923. Other magazines of news and political commentary soon followed, including *Newsweek*, *U.S. News*, and the *Nation*.

The development of radio communication early in the 1900's enabled the use of radio broadcasting for communicating news by about 1920. Network radio began during the 1920's with the founding of the National Broadcasting Company (NBC) and the Columbia Broadcasting System (CBS). Many print journalists moved to radio, changing their writing style to briefer reports made up of short sentences intended for the ear rather than the eye. Radio became a very important news medium for reporting the latest news during World War II, but its significance was reduced after the war by the rise of television.

Motion pictures were a popular news medium during the 1930's and throughout World War II, when newsreels of current news, sports, and general-interest events were shown in movie theaters. However, this use of movies was largely replaced by nationwide television broadcasts by the mid-1950's.

Television grew rapidly after World War II, and many radio journalists transferred their skills to the new medium. In the United States, television coverage of such major events as the Army-McCarthy hearings, the assassination of President John F. Kennedy, and the Vietnam War established television's position as an important journalistic medium capable of reaching millions of people at the same moment. News shows were broadcast every evening, and soon a majority of U.S. citizens were getting their news from television.

Beginning in the 1960's, communications satellites allowed worldwide transmission of television broadcasts. A more recent development in television news has been the establishment of the Cable News Network (CNN), offering round-the-clock news from every corner of the globe for the first time in history. Another has been C-Span, which covers entire government and public meetings throughout the United States, as they take place.

The Future of Journalism. Print media will always retain a key role in journalism, because newspapers, magazines, and newsletters are so portable and inexpensive. Increasingly, however, more and more news is received electronically. Both newspapers and magazines are beginning to experiment with electronic distribution through CD-ROM's (compact discs that can be read by computers) and computerized information networks. These **multimedia** technologies, combining text, sound, and images, are likely to play a role in the future of journalism.

With the growth of computer use, and the capability of users to communicate back and forth rather than just receive information, some predict that people will get their news more directly, in ways that they control more than the journalist does.

Regardless of changes in technology, the mission of journalism will still be to tell what is happening in the world as quickly, comprehensively, and truthfully as possible.

JUDITH D. HINES
OSCAR T. HINES
Communication Projects

JUÁREZ, BENITO (1806–1872)

Benito Juárez was a patriot, political reformer, and president of Mexico. His achievements had such an important effect on his country that he is considered one of the great statesmen of the Americas.

Juárez was born on March 21, 1806, in a small village in the state of Oaxaca. Both his parents were Zapotec Indians, and the family was very poor. At first, Juárez wanted to be a priest, but he felt that he could help the people of Mexico best by becoming a lawyer and entering politics. He served in both the state and national legislature, and in 1847 he became governor of Oaxaca state.

Juárez's hopes for the future of his country lay in the adoption of a constitutional form of government. Mexico at the time was engaged in a bitter political conflict between the conservatives and liberals. When the liberals came to power in 1855, Juárez was appointed minister of justice. He helped pass a measure, bearing his name, that gave all Mexicans equal justice under the law. He played a leading role in framing the historic Constitution of 1857, which limited the power of the church and called for freedom of worship, press, and assembly. The conservatives, in opposition to the new constitution, rose against the government in a war known as the War of the Reform. Juárez became provisional (acting) president and for three years struggled to hold together his government and to maintain the constitution. In 1863, Juárez was elected president under the constitution.

As president he faced many problems. Because the treasury was empty, Juárez suspended payments on debts owed to France, Britain, and Spain. Encouraged by the conservatives, Napoleon III of France used the debts as an excuse to establish a monarchy in Mexico. His troops occupied the capital, Mexico City, in 1863, forcing Juárez and his government to flee. In 1864, Archduke Maximilian of Austria was installed as emperor of Mexico. For the next three years, Juárez's determination held together the forces loyal to the republic, until, in 1867, the French had to withdraw from Mexico. Maximilian was executed.

Juárez introduced free primary education for all and encouraged the growth of industry. He was re-elected in 1871. He died in office on July 18, 1872. Juárez left behind him the beginnings of a modern Mexico, and today he is regarded as a national hero.

Reviewed by DAVID BUSHNELL
University of Florida

In the ceremony of Bar Mitzvah ("Son of the Commandment") a 13-year-old boy becomes an adult member of the Jewish community. One of the world's oldest living religions, Judaism was the first to teach monotheism, or the belief in one God.

JUDAISM

Judaism is the religion of the Jewish people, although both the people and its religion are older than the word "Judaism" itself, which did not come into use until many centuries after the beginning of Jewish history. It is a religion of many laws and customs that touch on every part of the life of the Jew. A Jew is a Jew not only because of what he or she believes but also and mainly because of what he or she does. The Jewish religion includes basic principles of ethics and human behavior. Jews are expected to shape their lives by these principles, to obey the requirements for daily behavior, to observe the Holy Days and festivals, and, most importantly, to feel themselves a part of the Jewish people, to learn and know its history and to be concerned with the welfare and security of Jews wherever they may be.

The laws and practices of Judaism, as well as its principles and values, are to be found in great literary works, written over centuries, that provide guidance and instruction for the Jewish people. The first of these writings is the Bible. As centuries passed and new laws

and customs emerged out of the old, they were written down in great bodies of literature called the **Talmud** and the **Midrash**. While these were completed many centuries ago, commentary and explanation have kept their teachings up to date.

For centuries, especially when Jews were required to live by themselves and not allowed to join freely in the lives of the people around them, there was general agreement on the practices and the life-style of Judaism. With the end of the 1700's, when Jews achieved freedom in the countries of Western Europe and the United States, many changes took place as Jews tried to interpret their religion and its requirements in a way that would enable them to participate as fully as possible in the lives of the people about them and to play a role in the societies of which they were a part. This period was called the Jewish Enlightenment. Some Jews clung desperately to the practices of the past while others initiated a great variety of changes. The Judaism of today reflects the difference, and sometimes the tension, between those who cling tightly to the past and those who try to come to terms with the present.

THE MAIN TEACHINGS AND BELIEFS

There is no formal creed that all Jews are obliged to accept, but certain basic teachings can be found in all periods of Jewish history, though they may not always have been understood in the same way. Foremost among these is the **Shema**, so called because it is the first word of the Hebrew sentence in Deuteronomy, "Hear O Israel, the Lord is our God, the Lord is One." Since ancient times this sentence has been recited by Jews every day in their prayer. It is spoken again before retiring and is the last utterance of one's life. It expresses the Jew's faith in a Creator of all that is. It is a way of saying that life is worth living no matter what difficulties have to be faced. It says that God is One and thereby rejects a belief in no god at all or a belief in two gods or three or many. This belief in one God is called **monotheism**.

A Covenant with God. According to the Bible an event took place at Mount Sinai that shaped the whole course of Jewish history. It was there that Moses—the leader of the Jewish people—spoke to the Children of Israel, in God's name, and presented to them all the laws by which they were to live. Among those laws are the Ten Commandments and many other laws and regulations covering every aspect of life for both the individual and society. According to the Bible, the Jewish people, or Children of Israel as they were then called, entered into a covenant, or agreement, with God, through which they were pledged to keep God's law. God, in turn, would look after them, making their land fertile and securing them from their enemies.

Because of the covenant, the Jewish people looked on themselves as a chosen people, not chosen for special advantage, but chosen for special responsibility: to obey God's law and to serve God always. So strong was this idea that even when the sacred city Jerusalem was destroyed by the Babylonians in 586 B.C., and again by the Romans hundreds of years later, the people did not rebel against God but said it was because of their sins that tragedy had come upon them. They looked on their exile from their land as punishment for their failures, not the failure of their God to care for them. In modern times this idea was modified by Reform Judaism, which looked on the scattering of the Jewish people as a call to teach the world about God, and it became the "mission" of the Jewish people to do so. More recently, the Reconstructionist movement removed from its prayer book any reference to the chosen people though they continued to believe that the Jew has a special obligation to study God's law and to live by it.

A Jew's Responsibility. It is the responsibility of the Jew to bear witness to God in everything he or she does, not only to observe the religious customs and practices of Judaism but to be examples of proper moral behavior. Almost a hundred years before the beginning of the Christian era, a great rabbi named Hillel was approached by a pagan who wanted to be taught all of Judaism in a brief statement. "What is hateful to you, do not do to another. This is the law, all the rest is commentary. Now go and study," was Hillel's prompt reply.

Failure to obey the law is a sin. To recover from sin, a person may repent, which in Hebrew means "to return" and try again. Repentance, therefore, is a way of recovering from doing something wrong and must be followed by an act of atonement, a way of making up for one's errors. So important is it for the Jew to be "at one" with God that the most important day of the religious calendar is called the Day of Atonement (Yom Kippur).

Life After Death. In its thinking about the future, Judaism presents a wide variety of beliefs. In biblical times there was no belief in any real life after death. The dead went to a place called Sheol for an eternity of silence and sleep. There was a belief that someday all the world would accept God and would be united in keeping God's law. This joyous future was to be in this life on earth. Shortly before the beginning of Christianity, the idea of a life after death gained popularity and has remained a part of traditional Jewish belief to this day, although the nature of that life after death is not presented in any detail. The idea of a coming great day is still held by most Jews but is interpreted in several ways. Traditionalists, or Orthodox Jews, believe that God will send his "anointed one" (Messiah) who will lead the world to a universal acceptance of God. When that time comes, say the Traditionalists, the righteous dead of all generations will be brought back to life. Liberal Jews still retain a faith in the triumph of goodness and truth and the coming of a better day, but they believe that it will be accomplished through human effort and cooperation.

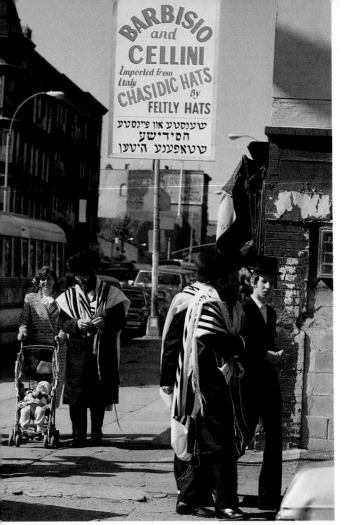

Hasidic (Chasidic) Jews are noted for their Orthodox beliefs and joyful worship, as well as for their distinctive dress. Two of the men are wearing prayer shawls.

▶DIFFERENCES IN JUDAISM

It is not surprising that a people as spiritually creative as the Jews would find that not all agreed on how the tradition was to be understood or the direction Jewish life was to take. Some of these differences were not of great consequence, but others, of great significance, left their imprint on the development of Judaism. Some differences today are broad and of great consequence, causing considerable tension among various groups in the Jewish world.

Orthodox Judaism

The differences in Jewish life today grow out of different approaches to the Jewish religious tradition. This tradition, including the Written law (the Bible) and the Oral law (the Talmud and the writings of the rabbis, or teachers), is accepted without question by those called Orthodox. Orthodox Jews accept the Revelation to Moses at Sinai as described in the Bible and accept as binding the decisions of the Talmud and later codes of Jewish law. (Non-Orthodox Jews consider the traditional texts to be of great importance but are prepared to make changes that will help adjust Jewish life to the modern world.) In spite of general agreement on basic religious ideas, some differences can still be found among the Orthodox, among whom are the **Sephardim**, descended from Jews who lived in Spain and Portugal until the end of the 1400's; **Ashkenazim**, Jews from Central and Eastern Europe; and **Hasidim**, a community that originated in Eastern Europe.

The Hasidim (the word *hasid* means "pious") are descended from Jews of the 1700's in Poland and the Ukraine who led a mystic revival and spiritual revolution in Judaism. While Orthodox in their beliefs, they stressed the importance of joy and enthusiasm in performing their religious obligations. The founder of the movement was Israel ben Eliezer, called the Baal Shem Tov ("Master of the good name"). Political and social conditions led to the rapid spread of the Hasidic movement. Numerous sects grew up around religious leaders, called *Zaddikim* ("holy men"), who dominated the life of their communities and frequently created dynasties of religious rule.

The Hasidic movement at first was rejected by the intellectuals who dominated Jewish life, but it attracted the masses who suffered from poverty and discouragement. While the followers of this movement held to the requirements of Jewish law (**Halakhah**), they appeared to their opponents as giving too much attention to the mystical and the emotional elements in Judaism. These opponents, called *Mitnaggedim*, were often violent in their denunciation of the Hasidim. Both groups felt threatened, however, by the Jewish Enlightenment at the end of the 1700's and the Reform movement that began to emerge.

After World War II, those Hasidim who escaped from Eastern Europe settled in Israel and the United States and have since moved as well to other parts of the world. They are frequently recognized by their traditional clothing and their close community life.

Reform Judaism

As Jews moved into the modern world, some felt the need to find a way of life closer to that of their neighbors. In 1818 a group of Jews in Hamburg, Germany, built a synagogue, which they called a temple. They introduced German in their prayer, shortened the service, and allowed instrumental music in their worship. A sermon was preached in German. They introduced Confirmation for boys and girls in place of Bar Mitzvah (see "Ceremonies and Rites"). They gave up a belief in a personal Messiah and the hope that all Jews would someday return to the land of Israel. They eliminated head covering and special dietary regulations and put great emphasis on ethical behavior.

The Reform movement did not grow rapidly until it was transplanted to the United States. In 1873, Rabbi Isaac Mayer Wise established the Union of American Hebrew Congregations, which today has more than 750 congregations in its membership. In 1875 he founded the Hebrew Union College, in Cincinnati, Ohio, for the training of rabbis. In 1889, Rabbi Wise organized the Central Conference of American Rabbis, which now has almost 1,500 members.

Among the sacred writings of Judaism are the Bible, of which the Torah (scroll at left) is the source of Jewish law, and the Palestinian and Babylonian Talmuds.

Conservative Judaism

Those who shared much of the spirit of Reform but were unhappy with some of its extreme positions created a Conservative movement. Members of this movement were willing to accept change, but only at a slower pace and in greater adherence to the tradition. Solomon Schechter, the head of the Jewish Theological Seminary in New York City, was one of the foremost spokespersons of the movement. Conservative congregations are joined in the United Synagogue, and the Rabbinical Assembly is the association of Conservative rabbis.

As is the case in Reform Judaism, there is tension within the Conservative movement between those who seek a more traditional expression of the Conservative philosophy and those who strive for a more liberal adjustment to the needs of Jewish life today.

Reconstructionist Judaism

In 1934, Rabbi Mordecai M. Kaplan published his *Judaism as a Civilization*, an attempt to apply modern thought to the Jewish religion. A movement grew out of this effort, and today there is a fellowship of Reconstructionist Congregations, and a Reconstructionist Rabbinical College in Philadelphia. The Reconstructionist movement publishes its own prayer books, as do the Reform and Conservative movements.

Diversity of Jewish Thought

The diversity of Jewish thought frequently gives rise to sharp exchanges among the various groups of Jews, especially between those who hold to strict orthodoxy and those who take a more liberal position. In Israel, the Orthodox enjoy government support and try to limit the development of any liberal form of Judaism. Of particular concern are such questions as "Who is a Jew?" "Who may be authorized to accept converts?" and "Which Jewish institutions should be given public and government support?"

▶ SACRED WRITINGS

Foremost among the sacred writings of Judaism is the Bible, a collection of books composed over a period of a thousand years, from the 1100's to the 100's B.C. It is what Christians called the Old Testament, although the arrangement of some of the books is dif-

The synagogue serves as a house of worship, as a place of learning, and as a community center. The Torah Scrolls are being carried from their place in the Ark.

ferent in the Hebrew Bible. Of especial importance is the **Torah**, comprising the Five Books of Moses—Genesis, Exodus, Leviticus, Numbers, and Deuteronomy—the main source for Jewish law.

Since the Bible was understood to contain all the laws necessary for personal and community life, it was continually studied and explained to make it applicable to change. Originally these explanations and comments were handed down orally from one generation of rabbis to the next. In the second century of the Christian era, this "Oral law" was arranged into a code and written down in a work called the **Mishnah**. Once written down, this code required interpretation and development, which was called **Gemara**. One Gemara was developed in Palestine and was joined to the Mishnah in the early 300's to produce the **Palestinian Talmud**. Another Gemara was developed in Babylonia and was joined, at the end of the 400's, to produce the **Babylonian Talmud**. These great collections of Jewish law and lore became the basis for all later development of the Jewish tradition.

Another body of literature, the **Midrash**, developed through the interpretation of the biblical texts. Largely nonlegal in character, it contains imaginative elaboration of the stories and ideas of the Holy Books.

After the completion of the two Talmuds, Jewish law continued to develop as inquiries were directed to the academies in Babylonia from the many places in which Jews lived. These questions and answers, in the hundreds of thousands, represent the **Responsa** literature. It tells us much about Jewish law and a great deal about the social, economic, and political conditions of Jewish life.

In the 1100's Moses Maimonides organized the vast body of Jewish law in a work called the **Mishneh Torah**. In the 1500's Joseph Caro used a different structure to produce the **Shulhan Arukh** ("The Prepared Table"), which became the standard text for Traditional Judaism.

Jewish mysticism, called **Cabala**, produced a work called the **Zohar** ("Splendor"). It was largely written by Moses De Leon, who died in 1305. The Zohar long was attributed to a rabbi of the 100's, Simeon ben Johai, who still is considered its author by some.

▶WORSHIP

The worship of God is an essential part of the Jewish faith. Originally, this worship was expressed in both prayer and sacrifice. Sacrifices were offered during the four centuries of its existence in the Temple of Jerusalem built by Solomon and after that, for another five centuries, in the Temple built after the return from Babylonian exile. In addition to sacrifices, administered by the priests, psalms and prayers were sung by the Levites, a tribe that since earliest times had been charged with the supervision of Jewish worship.

While the Temple was still in existence, a popular institution emerged that became a house of prayer, a place of study, and also a place for community gathering. This institution came to be known as the **synagogue**, and when the Temple was destroyed by the Romans in the year 70, it became the leading institution in Jewish life. It is found everywhere today and is the central institution of every Jewish community. It is the forerunner of the Christian church and the Muslim mosque.

The religious leader of the Jewish community is called a **rabbi**, which means "master" or "teacher." The position of the rabbi derives from Jewish tradition, which qualifies the rabbi to respond to all matters of Jewish law and ritual. Upon the completion of study, the rabbi is ordained by other rabbis who have supervised the instruction. In this way, the office has maintained a continuous history of more than 2,000 years. Until 1972 all rabbis were men, but in that year the Reform Hebrew Union College–Jewish Institute of Religion ordained its first woman rabbi. In 1986 the first woman rabbi was ordained at the Conservative Jewish Theological Seminary.

The leader of a congregation in prayer need not be a rabbi but may be a member of the congregation with a knowledge of the prayer service or liturgy. When the knowledge necessary for leading a worship service is accompanied by a fine voice and a familiarity with the musical tradition of the synagogue, such a person is called a **cantor**. Until recent times all cantors were men, but now female cantors serve in many Reform and some Conservative synagogues.

Jews are expected to pray three times each day: in the morning, afternoon, and evening. The prayers are read from a prayer book and may be recited either privately or with a congregation, which requires a group of at least ten worshipers, called a *minyan*. A Traditional service, which would count only males as part of the *minyan*, is entirely in Hebrew. In Conservative and Reform congregations women may be included in the *minyan*, and the prayers may contain varying amounts of English.

Additional prayers are recited on Sabbaths and Festivals, and a passage from the Torah Scroll (Five Books of Moses), appropriate to the occasion, is read to the congregation.

The festival of Sukkoth celebrates the last harvest of the year. Worshipers traditionally carry three plants and a citron (*ethrog*), symbolic of the harvest.

▶ SABBATH AND HOLY DAYS

Since biblical times the Sabbath has been a day of utmost importance. It was set aside because God completed the creation of the world in six days and made the seventh day a day of holiness and blessing. It is also a reminder that the Children of Israel were once slaves in the land of Egypt and that Jews were therefore obliged to free their servants and slaves from labor on the Sabbath. The day is also referred to as a "sign of the covenant" between God and the Children of Israel. While no work is to be done on the Sabbath, rest is not its main purpose. Its goal is holiness, and the day is set apart in each week for prayer and study.

The Sabbath begins with the setting of the sun on Friday evening. Following the service of welcome for the Sabbath, a Sabbath meal is shared by members of the family. Shortly before sunset, Sabbath candles are lit, generally by female members of the family. The Sabbath meal begins with a *kiddush* (the sanctification of the Sabbath over a cup of wine) and the breaking of a special loaf of bread called a *hallah*. Following the meal, grace is recited and Sabbath songs (*zemirot*) are sung.

Some Reform and Conservative congregations have their worship services following the Sabbath meal and include the lighting of the candles and the *kiddush* as part of the service. Following the service there is usually a congregational social hour called *Oneg Shabbat* ("Sabbath delight").

Passover is celebrated by a *seder* (*left*), during which the *Haggadah,* describing the Exodus from Egypt, is read and a symbolic meal is eaten. The *shofar,* or ram's horn (*right*), is blown on Rosh Hashanah and on Yom Kippur, the holiest day in the Jewish calendar.

The Torah Scroll is read on Saturday morning and again at the Sabbath afternoon service. The day is ended with a special service of *Havdalah* ("distinction"), which notes the difference between the sacred and the profane, between the Sabbath and the ordinary days of the week.

In the fall of the year the High Holy Days are observed. They are days of reverence and awe and a time to look into one's heart and to begin a new religious year as a better person. The first of these days is **Rosh Hashanah** ("new year"), and it is followed on the tenth day by **Yom Kippur** ("Day of Atonement"). To assist in the act of repentance on Yom Kippur, it is customary to fast during the whole 24-hour period. According to the tradition, these days provide forgiveness for sins against God, but sins against others can be forgiven only when one has repaired the damage that has been done.

Passover comes in the spring and commemorates the Exodus from Egypt (when Moses led the Jews out of slavery) and the beginning of the planting season. Seven weeks later the Festival of the First Fruits is observed and is called **Shabuoth**. The third festival, called **Sukkoth**, is observed at the time of the last harvest. The last day of the Sukkoth Festival is called *Simchat Torah* ("Rejoicing of the Torah"), and it notes the completion of the annual cycle of weekly scripture readings from the Torah Scroll.

There are two holidays that commemorate historical events. There are special prayers for these days, but the usual restrictions against work do not apply. **Hanukkah** is an eight-day Festival of Lights that begins on the 25th of Kislev (late November or December); it commemorates the "Rededication" of the Temple in Jerusalem by the Maccabees in 165 B.C. Candles are lighted in an eight-branched candelabrum (*menorah*). The closeness of Hanukkah to Christmas has encouraged the giving of gifts, especially in America. Three months later, on the 14th of Adar, the holiday of **Purim**, or Feast of Lots, commemorates the rescue of the Jews of Persia with the help of Queen Esther, the wife of King Ahasuerus, whose prime minister Haman had tried to destroy them. The Scroll of Esther (*Megillah*) is read, and the day is marked by merrymaking, costumes, and the exchange of food.

In the summer, on Tisha B'Av (the 9th of Av, or Ab), a fast day memorializes the destruction of the first and second Temples in Jerusalem and other sad occasions of Jewish history.

Three additional days marking recent events are observed by many Jews: Yom Ha-Shoah, or Holocaust day on the 27th of Nisan (usually in April); Yom Ha-Atzmaut, the anniversary of the founding (1948) of the State of Israel, on the 5th of Iyar (in April or May); and Yom Yerushalayim, the unification of Jerusalem (1967), on the 28th of Iyar (in May).

Life-cycle events are important in Judaism and reflect a striving toward *kedushah* ("sanctification"), which is the goal of Jewish religious living.

Birth

The birth of a child is regarded as a blessing from God and an occasion for deep gratitude. Traditionally, a daughter would be named in the synagogue on the first Sabbath following her birth. A son is named at the *Brit Milah* ("Covenant of Circumcision") on the eighth day. The circumcision is performed by an official called a *mohel*. Through the ceremony of circumcision the child is brought into the Covenant of Abraham and enters into the Community of Israel.

When young people reach the age of 13, there is a special ceremony among the Orthodox for boys only and among Reform and Conservative Jews for girls as well. The young person is called to the reading of the Torah and may be counted henceforth in the *minyan* for the congregational worship. A boy is called a **Bar Mitzvah** ("Son of the Commandment"), and a girl is called a **Bat Mitzvah** or **Bas Mitzvah** ("Daughter of the Commandment"). In many synagogues the Bar and Bat Mitzvah participate in the conduct of the service of worship, read out of the Torah, and chant the prophetic portion or *Haftarah*. This is an important day in the life of the family, and guests are invited to the synagogue to share the joy.

Early Reform congregations discarded Bar Mitzvah in favor of Confirmation for both boys and girls. The Confirmation service takes place on the Festival of Shabuoth, the anniversary of the giving of the Torah at Mount Sinai. Although Confirmation is still held in the Reform synagogues, it has not displaced Bar and Bat Mitzvah.

Marriage

The Jewish marriage ceremony takes place under a canopy (*chupah*), which is a symbol of the bridal chamber. The traditional ceremony begins with a blessing of betrothal (engagement) and is followed by the *kiddushin*, in which the groom places a ring on the index finger of the bride's right hand and says, "Behold, thou are consecrated unto me with this ring according to the Law of Moses and Israel." Liberal Jews will often use two rings, allowing the bride to recite her formula to the groom. A traditional marriage contract (*ketubah*) is then read. Written in Aramaic, it lists the responsibilities of the husband for the care and support of the bride. In Liberal ceremonies the traditional *ketubah* may be replaced by a personal statement of the bride and groom to each other.

Following the *ketubah*, seven benedictions are recited. The ceremony concludes with the breaking of a glass or other fragile object. For some the glass-breaking is a memorial to the destruction of Jerusalem; for others it may be a reminder of the fragile character of human happiness. An authorized official, usually the

A Jewish marriage ceremony traditionally concludes with the breaking of a glass underfoot by the groom. The ceremony itself takes place under a canopy, called a *chupah*, which symbolizes the bridal chamber.

rabbi, is required by state law; but Jewish law requires two witnesses and someone who is sufficiently learned to oversee the ceremony.

Civil law requires that divorce take place according to the laws of the state of residence. This is acceptable to Reform Jews, but Traditional Jews require that a *get*, a Jewish divorce, be signed by the husband before either party may remarry.

Death

Following death and burial, the immediate family enters a seven-day period of mourning (*shivah*) during which they remain at home except for the Sabbath, when they may attend the synagogue. After the seven days, and until the 30th day, the mourning customs are eased and the bereaved begin a return to normal life. During this time, and for the next ten months, it is customary to recite the *Kaddish* (mourner's prayer), which concludes every congregational service of worship.

On the anniversary of a death, a *yahrzeit* ("anniversary") candle is lighted and the *kaddish* prayer recited in the synagogue. On Yom Kippur and each of the Pilgrimage Festivals a memorial service (*yizkor*) is held.

Conversion to Judaism

Judaism welcomes those who wish to accept the Jewish faith. A ceremony of conversion (*gerut*) is conducted by three rabbis who determine the candidate's preparation. Traditional Jews require a visit to the ritual bath (*mikvah*) for a woman and circumcision for a male. Reform Judaism does not officially require either, although many Reform rabbis request this of those they have instructed. Upon conversion the new convert, or proselyte (*ger*), is considered a Jew in every respect.

▶DIETARY LAWS

The Bible declares certain animals, fowl, and fish as acceptable for food, while others are prohibited. An animal must chew the cud and have cloven hooves, while fish must have both fins and scales. Forbidden or acceptable fowl are listed by names. A further restriction says, "Thou shalt not boil a kid in the milk of its mother." This has led, in Traditional Judaism, to a complete separation of meat and dairy foods, which may not be served out of the same dishes or eaten at the same meal or in close proximity of time to one another.

The laws of the Talmud further extend dietary restrictions, and even an acceptable animal must be ritually slaughtered by an official trained to perform the task with a minimum of pain to the animal. Only the forequarters of a properly slaughtered animal may be eaten because of the presence of a forbidden sinew in the hindquarters. The flesh of meat and fowl must be soaked and salted to remove all traces of blood.

The prohibition of bread or leaven on the Passover requires further dietary precautions. An unleavened bread called *matzot* is eaten.

Food that is acceptable according to Jewish law and the utensils that may be used are *kasher*, or *kosher*. Foods not acceptable are called *terefah*.

Reform Judaism officially rejected the dietary laws although many Reform Jews keep some form of dietary restriction. Conservative Judaism accepts all the dietary restrictions, except for wine, which is no longer restricted. Traditional Jews observe the dietary regulations as a divine mandate, while Conservative and Reform Jews often observe the dietary laws for historical and psychological reasons.

▶SYMBOLS OF JUDAISM

Certain objects have a special meaning in Judaism. In the synagogue, the Ark is a large cabinet, usually highly decorated, that houses the Torah scrolls.

The menorah is a seven-branched candelabrum originally used in the Temple. Since the destruction of Jerusalem, it has brought to mind associations with ancient ritual. During Hanukkah an eight-branched menorah is used. It is called a *Hanukkiah*.

The *tzitzit* are fringes that appear on the four corners of the prayer shawl worn in the synagogue and by Traditionalists as part of their regular clothing beneath their outer garments. The prayer shawl is called a *tallit*.

In response to the verse in Deuteronomy 6: 8,9—"Bind them as a sign on your hand and let them serve as a symbol on your forehead; inscribe them on the doorposts of your house and on your gates"—two objects were developed. The first, *tefillin*, consists of two boxes containing passages from Exodus and Deuteronomy. These boxes are attached by straps to the left arm and the upper forehead during morning prayer, except on Sabbaths and holidays. The second, called *mezuzah*, consists of a narrow case containing a small parchment inscribed with verses from the Book of Deuteronomy. The *mezuzah* is put on the right doorpost leading into a home or a room.

The *shofar* ("ram's horn") was used in biblical times on ceremonial occasions. In today's synagogue it is sounded on Rosh Hashanah and at the end of Yom Kippur. In the State of Israel it is sounded on official occasions such as a presidential inauguration and in Orthodox neighborhoods to usher in the Sabbath.

On the festival of Sukkoth "four species" are brought to the synagogue and held during the prayer service. They are the palm branch (*lulav*), the myrtle (*hadas*), the willow of the brook (*aravah*), and the citron (*ethrog*).

Another common symbol, although without religious meaning, is the six-pointed star called the Magen David (Shield, or Star, of David). It is an ancient symbol and in the 1800's was selected as the symbol of the Zionist movement. It was later adopted by the State of Israel for its flag. During Nazi rule, Jews were compelled to wear the Magen David on their clothing.

While there is little basis in Jewish law for covering the head, even in prayer, custom requires a head covering for all Traditional Jews as a sign of reverence for God. Nontraditional Jews use the head covering less strictly. Its most common form is the skullcap called *kipah* in Hebrew and *yarmulka* in Yiddish.

▶A SUMMARY OF JUDAISM

Judaism is a religious faith, but it is also more. It is an ethical discipline, a cultural heritage, and a joyful experience of the beauty of life. Jews of different times and places may have developed different interpretations, but the flexibility of Judaism makes it possible to think and believe and practice within a broad framework. The vast cultural variety of Judaism and the breadth and depth of its teachings and practices indicate that Judaism should be considered—in Rabbi Mordecai M. Kaplan's term—as a "civilization."

JEROME R. MALINO, Rabbi Emeritus
United Jewish Center, Danbury, Connecticut

See also JEWS; HANUKKAH; PASSOVER; PURIM; TALMUD; TEN COMMANDMENTS.

JUDO

In 1882 the late Dr. Jigoro Kano opened the first school of judo in Japan. Dr. Kano's purpose in developing judo as a sport was to make available the physical and mental training of jujitsu without the techniques that could cause injury. Stripped of the deadly locks and throws of jujitsu, the new sport of judo became safe even for women and children.

Competitive judo, which demands the highest skill and stamina, is only one part of this sport. To those who know it well, it is an exciting study. To active men and women, judo is an enjoyable way to keep fit. Boys are enthusiastic students of judo and enter junior competition at an early age. Women and girls compete separately. They have also developed great skill in *kata*, the series of technical movements, and in *randori*, a type of free exercise.

What Judo Is

Unlike karate, which uses both foot and hand blows, judo basically depends upon the use of leverage and balance to overcome an opponent. A person under attack does not block or punch. He may resist for a moment and then let go suddenly. This forces his opponent off balance and makes it easy to throw him. The attacker's own lunging weight provides the force the opponent needs to control him. It is just as though someone were to push as hard as he could against a locked door, and you suddenly opened it. The person would probably fall through and land on the floor. This is one way that a judo player gains control over his opponent. As the attacker rushes in, the judo player either sidesteps or backs away. This catches the attacker off balance, and he may be pushed, pulled, or thrown to the ground.

Judo is a sport for two players. The sport is governed by strict rules of politeness. Before and after a match the players must bow to each other. A match is won on points or superior play. A player wins a point when he holds his opponent on his back so that he is unable to move for 30 seconds; when he forces his opponent to give up by using

TSURI-KOMI GOSHI (HIP THROW)

UCHI MATA (INNER-THIGH THROW)

strangleholds or armlocks; and when he makes a clean throw. A player wins a half point when he holds his opponent down for only 25 seconds. Kicking, hitting, and gouging are not allowed. A referee watches the players and decides who wins each point. A player who wins the necessary amount of points first wins the match. A contest or match may last up to 20 minutes.

Judo requires much physical training and instruction. Training takes place in a *dojo*, or gym area. In the Orient players practice on straw mats. In Western countries a canvas wrestling mat can be used. The players wear cotton jackets and trousers circled by colored belts. A beginner wears a white belt and a more accomplished player a brown belt. Experts wear the coveted black belt.

Kata

Most of the training a player is given is in *kata*. These are sets of exercises in which each move is arranged in much the same way that a ballet dancer's routine is planned. The entire series of moves must be done with grace and dignity. The illustrations above show the *Nage-No Kata*, or throwing technique. This is the *kata* most often shown or demonstrated. The *Nage-No Kata* is divided into five groups. Each group is named for the part of the body that is being used. There are three throws in each group.

The five groups are:

(1) Hand techniques
(2) Hip techniques
(3) Foot techniques
(4) Back techniques
(5) Side techniques

The *Nage-No Kata* must be mastered for promotion to First Degree Black Belt.

In addition to learning the *kata*, a *judoka*, or player, is taught a number of systems of throwing, pinning, locking joints, and so on.

The Kodokan in Tokyo establishes the most important rules for judo throughout the world.

Reviewed by PAUL V. HARPER, M.D.
Secretary, Olympic Judo Committee

See also KARATE.

JUGGLING

Juggling, the art of keeping several objects moving continuously in the air by alternately tossing and catching them, is an ancient practice that is today a popular form of recreation.

Juggling has a long history. Egyptian tomb paintings dating from 2600 B.C. depict women jugglers. Juggling was also popular in ancient Greece and Rome, as well as in China and other parts of Asia. The word "juggle" comes from the Latin word *joculari*, meaning "to joke." Entertainers of the ancient world often combined juggling with other forms of entertainment, including storytelling, acrobatics, and magic tricks. This tradition continued in Europe during the Middle Ages, when court jesters and traveling minstrels included juggling routines in their performances.

In the United States, juggling was part of almost every variety stage show from Civil War times until the 1920's. One of the greatest jugglers of this period was Russian-born entertainer Enrico Rastelli (1896–1931), who set records for juggling the most objects: ten balls or eight plates. After movies and radio and, later, television replaced live stage shows as pop-ular entertainment, juggling was performed mainly in circuses and by street performers. Beginning in the late 1970's, juggling surged in popularity. Today, international conventions draw thousands of participants each year, and local juggling festivals take place in many communities.

Jugglers use a variety of different tossing patterns. The most basic is the cascade, which is described in the feature below. Skilled jugglers can vary the pattern in a number of ways. For example, objects can be tossed under the leg, bounced off an elbow or knee, or caught and balanced on the forehead. Objects can also be tossed back and forth between partners. Balls, beanbags, hoops, and hollow clubs are the objects most commonly used for tossing. Beginners often start with scarves, which are lightweight and fall very slowly.

With practice, almost anyone can learn to juggle. It requires little special equipment and can be done almost anywhere. Those who juggle believe that it develops balance, eye-hand coordination, concentration, and timing. Many feel that it improves self-confidence and reduces stress. But most jugglers juggle mainly for fun.

DAVE FINNIGAN
Author, *The Complete Juggler*

Learning the Cascade

1. Using a scooping underhand throw, toss a ball from hand to hand in a smooth arc. Catch toward the outside, carry to the center, and toss diagonally to a point about a foot above the opposite shoulder. The ball traces a sideways figure-8 pattern in the air.

2. Next, hold a ball in each hand, keeping a third ball in reserve on the heel of your dominant hand. Toss Ball 1 along the figure-8 path and say "one." Just as it peaks and starts to fall, toss Ball 2 from the other hand and say "two." The two balls cross, ending up in opposite hands. Repeat until you can regularly exchange two balls without a drop.

3. Start again with two balls in your dominant hand and one in your other hand. Toss Ball 1 from the fingertips of your dominant hand and say "one." When it peaks, toss Ball 2 from the other hand and say "two." When Ball 2 peaks, say "one" again and toss Ball 3. Catch this third ball with the fingertips of your other hand.

4. To juggle continuously, always start tossing from the hand holding two balls and alternate your hands. Focus on the peaks rather than on your hands; every time a ball peaks, toss another. Counting will help you get a rhythm and keep you throwing alternately. Remember to keep your juggling pattern on a level plane in front of you and toss to the same height on each side.

July

Mark Antony, the Roman general and orator, named July after Julius Caesar. In the Northern Hemisphere, July is a vacation month as school children enjoy a long summer holiday. It is a time for picnics, camping, swimming, and sailing.

Place in year: 7th month.
Number of days: 31.
Flowers: Water lily and larkspur.
Birthstone: Ruby.
Zodiac signs: Cancer, the Crab (June 21–July 22), and Leo, the Lion (July 23–August 22).

1
- **Gottfried Wilhelm von Leibniz** born 1646
- The Battle of Gettysburg started and continued for three days, 1863
- British North America Act passed, uniting Canadian colonies under one confederation, 1867
- San Juan Hill in Cuba occupied by American troops, 1898
- Dominion Day (also called Canada Day or Confederation Day) in Canada
- Independence Day in Burundi; Rwanda

2
- **Christoph Willibald Gluck** born 1714
- President James Garfield fatally wounded by an assassin, 1881

3
- Champlain founded Quebec, 1608
- Idaho became the 43rd state, 1890

4
- **Nathaniel Hawthorne** born 1804
- **Giuseppe Garibaldi** born 1807
- **Stephen Collins Foster** born 1826
- **Calvin Coolidge** born 1872
- Continental Congress adopted the Declaration of Independence, 1776
- Erie Canal construction started, 1817
- Vicksburg surrendered to Union Army, American Civil War, 1863
- Statue of Liberty formally presented to U.S. by France, 1884
- *Independence Day*

5
- **David Glasgow Farragut** born 1801
- **Cecil Rhodes** born 1853
- Independence Day in Venezuela

6
- **John Paul Jones** born 1747
- British troops captured Fort Ticonderoga, 1777
- First state convention of the Republican Party held in Jackson, Michigan, 1854
- Independence Day in Comoros
- Republic Day in Malawi

7
- **Marc Chagall** born 1887
- Sandra Day O'Connor nominated to become first woman member of the U.S. Supreme Court, 1981
- *Independence Day in Solomon Islands*

8
- **John D. Rockefeller** born 1839

9
- **Elias Howe** born 1819
- *Independence Day in Argentina*

10
- **John Calvin** born 1509
- **James Abbott McNeill Whistler** born 1834
- **Mary McLeod Bethune** born 1875
- **Saul Bellow** born 1915
- Wyoming became the 44th state, 1890
- *Independence Day in Bahamas*

11
- **John Quincy Adams** born 1767
- **E. B. White** born 1899
- Alexander Hamilton fatally wounded in a duel with Aaron Burr, 1804
- *National Day in Mongolia*

12
- **Henry David Thoreau** born 1817
- **Sir William Osler** born 1849
- **George Eastman** born 1854
- **Amedeo Modigliani** born 1884
- *National holiday in Kiribati*
- *Anniversary of National Independence in Sao Tome and Principe*

13
- Northwest Ordinance adopted, 1787
- Blackout struck New York City, lasting until following day, 1977

14
- **Gerald R. Ford** born 1913
- *Bastille Day in France*

15
- **Rembrandt van Rijn** born 1606
- Manitoba became a province of Canada, 1870

16
- **Sir Joshua Reynolds** born 1723
- District of Columbia established, 1790

- First atomic bomb exploded in test at Alamogordo, New Mexico, 1945

17
- Spanish Civil War began, 1936
- Arco, Idaho, became first American town to have light furnished by atomic energy, 1955
- *17th of July Revolution Day in Iraq*

18
- **William Makepeace Thackeray** born 1811

19
- **Edgar Degas** born 1834
- First women's rights convention in U.S. held in Seneca Falls, New York, 1848
- France declared war on Prussia, 1870

20
- British Columbia became a province of Canada, 1871
- Neil A. Armstrong and Edwin E. Aldrin, Jr., on Apollo 11 mission became first humans to set foot on the moon, 1969
- Viking I landed on Mars, 1976
- *Independence Day in Colombia*

21
- **Ernest Hemingway** born 1899
- First Battle of Bull Run, American Civil War, 1861

22
- **Gregor Johann Mendel** born 1822
- *National Liberation Day in Poland*

23
- *Revolution Anniversary in Egypt*

24
- **Simón Bolívar** born 1783
- **Alexandre Dumas** (*père*) born 1802

- Mormons settled Salt Lake City, 1847

25
- Puerto Rico became a commonwealth, 1952
- First documented test-tube baby born in Oldham, England, 1978

26
- **George Bernard Shaw** born 1856
- New York ratified the Constitution, 1788
- *Independence Day in Liberia; Maldives*

27
- **Alexandre Dumas** (*fils*) born 1824
- First permanent Atlantic cable completed, 1866
- Armistice signed by United Nations and Communist delegates, ending Korean War, 1953

28
- **Beatrix Potter** born 1866
- Fourteenth Amendment to U.S. Constitution ratified, granting citizenship to U.S. blacks, 1868
- Austria-Hungary declared war on Serbia, starting World War I, 1914
- *Independence Day in Peru*

29
- **Benito Mussolini** born 1883
- Charles, Prince of Wales, and Lady Diana Spencer married in London, 1981

30
- **Emily Brontë** born 1818
- **Henry Ford** born 1863
- First representative assembly met in Jamestown, Virginia, 1619
- *Independence Day in Vanuatu*

31
- Christopher Columbus discovered island of Trinidad, 1498
- British attacked Spanish Armada, 1588

The calendar listing identifies people who were born on the indicated day in boldface type, **like this.** You will find a biography of each of these birthday people in *The New Book of Knowledge.* In addition to citing some historical events and historical firsts, the calendar also lists the holidays and some of the festivals celebrated in the United States. These holidays are printed in italic type, *like this.* See the article HOLIDAYS for more information.

Many holidays and festivals of nations around the world are included in the calendar as well. When the term "national holiday" is used, it means that the nation celebrates an important patriotic event on that day—in most cases the winning of independence. Consult *The New Book of Knowledge* article on the individual nation for further information on its national holiday.

June

The ancient Romans named the first month of summer June, probably in honor of the goddess Juno, patroness of women, marriage, and the home. In the Northern Hemisphere, summer begins on June 21 or 22—the longest day of the year.

Place in year: 6th month.
Number of days: 30.
Flower: Rose.
Birthstone: Pearl or alexandrite.
Zodiac signs: Gemini, the Twins (May 21–June 20), and Cancer, the Crab (June 21–July 22).

1
- **Jacques Marquette** born 1637
- **Brigham Young** born 1801
- Kentucky became the 15th state, 1792
- Tennessee became the 16th state, 1796
- Constitution Day in Tunisia
- Independence Holiday in Western Samoa

2
- **Thomas Hardy** born 1840
- **Sir Edward Elgar** born 1857
- Foundation of the Republic Day in Italy

3
- **Jefferson Davis** born 1808
- DeSoto claimed Florida for Spain, 1539
- Dutch West India Company chartered, 1621
- *Confederate Memorial Day* in Kentucky; Louisiana

4
- Massachusetts became first state to set a minimum wage, 1912

5
- **Charles Joseph Clark** born 1939
- Robert F. Kennedy shot by an assassin; died the following day, 1968
- Constitution Day in Denmark
- Liberation Day in Seychelles

6
- **Nathan Hale** born 1755
- YMCA (Young Men's Christian Association) organized in London, 1844
- Allied troops landed in Normandy on D-Day, 1944

7
- **Paul Gauguin** born 1848
- **John Napier Turner** born 1929

8
- **Robert Schumann** born 1810
- **Frank Lloyd Wright** born 1867

10
- **Maurice Sendak** born 1928
- National holiday in Portugal

11
- *Kamehameha Day* in Hawaii

12
- Baseball Hall of Fame in Cooperstown, New York, dedicated, 1939
- Independence Day in Philippines

13
- **William Butler Yeats** born 1865
- Yukon Territory organized, 1898

14
- **Harriet Beecher Stowe** born 1811
- Continental Congress adopted the U.S. flag, 1777
- Hawaiian Islands organized as Territory of Hawaii, 1900
- Argentine troops surrendered to British, ending fighting in Falkland Islands, 1982
- *Flag Day*

15
- **Edvard Hagerup Grieg** born 1843
- Magna Carta signed by King John, 1215
- Benjamin Franklin proved that lightning is electricity, 1752
- Arkansas became the 25th state, 1836
- *Pioneer Day* in Idaho

17
- **John Wesley** born 1703
- **James Weldon Johnson** born 1871
- **Igor Stravinsky** born 1882
- Mississippi River discovered by Louis Jolliet and Father Jacques Marquette, 1673
- Battle of Bunker Hill, 1775
- Reclamation Act passed by Congress, 1902
- Five men seized while apparently installing eavesdropping equipment in the Democratic National Committee Headquarters at the Watergate building in Washington, D.C., thus bringing about the Watergate Incident, 1972
- National Day in Federal Republic of Germany
- Independence Day in Iceland

18
- U.S. declared war on Great Britain, 1812
- Battle of Waterloo, in which Napoleon was defeated by Allied troops led by Wellington and Blücher, 1815

19
- First real baseball game on record with set rules played in Hoboken, New Jersey, 1846

20
- **Jacques Offenbach** born 1819

- Eli Whitney applied for patent on the cotton gin, 1793
- A patent for the telegraph granted to Samuel F. B. Morse, 1840
- West Virginia became the 35th state, 1863
- First oil from Alaska's north slope began flowing into the trans-Alaska pipeline, 1977

21
- New Hampshire ratified the Constitution, 1788
- Cyrus McCormick awarded a U.S. patent for his reaper, 1834
- U.S. armed forces captured Okinawa, 1945

22
- **George Vancouver** born 1757
- **Giuseppe Mazzini** born 1805
- U.S. Department of Justice established by Congress, 1870

23
- **Empress Joséphine** born 1763
- Treaty with Indian people signed by William Penn, 1683
- Taft-Hartley Act became law, 1947
- National holiday in Luxembourg

24
- **Henry Ward Beecher** born 1813

25
- **George Orwell** born 1903
- Virginia ratified the Constitution, 1788
- General Custer and troops killed by members of Sioux Indian tribe at Little Bighorn, Montana, 1876
- Fair Labor Standards Act became law, 1938
- Korean War began, 1950
- Independence Day in Mozambique

- First commercial color TV broadcast aired in New York by Columbia Broadcasting System, 1951

26
- **Sir Robert Laird Borden** born 1854
- **Pearl Buck** born 1892
- Fifty nations signed United Nations Charter in San Francisco, 1945
- Independence Day in Madagascar

27
- **Paul Laurence Dunbar** born 1872
- **Helen Keller** born 1880
- Independence Feast Day in Djibouti

28
- **Henry VIII** born 1491
- **Peter Paul Rubens** born 1577
- **Jean Jacques Rousseau** born 1712
- Assassination of Austrian Archduke Francis Ferdinand and his wife caused outbreak of World War I, 1914
- Treaty of Versailles signed, 1919

29
- Independence Day in Seychelles

30
- Pure Food and Drug Act became law, 1906
- Twenty-sixth Amendment to U.S. Constitution, extending full voting rights to 18-year-olds, ratified when Ohio legislature approved it, 1971
- Independence Day in Zaire

Second Sunday in June: *Children's Day.* **Third Sunday in June:** *Father's Day.* **June** (5th day of the 5th moon on Chinese calendar): Dragon Boat Festival in China.

The calendar listing identifies people who were born on the indicated day in boldface type, **like this.** You will find a biography of each of these birthday people in *The New Book of Knowledge.* In addition to citing some historical events and historical firsts, the calendar also lists the holidays and some of the festivals celebrated in the United States. These holidays are printed in italic type, *like this.* See the article HOLIDAYS for more information.

Many holidays and festivals of nations around the world are included in the calendar as well. When the term "national holiday" is used, it means that the nation celebrates an important patriotic event on that day—in most cases the winning of independence. Consult *The New Book of Knowledge* article on the individual nation for further information on its national holiday.

JUNE BUGS. See Beetles.

JUNG, CARL (1875–1961)

Carl Jung was a Swiss psychologist and psychiatrist whose life's work had a tremendous influence on the history of these sciences, and who is considered to be the founder of analytical psychiatry. Many of his discoveries and theories about the human personality are still taught, and his ideas have also been influential in philosophy, art, literature, and the theater.

Jung was born on July 26, 1875, in Basel, Switzerland. His father and grandfather were ministers. Jung himself was deeply religious, but he had a very independent and questioning mind. He also developed an interest in both mythology and spiritualism. All of these factors played a role in his later decision to become a psychiatrist.

Jung studied medicine at the University of Zurich. He became a lecturer in medicine after graduation, but his interest in psychiatry, begun at the university, deepened and he decided to pursue it. He joined the staff of the Burhölzi Asylum in the early 1900's. At Burhölzi he focused his studies on patients who had irrational, or unreasonable, reactions to

Jung in his study in Switzerland, where he continued his studies and his work until his death. Late in life he became known as the "Sage of Zurich."

particular words. These strange reactions happened, Jung discovered, because the words reminded the patients of thoughts and experiences that they were deeply ashamed of or were trying to force out of their minds. Jung developed his study into a theory about personalities with problems that he called **complexes**, a term that is still applied by many psychologists today.

Jung's work brought him into contact with Sigmund Freud, the creator of psychoanalysis (the scientific study of the human mind). From 1907 until 1912 they shared ideas about their work, particularly the influence of both the conscious and unconscious mind on behavior and mental health. In 1912, however, as Jung became critical of some of Freud's ideas, the two men quarreled and ended their friendship and their collaboration.

Jung went on to develop his own ideas, among them his theory of personality types. Jung focused his theory on what he felt were the most basic differences among individuals. He said people were predominantly **introverts**, inward-looking and strongly influenced by their own ideas and their unconscious, or **extroverts**, outward-looking and influenced by other people and the world outside themselves. Within these two categories people could be further described by characteristics based on which of four functions—thinking, feeling, sensations, or intuition—were most highly developed in the individual.

Jung also proposed that understanding thoughts buried in a patient's unconscious was essential to understanding and helping that patient. In his study of the unconscious, he developed a theory of what he called **archetypes** to express his ideas.

In their "personal" unconscious, people have memories, thoughts, and feelings about things that are specific to themselves. However, they also have what Jung called an inherited or "collective" unconscious. It is here that people have ideas, thoughts, and feelings about things that are basic and common to all human beings—their societies, cultures, religions, myths, dreams, and fantasies. These are archetypes—common images of people such as parents and children, and common understandings about ideas and concepts such as birth, death, power, magic, honor, the hero. The ways in which patients express their attitudes toward subjects in both their personal unconscious and their collective unconscious are carefully explored in the therapy Jung proposed as important to helping them become successful individuals.

Jung died at the age of 85 on June 6, 1961, in Küsnacht, Switzerland.

Rachel Kranz
Editor, Biographies
The Young Adult Reader's Adviser

Primitive transportation routes, such as this swinging bridge used to cross a Caribbean stream, make travel through the jungle difficult and sometimes dangerous.

JUNGLES

A jungle is a thick tangle of vegetation in tropical lands. It has denser undergrowth than tropical rain forests and fewer tall trees.

Travel in the jungle is difficult. Travelers must cut their way through the heavy vegetation. Jungle climate is generally hot and humid. Although there is dense undergrowth in some middle-latitude forests, these are not ordinarily called jungles.

Where Are the Jungles?

Most of the world's jungles are in tropical forest regions where the original trees have been cut down by man. The jungle growth is nature's way of healing the wound made by the forest clearing. In cleared areas and around the margins of rain forests more sunlight reaches ground level, so that jungle plants can grow. Riverbanks in the rain forest often have strips of jungle that extend only a short distance inland from the river. Thus, jungle is sometimes intermixed with rain forest in tropical lands. The main jungles are found in Central America, northern South America, and central Africa. There are others in southern Asia, in northern Australia, and on most of the world's tropical islands. In savanna grasslands and in sparse forests, dense jungles grow along the banks of rivers. The tree branches sometimes grow out over the river, hiding it from above. Such riverbank jungles are called **gallery forests**. On tropical coasts a special kind of jungle is made up of mangrove trees. The mangrove lives near a river mouth, in soil that is flooded by the tide. Mangrove seeds germinate while on the tree and are ready to grow when they fall into the mud. A mangrove jungle builds land by catching and holding mud washed in by the tide. In places it chokes the mouths of rivers, so that ships cannot enter.

Plant and Animal Life

Plant life in a jungle is a mass of trees, vines, creepers, bushes, and tall grasses. Fruits such as guavas, mangoes, bananas, and breadfruit sometimes grow wild. There are many kinds of palms. Some bear edible fruits or nuts. Others provide fibers from their bark or leaves. The rattan palm has long stems, which are used to make baskets and furniture. Another useful plant is bamboo. There are more than 200 kinds of bamboo. Some grow to heights of 120 feet (36 meters). Bamboo is used for houses, fences, water pipes, and containers. People of the jungle also make tools, weapons, and rafts of bamboo. Certain vines of the jungle are used for making mats and

This Philippine settlement is built on stilts along the water's edge. Since travel through heavy vegetation is difficult, rivers are the "roads" of the jungle.

ropes. Many kinds of tree and grass leaves furnish thatching for roofs.

Many birds, insects, reptiles, monkeys, and catlike mammals live in jungles. Grazing animals prefer the open grasslands. Animals such as the tiger of Asia or the jaguar of South America live in the jungle but move to grasslands in search of their prey. The elephants of Asia and Africa are also at home both in the jungle and on grassy plains. Other animals, like the crocodile and the hippopotamus, inhabit jungle rivers.

People of the Jungle

Few people live in the jungles. Most of them live in villages at the jungle's edge or in clearings. People of the jungle often use animal trails when hunting or gathering products of the forest. Sometimes they travel along the rivers in canoes. Their tools and weapons are crude and simple. Jungle houses are made of wood or bamboo and leaves. Clay is sometimes used to plaster the walls. People do not need much clothing in the hot climate. Some tribes weave their own cloth, which they dye bright colors. The art, music, and dances of the jungle people are often related to their worship of things in nature.

It is difficult to clear the jungle for farming. Trees can be cut and burned, but with simple tools it is almost impossible to remove the tough roots of grasses and bushes. For this reason, farming is not widespread in the true jungles. Some people who live on the fringes of the jungle practice **migratory agriculture**. They clear a patch of jungle land and plant vegetables or other crops. When their gardens become overrun by the jungle, it is easier to clear new land than to remove the tangle of weeds. A whole village may abandon a forest clearing and move to a new area. Migratory agriculture is also called **slash-and-burn agriculture** and **shifting cultivation**.

Tropical jungles have nearly hidden the ruins of some ancient civilizations, such as that of the Maya Indians in Central America. The famous ruins of the city of Angkor Thom and the temple of Angkor Wat were discovered deep in a jungle in Kampuchea.

In many places, the jungle has been conquered with modern machinery. People have established plantations to produce commercial crops, and timber and mineral deposits have been recovered from jungle lands. But the jungle is important in another way. Its trees take in carbon dioxide and release oxygen into the atmosphere, benefiting people in all parts of the world. Jungles also provide homes to the decreasing numbers of tropical plants and animals. Now many people are working to save jungles rather than to destroy them.

HOWARD J. CRITCHFIELD
Western Washington University

See also BIOMES; RAIN FORESTS.

JUNIOR COLLEGES. See UNIVERSITIES AND COLLEGES.

JUNIOR HIGH SCHOOLS. See EDUCATION; PREPARATORY SCHOOLS; SCHOOLS.

JUPITER

Imagine a planet so large that more than one thousand Earths could fit inside it. There is such a planet—Jupiter. The fifth planet from the sun, Jupiter is the largest and most massive planet in the solar system. With its huge size and its 16 moons, Jupiter is almost a miniature solar system in itself.

Although astronomers have observed Jupiter for more than 350 years, most of what we know about the planet comes from five space probes—*Pioneer 10* and *Pioneer 11* and *Voyager 1* and *Voyager 2*, which flew past it between 1973 and 1979, and *Galileo*, which began orbiting Jupiter in 1995. Cameras and sensitive instruments on board these probes have taken many close-up pictures and measurements of Jupiter and radioed this information back to Earth. After years of studying the information from these probes, astronomers have learned a great deal about Jupiter and its moons.

A World of Gases

Jupiter is a very different sort of planet from Earth. The Earth has a solid surface with an interior of molten rock. Jupiter, on the other hand, does not have a solid surface. Instead, it is an enormous ball of gases consisting of different elements. It is 82 percent hydrogen, 14 percent helium, and only 4 percent of all other elements combined. Because of its gaseous composition, Jupiter is sometimes referred to as a gas giant planet. Saturn, Uranus, and Neptune are the other gas giant planets in our solar system.

What would happen if you flew a spaceship to Jupiter and tried to land? First, you would be in for a big surprise. Jupiter does not have any place for you to land. If you flew your spaceship into the atmosphere and glided down through the clouds, the air would get warmer and denser. In Jupiter's upper atmosphere, hydrogen is a light gas as it is on Earth. But in the lower atmosphere, hydrogen and other gases become hotter and denser. Deeper and deeper you would go, and you would find nothing except more atmosphere. Finally you would go so deep that the pressure of the atmosphere would crush your spaceship flat.

Deep inside Jupiter's interior, the tremendous pressure of its atmosphere compresses

These images of Jupiter with four of its moons—Io, Europa, Ganymede, and Callisto—were taken by the *Voyager 2* space probe in July 1979.

hydrogen into a hot, molten metal. Jupiter's interior is extremely hot. Astronomers estimate that the deepest layers of the planet reach a temperature of 36,000°F (20,000°C). Compare this to the surface of the sun, which is 10,000°F (5500°C).

Although the very center of Jupiter may be a massive rocky core, astronomers believe that most of the planet's interior consists of the hot molten form of metallic hydrogen. Astronomers do not know for sure what happens when pressure causes gaseous hydrogen to become liquid, or when hydrogen becomes metallic. That mystery may have to be solved by future astronomers.

The Planet's Magnetic Field

When the *Pioneer* and *Voyager* space probes flew past Jupiter, special instruments called magnetometers measured the strength of the planet's magnetic field. Astronomers discovered that Jupiter's magnetic field is about ten times stronger than the magnetic field of the Earth. The magnetic field of both planets is caused by a similar process. As the molten material in each planet's interior

Jupiter

Position in the solar system	Fifth planet from the sun
Distance from the sun (average)	483,000,000 miles (778,000,000 kilometers)
Revolution around the sun	11.9 Earth years
Diameter	89,000 miles (143,000 kilometers)
	11 times the diameter of Earth
Mass	1,900 quintillion tons
	318 times the mass of Earth
Density	1.3 grams per cubic centimeter
Rotation on its axis	9 hours 55 minutes
Tilt of rotational axis	3.1°
Natural satellites known	16
Rings known	1
Surface	No surface; Jupiter is a gas giant
Atmosphere	Hydrogen, helium
Temperature (upper atmosphere)	–186°F (–121°C)
Symbol	♃
In mythology	Jupiter, king of the Roman gods

slowly circulates, it creates an electrical current. This flow of electrical current is what generates the magnetic field. The existence of a strong magnetic field on Jupiter is one of the reasons astronomers think that the planet's interior is composed of metallic hydrogen.

Jupiter's Incredible Winds and Clouds

When you look at a picture of Jupiter, what do you see? Views of Jupiter through large telescopes or in satellite photographs reveal a series of bright white and yellow-orange zones and dark red and brown belts circling the planet parallel to its equator. Small white oval clouds and hundreds of small swirls called **eddies** can also be seen. Jupiter's colorful belts and zones, which change in width and position over the years, trace the paths of clouds driven by powerful winds that blow around the planet. The strongest winds blow along the planet's equator at about 350 miles (560 kilometers) per hour. In the zones on either side of the equator, the winds blow at about 100 miles (160 kilometers) per hour in the opposite direction from those at the equator. Further north and south, the winds again blow in the same direction as at the equator.

Winds on Earth are produced when air is heated by light from the sun. As air gets warmer, it rises, and cooler air rushes in to take its place. This movement of air is what causes winds. Jupiter, however, is five times farther from the sun than the Earth is, and the sunlight there is very weak. Astronomers think that Jupiter's winds are caused by heat escaping from deep inside the planet. As warm plumes of gas rise from Jupiter's interior, the rotation of the planet causes each plume to swirl. Thousands of these swirling plumes combine to drive the winds in Jupiter's different belts and zones.

Jupiter's clouds are the most colorful in the solar system. They are composed mostly of tiny frozen crystals of ammonia and water. When these crystals are pure, they form white clouds. Other colors are formed when small amounts of compounds containing carbon, phosphorus, sulfur, and other elements are present, as they are in Jupiter's clouds. The strongest colors occur where gases from deep inside the planet rise to the top levels of the

WONDER QUESTION

What is the Great Red Spot on Jupiter?

The most amazing feature in Jupiter's clouds is an enormous orange-red, oval-shaped area called the Great Red Spot. The Great Red Spot is actually an intense disturbance in Jupiter's atmosphere made up of violently swirling gases that rise from deep inside the planet. In some ways it resembles a large hurricane that is more than twice as wide as the entire planet Earth. However, the Great Red Spot is not like storms on Earth, which last only a short time before they lose energy and die. Astronomers have watched the Great Red Spot through telescopes for more than 300 years. The *Voyager* space probe found

that the Great Red Spot gets energy continually from small eddies in Jupiter's atmosphere. Since it has a continuing source of energy to sustain it, the Great Red Spot may be a permanent feature of the planet.

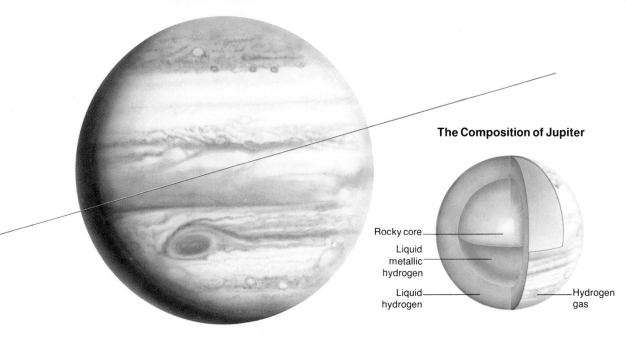

The Composition of Jupiter

Rocky core

Liquid metallic hydrogen

Liquid hydrogen

Hydrogen gas

clouds. The Great Red Spot may be just such a place. Fresh supplies of gaseous compounds from inside the planet may be what make Jupiter's Great Red Spot so vivid.

Radio Radiation

Jupiter generates and transmits powerful radiation in the form of radio energy, or radio waves. This radiation is generated by a vast invisible structure called the **magnetosphere**, which is formed by Jupiter's strong magnetic field. The magnetosphere contains magnetic lines of force that extend far into space and form a force field millions of times larger than Jupiter itself. When high energy particles (electrons and protons) from the sun stream past Jupiter, they are captured by the planet's magnetic field and spin around the magnetic lines of force in its magnetosphere. As the particles spin, they produce radio waves that can be detected by radio telescopes on Earth.

Jupiter's Satellites

In 1610, the Italian scientist Galileo pointed a telescope toward Jupiter and saw several tiny points of light beside the planet. At first he did not know what these lights were. Within a few weeks, however, he realized that they must be moons circling the planet. The four moons, or satellites, that Galileo discovered were named Ganymede, Callisto, Io, and Europa. In time, other satellites were also discovered in orbits around Jupiter. Until the two *Voyager* space probes flew past the planet, astronomers knew almost nothing about any of these satellites.

Today, they know some intriguing facts about each of them.

Ganymede. Jupiter's largest satellite, Ganymede, has a diameter of about 3,200 miles (5,200 kilometers). It is slightly larger than the planet Mercury. The icy surface of Ganymede is covered with peculiar craters and mountain ridges. The craters were formed when comets and asteroids crashed onto the satellite's surface. The mountains on Ganymede were formed billions of years ago as the satellite cooled and became frozen.

Callisto. Craters cover all of Callisto's frozen, icy surface. As on Ganymede, these craters have been formed by comets and asteroids crashing onto the satellite's surface over billions of years. Callisto is about 3,000 miles (4,800 kilometers) in diameter.

Io. Io's surface is covered with huge volcanoes and lava flows. Because Io is close to Jupiter, the planet's tremendous gravitational tidal forces have melted its interior. This

Ganymede

Callisto

Io

Europa

molten rock erupts continuously on Io's surface, causing sulfur dioxide to escape into space and form a gaseous ring, or **torus**, around Jupiter. Io is about 2,236 miles (3,600 kilometers) in diameter.

Europa. Europa is about 1,900 miles (3,100 kilometers) in diameter and has a slight atmosphere. Its interior is rocky, but its surface is covered with ice more than 60 miles (100 kilometers) thick. Images made by the *Galileo* spacecraft suggest that an ocean of liquid water may lie beneath the surface. Some scientists speculate that tidal forces caused by Jupiter's gravity could keep such an ocean warm enough to support life. Future space probes may provide more information.

Other Satellites. Astronomers know of twelve other small moons orbiting Jupiter. Two of these satellites are just a little more than 100 miles (160 kilometers) in diameter, and the remaining ten are 50 miles (80 kiloters) in diameter or less. Four of Jupiter's small satellites orbit very close to the planet, and astronomers think they may be fragments of a larger satellite that broke apart. The re-

Jupiter's Satellites		
Name	**Diameter***	**Year of Discovery**
Adrastea	22 miles (35 km)	1979
Amalthea	106 miles (170 km)	1892
Ananke	12 miles (20 km)	1951
Callisto	3,000 miles (4,800 km)	1610
Carme	19 miles (30 km)	1938
Elara	50 miles (80 km)	1905
Europa	1,900 miles (3,100 km)	1610
Ganymede	3,200 miles (5,200 km)	1610
Himalia	106 miles (170 km)	1904
Io	2,236 miles (3,600 km)	1610
Leda	6 miles (10 km)	1974
Lysithea	15 miles (24 km)	1938
Metis	25 miles (40 km)	1979
Pasiphae	22 miles (36 km)	1908
Sinope	17 miles (28 km)	1914
Thebe	62 miles (100 km)	1979

*Diameters are approximate.

maining eight small satellites orbit Jupiter far out in space in an opposite direction from the other moons. Astronomers think these distant satellites may be asteroids or comets that have been captured by Jupiter's gravity.

Jupiter's Ring

Soon after the *Voyager 1* space probe flew past Jupiter, its cameras took an amazing picture that showed a thin, delicate ring of fine particles circling the planet. Orbiting within this ring were two tiny moons, Metis and Adrastea. Astronomers think this ring was formed when meteors struck the surfaces of these moons. The ring is estimated to be about 18 miles (29 kilometers) thick and more than 4,000 miles (6,400 kilometers) wide. The discovery of the ring was remarkable because Saturn's famous rings were thought to be unique in the solar system.

In July 1994, ground-based telescopes, the Hubble Space Telescope, and instruments aboard the *Galileo* spacecraft focused on Jupiter as fragments of comet Shoemaker-Levy 9 struck the planet. In 1995, a probe released from *Galileo* into Jupiter's atmosphere found less helium than expected, very strong winds, and a new radiation belt above the clouds.

RICHARD BERRY
Former Editor-in-Chief, *Astronomy* magazine
Author, *Discover the Stars*

See also ASTRONOMY; PLANETS; SATELLITES; SOLAR SYSTEM; SPACE PROBES.

A striking picture of Jupiter's thin ring was taken by the *Voyager 2* space probe as the sun began to light it from behind.

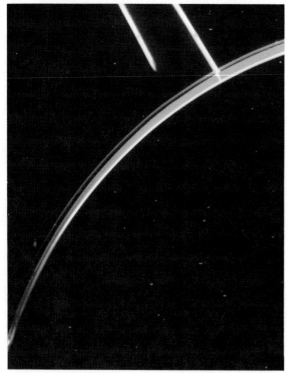

JURY

A jury is a group of people chosen by law and sworn to consider the facts of a case and decide upon the truth. A **grand jury** decides whether a suspected person should be brought to trial. A **trial,** or **petit** (small), **jury** decides whether the accused person is guilty or innocent. In United States law an accused person is considered innocent until proved guilty in a court.

In the United States arrested persons usually come before a lower-court judge called a magistrate. A person who clearly seems to be innocent can be released by the judge. A person who might be guilty is held for trial. In the case of lesser crimes (misdemeanors), the judge usually decides the question of guilt or innocence. But for serious, or major, crimes (felonies), the question of guilt may be settled by a trial jury.

History of Juries

Before jury trial existed, the main ways of deciding guilt or innocence were trial by battle, the ordeal, and compurgation. In **trial by battle** the accused person fought with the accuser or the accuser's representative. Winning showed innocence. Losing indicated guilt. The **ordeal** was a physical test. One ordeal required the accused to swallow a large piece of food. If the person could do it, the verdict was innocent. Choking on the food meant the verdict was guilty. **Compurgation** was a system in which an accused person could be proved innocent if twelve citizens (compurgators) swore to his or her honesty.

In the early 800's, Charlemagne, the Holy Roman Emperor, sent out royal officials to find out who was obeying or disobeying royal decrees. The officials made town leaders report on how well the royal laws were being obeyed. This was known as an inquisition. The people who made the report were called a *jurata,* from the Latin *jurare,* "to swear or promise." Their report was a *veredictum,* from *verus* ("true") and *dictum* ("saying"). The words "jury" and "verdict" come from these Latin words.

When William the Conqueror invaded England in 1066, he took Charlemagne's method with him. King Henry II developed the system further to create what is now called the grand jury. He also began to use trial juries. The Bill

After members of a trial jury have heard evidence from both sides, they are instructed by the judge on points of law. The jury decides matters of fact.

of Rights (1689) guaranteed the right of jury trial to all free English people. The English colonists brought the jury system to America. Trial by jury was among the rights guaranteed in the U.S. Constitution (1789).

How Juries Work in the United States Today

Almost any citizen over 21 can be a juror. Jurors serve for varying periods of time, often for two weeks. If they are workers, employers have to excuse them from their jobs. Some people (such as doctors) may be excused from jury duty.

There is no absolute limit on the number of people who may serve on a grand jury. As many as twenty-four jurors may be chosen or as few as one. A petit jury usually has twelve jurors. This custom comes from the days of compurgation, when there were twelve compurgators. A judge presides over a jury trial and decides points of law. Jurors are ordinary people and are not supposed to know about law. The jury's only task is to decide questions of fact.

In a criminal case the prosecutor presents the evidence "for the People" (society), to prove the accused is guilty. Then the attorney for the defense brings evidence of the accused's innocence. Each lawyer may also bring witnesses, and each may cross-examine (question) the other lawyer's witnesses.

When the jury has heard all the evidence,

the lawyers sum up their cases, both trying to persuade the jury that they are right. The judge instructs the jury about points of law in the case. Then the jury retires to discuss the case and reach a decision, or verdict. Jurors are not allowed to talk about the case with anybody, even other jurors, until this time. Nor are they supposed to make up their minds until they have heard all the evidence.

In the United States, verdicts in criminal cases must be unanimous (agreed on by all jurors). If the jurors cannot agree, a **hung jury** results. This means there must be another trial before a new jury. In civil cases some states permit verdicts that are not unanimous.

When the jury has decided, the foreman (leader) of the jury announces the verdict. If the jury gives a verdict of "innocent," the accused person goes free. If the verdict is "guilty," the judge sentences the accused.

In the United States, citizens called for jury duty go to their courthouse. There they are assembled in panels of up to thirty-six people. The lawyers usually choose twelve people from the panel to form the jury. Sometimes the jury may have only six members. Lawyers base their choice on their judgment of a juror's freedom from prejudice or personal interest in the case.

Jury verdicts represent the common-sense judgments of ordinary people. Some critics of the jury system believe that a jury trial is much like the old trial by combat. They claim that lawyers merely use clever courtroom tricks and psychology instead of the battle-ax and other weapons of the past.

Most people still think that a jury trial is the fairest way to decide guilt or innocence. Nevertheless, juries are being used less and less. This may be in part because there are more and more cases coming up, and jury trials usually take more time than trials decided by judges. The jury system is also being used less to decide civil cases, except some injury and accident cases.

HARRY ELMER BARNES
Co-author, *New Horizons in Criminology*
Reviewed by ROBERT MEIER
University of New Haven

See also COURTS.

JUSTICE, UNITED STATES DEPARTMENT OF

The Department of Justice is the largest law firm and law enforcement agency in the United States. With the assistance of thousands of lawyers, investigators, and agents, the department enforces federal laws, investigates federal crimes, operates federal prisons, and provides law enforcement assistance to states and local communities.

▶THE ATTORNEY GENERAL

The Justice Department is headed by the attorney general, who is the federal government's chief law enforcement officer and the president's chief legal adviser. The attorney general represents the United States in legal matters and may appear before the U.S. Supreme Court to represent the government in cases of exceptional gravity or importance.

The attorney general, who is a member of the president's cabinet, is appointed by the president with the approval of the Senate.

▶EXECUTIVE DIRECTION AND MANAGEMENT OFFICES

The **deputy attorney general** and the **associate attorney general** assist with program and policy development and also help direct the department's various organizations.

The **Justice Management Division** provides direct administrative services to the offices, boards, divisions, and, to a limited extent, the bureaus described below.

▶OFFICES AND BOARDS

Offices of the Justice Department include legal counsel; legislative affairs; policy and communications; professional responsibility; intelligence policy and review; community relations service; the solicitor general; the pardon attorney; and the executive offices for U.S. attorneys and U.S. trustees.

Justice Department boards include the Executive Office for Immigration Review; the United States Parole Commission; and the Foreign Claims Settlement Commission of the United States.

Attorneys General of the United States

Name	Took Office	Under President	Name	Took Office	Under President
Edmund Randolph	1789	Washington	Richard Olney	1893	Cleveland
William Bradford	1794	Washington	Judson Harmon	1895	Cleveland
Charles Lee	1795	Washington, J. Adams	Joseph McKenna	1897	McKinley
Levi Lincoln	1801	Jefferson	John W. Griggs	1898	McKinley
John Breckinridge	1805	Jefferson	Philander C. Knox	1901	McKinley, T. Roosevelt
Caesar A. Rodney	1807	Jefferson, Madison	William H. Moody	1904	T. Roosevelt
William Pinkney	1811	Madison	Charles J. Bonaparte	1906	T. Roosevelt
Richard Rush	1814	Madison, Monroe	George W. Wickersham	1909	Taft
William Wirt	1817	Monroe, J. Q. Adams	James C. McReynolds	1913	Wilson
John M. Berrien	1829	Jackson	Thomas W. Gregory	1914	Wilson
Roger B. Taney	1831	Jackson	A. Mitchell Palmer	1919	Wilson
Benjamin F. Butler	1833	Jackson, Van Buren	Harry M. Daugherty	1921	Harding, Coolidge
Felix Grundy	1838	Van Buren	Harlan F. Stone	1924	Coolidge
Henry D. Gilpin	1840	Van Buren	John G. Sargent	1925	Coolidge
John J. Crittenden	1841	W. H. Harrison, Tyler	William D. Mitchell	1929	Hoover
Hugh S. Legaré	1841	Tyler	Homer S. Cummings	1933	F. D. Roosevelt
John Nelson	1843	Tyler	Frank Murphy	1939	F. D. Roosevelt
John Y. Mason	1845	Polk	Robert H. Jackson	1940	F. D. Roosevelt
Nathan Clifford	1846	Polk	Francis Biddle	1941	F. D. Roosevelt, Truman
Isaac Toucey	1848	Polk	Tom C. Clark	1945	Truman
Reverdy Johnson	1849	Taylor	J. Howard McGrath	1949	Truman
John J. Crittenden	1850	Fillmore	James P. McGranery	1952	Truman
Caleb Cushing	1853	Pierce	Herbert Brownell, Jr.	1953	Eisenhower
Jeremiah S. Black	1857	Buchanan	William P. Rogers	1957	Eisenhower
Edwin M. Stanton	1860	Buchanan	*Robert F. Kennedy	1961	Kennedy, L. B. Johnson
Edward Bates	1861	Lincoln	Nicholas Katzenbach	1965	L. B. Johnson
James Speed	1864	Lincoln, A. Johnson	Ramsey Clark	1967	L. B. Johnson
Henry Stanbery	1866	A. Johnson	John N. Mitchell	1969	Nixon
William M. Evarts	1868	A. Johnson	Richard G. Kleindienst	1972	Nixon
Ebenezer R. Hoar	1869	Grant	Elliot L. Richardson	1973	Nixon
Amos T. Akerman	1870	Grant	William B. Saxbe	1974	Nixon, Ford
George H. Williams	1871	Grant	Edward H. Levi	1975	Ford
Edwards Pierrepont	1875	Grant	Griffin B. Bell	1977	Carter
Alphonso Taft	1876	Grant	Benjamin R. Civiletti	1979	Carter
Charles Devens	1877	Hayes	William French Smith	1981	Reagan
I. Wayne MacVeagh	1881	Garfield, Arthur	Edwin P. Meese III	1985	Reagan
Benjamin H. Brewster	1881	Arthur	Richard L. Thornburgh	1988	Reagan, Bush
Augustus H. Garland	1885	Cleveland	William P. Barr	1991	Bush
William H. H. Miller	1889	B. Harrison	Janet Reno	1993	Clinton

*Subject of a separate article in *The New Book of Knowledge*.

▶LITIGATING DIVISIONS

The **Antitrust Division** promotes and maintains competitive markets by enforcing laws that discourage unfair business practices.

The **Civil Division** represents all federal employees in cases concerning government-related activities.

The **Civil Rights Division** enforces federal laws prohibiting discrimination on the basis of race, national origin, religion, and disability.

The **Environment and Natural Resources Division** represents the United States in matters concerning public lands, natural resources, environmental quality, Indian lands and claims, and wildlife resources.

The **Tax Division** represents the Internal Revenue Service and other federal officials in cases regarding federal tax laws.

The **Criminal Division** enforces criminal laws that pertain to obscenity; the sexual exploitation of women and children; organized crime and racketeering; narcotics and dangerous drugs; national security; fraud; and other illegal activities (except those pertaining to the other litigating divisions).

▶BUREAUS

The **Immigration and Naturalization Service** authorizes the entry of legal immigrants and visitors into the United States and apprehends those who enter the country illegally.

The **Office of Justice Programs** (OJP) is intended to make the criminal justice system function more effectively. It carries out management responsibilities for the Bureau of Justice Assistance, the Bureau of Justice Statistics, the National Institute of Justice, the Office of Juvenile Justice and Delinquency Prevention, and the Office for Victims of Crime.

The **Federal Bureau of Investigation** (FBI), the department's principal investigative agency, gathers facts, locates witnesses, and compiles evidence in federal cases. (For more information, see the article FEDERAL BUREAU OF INVESTIGATION in Volume F.)

The **Drug Enforcement Administration** (DEA) enforces the laws and regulations concerning narcotics and controlled substances. Its main objective is to halt drug trafficking.

The **Federal Bureau of Prisons** protects society by confining convicts in federal penitentiaries, correctional institutions, and prison camps. Its correctional programs seek to rehabilitate as well as punish offenders.

The **United States Marshals Service** provides protection to judicial facilities and judges; apprehends federal fugitives; operates federal witness security programs; transports prisoners; executes court orders; and issues arrest warrants.

The **United States National Central Bureau —International Criminal Police Organization** (USNCB) represents the United States in INTERPOL, the International Criminal Police Organization. It provides an essential communications link between U.S. police and their counterparts in foreign countries.

The **Office of the Inspector General** promotes efficiency and economy within the department by enforcing laws and regulations concerning fraud, waste, and abuse.

▶**HISTORY**

The Department of Justice was formally established by an Act of Congress on June 22, 1870, although the office of the attorney general was created by the Judiciary Act of 1789, which also set up the federal court system.

Today the Justice Department employs approximately 86,000 people worldwide, including attorneys, investigators, border patrol agents, corrections officers, and a variety of other highly trained workers. Department headquarters are located at Pennsylvania Avenue at 10th Street, N.W., Washington, D.C. 20530.

Reviewed by the Justice Management Division
United States Department of Justice

See also FEDERAL BUREAU OF INVESTIGATION.

JUTE

Jute is a natural fiber that comes from a plant of the same name. It is strong, does not stretch, and is inexpensive. It has so many uses that, of all natural fibers, it is second only to cotton in the number of kilograms sold each year. Jute is the fiber used to make burlap bags. Jute yarn is woven into the backing of carpets. It is also used to make twine or string. Jute butts, the coarse ends of the plant's stalks, are manufactured into paper.

Most jute products are manufactured in India and Bangladesh, the two countries where most of the world's jute crop is grown. China is another important producer of jute and jute products.

Jute comes from two plant varieties: *Corchorus capsularis* and *Corchorus olitorius*. They require heavy, rich soil; a hot growing season; and gentle flooding to mature the stalks.

In India and Bangladesh, jute and rice are usually grown in rotation. The jute plants grow 2 to 4 meters (6½ to 13 feet) tall from seeds planted each spring in the rice fields. The stems are straight, branching only near the top. The leaves are light green. The flowers are yellowish white and grow in clusters opposite the leaves.

When the petals of the flowers begin to fall, it is time to cut the stalks. Bundles of stalks are stood on end until the leaves wilt and fall. Then they are stacked in water until the plant gums ferment and the fibers loosen.

The fiber is stripped off the stalk, washed, dried, and tied in bundles. The color of the fiber is either cream-to-straw or rusty brown-to-copper. When combed, the raw fiber looks and feels like doll's hair, for which it is sometimes used. The bundles of fiber are then sent to mills.

To make jute yarn, the fiber is first passed between heavy rollers and softened with water and oil. Then it is shredded and combed. Spinning frames twist the final slivers of fiber into yarn. Jute yarn is much coarser than the yarns of other fibers.

STUART J. HAYES
Fiber expert and textile consultant

JUVENILE CRIME

Juvenile crime occurs whenever a young person violates a law. Crime among juveniles is a serious problem in the United States and much of the world. When young people get involved in crime, parents and communities react with great concern.

Young people who break the law are sometimes called juvenile delinquents. In most states a person must be under 18 years of age to receive this designation.

Young people have to obey the same laws as adults. Activities such as scribbling graffiti on a wall, shoplifting, possessing illegal drugs, or driving a car without a license or the owner's permission violate local, state, or federal laws. Moreover, juveniles must follow some rules or laws that do not apply to adults. They may be required to attend school, for example. Age restrictions also prevent juveniles from purchasing guns or alcohol. Societies have more rules for young people because of the widespread belief that children require special protection and care until they become adults.

Ideally, young people are raised to respect the traditions and values of the family and community. When juveniles break laws, these traditions and values are threatened, and people look for ways to help youths become responsible adults. The juvenile justice system was created to deal with youths who disobey laws.

A young person who violates the law can be arrested by police and brought to court. However, the legal process for juveniles is different from that for adults. Early in the process, officials must determine whether a youth is in need of social welfare services or whether a juvenile court should handle the case.

▶ TYPES OF JUVENILE CRIME

Actions that are considered crimes for juveniles and not for adults—such as possessing alcoholic beverages, truancy, or running away from home—are known as **status offenses**. Status offenses account for many of the approximately 2.8 million juvenile arrests in the United States each year. However, young people who commit status offenses are not always formally arrested; they may be referred to the social welfare system. Various studies have found that about 40 percent of

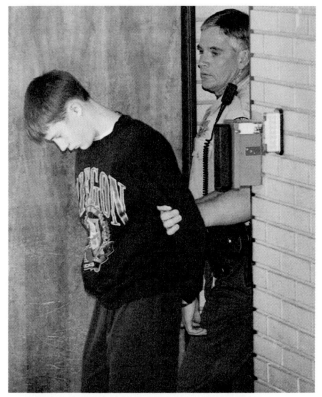

A 15-year-old boy is brought to court on charges of shooting classmates at his high school. Violent crime in schools is of growing concern in the United States.

young people who are detained (held in custody), whether or not they are arrested, are involved in status offenses.

Young people under 18 represent about one-fourth of the U.S. population, but they account for one in three arrests for **property offenses**. Larceny (acts such as shoplifting and purse snatching) is the most frequent property offense, followed by burglary (forced entry into a home or business), motor vehicle theft, and arson (deliberate burning of property). Juveniles account for fully half of all arsons and 40 percent of automobile thefts. They are also involved in many acts of vandalism (destruction of property).

Juveniles account for one in six arrests for **violent crime**. Aggravated assault (attacking someone with the intent to cause serious injury) is the violent crime for which juveniles are arrested most often, followed by robbery (using violence or threats to take something from a person) and, less often, rape and homicide. No more than one in about every 250 young people is arrested each year for a violent crime.

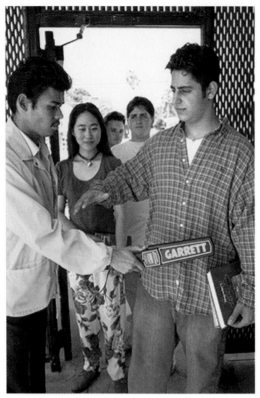

A security guard at a high school scans students for concealed weapons. Keeping firearms out of schools helps ensure the safety of students and teachers.

Juvenile crime rates in the United States decreased or held steady through the 1990's. For example, the juvenile arrest rate for murder declined by 39 percent from 1993 to 1997, and the rate for auto theft declined by 30 percent. However, school violence—particularly several cases of mass shootings by students—sparked intense debate about the accessibility of firearms and the responsibility of all citizens to help identify and find counseling for troubled youths before they resort to crime.

▶ OFFENDERS

Juvenile crime is highest among young people who live in city centers. It is next highest in the suburbs, and lowest in rural areas.

Boys are responsible for about three-fourths of all juvenile arrests.

Counselors from a community youth service talk with young gang members, who are at high risk for becoming involved in crime.

They are more likely to be arrested for murder and robbery than girls. Girls are more likely to be arrested for offenses such as prostitution (having sexual relations for money) and running away from home. Arrests of girls, especially for drug-abuse violations, increased in the early 1990's and thereafter declined more slowly than arrests of boys.

▶ WHY DO YOUNG PEOPLE COMMIT CRIMES?

There is no single explanation for youth involvement in crime. Experts in criminal justice believe that crime arises from a variety of sources, and the importance of various factors varies from child to child. Two children may grow up in similar families and go to the same schools, yet only one may break the law.

Home and Family. The quality of family life may have a lot to do with involvement in juvenile crime. Children raised by caregivers who are psychologically or physically abusive may be more likely to commit crimes. Although single-parent homes are sometimes viewed as a factor contributing to crime, in most such households the children grow up to be law-abiding citizens. What is most important in any home is the quality of care.

Peer Groups. A young person's peer group—people of the same age with whom he or she spends time—is an important influence on behavior. Young people want to be liked by their peers, and they tend to go along with the group. Some may get in trouble as a result.

The influence of peer groups can be seen at work in youth gangs. Gangs exist in every

state and many schools in the United States. Gang members may try to demonstrate their toughness and loyalty to the gang by breaking rules or fighting with other gangs. They are often involved in high-risk behavior, including crime, and they are also more likely to be victims of crime. A gang member may carry weapons, sell drugs, steal property, or commit other crimes to acquire money or as a condition of membership.

Some people believe that gangs make young people commit crimes, but others think that the young people who join gangs would get into trouble anyway. A young person may be attracted by the idea of belonging to a gang, or he or she may join a gang for protection.

Drugs and Alcohol. A great deal of juvenile crime is related to drugs and alcohol. In some places more than half of all arrested juveniles are under the influence of drugs or alcohol. These substances contribute to crime in several ways. Juveniles who are under the influence may commit criminal acts that they might not otherwise. They may harm themselves or others in accidents. Possessing or selling even small amounts of drugs is a very serious offense. Young people may commit crimes to get money to buy illegal drugs. They may also become victims of crime if others try to steal drugs from them.

▶ **JUVENILES AND LAW ENFORCEMENT**

In the United States, young people who violate laws enter the juvenile justice system in several ways. They may be referred by their families or schools. The most common way, however, is by police arrest.

Arrest. When the police suspect a youth of violating the law, they can deal with the situation in a variety of ways. They may warn the

youth or call his or her parents in to discuss the matter. But often the juvenile is arrested. To make an arrest, the police must have reason to believe that an offense occurred and that the juvenile committed it.

Like adults, juveniles who are arrested must be informed of their legal rights. They may be required to appear in a lineup, so that victims can identify them as offenders. They are then booked into a local detention center. Some juvenile cases are handled through local police diversion programs, which are intended to keep young people out of the official juvenile system. However, many cases are referred to the juvenile court system.

Juvenile Court. The first juvenile court in the United States was established in Illinois in 1899. Today there are juvenile courts in every state. The rules of juvenile court differ from those applied to adults. Juvenile court proceedings enable court workers—including probation officers, psychologists, social workers, and other trained

Juvenile offenders may be sent to detention centers or boot camps. Such facilities often promote rehabilitation by requiring inmates to study for their high-school equivalency certificates (*above*) and participate in physical exercise programs (*right*).

workers—to recognize and respond appropriately to the special needs of juveniles.

In court, juveniles have many of the same rights as adults. These include the right to legal counsel, the right to a hearing, the right to cross-examine witnesses, and the right to appeal court decisions. However, juveniles do not have the right to a jury trial, although some states allow it. Unlike adults, they can also be denied release from a juvenile detention center if a court determines that they would pose a danger to themselves. Juveniles can also be searched in school without a warrant or "probable cause" (reason to believe they may be involved in illegal activity).

Court Decisions. A juvenile court decision is called a **disposition**. The court looks closely at the offense, the circumstances surrounding it, the home life of the youth, and his or her prior problems with family, peers, schools, and the police. Based on this information the court tries to find the best ways to make the youth a responsible and productive citizen.

Juveniles can be sent to a detention center, a ranch or group home for children, a training center, or a similar facility. A few states are attempting to limit costs of holding juveniles in detention by setting up community-based programs for juvenile offenders.

Young people may also be placed on **probation**. They remain free but must meet certain conditions, such as participating in counseling or observing curfews (being home by a certain hour). They are closely monitored by probation officers to ensure that they behave appropriately. If probation is not successful, the juvenile will probably be placed in custody for treatment.

Juveniles cannot be sentenced to prison or jail, which are reserved for adults. Juveniles under 16 cannot be sentenced to death. Those 16 and older may face execution if they commit a capital crime, such as murder, in a state that allows the death penalty.

Rehabilitation (helping offenders become law-abiding citizens) is the primary goal of juvenile justice systems. However, in recent years states have imposed more rules on juvenile court judges. These rules require judges to give the same dispositions to juveniles with similar offenses and prior records, and to give sentences that are geared more toward punishment. Some states have passed laws that require juveniles who commit certain offenses to spend a minimum amount of time in an institution.

▶ QUESTIONS ABOUT JUVENILE JUSTICE

The juvenile court system has been criticized by people who feel that it is too easy on juvenile offenders. In response to this criticism, some states have passed or are considering laws that would lower the age at which juveniles can be tried as adults. These **waiver** procedures are generally restricted to older juveniles facing very serious charges. In a **judicial waiver** system, a juvenile court judge decides whether a youth is unfit for juvenile court services. The alternative is a **legislative waiver**, which automatically transfers juveniles to adult court for certain crimes.

It is important to remember that most young people do not get into trouble with the law, and that those who do usually do not grow up to be criminals. Juveniles who commit crimes hurt themselves, their families, and their communities. But communities attempt to deal with this by finding ways to help them become good citizens. That may involve providing opportunities for education, a job, the support of family, and involvement in community activities.

PATRICK JACKSON
Sonoma State University
Editor, *Western Criminology Review*

See also CRIME AND CRIMINOLOGY.

Supervised by a police officer, two youths paint over a graffiti-sprayed wall as part of a rehabilitation program for juvenile offenders.

K, the eleventh letter in the English alphabet, was also the eleventh letter in the ancient Phoenician and Hebrew alphabets, and the tenth letter in the classical Greek alphabet. The Phoenicians and Hebrews called it *kaph.* The letter *kaph* looked like this:

The Greeks borrowed their alphabet from the Phoenicians. So, although the Greeks changed the name of the letter to *kappa,* the form of the early letter looked very much like its Phoenician ancestor. Later, however, the Greeks changed the direction of their writing, and the *kappa,* like many other letters in the Greek alphabet, was reversed: **K**

The form of the letter K has remained generally the same since the time of the Greeks. The consonant sound of the letter, as in the word *king,* has remained unchanged, too. The Romans learned the Greek alphabet from the Etruscans, who used the letter C for the K sound. Thus the Romans also used the letter C for the K sound, and the letter K disappeared almost entirely. The English, in turn, inherited the Roman alphabet with its limited use of the letter K.

Many foreign words beginning with K have come into English; the word *ketchup* probably came to us from China, *kimono* came from Japan, and *Kremlin* came to us through French from Russia. English words of Greek origin, such as *kaleidoscope,* are also usually spelled with a K.

In the middle or at the end of a word, K generally follows a consonant, as in the words *ask* and *periwinkle.* It is also used after a long vowel, as in *leak, pike,* and *Quaker.* Before the letter N in words such as *know, knee, knit,* and *knife,* K is silent.

In chemistry, K stands for the element potassium. In weights and measures, K is the abbreviation for the prefix kilo-, which means 1,000—as in kilometer. K is also used to refer to a unit of computer storage capacity equal to 1,024 bytes.

Reviewed by MARIO PEI
Author, *The Story of Language*

See also ALPHABET.

SOME WAYS TO REPRESENT K:

The **manuscript** or printed forms of the letter (left) are highly readable. The **cursive** letters (right) are formed from slanted flowing strokes joining one letter to the next.

The **Manual Alphabet** (left) enables a deaf person to communicate by forming letters with the fingers of one hand. **Braille** (right) is a system by which a blind person can use fingertips to "read" raised dots that stand for letters.

The **International Code of Signals** is a special group of flags used to send and receive messages at sea. Each letter is represented by a different flag.

International Morse Code is used to send messages by radio signals. Each letter is expressed as a combination of dots (•) and dashes (––).

KALEIDOSCOPE

The kaleidoscope is a toy through which you can see brightly colored patterns. It was invented in 1816 by Scottish scientist Sir David Brewster to interest young people in the science of optics and, in particular, in *reflection*. The name he gave his invention is taken from three Greek words meaning "view beautiful forms."

A kaleidoscope looks rather like a telescope. There is an eyepiece at one end, through which the observer looks. At the other end is what is called an object box. This consists of two pieces of glass or plexiglass—the inside one clear, the outside one frosted. Sandwiched between them is a number of brightly colored shapes, such as beads or small pieces of transparent plexiglass.

The toy lives up to its name. When looking through the eyepiece, you see a symmetrical pattern in which all the colored objects are repeated several times in an arrangement that looks like a magnified snowflake. This symmetry is achieved by means of two mirrors, in the middle of the kaleidoscope, that are hinged together and reflect the pattern from one to another. The angle at which the mirrors are hinged determines the number of images you see.

Someone once calculated that if there were twenty colored objects in the kaleidoscope, and you changed the pattern ten times a minute by shaking the box, it would still take 462,880,899,576 years and 360 days to work through all the possible changes.

Carson I. A. Ritchie
Author, *Making Scientific Toys*

HOW TO BUILD A KALEIDOSCOPE

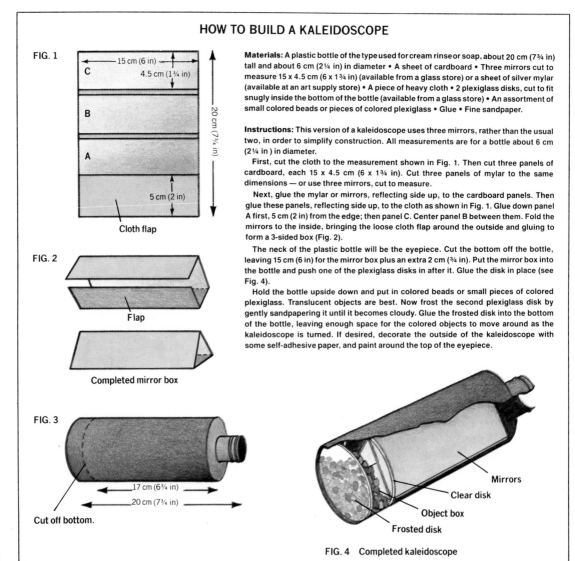

FIG. 1
C — 15 cm (6 in) — 4.5 cm (1¾ in)
B
A
20 cm (7¾ in)
5 cm (2 in)
Cloth flap

FIG. 2
Flap
Completed mirror box

FIG. 3
17 cm (6¾ in)
20 cm (7¾ in)
Cut off bottom.

Mirrors
Clear disk
Object box
Frosted disk
FIG. 4   Completed kaleidoscope

Materials: A plastic bottle of the type used for cream rinse or soap, about 20 cm (7¾ in) tall and about 6 cm (2¼ in) in diameter • A sheet of cardboard • Three mirrors cut to measure 15 x 4.5 cm (6 x 1¾ in) (available from a glass store) or a sheet of silver mylar (available at an art supply store) • A piece of heavy cloth • 2 plexiglass disks, cut to fit snugly inside the bottom of the bottle (available from a glass store) • An assortment of small colored beads or pieces of colored plexiglass • Glue • Fine sandpaper.

Instructions: This version of a kaleidoscope uses three mirrors, rather than the usual two, in order to simplify construction. All measurements are for a bottle about 6 cm (2¼ in) in diameter.

First, cut the cloth to the measurement shown in Fig. 1. Then cut three panels of cardboard, each 15 x 4.5 cm (6 x 1¾ in). Cut three panels of mylar to the same dimensions — or use three mirrors, cut to measure.

Next, glue the mylar or mirrors, reflecting side up, to the cardboard panels. Then glue these panels, reflecting side up, to the cloth as shown in Fig. 1. Glue down panel A first, 5 cm (2 in) from the edge; then panel C. Center panel B between them. Fold the mirrors to the inside, bringing the loose cloth flap around the outside and gluing to form a 3-sided box (Fig. 2).

The neck of the plastic bottle will be the eyepiece. Cut the bottom off the bottle, leaving 15 cm (6 in) for the mirror box plus an extra 2 cm (¾ in). Put the mirror box into the bottle and push one of the plexiglass disks in after it. Glue the disk in place (see Fig. 4).

Hold the bottle upside down and put in colored beads or small pieces of colored plexiglass. Translucent objects are best. Now frost the second plexiglass disk by gently sandpapering it until it becomes cloudy. Glue the frosted disk into the bottom of the bottle, leaving enough space for the colored objects to move around as the kaleidoscope is turned. If desired, decorate the outside of the kaleidoscope with some self-adhesive paper, and paint around the top of the eyepiece.

172

KAMEHAMEHA I (1758–1819)

Kamehameha I, also known as Kamehameha the Great, was the founder of the kingdom of Hawaii, which united all the Hawaiian islands under one government. He was born in Kohala, on the island of Hawaii, in 1758, the son of a chief. Originally named Kamehameha, which means "the lonely one," he was later given the name Pai'ea, meaning "hard-shelled crab," in honor of his tenacity and skill as a warrior.

When the English explorer Captain James Cook first visited the islands in 1778, the young Kamehameha was serving as an aide to his uncle Kalani'opu'u, ruler of Hawaii, the largest of the islands. On his deathbed in 1782, Kalani'opu'u willed his kingdom to his son Kiwala'o and the war god Ku—a powerful symbol—to his nephew Kamehameha. When Kiwala'o was killed in an uprising later that year, Kamehameha vied with two other high chiefs for control of Hawaii island. In

1791, having built a great temple to his war god, he defeated his rivals and united the island. Between 1791 and 1795 he conquered five more islands, bringing all eight Hawaiian islands under his control by 1805.

Kamehameha brought peace, stability, and prosperity to his realm. He encouraged profitable trading relationships with foreigners. But he also preserved traditional Hawaiian laws, customs, and religious beliefs. He died in Kailua on the island of Hawaii on May 8, 1819. The line of kings that he founded governed Hawaii until 1872.

Reviewed by LILIKALA KAME'ELEIHIWA
University of Hawaii at Manoa

KAMPUCHEA. See CAMBODIA.

KANDINSKY, WASSILY (1866–1944)

Wassily Kandinsky, a pioneer of abstract painting, was born in Moscow on December 4, 1866. When he was 30 he gave up a career in law and went to Germany to study painting.

Around 1908, Kandinsky painted his first important pictures. His dramatic landscapes in violent colors reflected the influence of both modern art and Russian folk art. In 1910 he conceived the idea of a completely abstract work of art—one with no subject. He felt that art should express the inner meaning of things. White might express silence. Orange might suggest the rich sound of church bells.

In 1911, Kandinsky and other painters formed a group called the *Blaue Reiter* "Blue Rider"). At this time his art was filled with lively lines and bright colors. When World War I began in 1914, he returned to Russia. But he felt that the Soviet government controlled art too closely, and he went back to Germany in 1921. There he taught at the Bauhaus school of art and design, and his paintings became more ordered and geometrical.

Kandinsky's many writings, such as *Concerning the Spiritual in Art* (1912), influenced the development of modern art.

Kandinsky's paintings do not tell a story. Instead, the artist uses colors and shapes to appeal directly to the viewer's feelings. *In the Black Circle* (1923).

When the Nazis forced the closing of the Bauhaus in 1933, Kandinsky went to Neuilly-sur-Seine, near Paris. He continued his work there until his death on December 13, 1944.

Reviewed by HAROLD SPENCER
University of Connecticut

Left: The growing joey returns eagerly to the snug, warm pouch to eat, sleep, and escape danger. *Above:* Traveling herds, or mobs, wander from place to place grazing on vegetation, including crops.

KANGAROOS

It stands up on its powerful hind legs, reaching almost 7 feet (2 meters) in height. For a moment it sniffs the air. Then it springs into action, hopping along with its long muscular tail swinging rhythmically. The gray kangaroo bounds across the plains of Australia at speeds of more than 40 miles (64 kilometers) per hour covering distances of up to 30 feet (9 meters) in a single hop!

Kangaroos range in size from the human-sized gray kangaroo, which weighs up to 200 pounds (91 kilograms), to the small kangaroo known as the rat kangaroo, which grows to about 13 inches (33 centimeters) in length and weighs about 2 pounds (1 kilogram).

All together there are more than fifty species, or kinds, of kangaroos living in Australia, New Guinea, and other neighboring islands. They can be found in many different environments, from deserts to grasslands to rain forests. Most kangaroos are ground dwellers, but a few of them live in trees.

The term "kangaroo" is usually applied to the large species of kangaroos, such as the gray kangaroo and the red kangaroo, that are most familiar to people and will be discussed in this article. Depending on size, other species of these furry mammals are also called wallabies, wallaroos, quokas, or pademelons.

▶CHARACTERISTICS OF KANGAROOS

All kangaroos belong to a group of mammals called **marsupials**. Marsupials differ from other mammals in the way their young develop and in how the young are cared for. The newborn marsupial, which is tiny and only partly developed, does most of its growing inside a pouch on its mother's stomach.

Along with the pouch of the female kangaroo, probably the best-known characteristic is the hopping locomotion of the kangaroo. Although they are the exception, hops as long as 43 feet (13 meters) and as high as 10½ feet (3 meters) have been recorded. The kangaroo's strong, muscular tail provides balance when the kangaroo hops and support when the kangaroo stands or walks.

Short fur covers the kangaroo's body. In most species, the fur is gray or brown. In some species, the male and female have different color fur. An example is the red kangaroo. The male red kangaroo has a reddish coat, while the female has a gray coat. Kangaroos use their short forelimbs to groom their fur.

Kangaroos have a varied plant diet. Some dine on soft plant matter such as mushrooms, others eat leaves and fruit. Others graze on grasses. Like other grazing animals, kangaroos have sharp cutting teeth, called incisors, for snipping plant stalks. They have broad, flat teeth, or molars, for crushing and grinding this tough food.

The kangaroo's digestive system, which includes a stomach separated into chambers, is also adapted for the animal's diet of tough grass and plant matter. After food is chewed and swallowed, it is forced back from the stomach into the mouth and is rechewed. Bacteria housed in one of the stomach's chambers helps to further break down the hard-to-digest plant fibers.

▶THE LIFE OF THE KANGAROO

Kangaroos, like all marsupials, give birth to tiny, undeveloped young. Birth occurs from three to five weeks after mating, depending on the species of kangaroo. In gray kangaroos, the young are born five weeks after mating, which occurs throughout the year.

At birth, a baby kangaroo, called a joey, is hardly an inch long. Its tail and hind legs are like tiny stumps. Its eyes are closed, and its ears are not fully formed. Its mouth is just a tiny hole. Only its front feet are well developed, with toes and nails.

Immediately after birth, the tiny baby kangaroo climbs from the birth canal up its mother's belly and into her pouch. Once inside, the joey quickly searches out a nipple and grabs on. The nipple swells inside its mouth, firmly attaching the little kangaroo to its mother. For several weeks, the young kangaroo remains attached, sucking its mother's milk. Within

The winner of this wrestling match will lead the mob. The match consists of pushing and shoving, interrupted with forceful kicks of the kangaroos' hind legs.

the pouch, the joey will complete its development. When the joey is about 8 months old, it is strong enough to jump out of the pouch and explore the world for the first time. By the time the joey is a year old, it no longer fits in the pouch. The young kangaroo stays with its mother, frequently returning to get milk. During this time, it also eats grass and other plant matter. By the time its diet consists of only plant matter, the kangaroo spends most of its waking hours in a search for food.

Kangaroos have life-styles that are as varied as their environments. Some kangaroos are primarily nocturnal—that is, they are active at night. Others are active during the day. Some kangaroos live alone, others live in groups. Several species of large kangaroos live in large groups called mobs.

Within the mob, there is usually one dominant male that leads the group and also mates with the most females. Male kangaroos fight to establish who will be the leader. The kangaroos support themselves on their hind legs and tails and wrap their forelimbs around each other. Then comes a wrestling match, with each kangaroo pushing and shoving. The wrestling is interrupted with kicks of the kangaroos' strong hind legs.

▶KANGAROOS AND THEIR ENVIRONMENT

Kangaroos are common in Australia's grasslands. The clearing of the forests has helped these animals spread and become increasingly abundant. The main natural enemy of the kangaroo is the dingo (wild dog). However, the kangaroo has always been hunted by humans. At one time, kangaroos were the main food of the aborigines (the first inhabitants of Australia). European settlers hunted kangaroos for sport.

Ranchers consider kangaroos a problem because they compete with cattle and sheep for grazing land. Limited hunting of the large kangaroos is permitted in order to keep their populations under control. More than a million kangaroos are killed each year. These animals are sold for meat and their skins are made into leather.

ELIZABETH KAPLAN
Author, *Biology Bulletin Monthly*
Reviewed by JAMES G. DOHERTY
Curator of Mammals
The Bronx Zoo

See also MARSUPIALS.

KANSAS

At the beginning of the 1800's, eastern Kansas was home to many different Native American tribes, including the Kansa (or Kaw), a name that means "wind" or "wind people." Kansas, as well as one of the region's principal rivers, was named after them.

Although Kansas has several nicknames, it is best known as the Sunflower State, a name that celebrates the tall, yellow prairie flowers that are native to the area.

Kansas lies in the midwestern United States. Before Alaska and Hawaii became states in 1959, Kansas occupied the center of the nation. A monument near Lebanon, in Smith County, still marks the exact geographic spot.

Kansas is thought of as a prairie state, but it is not as flat as people sometimes imagine. The land rises from about 700 feet (210 meters) above sea level in the east to more than 4,000 feet (1,220 meters) in the far west. The surface changes from wooded, rolling hills in eastern Kansas to high plains in the west. All of Kansas' major cities are located in the east. Wichita, on the Arkansas River, is the largest population center, followed by Kansas City and Topeka, the state capital.

In the mid-1800's, pioneers from the eastern United States and immigrants, primarily from Germany, Russia, Great Britain, and Scandinavia, began settling in Kansas, although some continued westward through Kansas on the Santa Fe and Oregon trails.

Tensions arose when the Kansas-Nebraska Act of 1854 allowed the settlers to decide whether or not they would allow the practice of slavery in the new territory. Bitterness led to bloodshed, and the land became known as Bleeding Kansas. After the Civil War (1861–65), the state became known for its rowdy cow towns of Abilene, Wichita, and Dodge City, the destinations of the legendary Texas longhorn cattle drives.

For most of the state's history, agriculture has been the backbone of Kansas' economy. Kansas usually leads the nation in the pro-

Clockwise from top left: Native produce is sold at roadside stands. Visitors can learn about the "cow town" era in Old Abilene Town. Kansas experiences more tornadoes per year than most other states. Sunflowers grow wild on the prairies.

State flag

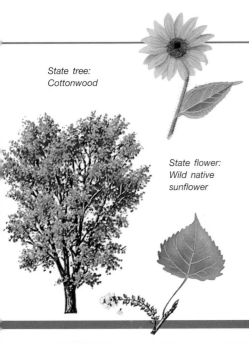

State tree:
Cottonwood

State flower:
Wild native
sunflower

FACTS AND FIGURES

Location: Central United States; bordered on the north by Nebraska, on the east by Missouri, on the south by Oklahoma, and on the west by Colorado.

Area: 82,277 sq mi (213,098 km^2); rank, 14th.

Population: 2,551,000 (1994 estimate); rank, 32nd.

Elevation: *Highest*—4,039 ft (1,231 m) at Mount Sunflower; *lowest*—680 ft (207 m) along the Verdigris River in Montgomery County.

Capital: Topeka.

Statehood: January 29, 1861; 34th state.

State Motto: *Ad astra per aspera* ("To the stars through difficulties").

State Song: "Home on the Range."

Nicknames: Sunflower State; Jayhawker State; Wheat State; Breadbasket of America; Midway, U.S.A.

Abbreviations: KS; Kan.; Kans.

State bird:
Western meadowlark

Left: Limestone ridges, known as the Flint Hills, lie between the Osage Plains and the Great Plains in central Kansas. The bluestem grass that grows there makes it an ideal place to graze cattle. *Right:* The northwestern part of the state is known as chalk country. The landscape at Monument Rocks National Landmark has eroded into fantastic shapes.

duction of wheat, which grows in the drier climate of central and western Kansas. Other important crops include corn and soybeans. Cattle grazing is concentrated in the Flint Hills of central Kansas.

Many industries in Kansas are tied to the production of crops and livestock, such as meatpacking and flour milling. Transportation equipment is important, too, with the manufacture of small airplanes and aircraft parts in the Wichita area, the assembly of motor vehicles in Kansas City, and the repair of railroad engines and cars in Topeka. Reserves of petroleum and natural gas and a large service industry further diversify the economy. Also, because the state has an older than average population, the number of health care services is proportionately high.

▶ LAND

Kansas is rectangular in shape except for its northeast boundary, which follows the course of the Missouri River. The state measures about 411 miles (661 kilometers) from east to west and about 208 miles (335 kilometers) from north to south.

Land Regions

Kansas is divided into three regions, the Dissected Till Plains and Osage Plains in the east and the Great Plains in the west.

The Dissected Till Plains, covering the area north of the Kansas River and east of the Big Blue River, belong to a larger region known

as the Central Lowland. This is the only part of Kansas that was covered by glaciers during the Ice Age. The melting ice left thick deposits of clay, sand, and gravel that filled in old stream valleys and smoothed the terrain. Today the landscape is made up of rolling hills and valleys.

The Osage Plains, located to the south of the Kansas River, also are part of the Central Lowland. They are made up of limestones, shales, and other rocks. Wind and streams have carved this region into a series of escarpments, which are long cliffs or steep hills. The highest of these are located in an area known as the **Flint Hills**. Between the escarpments are flat or gently rolling plains.

The Great Plains, in the central and western sections of Kansas, is a region of nearly flat uplands cut occasionally by stream valleys. Before and during the Ice Age, streams were eroding the Rocky Mountains and depositing huge loads of sand and gravel over what is now eastern Colorado and western Kansas. These deposits now form the surface of the plains as well as some of the sediments underground. One such layer, the Ogallala Formation, is of special value. From it comes large quantities of underground water that can be used for irrigation and for growing crops.

Rivers and Lakes

Many of the rivers and streams in Kansas have their source within the state. Exceptions are the Arkansas and the Cimarron rivers in the south and the Missouri, Big Blue, and Smoky Hill rivers in the northern half of the state. The Kansas River, commonly known as the Kaw, is only 169 miles (272 kilometers) long. It is formed by the joining of the Smoky Hill and Republican rivers at Junction City. None of these rivers can be navigated at present except for the Missouri.

Kansas has no important natural lakes, but the federal government has constructed about twenty large reservoirs to prevent the flooding of rivers. Most of them have become popular recreation areas and state parks. Tuttle Creek Lake on the Big Blue River is the largest among them.

Climate

Kansas is known for its sunshine. Daytime temperatures become truly hot in July and August, but a low relative humidity often makes these days more comfortable than the temperatures would indicate. Winters are generally dry and sunny throughout the state. In Topeka, the temperature averages 78°F (26°C) in July and 28°F (-2°C) in January.

Most of the moisture that comes to Kansas originates in the Gulf of Mexico. The southeastern section of the state receives about 40 inches (1,016 millimeters) of precipitation annually. Total amounts decrease gradually from east to west. Greeley County, on the Colorado border, averages about 16 inches (406 millimeters) annually. Kansas is fortunate in that most of the rainfall comes during the growing season, which extends from April through September. January is usually the driest month. Severe storms, such as blizzards, tornadoes, and blowing dust, occasionally plague the state, but such outbreaks usually cover only a small area and last a short time.

Plant and Animal Life

Kansas is known for its grasses. Tall prairie species called bluestem and Indian grass are found in the eastern third of the state. Western Kansas has short buffalo and grama grasses.

Kansas has no true forests, but wooded areas are plentiful, especially in the eastern part of the state. These include a mixture of oak, hickory, ash, and other trees. The cottonwood thrives along streams.

Great herds of bison once roamed the Kansas plains, and a small number still graze in Kansas on private landholdings and state game reserves. Other survivors from the prairie days include white-tailed deer, antelope, jackrabbits, prairie dogs, and coyotes. Cheyenne Bottoms in Barton County and the Quivira National Wildlife Refuge in Stafford

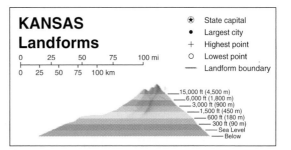

KANSAS Landforms

State capital
Largest city
Highest point
Lowest point
Landform boundary

0 25 50 75 100 mi
0 25 50 75 100 km

15,000 ft (4,500 m)
6,000 ft (1,800 m)
3,000 ft (900 m)
1,500 ft (450 m)
600 ft (180 m)
300 ft (90 m)
Sea Level
Below

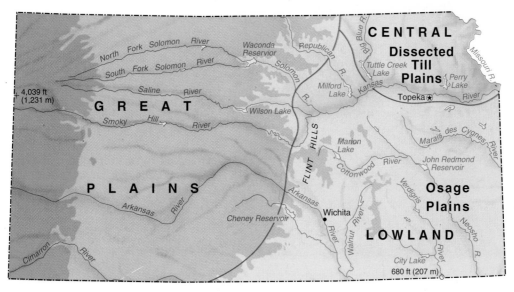

County are major stopping points for migratory water birds.

Natural Resources

The Kansas economy depends heavily on groundwater, soil, and mineral resources. The first two of these help to make the state a leader in agricultural production. The minerals supply fuel for use in industry, transportation, and homes.

Groundwater, pumped from a vast underground deposit known as the Ogallala aquifer, is used to irrigate the dry western part of the state. Recently, however, some of the wells have gone dry, causing great concern. Conservation measures, including the use of more efficient sprinklers, are now being used.

Almost all of the soils in Kansas are suitable for growing crops. The most productive section is in the northeast, where the soils are usually thick, dark brown, and fertile. Greater rainfall in eastern Kansas also favors a wider variety of crops than can be grown in the central and western parts of the state. Soils in much of western Kansas are formed from loess, a rich, windblown material composed of sand, silt, and clay. Soil conservation is important in Kansas because water and wind have eroded large areas. Today the most erosion-prone land is protected by a cover of grass. Also, new methods of plowing leave some of the old crop on the surface to help hold the soil in place.

Petroleum and natural gas, the state's most important minerals, are found throughout Kansas. From mines near Hutchinson, Kansas also supplies the nation with much of its salt. In 1903, helium gas was found in natural-gas deposits near Dexter in the Flint Hills. This was the first discovery of helium in the United States.

▶ PEOPLE

Eastern Kansas was once inhabited by the Kansa, Osage, Pawnee, and Wichita Indians. The Arapaho, Cheyenne, Comanche, and Kiowa hunted bison on the western plains. In the 1820's and 1830's, they were joined by some 10,000 displaced Native Americans from the Great Lakes region, including the Delaware, Kickapoo, Potawatomi, Sauk (or Sac), Mesquakie (or Fox), Shawnee, and Wyandot. Today only three small reservations remain in Kansas. Most of the state's 23,000 Native Americans live in Lawrence, Topeka, and other urban areas.

When the territory of Kansas was first created in 1854, it attracted settlers primarily from Illinois, Indiana, Missouri, and Ohio. In addition, an antislavery organization in New England sponsored several thousand migrants to settle in Kansas to head up a movement against slavery there. Antislavery forces were successful, and Kansas entered the Union as a free state in 1861. After this, approximately 12,000 African Americans migrated to Kansas. Most of them had escaped slavery in Missouri. They were joined in 1879 and 1880 by about 6,000 other former slaves from Mississippi and Texas, who came to escape racial violence.

The central and western parts of Kansas were not settled extensively until enterprising businessmen built the Kansas Pacific and the Atchison, Topeka, and Santa Fe railroads across the state after the Civil War. Iowans dominated the settlement in the northern tier of counties. Mostly

Using wheat fields as canvases and plows as pencils, Kansas artists create "crop art," such as *Sunflower Still Life* by Stan Herd.

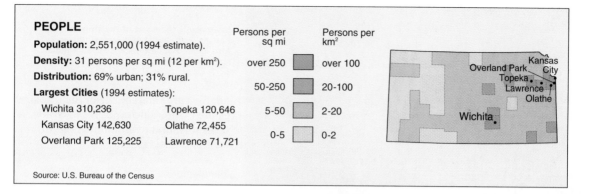

PEOPLE

Population: 2,551,000 (1994 estimate).

Density: 31 persons per sq mi (12 per km²).

Distribution: 69% urban; 31% rural.

Largest Cities (1994 estimates):

Wichita 310,236	Topeka 120,646
Kansas City 142,630	Olathe 72,455
Overland Park 125,225	Lawrence 71,721

Persons per sq mi		Persons per km²
over 250		over 100
50-250		20-100
5-50		2-20
0-5		0-2

Source: U.S. Bureau of the Census

Missourians occupied the extreme south. In between, along the lines of the two railroads, settlers came from many places. They included some 30,000 Germanic peoples from Russia, recruited by Santa Fe officials, and several thousand immigrants each from Germany, Sweden, England, Ireland, and French Canada. In the 1900's, immigrants from Croatia, Italy, Mexico, Poland, Slovenia, and Vietnam added even more diversity to the population.

Education

In 1855, the first Kansas territorial legislature passed laws for the free public education of white children. This right was extended to other races in 1859. Public high schools began in Leavenworth in 1865. Today Kansans are among the best educated citizens in the nation. Of residents age 25 or older, 81 percent have earned a high school diploma.

The present Kansas State University, located in Manhattan, was the first state-supported institution of higher education in Kansas. It was founded in 1863. At about the same time, Lawrence was selected as the site for the University of Kansas, but the university did not open until 1866. It was one of the first state universities in the United States to accept women students on the same basis as men. Other state universities are located in Emporia, Hays, and Pittsburg. These three were founded originally for the training of teachers. In 1963 the legislature voted the University of Wichita into the state system and renamed it Wichita State University.

Three private colleges chartered when Kansas was still a territory are still in existence. They are Baker University in Baldwin City, Benedictine College in Atchison, and

Kansans are avid college sports fans. Among the teams they cheer for are the Jayhawks of the University of Kansas (*above*) and the Wildcats of Kansas State.

Highland Community College in Highland, although the latter is now a public institution. Other private institutions include Bethany College (1881) in Lindsborg, Bethel College (1887) in North Newton, Friends University (1898) in Wichita, McPherson College (1887) in McPherson, Ottawa University (1865) in Ottawa, and Southwestern College (1885) in Winfield. Haskell Indian Nations University, founded in Lawrence in 1884, is financed by the federal government.

Libraries, Museums, and the Arts

About 320 public libraries serve the cities of Kansas. Major research libraries are located at Kansas State University and at the University of Kansas. The Kansas State Historical Society in Topeka maintains extensive holdings on state history. It also has one of the largest collections of newspapers in the country. Another important specialized collection is in the Eisenhower Library and Museum in Abilene. It contains the personal and state papers of the former president.

Lawrence is the home of the University of Kansas (*left*), the state's largest university. Also located in Lawrence is Haskell Indian Nations University.

Significant history and natural history museums in Kansas include the Dyche Museum of Natural History in Lawrence, the Eisenhower Center in Abilene, the Santa Fe Trail Center in Larned, the U.S. Cavalry Museum at Fort Riley, and the Sternberg Museum in Hays, which has a world-famous fossil collection. Major art collections are housed at the Spencer Museum in Lawrence, known for its European baroque paintings, and at the Wichita Art Museum.

▶ **ECONOMY**

For many years Kansas has ranked among the 15 most productive agricultural states. Nevertheless, the various service and manufacturing industries far surpass farming and ranching in value and in the number of people they employ.

Services

More than 70 percent of all Kansans are employed in the service industries, including health care, finance, insurance, real estate, wholesale and retail trade, transportation, communication, utilities, and government.

Manufacturing

Transportation equipment, especially small airplanes and aircraft parts, ranks first among the products manufactured in Kansas. Workers also create railroad cars, trailers for trucks and passenger cars, and rubber tires. The second most important manufacturing industry is food processing. Southwestern Kansas is noted for its meatpacking plants, and several cities statewide specialize in the milling of flour. Other manufactured goods include gasoline and lubricating oils derived from the state's petroleum fields, nonelectrical machinery, and chemicals.

Agriculture

Good soil, level terrain, and progressive farming methods make Kansas an important agricultural state. More than 90 percent of the land is devoted to farming.

In most years, Kansas farmers produce more wheat and grain sorghum than are grown in any other state. Wheat is planted widely but with a concentration in the central and western sections. Sorghum, like corn, is used chiefly as feed for livestock. It has become a popular crop in Kansas because it is resistant to drought. Corn, soybeans, and alfalfa (grown for hay) are other important crops. Soybeans are usually grown in the moister, eastern section. Corn and alfalfa are eastern

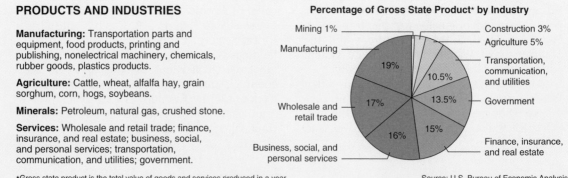

PRODUCTS AND INDUSTRIES

Manufacturing: Transportation parts and equipment, food products, printing and publishing, nonelectrical machinery, chemicals, rubber goods, plastics products.

Agriculture: Cattle, wheat, alfalfa hay, grain sorghum, corn, hogs, soybeans.

Minerals: Petroleum, natural gas, crushed stone.

Services: Wholesale and retail trade; finance, insurance, and real estate; business, social, and personal services; transportation, communication, and utilities; government.

*Gross state product is the total value of goods and services produced in a year.

Percentage of Gross State Product* by Industry

Mining 1%
Manufacturing 19%
Wholesale and retail trade 17%
Business, social, and personal services 16%
15%
13.5%
10.5%
Construction 3%
Agriculture 5%
Transportation, communication, and utilities
Government
Finance, insurance, and real estate

Source: U.S. Bureau of Economic Analysis

crops, too, but they also are popular choices for the irrigated fields in western Kansas.

The raising of beef cattle has been important in Kansas for more than one hundred years. The choicest pastureland lies in the Flint Hills and in the Smoky Hills of north central Kansas. In the past, most cattle were shipped into these pastures and grazed only seasonally. Today, permanent herds are the rule, with mature animals being sent to feedlots for fattening on corn or sorghum. Hogs and dairy cattle are of moderate importance to Kansas' economy.

Mining and Construction

Natural gas and petroleum are the most important minerals in the state. Natural gas production is concentrated in the Hugoton Field in the southwest. Petroleum is widespread across the southern two-thirds of the state. Both products are transported to distant cities by pipeline.

The ongoing construction of homes, shopping centers, and office buildings, as well as the building and maintenance of roads and other public facilities, accounts for about 3 percent of the state's economy.

Transportation

Two of the most famous early routes to the West, the Santa Fe

Trail and the Oregon Trail, crossed Kansas. The route of the Pony Express and many stagecoach and wagon roads also passed through the area. These routes linked the eastern states with the mining, trading, and agricultural centers

Top: Beef cattle are Kansas' most profitable agricultural product. *Above:* Kansas is often called the Wheat State because it is the nation's largest producer of wheat. *Below:* One of Kansas' most important industries is aircraft manufacturing.

Places of Interest

Kansas Cosmosphere and Space Center, in Hutchinson

Fort Larned National Historic Site and Santa Fe Trail Center

Front Street, in Dodge City

Eisenhower Center, in Abilene

Boot Heel Museum and Front Street, in Dodge City, is a re-creation of the downtown as it was at the time of the cattle drives in the early 1880's. Attractions include the original Boot Heel Cemetery, a saloon, a jail, stagecoach rides, and reenacted gunfights.

Cimarron National Grasslands, near Elkhart, is maintained by the National Forest Service. It was established on land purchased from dust bowl farmers and features Point of Rocks, a landmark on the Santa Fe Trail.

Council Grove became famous as the last supply center for west-bound travelers on the old Santa Fe Trail. The town features a museum dedicated to Kansa Indian life.

Eisenhower Center, in Abilene, includes the boyhood home and burial site of President Dwight D. Eisenhower. A museum depicts his military and civilian career, and a presidential library maintains his personal papers and official state documents.

Fort Larned National Historic Site and Santa Fe Trail Center, near Larned, are separate but related sites. Soldiers at the fort guarded the trail from 1859

through 1878. An excellent restoration of the 1860's period features nine sandstone buildings. The center is a combined museum and library. Nearby, trail ruts carved by the pioneers' wagon wheels are still visible.

Fort Leavenworth, adjacent to Leavenworth, is the oldest active army base west of the Mississippi River. Today it is home to the Command and General Staff College, an elite training facility for officers. A transportation museum on the base contains an extensive collection of horse-drawn vehicles. A maximum-security prison is located just west of the fort.

Kansas Cosmosphere and Space Center, in Hutchinson, chronicles the history of the U.S. space program. The exhibits include a planetarium and moon rocks brought back by the astronauts of *Apollo 11.*

Lucas, in Russell County, is a center for visionary art. Its Garden of Eden is an elaborate series of concrete sculptures intended as a critique of modern civilization by S. P. Dinsmoor. Two blocks away, the Grassroots Arts Center provides interpretations of the artwork and houses

additional creations made out of concrete and limestone.

Pawnee Indian Village Museum, near Republic, is a modern interpretive center built over and around an archaeological excavation of a dwelling dug into the earth. The site is administrated by the Kansas State Historical Society.

Victoria is the core of a large Volga German settlement. The cemeteries here and in neighboring villages feature large, carefully designed iron crosses. Catholic churches built out of local limestone are even more impressive. Victoria's Saint Fidelis, completed in 1911, is known as the Cathedral of the Plains.

Z-Bar Ranch, north of Cottonwood Falls, is in the process of development as a national park to preserve and interpret the ecosystem, or natural balance, of the tall-grass prairie. The park headquarters is in an elaborate stone house built in 1881. Buffalo, antelope, and other native species graze on adjacent land.

State Parks. For more information about state parks and recreation areas, contact the Kansas Department of Wildlife and Parks, 900 Southwest Jackson Street, Topeka, Kansas 66612.

in the Rocky Mountains and points farther west.

The railroads, highways, and airfields of today continue to focus on east–west connections and are a more important part of the economy in Kansas than in most other states. Kansas' busiest airport is located in Wichita.

Communication

Kansas' first newspaper was the *Shawnee Sun*, a monthly paper published in 1835 at the Shawnee Indian mission near present-day Kansas City. The first English-language newspaper was the *Kansas Weekly Herald*, published at Leavenworth in 1854. Today Kansas has 45 daily newspapers, led in circulation by the *Wichita Eagle* and the *Topeka Capital-Journal*. Broadcast media outlets include approximately 124 radio stations and 22 television stations.

▶ CITIES

All of Kansas' largest cities are located in the eastern and central parts of the state, mostly along the main rivers.

Topeka, the state capital, is located on the Kansas River in the northeastern part of the state. The city was founded in 1854 by Cyrus K. Holliday, a young Pennsylvanian, and others who hoped to build a railroad. Construction of the Santa Fe Railway was begun westward from Topeka in 1868.

Today Topeka is known for its printing and publishing businesses. It is also a repair center for the Burlington Northern Santa Fe railroad system and the location of several flour mills and foundries. Points of interest include the state capitol and the Kansas State Historical Society. The Menninger Foundation, a world-famous center for the treatment of mental illnesses, is also located there.

Wichita, Kansas' largest city, is located on the Arkansas River in the south central part of the state. It was founded in the late 1860's as a trading post along the Chisholm Trail. When the Santa Fe Railway

Wichita, the largest city in Kansas, was named after the Wichita Indians. Known for the production of aircraft, it is often called the Air Capital of the World.

reached the settlement in 1872, Wichita boomed as a cattle distribution center.

Today Wichita is known for the production of private and military aircraft. The level land around the city is useful for test takeoffs and landings. Wichita is also considered the state's petroleum capital because it contains a major refinery and is the headquarters of several oil companies. Flour milling is another large industry. Wichita is the home of Wichita State University, Friends University, and Kansas Newman College.

Kansas City, the state's second largest city, is located where the Kansas River meets the Missouri River. Although the Wyandot Indians were the first to settle there in the 1840's, Kansas City was not formally established until 1886, when leaders from several smaller communities decided to join their towns together. Once noted for stockyards and meat-packing plants, Kansas City today is a major hub for health services and for the manufacture of motor vehicles, soap, fiberglass insulation, chemicals, and food products.

▶ GOVERNMENT

Kansas is governed under one of the oldest state constitutions still in use. Although amended, it has been the basic law of the land since 1861.

The government of Kansas has three divisions, each similar to those in the federal system. Laws are made by the legislature, which consists of a senate and a house of representatives. The executive branch is headed by a governor, and the judicial branch has a chief justice and six associate justices.

Kansas established a special legislative agency in 1933 known as the Legislative Coordinating Council. It is made up of leading

The state capitol building in Topeka, modeled after the U.S. Capitol, was completed in 1903. It contains murals by the Kansas-born artist John Steuart Curry.

representatives of both houses of the legislature. Council members meet to study and prepare bills that will be introduced in the full legislature. Many other states have since adopted similar councils.

▶ HISTORY

Eastern Kansas was once settled by four major Native American tribes—the Kansa, Osage, Pawnee, and Wichita. Probably the first Europeans to come to Kansas were a group of Spanish explorers led by Francisco Vásquez de Coronado in 1541. French explorers and traders came in the early 1700's.

In 1803, the United States acquired Kansas as part of the Louisiana Purchase. Soon afterward, the U.S. government sponsored expeditions, led by explorers Lewis and Clark (1804), Zebulon Pike (1806), and Stephen Long (1820), to learn about the region. Their descriptions caused many people to believe that Kansas was a desert. Based in part on their negative reports, federal officials decided in the 1820's to reserve Kansas as a permanent "Indian Country," a place to relocate Native Americans from the east. Later, as pioneers began moving west along the Santa Fe and Oregon trails, it became obvious that Kansas was not desert but productive land. People demanded that the Indians be removed and the land opened for general settlement.

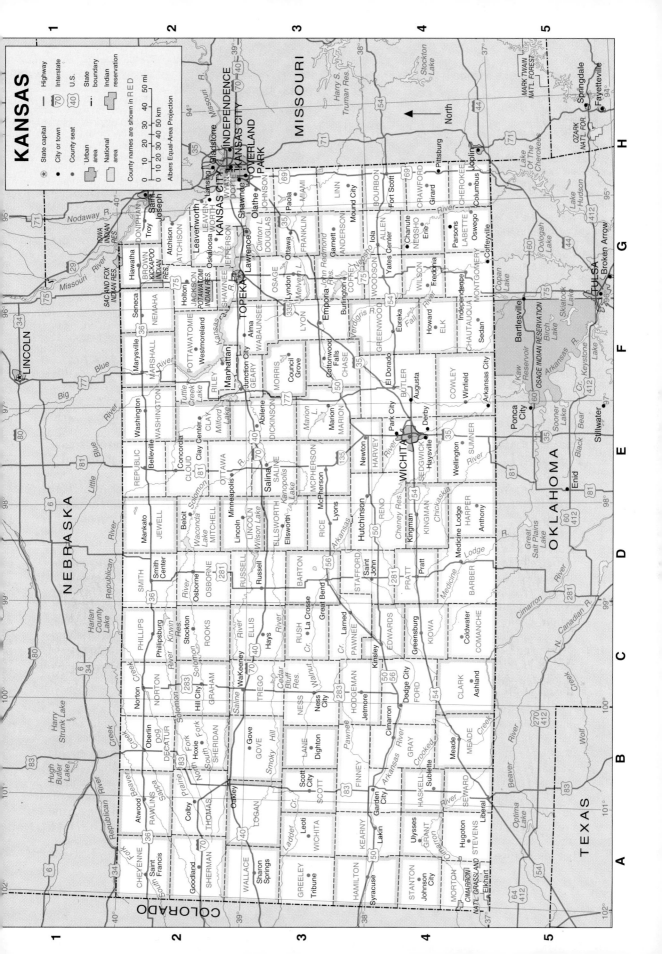

Famous People

Consult the Index to find more information in *The New Book of Knowledge* about the following people who were born in or are otherwise associated with Kansas: abolitionist John Brown (1800–59); gunfighter and lawman Wyatt Earp (1848–1929); Vice President Charles Curtis (1860–1936); baseball pitcher Walter Johnson (1887–1946); President Dwight D. Eisenhower (1890–1969); aviator Amelia Earhart (1897–1937?); author Langston Hughes (1902–67); and football running back Gale Sayers (1943–).

Susanna Salter

John Steuart Curry

Walter Percy Chrysler (1875–1940), the founder of the major automobile corporation that bears his name, was born in Wamego and grew up in Ellis. In 1912, Chrysler went to work for the Buick Motor Company, the principal division of General Motors, and four years later became president of the organization. He retired as a millionaire at the age of 45 but soon returned to the workplace and developed the six-cylinder automobile. In 1925 he cofounded the Chrysler Corporation, which became one of the nation's largest automobile manufacturers. Chrysler's boyhood home in Ellis is now a museum.

John Steuart Curry (1897–1946), an artist known for his dramatic portrayals of rural life in the Midwest, was born near Dunavant. A student at the Kansas City Art Institute (1916) and the Art Institute of Chicago (1916–18), Curry's first significant work was entitled *Baptism in Kansas* (1928). During the Great Depression of the 1930's, Curry became associated with an art movement called regionalism and was hired by the Works Progress Administration (WPA) to paint murals for the Department of Justice in Washington, D.C. His most famous work, a portrait of the abolitionist John Brown, was done as a mural panel in the state capitol building in Topeka.

Robert Joseph (Bob) Dole (1923–), a native of Russell, was the Republican candidate for president in 1996. A longtime leader in the Republican Party, Dole served as the national chairman of the Republican Party (1971–73) and as U.S. Senate majority leader (1985–87; 1995–96) and minority leader (1987–95). He earned a reputation for being a practical and effective mediator, capable of build-

Bleeding Kansas

From 1812 to 1821, most of what is now Kansas was governed as part of the territory of Missouri. When Missouri became a state in 1821, Kansas no longer fell under Missouri's jurisdiction.

In 1854, all the plains country west of Missouri and north of 37 degrees latitude was divided into two parts. The southern section was called Kansas, the northern one Nebraska. The Kansas-Nebraska Act (1854), which created the new territories, gave the people living in each place the right to choose whether their territory would become a slave state or a free state. (For more information, see the article KANSAS-NEBRASKA ACT in this volume.)

During the 1850's, it was an unstated but rigid policy of the United States to keep the number of free states equal to the number of slave states. People therefore expected Nebraska to enter the Union as a free state and Kansas as a slave state. This process went as expected in Nebraska, but the fate of Kansas was less certain. Many people came to the territory to try to influence the votes. Fights broke out between the two sides, and many towns were raided and burned. The region became known as Bleeding Kansas.

The exact origin of the Kansas nickname Jayhawk, or Jayhawker, is not known, but it goes back to this time, when the bands of antislavery guerrilla fighters in Kansas were called jayhawkers. Gradually the name came to be applied to Kansas and to Kansans.

Kansas Becomes a State

For a time, the antislavery forces and the proslavery forces had separate legislatures that passed laws in opposition to each other. Several constitutions were drawn up and rejected. Finally, in 1859, the Free State Party gained control, and delegates drew up a constitution that was approved by a majority of all the voters. On January 29, 1861, Kansas was admitted to the Union as a free state.

The Late 1800's

A few months after Kansas became a state, the Civil War (1861–65) began. Kansas contributed a large number of soldiers to the Union army. Few skirmishes actually took place in the area. The most infamous incident occured on August 21, 1863, when Confederate outlaw William Quantrill and his band raided and burned the town of Lawrence, killing 150 townspeople. After the war, settlement resumed. Because most of the male set-ing coalitions to achieve legislative goals. Dole was the unsuccessful Republican candidate for vice president in 1976 and a contender for the Republican presidential nomination in 1980 and 1988.

Alfred Mossman Landon (1887–1987), born in West Middlesex, Pennsylvania, served two terms as governor of Kansas (1933–1937). During that time he became known for reducing taxes and balancing the budget. In 1936 he was the Republican candidate for president of the United States. Governor Landon gained prominence in the oil industry as well as in politics. His daughter, **Nancy Landon Kassebaum** (1932–), served as a U.S. senator from Kansas (1978–). In 1996 she coauthored the Health Insurance Reform Bill that guarantees coverage to people who quit, lose, or change jobs.

Charlie Parker

Bob Dole

Charlie Parker (Charles Christopher Parker, Jr.) (1920–55), one of the most influential figures in American jazz, was born in Kansas City. Nicknamed Bird or Yardbird, Parker was an alto saxophonist and composer who teamed with trumpeter Dizzy Gillespie and others in the 1940's to create and popularize a rhythmic style known as bebop (modern jazz). Parker's most famous compositions include *Now's the Time*, *Yardbird Suite*, *Ornithology*, and *Confirmation*. A long-time addiction to heroin cut his life short.

Susanna Madora Salter (1860–1961), born in Lamira, Ohio, was a Woman's Christian Temperance Union officer, dedicated to prohibiting the use of alcoholic beverages. While a resident of Argonia, Kansas, anti-prohibitionists jokingly put her name on the ballot for mayor. She won the election and became the first woman mayor in the United States. She served one year (1887).

William Allen White (1868–1944), publisher and editor of the *Emporia Gazette*, was born in Emporia. In 1896, White wrote an editorial entitled "What's the Matter with Kansas?" that attracted national attention and made him a spokesman for small-town America. His autobiography, published after his death, won a Pulitzer Prize in 1947.

---

tlers were veterans of the Union army, the majority of Kansas' western counties were named after war heroes.

As the railroads pushed their way across the state, longhorn cattle from Texas were driven along the cattle trails to the "cattle towns" of Abilene, Dodge City, and Wichita for railroad shipment to eastern markets. By the mid-1880's, the railroads had reached as far as Texas, putting an end to the overland cattle drives. Along the old cattle trails, Kansas farmers planted corn and wheat.

Gradually, Kansas City became the regional leader in agricultural marketing, wholesaling, and manufacturing. Kansas City's stockyard was one of the largest in the world. Major deposits of coal, petroleum, and natural gas were discovered in the southeastern counties.

The Early 1900's

When the United States entered World War I in 1917, Kansas farmers responded to a call for more grain by plowing up much of the state's western rangeland. This effort did supply huge quantities of wheat, but it also left the soil vulnerable to wind erosion. When a series of dry years began in the early 1930's, much of the plains became a "dust bowl." The dust of dried-out soil filled the air, and many farms had to be abandoned.

The United States' participation in World War II (1941–45) boosted Kansas' economy. Rising prices helped farmers, and the demand for manufactured goods hastened the move of people from farms to cities. Munitions factories hired many workers, and Wichita's airplane industry grew tremendously.

Recent Decades

Kansas today is poised between a rural past and an urban future. For many outsiders, Kansas maintains an image as a land of healthy small towns, but the reality is far different. Most of the counties in the state have been losing population for decades. Nevertheless, a few regions of the state have gained population and are doing well economically. For example, since the 1960's, southwest Kansas has been transformed from a dryland farming economy into a more urban one based on irrigated farming and industry. But other than the southwest, most of the state's recent economic growth has been concentrated in Wichita and in the cities of the Kansas River valley.

JAMES R. SHORTRIDGE
University of Kansas

KANSAS CITY (MISSOURI)

Kansas City is located in western Missouri at the junction of the Missouri and Kansas rivers. It is Missouri's largest city, both in population and in land area. Approximately 435,000 people live in the city proper, which covers 316 square miles (818 square kilometers). The greater metropolitan area—which includes Kansas City, Kansas, on the opposite side of the Kansas River—is home to nearly 1.6 million people.

Kansas City began as a trading post for French fur traders in 1821. Promoters incorporated the Town of Kansas in 1850 and reincorporated it three years later as the City of Kansas. Residents adopted the name Kansas City in 1889. Construction of a railroad bridge across the Missouri River in 1869 transformed the sleepy western town into an industrial city, linking it to Chicago, St. Louis, and other commercial centers to the east.

Today, Kansas City maintains its importance as a western center of commerce and industry. A variety of farm-related items, such as machinery, chemicals, and barbed wire, are produced there, and a significant amount of the nation's wheat, corn, and soybeans passes through the city's grain elevators and mills. Three car and truck assembly plants make Kansas City an important automotive center. It is also the location of one of the nation's twelve Federal Reserve banks, and the federal government is a large regional employer.

Visitors expecting to see flat prairie land will be surprised by Kansas City's rolling terrain. The lovely hills of Swope Park, the city's largest recreational area, hold a number of attractions, including a zoo, golf courses, picnic areas, and playgrounds.

An educational center, Kansas City is home to more than a half dozen colleges and universities. Performance arts centers include the Kansas City Symphony Orchestra; Lyric Opera; Starlight Theater; Kansas City Ballet; and Missouri Repertory Theater. Cultural centers include the Nelson-Atkins Museum of Art, with its world-famous collection of Asian art, and the Kansas City Museum, featuring regional and natural history exhibits. Another landmark is the Harry S. Truman Sports Complex, home of the Kansas City Royals baseball team and the Kansas City Chiefs football team.

DARRYL LEVINGS
Kansas City Star
Reviewed by LAWRENCE O. CHRISTENSEN
University of Missouri, Rolla

Kansas City, Missouri, is situated at the junction of the Missouri and Kansas rivers. Established as a fur-trading post in 1821, it is now a major distribution center for a vast agricultural region.

KANSAS-NEBRASKA ACT

The Kansas-Nebraska Act of 1854 created two territories west of Iowa and Missouri. It was drawn up to prepare for a transcontinental railroad. It also reopened the question of slavery in U.S. territories and led to tension between the North and the South.

When California became a state in 1850, it was so far away that people realized a railroad was needed to bind it to the rest of the country. A southern route appeared practical because routes to the north would pass through Nebraska, an unsettled land without a government. Bills were introduced to organize Nebraska as a territory free of slavery, as required by the Missouri Compromise of 1820. But the bills were blocked by Southerners. They wanted a southern route. They also wanted to prevent an increase in the number of free states.

Senator Stephen A. Douglas of Illinois backed a central route that would enrich his home city, Chicago. He used the idea of popular sovereignty to win Southern support for his Nebraska bill. (Popular sovereignty allowed settlers themselves to permit or outlaw slavery.) Douglas agreed to divide Nebraska into two territories, Kansas and Nebraska, and to repeal the Missouri Compromise. Kansas, west of the slave state of Missouri, presumably would become a slave state. Nebraska, west of Iowa and the Minnesota territory, would be free.

The bill passed, but there was intense opposition. Charles Sumner, an antislavery senator from Massachusetts, said the bill "puts Freedom and Slavery face to face, and bids them grapple. Who can doubt the result?"

Sumner predicted correctly. Opponents of the new law organized the Republican Party to stop the spread of slavery. Proslavery and antislavery settlers fought to control what became known as bleeding Kansas. Freedom won in the end. But the strife increased the hostility between Northerners and Southerners and helped bring on the Civil War.

ARI HOOGENBOOM
City University of New York, Brooklyn College
See also MISSOURI COMPROMISE.

KANT, IMMANUEL (1724–1804)

The German philosopher Immanuel Kant was born in Königsberg on April 22, 1724. His father was a master harness-maker. Both his parents were good, upright people who taught their children to be the same.

Immanuel was so bright that in 1732 he entered the Collegium Fredericianum, where he could study theology, as his mother wished. He entered the university in 1740.

Kant helped support himself by coaching other students. He left Königsberg in 1747 to earn his living as a private tutor. He returned in 1754. The next year he presented his doctor's thesis at the university and received his degree. He taught at the University of Königsberg for the next 42 years.

His schedule of lectures on logic, metaphysics, mathematics, the natural sciences, and physical geography was heavy. But Kant also published many scientific works. He refused all offers to teach elsewhere because he wished to stay in his hometown. After 15 years he was made a full professor, and in 1786 he became rector of the university. In his teaching he was concerned that his students learn to think for themselves. His most influential writings were *Critique of Pure Reason* (1781), *Critique of Practical Reason* (1788), and *Critique of Judgment* (1790).

Kant's belief that the human mind is a creative force has had an important influence on the history of ideas. He lived what he taught, and he put great value on moral duties and on human dignity. When he died on February 12, 1804, he was honored for his uprightness as well as for his service to philosophy. A bronze tablet was put on his house 100 years later. The words on it came from his *Critique of Practical Reason:*

Two things fill the heart with ever renewed and increasing wonderment and reverence, the more often and the more lastingly we meditate upon them: The starry firmament above me and the moral law within me.

Reviewed by HOWARD OZMON
Author, *Twelve Great Philosophers*

Kapok trees often grow to enormous size. This old giant is in Kingston, Jamaica.

KAPOK

Kapok is a lightweight fiber used to stuff life preservers, cushions, pillows, mattresses, and toys. It is also sometimes used for insulation. The fiber is taken from the ceiba—silk cotton, or kapok—tree, which grows in many tropical regions.

Most commercial kapok comes from the tree known as *Ceiba pentandra,* which is grown mostly in Southeast Asia. But this tree grows also in the American and African tropics.

Flowers and pods grow on the tree during the dry season. The pods are 3 to 6 inches (8 to 15 centimeters) long. Inside the pods are many seeds surrounded by fibers. Each fiber is about 1 inch (2.5 centimeters) long. They are silky and light. They resemble cotton fibers, but they are too brittle to spin or weave. Kapok fibers are usually white. Some types of kapok trees produce pale gray or brown fibers.

Each fiber is a single cell with thin walls. Unlike most other plant fibers, the cell walls of kapok fibers do not absorb moisture. Water cannot enter the cells unless the cell walls are broken. This makes kapok a good material for filling life preservers. When it is properly processed, kapok is more buoyant than cork.

Kapok fibers are not harmed when they are sterilized by heat. Because the fiber remains light and fluffy, it makes good filling for pillows and cushions. Pillows filled with kapok are often used by people who are allergic to feathers or down.

Kapok does not conduct heat well. For this reason, it is also useful for insulation. But it has been largely replaced for this purpose by synthetic materials.

Kapok pods are usually harvested when they dry out and start to crack open. They are cut from the tall trees with knives attached to long poles. The seeds and fibers are separated from one another either by hand or by machines. An oil similar to cottonseed oil is pressed from the seeds. The oil is used in margarine and soap. The crushed seeds are used for cattle fodder and fertilizer.

Kapok trees in the tropics of the Western Hemisphere and Africa are somewhat larger than those grown in Asia. In the West Indies, kapok trees reach 80 to 100 feet (24 to 30 meters) in height and about 8 feet (2.5 meters) in diameter. Some of these giant trees are extremely old. There is one on the island of Puerto Rico that is said to have been a large tree when Columbus landed there in 1493. The fiber from these trees is not used commercially as much as that from the Asian trees, which are cultivated especially for their fiber. Indonesia is the chief exporter of kapok.

HAROLD F. WINTERS
United States Department of Agriculture

See also FIBERS.

KARACHI

Karachi is the largest city in Pakistan and the capital of Sind Province. It is the center of the country's trade, industry, banking, transportation, and communications and its most important seaport. The great bulk of Pakistan's exports and imports pass through the city of Karachi.

Located in southern Pakistan, Karachi is situated on the coast of the Arabian Sea and on the western edge of the great Indus River delta. It is a crowded, bustling city. Its over 5,000,000 people represent almost one fifth of Pakistan's total urban population. No other city reflects the economic, ethnic, and regional diversity of Pakistan as well as Karachi. It has offices of major industrial and commercial corporations, residences of the wealthy, as well as squatter settlements of the poor. A majority of the people are Muslim refugees from India who settled in the city after the creation of the separate states of Pakistan and India in 1947. The next largest group is composed of native Sindhis. But Karachi also is home to a million or more Pathans, who have come from such areas as the North-West Frontier Province, and thousands of Baluchis from the province of Baluchistan.

The city's architecture is a mixture of the old and the new. Modern multi-storied structures share the skyline with buildings dating from the period of British rule. One of Karachi's most notable landmarks is the mausoleum (tomb) of Mohammed Ali Jinnah, the founder of Pakistan. Others include the National Museum and the University of Karachi.

Karachi's prosperity is based largely on manufacturing and trade, which employ close to half the labor force. Textiles and footwear are the principal industries, followed by iron and steel, food and beverages, paper and printing, machinery, chemicals, petroleum, and electrical goods.

History. Karachi is a fairly young city by Asian standards. Starting as a small fishing village in the early 18th century, it emerged as a commercial center and military headquarters under the British during the middle of the 19th century. Its present importance dates from 1947, when Pakistan was founded and Karachi became the first capital of the new nation. Its population swelled with the arrival of refugees from India. In 1959, Pakistan's capital

As an industrial and trading center, Karachi is a busy and very crowded city. Its population has increased nearly tenfold since the founding of Pakistan in 1947.

was transferred to Rawalpindi and in 1967 to the newly built city of Islamabad, the present capital. Karachi, however, remains a magnet that continues to draw people to it from all over Pakistan. As the country itself grows, Karachi, too, will continue to grow.

KHALID BIN SAYEED
Queen's University (Ontario)
Author, *Politics in Pakistan*

KARATE

It seems impossible that people could punch through bricks with their bare hands. But for masters of karate, that would be easy.

Karate is a spectacular and powerful method of unarmed self-defense. It combines kicking and punching with knowledge of weaknesses in the human body. Karate students can fight back against muggers and bullies with their hands, feet, elbows, knees, fingers, and other parts of the body—even the head. Using karate, it is possible to overcome an attacker with a single blow.

Besides being a means of self-defense, karate is a popular sport. It is also a system of exercise that builds agility, flexibility, and strength.

Karate masters place great importance on controlling their fighting ability, since it would not be fair for them to fight with untrained people. They live by a strict code of morals and do not fight unless attacked.

▶ HISTORY OF KARATE

In ancient times, a method of fighting began to develop in Okinawa. Around 1600, Japanese warriors invaded the island. To maintain control of the Okinawans, the Japanese made it a crime to own any weapon. From that time on, secret training in unarmed fighting increased among Okinawan farmers and their families. The Okinawans were also helped by Chinese visitors who knew many different ways to fight. They taught the Okinawans the points on the body that could be easily hurt—the eyes, the spine, the groin, the joints, and so on. The Okinawans toughened their hands by hitting hard posts and punching sand or gravel.

The Okinawans also invented ways to use their farm tools as weapons. Some karate schools still teach students how to fight with the *kama* (sickle), the *nunchaku* (flail), the *tonfa* (a short stick), the *bo* (a long wooden staff), the *sai* (a short pitchfork), and the *eku* (a long club).

These Okinawan fighting arts were taught secretly for over 300 years. Then, about 1920, an Okinawan, Gichin Funakoshi, first taught karate to the Japanese. Funakoshi, who is known as the "father of karate," started to learn the different Okinawan ways of fight-

ing at the age of 11. He combined those methods into one style before he began teaching in Japan. He also taught the idea that karate students do not attack anyone. They use karate only to defend against wrongdoers.

Today, karate is taught worldwide. Karate was introduced to the United States in the early 1950's, and many people have become highly skilled in this martial (fighting) art.

▶ LEARNING KARATE

A karate student is called a **karate-ka**. The practice gym is called a **dojo**. Most dojos have mats on the floor for barefoot practice and mirrors on the walls so that the students can check their form as they practice their punches and kicks.

A lesson usually begins with stretching exercises. Other exercises, including push-ups and sit-ups, are for strength and stamina.

As students progress, they learn **katas.** These are complex, dancelike patterns of imagined attacks and defenses, often performed with great speed. Like shadowboxing, katas are performed alone and are an excellent way of maintaining overall fitness. A well-performed kata—with its flowing, rhythmic movements—is also an art form, like ballet dancing or gymnastic routines.

Just as boxing does, karate stresses keeping one's balance during movement and co-ordinating one's breathing with punching.

▶ SPARRING

A beginning student is taught to punch or kick at a certain spot on a partner's body. The partner practices by blocking the attack. This kind of sparring is done carefully and slowly to prevent injuries. More advanced students spar more freely, at almost full speed, but without actually hitting each other hard. They learn to pull the punch or kick at the last instant so that their practice partners do not get hurt.

What is the difference between karate and judo?

Karate uses a variety of blocks, kicks, and punches for self-defense. Judo basically depends upon the use of balance and leverage to pull, push, or throw an opponent to the ground. Both words come from the Japanese. Karate means "empty hand," and judo means the "gentle art."

Karate was originally developed on Okinawa, an island near Japan. Other Asian fighting methods that resemble karate have their own names. Kung fu is Chinese; tae kwon do is Korean.

Left: A black-belt karate-ka demonstrates a high front kick. Right: a black-belt karate-ka tests the power of his blows by breaking a wooden board with his bare hand.

▶ SPORT KARATE

In sport karate, two contestants spar with each other. Sometimes the rules allow only light contact. But sometimes they allow the fighters to spar with full contact. In this case they wear padded gloves and footwear. Points are scored by landing blows.

Karate tournaments may also have kata competitions. Kata competitors are judged on such things as form, correct focus of kicks and punches, power, and proper rhythm and breathing.

▶ BREAKING

The kicks and punches of a trained karate-ka are dangerously powerful. For this reason, students never strike each other bare-handed with full force. Those who wish to test the power of their blows do so by hitting objects. Boards, bricks, rocks, concrete slabs, and roofing tiles are commonly broken by karate-kas to test strength—or just to provide a show. More unusual objects have also been broken by karate masters—cast-iron pump handles and large blocks of ice.

▶ THE BLACK BELT

Beginning students wear white belts in the dojo. The instructor keeps track of the stu- dents' progress by the color of their belts. A new belt is awarded after every test and pro- motion. The white belt is usually followed by a yellow belt, then a green belt, then a brown belt. It might be necessary to pass five tests to earn a green belt, then perhaps nine tests to earn the brown belt. After passing the tenth test, students would be allowed to wear a black belt, the symbol of mastery of the basic skills and ideals of karate. To earn a black belt, students must perform a number of katas well and spar confidently with trained attackers. They must also have developed the ability to control themselves and their fighting techniques. After earning a black belt, a stu- dent may become an instructor and teach the art of karate to other students.

Earning a first-degree black belt usually takes two to four years of hard practice. There are ten degrees of black belts. Second- and third-degree belts are awarded to conscien- tious karate-kas who have been dedicated in their training and teaching. Higher rankings are given to honor advanced martial artists who demonstrate exceptional dignity and ded- ication to the art of karate.

JOHN H. STEWART
Media consultant, martial arts subjects

KARL (Kings of Sweden). See CHARLES.

A young kart driver concentrates on the race. Karts can reach high speeds, and the driver wears the appropriate safety gear—crash helmet with visor, flame-resistant suit and gloves.

KARTING

The sport of karting came tearing out of the parking lots of southern California in the mid-1950's. Within a few years, adults and children in many countries were taking up the sport of kart racing. It is still popular in many places.

A kart is a tiny racing car, made of a frame, four wheels, a seat, and an engine. Depending on the type of racing, drivers either sit up or recline (lie back).

You can buy a competitive kart from a manufacturer or dealer. For safety, it is important to keep the kart in good condition. You should make sure that it is checked often by a mechanic.

Before buying a kart, you should be certain that you can drive it safely. You should also find out whether there is a place where you can drive it legally. Karts are not permitted on streets and highways.

▶ RACING

There are three types of kart racing—sprint, speedway, and road racing. Most events are for adults. But children at least 9 years old may drive in the Rookie Junior Class in sprint and speedway events.

Sprint racing takes place on specially built courses with many turns. A lap, or circuit, is usually 0.4 to 0.8 kilometer (¼ to ½ mile) in length. Speeds can reach 95 kilometers (60 miles) per hour. In sprint racing, the karts are driven in the sit-up position.

Sprint races are run in three events, or heats, of ten laps each. The driver with the best combined record in the three heats becomes the overall winner. There are 15 classes of competition, based on such factors as weight, driver's age and experience, engine size, and engine modification.

Speedway racing is done on an oval dirt track. The length of each lap is usually 0.2 or 0.4 kilometer (⅛ or ¼ mile). Speedway karts use the same sit-up style of frame used in sprint racing. There are seven speedway classes. As with sprint racing, speedway racing uses the three-heat system to determine winners.

Road racing takes place on long tracks. Lap lengths are usually between 3 and 5 kilometers (2 and 3 miles). The driver who completes the greatest number of laps in an hour is the winner. There are 15 classes in kart road racing. Drivers usually race in a reclining position. This reduces air resistance and helps their karts go faster. Road-racing karts can reach speeds of 195 kilometers (120 miles) per hour.

▶ RACING COMPETITIONS AND AWARDS

Local, regional, and national competitions are held at various times during the year to test the skills of drivers and mechanics. Trophies are awarded at most events. Some professional events offer cash prizes.

The International Kart Federation (IKF) in Covina, California, and the World Karting Association in North Canton, Ohio, govern kart racing in the United States. In Canada, the Canadian Automobile Sports Clubs in Toronto, Ontario, has a national karting director. National and regional karting organizations provide information about karting events and set the rules for competitions.

RON BLACK
Consultant, International Kart Federation

KASHMIR

Few places in the world can equal the scenic beauty of Kashmir, which is also known as the state of Jammu and Kashmir. It is a region of sparkling rivers and lakes, lush forests and meadows, and towering snowcapped mountains. Poets and artists have described it in verse and in paintings. In the past the emperors of India spent their summers in Kashmir. In more recent times it has attracted tourists and vacationers from many countries. Today Kashmir is divided. It is claimed by both India and Pakistan, and part of it is occupied by China.

▶ THE PEOPLE

Kashmir has a population of approximately 6,000,000. About half of the people live in the Vale of Kashmir, a beautiful valley that is the best-known part of the region.

Most of the people of Kashmir are Muslims. There are also Hindus, some Christians, Buddhists, and members of tribal religious groups. The people who live in the Vale, known as Kashmiris, are mainly Muslims. The Hindu people to the south, in the district of Jammu, are known as Dogras. In the Pakistani part of Kashmir most of the people have the same traditions and religion (Islam) as the people of Pakistan. In Ladakh on the eastern border of Kashmir the people are related to the Tibetans in customs, language, and religion (Buddhism).

Agriculture is the main occupation of the people. Crops are grown in the valleys and on the terraces along slopes. The main crops are rice, corn, and wheat. Fruits and vegetables are grown in the Vale, the most fertile area. Sheepherding and goat-herding are important activities.

Because of its spectacular mountain scenery Kashmir is sometimes called the Switzerland of the Orient. The Vale of Kashmir is famous as a tourist center in Asia. Visitors to the Vale and nearby areas enjoy the region's natural beauty and such sports as skiing, hunting, hiking, boating, and horseback riding.

Srinagar is the heart of Kashmir. This city is the center of a world-famous handicraft industry. The Kashmiris have a long tradition of making woolen rugs, embroidered shawls, cashmere sweaters, wood carvings, papier-

KASHMIR

Srinagar

mâché articles, jewelry, and furniture. The Jhelum River winds through the heart of Srinagar. Picturesque wooden homes with balconies line the sides of the river. Tourists who wish to do so may live in the delightful houseboats moored in the lakes around Srinagar. An unusual attraction of Srinagar is the floating gardens on Dal Lake. These gardens are actually long rafts covered with soil, on which vegetables are grown.

▶ THE LAND

Kashmir has an area of about 223,000 square kilometers (86,000 square miles). It is located in the Himalaya mountains where Pakistan, India, and China meet.

Entering Kashmir from the south, one first crosses a narrow plain called the Punjab plain. Beyond the plain is a hilly area known as the Outer Himalayas, where elevations range from 600 to 1,200 meters (2,000 to 4,000 feet). Farther north is a higher range known as the Lesser Himalayas. Still farther north are the Great Himalayas, where some peaks are over 7,600 meters (25,000 feet) high. The Vale of Kashmir lies in a broad valley between the Lesser and Great Himalayas, at an elevation of about 1,600 meters (5,200 feet). In northern Kashmir are great plateaus and the towering, snowcapped peaks of the Karakoram range. In the Karakoram range in Kashmir is the famous K2 (Mount Godwin Austen), the world's second highest mountain after Mount Everest. It rises to a height of 8,611 meters (28,250 feet) near the Chinese border.

A number of the great rivers of India and Pakistan have their origins in Kashmir or pass through the region. The most important of these are the Indus, Jhelum, Ravi, and Chenab rivers.

Wular and Dal lakes in the Vale are used for fishing and boating. Most of the other lakes in Kashmir are located in high mountains and are difficult to reach.

Climate. The Punjab plain and southern mountains have a humid subtropical climate. In the high parts of the Himalaya and Karakoram mountains the climate ranges from subarctic to arctic. Between these extremes are many variations in temperature, rainfall, and snowfall. The main causes of such variations are differences in elevation and the shielding effects of mountains.

The wettest sections of Kashmir are along the southern slopes of the Outer and Lesser Himalayas. They receive 1,000 to 1,800 millimeters (40 to 80 inches) of rainfall annually. Nearly all of it occurs in the summer monsoon season. The Vale of Kashmir receives more moderate precipitation. Much of it falls in the winter in the form of snow. The rest of Kashmir is quite dry.

Natural Resources. Over 10 percent of Kashmir's area is covered with forests. Among the more important trees are the chir pine, which is tapped for turpentine, and the deodar, used for building houseboats and making railway ties. Chinar, fir, spruce, juniper, and walnut trees are used in a variety of industries, such as furniture-making, wood carving, and construction. A number of medicinal plants grown in Kashmir are useful in the making of drugs. Sericulture—raising silkworms to produce raw silk—is second in importance to lumbering as an export industry. Sericulture dates back to the 16th century.

Among the many wild animals that live in Kashmir are mountain goats and sheep, deer, antelope, bears, and snow leopards. There are also ducks, geese, pheasant, and other game birds.

Minerals of commercial value found in Kashmir include rock salt, limestone, gold, coal, bauxite, sapphire, gypsum, and china clay.

▶**HISTORY**

The Khasis, who were among the first inhabitants of this region, called it Kasmir. The modern name Kashmir derives from this. Hindus controlled parts of Kashmir from ancient times until the 14th century, when it was conquered by the Muslims. Under the Muslim sultans many of the people were converted to the Islamic faith. In the 16th century, Kashmir became a part of the Indian Mogul Empire. In later periods, Kashmir was ruled by the Afghans and the Sikh kingdom of the Punjab. During that time additional territory was added to Kashmir through wars of conquest. Later, in the 19th century, the British moved into the area and established their authority. In 1846 they granted hereditary rule to the male heirs of Gulab Singh, a Dogra prince. But British influence continued until 1947. In that year the Indian subcontinent, which had been ruled by the British Government since 1858, was divided into two independent countries, India (Hindu) and Pakistan (Muslim).

The Kashmir Dispute. The Indian subcontinent was divided because of the long history of strife between its Hindu and Muslim populations. This strife carried over into Jammu and Kashmir. The ruler, Maharajah Sir Hari Singh, was a Hindu. But most of the people were Muslims. Pakistan's leaders expected the territory to become part of their country. But when Pakistani hill tribes invaded Jammu and Kashmir, the Maharajah chose to join India. Pakistani soldiers then joined in the attempt to take control of the territory. Indian troops were rushed to the area as the undeclared war ignited. With the help of the United Nations, a truce was arranged early in 1949.

As a result of the war, Pakistan occupied about one third of the region. India controlled the remaining territory. India's claim to the territory was based on the right of

Above: Water taxis and a picturesque houseboat on one of the many scenic lakes in Kashmir. *Right:* Rugs for sale are displayed on the side of a merchant's house in Srinagar.

its ruler to join the nation of his choice. Pakistan's claim was based on the region's Muslim majority.

In 1952 the princely status of Jammu and Kashmir was abolished. China occupied the eastern part of the region as a result of border wars with India in 1959 and 1962. The Kashmir dispute led to renewed hostilities between India and Pakistan in 1965. The fighting was ended in 1966 by the Declaration of Tashkent, but there again were armed clashes during the brief India-Pakistan war of 1971. The Simla Agreement of 1972 slightly modified the cease-fire lines.

The issue remains unresolved. The Indian-controlled part of the region is governed as a state of India. The Pakistani-controlled section is called Azad ("Free") Kashmir and has its own government. Direct talks between Indian and Pakistani leaders on the Kashmir dispute were held in the 1990's, but little real progress was made.

DAVID FIRMAN
Towson State University

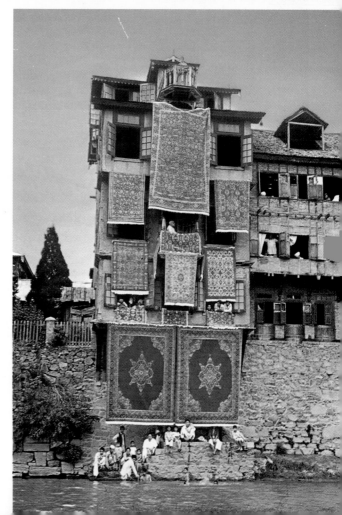

KAZAKHSTAN

Kazakhstan

Kazakhstan (or Kazakstan) is the second largest in area of the 15 republics that formerly made up the Soviet Union. It is exceeded in size only by the vast Russian Federation. Kazakhstan, which means "land of the Kazakhs," gained its independence in 1991, as the Soviet Union was breaking apart. Situated in north central Asia, Kazakhstan is bordered on the west by the Caspian Sea, on the north by the Russian Federation, on the east by China, and on the south by the other former Soviet Central Asian republics —Uzbekistan, Kyrgyzstan, Tajikistan, and Turkmenistan.

People. The Kazakhs were originally nomads and herders of livestock who lived in felt tents and depended for their food on the meat and milk of their animals. Today, most lead a more settled existence. However, they still define themselves first as members of a group, then a tribe, and only after that as a nation. The Kazakhs are a mixture of Turkic and Mongol stock and look more Asian than their Uzbek neighbors to the south. Their language is related to Turkish. In religion, the Kazakhs are Muslims.

Top: A Kazakh man offers his peppers for sale at an open-air market. Ethnically, the Kazakhs are a mixture of Turkic and Mongol peoples. *Left:* Kazakhstan's land, although vast in area, includes large semi-desert regions, suitable only for grazing livestock. Other areas, if irrigated, can produce cotton and food grains. The climate is often extreme, with long, cold winters and short, hot summers.

Kazakhs are a minority in their own country. They make up about 40 percent of the total population, although they predominate in the south. Russians form another 40 percent of the population and are concentrated in the north and in the cities. They are a majority in Almaty (formerly Alma-Ata), the largest city. There are also significant numbers of Ukrainians as well as Belarusians and Volga Germans. The Germans were deported to Kazakhstan, along with some other "punished" nationalities in the years before and during World War II. The Russians and other Slavs have traditionally belonged to the Eastern Orthodox Church.

Land. Enormous in size, Kazakhstan includes several different regions. These include the steppe, or grassland, in the north; the semi-desert plain in the center and southwest; the fertile valleys bordering on the mountains of Tien Shan in the southeast; and the desolate Caspian Sea coast. The Aral Sea lies on the border with Uzbekistan. Overall, the climate is dry, with limited rainfall. Winters are long and cold and frequently snowy. Summers are short and hot.

Economy. Kazakhstan is rich in mineral resources. It is a major producer of lead, zinc, and copper, as well as coal, oil, iron ore, and gold and other rare metals. Kazakhstan was the leading cattle-breeding region of the Soviet Union and an important producer of wheat and other grains, cotton, and tobacco. The Soviets developed its industry, which includes the manufacture of machinery, steel, and textiles, and other products.

History and Government. The early history of southern Kazakhstan, like that of Uzbekistan, was marked by successive waves of invaders. The Turkic and Mongol invasions were to have the most lasting effect. The Muslim religion was probably first brought by Arab traders in the 800's, but it did not become firmly rooted until the 1300's.

Russian penetration began in the 1700's and was completed by 1864, as one Kazakh community after another swore allegiance to the Russian czar, or emperor. A revolt in the 1800's against Russian rule failed, as did one in 1916. An attempt to form a Kazakh nationalist government after the overthrow of the Russian Empire in 1917 was short-lived.

Under the new government of the Soviet Union, Kazakhstan first became an autono-

FACTS and figures

REPUBLIC OF KAZAKHSTAN is the official name of the country.

LOCATION: North central Asia.

AREA: 1,049,000 sq mi (2,717,300 km²).

POPULATION: 17,000,000 (estimate).

CAPITAL: Astana.

LARGEST CITY: Almaty.

MAJOR LANGUAGES: Kazakh, Russian.

MAJOR RELIGIOUS GROUPS: Muslim, Eastern Orthodox Christian.

GOVERNMENT: Republic. **Head of state**—president. **Head of government**—prime minister (appointed by the president). **Legislature**—Parliament (made up of the Senate and the Majilis).

CHIEF PRODUCTS: Agricultural—wheat and other grains, cotton, tobacco, cattle and other livestock. **Manufactured**—machinery, steel, textiles. **Mineral**—lead, zinc, copper, coal, iron ore, gold.

MONETARY UNIT: Tenge (1 tenge = 100 tein).

mous republic within the Soviet republic. It received the status of a separate union republic in 1936. The Kazakhs suffered greatly from 1929 to 1931 when agriculture was brought under state control. In the resulting famine, the Kazakhs lost most of their cattle and saw their population decline by one-quarter.

During the late 1980's, the Kazakh Communist party head, Nursultan Nazarbayev, became a key associate of Soviet leader Mikhail Gorbachev. In 1991, Kazakhstan joined other Soviet republics in declaring its independence, with Nazarbayev as its president. Kazakhstan was admitted to the United Nations in 1992.

Kazakhstan adopted its present constitution in 1994. It provides for an elected president as head of state and chief executive who appoints a prime minister to lead the Council of Ministers and the legislature. A referendum in 1995 increased the powers of the president, and the capital was moved from Almaty to Astana (formerly Aqmola). Nazarbayev was re-elected president in 1999.

MICHAEL RYWKIN
Author, *Moscow's Muslim Challenge: Soviet Central Asia*

KEATS, JOHN (1795–1821)

John Keats, one of England's great poets, was born in London on October 31, 1795, the eldest of four children. His father worked in John's grandfather's livery stable. When John was 8, his father died in a fall from a horse. Six years later, his mother died of tuberculosis, leaving the children in the care of their grandmother. She appointed Richard Abbey, a tea merchant, as their guardian.

In 1803, John entered school at Enfield, near London, where at first he showed more interest in games and fighting than in his books. But under the influence of the headmaster's son, Charles Cowden Clarke, Keats learned to love reading, especially poetry. His guardian, however, cared little for book learning. He removed Keats from school in 1811 and apprenticed him to a surgeon.

Although Keats completed his medical training at Guy's Hospital in 1816, he never practiced medicine. The same year, he wrote

I HAD A DOVE

I had a dove and the sweet dove died;
And I have thought it died of grieving:
O what could it grieve for? Its feet were tied,
With a silken thread of my own hand's weaving;
Sweet little red feet! why should you die—
Why should you leave me, sweet bird! Why?
You lived alone in the forest-tree,
Why, pretty thing! would you not live with me?
I kissed you oft and gave you white peas;
Why not live sweetly, as in the green trees?

From ENDYMION

A thing of beauty is a joy for ever:
Its loveliness increases; it will never
Pass into nothingness; but still will keep
A bower quiet for us, and a sleep
Full of sweet dreams, and health, and quiet
    breathing.
Therefore, on every morrow, are we wreathing
A flowery band to bind us to the earth,
Spite of despondence, of the inhuman dearth
Of noble natures, of the gloomy days,
Of all the unhealthy and o'er-darken'd ways
Made for our searching: yes, in spite of all,
Some shape of beauty moves away the pall
From our dark spirits. Such the sun, the moon,
Trees old and young, sprouting a shady boon
For simple sheep; and such are daffodils
With the green world they live in; and clear rills
That for themselves a cooling covert make
'Gainst the hot season; the mid-forest brake,

Rich with a sprinkling of fair musk-rose blooms:
And such too is the grandeur of the dooms
We have imagined for the mighty dead;
All lovely tales that we have heard or read:
An endless fountain of immortal drink,
Pouring unto us from the heaven's brink.
    Nor do we merely feel these essences
For one short hour; no, even as the trees
That whisper round a temple become soon
Dear as the temple's self, so does the moon,
The passion poesy, glories infinite,
Haunt us till they become a cheering light
Unto our souls, and bound to us so fast,
That, whether there be shine, or gloom o'ercast,
They always must be with us, or we die.

WHEN I HAVE FEARS . . .

When I have fears that I may cease to be
    Before my pen has glean'd my teeming brain,
Before high piled books, in charact'ry,
    Hold like rich garners the full-ripen'd grain;
When I behold, upon the night's starr'd face,
    Huge cloudy symbols of a high romance,
And think that I may never live to trace
    Their shadows, with the magic hand of
    chance;
And when I feel, fair creature of an hour!
    That I shall never look upon thee more,
Never have relish in the faery power
    Of unreflecting love;—then on the shore
Of the wide world I stand alone, and think
Till Love and Fame to nothingness do sink.

his first great poem, "On First Looking Into Chapman's Homer," which was published in his first book, *Poems*, in 1817. Keats's genius lay in his ability to identify intensely with the subjects he wrote of and to convey his feelings in words. He grew rapidly in skill, writing the 4,000-line *Endymion* in 1817 and *Isabella* and *Hyperion* in 1818.

In 1818, Keats's younger brother Tom was dying of tuberculosis. While nursing Tom, who died on December 1, Keats met Fanny Brawne and soon declared his love for her. But they were never to marry, for Keats caught tuberculosis from his brother.

Before his illness became apparent in 1819, Keats wrote his greatest works—*The Eve of St. Agnes* in January; the odes "To a Nightingale," "On a Grecian Urn," and "On Melancholy" in May; *Lamia* and *The Fall of Hyperion* in the summer; and the ode "To Autumn" in September. All the while, he was also writing many of his most wonderful letters, which show his depth of self-knowledge and feeling.

The next year was filled with increasing illness and unhappiness. Fearing that close contact with Fanny would infect her with tuberculosis, and suffering from the belief that he was a failure, Keats left for the warmer climate of Italy in September 1820. He died in Rome on February 23, 1821, at the age of 25.

RANDEL HELMS
Arizona State University

KELLER, HELEN (1880–1968)

Helen Keller was known and admired throughout the world. Although blind and deaf, she lived a full life and brought hope, courage, and help to other disabled people.

She was born on June 27, 1880, on a farm near Tuscumbia, Alabama. For the first 18 months, she was a normal infant, but then an illness erased her sight and hearing, and, as a result, her speech. If it had not been for Anne Sullivan—who came in 1887 from the Perkins Institution for the Blind, in Boston, Massachusetts—Helen's world might have been forever dark and silent. As her teacher, Miss Sullivan helped Helen begin a life of purpose and achievement. The story is told in Miss Keller's book, *The Story of My Life* (1902).

Helen was eager to learn and had a remarkable mind. She entered Radcliffe College in 1900. Miss Sullivan sat beside her in the classroom and, through a system of touch signaling into Helen's hand, spelled out everything that was said. She read endlessly in this way to Helen, for few of the books that Helen needed were in braille (the writing system, which has characters made up of raised dots, used in books for the blind).

Helen graduated with honors in 1904. She continued to write and went on lecture tours with Miss Sullivan. She had learned to speak, but her speech was hard to understand, and Miss Sullivan would repeat to the audience all that Helen said. Helen worked for the American Foundation for the Blind and was active in social movements. Her later books include *Helen Keller's Journal* (1938) and *Teacher: Anne Sullivan Macy* (1955).

A tireless traveler, Helen Keller was honored throughout the world for her work on behalf of blind people. She died on June 1, 1968, in Westport, Connecticut.

Reviewed by ALLEN F. DAVIS
Temple University

KELLOGG, W. K. See MICHIGAN (Famous People).

KENNEDY, ANTHONY. See SUPREME COURT OF THE UNITED STATES (Profiles).

KENNEDY, EDWARD M. See KENNEDY, ROBERT F. AND EDWARD M.

Helen Keller (right), blind and deaf herself, devoted her life to helping disabled people. Polly Thompson (left) became her companion after Anne Sullivan died.

JOHN F. KENNEDY (1917–1963)

35th President of the United States

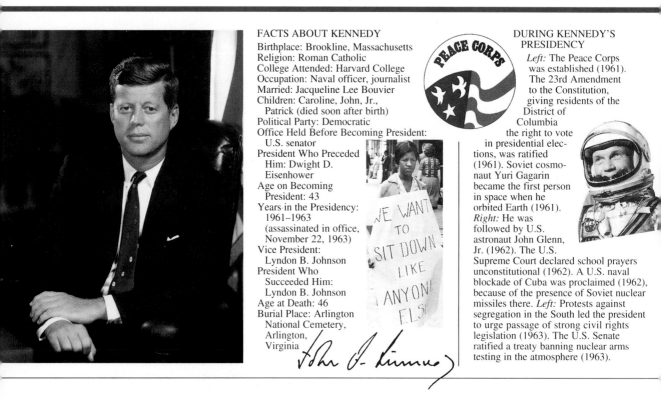

FACTS ABOUT KENNEDY

Birthplace: Brookline, Massachusetts
Religion: Roman Catholic
College Attended: Harvard College
Occupation: Naval officer, journalist
Married: Jacqueline Lee Bouvier
Children: Caroline, John, Jr.,
  Patrick (died soon after birth)
Political Party: Democratic
Office Held Before Becoming President:
  U.S. senator
President Who Preceded
  Him: Dwight D.
  Eisenhower
Age on Becoming
  President: 43
Years in the Presidency:
  1961–1963
  (assassinated in office,
  November 22, 1963)
Vice President:
  Lyndon B. Johnson
President Who
  Succeeded Him:
  Lyndon B. Johnson
Age at Death: 46
Burial Place: Arlington
  National Cemetery,
  Arlington,
  Virginia

DURING KENNEDY'S PRESIDENCY

Left: The Peace Corps was established (1961). The 23rd Amendment to the Constitution, giving residents of the District of Columbia the right to vote in presidential elections, was ratified (1961). Soviet cosmonaut Yuri Gagarin became the first person in space when he orbited Earth (1961). *Right:* He was followed by U.S. astronaut John Glenn, Jr. (1962). The U.S. Supreme Court declared school prayers unconstitutional (1962). A U.S. naval blockade of Cuba was proclaimed (1962), because of the presence of Soviet nuclear missiles there. *Left:* Protests against segregation in the South led the president to urge passage of strong civil rights legislation (1963). The U.S. Senate ratified a treaty banning nuclear arms testing in the atmosphere (1963).

KENNEDY, JOHN FITZGERALD. John F. Kennedy, whose ancestors came from Ireland, was the first Roman Catholic to become president of the United States. Aged 43 at the time of his election in 1960, he was also the youngest person ever elected to the country's highest office, although he was not the youngest to serve in it. Theodore Roosevelt was not quite 43 when the assassination of President William McKinley in 1901 elevated him to the presidency. Like McKinley, Kennedy was to die at the hands of an assassin.

A confrontation with the Soviet Union in Berlin and the discovery of Soviet nuclear missiles in Cuba brought the United States close to the brink of war during Kennedy's presidency. His support of demands by blacks for equality in civil rights shook the Democratic Party's long-standing grip on the South and tested his political leadership. Racial integration, economics, and other issues stirred fierce antagonisms throughout the United States. But for millions of Americans, the young president held great charm and even

greater hopes, and his violent death in 1963 brought many people to tears.

▶**EARLY LIFE**

John Fitzgerald Kennedy was born on May 29, 1917, in Brookline, Massachusetts, a suburb of Boston, into a family of wealth and strong political tradition. Both his grandfathers, Patrick J. Kennedy and John F. Fitzgerald, had been elected to public offices. Fitzgerald, in fact, had been mayor of Boston and had served in Congress.

Joseph P. Kennedy, father of the future president, was a financier and businessman who built one of the great private fortunes of his time. He was active in politics, too, holding several important posts, including ambassador to Great Britain. He and his wife, Rose Fitzgerald Kennedy, raised a family of nine children. John was the second born.

The family circle was close and warm, although the boys, four in all, were competitive, a trait that would distinguish them all their lives. The slightly built John (or Jack, as he was usually called) was often overshadowed by his older, sturdier brother, Joseph, Jr., who was likeable, outgoing, and aggressive. When Joseph, Jr., was born, his father was reported to have remarked that he would be the first Kennedy to become president.

However, young Joe would be killed while piloting a bomber in World War II, leadership of the new generation of Kennedys passing to John, who would also serve in the war, but survive it. The two younger brothers, Robert and Edward, would also have impressive political careers, although Robert's life, like John's, was to end tragically. An article on Robert and Edward Kennedy can be found following this article.

As a boy, Kennedy attended private schools in Brookline and New York City and went on to Choate School, a college preparatory school in Connecticut. Although his father was a graduate of Harvard and his brother Joe was studying at Harvard, John decided to continue his education at Princeton University. Joseph, Sr., kidded John about fleeing his older brother's shadow, but John simply said that he wanted to be with his Choate friends, who were going to Princeton. First, though, at his father's urging, he left for London in the summer of 1935 to attend a session of the London School of Economics. Soon after arriving, however, he came down with jaundice, a liver ailment, and had to return home. He entered Princeton as planned the following fall, but a

second attack of jaundice forced him to leave school. He spent months recuperating and the following year re-entered college, this time choosing Harvard.

▶ YOUNG MANHOOD

Harvard professors found John Kennedy "a pleasant, bright, easygoing student," although his grades were seldom higher than C in his first two years. He worked on the college newspaper and went out for swimming, football, sailing, and other sports. One day, he hurt his back in a junior varsity football game. It was the beginning of a painful injury that would bother him for the rest of his life.

Politics apparently did not concern him at first, but a visit to Europe in the summer of

The Kennedy family in 1934. Standing, from left: Joseph, Jr., John, Mrs. Joseph Kennedy, Jean, Patricia. Seated, from left: Robert, Edward, Mr. Joseph Kennedy, Eunice, Rosemary, Kathleen.

1937 increased his interest in world affairs. Another trip, this time to Eastern Europe in 1939, sharpened his intellectual interests noticeably. His grades improved dramatically in his senior year, and in 1940, he graduated from Harvard *cum laude* ("with honor"). World War II had already begun in Europe. Kennedy's senior thesis reflected his earlier observations so well that he turned it into a successful book, *Why England Slept*. It was his explanation of the inaction of democratic nations in the face of the early threats of war from Nazi Germany.

Kennedy commanded a torpedo boat in the Pacific during World War II. He became a hero for saving his crew after a Japanese destroyer cut his boat in half.

▶ THE WAR YEARS

Out of college, Kennedy was uncertain about his future. He thought about attending Yale Law School, went to business school at Stanford University for six months instead, then toured South America. In 1941 he tried to enlist in the Army but was rejected because of his old back injury. After five months of exercise to strengthen his back, he was accepted for service by the Navy.

Kennedy found his assignments, mostly paperwork, dull. When the United States entered World War II in December 1941, he applied for sea duty, underwent torpedo boat training, and was commissioned an ensign. The next year he shipped out for the South Pacific. There he became the central figure in one of the dramatic episodes of the war.

Exploits of PT-109. In the early hours before dawn on August 2, 1943, Kennedy, now a lieutenant (junior grade), was in command of the torpedo boat PT-109 on patrol near the Solomon Islands. Suddenly a Japanese destroyer plowed through the darkness and cut Kennedy's boat in half. Two of the twelve-man crew disappeared, one was badly burned, and others were less seriously hurt. Kennedy himself was thrown to the deck and his back re-injured, but he gathered his men on the bobbing bow, all that remained of his boat. When it seemed as if the bow would sink, Kennedy ordered everyone to make for an island about 3 miles (5 kilometers) away. Those who could not swim were told to hang onto a plank, once part of the gun mount, and push. Kennedy took charge of the burned crew member, and holding the straps of the man's life vest with his teeth, he towed him to the island.

Kennedy swam to other islands to try to find help but got caught in an ocean current and passed out, only his life vest saving him. Eventually, he and another officer found two natives in a canoe. Scratching a message on a coconut, Kennedy handed it to the natives, who carried it to a U.S. naval base. The men were rescued five days later. For his courage and leadership, Kennedy won the Navy and Marine Corps Medal.

He refused a chance to leave active duty, but malaria and his old back injury finally forced him into the hospital in 1944. After back surgery, he was discharged from the Navy in 1945.

▶ JOURNALISM, POLITICS, AND MARRIAGE

Still searching for a career, Kennedy went to work for the Hearst chain of newspapers. He covered the San Francisco conference that established the United Nations, British elections, and the Potsdam Conference held by the victorious Allied leaders at the end of World War II. Deciding that journalism was not for him, however, Kennedy turned to politics.

In 1946 he ran for the Democratic nomination for the U.S. House of Representatives from a Boston district. By hard campaigning, he defeated a large field of rivals for the nomination and easily won the election. After twice

other welfare benefits also stamped him as a liberal. But when some liberals resisted union reform legislation, Kennedy disagreed. He did not join the anti-union reformers, but took a moderate position. Only a master of the art of politics could, in those days, insist on any union reforms at all and still command the support of labor leaders, as Kennedy did.

winning re-election, in 1952 he sought the U.S. Senate seat from Massachusetts held by Republican Henry Cabot Lodge. Lodge was considered unbeatable and it was a banner year for Republican candidates, generally, but Kennedy won by a comfortable margin.

In 1953, Kennedy married Jacqueline Lee Bouvier in Newport, Rhode Island. They had a daughter, Caroline (1957–), and a son, John, Jr. (1960–99). Another child, Patrick, was born in 1963 but lived only a few days.

▶ HIS CONGRESSIONAL RECORD

Kennedy's record in Congress—six years in the House of Representatives and eight in the Senate—defied easy labeling. His strong liberal streak led him, for instance, to oppose the loyalty oath that college students had to take to get a loan. His support of labor's demands for higher-minimum-wage laws and

The McCarthy Issue. Kennedy displeased the liberals, however, by failing to take a strong position against McCarthyism. He was in the hospital, suffering from a recurrence of his old back ailment, when the Senate voted on December 2, 1954, to censure (reprimand) its Wisconsin Republican member, Joseph R. McCarthy. McCarthy's methods of investigating Communist influence in the United States during the early 1950s had caused great controversy. It was generally felt that his methods had violated rules of fair play and had unjustly damaged reputations. Liberals, in particular, criticized Kennedy for what they considered evasion of a difficult issue.

▶ CAMPAIGN FOR THE PRESIDENCY

Kennedy missed being nominated for vice president by a few votes at the National Democratic Convention in Chicago in 1956. But he gained an introduction to the millions of Americans who watched the convention on television, and when he decided to run for president in 1960, his name was widely known. Many people thought that his religion and his youthful appearance would handicap him. Kennedy faced the religion issue frankly, declaring his firm belief in the separation of church and state. He drew some criticism for his family's wealth, which enabled him to assemble a large staff and to get around the

Kennedy easily defeated his Republican opponent, Vice President Richard M. Nixon (on right), in electoral votes, but his popular vote margin was extremely close.

Left: President Kennedy signed a bill into law in 1961 naming Vice President Lyndon Johnson (right) chairman of the National Aeronautics and Space Council. *Top:* Soviet leader Nikita Khrushchev (right) tested Kennedy's resolve during the 1962 Cuban missile crisis. *Above:* The President and First Lady honored Nobel Prize winners at the White House in 1962. Novelist Pearl Buck is at left, and poet Robert Frost stands at right.

country in a private plane. But he attracted many doubting Democratic politicians to his side by winning delegate contests in every state primary he entered.

On gaining his party's nomination, Kennedy amazed nearly everybody by choosing Lyndon B. Johnson, who had opposed him for the nomination, as his vice-presidential running mate. Again, he used his considerable political skills to convince doubting friends that this was the practical course.

Kennedy's four television debates with the Republican candidate, Richard M. Nixon, were a highlight of the 1960 campaign. In the opinion of one television network president, they were "the most significant innovation in Presidential campaigns since popular elections began." The debates were important in Kennedy's victory—303 electoral votes to 219 for Nixon. The popular vote was breathtakingly close: Kennedy's winning margin was a fraction of 1 percent of the total vote.

▶HIS ADMINISTRATION

Kennedy's major problems as president were the Cold War with the Soviet Union and its Communist allies, the resistance of southerners in his own party to the demands of blacks for full civil rights, and unemployment. Soon after taking office in 1961, he had to deal with two dangerous confrontations with the Soviet Union.

Berlin. As if to test the new president's courage, the Soviets chose to make Berlin, the capital of pre-war Germany, a chief battleground of the Cold War. In the summer of 1961, they intensified their pressures on West Berlin, which was under the protection of the United States, Britain, and France and was entirely surrounded by Communist East German territory. Kennedy insisted on the Western Allies' right of access to West Berlin, and when the Communist authorities built a wall separating the city's eastern and western sectors, he responded by increasing U.S. military forces. The Soviet threat subsided in Berlin by 1962 but soon flared elsewhere.

Cuban Crisis. It struck closer to home, on the island of Cuba. Earlier, in April 1961, a group of Cubans, trained by the U.S. Central Intelligence Agency (CIA), had launched an unsuccessful invasion of the island in an attempt to overthrow the Communist regime of Fidel Castro. Kennedy accepted responsibility for the affair, although its planning had begun under the previous administration of President Dwight Eisenhower. The Cuban issue became far more serious in the fall of 1962, when aerial photographs revealed the presence of Soviet missiles and troops on the island. Kennedy insisted on their withdrawal, proclaiming a naval blockade of the island. The crisis lasted for more than a week, ending when Soviet leader Nikita Khrushchev agreed to the U.S. demand. See the article on the Cuban Missile Crisis in Volume C.

Other Foreign Policy Measures. Relations between the United States and the Soviet Union improved after the end of the Cuban missile crisis, at least on the surface, but Cold War tensions continued. Increased Communist guerrilla activity in South Vietnam and other parts of Southeast Asia led Kennedy to greatly increase the number of U.S. military advisors there. To counter Communist influence in Latin America, he established in 1961 the Alliance for Progress, a program of aid and cooperation between the United States and the countries of the region. A hopeful step was a treaty banning nuclear testing in the atmosphere, signed in 1963, by the United States, the Soviet Union, and Britain.

Civil Rights. The civil rights issue presented the most difficult challenge to the president at home. Demonstrations by blacks in the South for an end to segregation led Kennedy to declare a "moral crisis" and call for legislation providing equal rights for all. When rioting broke out at the University of Mississippi in 1962 over the enrollment of a black, James Meredith, the administration sent federal marshals backed by national guardsmen to the scene to restore order. This resulted in a white

The First Family: The president and Mrs. Kennedy celebrated Easter 1963 with their two children, John, Jr. (left) and Caroline (right).

anti-Kennedy backlash in the South, directed not only at the president but also at his brother Robert, who was attorney general.

Other Domestic Issues. Kennedy called his domestic program the New Frontier. Delaying tactics, more than actual rejections, by Congress hampered his record of legislative achievements. His hopes for new civil rights laws and a tax cut to help provide more jobs were unfulfilled at the time of his death. However, Congress did pass the Trade Expansion Act, which enabled the president to lower tariffs, or taxes on imports, to compete with nations of the European Community (now the European Union). One of Kennedy's most popular achievements was the Peace Corps, a volunteer organization that brought education and skills to developing countries of the world. See the article on the Peace Corps in Volume P.

Kennedy also appointed two new justices to the U.S. Supreme Court, Byron R. White and Arthur J. Goldberg. Goldberg had served as his secretary of labor.

Kennedy's flag-draped coffin was carried past a mourning crowd in Washington, D.C., in 1963. The president's accused assassin, Lee Harvey Oswald (*below*), was himself shot and killed soon after.

▶ **LIFE AND DEATH**

During all this, pain from his old back injury returned. Kennedy wore a small brace and suffered more than the public knew. Yet he loved life and politics. The image of vigor, friendliness, and humor that he gave to the country was real. Even with the burden of the presidency, he found time to read both for information and for pleasure. He wrote two books after he had entered politics, *Profiles in Courage* in 1956, which won the Pulitzer Prize, and *Strategy of Peace* in 1960. He had a deep sense of history and an appreciation of scholarship and was able to convey his thoughts in clear, forceful language.

On November 22, 1963, Kennedy was in Dallas, Texas, on a political tour of the state. Accompanied by Mrs. Kennedy and Texas governor John B. Connally, he was riding in an open car in a motorcade when shots rang out, striking the president in the head and neck. Kennedy was rushed to the hospital, but he died soon after without regaining consciousness. Governor Connally was also wounded but he recovered. As the news was relayed to a shocked nation, Vice President Lyndon Johnson was sworn in as president and flown to Washington, D.C.

Police arrested a man named Lee Harvey Oswald for the murder. Two days later, while being transferred from one jail to another, Oswald himself was shot to death by Jack Ruby, a Dallas nightclub owner.

A seven-member commission, headed by U.S. Chief Justice Earl Warren, was appointed by President Johnson to investigate the assassination. It reported that Oswald, alone, had fired the shots that killed the president, although questions surrounding Kennedy's death have continued to arouse speculation ever since. See the article on the Warren Report in Volume W-X-Y-Z.

JOSEPH A. LOFTUS
The New York Times Washington Bureau

WONDER QUESTION

Who was Lee Harvey Oswald?

Lee Harvey Oswald, the accused assassin of President John F. Kennedy, was born in New Orleans, Louisiana, on October 18, 1939, and spent his early life in various U.S. cities. He dropped out of school at the age of 16, and at 17, joined the Marine Corps. After his release from the Marines in 1959, he traveled to the Soviet Union, where he tried and failed to gain Soviet citizenship. Although sympathetic to Communism, he disliked life there, and in 1962, he returned to the United States with his Russian-born wife, Marina, and a baby daughter. In 1963 he sought but was denied permission to visit Cuba.

Oswald was in Dallas, Texas, working at the Texas School Book Depository, on November 22, 1963, when Kennedy's motorcade passed. According to the evidence of the Warren Commission, he fired the shots that killed the president from a sixth-floor window of the building. The weapon, an Italian-make rifle, had been purchased by mail. Oswald was also charged with killing a police officer, J.D. Tippit, who was trying to arrest him. Oswald's own murder by Jack Ruby, on November 24, while in police custody, heightened the air of conspiracy that some found in the president's assassination. Ruby died in prison in 1967.

KENNEDY, ROBERT F. (1925–1968) and EDWARD M. (1932–)

Robert F. (Bobby) Kennedy and Edward M. (Ted) Kennedy were the younger brothers of President John F. Kennedy. Both became well-known political leaders in their own right, and both were at one time considered candidates for the presidency. But Robert Kennedy's life, like that of John Kennedy, ended in assassination, and the career of Edward Kennedy was also marred by personal tragedy.

Robert Francis Kennedy was born on November 20, 1925, in Brookline, Massachusetts. After graduating from Harvard College (1948) and the University of Virginia Law School (1951), he served as an attorney in the Department of Justice and as a legal counsel to two U.S. Senate subcommittees. He also managed John F. Kennedy's successful campaign for the Senate in 1952 as well as his campaign for the presidency in 1960. Appointed attorney general by his brother in 1961, he aggressively prosecuted cases of civil rights violations against blacks and emerged as the president's closest adviser.

He continued as attorney general after Kennedy's assassination in 1963, but in 1964 he resigned to run for the Senate, winning a seat from New York. There, his support of civil rights and social welfare measures and his criticism of the Vietnam War won him a wide following among liberal Democrats. Kennedy was in Los Angeles, California, campaigning for the 1968 Democratic presidential nomination, when he was shot by Sirhan B. Sirhan, a Jordanian immigrant, and died on June 6, 1968.

Robert F. (Bobby) Kennedy was attorney general under his brother President John F. Kennedy and served in the U.S. Senate. He was assassinated in 1968, while campaigning for the Democratic presidential nomination.

Edward Moore Kennedy was born in Brookline on February 22, 1932. Like his brother Robert, he graduated from Harvard College (1956) and the University of Virginia Law School (1959). In 1962 he was elected to the U.S. Senate seat formerly held by President John F. Kennedy. At 30, he was the minimum age allowed for a senator.

Re-elected regularly thereafter, Kennedy became an influential figure in the Senate and a leader of its liberal Democratic wing. He has served as assistant majority leader and as chairman of the Judiciary and the Labor and Human Resources committees. Although often mentioned as a possible presidential candidate in the 1970's, his career was set back by an automobile accident, in 1969, at Chappaquiddick Island, Massachusetts, in which a woman companion was drowned. Kennedy also cited the deaths of his brothers, which made him head of the family, for his reluctance to run for higher office. He did seek the 1980 Democratic presidential nomination but lost to Jimmy Carter. Kennedy won re-election for a sixth time in 1994.

Reviewed by RICHARD S. KIRKENDALL
Iowa State University

KENNEDY SPACE CENTER. See SPACE AGENCIES AND CENTERS.

The youngest of the Kennedy brothers, Edward M. (Ted) Kennedy continued the family's political tradition with a long and influential career in the U.S. Senate.

KENTUCKY

The name "Kentucky" comes from a Native American word that scholars believe meant "great meadow" or "land of tomorrow."

Kentucky is nicknamed the Bluegrass State, after a type of grass that grows in the state's rich limestone soil. Kentucky bluegrass is not really blue, although in the spring, the new growth blooms in a distinctive blue tint.

State flag

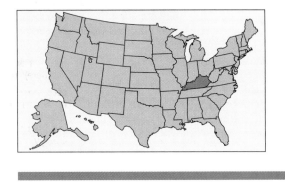

Located in the east central United States, Kentucky lies between the Appalachian Mountains in the east and the Mississippi River in the west. The Ohio River forms the northern border of the state. Kentucky is one of only four states officially called a commonwealth, which in this instance means the same as a state. The others are Massachusetts, Virginia, and Pennsylvania.

Kentucky's landscape is dramatic in its contrasts. Majestic mountains in the eastern part of the state are covered with hardwood and pine forests. Gentle hills and lush, level pastures dominate the central regions, while western Kentucky has large areas of level farmland, where burley tobacco, corn, soybeans, and wheat are grown. Cattle, hogs, and horses also are raised in large numbers.

Industry was slow to develop in Kentucky. In the 1800's, the state supported a small iron industry. Rope making was also important to the economy until vast coal deposits were discovered and coal mining became Kentucky's primary source of income. Coal mining, farming, and manufacturing are still important to the economy. One of Kentucky's most famous products is bourbon whiskey. Tourism has also become a thriving industry.

Each year, many visitors come to see what might be the state's most familiar symbol—the prized Thoroughbred horses that are raised on Kentucky's lush bluegrass pasturelands. Every spring since 1875, thousands of people have traveled to Churchill Downs racetrack in Louisville, Kentucky's largest city, to witness the thrill of the Kentucky Derby, the nation's most prestigious horse racing event. Other popular tourist attractions include the birthplaces of the two presidents of the Civil War, Jefferson Davis of the Confederate States and Abraham Lincoln of the United States.

▶ **LAND**

Kentucky is located midway between Canada and the Gulf of Mexico. The land slopes greatly from east to west. At 4,145 feet (1,263 meters), Black Mountain in eastern Kentucky is the highest point in the state. The lowest point is 257 feet (78 meters) above sea level, in the west along the Mississippi River.

Land Regions

Kentucky is divided into three major landforms—the Appalachian Plateau, the Interior Low Plateaus, and the Coastal Plain.

The Appalachian Plateau, which extends from New York to Alabama, covers the eastern third of Kentucky, where it is known as the Cumberland Plateau. Valleys and steep ridges characterize the eastern edge of this region. The highest and longest ridges are in the Cumberland and the Pine mountain systems. The western part of the Cumberland Plateau is lower in elevation. Much of the land there is gently rolling. Rich deposits of coal are found here in an area known as the Eastern Coal Field.

The Interior Low Plateaus extend from the Cumberland Plateau in the east to the Tennessee River in the west. The surface of the land varies from level to hilly. The northeast-

Opposite page, clockwise from left: Louisville, on the Ohio River, is Kentucky's largest city. Kentuckians are renowned for their love of horses. Most of the state's horse farms are located in north central Kentucky, near Lexington.

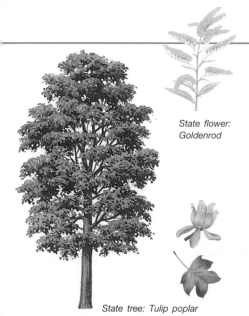

State flower: Goldenrod

State tree: Tulip poplar

FACTS AND FIGURES

Location: East central United States; bordered on the north by Illinois, Indiana, and Ohio, on the east by West Virginia and Virginia, on the south by Tennessee, and on the west by Missouri and Illinois.

Area: 40,409 sq mi (104,660 km²); rank, 37th.

Population: 3,828,000 (1994 estimate); rank, 24th.

Elevation: *Highest*—4,145 ft (1,263 m) at Black Mountain; *lowest*—257 ft (78 m) along the Mississippi River in Fulton County.

Capital: Frankfort.

Statehood: June 1, 1792; 15th state.

State Motto: *United we stand, divided we fall.*

State Song: "My Old Kentucky Home."

Nickname: Bluegrass State.

Abbreviations: KY; Ky.

State bird: Cardinal

Above: Horses graze on the lush rolling hills of the Bluegrass Basin. **Left:** Kentucky's first pioneers came through the Cumberland Gap, a natural passage through the Cumberland Mountains.

ern part of this region is known as the Bluegrass, or Lexington, Basin. It is one of the most beautiful parts of Kentucky. Most of the land is gently rolling, although a rough, hilly area, known as the Knobs Region, surrounds the basin.

Also in this area is the Pennyroyal region (pronounced "Pennyrile"), which extends southwestward from the Bluegrass Basin to the Tennessee River. This part of Kentucky gets its name from a small plant of the mint family that grows abundantly there. The region is known for its sinkholes, underground streams, and fascinating rooms of shimmering underground caves, including the famous Mammoth-Flint Ridge, the longest system of caves in the world. At the center of the Pennyroyal region is a treeless area known as the Barrens. To the north and west lies the Western Coal Field, which contains more than half of the state's tremendous coal reserves.

The Coastal Plain, known in Kentucky as the Jackson Purchase Region, is bounded on three sides by rivers, which have smoothed the surface to a rolling plain. The only hills are in a narrow strip near the Tennessee River. The low, flat land in the southwest has marshes and sluggish streams.

Rivers and Lakes

The Ohio River flows along the entire northern border of Kentucky, where its tributaries include the Kentucky, Green, Licking, and Salt rivers. The Cumberland River flows westward from the Cumberland Mountain Ridge in southeastern Kentucky southward into Tennessee before re-entering western Kentucky. The Tennessee River forms part of the Kentucky and Tennessee border. The Mississippi loops through the western part of the state.

Most of Kentucky's many lakes are reservoirs, created by dams on the rivers. The largest is Lake Cumberland in the southeast. The lakes are an important source of income. Fishing and boating bring many visitors to

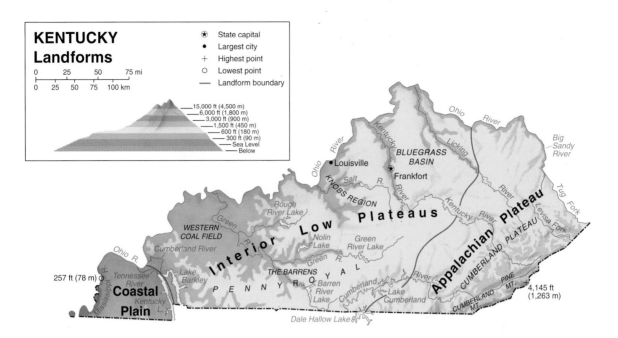

KENTUCKY Landforms

✪	State capital
•	Largest city
+	Highest point
○	Lowest point
—	Landform boundary

15,000 ft (4,500 m)
6,000 ft (1,800 m)
3,000 ft (900 m)
1,500 ft (450 m)
600 ft (180 m)
300 ft (90 m)
Sea Level
Below

0 25 50 75 mi
0 25 50 75 100 km

the state. The dams that form the lakes also provide electrical power and water supplies.

Climate

Kentucky's climate is generally mild. January is the coldest month, with temperatures averaging 36°F (2°C) in the south and 29°F (–2°C) in the north. In July, temperatures average 78°F (26°C) in the south and 75°F (24°C) in the north.

Precipitation in Kentucky falls in the form of rain and melted snow. Average rainfall is 41 inches (1,041 millimeters) in the north and about 52 inches (1,320 millimeters) in the south. Winter and spring are the wettest seasons of the year.

Plant and Animal Life

Vast forests once covered most of Kentucky, and the extensive hardwood forests of oak, hickory, beech, maple, and poplar trees were invaluable to the early pioneers. They used

the timber for fuel and to build houses, furniture, and boats, whiskey barrels, and railroad ties. By the early 1900's, much of the virgin woodlands had been cut down. While Kentucky remains heavily wooded, some areas still are in need of replanting.

Kentucky has an abundance of wildlife. Many species of birds and small animals inhabit the forests of the state. The most common are squirrels, deer, groundhogs, raccoons, foxes, opossums, and rabbits. Wild turkeys, ducks, and geese were found in

The Cumberland Falls on the Cumberland River is the second largest waterfall east of the Rocky Mountains. Only Niagara Falls is larger.

countless numbers. Rarer birds include the American egret and great blue heron. Rivers and streams are stocked with bass, bluegill, trout, catfish, and many other fish.

Natural Resources

Kentucky is rich in natural resources. Large amounts of timber, water, coal, natural gas, oil, limestone, gravel, clay, and fluorspar can be found throughout the state. Kentuckians realize the importance of these resources and are making progress in conservation. Laws have been passed to help reduce water pollution and to reclaim land that has been eroded, deforested, or damaged, particularly by extensive coal mining.

▶ PEOPLE

Mounds, cave shelters, and campsites show that many prehistoric Indian peoples once occupied Kentucky. By the time the first

white settlement was established in 1774–75, no Indian settlements remained, although the Cherokee and Shawnee still hunted on the land.

By the time the Revolutionary War began in 1775, the population of the eastern colonies had grown rapidly. Farmland had become scarce and taxes were high, so many people moved west in search of new land. Families from the Carolinas and Virginia moved through the Cumberland Gap into the Appalachian Plateau and the Bluegrass Basin. Settlers from Pennsylvania and Maryland traveled down the Ohio River and then spread southward. Most of these early pioneers were of English, Scottish, Irish, and German descent. Settlers also came from the southern states, and many brought slaves. The African American population increased as laborers were needed on the farms that grew hemp and tobacco.

Education

Kentucky's first school was opened in the fort at Harrodstown in 1775. Some children did not attend school and were taught the basics of reading, writing, and arithmetic at home. Many young Kentuckians did not receive any education at all. As the state became more populous, wealthier Kentuckians sent their children to private academies and church schools.

Annual festivals are popular in many regions of Kentucky, including Paducah, where the Dogwood Trail Celebration is held every April.

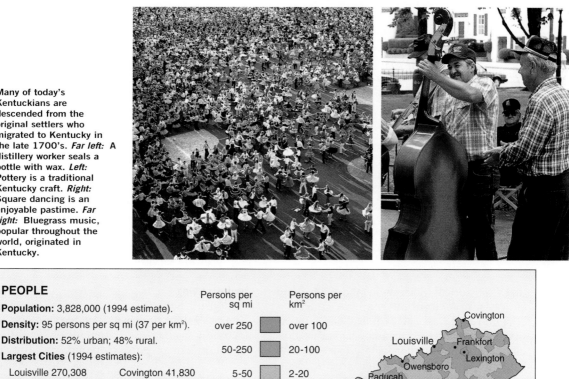

Many of today's Kentuckians are descended from the original settlers who migrated to Kentucky in the late 1700's. *Far left:* A distillery worker seals a bottle with wax. *Left:* Pottery is a traditional Kentucky craft. *Right:* Square dancing is an enjoyable pastime. *Far right:* Bluegrass music, popular throughout the world, originated in Kentucky.

PEOPLE

Population: 3,828,000 (1994 estimate).

Density: 95 persons per sq mi (37 per km^2).

Distribution: 52% urban; 48% rural.

Largest Cities (1994 estimates):

Louisville 270,308	Covington 41,830
Lexington 237,612	Hopkinsville 32,283
Owensboro 53,645	Frankfort 28,708
Bowling Green 45,451	Paducah 26,749

Source: U.S. Bureau of the Census

Persons per sq mi	Persons per km^2
over 250	over 100
50-250	20-100
5-50	2-20
0-5	0-2

In 1838 the Kentucky legislature enacted the first statewide school law, providing for a tax-supported public school system. The law was enforced after 1847 due to the capable leadership of State Superintendent of Public Instruction Robert J. Breckinridge.

The oldest institution of higher learning west of the Allegheny Mountains is Transylvania University in Lexington. Chartered in 1780 and opened as Transylvania Seminary near Danville in 1783, it was moved to Lexington in 1788. The University of Louisville was founded as Jefferson Seminary in 1798 and is now a state university. Also well known is Berea College, in Berea, founded in 1855 to provide a college education for young people from the mountain areas. Students work at the school to pay for some of their expenses.

The University of Kentucky, chartered in Lexington in 1865, is the largest university in the state. It includes the main Lexington campus and a dozen community colleges, located throughout Kentucky. Other state universities are Western Kentucky University in Bowling Green, Eastern Kentucky University in Richmond, Murray State University in Murray, Morehead State University in Morehead, and Northern Kentucky University in Highland Heights.

Libraries, Museums, and the Arts

Libraries are located in all of the cities and most of the small towns. The University of Kentucky has the largest of the university and college libraries. Libraries with special collections on the history of Kentucky include the Kentucky Historical Society in Frankfort, the Kentucky Library at Western Kentucky University in Bowling Green, and the Filson Club Historical Society in Louisville. The library at Transylvania University in Lexington is noted for its collection of rare books.

Kentucky has several notable museums. The J. B. Speed Art Museum in Louisville contains the finest collections of art from the 1800's and modern art in the state. The Ken-

Students enjoy an outdoor lecture at the University of Kentucky in Lexington, the state's largest institution of higher learning.

tucky Historical Society in the Old State House in Frankfort houses a large collection of state-related art and artifacts. The University of Kentucky in Lexington has museums of fine arts and anthropology. The National Corvette Museum in Bowling Green is dedicated to the famous Corvette sports car. Also in Bowling Green is the Kentucky Museum, located on the campus of Western Kentucky University. It displays artifacts from Kentucky's past. The Kentucky Life Museum, housed in the Waveland State Historic Site near Lexington, portrays life on a Kentucky plantation in the 1800's. Other museums include the Barton Museum of Whiskey History near Bardstown and the Patton Museum of Cavalry and Armor at Fort Knox, which contains World War II firearms, vehicles, and other items collected by General George S. Patton, Jr.

▶ ECONOMY

Kentucky's economy, once based primarily on agriculture, is becoming increasingly diversified. Services, manufacturing, mining, and the timber

industry now play vital roles in the state's economic life.

Services

Services account for nearly two-thirds of Kentucky's economy. They include a wide range of activities, including banking and real estate, government, transportation, utilities, and personal services. Thousands of jobs are supported by Kentucky's growing tourism industry. Health care is also one of the fastest-growing service industries in the state.

Manufacturing

Industry has expanded at a rapid pace in Kentucky since the 1970's. Automobile manufacturing has increased dramatically with the establishment of Ford, Corvette, and Toyota factories. Tobacco goods and alcoholic beverages, particularly bourbon whiskey, have long been important products. Grain, lumber, meatpacking, and the textile industry are also vital to the state's economy. Other notable industries include chemical and electrical products, office machinery, and transportation equipment.

Agriculture

Although the number of Kentucky farms has decreased in recent decades, agriculture

In recent years, automobile manufacturing has become an important segment of Kentucky's economy.

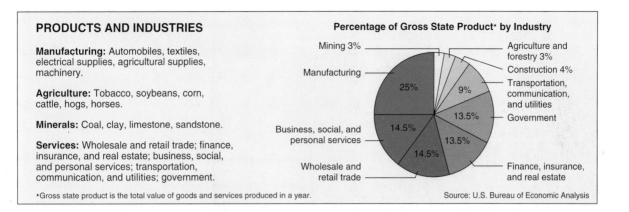

PRODUCTS AND INDUSTRIES

Manufacturing: Automobiles, textiles, electrical supplies, agricultural supplies, machinery.

Agriculture: Tobacco, soybeans, corn, cattle, hogs, horses.

Minerals: Coal, clay, limestone, sandstone.

Services: Wholesale and retail trade; finance, insurance, and real estate; business, social, and personal services; transportation, communication, and utilities; government.

Percentage of Gross State Product* by Industry

Mining 3%
Manufacturing 25%
Business, social, and personal services 14.5%
Wholesale and retail trade 14.5%
Agriculture and forestry 3%
Construction 4%
Transportation, communication, and utilities 9%
Government 13.5%
Finance, insurance, and real estate 13.5%

*Gross state product is the total value of goods and services produced in a year.

Source: U.S. Bureau of Economic Analysis

---

remains important to the economy of the state. Tobacco, the most valuable crop, is grown in all parts of the state except the mountains. Other major crops include corn and soybeans. Farmers also produce rye, oats, barley, fruits, and vegetables. Cattle, hogs, dairy products, poultry, and eggs also contribute to the farmers' income.

Kentucky's world-famous horse farms specialize in raising Thoroughbred race horses. Standardbred horses, used for harness racing, and American saddle horses are also raised.

Mining and Construction

Mining has a long history in Kentucky. Saltpeter (potassium nitrate) was mined to make gunpowder during the War of 1812. Coal, however, has long been the dominant mining industry in the state. Kentucky is a leader in coal production. Kentucky also has plentiful deposits of petroleum and natural gas.

Stone is quarried in more than 55 counties. Limestone and sandstone are used in building materials and in road construction. Large clay deposits produce a variety of clays for firebricks and pottery. Fluorspar is used in the manufacture of ceramics, glass, and acids.

Transportation

Kentucky's first highway was the famous Wilderness Road through the Cumberland Gap, cleared by Daniel Boone in the 1770's. Today more than 70,000 miles (112,650 kilometers) of highways makes every part of the state accessible.

River transportation is important to Kentucky's economy. More than 1,300

Tobacco leaves are hung up to dry in curing barns. Tobacco is Kentucky's most valuable cash crop. In the United States, only North Carolina outranks Kentucky in its production.

Places of Interest

Abraham Lincoln Birthplace National Historic Site, near Hodgenville

Fort Knox, near Louisville

Abraham Lincoln Birthplace National Historic Site, located near Hodgenville, commemorates the place of the president's birth. At the site is a monument containing a small log cabin that is symbolic of the one in which he was born in 1809.

Blue Licks Battlefield State Park, northeast of Lexington, commemorates the last battle of the Revolutionary War in the west. The battle was fought in August 1782. A museum in the park contains Native American and pioneer relics.

Churchill Downs, one of the nation's most famous race tracks, is located in Louisville. For more information, see KENTUCKY DERBY in this volume.

Cumberland Gap National Historical Park, near Middlesboro, is shared by Kentucky, Virginia, and Tennessee. The Cumberland Gap marked the beginning of the historic Wilderness Road, through which many scouts and early settlers moved westward.

Fort Knox, named for Henry Knox, the first U.S. secretary of war, is located near Louisville. It is the home of the United States Armor Center. Since 1936 it has also been the depository for the nation's largest gold reserves. More than $6 billion in gold bars are stored there.

John James Audubon State Park, near Henderson, was established as a memorial to John James Audubon, the famous naturalist and painter of North American birds. The park contains nature trails, lakes, a bird sanctuary, and the Audubon Memorial Museum.

Mammoth Cave National Park, Kentucky's only national park, covers a large area in Hart, Barren, and Edmonson counties. The cave contains 194 miles (312 kilometers) of explored passageways on five levels. The strange rock and crystal formations have such names as

Churchill Downs, in Louisville

Giant's Coffin, Frozen Niagara, and Fat Man's Misery.

My Old Kentucky Home State Park, near Bardstown, is a historic mansion, also known as Federal Hill. It was built by Judge John Rowan, a lawyer and United States senator and representative. It is said that Stephen Foster composed "My Old Kentucky Home" during a visit to Federal Hill in 1852.

Natural Bridge State Park, in eastern Kentucky, includes a large area of rugged mountains in the Daniel Boone National Forest. The main feature is Natural Bridge, a spectacular rock formation 65 feet (20 meters) high.

Old Fort Harrod State Park, at Harrodsburg, commemorates the first permanent English settlement west of the Allegheny Mountains. It contains a com-

plete reproduction of the old Fort Harrod, including the first school in Kentucky.

State Recreation Areas. The Daniel Boone National Forest covers heavily wooded mountains in eastern Kentucky. A small part of the Jefferson National Forest extends into Kentucky from Virginia. The Big South Fork National River and Recreation Area (shared with Tennessee) is in the southeastern part of Kentucky. The strip of land between Kentucky and Barkley lakes, in western Kentucky and Tennessee, is called the Land Between the Lakes. It is managed by the Tennessee Valley Authority as a recreation area. For more information on these and Kentucky's numerous state parks, write to Kentucky Department of Parks, 500 Nero Street, Capitol Plaza Tower, 10th Floor, Frankfort, Kentucky 40601.

miles (2,100 kilometers) of the state's rivers are navigable. Barges carrying bulky cargoes of coal and automobiles travel on the Ohio and Mississippi rivers. The Cumberland and Tennessee rivers are also used to transport freight.

Railroads have played an important part in the transportation of goods in Kentucky. About 3,300 miles (5,300 kilometers) of track crisscross the state. The major railroads include CSX Transportation, Inc., Norfolk Southern Corporation, Illinois Gulf Central, and Amtrak.

A number of airlines serve Kentucky's larger cities. There are more than 80 commercial and public access airports in the state. The largest airports are Standiford Field in Louisville, Bluegrass Field in Lexington, and Cincinnati International at Erlanger, servicing the Covington-Cincinnati area.

Communication

The first newspaper in Kentucky was the *Kentucky Gazette*, published in Lexington in 1787. Kentucky now publishes 25 dailies and more than 125 weekly and semiweekly newspapers. Those with the largest circulations include *The Courier-Journal*, published in Louisville, and the *Lexington Herald-Leader*. More than 270 radio and 40 television stations broadcast in the state.

▶ CITIES

For most of its history, Kentucky's population was predominantly rural. Kentuckians lived on farms or in small communities. But in 1970, the number of residents living in urban areas surpassed those living in the country. The densely populated sections of Kentucky are along the Ohio River.

Frankfort, the state capital, is located on the Kentucky River. Established in 1786, the site was originally named Frank's Ford for Stephen Frank, a pioneer who was killed by Indians. In 1792, Frankfort was chosen as Kentucky's capital.

Frankfort today is a small industrial city with distilleries, electronics plants, and textile factories. Among its points of interest are the Old State House, the Kentucky Historical So-

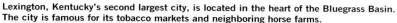

Lexington, Kentucky's second largest city, is located in the heart of the Bluegrass Basin. The city is famous for its tobacco markets and neighboring horse farms.

ciety, the present capitol building, the graves of Daniel Boone and his wife, and Liberty Hall, a beautiful mansion that dates back to the late 1700's.

Louisville, pronounced LOO-ee-vil or LOO-ih-vul, is Kentucky's largest city. It was founded in 1778 during the Revolutionary War as a supply depot for frontier expeditions against the British and their Indian allies. Originally called the Falls of the Ohio, Louisville was later named in honor of King Louis XVI of France, who helped the Americans during the war.

Throughout its history, the city has been an important river port for the southeastern United States as well as a vital commercial center. Among the goods manufactured there are automobiles, tobacco products, whiskey, leather goods, and farm tools. The city is known for its beautiful public parks and as the home of the famous Kentucky Derby Thoroughbred horse race. It is also the home of the University of Louisville, one of the state's oldest universities.

Lexington is Kentucky's second largest city. Founded in 1775, it was named after the first battle of the Revolutionary War that took place that year. Lexington's surrounding area is the home of the world's most famous horse farms. Keeneland Race Course is within a short distance of the city. The city has one of the largest loose leaf tobacco markets in the world. Also located in Lexington is the University of Kentucky and Transylvania University. Also, the Festival of the Bluegrass is held in Lexington every summer.

Covington is located on the Ohio River, just south of Cincinnati, Ohio. Founded in 1814, it is the site of petroleum refineries and food-processing plants.

Owensboro, also located on the Ohio River, was founded in 1816. Owensboro has a large

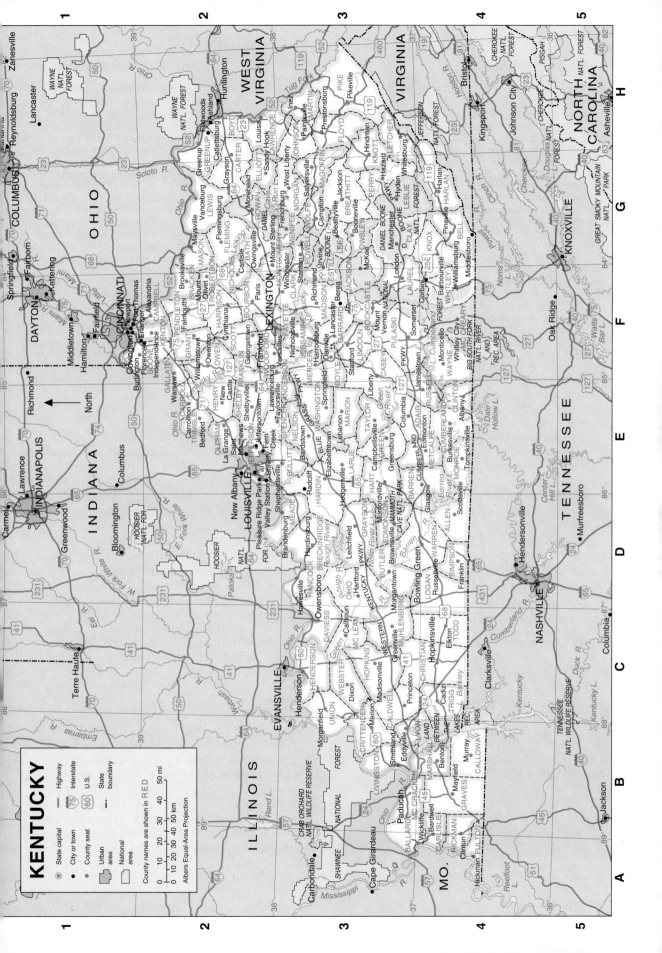

Famous People

Consult the Index to find more information in *The New Book of Knowledge* about the following people who were either born in or are associated with Kentucky: frontiersmen and explorers Daniel Boone (1734–1820) and Kit Carson (1809–68); statesman and three-time presidential candidate Henry Clay (1777–1852); Vice Presidents Richard M. Johnson (1781–1850), John C. Breckinridge (1821–75), Adlai Stevenson (1835–1914), and Alben Barkley (1877–1956); Presidents Zachary Taylor (1784–1850) and Abraham Lincoln (1809–65); First Lady Mary Todd Lincoln (1818–82); naturalist John James Audubon (1785–1851); Confederate president Jefferson Davis (1808–89); prohibitionist Carry Nation (1846–1911); civil rights activist Whitney M. Young, Jr. (1897–1975); and author Robert Penn Warren (1905–89).

Daniel Boone

Mary Breckinridge

Muhammad Ali (1942–), known as the Greatest, was one of boxing's most celebrated and flamboyant heavyweight champions. Born Cassius Marcellus Clay, Jr., in Louisville, he first became known when he won the lightweight-heavyweight championship at the 1960 Summer Olympic Games in Rome. Later, as a heavyweight, Ali won the championship title four times, beating Sonny Liston (1964), Ernie Terrell (1967), George Foreman (1974), and Leon Spinks (1978). In 1967 during the Vietnam War, Ali was convicted of dodging the draft, although he had done so due to his religious beliefs. He was stripped of his title and did not box again until 1971, when the U.S. Supreme Court overturned his conviction. Ali retired in 1980. In 1996 he was the honored person to light the Olympic flame at the Summer Games in Atlanta, Georgia.

Louis Dembitz Brandeis (1856–1941), born in Louisville, was an author, educator, and jurist. The first Jew to serve as a justice of the U.S. Supreme Court (1916–39), Brandeis was known for his liberal rulings that often favored the interests of the common man over those of giant corporations. He was one of the few justices to support President Franklin Roosevelt's New Deal legislation. After his retirement, Brandeis devoted his energies to the Zionist movement, which called for

tobacco market and several distilleries as well as other industries. It is the home of Kentucky Wesleyan University.

▶ GOVERNMENT

The Commonwealth of Kentucky is governed under its fourth constitution, which was adopted in 1891. The executive branch of the government is headed by the governor, who cannot be elected to two consecutive terms. Other executive administrators include a lieutenant governor, secretary of state, attorney general, treasurer, auditor, and commissioner of agriculture.

The state's legislative branch is called the General Assembly. It is divided into a senate and a house of representatives. Senators and representatives come together in January of even-numbered years, and sessions may not last beyond April 15, although special sessions may be called by the governor.

The state's supreme court heads the judicial branch of state government. Seven justices are elected to 8-year terms. The next highest court is the court of appeals. Below it are the circuit and district courts. All the judges in Kentucky are elected by popular vote.

▶ HISTORY

By the time European explorers came to Kentucky in the 1600's, there were no Native American settlements. However, a rich archaeological heritage of arrowheads, pottery, and sandals woven from grasses shows that prehistoric peoples had inhabited the Kentucky region for thousands of years. They lived by hunting, fishing, and gathering wild berries, roots, and other edible plants. No one, however, knows what became of them.

The seat of government of the Commonwealth of Kentucky is located in Frankfort, the capital since 1792. Government is the city's largest employer.

the establishment of a Jewish homeland in Israel. Brandeis University, in Waltham, Massachusetts, was named for him.

Mary Breckinridge (1881–1965), a granddaughter of Vice President John C. Breckinridge, was born in Memphis, Tennessee. In 1925, after discovering that nearly 10,000 people living in Kentucky's remote eastern mountain regions had no access to a doctor or nurse, Breckinridge founded the Frontier Nursing Service. She trained nurse midwives, who for years had to journey to the rural mountain homes on horseback. Today the Mary Breckinridge Hospital in Hyden administers three additional branches as well as a Women's Health Care Center.

Laura Clay (1849–1941), a daughter of the famous Kentucky abolitionist Cassius M. Clay, was born in Richmond on a 2,500-acre estate known as White Hall. A feminist, Laura Clay became one of the best-known advocates of women's rights in the South. Dedicated to the cause of equal rights, she cofounded and was the first president of the Kentucky Woman Suffrage Association.

Albert Sidney Johnston (1803–62), born in Washington, was a Confederate general during the Civil War. A graduate of West Point (1826), he served as a commander of the Texan army (1837–38) and fought in the Mexican War (1846–48). In 1861 he was given the impossible task of defending the area between the Appalachian Mountains and the Mississippi River. He was killed at the Battle of Shiloh.

Bill Monroe (1911–96), born in Rosine, is considered the father of bluegrass, a distinctive form of American music that merges traditional folk music with elements of blues, country, and gospel. With his band, the Blue Grass Boys, Monroe established the classic bluegrass sound: high, closely harmonized vocals accompanied by mandolin, guitar, fiddle, banjo, and bass. He was elected to the Country Music Hall of Fame in 1970.

Thomas Hunt Morgan (1866–1945), born in Lexington, was a renowned zoologist. In 1933 he won the Nobel Prize for physiology or medicine for his work in genetic research. By breeding fruit flies, he developed the chromosome theory of heredity, in which he concluded that genes—the individual units of heredity—are arranged in a line on the chromosome.

Muhammad Ali

Exploration and Settlement

In the 1600's, both the French and the English explored and claimed Kentucky. The French did not attempt to settle the area, and the English did not establish claims there until the mid-1700's.

In 1750, Dr. Thomas Walker, representing the Loyal Land Company of Virginia, led a group of explorers into what are now Kentucky and Tennessee. Dr. Walker named the Cumberland Gap (originally called Cave Gap) and the Cumberland River in honor of the English duke of Cumberland. Other explorers around this time included Christopher Gist, a representative of the Ohio Land Company, who sailed down the Ohio River toward present-day Louisville, and Daniel Boone, the now-famous trail blazer and frontiersman. In 1775, Boone was employed by the Virginia-based Transylvania Land Company to blaze a trail from the Cumberland Gap to the present site of Boonesboro in Madison County. The route Boone took, known as the Wilderness Road, became one of the principal routes into Kentucky.

In 1774, James Harrod and a company of surveyors from Virginia established Harrodstown, Kentucky's first permanent settlement. It was quickly abandoned due to attacks from the Native Americans, who claimed the area as a hunting ground, but it was rebuilt the following year. At the same time, the Transylvania Land Company, founded by Richard Henderson, obtained Kentucky land from the Native Americans through the treaty of Sycamore Shoals. The treaty, however, was declared illegal and Kentucky came under the control of Virginia. It was established as a county in 1776.

Meanwhile, the Shawnee Indians, who lived across the Ohio River, claimed Kentucky for themselves. They waged war against the new settlers, and many people on both sides were killed. During the American Revolution (1775–83), the Shawnee allied themselves with the British and attacked a number of Kentucky forts. The last major battle occurred in 1782 at the Battle of Blue Licks. The Indian raids ceased when the war ended.

Statehood

On June 1, 1792, Kentucky became the 15th state to enter the union. Its present-day boundaries were decided in 1818, when President Andrew Jackson and Kentucky's first governor, Isaac Shelby, bought the land west of the Tennessee River from the Chickasaw Indians.

Coal has dominated Kentucky's mining industry for more than one hundred years. Coalfields in the east and west cover nearly 40 percent of the state.

By 1820 the population of Kentucky had grown rapidly along the Ohio River and in the Bluegrass Basin. Settlers established farms and plantations to grow tobacco, corn, and wheat. Hemp plantations were developed to provide material for rope and cloth. Kentuckians sent their produce to the ports along the Ohio and Mississippi rivers to be sold.

After 1830, steamboat and railroad transportation increased Kentucky's commerce. Coal mining began, providing fuel for industry, especially the iron and steel industry at Ashland. The development of the timber industry also added to the state's prosperity, and Kentucky became one of the wealthiest states in the union.

The Civil War (1861–65)

Kentucky's location between the North and the South placed it in a difficult position when civil war divided the nation. Kentucky was a slave state, but it had strong economic ties to both sides. While some Kentuckians, such as Cassius M. Clay, were abolitionists, devoted to ending slavery in their state, others felt that the federal government was trying to interfere with their right to property, which at that time included their right to own slaves.

When war broke out in April 1861, Kentucky was one of four "border" states to declare itself neutral. Eventually, Kentucky officially sided with the Union, but some Kentuckians broke away and sent delegates to the Confederate Congress. More than 45,000 Kentuckians joined the Confederate Army, and over 90,000 joined the Union forces. This division of loyalties brought particular tragedy to Kentucky, for it was not uncommon for members of the same family to find themselves on opposite sides in battle.

Many skirmishes and some major battles took place in Kentucky during the course of the war. The most notable was the Battle of Perryville on October 8, 1862. After their defeat at Perryville, the Confederates ceased in their attempts to take Kentucky.

The World Wars

When the United States fought in World War I from 1917–18 and World War II from 1941–45, Kentucky industries contributed heavily to the war efforts, and many Kentuckians served in the armed forces. Fort Knox, near Louisville, was established in 1918 as a World War I military training post. Later it became the depository for much of America's gold reserve.

Kentuckians were deeply affected by the economic collapse known as the Great Depression of the 1930's. The federal government provided many jobs and built numerous public buildings in the state to help the economy. The Tennessee Valley Authority (TVA), created by Congress in 1933, built a series of dams in the region. The electric power that was made possible by the dams attracted new industries to Kentucky, and the lakes that resulted from damming the rivers eventually made Kentucky an attractive vacation destination, helping to boost its economy.

The Future

In recent decades, many Kentuckians have moved to the cities as small farms have become unprofitable and mines have closed down. Although agriculture and the coal mining industry have faced difficult times, tourism and manufacturing, particularly the production of automobiles, continue to grow. In order to keep up with the shift in the workplace, schools have focused their attention on teaching job skills that are more suitable for today's employment opportunities.

RON D. BRYANT
The Kentucky Historical Society

KENTUCKY AND VIRGINIA RESOLUTIONS

In 1798, the state legislatures of Kentucky and Virginia passed a series of resolutions in opposition to the Alien and Sedition Acts, which the U.S. Congress had passed earlier in the year. These acts had placed many new restrictions on people living in the United States. Aliens (foreigners) had to wait 14 rather than 5 years before they could apply for naturalized citizenship, and it became a crime for anyone to publish anything about the government that was critical or untrue. These laws were supported by the Federalist Party and the president, John Adams.

Those who opposed the Alien and Sedition Acts included members of the Democratic-Republican Party, such as Thomas Jefferson and James Madison. Jefferson and his followers believed that the states were more important than the federal government and therefore should have more rights. This principle came to be known as **states' rights**.

Resolutions against the Alien and Sedition Acts were passed in Kentucky and Virginia in 1798 and again in Kentucky in 1799. One of the Kentucky resolutions, secretly written by Jefferson, claimed that the states had the right to disobey any federal law they felt was unconstitutional, or not in the best interests of the states. In other words, a state could nullify (do away with) a law it did not think appropriate. This political philosophy is called **nullification**.

Largely due to the unpopularity of the Alien and Sedition Acts and the limitations they placed on freedom of the press, the Federalists lost the presidential election of 1800 to the Democratic-Republicans. Under the new administration of President Thomas Jefferson, the Alien and Sedition Acts were soon repealed.

In later years, the doctrine of nullification, first stated in the Kentucky and Virginia Resolutions, was the principle on which eleven Southern states seceded (1860–61) from the Union, leading to the Civil War.

RON D. BRYANT
The Kentucky Historical Society

See also ADAMS, JOHN (The Alien and Sedition Acts).

KENTUCKY DERBY

The Kentucky Derby is the most famous horse race in the United States and one of the oldest and most anticipated racing events in the world. Also known as the Run for the Roses, this 1 1/4-mile (2.01-kilometer) race for 3-year-old Thoroughbreds is run on the first Saturday of every May at Churchill Downs in Louisville, Kentucky. It is part of the famous Triple Crown series of races held each year in the United States. The second and third races are the Preakness and Belmont Stakes, respectively.

The founders of the Kentucky Derby, Colonel M. Lewis Clark, Jr., and Colonel Matt J. Winnare, were impressed with the famous English racing events, especially the Epsom Derby, and wished to establish a similar race in Kentucky. The winner of the first Kentucky Derby, which was run on May 17, 1875, was a small red colt named Aristides. More than 10,000 people attended the race.

The Kentucky Derby is not only a great horse race but a great social occasion. The

city of Louisville stages a Derby Festival leading up to the Kentucky Derby. Events include the Pegasus Parade (named for the winged horse of Greek mythology); Thunder Over Louisville, one of the nation's largest fireworks displays; and the Great Steamboat Race, a contest between the paddlewheelers the *Belle of Louisville* and the *Delta Queen*.

RON D. BRYANT
The Kentucky Historical Society

See also HORSE RACING.

KENYA

Kenya, a nation in East Africa, is a land of striking contrasts. It lies astride the equator, yet it has mountains that are permanently capped with snow. Lions, giraffes, and other wild animals roam freely in a huge national park not far from the modern capital city of Nairobi. Kenya retains many of its African traditions, but it also has inherited many European customs from its years as a British colony before gaining its independence in 1963.

▶THE PEOPLE

Most of the people of Kenya live in the southwest, where the soils are good and there is enough rainfall for farming. Few people live in the arid northern region.

Ethnic Groups, Language, and Religion. Almost all Kenyans are black Africans. There are small communities of Asians (whose ancestors came from what is now India and Pakistan), Europeans, and Arabs. Kenya's official language is Swahili, which is widely spoken along much of the East African coast. But many Kenyans speak English, and the people in rural areas speak tribal languages. Many Kenyans are Christians, including Roman Catholics and Protestants. Others follow traditional African religions. About 6 percent of the people are Muslims.

The Kikuyu Way of Life. The Kikuyu are Kenya's largest single ethnic group. Making up slightly more than one fifth of the population, they have played a major role in the political development of the country. Their traditional homeland is in the fertile highlands. Kikuyu farmers grow food crops of corn, beans, and millet. They also keep large herds of sheep and goats and some cattle.

The one great wish of almost every Kikuyu is to own a piece of land on which to build a

Traditional village homes of the Kikuyu, Kenya's largest ethnic group, are round with conical grass roofs. Older children help care for their younger brothers and sisters.

house and plant a garden. Kikuyu children play an important part in the economic life of the family. Small children are left at home to care for infant brothers and sisters while parents work in the fields. As soon as children are old enough to hold digging sticks, they are given little pieces of land on which to practice. Their parents help them plant seeds and teach them how to tell corn from weeds. As the children grow older, they are given larger plots to plant. Even after marriage, they continue to cultivate their childhood gardens. Children also help in many other ways. They collect firewood, do housework, and herd livestock.

Although the Kikuyu have preserved many traditional customs, their way of life has changed with changing times. Most of them still live in round houses with mud walls and grass roofs. But the wealthier Kikuyu now build Western-style houses equipped with television sets and modern furniture. Kikuyu farmers have adopted scientific agricultural methods, and some of them grow export crops such as coffee and tea. Many Kikuyu have become traders, skilled workers, lawyers, doctors, and government officials in the cities. Others leave their farms to work for a time in the cities.

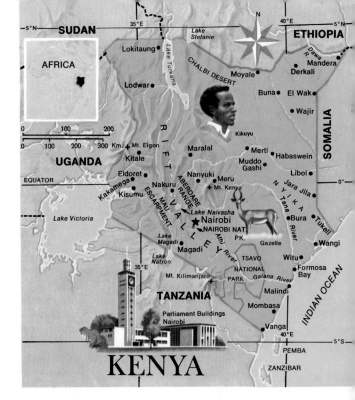

KENYA

A proud, handsome people, the Masai were renowned as warriors and lion hunters. Most now live as cattle herders. Masai men use a red clay to decorate their hair.

The Masai. The Kikuyu's southern neighbors are the Masai. A tall, proud people, famed as warriors and lion hunters, the Masai live primarily as herders of cattle. They travel with their herds over large areas of southern Kenya. During the rainy season their herds graze in the valleys, and during the dry season they move to higher land. Because the Masai are always moving with their livestock, they do not have permanent homesteads. Their cattle provide the Masai with milk, but since the animals are considered a source of wealth, they are rarely killed for food. Instead, the Masai obtain millet and beans from other, more settled tribes.

Masai men sometimes decorate their bodies with a red clay. Carrying their long spears and shields they present imposing figures. The Masai women traditionally shave their heads and adorn their arms with many bracelets.

The traditional life of the Masai is gradually changing. Like the Kikuyu, some are now moving to the cities, sending their children to schools, and using modern medicine.

Other Peoples. Other important African groups in Kenya include the Luhya, the Kisii, and the Luo. The Luo, who live in the Lake Victoria region, catch fish that they sell throughout Kenya. They also grow corn and other grains and raise cows and goats for meat and milk.

Most of the Arabs in Kenya are farmers and traders living on the coast. Asians have traded for centuries along the eastern coast of Africa. Many of them settled in the towns of Kenya, where they opened shops. Most of the Europeans also live in cities and towns. Since independence, black Africans have taken over many of the jobs once held by Europeans, Asians, and Arabs. While the great majority of the people still live in the countryside, Kenya's cities have grown due to a slow but steady movement of people from rural areas.

Education. Although education is not compulsory (required by law) in Kenya, it is highly valued, and the government encourages schooling for both boys and girls. Primary education is free, and about 80 percent of children in the primary grade age group attend school. In addition to the government schools, Kenya also has *Harambee,* or self-help, schools. *Harambee,* the national motto of Kenya, is a Swahili word meaning to "pull together." These schools are built and staffed by volunteers to provide additional classrooms for children who otherwise would be unable to attend regular schools.

Kenya has several colleges and technical schools and one university, the University of Nairobi. Many Kenyan students earn scholarships to universities abroad.

▶THE LAND

Highlands. Kenya's most important physical feature is the large area of highlands in the southwestern part of the country. These highlands have more rainfall, lower temperatures, and richer soils than other parts of the country. For these reasons many Europeans settled there, and the area became known as the White Highlands. Most of Kenya's export crops are grown on large farms in the highlands.

Kenya's chief mountains are also located in this area. Mount Kenya, which gives the country its name, is an extinct snowcapped volcano rising to 17,040 feet (5,194 meters). The Kikuyu people who practice traditional African religions believe that their god, Ngai, dwells on Mount Kenya, and they turn toward it when they pray. Mount Elgon and the Aberdare Range are also found here.

The Great Rift Valley. One of the most spectacular geographical features on the earth's surface—the Great Rift Valley—crosses Kenya from north to south. This gigantic valley runs from Southwest Asia through the Red Sea and crosses eastern Africa as far as the nation of Mozambique in the south. In northern Kenya the Great Rift Valley forms a wide shallow basin, in which Lake Turkana (Lake Rudolf) lies. In the south it forms a deep,

The highlands are Kenya's most fertile and productive region and the source of most of its export crops. In the distance is Mount Kenya, the country's highest peak.

Coffee, Kenya's chief export, is loaded for shipment abroad at the port of Mombasa. Coffee and tea together account for close to half of Kenya's foreign exchange earnings.

steep-walled valley, broken by a series of small lakes. The floor of the Great Rift Valley is dotted with small extinct volcanoes. Great outpourings of lava that once came from these volcanoes formed the surrounding highlands, as well as Mount Kenya and Mount Elgon.

The Nyanza and Nyika Regions. To the west of the highlands is a hilly region that slopes down to Lake Victoria, the largest lake in Africa, which forms a part of Kenya's western border. This is part of the Nyanza (lake) region, one of the most important corn-producing regions of eastern Africa. To the east of the highlands the land falls in a series of steps down to Kenya's coast on the Indian Ocean. This region is known as *Nyika*, a Swahili word meaning "wilderness."

The two largest rivers in Kenya are the Tana and the Athi. Both of these rivers flow eastward into the Indian Ocean.

▶THE ECONOMY

Agriculture. Kenya's economy is based mainly on agriculture, including the raising of livestock, which employs about 75 percent of the work force. Most of these are subsistence

FACTS AND FIGURES

REPUBLIC OF KENYA (Jamhuri ya Kenya) is the official name of the country.

THE PEOPLE are known as Kenyans.

LOCATION: East Africa.

AREA: 224,960 sq mi (582,646 km²).

POPULATION: 20,000,000 (estimate).

CAPITAL AND LARGEST CITY: Nairobi.

MAJOR LANGUAGES: Swahili (official), other African languages, English.

MAJOR RELIGIONS: Christian (Roman Catholic, Protestant), traditional African religions, Muslim.

GOVERNMENT: Republic. **Head of state and government—** president. **Legislature—**National Assembly.

CHIEF PRODUCTS: Agricultural—coffee, tea, sisal, corn, millet, beans, other vegetables, pyrethrum, sugarcane, cotton, livestock. **Manufactured—**processed food, livestock products, textiles, cement. **Mineral—**soda ash, limestone, salt, fluorspar, iron ore, gold.

MONETARY UNIT: Kenya shilling (1 shilling = 100 cents).

NATIONAL ANTHEM: *Wimbo Wa Taifa* (National Anthem), beginning *Ee Mungu nguvu yetu* ("Oh God of all creation").

Elephants roam freely in one of Kenya's national parks. Tourism, one of the country's most important industries, depends largely on Kenya's varied wildlife.

to visit Kenya's beaches on the Indian Ocean and to see the many animals that roam in the nation's tropical grasslands. A golf club at Kisumu, near Lake Victoria, has a club rule that when a ball falls dangerously near a hippopotamus or a crocodile, the player should use another ball. Ostriches are found in the bush grassland, and the Rift Valley lakes are the home of large flocks of flamingos. To preserve this rich wildlife, large tracts of unpopulated country have been set aside as national parks.

Mining. Kenya's known mineral resources are limited. They include soda ash (used in making soap), limestone, salt, fluorspar, and some iron ore. Small amounts of gold also are mined.

▶CITIES

Nairobi is Kenya's capital, largest city, and its center of industry and commerce. Located in south central Kenya, in the highlands area, its elevation of almost 5,500 feet (1,600 meters) above sea level gives it a pleasant climate. A modern city, it has grown rapidly in recent years and now has a population approaching 1,000,000. The city is only a few miles away from Nairobi National Park, a wildlife refuge.

Mombasa is Kenya's second largest city and its principal seaport. The city is situated on an island off the Kenya coast. It has had a long history as a port and trading city.

▶HISTORY AND GOVERNMENT

Early History. Kenya was one of the earliest homes of prehistoric people. Scientists have discovered the remains of humanlike creatures called australopithecines who lived in Kenya as long as 3,000,000 years ago. Bones of *Homo erectus*, a more advanced human ancestor who may have used simple tools, have also been found in Kenya.

Kenya's earliest recorded history tells of various herding and farming tribes that migrated into the area from other parts of Africa. Some 2,000 years ago, merchants from Arabia sailed along the coast of Kenya in search of gold. From the 7th century on, Arabs built trading centers at places like Mombasa and what is now the town of Malindi. In 1498 the Portuguese navigator Vasco da Gama sailed around the Cape of Good Hope and landed at Malindi. The Portuguese established coastal

farmers, who grow only enough food for their own needs. Kenya has been largely self-sufficient in food production, although a drought in 1984 affected this vital aspect of the economy.

About one third of Kenya's agriculture is devoted to cash crops, intended for export. Coffee is the leading export crop, followed by tea. Other important cash crops are sisal (a fiber used to make cord and twine) and pyrethrum (a flower used in making insecticides). Cotton, sugarcane, and various vegetables, fruits, and grains are also grown, both for domestic use and for export.

Industry. Textiles, processed foods, livestock products, cement, and textiles are among the leading manufactured goods. Tourism has long been an important industry in Kenya, traditionally second only to coffee as a source of income. People come from all over the world

trading posts and held them until 1740, when the Arabs drove them out.

British Rule. The British first entered the area mainly to stop the slave trade. In 1895, Britain began to build a railroad from the coast to Lake Victoria. That same year, to safeguard the railroad, the British government made most of what is now Kenya a protectorate known as the East Africa Protectorate. It was later given its present name and boundaries.

The British government encouraged Europeans to settle in the Kenya highlands. The whites aroused bitter hatred when they forced the Africans, mostly Kikuyu, off the land. In the 1950's, a secret Kikuyu movement called Mau Mau tried to frighten the whites away and force Britain to grant Kenya independence.

Independence. Kenya gained independence in 1963 and became a republic in 1964. The head of state and government is the president. The president and most members of the legislature, the National Assembly, are elected directly by the people for a term of 5 years, although new elections may be called earlier.

Jomo Kenyatta, the Kikuyu political leader, became Kenya's first president and one of Africa's best-known leaders. Many feared that an old rivalry between the Kikuyu and the Luo would cause turmoil after Kenyatta's death. Tensions increased in 1969, when the Luo leader Tom Mboya was assassinated. All political parties except Kenyatta's Kenya African National Union were then banned.

Recent History. Kenyatta died in office in 1978 and was succeeded by Vice President Daniel arap Moi, who was elected president in 1979. In 1982 the constitution was changed to make Kenya a one-party state, and Moi was automatically reelected in 1983 and 1988. Forced to reintroduce a multiparty system, Moi won narrow and disputed victories in elections held in 1992 and 1997. He has resisted domestic and international demands for further political reforms.

Once one of Africa's more politically stable and prosperous nations, Kenya has become increasingly troubled by violence and by economic problems. In 1998, a terrorist's bomb exploded outside the U.S. embassy in Nairobi, killing approximately 200 people.

W. Senteza Kajubi
Makerere University (Uganda)

Modern Nairobi is Kenya's capital and largest city. It is also one of Africa's primary centers of commerce.

KEPLER, JOHANNES (1571–1630)

Johannes Kepler was one of the outstanding astronomers of all time. His work helped explain the motion of the planets around the sun.

Kepler was born in Weil, Germany, on December 27, 1571. His childhood was an unhappy one. He was a weak, sickly child. His parents were poor, and they quarreled quite often. The father, Heinrich, did not want to support his wife and children. When Johannes was 3 years old, his father left home and hired himself out as a soldier. A few years later Heinrich deserted the family altogether.

From the time he was a boy, Johannes wanted to study to become a Protestant clergyman. But his family was too poor to pay for his education. Because he was a good student, he earned scholarships that took him through school. In 1589 he entered the University of Tübingen to study to become a clergyman.

Kepler studied religion, and other subjects as well. One of these subjects was mathematics. He was tremendously impressed by the order and exactness of mathematics. He thought that God surely must have used mathematics in designing the universe.

By the time Kepler left the university he had decided on a change in his life's work. He felt there were other ways of serving God than by being a clergyman. One such way was to become an astronomer and use mathematics to study the motions of the planets.

Kepler became a teacher of mathematics. In his spare time he did research in astronomy. By now he had already accepted the Copernican theory. This theory stated that the earth is only one of a group of planets, all moving around the sun.

Over many years Kepler created a number of mathematical laws about the motion of the planets. Among these laws are the three called **Kepler's laws of planetary motion**. These three laws describe the speed of motion of the planets, and their paths around the sun.

He wrote a number of books on astronomy and on subjects related to it. These books were in Latin, which was the scientific language of that time. Three of his most impor-

Johannes Kepler studying the motion of planets.

tant books are *Mysterium Cosmographicum* ("Cosmic Mysteries"), *Astronomia Nova* ("New Astronomy"), and *Harmonices Mundi* ("The Harmony of the Universe"). His laws of planetary motion are explained in these books.

Kepler became famous as an astronomer during his lifetime. In 1601 the Holy Roman Emperor Rudolph II appointed him court mathematician. This post brought him a good living, as well as great honor. After Rudolph's death in 1612 Kepler returned to teaching.

Kepler's work was important to the scientists who later developed the theory of gravitation. His laws of planetary motion, added to the Copernican theory, gave scientists more accurate knowledge of our solar system.

Kepler died in Regensburg, Germany, on November 15, 1630.

DUANE H. D. ROLLER
The University of Oklahoma

KEROSENE

Kerosene is a colorless liquid fuel. Chemically, it is a mixture of hydrocarbons. That is, it is made up of hydrogen and carbon atoms.

Kerosene is sometimes spelled kerosine, similar to gasoline. The name comes from the Greek word *kēros,* meaning "wax." Perhaps this name was given because kerosene dissolves wax, as well as fats and other substances. For example, kerosene is used as a solvent in weed killers and insecticides. It helps remove the waxy coatings on weeds and insects, thus increasing the chemicals' effectiveness.

▶ SOURCES OF KEROSENE

Kerosene was first made in the 1840's and 1850's by researchers in Europe and North America. They learned how to extract it from coal tar and shale.

Kerosene is also one of many products made from petroleum. In 1859 the first successful petroleum well in the United States was drilled. This resulted in large-scale petroleum production and provided an abundant source of kerosene.

Kerosene and the other components of petroleum are separated from one another by the process of distillation. This depends on the fact that the various hydrocarbons that make up petroleum boil (and condense) at different temperatures. The kerosene portion boils (and condenses) between 175 and 260°C (350 and 500°F). The actual temperature depends on the mixture of hydrocarbons in that specific kerosene.

Today, petroleum is still our major source of kerosene. But in recent years, scientists have been developing ways to gasify coal efficiently, turning it into kerosene and other products. This is part of the effort to find sources of energy other than petroleum.

▶ THE USES OF KEROSENE

Kerosene was first used to light lamps. Kerosene lamps were a great improvement over tallow candles and whale-oil lamps, which gave little light. In a kerosene lamp the fluid is stored in a lower compartment. One end of a woven wick dips into the kerosene. The other end is lighted to provide light. The kerosene moves up the wick by capillary action, much as water moves in a blotter.

Kerosene was also used widely in stoves and heaters. Gradually, it was replaced by natural gas and electricity for cooking and lighting. Today kerosene lamps and stoves are used only in places where gas and electricity are not available.

For years kerosene was used as a cheap fuel for tractors and in railroad lamps. Then special mixtures of kerosene were found to have tremendous power when burned in jet airplane engines. Today over 53,000,000,000 (billion) liters (14,000,000,000 gallons) of kerosene are used in the United States every year for jet fuels alone. One advantage of kerosene over gasoline as a jet fuel is that it must be heated to a higher temperature before it ignites. This makes it safer to use. It also has a higher weight per unit volume. This means it enables the plane to fly farther than an equal volume of gasoline would permit.

Large producers of kerosene include the United States, the Netherlands Antilles, Canada, the United Kingdom, Iran, Japan, Venezuela, and the Netherlands.

A. L. McCLELLAN
Chevron Research Company

See also FUELS; LIGHTING; PETROLEUM AND PETROLEUM REFINING.

Jet planes use a special mixture of kerosene. Here military jets demonstrate their flying maneuvers.

KETTERING, CHARLES FRANKLIN
(1876–1958)

"The only time you don't want an experiment to fail is the last time you try it." So said a sign that hung in Charles F. Kettering's office. The motto summed up Kettering's patient way of going about his work.

Charles Kettering was an inventor, engineer, and businessman. He did perhaps more than any other person to make the automobile easy and convenient to operate.

Kettering was born August 29, 1876, on a farm near Loudonville, Ohio. While he was in school, he worked for a telephone company on country telephone lines. At 19 he taught for a year at a country school. After that he studied mechanical and electrical engineering at Ohio State University.

After graduating, Kettering went to work for the National Cash Register Company in Dayton, Ohio. In 1905 he married Olive Williams. They had one son.

While at the National Cash Register Company, Kettering invented a cash register that was driven by an electric motor, instead of a hand crank; and he also invented an automated inventory-control system. Kettering became chief of the inventions department of the National Cash Register Company but resigned in 1909 to help form the Dayton Engineering Laboratories. This company, which was later called Delco, worked on inventing and improving electrical equipment for automobiles.

Kettering worked out an improved ignition and lighting system, and he invented the first automobile self-starter, which made him famous.

In 1916, Delco was purchased by the United Motors Corporation. This company was later bought by the General Motors Corporation. Kettering also formed a research company that was later bought by General Motors and an airplane company. During World War I, Kettering worked on many improvements on airplanes. In 1917 he and Orville Wright, one of the inventors of the airplane, developed a guided missile.

In 1920, Kettering became president and general manager of the General Motors Research Corporation. There he was responsible for many important developments, including improvement of engines, especially diesel engines; invention of a quick-drying paint for cars; development of safety glass; and development of an antiknock gasoline.

Kettering was interested in many different fields of engineering and science. He established an institute for the study of photosynthesis at Antioch College. In 1945, with Alfred P. Sloan, Jr., chairman of the board of General Motors, he founded the Sloan-Kettering Institute for Cancer Research in New York City.

Charles Kettering died at his home in Dayton, Ohio, on November 25, 1958.

Reviewed by Terry S. Reynolds
Michigan Technological University

KEYBOARD INSTRUMENTS

A keyboard is a device for playing musical instruments such as the piano and organ. It consists of a system of levers, or keys, on which the player selects the particular notes to be played. Keyboards have been used since ancient times. The Roman hydraulus, a simple type of organ, was played by means of a keyboard.

The player strikes the keys to make the instrument sound. The pitch for each note is fixed and cannot be changed by the player. All the player can do is stop the sound by releasing the key. Many of the great composers wrote some of their finest music for keyboard instruments.

▶ORGAN

The oldest keyboard instrument is the organ. From early, simple beginnings it developed into the large, complex instrument we know today. Organ keyboards are called manuals. Though modern organs usually have several keyboards, the first organs had only one. On the bigger instruments the keys were large levers. The player had to pound them with his fist to push them down. Little by little, organs were improved. The keys were made smaller and could be played with the fingers.

When an organ key is pressed down, it opens a valve that lets air into a pipe. When

This electrically operated organ was designed specially for use in the home.

the player lets go of the key, the valve closes and shuts the air off. In modern organs the air is provided by large electric blowers. Before electricity was used, the air had to be pumped by hand.

Organs were used in Christian churches as early as the 10th century. Within a few hundred years they became an essential part of most church services. In the 12th century pedal levers began to be used to play some of the low notes. These levers were developed into pedal boards for the feet, similar to the finger keyboards. The foot pedals play the lowest notes on the organ.

▶ CLAVICHORD

The clavichord is the earliest stringed keyboard instrument. It developed from the ancient monochord, a single string stretched on a wooden frame. Before 500 B.C. the Greek philosopher Pythagoras had used the monochord to experiment with sound.

The clavichord has from 20 to 30 strings, all of about the same length, stretched over an oblong sounding board. For each string there are one or more short metal blades called tangents. The tangents are mounted inside the instrument, on the rear ends of the keys. They have two functions. First, when the key is pressed down, the tangent rises up and strikes the string. Second, it determines the pitch by striking the string at the right point. Because the tangent must remain on the string while making the sound, the string cannot vibrate freely. Thus the clavichord can produce only a very soft sound.

The clavichord was an important instrument in the 17th and 18th centuries.

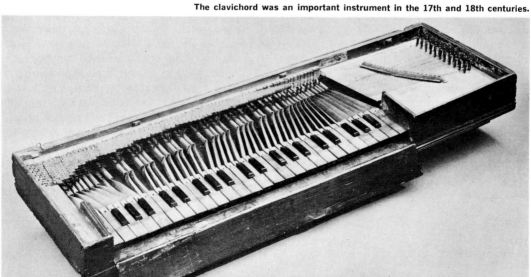

A 17th-century harpsichord with two keyboards.

The clavichord was the first keyboard instrument in which the volume of the sound could be controlled by the player's touch. The clavichord was therefore the forerunner of the piano. It was popular in Germany during the 17th and 18th centuries. Johann Sebastian Bach (1685–1750) wrote many works for his children to play on the clavichord. His son Karl Philipp Emanuel (1714–1788) became clavichordist to Frederick the Great, who was very fond of the instrument.

▶ HARPSICHORD

More important keyboard instruments began to be used in the early 1500's. They were either rectangular or triangular in shape, and light enough to be carried by one person. In England they were called virginals, and in Germany, spinets. Later larger models were developed with more than one keyboard. Their shape resembled today's grand piano. These larger instruments were called harpsichords. The Italian name was *clavicembalo,* or just *cembalo.*

The harpsichord developed from an early stringed instrument called a psaltery. The psaltery's strings were of unequal length, with one, two, or three strings for each note, and were stretched on a triangular or rectangular frame. The psaltery's strings were plucked either with a pick or by the fingers. In the harpsichord a key operates a pick for each string. The pick is fastened to a hinge in an upright wooden rod called a jack. Each jack is mounted on the end of the key, inside the instrument. When the key is pressed down, this end goes up. It lifts the jack, and the pick plucks the string. When the key is released, the hinge allows the pick to swing back, thus avoiding a repetition of the tone. The jack then returns to its resting place. The damper, a small felt pad at the top of the jack, stops the string from vibrating.

As harpsichords were improved, their keyboards were enlarged to include five octaves, or 61 keys. Other sets of strings were added. These gave the instrument brilliance and variety of sound. Each set of strings, called a stop, could be used at the player's will. In this respect the harpsichord resembled the organ. Also, like the organ, harpsichords frequently had two keyboards.

From about 1550 to 1775 the harpsichord was a favorite instrument of European noble families. Queen Mary Tudor of England was an excellent virginal player; so was Queen Elizabeth I, who owned a number of virginals. The harpsichord was sometimes considered more than just an instrument for making music. It was thought of as an object of art and was often decorated with wood carvings, elaborate paintings, and inlay work. Many of the greatest composers wrote for the harpsichord. Among them were Johann Sebastian Bach, George Frederick Handel (1685–1759), and Domenico Scarlatti (1685–1757).

The sound of the harpsichord was rich and brilliant, but never very loud. The tone could not be varied by the stroke of the player's finger, as on the clavichord or piano. However, the stops could be used to make the different sections of a composition louder or softer. The picks of the harpsichord were made from birds' quills or hard leather, and had to be replaced often. The harpsichord was easily tuned, but it would not stay in tune for very long.

Since the beginning of the 20th century there has been a renewed interest in the harpsichord, and it is now frequently heard in

The modern grand piano is used in concerts and in solo piano recitals.

concert halls. Occasionally it is found in private homes. Several 20th-century composers have written music for it, and it is used by some jazz musicians.

▶ PIANO

During the middle of the 1700's many people became somewhat dissatisfied with the harpsichord. They wanted an instrument that could respond to the finger's pressure on the key, like the clavichord. But they also wanted an instrument that had the brilliance of the harpsichord. Such an instrument had already been invented in Italy about 1709 by Bartolommeo Cristofori (1655–1731). It was called a *pianoforte,* the Italian word for "soft-loud." Today it is usually called simply the piano.

The strings of the piano are not plucked, as in the harpsichord, but struck by felt-covered wooden hammers. The hammers hit and bounce off the strings, so the strings can vibrate freely after being struck. The player's fingers control the loudness of the sound.

Pianos, like harpsichords, have dampers to cut off the sound as soon as the key is released. A foot pedal was developed to work the piano dampers. With the pedal the player can lift all the dampers at once. This permits a variety of effects without having to use the fingers.

It was not long before the piano was widely accepted. By 1780 it had replaced the harpsichord as the favorite keyboard instrument.

The accordion is a popular folk instrument.

Soon it became the very popular instrument that we know today. The modern piano keyboard has 88 keys.

The first pianos resembled the harpsichord in shape. These are now called grand pianos. During the 19th century a square, or box-shaped, piano was popular. Two other types of pianos used in today's homes are the upright and the small spinet pianos.

▶ OTHER KEYBOARD INSTRUMENTS

Keyboards are also used for playing some wind, percussion, and electronic instruments. Foremost in the wind group are the reed organs. These include the harmonium, equipped with foot pedals. These pedals pump the bellows, driving air through the reeds. The accordion is a small reed organ; here the player's arms pump the bellows.

The most important of the percussion keyboard instruments are the carillon and celesta.

The bells of a carillon are played by keys struck with the closed hand. The celesta looks like a small upright piano. Hammers strike metal bars that give off bell-like sounds. It is used mainly as an occasional instrument in the symphony orchestra. "The Dance of the Sugarplum Fairy" from Tchaikovsky's *Nutcracker Suite* is a famous piece with a solo celesta part.

The electronic organ has been developed in the 20th century. It is capable of producing a variety of sounds, including imitations of many kinds of instruments. Compared to other types of organs, electronic organs can be less costly to build and take up very little space. For this reason they are popular in small churches and in homes.

Reviewed by KARL GEIRINGER
Professor of Music
University of California (Santa Barbara)

See also ORGAN; PIANO.

KEYNES, J. M. See ECONOMICS.

KEYS. See LOCKS AND KEYS.

KHRUSHCHEV, NIKITA (1894–1971)

Nikita Sergeyevich Khrushchev, former premier of the Soviet Union, was born in Kalinovka, Russia, on April 17, 1894, the son of a miner. The family was very poor, and Nikita received little education. In his late teens he went to work as a mechanic in the Donets coal mines in the Ukraine. At the time, he was a rough, jolly fellow and a great talker. He

Nikita Khrushchev, former premier of the Soviet Union.

joined the Communist Party in 1918 and served in the Red Guards during the Russian Civil War. He then went to a workers' academy to learn to be a party organizer. From here he started his long rise to supreme power in the Soviet Union. During this period he married Nina Petrovna, a schoolteacher. They had two sons and three daughters.

Khrushchev's success was largely due to his ability as a politician. His career might be compared to that of a man in the United States who started as a worker in city politics and worked his way up to become mayor, governor, member of the cabinet, and finally president. Khrushchev began as Communist Party secretary in a tiny district in the Ukraine. He rose to become second secretary of the party in Moscow, then party boss in the Ukraine. Eventually he became a member of the Presidium, the small group that rules the Communist Party, and a favorite of the Soviet dictator, Joseph Stalin.

When Stalin died in 1953, the Presidium appointed Khrushchev first secretary of the Communist Party. (The position is now called general secretary.) This was the most important position in the Soviet Union because the general secretary could control the party and the government. Between 1954 and 1958 Khrushchev replaced most of the local party secretaries with his own men. He also secured the removal of those on the Presidium who opposed him. Finally, he took the title of premier (while keeping the all-important post of first secretary of the party), to gain the same position of power that Stalin had held.

At the same time, Khrushchev announced that Stalin had been a great villain. The former dictator's body was removed from its tomb near the Kremlin, and all pictures and statues of him were taken down. Cities and streets that had been named for Stalin were renamed.

Khrushchev's rise was due to his political ability. But he was more than a politician. He was a great organizer and a hard-hitting, hard-working executive. As a diplomat his methods were crude, but he kept the best statesmen of the West off balance for 10 years.

In international relations Khrushchev often confused diplomats of the West. Though he talked about peaceful coexistence, with Communism and democracy living side by side, he insisted that his smiles did not mean that he had given up the anti-capitalist principles of Karl Marx and Lenin. "They who wait for that," he would add, "will have to wait until the shrimp learns to whistle."

Under Khrushchev, the Soviet Union's agricultural and industrial problems were far from solved. But there were more consumer goods to be had, and the Soviet people were better off than they had been before.

Nevertheless, Khrushchev was removed from power in 1964. A book said to be his memoirs was published in the West in 1970 under the title "Khrushchev Remembers." Khrushchev dissociated himself from the book. He died on September 11, 1971.

FRANK R. DONOVAN
Author, *Famous Twentieth Century Leaders*
See also STALIN, JOSEPH.

KIDD, CAPTAIN WILLIAM (1645?–1701)

Though Captain Kidd is probably the most famous of all pirates, he hardly deserves his celebrated reputation. Many accounts of his exploits and buried treasures are merely legends.

Kidd was born about 1645 in Greenock, Scotland. He went to sea as a young man, eventually becoming a ship's captain. About 1690 he settled in New York. He married the widow of a sea captain and acquired considerable property, including a house near Wall Street. In 1695 the British Government, aroused by attacks of pirates against its ships, decided to send an expedition against them. Because of his reputation as a skillful captain, Kidd was put in command. On April 23, 1696, he sailed from Plymouth, England, in the *Adventure Galley,* a ship of 34 guns.

Almost from the start Kidd's voyage was plagued by bad luck. England and France were at war (King William's War). And part of Kidd's crew was impressed—forced into service—by an English man-of-war. The replacements were mostly ruffians and criminals. Some may have been pirates themselves.

A third of his new crew died from cholera, a dread disease, and the *Adventure Galley* began to leak. The expedition was a private business venture, and the crew were to be paid only if they took prizes—captured French or pirate vessels. So when only one small French ship fell to them as a prize, they became rebellious. Finally, after Kidd refused to attack a friendly Dutch ship, they threatened mutiny. One crewman attacked Kidd, who killed him with a bucket. It was probably at this point that Kidd, threatened by his crew and desperate because of the failure of his expedition, turned to piracy. He attacked several ships and soon became friendly with the pirates he had been sent to capture.

In 1699, Kidd arrived in the West Indies. He was charged with piracy and sent to England for trial. Kidd claimed that some of the ships he had taken had been sailing under French papers, making them legal prizes of war. Nevertheless, he was found guilty, and on May 23, 1701, he was hanged.

Reviewed by EDITH MCCALL
Author, *Pirates and Privateers*

KIDNEYS

The kidneys are only about as big as a fist, but they are giants when it comes to their ability to work. They filter and clean the blood, producing the urine that carries liquid waste out of the body. Each minute more than 1 quart (about 1 liter) of blood passes through the kidneys as it is cleaned and recycled—that adds up to about 425 gallons (1,609 liters) of blood each day!

The two kidneys are the major organs of the urinary system, which also includes the ureters, bladder, and urethra. Located below the middle of the back on each side of the spine, the kidneys are reddish-brown, bean-shaped organs about 4 inches (10 centimeters) long. Each kidney is covered by a thin, tough transparent membrane. A layer of fat surrounding the kidneys helps to hold them in place as well as cushion and protect them.

The Structures of the Kidney

The bean-shaped kidneys are the waste-purification units of the urinary system. As they produce urine, they remove wastes from the blood and regulate the fluid balance of the body.

Along with their main task, producing urine, the kidneys also constantly check and adjust the amounts of water, acids, salts, and other chemicals in the body.

▶ THE PARTS OF THE KIDNEY

When a cross section of the kidney is examined, three distinct regions can be seen. The **cortex**, the outer region, has a grainy appearance and contains the kidney's filtering units. The **medulla**, the middle region, is streaked by pyramid-shaped structures. These pyramids drain urine into cup-shaped tubes, called **calyxes**, that make up the funnel-shaped **pelvis**, the inner region. From the calyxes, urine travels to the ureter.

Large blood vessels enter each kidney at its inner curve. The **renal arteries** bring fresh blood to the kidneys, and the **renal veins** carry blood back toward the heart. It is the rich blood supply to the kidneys

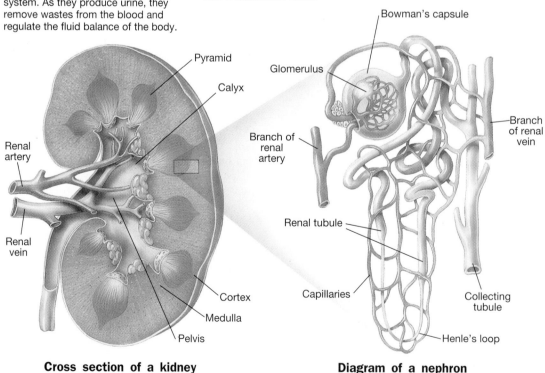

Cross section of a kidney

Renal artery
Renal vein
Pyramid
Calyx
Cortex
Medulla
Pelvis

Diagram of a nephron

Bowman's capsule
Glomerulus
Branch of renal artery
Branch of renal vein
Renal tubule
Capillaries
Collecting tubule
Henle's loop

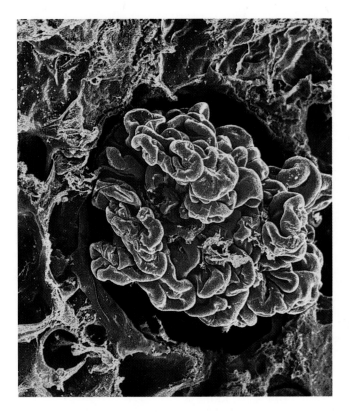

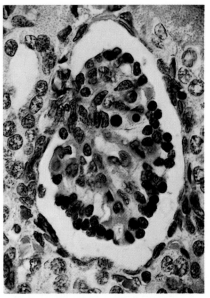

Blood enters a nephron through a ball of capillaries called a glomerulus (*left*). Within the glomerulus (*above*), the capillary network surrounded by Bowman's capsule can be seen.

that gives them their dark red color. The ureters, the tubes that carry urine to the bladder, also enter the kidneys at their inner curves.

Each kidney contains about a million microscopic filtering structures, called **nephrons**. A nephron begins with a tiny, fluffy tangle of capillaries (the smallest, thinnest blood vessels) that looks like a ball of cotton and is called the **glomerulus**. This is surrounded by a double-walled cup-shaped structure called **Bowman's capsule**. This capsule leads into a narrow **renal tubule** that twists and turns, dips downward and up to form **Henle's loop**, and finally feeds into a slightly thicker **collecting tubule**. A network of capillaries, formed from a blood vessel that branches out from the glomerulus, surrounds the various portions of the renal tubule.

▶ HOW THE KIDNEYS WORK

Together the two kidneys function like a tireless, nonstop machine. They produce urine in a three-step process of filtration, reabsorption, and secretion.

The filters in the nephrons are the thin walls of the capillaries that make up the glomeruli (plural of glomerulus). Small molecules in the blood, such as water and salts, can pass easily through the capillary walls into Bowman's capsule, but larger molecules, such as proteins, stay inside the glomerulus. So the blood that flows on through the capillary network is thicker, and a thin, watery fluid, called the glomerular filtrate, collects in the coiled tube of the nephron.

If all the kidneys did was filter liquids from the glomeruli, hundreds of pounds of water would be lost each day! But a process called **selective reabsorption** takes place. In this process, substances are transported out of the glomerular filtrate through the membrane of the renal tubule and into the blood of the surrounding capillaries. About 99 percent of the water in the glomerular filtrate is selectively reabsorbed into the blood. Nearly all the sugar, amino acids, vitamins, and any protein that has leaked through, along with various amounts of salts, are also taken back. In this way, the amount of water lost is reduced and the kidneys are able to adjust the concentrations of various chemicals in the body fluids. For example, if the body reserves of sodium or calcium are low, sodium or cal-

Can a person survive with only one kidney?

Some people are born with only one kidney. Others can lose a kidney because of a disease. And even though the fragile kidneys are protected by thick layers of fat, they can be injured by a hard blow to the body. That is why kidney punches are illegal in boxing. But whichever way a kidney is damaged, it is possible to live a normal, healthy life with only one kidney.

Both kidneys do exactly the same jobs of removing waste and toxins from the body, regulating the balance of body fluids, and maintaining the proper range of blood pressure. In a lifetime, these remarkable organs clean more than 1 million gallons of liquid—enough to fill a small lake! But one kidney can handle this gigantic task. In fact, if one kidney is removed, the remaining kidney can increase in size by 50 percent within two months to take over the whole job.

cium is reabsorbed from the filtrate. If the body has an oversupply of a particular substance, that substance remains in the filtrate and is carried out of the body along with waste products, such as ammonia.

During secretion, the tubule cells remove substances from the blood and secrete them into the urine. This is how the body gets rid of some drugs and other chemicals. When people take penicillin for an illness, traces of the drug will soon appear in their urine. In fact, if nonsmokers spend time in a room where people are smoking, their urine might test positive for the chemicals in cigarette smoke.

As they produce urine, the kidneys make constant adjustments in the body's fluids, fine-tuning their composition and concentration so that conditions are just right for all the body's organs. For instance, if too many salty foods have been eaten, the kidneys help to bring the inner environment back to normal by getting rid of extra salt and retaining extra water.

While ridding the body of waste products, the kidneys perform other tasks that help regulate body functions. They produce a hormone, **erythropoietin**, that stimulates the production of red blood cells. They also work to keep the blood pressure within a normal range. The kidneys adjust the blood pressure by changing the blood volume (if more urine is excreted, the blood volume and pressure decrease) and by secreting an enzyme called **renin**. This enzyme activates chemicals that cause the blood vessels to narrow, which raises the blood pressure.

▶ DISORDERS OF THE KIDNEYS

The most common kidney disease is an infection called **pyelonephritis**. However, the infection does not usually start in the kidneys but in the bladder. Once in the bladder, the infection may spread up into the kidneys. This kind of infection does not usually lead to kidney failure, unless there is a blockage in the urinary tract.

Glomerulonephritis is an inflammation of the glomeruli. It may develop when antibodies produced to fight bacteria or viruses somewhere else in the body mistakenly attack the kidneys.

Calcium salts in the urine sometimes form solid crystals, or stones, which may grow too large to pass out of the kidneys. These **kidney stones** block the flow of urine and may be very painful. They can be removed by surgery or with a device called an extracorporeal shock-wave lithotripter, which is used to pulverize the stones into tiny particles that can pass out in the urine.

The kidneys can be seriously damaged by disorders such as high blood pressure or diabetes, as well as by various poisons and drugs. Stones, tumors, or other problems that block urine flow can also damage the kidneys so that they are no longer able to perform their vital functions adequately. If both kidneys fail, poisonous wastes build up in the body and can lead to coma and death. **Hemodialysis** is a method of cleaning the blood of wastes by pumping blood through a filter system, then returning the cleaned blood to the body. Damaged kidneys can also be replaced surgically. A **kidney transplant** replaces a person's injured kidneys with an organ from a donor.

ALVIN SILVERSTEIN
VIRGINIA SILVERSTEIN
Coauthors, *The Excretory System*

See also BODY, HUMAN.

KIEV

Kiev is the capital and largest city of Ukraine. Situated on the Dnieper River, in the north central part of the country, it is an important river port and manufacturing center, with a population of more than 2.6 million. A handsome and historic city, one of the oldest in Europe, it has long been at the heart of Ukrainian cultural life. Present-day Kiev lies on both banks of the Dnieper, having expanded from its original site on the high cliffs above the right bank of the river.

The City. Probably the most notable of Kiev's surviving historical landmarks is the Cathedral of St. Sophia, which dates from approximately the 1040's and is now a museum. Nearby are the ruins of the Golden Gate, once the main gate of the city, which dates from the same period. The principal church still in use, the Cathedral of St. Vladimir, was built in the 1800's and is named for Prince (later Saint) Vladimir of Kiev, who in the late 900's began the conversion of the people to Christianity. His statue stands on a height overlooking the Dnieper.

One of the city's most distinctive historic sites is the Pechersky Lavra, or cave monastery, first constructed between the mid-1000's and 1100's. A vast enclosed area, it consists of numerous churches, belfries, and other structures, as well as a network of catacombs, or underground tombs.

St. Andrew's, built in the 1700's, is one of several historic churches in Kiev, capital and largest city of Ukraine. Blue and yellow are national colors.

Much of Kiev was destroyed or badly damaged during World War II, including the city's main thoroughfare, the Kreshchatik, which was rebuilt afterward at twice its original width. In a northwest suburb of the city, the Babi Yar monument commemorates the slaughter of some 100,000 Jews and other Kievans by the Germans during the war.

Population increases led to the expansion of the city, chiefly to the low-lying left bank of the Dnieper. The district, known as Darnitsa, consists of both residential suburbs and industrial areas.

Economic Activity. Kiev's location has made it a hub of transportation, with air, ship, and rail connections linking it to the rest of the country. As a major industrial city, it produces a variety of manufactured goods, including precision instruments, machine tools, aircraft, chemicals, and processed foods. It is also the country's publishing center and produces many of its consumer goods.

History. According to legend, Kiev was founded in the A.D. 400's by Prince Kii, although the city first appears in historical chronicles of the 800's. For more than 300 years it was the capital of the Eastern Slavic state known as Kievan Rus and a center of trade, religion, and culture. The city declined thereafter, and in 1240, it was destroyed by invading Mongols, beginning the pattern of destruction followed by rebuilding that is part of its long history.

Along with the rest of Ukraine, Kiev was absorbed by Russia in the 1600's and the Soviet Union in the 1900's. It was one of the leading cities of both the Russian Empire and its successor, the Soviet Union. With the breakup of the Soviet Union in 1991, it became the capital of an independent Ukraine.

ARTHUR CAMPBELL TURNER
University of California, Riverside

An important activity in kindergarten and nursery school is learning the different letters of the alphabet.

Although there is a lot of variation, 2- and 3-year-old children usually attend nursery school for several half days a week and move up to five half days a week when they turn 4. Some children whose parents work long hours may spend more time in these early childhood programs.

▶ ACTIVITIES IN KINDERGARTEN AND NURSERY SCHOOLS

KINDERGARTEN AND NURSERY SCHOOLS

It may seem to us that small children, under the age of 6, have little to learn at school. In fact, however, there are many things that young children can find out about before they enter the first grade. Even 3- and 4-year-old children can attach names to colors and shapes; they can discover which things float and which things sink; they can begin to draw and paint, do puzzles, and much more.

Young children also learn how to make choices, get along with other children, follow instructions, and finish projects that they begin. They learn most easily through working directly with materials such as clay and blocks rather than worksheets and workbooks. The methods, materials, and teaching practices used with young children is called **early childhood education**.

Two settings in which early childhood education takes place are nursery school and kindergarten. Generally, kindergarten is for 5-year-old children who will enter first grade the following year. Nursery schools serve children from age 2 to 4. Kindergarten classes are often taught in the public schools and may be half-day or full-day programs. Nursery schools are often located away from schools in their own buildings, in churches and synagogues, and sometimes even in factories and office buildings.

Young children learn best through doing. In nursery school and kindergarten, for example, young children learn the letters of the alphabet by playing with blocks that have the letters printed on them for easy recognition. The letters on the blocks are also raised so children can touch and feel, as well as see, their shapes. In kindergarten, they also begin to print letters. They also identify sight words like "Stop" and "Go," thus taking their first steps toward learning to read.

In the same way, children learn numbers and the basic operations of arithmetic. Most classrooms have cards with large numbers that are printed on them. Children learn to match the cards with the correct number of beads, sticks, buttons, or other objects—putting the number 2 next to two blocks, the number 3 next to three blocks, and so on. Young children also learn the basics of arithmetic through handling materials. They observe, for example, that if you take one block away from three blocks, then you have two blocks left. Although this seems obvious to adults, it is an exciting discovery for young children.

Young children are given opportunities to paint with watercolors, to cut with scissors, to draw with crayons, and to make animals out of clay and modeling dough. They also enjoy singing and playing simple instruments, such as bells, tambourines, and drums. Young children have a good sense of rhythm and like to move to music.

Other activities include sitting in a circle while the teacher reads a favorite story. Children also develop their language skills by telling stories about a vacation, a family pet, or other topics familiar to them.

Children may also take trips outside the school. For example, they may visit the local fire station or go to a doughnut shop, where they may be allowed into the kitchen to watch the bakers at work.

A common and frequent learning activity for young children is a cooking project such as making soup or baking bread. When they are engaged in such a project, children learn many different skills. In making soup, for example, children have to peel and slice the vegetables and in so doing learn the names of the vegetables, as well as the names of their colors and shapes. Children also have to measure the water, salt, and spices, which is a lesson in basic math. While watching the soup cook, they find that putting potatoes and carrots into a pot of boiling water makes them soft even though doing the same thing with eggs makes them hard. In this way, children acquire a few basic facts of chemistry as well.

One of the more important benefits of these projects is the development of children's social skills, such as sharing responsibility, cooperating, and interacting with others. In the particular project above, children also learn about good hygiene and safety practices.

The project method of teaching is well suited to the way young children learn best: through play activities that are fun and provide important learning experiences.

▶ THE CLASSROOM

Kindergarten and nursery school rooms do not have desks. Children usually work at tables or on a carpeted floor.

The rooms are typically arranged into different activity areas. There is generally a block corner with a full set of wooden blocks of different sizes and shapes. Nearby there is often a math area that will have varied sets of objects, such as buttons, to be counted. Other sets, such as sticks of different lengths, can be put in order according to their sizes.

In another part of the room, there is usually a group of science instruments such as magnets, magnifying glasses, and scales. Sometimes this area includes a water table

Children enjoy finding out how musical instruments make their various sounds, especially when they can play them while marching around the classroom in a make-believe parade.

with a tub of water for exploring objects that sink and float.

Many kindergartens and nursery schools have animals such as rabbits, gerbils, or guinea pigs as well as plants. There is also a reading corner with many different picture books, story books, and books of poetry. This corner usually has lots of soft pillows and is usually outfitted with a phonograph or tape recorder with records or tapes of stories and songs.

There is also usually a housekeeping area with pots and dishes, child-size appliances, brooms, and other items, and a workshop area with a workbench, and toy hammers, wood saws, and other tools.

What is Project Head Start?

Project Head Start is a program of the United States government that provides educational and social services to economically disadvantaged children and their families. The program, which started in 1965, is run by the Administration for Children, Youth and Families, of the United States Department of Health and Human Services.

Head Start aims to improve the health, intellectual performance, emotional adjustment, and social attitudes of the preschool child by providing day care, meals, and medical and dental care. In addition, Head Start provides educational services for parents of children in the program.

Most nursery schools and kindergartens open directly onto an outdoor play area. This outside area is usually outfitted with a track for tricycles, a large sandbox, swings, and a jungle gym. Many outdoor play areas have sheds with a variety of play materials such as tricycles and wagons, as well as shovels and pails. Many children bring their own toys to school and can play with these in the sandbox or elsewhere.

▶ **THE TEACHER**

Young men and women who want to teach young children can choose from a large number of excellent training programs in colleges and universities around the country.

In addition to taking the necessary courses in language, mathematics, science, social science, and the arts, students also take courses in education and child development to learn methods for teaching young children. Most training programs require that student teachers spend some time in the classroom working with young children under the supervision of an experienced teacher.

Teachers of young children must be prepared to work with children who are new to the country and who may not yet speak English. They also take courses in teaching children who have special needs—children who have limited hearing, limited vision, or other disabilities.

In order to be a kindergarten or nursery school teacher, one must enjoy being with young children. Unlike older children, children under 6 cannot be taught with textbooks or lectures. They also need physical contact. They may want to sit on the teacher's lap and may need an occasional hug. Young children also have less control over their emotions and are more apt to cry and quarrel. The teacher of young children must be prepared to be more of a substitute parent than is true for teachers of older children.

The majority of teachers for young children are women. Nursery school teachers are almost totally women, but there are male kindergarten teachers.

▶ **HISTORY**

Early childhood education has a relatively short history. Although children over the age of 6 have been schooled since ancient times, educational programs for children under 6 were not introduced until the Industrial Revolution of the 1700's.

As a result of the Industrial Revolution, families moved to the cities, where parents got work in factories. Because both men and women worked in factories, there was no one to stay at home and care for the children. The first early education programs were created to care for the children of working parents.

In 1816, the most famous, and possibly the first, infant school was started by Robert Owen (1771–1858), a Welsh cotton-mill owner. In 1816, Owen set up a system of schools for all the children under 12 in the mill town of New Lanark, Scotland. (Those who were 12 could work in the mill.) The very youngest children were placed in an infant school as soon as they could walk. In this school, the children were treated kindly and they played together.

A number of infant schools grew up in England. Infant schools also became popular in France.

Growth of Ideas

One of the first early childhood educators was Heinrich Pestalozzi (1746–1827), a Swiss teacher and writer. Pestalozzi started a number of schools for young children and also wrote books for mothers on how to teach basic concepts to young children. A student of Pestalozzi, Friedrich Froebel (1782–1852), created a school for young children in Germany. He called the school kindergarten, from the German words *kinder* ("children") and *garten* ("garden").

Froebel believed that children express their interests through their play. He developed a set of play materials, called gifts. A ball, for example, can be used to teach a child the idea of roundness, as well as of texture and color. In addition, Froebel believed that the ball could help children appreciate more general concepts such as the roundness of the Earth.

Perhaps the best known and most influential of early childhood educators was Maria Montessori (1870–1952). After receiving her medical degree, Montessori worked with children who had special needs. After several years, she was asked to design an educa-

Story time helps young children develop their listening skills and stimulates their imaginations.

tional program for disadvantaged children who were living in a housing project in one of the poorer sections of Rome.

Drawing on her work with children with special needs, Montessori felt that children become independent by doing things for themselves. She believed that there are what she called sensitive periods in early childhood when children learn best through one or another of the senses. Her materials were designed to provide the kind of stimulation children need during these periods. Many of the materials were what she called self-teaching. For example, she introduced a board with holes of different sizes and a series of pegs that were different sizes as well. The child had to put the pegs in the holes. If the child put a small peg in a large hole, there would be no place for the large peg, and the child could not get all the pegs in.

Montessori placed a great deal of emphasis on the learning environment. She had craftspeople make child-size chairs, tables, plates, glasses, and utensils. With objects suited to their small bodies and hands, children could care for themselves and also learn a great deal on their own.

A method of teaching known as the progressive method was developed by John Dewey (1859–1952), an American philosopher. In 1896, Dewey started an experimental

children who had not yet reached first-grade age. In 1918, an act was passed allowing the establishment of nursery schools for children aged 2 to 5 within the English school system.

In the United States in the early 1920's, a number of universities established centers to study the growth and development of children. Nursery schools grew up around many of these centers. They were run privately or as co-operatives and did not become part of the public school system.

In the 1930's and early 1940's, the federal government supported nursery schools. But the funding ended in 1946. However, in 1965, President Lyndon B. Johnson announced funding for an antipoverty preschool program named Head Start.

In the 1960's, many mothers of young children began to enter the workforce. The fact that large numbers of young children were being cared for outside the home for many hours a day changed society's perceptions of early childhood education. It was recognized that early childhood programs should be more than babysitting and that the child care center should provide an educational program. Today, most nursery schools, kindergartens, and day care centers provide the kinds of learning environments described above.

The growth of early childhood education reflects our new appreciation of the fact that young children learn an enormous amount during the first years of life. Nonetheless, young children have different things to learn than children in grade school, and they learn them best in an environment that is in keeping with their size, interests, and abilities. We recognize today that early childhood education is not a smaller-size model of elementary education. Rather, we appreciate that it is a unique form of education equal in importance to higher levels of education.

DAVID ELKIND

Professor of Child Study, Tufts University

See also DAY CARE.

school, the University of Chicago Laboratory School. Dewey felt that the school should focus on the child rather than the teacher. He also believed that children learn by doing. In his school, children did not simply sit in the classroom and learn from books. The group also learned from taking part in experiences.

Later Developments

The kindergarten movement began in the United States in the mid-1800's. The first kindergarten in the United States was opened at Watertown, Wisconsin, in 1856.

Modern nursery schools began in England almost 75 years after the kindergarten was established. A leader in the development of nursery school was Margaret McMillan (1860–1931). She saw a need for schools for

KING, MARTIN LUTHER, JR. (1929–1968)

"I still have a dream. It is a dream deeply rooted in the American dream . . . a dream that my four little children will one day live in a nation where they will not be judged by the color of their skin but by the content of their character."

These were the words of Martin Luther King, Jr., a black Baptist minister, speaking at the Lincoln Memorial in Washington, D.C. The occasion was the largest civil rights rally in the history of the United States. More than 200,000 people filled the grassy area around the monument on that sizzling August day in 1963. Since that day the words "I have a dream" have become the symbol of Martin Luther King, Jr., and his nonviolent efforts to secure justice for black Americans.

King was born in Atlanta, Georgia, on January 15, 1929, to Alberta and Martin Luther King. His father was the pastor of Ebenezer Baptist Church. As a member of a black middle-income family, young Martin never felt the pinch of poverty. But his family could not protect him from the cruelties of racism. As Martin grew up, he kept his mother's words in mind: "You are as good as anyone."

King earned degrees from Morehouse College in Atlanta and Crozer Theological Seminary in Pennsylvania. He then went to Boston University, where he earned a doctorate. In Boston he met Coretta Scott. They married in 1953 and settled in Montgomery, Alabama, where King had been appointed pastor of the Dexter Avenue Baptist Church.

Not long after King arrived in Montgomery, he was asked to lead a black boycott of the city buses. The black people of Montgomery had decided that they would not ride in segregated buses. They appealed to the courts for support of their efforts. The boycott, which lasted 381 days, ended in victory in 1956, when the U.S. Supreme Court declared segregation of buses to be in violation of the Constitution.

Soon after the boycott, King was asked to lead a new organization called the Southern Christian Leadership Conference (SCLC). In 1959, he returned to Atlanta as co-pastor, with his father, of the Ebenezer Baptist Church. He continued his work with the SCLC there.

The goal of SCLC was to win equality for black people. SCLC members pledged to avoid violence in striving for their aims. Despite jailings, threats, and violent acts against them, they never wavered from this policy. All of SCLC's many victories for equality were won through nonviolent techniques such as boycotts, marches, and sit-ins. SCLC campaigns in Birmingham and Selma, Alabama, helped to bring about the Civil Rights Act of 1964 and the Voting Rights Act of 1965.

It was King's leadership that inspired SCLC's nonviolent policy. King based his philosophy on the teachings of Jesus and those of the Indian leader Mohandas Gandhi. To those who opposed SCLC's efforts, King said: "We will match your capacity to inflict suffering with our capacity to endure suffering. . . . We will not hate you, but we cannot . . . obey your unjust laws . . . we will so appeal to your heart and conscience that we will win you in the process." These words summed up King's philosophy. His pursuit of justice won him the Nobel peace prize in 1964.

In the spring of 1968, Martin Luther King, Jr., went to Memphis, Tennessee, to help sanitation workers win better wages and working conditions. On April 4, the day before a mass march, he was shot and killed by an assassin. King's death, at the age of 39, was mourned not only by his wife and four children but by the whole world. He is buried in Atlanta. Since 1986 his birthday has been a national holiday in the United States, celebrated on the third Monday in January.

JACQUELINE L. HARRIS
Co-author, *Marching to Freedom: The Life of Martin Luther King, Jr.*

KING, WILLIAM LYON MACKENZIE
(1874–1950)

William Lyon Mackenzie King was one of Canada's greatest leaders. He was prime minister for 21 years, longer than any other prime minister in his country's history. He served longer, in fact, than any prime minister in the history of the Commonwealth. King led Canada through the difficult years of World War II to an important role in world affairs. He has been called "the rock upon which . . . modern Canada was built."

King was a shy, retiring man. He never married and devoted most of his life to his work. His long career in politics followed his earlier interest in social work and industrial labor relations.

King was born on December 17, 1874, at Berlin (now Kitchener), Ontario. His father was a lawyer. King was named after his maternal grandfather, William Lyon Mackenzie, a political activist who in 1837–38 had led a rebellion against the colonial government. King studied at the University of Toronto, from which he received a law degree in 1896. He attended the University of Chicago, where he became involved in social work, and later received a doctor of philosophy degree from Harvard University. In 1900, he helped organize Canada's new Department of Labor and became deputy minister of labor, a post he held for eight years.

In 1908, King won election to Parliament as a Liberal. A year later he became minister of labor under Prime Minister Wilfrid Laurier. The Liberals were defeated in the election of 1911, and King lost his own seat in Parliament. After working for the Liberal Party until 1914, he accepted a position as a labor-relations consultant with the Rockefeller Foundation in New York City. He helped settle a coal miners' strike in Colorado, and his services were used by several other American companies to solve labor disputes.

But King's heart was in Canadian politics. When Laurier died in 1919, King was chosen to head the Liberal Party. In 1921 the Liberals won an election, and King became prime minister, the first of his three periods in that office. He resigned in 1926 during a constitutional crisis, but he returned as prime minister when his party won later that year.

A portrait in oil of William Lyon Mackenzie King, painted by the British artist Sir William Orpen.

King's party was defeated by the Conservatives in 1930, and King spent five years out of office. He became prime minister again in 1935. After that he won every election until he retired in 1948. He was succeeded as prime minister by Louis St. Laurent. St. Laurent, with the Liberal Party, remained in power until 1957. King died on July 22, 1950.

As prime minister, King won recognition for Canada as an independent nation within the Commonwealth. He generally followed a policy of avoiding foreign involvement. But when World War II broke out in 1939, he brought Canada into the war on the side of Britain and France. His friendship with U.S. President Franklin D. Roosevelt led to a period of close Canadian-American co-operation. One of King's greatest contributions was to Canadian unity. His policies united Canadians by overcoming the differences between various parts of the country.

King was not a great debater in Parliament, and his quiet personality did not make him a popular leader. Perhaps his greatest gift was his ability to understand what had to be done and, by compromise, to accomplish it.

JOHN MOIR
University of Toronto

See also MACKENZIE, WILLIAM LYON.

KING, WILLIAM RUFUS. See VICE PRESIDENCY OF THE UNITED STATES.

KINGDOMS OF LIVING THINGS

Living things—organisms—are found in a variety of environments almost everywhere on Earth: from deep in the oceans to high in the air, from the ice-covered poles to the tropical forests of the equator. **Biologists**, scientists who deal with organisms, have identified 1.5 million species, or kinds, and estimate that as many as 50 million now exist. To help make sense of this complex world of living things, scientists have developed a classification system that puts all living things within large groups of closely related organisms called kingdoms.

▶ **CLASSIFYING LIVING THINGS**

Since early times, people have tried to classify living things in an orderly manner. The Greek philosopher and scientist Aristotle, who is often called the father of biology, developed the first all-encompassing system of biological classification. He divided the living world into two kingdoms—animals and plants. For more than 2,000 years, Aristotle's system endured.

As biologists learned more about living things, they realized that some organisms, such as bacteria and fungi, could not readily be classified as either plants or animals. It was not until the 1960's that biotechnological techniques allowed researchers to distinguish between some closely related species with similar appearances. With this ability, new groupings were suggested. Some proposed separating living things into as many as 13 kingdoms! However, it was the proposal of American biologist Robert H. Whittaker that gained acceptance and is recognized by most scientists today. Whittaker developed a system that divides living things into five kingdoms: animals, plants, fungi, protists, and monerans. All the members of each kingdom share characteristics that make them different from members of the other kingdoms. These characteristics include the way they are built, how they get food, and how they reproduce.

The incredible variety of living things found on the surface of the Earth, including those organisms that have become extinct, are classified by most scientists into five major groups, or kingdoms (*from top*): animals, plants, fungi, protists (such as amoebas), and monerans (such as bacteria).

Animals

Animals make up the largest kingdom of living things—Kingdom Animalia. Biologists have identified more than 1 million species of animals. The many kingdom members exhibit great variety of shape, size, and structure. But however different animals such as elephants, mice, whales, pigeons, snakes, fish, sponges, insects, lobsters, worms, jellyfish, and even humans might appear, they share important similarities.

Animals are complex, multicelled organisms. Each cell in an animal's body is bounded by a delicate skinlike covering called the cell membrane. This protects the inner parts of the cell and gives the cell its shape. Within the cell are various structures, each of which has certain functions. Perhaps the most important structure is the nucleus, which is the cell's command center. It directs the cell's activities.

The cells of most animals are arranged in groups or layers called tissues. All the cells in a tissue look alike and do the same job. For example, muscle tissue is made up of muscle cells and makes movement of the

Whether great or small, every member of the animal kingdom is a multicellular organism that begins life as a single cell. Within that single cell is all the genetic information necessary for development. The single cell divides again and again as the developing organism, or embryo (nine-day-old chicken embryo *at left*), moves rapidly through the stages of early growth to maturity.

body or of certain parts of the body possible. Nervous tissue is built of nerve cells and is responsible for carrying nerve signals throughout the body. An organ, such as the heart,

Did you know that...

binomial nomenclature—the method of naming living things—was introduced in 1735 and is still used today? Swedish biologist Carolus Linnaeus established the practice of giving each kind of organism a unique two-part name, which was Latin in form, as he worked to develop a system of classifiying

all living organisms. The first part of the name is the same for all organisms in the same genus, or group; the second part is the species, or kind, within the genus. For example, *Acer saccharum, Acer nigrum,* and *Acer rubrum* are the scientific names of the sugar maple, the black maple, and the red maple.

Because animals cannot make their own food, they must find food. The type of food that each kind of animal seeks out to eat varies. Some animals, such as caribou (*above*), eat only plant matter, while others, including hyenas (*right*), eat only meat. Bears (*above right*) are among the animals that will eat both plant substances and meat.

stomach, or brain, is formed when different kinds of tissue are combined. An organ performs special tasks for the body.

An animal's life cycle includes a distinctive early stage of rapid growth as a tiny, multicellular form called an embryo. As an animal grows, it follows a definite growth pattern. When it reaches a certain size, it stops growing. Its shape is like that of all animals of its kind. For example, all eels have a slithery snakelike form, all spiders have eight legs, all bats have two wings.

In order to live, animals must take in food. Some animals, such as deer, eat only plants. Other animals, such as tigers, eat meat. Still others, such as humans, eat both plant and animal matter. Animals digest, or break down, the food they eat to provide the energy to power life-sustaining body functions. They take in oxygen to help them obtain energy from the

The sea anemone, unlike most animals, stays in one place for most of its life, moving only those body parts necessary to capture food, reproduce, or defend itself.

food. And they excrete, or release, carbon dioxide and other body wastes.

Most animals can move. They swim, walk, crawl, or fly from one place to another, sometimes covering great distances. This ability allows them to find food, escape enemies, or search for mates. Even animals that remain in one place are able to move parts of their bodies. For example, a sea anemone swims only during an early stage in its life. Then it settles onto the seafloor, where it spends the rest of its life anchored to a rock or shell. It waves its tentacles back and forth in the water, capturing prey and dragging it into its mouth.

Plants

Kingdom Plantae contains more than 350,000 known species. These include ferns, mosses, liverworts, trees, grasses, and flowering herbs. Plants are multicelled organisms, as are animals, with cells organized into tissues. But a plant cell has an additional structure. Outside the cell membrane is a thick cell wall composed of a material called cellulose.

Plant tissues also are different from animal tissues. Plants do not have muscle, nerve, skin, or blood tissues. But their specialized tissues accomplish many of the same kinds of tasks—transport tissue carries water, minerals, and other materials to various parts of the plant; growth tissue produces new parts as well as increases in the plant's size; and protective tissue covers parts of the plant to keep the insides safe from injury.

The life cycle of a plant, which includes an embryo stage, ranges from days to centuries. Unlike most other living things, plants grow throughout their lives. They do not stop when they reach a certain size. Some sequoias and bristlecone pines are thousands of years old and still growing! Most growth takes place at the ends of roots and stems, producing new branches, leaves, roots, and other parts.

Like all plants, the delicate rose (*left*) and the formidable sequoia (*above*) share the same growth pattern. That is, they continue to grow as long as environmental conditions are favorable.

Plants occupy a unique role in nature. Most plants make their own food in a process known as photosynthesis. A plant's food-making factories are cellular structures called chloroplasts, which are usually located in the cells of a plant's leaves. Inside the chloroplasts is the substance chlorophyll, a green light-absorbing pigment. Through the action of chlorophyll, carbon dioxide, water, and light energy are combined to produce a plant's food. Some of the food is used immediately by the plant for activities such as growth. Any excess is transformed into other food products or stored for future use. Plants are essential to the survival of most other living things because they provide food for animals and other organisms.

Even though plants do not move about, they are capable of some movement. A geranium turns its leaves toward light. Sweet peas wrap tendrils around fence posts. The leaves of a mimosa tree fold up when touched.

Plants respond to their environments with movement—a grapevine encounters a wire support and wraps its tendrils tightly around it.

Fungi

Scientists have identified more than 100,000 species of fungi. Members of the Kingdom Fungi, which are mostly land dwellers, include mushrooms, molds, rusts, mildews, truffles, puffballs, and yeasts. A yeast consists of only one cell. But the majority of fungi are multicelled.

Each fungal cell has a cell wall, which gets its stiffness from cellulose or a material called chitin or both. The body, or mycelium, of a fungus consists of a mass of slender branching tubes called hyphae. In some species, a hypha consists of one long cell. In other species, each hypha is divided into many cells by walls called

Although yeasts (*left*) are single-celled organisms that can be seen only with a microscope, most fungi, including the white mold that grows on strawberries (*below left*), are multicelled organisms of varying sizes that can be seen with the naked eye.

septa (plural of septum). Each cell contains at least one nucleus, but in some species, cells have two or more nuclei.

Unlike animals and plants, fungi do not have an embryo stage. A fungus begins life as a spore that develops into a hypha. The hypha, which grows at its tip, branches and eventually forms the mycelium. Hyphae grow mostly underground or within the object on which the fungus feeds. Thus, the mycelium of a fungus usually is invisible. The part of a mushroom or other fungus commonly seen by people is the reproductive structure. It is a dense, tangled mass of special hyphae.

The fungal cell lacks chlorophyll, so a fungus cannot make its own food. Instead, fungi secrete powerful chemicals that break down food into molecules that can be absorbed. Some fungi feed on living organisms. For example, corn smut grows on the ears of corn. Other fungi feed on dead organisms or on products of organisms, including their wastes. For example, bread mold gets its nutrients from bread, which is made from plant grains.

Still other fungi absorb nutrients from a variety of foods. Honey mushrooms usually feed on dead tree branches. But under certain conditions they will feed on living trees.

A fungus spends its entire life in one spot. It does not move about, but it can react to changes in its environment. For example, when a hypha of one fungal species touches hyphae of another species, it will turn away and grow in a different direction.

Fungi get their food and energy from the living organisms, such as trees (*above*), or the decaying matter they live on.

Spores ejected from a puffball (*right*) drift on air currents to new homes where, if conditions are suitable, they will grow.

As a group, protists exhibit a number of diverse traits. For example, algae (*far left*) are able to manufacture their own food through photosynthesis, and paramecia (*left*) have hairlike structures that allow them to move. However, there is one characteristic that protists share—all live in watery environments.

Protists

Kingdom Protista contains more than 100,000 known species, including most kinds of algae and one-celled organisms commonly called protozoans, meaning "first animals." These include paramecia (plural of paramecium), amoebas, and many other tiny organisms, most of which can be seen only when viewed through a microscope.

Most protists consist of a single cell, with a cell membrane. Some also have a cell wall. Within its one-celled body, the organism carries out the same basic life processes that are carried out by multicelled organisms. The cell has many specialized structures, including at least one nucleus.

There is great variety among these organisms that can be found wherever there is water or moisture. Some contain chloroplasts and can make their own food, while others must find food. Some protists live in one spot, but many have parts that help them move and gather food. A paramecium, for example, has many hairlike extensions called cilia. As the cilia beat back and forth, the paramecium is propelled through the water. A euglena swims using a long, whiplike flagellum (singular of flagella) that it swings back and forth as it moves.

Many species of protists form colonies. The colonies have a definite shape. For example, *Volvox* cells join together in a ball-shaped colony, while a spirogyra colony is threadlike, consisting of cells joined end to end. These colonies may be large enough to be seen with the unaided eye.

Volvox colonies (*left*) are formed by hundreds of thousands of the single-celled algae linked together. Many kelps (*below*) may grow together to form huge undersea forests.

Monerans

The Kingdom Monera includes all the one-celled organisms known as bacteria. Scientists have identified more than 10,000 species of bacteria. They are very ancient organisms. In fact, they were probably among the first living organisms.

Bacteria are extremely tiny organisms. It would take as many as 50,000 average-sized bacteria, placed end-to-end in a row, to equal a distance of 1 inch (2.5 centimeters). While

How many kinds of living things are there?

Scientists have identified about 1.5 million species, including some that lived long ago but are now extinct. The actual number of species is believed to be much higher. Scientists estimate that at least 9 million and perhaps 50 million species of living organisms now exist!

Each year, hundreds of previously unknown species are discovered, as remote areas such as tropical rain forests and ocean bottoms are explored, rock formations are examined for fossils, and living things are re-examined. New species are also revealed as scientists gain new tools. No one knew of the existence of bacteria until microscopes were invented. One of the latest tools used in identifying species is DNA (deoxyribonucleic acid). This is the material in cells that carries an organism's hereditary information. Different species, even if they look alike and are closely related, have very different DNA. DNA tests will help scientists determine if a barking deer found recently in Laos is a new species altogether or a species from China that has traveled to Laos.

bacteria are single-celled creatures, some kinds of cyanobacteria (also known as blue-green algae) form colonies. The colonies are clumps of cells inside a blob of slime or cells arranged end to end, in threads.

A cell wall, usually surrounded by a layer of slime, encloses the cell. But monerans differ from all other living things in that their cells do not have nuclei or other specialized

There are more bacteria in our world than any other life-form. These small, simple creatures are classified according to whether they are round (*below*), rod shaped (*bottom left*), or spiral (*bottom right*).

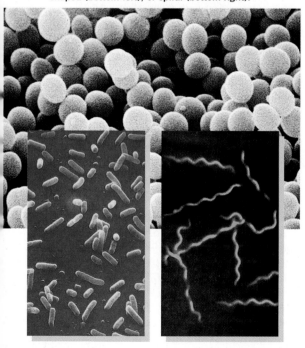

structures. Most bacteria do not contain chlorophyll or other chemicals that allow them to make their own food. They must obtain their food from other organisms or from nonliving matter. The only bacteria that contain chlorophyll and can carry out photosynthesis are the cyanobacteria. Cyanobacteria also can absorb food from their surroundings.

Bacteria are simple creatures that live in some of the harshest environments. They can survive freezing temperatures for years. Some species thrive in hot springs and others in very hot acids. Most scientists now classify many of these extreme species as archaea, a branch of life separate from bacteria.

Many kinds of bacteria make their home in the human body. Some are harmful, others are not. They cover the skin, pack the digestive tract, and live in the mouth. For example, more than one hundred species of bacteria may live in your mouth, with their total number greater than the number of people who have ever lived!

Most bacteria cannot move from place to place on their own. A few species move by twisting the entire cell. Species that live in water or other liquids often have flagella. The number of flagella depends on the species.

JENNY TESAR
Author, *Patterns in Nature:
An Overview of the Living World*

See also ANIMALS; FUNGI; LIFE; PLANTS.

KINKAJOUS. See RACCOONS AND THEIR RELATIVES.

KIPLING, RUDYARD (1865–1936)

The English writer Rudyard Kipling also belongs to India, America, and South Africa. He was born on December 30, 1865, in Bombay, India, where his father was the principal of a school of art. He was named Rudyard after the lake in England where his parents first met.

When he was 5, Rudyard was taken to England and left in the care of a retired naval officer and his wife. He was not well treated and was very unhappy. When he was 12, he was sent to the United Services College in North Devon. *Stalky and Co.* (1899) describes his life at school. He performed in plays and read constantly. The headmaster let him borrow freely from his own library. Since many of his parents' friends and relations were writers and artists, Rudyard knew books and

art at an early age. He especially liked the work of Americans writing at that time— Emerson, Poe, Longfellow, Whitman, Harte, Twain, and Harris. He tried writing in the style of different authors. In 1881 his parents had his *Schoolboy Lyrics* printed in India.

After 5 years of school Rudyard returned to India and became the assistant editor of the *Civil and Military Gazette* of Lahore. His father was then principal of Lahore's school of art and curator of its museum, later described in *Kim* (1901). Work on the newspaper was done at night. Afterward Kipling would wander through the old walled city of Lahore. He began writing stories and verses for the paper. In 1887 he was transferred to the staff of the *Pioneer* at Allahabad and traveled through northern India. His stories for the *Pioneer* were published as paperback books in the Indian Railway Library. They were carried by travelers all over the world. When Kipling left India and arrived in London in 1889, he found he was already famous. His stories were read eagerly, and people were talking about his "Ballad of East and West," which had just appeared in *Macmillan's Magazine.*

In London, Kipling went into the barrooms, barrack-rooms, and music halls to listen to the songs the people were singing. He put new words to them. His *Barrack-Room Ballads* (1892) were an entirely new kind of verse. He wrote a novel, *The Light That Failed* (1891), and then took off for America, South Africa, New Zealand, Australia, and India. He returned to England in 1892 to marry Carrie (Caroline Starr) Balestier. The writer Henry James gave her away at the wedding. He remained a close family friend.

The Kiplings settled near Brattleboro, Vermont, Carrie's home. When their first child was on the way, Kipling began writing stories for children. He continued writing them until their last child was too old for stories. The *Jungle Books* (1894–95) were about a boy brought up by animals in the jungle. *Captains Courageous* (1897) was composed of sea tales told by the Kiplings' Vermont doctor. Kipling also went to Gloucester to talk with former sea captains and look at ships. He told the *Just So Stories* (1902) to his "Best Beloved" daughter Josephine, who died in 1900. *Puck of Pook's Hill* (1906) and *Re-*

wards and Fairies (1910) were inspired by the ancient history of the area near the Kiplings' house in Sussex, England.

The Kiplings left Brattleboro for England in 1896. In 1898 they traveled to Cape Town, South Africa. There they met Cecil Rhodes, the founder of Rhodesia. On a visit to Rhodesia, Kipling saw the "great grey-green greasy Limpopo River all set about with fever-trees" that appears in his *Just So Stories*. Between 1901 and 1908 the Kiplings spent each winter near Rhodes's house in South Africa.

Near the end of the 1800's, Kipling published a number of poems in the *London Times* that dealt seriously with political subjects. Some poems reflected Kipling's belief in the duty of powerful nations to promote their forms of government, religion, and culture throughout the world. Today, many people consider these ideas to be wrong. But Kipling's views were popular in their day and influenced political leaders such as U.S. President Theodore Roosevelt. Kipling and Roosevelt wrote many letters to each other. Their correspondence is now in the U.S. Library of Congress.

In 1907 Kipling was awarded the Nobel prize for literature. In 1923 he was elected lord rector of the University of St. Andrews. He was also a trustee of the Rhodes scholarships and met annually with the Rhodes scholars at Oxford. He received many honors from universities and literary societies, among them the gold medal of the Royal Society of Literature, which only Scott, Meredith, and Hardy had received before him. He refused all royal honors, however, even though he was a good friend of King George V. Kipling wished to be free to write as he chose.

Kipling always carried two books with him on his journeys—*Flowers of the Field*, by C. A. Johns, and a volume of poetry by Horace. He was interested in botany, and he made notes in the margins of Johns's book about flowers he saw.

Kipling died on January 18, 1936. He was buried in the Poets' Corner of Westminster Abbey. His autobiography, *Something of Myself*, was published the following year.

Reviewed by REGINALD L. COOK
Middlebury College

"The Elephant's Child," one of Rudyard Kipling's *Just So Stories*, follows.

▶THE ELEPHANT'S CHILD

In the high and Far-Off times the Elephant, O Best Beloved, had no trunk. He had only a blackish, bulgy nose, as big as a boot, that he could wriggle about from side to side; but he couldn't pick up things with it. But there was one Elephant—a new Elephant—an Elephant's Child—who was full of 'satiable curtiosity, and that means he asked ever so many questions. *And* he lived in Africa, and he filled all Africa with his 'satiable curtiosities. He asked his tall aunt, the Ostrich, why her tail-feathers grew just so, and his tall aunt the Ostrich spanked him with her hard, hard claw. He asked his tall uncle, the Giraffe, what made his skin spotty, and his tall uncle, the Giraffe, spanked him with his hard, hard hoof. And still he was full of 'satiable curtiosity! He asked his broad aunt, the Hippopotamus, why here eyes were red, and his broad aunt, the Hippopotamus, spanked him with her broad, broad hoof; and he asked his hairy uncle, the Baboon, why melons tasted just so, and his hairy uncle, the Baboon, spanked him with his hairy, hairy paw. And *still* he was full of 'satiable curtiosity! He asked questions about everything that he saw, or heard, or felt, or smelt, or touched, and all his uncles and his aunts spanked him. And still he was full of 'satiable curtiosity!

One fine morning in the middle of the Precession of the Equinoxes this 'satiable Elephant's Child asked a new fine question that he had never asked before. He asked. "What does the Crocodile have for dinner?" Then everybody said, "Hush!" in a loud and dretful tone, and they spanked him immediately and directly, without stopping, for a long time.

By and by, when that was finished, he came upon Kolokolo Bird sitting in the middle of a wait-a-bit thorn-bush, and he said, "My father has spanked me, and my mother has spanked me; all my aunts and uncles have spanked me for my 'satiable curtiosity; and *still* I want to know what the Crocodile has for dinner!

The Kolokolo Bird said, with a mornful cry, "Go to the banks of the great grey-green, greasy Limpopo River, all set about with fever-trees, and find out."

That very next morning, when there was

nothing left of the Equinoxes, because the Precession had preceded according to precedent this 'satiable Elephant's Child took a hundred pounds of bananas (the little short red kind), and a hundred pounds of sugarcane (the long purple kind), and seventeen melons (the greeny-crackly kind), and said to all his dear families, "Good-bye. I am going to the great grey-green, greasy Limpopo River, all set about with fever-trees, to find out what the Crocodile has for dinner." And they all spanked him once more for luck, though he asked them most politely to stop.

Then he went away, a little warm, but not at all astonished, eating melons, and throwing the rind about, because he could not pick it up.

He went from Graham's Town to Kimberley, and from Kimberley to Khama's Country, and from Khama's Country he went east and north, eating melons all the time, till he at last came to the banks of the great grey-green, greasy Limpopo River, all set about with fever-trees, precisely as Kolokolo Bird had said.

Now you must know and understand, O Best Beloved, that till that very week, and day, and hour, and minute, this 'satiable Elephant's Child had never seen a Crocodile, and did not know what one was like. It was all his 'satiable curiosity.

The first thing that he found was a Bi-Coloured-Python-Rock-Snake curled round a rock.

" 'Scuse me," said the Elephant's Child most politely, "but have you seen such a thing as a Crocodile in these promiscuous parts?"

"*Have* I seen a Crocodile?" said the Bi-Coloured-Python-Rock-Snake, in a voice of dretful scorn. "What will you ask me next?"

" 'Scuse me," said the Elephant's Child, "but could you kindly tell me what he has for dinner?"

Then the Bi-Coloured-Python-Rock-Snake uncoiled himself very quickly from the rock, and spanked the Elephant's Child with his scalesome, flailsome tail.

"That is odd," said the Elephant's Child, "because my father and my mother, and my uncle and my aunt, not to mention my other aunt, the Hippopotamus, and my other uncle, the Baboon, have all spanked me for my 'satiable curiosity—and I suppose this is the same thing."

So he said good-bye very politely to the Bi-Coloured-Python-Rock-Snake, and helped to coil him up on the rock again, and went on, a little warm, but not at all astonished, eating melons, and throwing the rind about because he could not pick it up, till he trod on what he thought was a log of wood at the very edge of the great grey-green, greasy Limpopo River, all set about with fever-trees.

But it was really the Crocodile, O Best Beloved, and the Crocodile winked one eye—like this!

" 'Scuse me," said the Elephant's Child most politely, "but do you happen to have seen a Crocodile in these promiscuous parts?"

Then the Crocodile winked the other eye, and lifted half his tail out of the mud; and the Elephant's Child stepped back most politely, because he did not wish to be spanked again.

"Come hither, Little One," said the Crocodile. "Why do you ask such things?"

" 'Scuse me," said the Elephant's Child most politely, "but my father has spanked me, my mother has spanked me, not to mention my tall aunt, the Ostrich, and my tall uncle, the Giraffe, who can kick ever so hard, as well as my broad aunt, the Hippopotamus, and my hairy uncle, the Baboon, *and* including the Bi-Coloured-Python-Rock-Snake, with the scalesome, flailsome tail, just up the bank, who spanks harder than any of them; and *so*, if it's quite all the same to you, I don't want to be spanked any more."

"Come hither, Little One," said the Crocodile, "for I am the Crocodile," and he wept crocodile-tears to show it was quite true.

Then the Elephant's Child grew all breathless, and panted, and kneeled down on the bank and said, "You are the very person I have been looking for all these long days. Will you please tell me what you have for dinner?"

"Come hither, Little One," said the Crocodile, "and I'll whisper."

Then the Elephant's Child put his head down close to the Crocodile's musky, tusky mouth, and the Crocodile caught him by his little nose, which up to that very week, day, hour, and minute, had been no bigger than a boot, though much more useful.

"I think," said the Crocodile—and he said it between his teeth, like this—"I think today I will begin with Elephant's Child!"

At this, O Best Beloved, the Elephant's Child was much annoyed, and he said, speaking through his nose, like this, "Led go! You are hurtig be!"

Then the Bi-Coloured-Python-Rock-Snake scuffled down from the bank and said, "My young friend, if you do not now, immediately and instantly, pull as hard as ever you can, it is my opinion that your acquaintance in the large-pattern leather ulster" (and by this he meant the Crocodile) "will jerk you into yonder limpid stream before you can say Jack Robinson."

This is the way Bi-Coloured-Python-Rock-Snakes always talk.

Then the Elephant's Child sat back on his little haunches, and pulled, and pulled, and pulled, and his nose began to stretch. And the Crocodile floundered into the water, making it all creamy with great sweeps of his tail, and *he* pulled, and pulled, and pulled.

And the Elephant's Child's nose kept on stretching; and the Elephant's Child spread all his little four legs and pulled, and pulled, and pulled, and his nose kept on stretching; and the Crocodile threshed his tail like an oar, and *he* pulled, and pulled, and pulled, and at each pull the Elephant's Child's nose grew longer and longer—and it hurt him hijjus!

Then the Elephant's Child felt his legs slipping, and he said through his nose, which was now nearly five feet long, "This is too butch for be!"

Then the Bi-Coloured-Python-Rock-Snake came down from the bank, and knotted himself in a double-clove-hitch round the Elephant's Child's hind legs, and said, "Rash and inexperienced traveller, we will now seriously devote ourselves to a little high tension, because if we do not, it is my impression that yonder self-propelling man-of-war with the armour-plated upper deck" (and by this, O Best Beloved, he meant the Crocodile), "will permanently vitiate your future career."

That is the way all Bi-Coloured-Python-Rock-Snakes always talk.

So he pulled, and the Elephant's Child pulled, and the Crocodile pulled; but the Elephant's Child and the Bi-Coloured-Python-Rock-Snake pulled hardest; and at last the Crocodile let go of the Elephant's Child's nose with a plop that you could hear all up and down the Limpopo.

Then the Elephant's Child sat down most hard and sudden; but first he was careful to say "Thank you" to the Bi-Coloured-Python-

Rock-Snake; and next he was kind to his poor pulled nose, and wrapped it all up in cool banana leaves, and hung it in the great grey-green, greasy Limpopo to cool.

"What are you doing that for?" said the Bi-Coloured-Python-Rock-Snake.

" 'Scuse me," said the Elephant's Child, "but my nose is badly out of shape, and I am waiting for it to shrink."

"Then you will have to wait a long time," said the Bi-Coloured-Python-Rock-Snake. "Some people do not know what is good for them."

The Elephant's Child sat there for three days waiting for his nose to shrink. But it never grew any shorter, and, besides, it made him squint. For, O Best Beloved, you will see and understand that the Crocodile had pulled it out into a really truly trunk same as all Elephants have to-day.

At the end of the third day a fly came and stung him on the shoulder, and before he knew what he was doing he lifted up his trunk and hit that fly dead with the end of it.

" 'Vantage number one!" said the Bi-Coloured-Python-Rock-Snake. "You couldn't have done that with a mere-smear nose. Try and eat a little now."

Before he thought what he was doing the Elephant's Child put out his trunk and plucked a large bundle of grass, dusted it clean against his fore-legs, and stuffed it into his own mouth.

" 'Vantage number two!" said the Bi-Coloured-Python-Rock-Snake. "You couldn't have done that with a mere-smear nose. Don't you think the sun is very hot here?"

"It is," said the Elephant's Child, and before he thought what he was doing he schlooped up a schloop of mud from the banks of the great grey-green, greasy Limpopo, and slapped it on his head, where it made a cool schloopy-sloshy mud-cap all trickly behind his ears.

" 'Vantage number three!" said the Bi-Coloured-Python-Rock-Snake. "You couldn't have done that with a mear-smear nose. Now how do you feel about being spanked again?"

" 'Scuse me," said the Elephant's Child, "but I should not like it at all."

"How would you like to spank somebody?" said the Bi-Coloured-Python-Rock-Snake.

"I should like it very much indeed," said the Elephant's Child.

"Well," said the Bi-Coloured-Python-Rock-Snake, "you will find that new nose of yours very useful to spank people with."

"Thank you," said the Elephant's Child, "I'll remember that; and now I think I'll go home to my dear families and try."

So the Elephant's Child went home across Africa frisking and whisking his trunk. When he wanted fruit to eat he pulled fruit down from a tree, instead of waiting for it to fall as he used to do. When he wanted grass he plucked grass up from the ground, instead of going on his knees as he used to do. When the flies bit him he broke off the branch of a tree and used it as a fly whisk; and he made himself a new, cool, slushy-squshy mud-cap whenever the sun was hot. When he felt lonely walking through Africa he sang to himself down his trunk, and the noise was louder than several brass bands. He went especially out of his way to find a broad Hippopotamus (she was no relation of his), and he spanked her very hard, to make sure that the Bi-Coloured-Python-Rock-Snake had spoken the truth about his new trunk. The rest of the time he picked up the melon rinds that he had dropped on his way to the Limpopo—for he was a Tidy Pachyderm.

One dark evening he came back to all his dear families, and he coiled up his trunk and said, "How do you do?" They were very glad to see him, and immediately said, "Come here and be spanked for your 'satiable curtiosity."

"Pooh," said the Elephant's Child. "I don't think you peoples know anything about spanking; but I do, and I'll show you."

Then he uncurled his trunk and knocked two of his dear brothers head over heels.

"O Bananas!" said they, "where did you learn that trick, and what have you done to your nose?"

"I got a new one from the Crocodile on the banks of the great grey-green, greasy Limpopo River," said the Elephant's Child, "I asked him what he had for dinner, and he gave me this to keep."

"It looks very ugly," said his hairy uncle, the Baboon.

"It does," said the Elephant's Child. "But it's very useful," and he picked up his hairy uncle, the Baboon, by one hairy leg, and hove him into a hornet's nest.

Then that bad Elephant's Child spanked all his dear families for a long time, till they were very warm and greatly astonished. He pulled out his tall Ostrich aunt's tailfeathers; and he caught his tall uncle, the Giraffe, by the hind-leg, and dragged him through a thorn-bush; and he shouted at his broad aunt, the Hippopotamus, and blew bubbles into her ear when she was sleeping in the water after meals; but he never let any one touch Kolokolo Bird.

At last things grew so exciting that his dear families went off one by one in a hurry to the banks of the great-grey-green, greasy Limpopo River, all set about with fever-trees, to borrow new noses from the Crocodile. When they came back nobody spanked anybody any more; and ever since that day, O Best Beloved, all the Elephants you will ever see, besides all those that you won't, have trunks precisely like the trunk of the 'satiable Elephant's Child.

KIRIBATI

Kiribati is a nation of islands located in the central Pacific Ocean. Although the islands are lightly populated and small in area, they are scattered over a vast expanse of the Pacific measuring approximately 2,000,000 square miles (5,000,000 square kilometers). Kiribati was formerly a British colony, first as part of the Gilbert and Ellice Islands and then as the Gilbert Islands, before gaining its independence in 1979.

▶ THE PEOPLE

The people of Kiribati are mostly Micronesians, but a few are of Polynesian, mixed Micronesian and Polynesian, and European ancestry. The most populous island is Tarawa, the site of the government. A distinct ethnic group known as the Banabans once lived on Banaba (Ocean Island). They were resettled on Rambi, in the Fiji islands, because phosphate mining had made their home island uninhabitable.

Religion, Language, and Education. Most Kiribatians are Christians, divided about equally between Roman Catholics and Protestants. English is the official language, but most of the people speak Gilbertese (I-Kiribati), a Micronesian language. Primary education is free for all children between the ages of 6 and 15. Most schools were once run by missionaries, but the schools have been gradually taken over by the government. There is a branch of the University of the Pacific at Bikenibeu, on the island of Tarawa. Many students attend colleges abroad on government scholarships.

Way of Life. Most of the people live in small villages built around a community meeting house. Several generations of a family normally live together, and people usually own the land on which they live. Houses on the more urbanized island of Tarawa are often built of concrete blocks, with aluminum roofs.

▶ THE LAND

The islands of Kiribati are atolls, coral islands made up of a reef surrounding a lagoon. There are three groups of islands—the 17 Gilbert Islands (including Banaba), the 8 Line Islands, and the 8 Phoenix Islands. Many of the Phoenix and Line islands are uninhabited. Christmas Island (Kiritimati), in the Line Islands, is the largest island of Kiribati and one of the largest atolls in the world.

The climate is pleasant, with an average annual temperature of about 80°F (27°C). Rainfall usually comes in brief, violent showers and varies widely from island to island, with some islands suffering periods of drought.

▶ THE ECONOMY

Most of the people of Kiribati catch fish or grow food for their own needs. The chief crops are coconuts, breadfruit, bananas, and papayas. Pigs and poultry are raised. Copra (dried coconut meat) is the chief export.

The government is encouraging the growth of commercial fishing. Kingfish, snapper, and tuna are among the many varieties of fish that are plentiful in the waters around the islands. Shrimp are raised commercially on Christmas Island. Local industries include the processing of foods and beverages, construction, furniture making, handicrafts, and boatbuilding.

Phosphate rock, a source of fertilizer, was mined for export on Banaba for nearly 75

Weighing copra for sale is a community affair in a Kiribatian village. The dried meat of coconuts, copra is Kiribati's most important export.

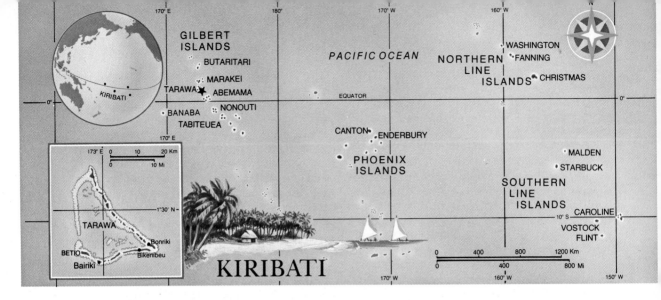

KIRIBATI

years. The last shipments of phosphate were made in 1979. Phosphate is believed to exist on other islands but has not yet been tapped.

▶ **HISTORY AND GOVERNMENT**

Kiribati was probably settled by people from the nearby Marshall Islands and from other Pacific islands. The first Europeans to sight what are now the islands of Kiribati were Spanish explorers in the 1500's and 1600's. The British rediscovered them in the 1700's. The islands of the Gilbert group were named after a British sea captain, Thomas Gilbert.

The first non-native settlers were sailors from American and British whaling ships, which arrived in the area in the mid-1800's.

They were followed by missionaries who converted the people to Christianity. A flourishing trade in coconut oil and copra was soon established. In 1877 the Office of the British High Commissioner for the Western Pacific was created to administer the islands. Britain formally annexed the various islands over a period of years. The Gilbert and Ellice Islands Colony was created in 1916. Several of the islands were occupied by the Japanese during World War II. Tarawa was the scene of a major battle in that war.

During the 1970's the islanders were given control over their own affairs. The Ellice Islands were separated from the Gilberts in 1974 at their request and were renamed Tuvalu, which became independent in 1978. (An article on Tuvalu appears in Volume T.) The remainder of the former Gilbert and Ellice Islands Colony, the Gilbert Islands, won independence as the Republic of Kiribati in 1979.

In 1983 the Kiribati Government purchased the land on the islands of Washington (Teraina) and Fanning (Tabuaeran) in the Northern Line Islands. The land formerly had been owned by a private copra company.

The government of Kiribati includes an elected president (Beretitenti) and legislature. The president, who serves as both head of state and government, appoints a cabinet from among the members of the legislature, the House of Assembly (Maneaba ni Maungatabu). One seat in the legislature is reserved for the Banaban community.

HAROLD M. ROSS
St. Norbert College

FACTS AND FIGURES

REPUBLIC OF KIRIBATI is the official name of the country.

THE PEOPLE are known as Kiribatians.

LOCATION: Central Pacific Ocean.

AREA: 281 sq mi (728 km²).

POPULATION: 62,000 (estimate).

CAPITAL: Tarawa.

MAJOR LANGUAGES: English (official), Gilbertese (I-Kiribati).

MAJOR RELIGIONS: Roman Catholic, Protestant.

GOVERNMENT: Republic. **Head of state and government**—president (Beretitenti). **Legislature**—House of Assembly (Maneaba ni Maungatabu).

CHIEF PRODUCTS: Coconuts, copra (dried coconut meat), breadfruit, papayas, bananas, pigs, poultry, fish, handicrafts.

MONETARY UNIT: Australian dollar (1 dollar = 100 cents).

NATIONAL ANTHEM: *Teirake Kain, Kiribati* ("Stand, Kiribati").

KIRKPATRICK, JEANE (1926–)

Jeane Kirkpatrick was the first woman to serve as a United States delegate to the United Nations (1981–85). Born Jeane Duane Jordon on November 19, 1926, in Duncan, Oklahoma, Kirkpatrick received her masters (1950) and doctoral (1968) degrees from Columbia University in New York City. After raising a family of two sons with her husband Evron, Kirkpatrick began teaching political science in 1967 at Georgetown University in Washington, D.C. She wrote numerous books, including *Political Women* (1974) and *The New Presidential Elite* (1976).

Kirkpatrick, a former Democrat, switched her allegiance to the Republican Party in the late 1970's and became a strong supporter of conservative policies. In 1980 she advised Republican presidential candidate Ronald Reagan, and he appointed her to the U.N. post in 1981, following his election.

Reviewed by CHARLES MORITZ
Editor, *Current Biography*

KISSINGER, Henry (1923–)

"What interests me is what you can do with power," Henry Kissinger once said. Intense, incisive, and strong willed, this former Harvard University professor dominated American foreign policy for eight years, as both national security adviser (1969–75) and secretary of state (1973–77) under presidents Richard Nixon and Gerald Ford.

Henry Kissinger steered the United States on a conservative course regarding international relations. He opposed political change in developing nations, and he sought détente (an easing of tensions) with the Soviet communist powers. He tried to apply American political and military power to achieve his ideal of a secure world order.

Henry Kissinger was born Heinz Alfred Kissinger on May 27, 1923, in the German city of Fürth, a few miles from Nuremberg. In 1938 anti-Semitism in Germany forced Louis and Paula Kissinger and their two teenage sons, Henry and Walter, to flee the persecution of the Nazis and seek refuge in the United States. The family settled in New York City, and Henry became a U.S. citizen in 1943. The tumult during his youth profoundly affected Kissinger's later views on foreign policy, producing a deep suspicion of political upheavals and a tendency toward compromise.

In the United States, Kissinger had a successful career as a professor of government at Harvard University and as an author and governmental adviser. His work drew the attention of Richard Nixon, who became president in 1969.

As a member of Nixon's administration, Kissinger earned a reputation as a skillful ne-

Henry Kissinger served as secretary of state under presidents Nixon and Ford. In 1973 he shared the Nobel peace prize for negotiating a cease-fire during the Vietnam War.

gotiator. He arranged a cease-fire between the Arabs and the Israelis in the Arab-Israeli War of 1973; he helped restore America's relations with the People's Republic of China; and he secured the 1973 cease-fire with North Vietnam, for which he shared the 1973 Nobel peace price with North Vietnam's negotiator, Le Duc Tho. (Kissinger was the fifth American secretary of state to receive the coveted Nobel peace prize, but the first to receive the award while still in office.)

Kissinger had his share of critics, especially those who opposed America's involvement in the Vietnam War. Many considered him a chief advocate of American aggression there.

After leaving government office, Kissinger continued his work as a consultant, lecturer, and writer on world politics and international relations. In 1982, he founded Kissinger Associates, a consulting firm that helps corporations evaluate foreign policy issues that affect their interests. His memoirs appeared in two volumes, *White House Years* (1979) and *Years of Upheaval* (1982).

FRED L. ISRAEL
Department of History
The City College of New York

KITES

People have enjoyed making and flying kites for at least 2,000 years. It is fun to watch a kite lift in the breeze and rise until it is just a speck of color in the sky. The word "kite" is the name of a bird of the hawk family, known for its grace in the air.

A kite may be a simple arrangement of two sticks, crossed and covered with paper or cloth and flown at the end of a string, also known as a **flying line**. Or the kite may be a more elaborate shape, such as a box or a pyramid. Kites may be made of paper, light plastic, or cloth. Sticks may be made of wood, plastic, or fiberglass.

In Asia, kites are made in the shapes of birds, fish, and butterflies. Many are beautifully decorated. One of the largest kites is the Chinese dragon kite. It is a long train of individual kites connected by lines. The first kite represents the dragon's head, and a number of circular kites behind it represent the dragon's body. This kite is so long that it must be launched by several people.

Types of Kites

Kites come in an enormous number of colors and styles. Some of the most common kites include the flat kite, the bowed kite, and the box kite.

The Flat Kite. The flat kite with a tail is the oldest and most familiar kind of kite. The weight of the tail helps keep the bottom of the kite down and the nose tilted up. The tail also steadies the position of the kite in the air. It acts somewhat like the rudder of a ship. When the wind pushes the kite too hard in one direction, the surfaces of the tail act as an opposing force to the wind, so the kite can remain steady.

The Bowed Kite. One of the best fliers, this kite is built on a framework of two sticks crossed in a T, with the cross stick bent like an archer's bow. This creates an angle to the wind, so that the kite does not need a tail. One kind of bowed kite was invented in 1898 by an American, William A. Eddy, which is why this type of kite is also called the Eddy kite.

The Box Kite. This type of kite is shaped like a long box with open ends. The sides are covered except for an open section in the center. This kite was invented by Lawrence Hargrave, an Australian, about 1892.

Other Types of Kites. The delta kite is shaped roughly like a triangle. This type of kite has wide wings and is supported by a flap of material called a **keel** underneath the wings. The keel guides the kite and steadies it. Another type is the flexible kite, which has no supporting rods. These kites form different shapes—an airplane, for example—when they are filled with wind.

Another example is the parafoil, which looks somewhat like a parachute. Stunt kites are able to dip, spin, loop, and twirl in the sky with the operator manipulating one or more strings. Some kites look like dragons or other animals. Others may have various geometric shapes.

Beautifully decorated kites fly at a kite festival in Mitsuke, a city on the island of Honshu in Japan. Although no one is sure who invented the kite, we do know that making and flying kites have been popular pastimes in many Asian countries for hundreds of years.

How does a kite fly?

Two opposing forces act on a kite. One is the lifting force of the wind. The other is the pull of the kite string back to the ground. When these two forces are balanced or nearly equal, a kite remains in the air.

The force of the wind on a kite is similar to the force of the wind on a sail. When a kite is launched correctly, it should be at an angle to the horizontal movement of the air. This angle, called the angle of attack, forces the air to strike the underside of the kite and be deflected downward. In reaction to this downward force, the air pushes back up on the underside of the kite. This upward force is a kite's main source of lift.

In some designs, such as those of bowed kites, the kite billows slightly upward, in much the same way that an airplane's wings are curved on top. The wind blowing over this curved surface travels faster than the wind blowing underneath, creating a lower pressure above the kite than below it. This difference in pressure produces an upward force, which is a second source of lift.

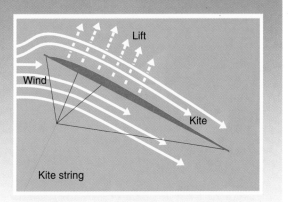

History

No one is sure who invented the kite. Some historians believe it was invented by a Greek named Archytas about 400 B.C. Others believe it was invented 200 years later by Han-Sin, a Chinese general. But we do know that making and flying kites have been popular pastimes in China, Japan, Korea, and other countries of the Far East for many hundreds of years and still are today.

In China, the ninth day of the ninth month is known as Kites' Day, or the Festival of Ascending on High. It is the tradition for people of all ages to fly kites on that day.

In Japan, Children's Day is celebrated on May 5. Each family flies a fish kite from a bamboo pole in front of the house for each

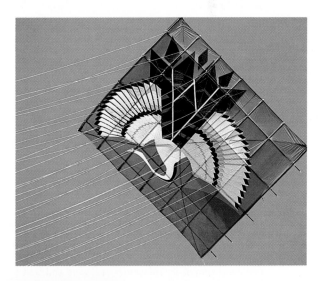

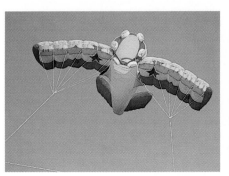

Kites can take many forms. *Far left:* This whimsical "airplane" is a type of flexible kite, which takes shape when filled with wind. *Left:* A bird kite and flower kite are examples of creative kite design. *Top:* A complex geometric box kite requires many strings to be flown properly.

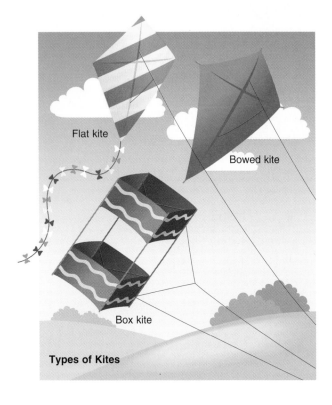

Flat kite

Bowed kite

Box kite

Types of Kites

boy in the family. The Japanese and other Asians also enjoy a sport known as kite fighting. Large numbers of people play at one time. Each kite flier coats a portion of his kite string near the kite with a mixture of powdered glass and glue. When all the kites are in the air, a player tries to cross and cut the string of another kite with a sharp, glass-coated part of his own string.

Kites have been used in scientific experiments. In 1749 two Scottish scientists, Alexander Wilson and Thomas Melville, sent up a train, or connected series, of kites with a thermometer attached to each in order to find out the temperature of different altitudes.

In 1752, Benjamin Franklin used a kite in his famous experiment with lightning. He wanted to prove that it was a form of electricity. To do this, he had to find a way to attract lightning. He decided to fly a kite into a thundercloud during a storm. Franklin had attached a metal key on the flying line. He hoped the lightning flashing in the thundercloud would travel along the kite string to the

See For Yourself

How to Fly Your Kite

A day of clear skies and winds of 8 to 15 miles (13 to 24 kilometers) per hour is ideal for kite flying. The best place to launch a kite is a level field with no trees.

Stand with your back to the wind. With one arm raised, hold your kite upright by the lower corner. The cover of the kite should be facing the wind, and the nose should be tilted slightly toward you. This is the angle at which the kite will fly. The tail should be straight out on the ground in front of you. With your other hand, hold the reel of string. When the wind blows steadily, let go of the kite, giving it a little push into the stream of air. Then move backward and start to let out the line.

You can also launch your kite with the help of a friend. Have your friend face the wind and hold the kite while you walk backward into the wind, letting out string as you walk. Let out about 75 feet (23 meters) of string. Do not let any of it rest on the ground. Now have your friend lift the kite and hold it in the launching position described above. When the wind tugs at the kite, your helper will feel the kite string tighten and should then release the kite gently. As it begins to rise, walk backward, letting out more line.

To bring your kite down, walk toward the kite, in the direction in which the wind is blowing, and reel in line as you walk.

A clear day with light winds is best for kite flying. Look for a level, open area such as a field or stretch of beach.

How to Make a Flat Kite

The flat kite is easy to make. You will need one stick 36 inches (91 centimeters) long and one 30 inches (76 centimeters) long. The sticks may be round dowel sticks $\frac{1}{4}$ inch (6 millimeters) thick or strips of wood $\frac{3}{8}$ inch (10 millimeters) wide and $\frac{1}{4}$ inch (6 millimeters) thick. It is best to use sticks of pine or spruce to keep the kite lightweight.

Using a pencil, mark the center of the smaller stick and a point 9 inches (23 centimeters) from one end of the longer stick. The longer stick will be the upright, or **spine**. Place the two sticks in a t-shape so that the two pencil marks meet. Wind string tightly around them, then coat the string with glue. (You can use special kite string, fishing line, or cotton twine both in making the kite and in flying it later.)

Ask an adult to cut a notch in the end of each stick. Outline the kite by slotting the string into the notches and pulling it tight. Knot it firmly. Put a drop of glue in each notch. This will help keep the string in place.

Place the framework of the kite on a large piece of tissue paper, gift wrapping paper, newspaper, or thin plastic. Cut the covering so that it is 2 inches (5 centimeters) larger than the framework. Fold the margin of the covering over the string and glue or tape it down. Trim the corners of the kite.

To decorate a paper kite, paint it with poster paints or watercolors. Be careful not to tear the paper.

Now you are ready to attach the kite to the string. The string is not fastened directly to the kite, but to two slack strings called the **bridle**, which helps keep the kite tilted upward at a good flying angle. To make the bridle, put the

A flat kite is fun to make. After you finish, take it outside for a test flight. Be sure to hang on tightly to the string!

kite on the floor with the paper covering facing you. Tie one end of a piece of string 42 inches (107 centimeters) long to the top and the other end to the bottom of the upright kite stick. Tie a second piece of string 36 inches (91 centimeters) long to the two ends of the cross stick.

Pick up the two strings of the bridle where they cross, and attach the end of your reel of kite string at this point. After trying out your kite, you may find that you need to adjust the length of the bridle string so that the kite flies well.

To make a tail for your kite, you will need a piece of string at least 8 feet (2.4 meters) long. (After you have flown the kite, you can adjust the length of the tail if necessary.) Cut some cloth into 6- by 2-inch (15- by 5-centimeter) pieces. Attach each piece of cloth, at its center, to the tail string. Leave 6 inches (15 centimeters) between pieces. Tie the tail to the bottom of your kite.

key. This happened, and Franklin got an electric shock. We realize today that Franklin's experiment was extremely dangerous. A person who comes into contact with electricity while he or she is wet could be killed.

Many years later, kites also played a part in the development of the airplane. Before they built and flew the first airplane in 1903, Wilbur and Orville Wright experimented with huge box kites strong enough to lift an adult into the air.

Kites have also been used for other purposes. They have been equipped with cameras in order to take pictures from the air. During the Spanish-American War (1898), a kite was used when a photographer stood on the ground and clicked the shutter of the camera by pulling a string that was attached to it.

In the early part of the 1900's, the United States Weather Bureau (now the National Weather Service) used box kites that were equipped with instruments to obtain various information for weather forecasts.

Kites of all shapes and sizes can be seen at kite festivals. *Right:* A lizard-shaped kite soars in the air in Rome, Italy. *Below:* Onlookers surround a huge fish kite in Castiglione de Lago, Italy.

During the Boer War in South Africa (1899–1902), large kites carried British soldiers over enemy territory so that the soldiers could report on the movements of the enemy. In World War I (1914–18), the Germans developed a kite that could be used to fly people from a submarine.

Kites were used as targets in gunnery practice by the United States military during World War II (1939–45). Life rafts were also equipped with kites. These kites were used to fly wire radio antennae into the air. In this way radio signals could easily be transmitted long distances.

Today kites are flown mostly for enjoyment and recreation. Kite festivals are held in a number of cities and towns around the world. In the United States, popular kiting events include the annual Smithsonian Kite Festival in Washington, D.C. At a kite festival, you can see kites of all shapes and sizes flying in the air, many of them handmade. Games and contests offer something of interest for every kite flier.

Reviewed by LARRY KETTELKAMP
Author, *Kites*

KLEE, PAUL (1879–1940)

Paul Klee was one of the most original artists of the 20th century. He followed no movement, and there is no single term that describes his style. In his paintings Klee created a world of his own—a dreamy world that suggests poetry and the rhythms of music.

Klee was born on December 18, 1879, in Münchenbuchsee, Switzerland. He learned to love music from his father, a German music teacher. Paul chose painting as a career, but music had a great influence on his work.

In 1898, Klee went to Munich to study art. Four years later, he moved to Bern and produced a series of etchings. In 1906, he settled in Munich and married Lily Stumpf, a piano teacher. The couple had a son, Felix.

In 1912, Klee exhibited his paintings with German artists known as the Blue Rider group. A short trip to Tunisia in 1914 proved to be a turning point in Klee's art. Up to this time, he had worked mostly in black and white. In Tunisia, Klee "discovered" color. The brilliant red sun there seemed to make all colors brighter and deeper. Color then became the basis of his art. "Color and I are one," he wrote in his diary.

Klee was a quiet, thoughtful man. He took long walks alone and loved to watch the flowers and leaves moving in the breeze. He painted with great precision on small canvases. His subjects included yellow birds resting on purple branches, floating cities of squares and rectangles, and mazes of lines.

After 1921, Klee taught at the Bauhaus, an art school in Germany. In 1930, he left to become a professor at the Academy of Fine Arts in Düsseldorf. Disagreeing with Nazi policies, Klee left Germany in 1933. He returned to Switzerland, where he lived until his death on June 29, 1940.

Reviewed by HAROLD SPENCER
University of Connecticut

KLIMT, GUSTAV (1862–1918)

Gustav Klimt was a leader of modern painting in Austria. Klimt was born on July 14, 1862, in Baumgarten near Vienna. Between 1876 and 1883, he studied at the Vienna School of Decorative Arts and painted murals for theaters with his brother Ernst. Klimt was saddened by the death of Ernst in 1892, and for five years his public works dwindled to almost nothing. In 1900, Klimt completed the first of three ceiling murals for the University of Vienna. These works were controversial because they illustrated somber aspects of life, such as death and disease.

Between 1897 and 1905, Klimt was the leader of the Secession, a group of Austrian artists dedicated to artistic freedom and a style of art known as art nouveau. He began painting landscapes and portraits of wealthy Viennese ladies, receiving the support of loyal patrons. The radiant women in his portraits seem to appear in a kaleidoscope of geometric shapes, spirals, flowers, and golden decorations. Although their faces and hands are painted realistically, their fanciful dresses blend into a background of decorative patterns inspired by medieval, Byzantine, and Oriental art.

Klimt also painted pictures of women that symbolized the cycles of life and death. His art celebrated love, beauty, and motherhood, but it also showed sadness, illness, and tragedy. His last two murals, *Beethoven Frieze* (1902) and the *Stoclet Frieze* (1905–09), showed figures set against luxurious patterns of golden designs. Two of his most famous paintings are *Portrait of Adele Bloch-Bauer I* (1907) and *The Kiss* (1907–08; pictured).

Klimt died on February 6, 1918, in Vienna. His work influenced the younger Austrian artists Oskar Kokoschka and Egon Schiele, who helped create a style of art known as expressionism.

JOYCE RAIMONDO
Department of Education
The Museum of Modern Art

KNIGHTS, KNIGHTHOOD, AND CHIVALRY

Knights were the highest class of fighting men in Europe during the Middle Ages. There were other classes of fighting men, such as the lowly foot soldiers. But the knights, who fought on horseback, were the aristocrats of the battlefield. Their whole way of life was based on warfare. The great heroes of the time, both in story and in fact, were knights. Songs and verses told of the brave deeds of the great mounted warriors—Roland, King Arthur, Lancelot, and Edward the Black Prince.

The high position of the knights was partly due to the fact that during the early Middle Ages, kings and central governments had little real authority. Power belonged to the best fighters. The man who had horses and heavy arms and knew how to use them had a great advantage. For these reasons knights were usually the most powerful men in every neighborhood. Weaker men had to put themselves under the protection of knights. Even kings depended on their services.

From their walled and moated castles the more powerful knights ruled the nearby countryside. They honored no law but their own, and they freely made war against their neighbors. A knight did as he wished because no one else was powerful enough to stop him. At best, a knight-lord might keep some sort of order in his land and protect his people from bandits. At worst, a knight himself was little better than a bandit.

The Knight's Horse

A knight's horse was probably the most valuable thing he owned, for his skill as a fighting man depended on a good mount. A well equipped knight had several horses. He might have a heavy charger for tournaments, a fast courser for battle, a palfrey for travel, and a packhorse to carry his arms and other equipment. The war-horse was the important one. Knights gave their horses names and regarded them almost as companions-in-arms. Stories about the great hero-knights almost always tell of their horses. Poets composed verses about the beauty and strength of the knights' good steeds.

The Knight's Arms

The armor worn by knights differed from one century to another during the Middle Ages. A knight in the year 1100 had much lighter armor than one in 1400. In the earlier time a well-armed knight wore a long, heavy cloth or leather garment, which covered most of his body. Over this he wore chain mail—a network of linked iron rings—called a **hauberk.** It had a hood that fitted over the head and protected the neck. On his head a knight wore a steel helmet, which sometimes had a metal nose protector. In later times the body armor was made of strong metal plates. The helmets had heavy visors that could be lowered to cover the face. The body armor weighed at least 55 pounds (25 kilograms).

Knights carried light wooden shields for protection. These were covered with hide and edged with metal. Each knight had his own emblem—sometimes a beast, such as a dragon, bear, or lion—painted on his shield.

The gallant knight, who lived by the code of chivalry, is one of history's most romantic figures. In reality, knights did not always live up to this idealized image.

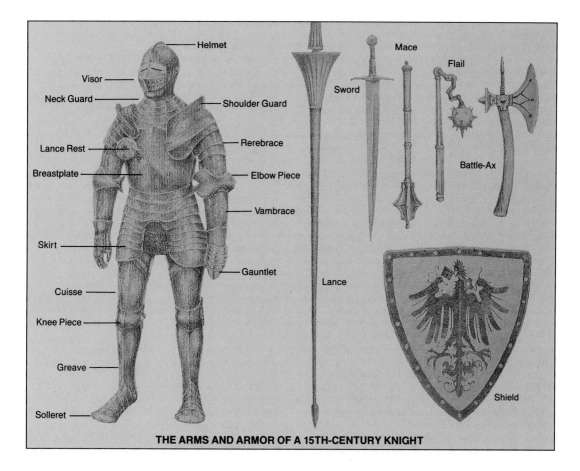

Helmet
Visor
Neck Guard
Shoulder Guard
Lance Rest
Rerebrace
Breastplate
Elbow Piece
Vambrace
Skirt
Gauntlet
Cuisse
Knee Piece
Greave
Solleret

Sword
Mace
Flail
Lance
Battle-Ax
Shield

THE ARMS AND ARMOR OF A 15TH-CENTURY KNIGHT

This emblem was called his **coat of arms.** A young knight hoped to make his coat of arms famous by showing it on many battlefields.

The knight's chief weapons were his lance and sword. The lance, a long pole with a pointed steel head, was for use when the knight was on horseback. The knight pointed his lance straight ahead and rode at full speed against his enemy, trying to run him through or to knock him off his horse. When two knights rode at full speed against each other, their lances struck with such force that the weapons were often shattered.

A knight valued his large, heavy sword almost as much as he did his horse. He used his sword after his lance had been shattered or when he had been forced to dismount. The blade was made of fine, hammered steel. The handle, or hilt, often was decorated with gold and precious stones. The hilt might also contain a relic of some saint. This might be a thread from his robe, a lock of hair, or even a fragment of his bones. Such relics were re-

garded as holy, and the knight hoped they would bring him special protection.

In addition to their lances and swords, knights fought with battle-axes, iron-headed war clubs called **maces,** and iron balls swung on chains, called **flails.** All these weapons required the use of a great deal of strength.

Making Warfare Pay

Battles among the knights were not as frightful as one might think. For one thing, many of the battles were between small groups, often just a few hundred men, and the fighting lasted only a few hours. A knight was less interested in killing his enemies than in capturing them. A captured enemy could be held for **ransom** (payment of a stated price). It was by capturing enemies rather than by killing them that knights made war pay.

The amount of ransom varied according to the wealth and importance of the captive. When King John II (1319–64) of France was taken prisoner at the battle of Poitiers (1356)

Knights sharpened their fighting skills in tournaments, or mock battles. In a contest called tilting, each opponent attempted to knock the other off his horse.

during the Hundred Years War, his English captors quarreled about who had taken him. But the king assured them that there was no need for argument, ". . . for I am so great a lord as to make you all rich."

Because knights were professionals fighting for profits, warfare was something like a game in which the opponents probably knew each other well. An account of the battle of Brenville in 1119 explains that although 140 men were taken prisoner, only three lost their lives. This was partly because they were well protected by armor. But it was also because the knights on each side were known to each other as old comrades, and so "there was no slaughter."

The common soldiers, however, did not always treat war in this spirit, perhaps because they had so little to gain from it. When the English defeated the French at the battle of Crécy in 1346, the English king and his knights were distressed because "certain rascals" had killed the French knights as they lay helpless on the ground, weighed down by their heavy armor. The English knights would much rather have taken them alive and held them for ransom.

The Sport of the Knights

The warfare of the knights was like a game, and their games were like war. Hunting was probably their most common sport. Riding through forest or swamp after deer, wolves, and wild boars was good training for a fighting man. Spearing a boar while riding horseback was somewhat like tilting with a lance.

Chess was a popular indoor game. Perhaps it appealed to the knights because it called for making moves like those on a battlefield.

The sport most like battle was the **tournament,** or tourney. For many years it remained more like a battle than a sport. Tournaments later became mock battles in which knights fought with flattened lances and blunted swords. Gaily dressed crowds of ladies and gentlemen cheered on the knights as brightcolored banners fluttered over the field. The object of a tournament was about the same as that of a battle—to capture an enemy and collect ransom. Knights were not supposed to injure their opponents, but in a sport so much like battle, accidents occurred and serious injuries were not uncommon. From time to time churchmen tried to do away with tournaments. Most people, however, thought that a knight could not shine in war if he had not been prepared for it in tourneys.

Chivalry—the Knight's Code

Both tournaments and wars had certain rules and customs, which knights were expected to follow. When one knight took another one captive, he was supposed to treat his captive as an honored guest even if they had been bitter enemies. During the Hundred Years War, King Edward III (1312–77) of England captured a group of French knights on the last day of the year 1348. That very night he entertained them with a New Year's Eve party.

According to custom, one knight was not supposed to attack another without warning. This enabled his opponent to prepare himself for battle. Thus King Robert Bruce of Scotland was following knightly practice when he sent word to King Edward in 1327 that he would "enter England and devastate the country by fire." A surprise attack would have been unworthy of a true knight.

Why did knights pay attention to these rules and customs? It was mostly a matter of mutual advantage. The knight who held a captive today might himself be captured on another day. It was to every knight's advantage that warning be given before an attack. If this had not been the custom, no knight could have left his castle without wearing his heavy, uncomfortable armor.

These rules of behavior were called the Code of Chivalry. The word **chivalry** comes from the French word *chevalier,* which means "horseman." Chivalry simply means the rules and customs of the horsemen or knights.

The Growth of Chivalry

Chivalry in time came to include many things besides the customs of warring knights. The church taught that a knight should observe the commandments of the Christian faith. A knight, for example, should be generous to the needy. He should protect the church, women, and all who were unable to defend themselves.

The church had only partial success with the knights. Not all of them protected the poor and helpless, yet some changes were made. By the end of the Middle Ages, chivalry was partly a Christian code and partly a warrior's code.

Ladies, too, had ideas about what was proper behavior for a knight. They helped to tame this rough class of fighting men, and politeness became part of the code. Knights curbed their coarse ways in the company of ladies. They accepted the idea that a truly chivalrous knight honored ladies, particularly the one to whom he had given his love and to whom he had sworn devotion. He remained true to her and for her sake performed great deeds.

But not all knights observed these rules. There was a great difference between the ideal knight and the knight as he really was. The code of chivalry set forth what ought to be, and the idea of what ought to be generally has some effect on actual behavior. The knight in the year 1350 was much better mannered and more civilized than the knight in the year 1050. The church and the ladies had had some success in changing a class of rough fighters into gentlemen.

The skills practiced in tournaments were put to good use in battle. But the victorious knight often spared his enemy's life, preferring to hold him for ransom.

The vigil was part of a young man's initiation into knighthood. After a ceremonial bath, he spent the night in church praying and thinking about his duties.

Gentleman by Birth Only

During the Middle Ages only a knight was called a gentleman. This word applied only to one who belonged to an old family. Thus, every knight was of noble birth. Common men were not thought to be gentlemen, nor were they thought to be capable of brave deeds. A knight did not think the promise of a common man worth much, because "low fellows" were not expected to keep their word. Only the word of a gentleman—a knight—was to be trusted.

Knights treated other classes as inferiors. A young knight was warned never to treat a servant as an equal, for the more he did so, the more the servant would despise him. In war, knights did not show the same consideration for common people that they showed to members of their own class. Foot soldiers were not captured for ransom, so there was little hesitation about slaying them. Even those who did not fight might be put to the sword. Edward the Black Prince, the son of King Edward III of England, is often thought of as an ideal knight. But when he captured and sacked the French city of Limoges in 1370, he had more than 3,000 of the citizens killed.

The Training of a Knight

Although noble birth was important for knighthood, it was not the only requirement. A knight had to master the art of war and the code of chivalry. This training began early.

The Page. At the age of 7 a boy was sent away from home to the household of another knight, to get him away from his mother and sisters, who might spoil him. This does not mean that ladies had nothing to do with his training. For 6 or 7 years he served as page to the ladies of the household to which he was sent. They taught him manners and how to make himself agreeable in company. Sometimes they taught him to sing or to play a lute or some other musical instrument. Only a few pages learned to read. Reading was not considered necessary for knights.

Even as a page a boy learned to ride and to handle arms. He rode with the ladies when they hunted with falcons. He dueled with other boys, using blunt swords.

The Squire. Stricter training began when a boy reached 14 and became a knight's squire, or shield bearer. It was his job to look after the knight's arms. He had to keep the helmet, chain mail, and sword polished and free from rust. He cared for the knight's horses. He accompanied his lord in battles and tournaments.

The young squire spent a great deal of time with sword and lance. He accustomed himself to wearing armor. He ran, jumped, and even turned somersaults while wearing a coat of mail. He practiced leaping into the saddle while fully armed.

The squire, like the page, continued to serve the lord and ladies of the household. He helped his lord to dress. He waited on table, carrying dishes and carving meat. Such services were not thought to be beneath the dignity of a young gentleman. On the contrary, people believed that it was proper that the squire should learn to obey before he governed. Otherwise he would not be able to appreciate the nobility of his rank when he became a knight.

Receiving the Knighthood. When a squire reached the age of 20, he might be made a knight. If he had shown himself especially worthy, the ceremony would take place on a battlefield. In such cases the squire knelt before his lord, who pronounced him a knight and then gave him a stout blow with his open hand or the flat side of his sword. Perhaps the blow was a sign that the new knight was able to take the blows of battle.

Less often a squire might receive the title of knighthood in another way—one that, by the 14th century, had become an elaborate ceremony. It began with a ceremonial bath, a sign that he was washed clean of all past misdeeds. Those knighted in this fashion were known as knights of the bath. After bathing, the young man went to church, where he spent the night praying and thinking about his duties.

The next morning he returned to the castle for the main ceremony. Older knights helped him put on his new armor and fasten on his sword. He knelt before his lord, who declared him a knight and gave him the blow. The new knight then gave a demonstration of his ability to ride and use arms. Often a tournament was held in which the young man had a chance to show what he could do.

Celebrations like this were very expensive and were paid for by the family of the young knight. They also were expected to give him a landed estate. If a family could not provide a knighthood and land for their son, he had to remain a squire all his life. Some squires sought service with rich knights. Others wandered about seeking their fortunes. A number became **mercenaries,** or hired soldiers, who played an important part in the wars of the later Middle Ages.

To this day, tales are told about the heroic deeds of knights. One of the most popular is that of a knight who slays a dragon to rescue a damsel in distress.

Chivalry Lives On

By the year 1500 the time of the knight as a fighting man was over. Hired foot soldiers with firearms replaced the man on a horse. But knighthood and chivalry did not die out altogether. Knighthood remained an honor that rulers bestowed on worthy men. This custom is still followed in Great Britain today. Membership is an order of knighthood, which gives the holder the right to the title of ''Sir.'' His wife is called ''Lady.'' A woman with the rank of knight is called ''Dame.''

Chivalry, the code of a gentleman, lived on. The idea of a gentleman changed, however. It came to mean more than belonging to an aristocratic family. A gentleman was a man of any class who did gentlemanly deeds. King James I (1566–1625) of England once said that although he could make a certain man a knight, ''only God Almighty can make a gentleman.'' This idea of chivalry—gentlemanly behavior—still remains an important idea in the world today.

KENNETH S. COOPER
George Peabody College

See also ARMOR; CASTLES; FEUDALISM; HERALDRY.

KNITTING

Making a piece of material by using two needles and yarn, string, or even rope is called knitting. No one knows exactly when knitting was invented. In the beginning knitting may have stemmed from the working of grasses into fishing nets, mats, and baskets. The oldest known knitted fabric dates from the 300's A.D.

In many countries, boys and girls learn to knit as part of their education. Knitting lessons begin in first grade along with reading and writing.

▶ HOW TO KNIT

There are three basic techniques to learn in order to knit. The first is how to get the first loops on the needle. This process is called **casting on**. The second is how to pull one loop through another loop to make a stitch. There are many ways to accomplish this, but two basic methods are called **knitting** and **purling**. Third, you must learn how to take the stitches off the needle when you are done. This is called **binding off**. This article will teach you how to cast on, knit, purl, and bind off as well as a few other techniques to make your knitting projects successful.

Knitting Needles

Knitting needles come in many different sizes and styles. They are most often made from metal, plastic, or wood. In the United States, size is indicated by numbering needles from 0 to 50. The higher the number, the fatter the needle. There are three different styles of knitting needles—double-pointed, circular, and straight. Double-pointed needles come in sets of four and are used mainly for knitting small tube-shaped items such as socks or mittens. Circular needles are flexible with a metal or plastic point at each end. They are primarily used for large tubular items such as skirts or sweater bodies. The most common type of needles are straight needles. They always come in pairs, usually in lengths of 10 or 14 inches. A beginner will find 10-inch metal needles easiest to use because they are a comfortable length and are not likely to bend.

Casting On

Putting the first stitches on the needle is called casting on. Practice with a pair of medium-sized 10-inch needles (size 8, 9, or 10) and a ball of worsted-weight knitting yarn.

1. You will be casting on 20 stitches. Each stitch will use about an inch of yarn, so measure off about 25 inches and make a slip knot at that point. Put the loop on one of your needles. This loop is the first stitch (Diagram 1a). Give the yarn end a tug to tighten the stitch on the needle.

2. Hold the needle in your right hand. Bring the yarn that is coming from the ball over your left index finger (Diagram 1b).

3. Wrap the 25-inch loose end of the yarn around your left thumb (Diagram 1c).

4. Put the tip of the needle under the yarn in front of your thumb (Diagram 1d).

5. Scoop the yarn from the index finger, drawing a loop onto the needle (Diagram 1e).

6. Slide your thumb out of the loop and tighten the new stitch by pulling the loose yarn forward with the thumb (Diagram 1f).

Repeat steps 4 through 6 until there are 20 stitches on the needle.

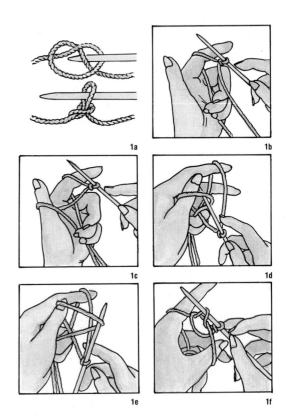

1a

1b

1c

1d

1e

1f

Knit Stitch

Hold the needle with the cast-on stitches in your left hand. This is the left-hand needle. Hold the other needle in your right hand. This is the right-hand needle (Diagram 2a).

1. Holding the yarn behind the work, put the point of the right-hand needle into the front of the first stitch on the left-hand needle (Diagram 2b).

2. With your right hand, bring the yarn from the back and around the point of the right-hand needle (Diagram 2c).

3. Hold yarn and right-hand needle firmly. With the point of the right-hand needle, pull the yarn through the stitch, forming a new loop on the right-hand needle (Diagram 2d).

4. Slip the stitch off the left-hand needle (Diagram 2e). You have knitted the first stitch. Repeat steps 1, 2, 3, and 4 on every stitch on the left-hand needle.

Keep pushing the stitches up toward the tip of the left-hand needle. Be careful not to push the stitches too far or they will slip off the end.

To knit the next row, put the needle holding all the stitches in your left hand. Work as you did before. When finishing one row, you must switch the needle holding the stitches back to your other hand in order to start the next row.

Count the stitches each time a row is completed to be sure you still have the original number. Photo A shows the knit side of a knitted article.

2a

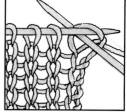
2b

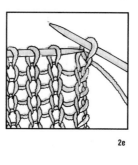
2c

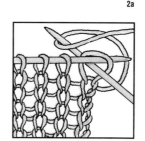
2d

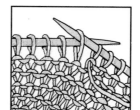
2e

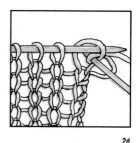
A

Purl Stitch

1. Hold the needle with the knit stitches in your left hand. Keeping the yarn in front of the work, put the tip of the empty right-hand needle into the first stitch on the left-hand needle, from back to front (Diagram 3a).

2. With your right hand, pick up the yarn from in front. Bring the yarn in back of and around the right-hand needle as indicated by the arrows in Diagram 3b.

3. Catch the yarn with the point of the right-hand needle and pull it through the first loop. Slide the stitch off the left-hand needle (Diagram 3c).

Work each stitch this way, and remember that the yarn should always be in front of the needle to purl.

Photo B shows the purl side of a knitted article.

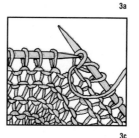
3a

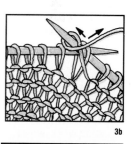
3b

3c

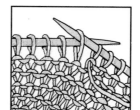
B

Binding Off

Binding off is the last step in knitting. It locks the stitches in place to prevent raveling.

Begin by knitting the first two stitches from the left-hand needle.

1. Hold the left-hand needle firmly. Put the point of that needle into the first stitch on the right-hand needle (Diagram 4a). The first stitch is the one you started with.

2. Pull this stitch over the stitch next to it and over the point of the right-hand needle (Diagram 4b). Let it drop off. Just one stitch will be left on the right-hand needle (Diagram 4c).

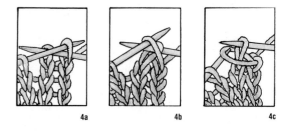

4a   4b   4c

Knit another stitch from the left-hand needle and repeat steps 1 and 2. Work all of the stitches this way until only one stitch remains on the right-hand needle.

Cut the yarn 3 or 4 inches from the needle. Pull the cut end through the last stitch firmly and slip off the needle.

Decreasing

To make your work narrower, you decrease the number of stitches on the needle by knitting or purling two stitches together to make one stitch. Decreasing may be done anywhere along a row. To decrease on a knit row:

1. Insert the right-hand needle, from *left to right*, into the *second* and then the *first* stitch on the left-hand needle. Wrap the yarn around the right-hand needle as you would to knit (Diagram 5a).

2. Pull the new loop through both stitches at the same time, forming one new knit stitch from two (Diagram 5b).

To decrease on a purl row:

1. Put the right-hand needle from *right to left* in the *first* then the *second* stitch on the left-hand needle. Wrap the yarn around the needle as you would to purl (Diagram 6a).

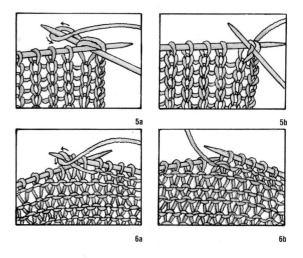

5a   5b

6a   6b

2. Pull the new loop through both stitches at the same time (Diagram 6b).

Increasing

To increase in knitting means to add more stitches to those already on the needle to make your work wider. There are many ways to increase, but this way is the easiest:

1. Put the point of your right-hand needle into a stitch (Diagram 7a). Knit it, but do not slip the old stitch off the left-hand needle (Diagram 7b).

2. Knit into the back of the same stitch (Diagram 7c).

3. Drop the old stitch off the left-hand needle (Diagram 7d).

Increasing may be done at the beginning or end of a row or at any place along a row.

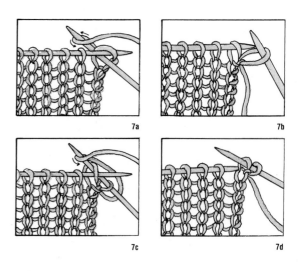

7a   7b

7c   7d

PATTERN STITCHES

All knitting pattern stitches are combinations of the knit stitch and the purl stitch. Here are some instructions for the most frequently used patterns.

Garter Stitch. The easiest stitch to form is the garter stitch. This pattern will emerge if you knit every row. (The same pattern will form if you purl every row.) The garter stitch looks the same on both sides (Photo C).

Stockinette Stitch. On page 279, the photographs show both sides of one of the most popular combinations of knitting and purling —the stockinette stitch. This pattern is formed by alternating one row of knit stitch with one row of purl stitch. The smooth side, shown in Photo A on page 279, is the knit side. All of the purl bumps appear on the reverse side as shown in Photo B.

Ribbing. Ribbing is made by alternating knit and purl stitches on the same row. Because ribbing is stretchy, it is often used to make a sweater fit snugly at the bottom, for cuffs, and around necklines.

Every row is the same, starting with a knit stitch and ending with a purl stitch, always with an *even* number of stitches. Ribbing can be as narrow or as wide as you like. The most common ribbing is either Knit 1, Purl 1 (Photo D), or Knit 2, Purl 2 (Photo E).

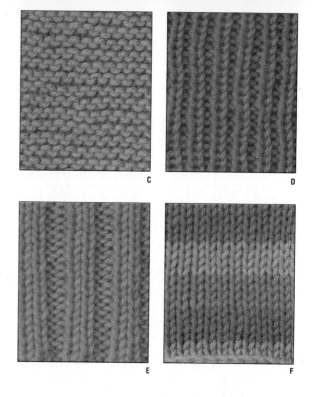

Stripes. Colorful stripes are easily knit in the stockinette stitch simply by changing yarn colors at the end of a row. See Joining New Yarn on page 282 for instructions. You can choose to knit any number of rows of each color. It is best to knit at least two rows of a color before changing (Photo F).

SEWING THE PARTS TOGETHER

Backstitching is one way of connecting the parts of a knitted article. In this method, the stitches do not show on the right side of the article.

Lay the pieces on a table the way you want them to look after they are sewn together. Pin them (be sure to use rust-proof straight pins). Thread a big-eyed, blunt-pointed yarn needle with matching yarn. Sewing from *right to left* (left to right for left-handers), leave a 3- or 4-inch tail. Fasten the yarn at the edge by putting the sewing needle through *both* pieces at the same time, then back through again. Come up from *back to front*, about ½ inch forward from the edge. Insert the sewing needle from *front to back* at the end of the last stitch and draw the yarn through (Diagram 8a). Continue until the seam is completed. Take care not to pull or stretch the material or work the stitches too tightly. Finish off by putting the sewing needle

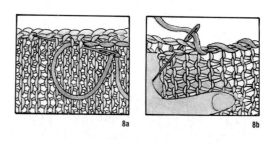

in and out of the last stitch one or two times. Leave a short end and cut the yarn.

Overcasting. Fasten the sewing yarn at the outer edge of the seam as for backstitching. Hold the pieces firmly. Insert the sewing needle into both pieces at the same time, from *back to front*, and pull it through. Again, insert the needle from *back to front*, about ¼ inch forward of the first stitch. Continue this way until the seam is completed (Diagram 8b). Fasten off as for backstitching. Use this stitch on either side of your work.

PICKING UP STITCHES

Sometimes stitches are picked up to add sleeves or to make a ribbed neckband. Holding the bound off sample in your left hand, put the point of the right-hand needle into the first edge stitch (Diagram 9a). Catch the yarn a few inches from the end with the needle and pull it through. The loop on your right-hand needle is the first new stitch. Work this way, from right to left, until you reach the opposite edge. Diagram 9b shows stitches being picked up

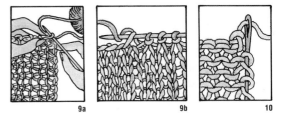

9a   9b   10

along a cast-on edge. Be sure to weave in the loose end when you are finished (Diagram 10).

JOINING NEW YARN

If possible, start a new ball of yarn at the beginning of a row. Leave about a 3-inch length of the old yarn and the same amount of new yarn and just start knitting with the new yarn. Tie the yarn ends together loosely, up close to the needle. Later on, after you have completed your work, untie the knot and weave in the ends right along the seam.

SQUARED-OFF SWEATER

For a boy's or girl's sweater, you will need:

6 2-ounce balls worsted-weight knitting yarn (4 balls if you prefer to make a vest)
1 pair size 10 knitting needles
1 big-eyed yarn needle for sewing up
straight pins and tape measure

Gauge: 4 stitches = 1 inch (each square will measure about 9 inches both ways). After connecting the parts, the chest measurement will be about 17½ inches.

To make your sweater longer or wider just add more stitches to the squares in either direction.

Cast on 36 stitches. Work in the garter stitch until your work measures the same across and up and down. Measure your gauge. If you are getting more than 4 stitches to the inch, change to a larger needle—if fewer stitches to the inch, change to a smaller needle. Bind off. Make 7 more squares the same size for a vest—11 more if you want sleeves.

Sewing up: Following the diagram to the right, pin then sew 4 squares together for the back. Sew the other 4 squares together for the front.

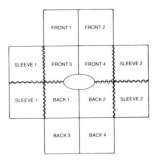

For shoulders, pin front and back squares together. Starting at the outside edge, sew halfway across each shoulder, or far enough to leave room for your head to slip through easily. Pin the side seams from the bottom up the length of one square. Sew together. Weave in loose ends along each seam.

To add sleeves, make 2 more squares the same size for each sleeve. Pin then sew 2 squares together for each sleeve. Match the sleeve seam with the shoulder seam, then pin and sew them together.

Pin and sew the underarm and side seams. Weave in loose ends. Place the sweater on a terry towel and lightly spray the seams with water. Do not soak them. Press the damp seams with the palm of your hand and leave the sweater in place until completely dry. Try decorating your sweater with fringe around the neck or along the bottom. Wear it with pleasure!

FERNE GELLER CONE
Author, *Classy Knitting,*
Knutty Knitting for Kids

Silver flatware helps make an elegant table setting.

KNIVES, FORKS, AND SPOONS

To many people in Western countries, nothing seems more common than a table set with knives, forks, and spoons. Yet these table implements are not commonly used in many parts of the world. And most types of knives, forks, and spoons used today are not more than 100 or 200 years old. For centuries, people picked up their food with their fingers. They used knives mainly to spear and cut up meat. Spoons were used to dip juices, or sauces, from the cooking pot.

Today, the manufacture of knives, forks, and spoons is often divided between two separate industries. One of them produces **flatware**—the different kinds of knives, forks, and spoons used in table settings. The other

specializes in **cutlery,** which includes a wide variety of implements—knives of many kinds, scissors and shears, and the like. This article deals mainly with the history and manufacture of flatware.

▶ORIGINS

The knife is one of the earliest tools. People hunted with it, used it to cut skins into clothing, and sliced their food with it. One knife served every need. It was made of slate, flint, bone, or other materials.

The spoon was the first tool made solely for eating. Clay spoons that date from about 5000 B.C. have been found. Archeologists believe that the spoon was invented when early people began to stew their meat. The natural bowl shape of shells probably inspired them to

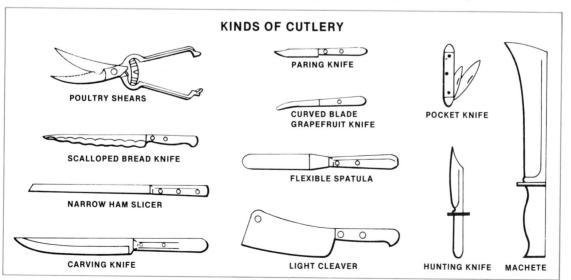

KINDS OF CUTLERY

POULTRY SHEARS

SCALLOPED BREAD KNIFE

NARROW HAM SLICER

CARVING KNIFE

PARING KNIFE

CURVED BLADE
GRAPEFRUIT KNIFE

FLEXIBLE SPATULA

LIGHT CLEAVER

POCKET KNIFE

HUNTING KNIFE   MACHETE

A knife of the 1500's.

A spoon of the 1500's.

make a ladle. They shaped and smoothed a thick piece of clay until they had hollowed a bowl in one end.

The spoon in a more developed form was used in ancient Egypt. Egyptian spoons were made out of wood, slate, ivory, and other materials. Many were richly ornamented. Some even had precious stones set into the handles. Not all spoons were used for eating. Incense, oils, and perfume were burned in special spoons, as sacrifices to the gods.

Greek and Roman knives were made of bronze, copper, and iron. Spoons were made of silver and bronze. At an elaborate Roman dinner, guests used three different kinds of spoons. They had ladles to spoon out sauces, smaller spoons for general use, and tiny pointed spoons for eating eggs and shellfish. Guests had knives, too, but knives were used mainly for spearing and cutting food. Most of the food was eaten with the hands. The Romans did have a few specialized knives. They used a small knife, usually made of bone, for peeling fruit. The most interesting Roman knives were folding knives, which worked much the way our present pocketknives do.

Forks appeared very late and were not common for centuries to come. Archeologists have found several small forklike tools in the ruins of Pompeii, but their use is unknown.

▶**FLATWARE THROUGH THE AGES**

Guests brought their own eating tools with them during the Middle Ages. People were seated in order of their importance, and their flatware matched their rank. Nobles sat on raised platforms and ate with silver spoons. Below them, lesser guests ate with spoons made out of latten (hammered brass or tin-plated iron). At the foot of the table sat people so poor they had only wooden spoons. The quality of the knives, too, varied with the wealth of their owners. People wore their knives on their belts when they were not using them. They held their food on the plate with one hand and cut it with a knife held in the other. The meat was cut into chunks or very thick slices. Knives were broad enough to scoop up peas and other foods that could not be picked up in the hand. When the food was very hot, people wore gloves to protect their fingers while they held it. Some even used metal finger guards. Since there were no napkins, diners usually wiped their hands on the tablecloth. The company sat in couples. Each couple ate from one plate and drank from one cup. The plate often was a large piece of bread, which was either eaten at the end of the meal or thrown to the dogs in the dining hall.

During the latter part of the Middle Ages lavishly decorated knives became popular. Wealthy people had different knives for different occasions. They used ebony-handled knives during the sober season of Lent. They brought out ivory-handled knives to celebrate Easter, and they had gilt-and-enamel knives for state occasions.

During the 1300's, brides began to receive knives as wedding gifts. The custom took firm hold in England during the 1400's and 1500's. The knives were often lavishly decorated and encased in sheaths of gold studded with precious stones. The handles were ivory, amber, agate, or gold and were sometimes etched with Biblical scenes. By the end of the 1500's, almost every wife wore her wedding knives attached to her belt. The custom of giving and wearing wedding knives faded out by the end of the 1600's.

After knives and spoons began to be designed for special purposes, knives for table use were made with straight blades and rounded ends. Curved blades were made for whittling, and the dagger shape was made for combat. In the 1400's, two kinds of knives were often used at the table. A large carving knife was used for cutting up the meat. A small pointed knife, like a present-day fruit knife, was used for picking up pieces of food.

Authorities believe that forks came to Italy from Byzantium. The forks were small and two-pronged. They probably were used in Byzantium to eat sweetmeats or fruits preserved in heavy syrups. At first the Italians used these forks only in the kitchen or to take food from the pot to put on the plate. Gradually the wealthier people of Italy began to eat with forks at the table. By the 1500's, forks were common throughout Italy. At the start of the 1600's, the nobility in most European countries owned forks.

Most forks were made of steel or tin, with two straight prongs. The handles often were designed in odd shapes and were brightly colored. Forks were sometimes made with a spoon on the other end. The diner could spoon up the gravy after eating the solid food. In England these fork-spoons were called **sucket forks.** Some could be folded up and pocketed when the meal was over. But most people did not really adopt the fork until the end of the 1600's. Some ministers even preached against the fork because it was a substitute for a person's God-given fingers.

During the 1600's, spoons began to be set on the table. Finally, knives took their place on the table beside the spoons. By the 1700's, forks had joined knives and spoons as a common setting. The three-pronged fork replaced the two-pronged fork.

▶ MANUFACTURE OF FLATWARE

Once people began to use knives, forks, and spoons at the table, they had to have enough place settings for everyone. Makers of cutlery and other metalware began to design and produce knives, forks, and spoons for use in eating, along with pieces for carving and serving.

People who could afford silver chose it because of its natural beauty and the elaborate designs that could be cut on it. Queen Elizabeth I of England set the official standards for **sterling silver,** which have remained the same to this day. Sterling silver must be 92.5 percent silver and 7.5 percent copper. Because sterling silver was too expensive for many people, makers of flatware were continually looking for cheaper substitutes.

Silver had been used as a thin plating, or covering, over cheaper metals since ancient days. But in 1742 a maker of cutlery and other metalware in Sheffield, England, discovered a new way to plate silver. He found that copper and silver fuse together when they are heated at very high temperatures. By sandwiching copper between layers of silver, he produced an attractive plate. The plate became known as **Sheffield plate,** and it was widely used.

This method of producing silver plate was used until about 1840, when it was replaced by **electroplating.** In electroplating, a bar of silver and a metal article, such as a fork made of nickel, are placed in a chemical solution containing silver. When an electric current is passed through them, silver in the solution is deposited on the fork. At the same time silver from the bar gradually dissolves and replaces the silver in the solution.

A base made of **nickel silver,** or so-called **German silver,** was often used in electroplating after 1850. Nickel silver is an alloy of nickel, copper, and zinc. It is harder than brass, is silver-colored, and does not tarnish easily. Many cheaper forks and spoons were made of nickel silver with no silver plating.

Pewter and **Britannia metal,** also known as white metal, were also used as silver substitutes. Pewter, an alloy of lead and tin, was used for making spoons from the Middle Ages until the end of the 1800's. It began to be replaced by Britannia metal in the 1800's. Britannia metal is stronger than pewter, and it takes a better polish. It is an alloy of tin, copper, and antimony.

Stainless steel, which was introduced in England before World War I, caused a revolution in the manufacture of both cutlery and flatware. Because stainless steel does not tarnish, it is much easier to care for than silver. It is also cheaper. And it can easily be worked into the simple, curving lines of the most popular patterns.

Stainless steel is an alloy of steel and chromium. The chromium makes the steel strong, flexible, and rust-resistant. The best-quality steel had always been hammered by hand, but stainless steel needs the harder blows of a mechanical hammer. It also does not grind well on the older grindstones.

In the 1900's the manufacture of flatware and cutlery turned from a handicraft to a mechanized industry. Ivory, horn, and other natural materials that had been shaped into handles with fine tools gave way to mass-produced synthetic materials.

For many informal uses today, plastic knives, forks, and spoons are often used instead of metal flatware.

Reviewed by Louis M. Hovey, Jr.
Utica Cutlery Company

KNOTS

Ever since early people first made an ax by tying a stone to a stick, knots have been used to join things together. Early hunters and fishermen made their traps and nets by knotting together ropes that they had wound from vines or animal muscle and hair. In ancient Egypt knot making was employed in building rope bridges and in making ships' rigging. The Egyptians tied knots in series to make their fishing nets.

Knots have also been thought to possess magical powers. In Rome, in the 1st century A.D., it was believed that a wound would heal faster if the bandages applied to it were tied in a ''Hercules knot'' (now known as the reef knot). Knots could have harmful as well as healing powers. In some parts of 18th-century Europe it was thought that a person could be bound under a spell by tying certain knots near him. The victim would be unable to move any part of his body.

Until the 20th century, in parts of northern Europe, people believed that wizards could capture the wind and hold it in knots tied in rope. Sailors bought knotted charm cords from these wizards. The cords had three knots, which could be untied at sea when the wind died down and the ship could not move. When the first was untied, it would release a moderate breeze. A half-gale could be untied from the second. And the third would loose a blast of hurricane force.

Before people knew how to write, they tied knots in ropes as a way of keeping records. The Incas (Indians of South America) used knotted ropes called *quipus*. These were not a substitute for a written alphabet but an elaborate system for keeping records of nearly everything that happened in the vast Incan Empire.

The word ''knot'' stands for the sailor's measurement of ship speed. Knots were tied at regular intervals in what was called the ship's log line. To this line was attached a log chip that was cast off the ship to float in the water. As the ship moved forward, the line began to unreel into the water, and the knots on the line were counted and their departure timed with a sandglass. A knot is still standard measurement for 1 nautical mile (6,076 feet, or 1,852 meters) per hour. Sailors also measured the depth of the water beneath their ship

The **overhand knot** is the simplest stopper and is used as a first step in many other knots. It can jam, making it difficult to untie.

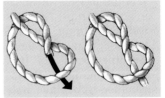

The **figure-eight** is the stopper most often used by sailors. It is the most effective stopper in a tackle or pulley.

The **bowline,** a loop knot, can be used to secure a boat to a piling. It is easy to untie and will not slip or jam.

The **honda** is another kind of loop knot. It is one of the oldest knots in the world, used since ancient times to tie the bowstring to the archer's bow. It is also used to make the cowboy's lariat, or lasso.

The **square knot** is the most common binding knot. It is useful for tying packages, because it can be untied easily.

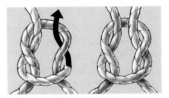

by counting the knots in a weighted line that they lowered into the water.

Uses of Knots

The same knot may be called by different names when used for different purposes. Usually one cannot tell from the names of knots where they were first tied. Most were in common use before they were given the names by which we know them.

Knots can be employed to lift, pull, or support almost anything—from a man to a much heavier or lighter load. A knot can fasten two things together. It can shorten a rope or join two ropes. Knots are used for various tasks in a great many occupations. They are most typically linked with sailors and sailing.

The bow knot with which you tie your shoelaces is simple. An example of a complex knot is the "monkey fist." It is tied by sailors at the end of a rope that will be thrown from one ship to another. This knot must be heavy, or the wind will take the thrown rope away from its target. So the sailor joins many knots together in a large knot that looks something like a monkey's fist.

The "monkey fist" is a difficult knot to tie. There are other knots that are easy to learn and almost as simple as the bowknot, which is used in tying shoelaces, string, and ribbon. In knot-tying there are a few essential things to keep in mind. Do you want the knot to be permanent or temporary? Will it hold fast under heavy strain or come easily undone? You would not try to tie a ship to a pier with the same knot you use to tie your shoes. You must use the knot that is right for the job. And a knot should be easy to untie.

Types of Knots

The family of knots is large and varied. It can be broken down into groups of knots that are used for similar jobs. These include stoppers, bends, and hitches as well as binding knots and loop knots. There are also ornamental knots, which are not grouped according to function.

A **stopper** is a knot made in the end of a rope to prevent the rope from slipping out of an eyebolt, a hole, or the loop of another knot. Many of the knots that we first learned to tie are stopper knots. For example, the knot that secures a piece of thread in the fabric as you begin sewing is a stopper.

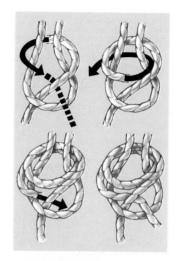

Sheet bends are used mainly to tie two different ropes to each other. The knots do not slip and are easy to untie. The broken line (above left) shows how to complete a **single sheet bend.** Following the solid arrows will produce a **double sheet bend.**

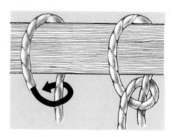

The **Carrick bend** is one of the strongest knots. It is the bend most often used to tie heavy ropes and cables. It unties easily and rarely jams.

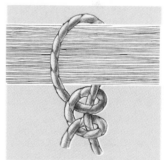

The **half hitch** is quickly fastened but is not the most reliable hitch. It is the first step in making many other hitches.

Two half hitches are more secure. Ships are often moored with two half hitches. The hitches are also used to hang or hoist barrels and other large loads.

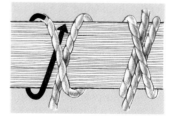

The **clove hitch** has many uses but sometimes tends to slip. It is used for lifting planks of wood and for making fishing nets.

The **round turn** and **two half hitches** are the best knots to use when fastening a tow rope to pull one automobile with another.

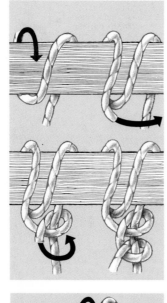

The **cat's paw** is made by putting two loops of rope over a hook. It is the hitch most often used to attach a rope sling to a hook to hoist heavy loads. The most practical of all hook hitches, it never slips or jams, and it falls apart as soon as the hook is removed.

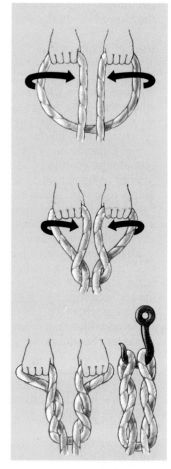

The **rolling hitch** is used in sailing. It is very secure and will not slip even when tied to something smooth, such as wire.

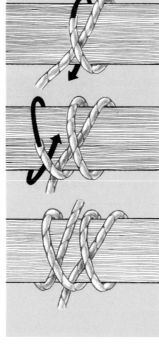

Bends are knots used to tie together two ropes or two ends of the same rope. A bend is a temporary way of joining rope. (A much stronger and more permanent method is splicing, or weaving together, two rope ends. A splice is not a knot.)

Hitches are knots tied directly onto something, such as a pole or a hook. Hitches are widely used as a temporary way of tying things—a horse to a post, for instance. They can be easily untied.

The knots mentioned here are simple and basic. They can be easily learned, with practice. A well-tied knot is one that does its job well.

DAVID M. JOHNSON
Editor, *Third Naval District Reserve Bulletin*
See also MACRAMÉ.

KNOW-NOTHING PARTY. See FILLMORE, MILLARD.

A **loop knot** is tied in the hand to form a loop that can then be slipped around an object and tightened. The bowline is the most widely used of the loop knots.

Binding knots are used to fasten two or more objects tightly together or to hold one object in place. A binding knot will also hold together a bundle or the stitches in a wound.

KNOX, JOHN (1514?–1572)

The brilliant revolutionary and theologian John Knox was the spiritual leader of the Protestant Reformation in Scotland and the founder of Scottish Presbyterianism. Knox was born near Haddington in Southeast Scotland, although the exact year is not known. He was ordained a priest in 1536, at a time when Scotland was plagued with civil disorder and its Roman Catholic Church was exceptionally corrupt. Clergymen and nobles had plundered the church's considerable wealth and bankrupted many parishes.

In 1543, while working as a country lawyer and tutor, Knox came under the influence of the charismatic preacher George Wishart, who converted Knox to the new Protestant beliefs. When Wishart was burnt for heresy in 1546, the outraged Knox joined a band of radical Protestants, who had assassinated Wishart's judge, Cardinal Beaton. They then held St. Andrew's Castle hostage from the Catholic-controlled Scots government and its French allies. There Knox preached his first sermon, characteristically declaring that the popes were Antichrists and that the Catholic Mass worshiped idols and was wicked.

After the Scots government recaptured St. Andrews, Knox served two years hard labor (1547–49) as a French galley slave, but all the while he remained spiritual adviser to his fellow Scots prisoners. With deep-set eyes and long beard, John Knox looked, as well as acted, like an Old Testament prophet.

Upon his release, Knox took refuge in Edward VI's England, where he became a leader of the radical Protestant movement (1549–53). When Edward died and his Catholic sister, Mary I, inherited the throne, Knox fled from England and spent the next six years (1553–59) among exiled Protestants in France, Germany, and Switzerland. In Geneva he studied under the great theologian John Calvin and adopted the stern Calvinist doctrine of predestination, which held that some people are destined for salvation and others to damnation. Knox also developed his own revolutionary doctrines, teaching that people might lawfully resist unjust rulers, by which he meant Catholic monarchs. He also preached that a person's first duty was to obey not governments but the word of God as embodied in the Bible.

John Knox (*right*) led the Protestant Reformation against Roman Catholicism in Scotland. The chief target of his attack was Mary, Queen of Scots.

Equally infamous was his 1558 publication, *First Blast of the Trumpet against the Monstrous Regiment of Women*, in which Knox declared that rule by female monarchs was unnatural and contrary to God's law. Although aimed at Mary I of England, this book deeply offended her successor, Queen Elizabeth I, the chief ally of Scots Protestantism.

Knox returned to Scotland in 1559 to lead a spiritual revolution to overthrow the Catholic government. The following year he succeeded in establishing the Presbyterian Church of Scotland, making Calvinist Protestantism the country's official religion. As minister of St. Giles, Edinburgh, he established a church that controlled the politics, education, law, morals, and spiritual life of the nation.

In 1561, Knox came into conflict with Scotland's new Catholic queen, Mary, Queen of Scots, whom he opposed relentlessly. Knox condemned Mary's private Catholic masses. In 1567, in a final confrontation, he demanded Mary's execution for her supposed participation in the murder of her husband, Lord Darnley. Mary was forced to give up the throne in favor of her baby son and heir, James, who was baptized a Protestant.

Fearless and utterly convinced of his own moral integrity, John Knox died in 1572, content to have seen Protestantism firmly established in Scotland.

DR. CHARLES KIGHTLY
Contributor, *The Illustrated Dictionary of British History*

The koala and her offspring share a close bond. The youngster spends most of its first year either snug in its mother's pouch or riding comfortably on her back.

KOALAS

With its large, rounded ears, leathery black nose, and stout body covered with woolly gray-brown fur, the koala looks like a small bear. Sometimes it is even called the koala bear. But this gentle creature that lives in the forests of eastern Australia is not a bear. Along with its relatives, the kangaroo and opossum, the koala belongs to a group of mammals called **marsupials**.

▶ KOALAS AND THEIR YOUNG

Like other marsupials, koalas raise their young in a pouch on the underside of the mother's body. At birth, koalas are tiny, hairless creatures weighing only about ¹⁄₅₀ ounce (0.5 gram). The single newborn crawls into the pouch and attaches itself to one of two nipples there. It spends the next several months nursing and growing.

At about 5 or 6 months old, the baby koala climbs out of the mother's pouch for the first time. It still returns there to sleep, nurse, and hide when frightened. At 7 or 8 months old, most koalas are too large for the pouch. The youngster climbs onto its mother's back, holding onto her for safety and comfort. It does this until it is about a year old. During this time the young koala starts to eat eucalyptus leaves in the form of partially digested food from the mother's digestive tract.

By the time it is 18 months old, the koala goes off to live on its own. When the male koala is full grown, it may weigh up to 30 pounds (14 kilograms). A female may weigh up to 20 pounds (9 kilograms). By age 2 or 3 they are mature enough to mate.

▶ THE LIFE OF A KOALA

Koalas live relatively long lives for a small mammal. Their life span is about 15 years. They spend most of their lives in eucalyptus trees, feeding on the leaves and sleeping up to 18 hours a day. They are mainly nocturnal, meaning that they are active at night.

The koala's diet is among the most specialized of any mammal. Although there are about 350 species, or kinds, of eucalyptus trees in Australia, koalas eat leaves from only about 20 species and actually may prefer only about 5. An adult eats about 2½ pounds (1 kilogram) of eucalyptus leaves each day. But koalas must be careful. Young leaves of eucalyptus trees contain an acid that can be poisonous. Koalas can digest small amounts of this poison but will become very sick if they eat too many young leaves.

▶ KOALAS AND THEIR ENVIRONMENT

Koalas are slow-moving, gentle creatures. They were easy targets in the 1800's and early 1900's when European hunters killed hundreds of thousands of koalas for their fur.

Zoos have tried to keep koalas but have had limited success because fresh eucalyptus leaves are not easy to provide, especially in northern climates. The zoos in the United States that have housed koalas for the longest time all are in California. These zoos plant eucalyptus forests so they will have enough leaves to feed their koalas.

Koalas are no longer threatened by hunting and, in fact, are now protected by conservation laws. But they are vulnerable to disease, to forest fires, and to clearing of their forest homes. This leaves the koalas with only small areas in which to live and breed. In time, the dwindling habitat could greatly reduce the number of Australia's koalas.

ELIZABETH KAPLAN
Author, *Biology Bulletin Monthly*

See also MARSUPIALS.

KOCH, ROBERT (1843–1910)

One of the milestones of science was the discovery that germs cause disease. This was proved in 1876 by Robert Koch, a little-known German country doctor. Koch proved that a certain microbe (germ) caused the cattle disease anthrax. The science of bacteriology—the study of microbes—is based mainly on his work. Koch's methods have since led to the discovery of dozens of disease-causing microbes and ways to fight them.

Robert Koch was born in Klausthal, Germany, on December 11, 1843. He was the son of a mining official and the third of 13 children. As a boy he became interested in nature and the wildlife of the nearby countryside. He was a good student in high school and decided to study medicine. He went to the University of Göttingen, graduating in 1866.

Koch spent the next few years in hospital work. During this period he married. In 1869 he settled with his wife in eastern Germany, near Breslau. Over the next ten years Koch served as a doctor in that region.

But Koch was not satisfied just treating patients. He was interested in laboratory work as well. Often he studied tiny organisms with his microscope late into the night.

Then an epidemic of the cattle disease anthrax broke out. Koch noticed that the blood of the animals that died turned black. Using his microscope, he saw that their blood always contained the same kind of particles. They looked like tiny rods and threads. Koch never saw them in the blood of healthy animals, however. Were these rods and threads alive? Could they cause anthrax?

For long periods Koch watched the tiny particles with his microscope. Finally he saw a rod-shaped particle divide in two. Then another divided, then another. Now, using a needle, he put a tiny amount of the fluid containing the germs on a drop of jelly. The jelly was from the inside of the eye of a cow. Under his microscope he watched the organisms grow. Then, using a sterilized sharp sliver of wood, he injected the germs into a mouse. The next day the mouse was dead. Its blood was full of the same type of germs he had injected into it.

Eventually Koch traced the complete life cycle of the rod-shaped germ and proved that it caused anthrax. For the first time in history a disease-causing germ had been identified.

Koch, always a painstaking worker, checked his results many times. Then he reported them to scientists studying microbes at the Botanical Institute in Breslau. Over the next few years the value of Koch's work was recognized. By 1880 his work as a researcher had earned him a position on the Imperial Board of Health in Berlin.

Koch could now work in a well-equipped laboratory. He had assistants to help him. Within two years Koch discovered the microbe that caused tuberculosis. He spent many years trying to find a cure for this disease. Although he did not find it, he found a way to test whether or not a person had the disease. His method is still in use today.

While studying tuberculosis, Koch also found better ways to light slides in a microscope. He found new dyes for staining microbes and body tissues placed on the slides. And he discovered a way to grow colonies of microbes on gelatin so that each colony contained only one type of microbe. Because of his discoveries Koch is often called the father of bacteriology.

In 1883 the disease cholera seemed likely to break out in Europe. The German government sent Koch to Egypt and India to examine cholera victims. There he discovered the microbe that causes the disease. He then suggested ways to keep the cholera microbe from spreading. By this time Koch had become famous.

In Berlin, Koch headed the Institute for Infectious Diseases. Students came from all over the world to study bacteriology under him there. Using Koch's methods, they studied the microbes that cause diphtheria, tetanus, and other diseases.

Koch received many honors throughout his career. The greatest of these was the 1905 Nobel Prize for physiology or medicine. The award was given for his work on tuberculosis.

Soon after this Koch gave up most of his scientific work. In 1910, while on a trip to southern Germany, Koch died peacefully in Baden-Baden.

Reviewed by MORRIS C. LEIKIND
National Institutes of Health

See also MICROBIOLOGY.

KONIGSBURG, E. L. See CHILDREN'S LITERATURE (Profiles).

KORAN

The Koran is the holy book of the religion of Islam. Islam was founded in Arabia in the 7th century by the prophet Mohammed. For this reason Islam is often called Mohammedanism. It now has about 400,000,000 believers, who call themselves Muslims. It is the chief religion of North Africa, the Middle East, Pakistan, and Indonesia. There are many different groups of Muslims with slightly different beliefs, but all of them consider the Koran to be the source of their religion.

The Arabic word *qur'ān,* or koran, means "recitation." The book is made up of the recitations, or talks, the prophet Mohammed made to his people in order to teach them his new religion.

Mohammed

Mohammed was born in Mecca in west central Arabia about the year 570. Arabia was then, and still is, a tribal society. Most of the tribes had special gods of their own. Mohammed's tribe was called the Quraish. Its members were settled mainly in the city of Mecca. They worshiped their gods in several shrines. The most important shrine, in the center of the city, was called the Kaaba. For many years before Mohammed's birth the gods of the Kaaba had been worshiped by other tribes, too, because Mecca was an important center of trade and commerce. One branch of Mohammed's tribe had charge of the Kaaba, and nearly all benefited from the business that came into the city.

As he grew older, Mohammed became dissatisfied with the religion of his tribe. He felt that it was too interested in moneymaking. He objected to the many social injustices and immoral practices that it allowed. He began to study and think about the religions of the Jews and Christians who lived in small groups in and around Mecca. Gradually he became convinced that the religion of his tribe was completely false. He came to believe that there was only one true God, the God of the Jews and Christians. He had heard that that God had revealed Himself and His truths to the Jews and Christians through the prophets.

One night, when he was about 40 years old, he was thinking about these matters in a little cave on a hill outside Mecca. Suddenly he felt that he himself was called to be a prophet of God. He said the angel Gabriel came and commanded him to recite the words of God to the Arabs in their own language. When he asked the angel what words he should recite, the angel replied, "Recite: In the name of your God who has created, created man from a clot. Recite: And your Lord is most generous, who taught by the pen, taught man what he did not know."

At first Mohammed was not certain that he was receiving the revelations of God, but soon he was sure of it. He received revelations at intervals for the rest of his life. The Koran is the collection of all those revelations.

The Koran

The Koran consists of 114 chapters (called suras) divided into verses (called ayahs). The titles are taken from a passage within the chapter, and some of the chapters begin with a mysterious combination of letters. The Koran is written in a style that is between prose and poetry—a melodic sing-songy prose. Many Muslims memorize the whole Koran, and schoolchildren throughout the Arab world use it as a textbook for the Arabic language.

The Koran's chapters are not equal in length, since they were recited by Mohammed over a period of more than 20 years. Except for the first chapter, they are arranged in order of length, from the longest to the shortest. Since nearly all the shorter chapters date from earlier times than the longer ones, the order of the book is almost the reverse of the way it was given by Mohammed. However, the chapters are meant to stand by themselves without any particular connection between them, so their arrangement is not regarded by Muslims as very important.

Muslims believe the Koran is the direct word of God. They do not believe that Mohammed wrote it all. In fact, most of them say that Mohammed could not read or write. They say that he memorized the Koran as it was told to him by the angel Gabriel and then recited it to his early followers, who also

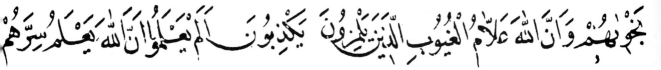

memorized it. It was put together in written form after Mohammed's death.

Mohammed's Religion

For about 12 years Mohammed recited chapters of the Koran and preached a religion that was quite simple. He spoke of one God who had created all mankind, who had blessed mankind with the good things of this world, who had revealed Himself first through the Jewish prophets and then through Jesus, and who intended to reward good and punish evil in a life to come. Mohammed believed that God wished to confirm the religion of the Jews and Christians through him and to establish it among the Arabs. The chapters he recited during this period reflect this simplicity. They are short and uncomplicated. They often begin with an oath, swearing "by the daylight" or "by the fig and the olive." Then they point out some form of wickedness ("those who do not want the poor to eat," "those who shove the orphan aside," or "witches who cast spells"). Finally they call on mankind to repent, and they present frightening descriptions of hell ("the wicked will be roasted in columns of fire" or "the wicked will eat dry branches and drink boiling water").

Later on, Mohammed frequently included stories from the Bible in his chapters. He told about Adam and Eve, Noah and the Flood, Abraham and his sons, Jacob, Joseph and his brothers, Moses, and the later prophets. All the stories were told in the style of the Koran, and some of them were given a new slant to make them understandable and appealing to the Arabs. Mohammed claimed that Abraham's son Ishmael was the ancestor of the Arabs. He accepted Jesus as a prophet, but he denied that he was God. He believed that the Gospel was revealed to Jesus and recited by him in the same way that the Koran was being revealed and recited.

Mohammed's message was not warmly received in Mecca. Most of the Meccans, especially those of Mohammed's relatives who were involved in the Kaaba, found his new religion highly irritating. They may even have been plotting to murder him. But just at this time Mohammed received a request from two tribes in Medina to come and settle a feud between them. He immediately sent his followers there and then escaped himself.

Medina

The year of Mohammed's move from Mecca to Medina, 622, became the first year of the Muslim calendar. At Medina, Mohammed was able to establish his religion firmly and to expand it rapidly. When his efforts to win over some neighboring Arab tribes and Jewish communities failed, he took strong measures against them and turned to a more military strategy.

Mohammed's character and the character of the Koran changed at Medina. The chapters were long lists of rules and regulations for his growing community. Divorce and polygamy (marriage with more than one wife) were established. Many Jewish customs, including the direction to be faced while praying, the forbidding of pork, and the circumcision of boys, were introduced.

The religion of Islam took on its permanent form at Medina. Mohammed's basic teachings were later termed the "five pillars" of Islam. The first is the profession of faith: "There is no god but God, and Mohammed is his messenger." The second is prayer. Muslims pray five times a day. Originally they faced in the direction of Jerusalem, but later they turned toward Mecca. The most formal prayers take place in the central churches (called mosques) at noon on Fridays. Almsgiving, or help to the poor, is the third pillar. Alms were given privately at first, but later they became the official taxes of the Muslim empire. The fourth pillar is fasting. A separate month, called Ramadan, was set aside for it. The fifth pillar is the pilgrimage to Mecca. This duty is required only of those who have the health and money for it.

Mohammed conquered Mecca finally in 630 and included the Kaaba and other items of his tribe's religion in his new religion. After he died in 632, Muslims began their remarkable conquest of much of the world.

JAMES KRITZECK
Princeton University

See also ISLAM; MOHAMMED.

KOREA

Left: Democratic People's Republic of Korea (North Korea)
Right: Republic of Korea (South Korea)

The divided country of Korea lies on a peninsula in East Asia, situated between China and Japan. The name Korea comes from the Koryo dynasty, which ruled it from the A.D. 900's to the late 1300's. The Koreans more often call their country *Choson*, meaning "land of the morning calm."

Korea was freed from 35 years of Japanese colonial rule in 1945, at the end of World War II. Three years later the country, which had been occupied by Soviet troops in the north and by United States forces in the south, was divided into two states—the Republic of Korea (South Korea) and the Democratic People's Republic of Korea (North Korea). Since the Korean War (1950–53), fought between the two states and their allies, North and South Korea have been separated by a demilitarized zone. Although talks about the possibility of reuniting the country have sped up over the past several years, major differences still separate the two Koreas.

▶THE PEOPLE

Where They Live. Although North Korea is the larger of the two states in area, South Korea has nearly twice as many people. Both North and South Korea are quite mountainous, and most of the population is concentrated in lowland areas in the west and south. There has been a rapid growth of cities, where the great majority of the people now live.

Koreans are also found outside their homeland. Many live in Manchuria, a part of China bordering northern Korea, and some in Siberia, a part of the Russian Federation. Koreans make up an important minority in Japan, while substantial numbers have emigrated to the United States.

Language and Religion. Korean is one of the Altaic languages, which also include Turkish and Mongolian. Korean was originally written in Chinese characters, but around 1442 a Korean alphabet, now called *hangul*, was invented. Today a script that combines *hangul* and Chinese characters is used in South Korea. Only *hangul* is used in the North.

The main organized religions of Korea are Buddhism, Christianity, and a native Korean religion called *Chondokyo*, or "religion of the heavenly way." Many Koreans also follow the teachings of Confucius, called Confucianism, introduced from China, which stresses proper ethical behavior and human relations. Some

The many faces of Korea include (*from left to right*) a North Korean factory worker holding a rare bouquet of flowers, a reward for exceeding her work quota; a South Korean boy in Little League uniform; a girl in traditional Korean dress; and a village elder who has enhanced his robes with a Western-style hat.

Koreans maintain the ancient folk religious beliefs known as shamanism. About one quarter of South Koreans are Christians, mainly Protestant. Many Koreans combine elements of various religions in different aspects of their lives. In North Korea, where a Communist government holds power, all forms of religion are strongly discouraged.

Education. In South Korea, most students complete the ninth grade, and increasing numbers are continuing on to high school. Many South Korean parents make great sacrifices to send their children to universities, which enroll some 1.3 million students. There are more college students in South Korea as a percentage of their age group than in any other country except the United States. In North Korea, most children attend school for eleven years. Students completing primary school usually go on to vocational schools and receive training on farms and in factories. The costs of higher education in the North are paid by the government.

Foods. Koreans have traditionally used chopsticks for eating solid food. Brass spoons with long, straight handles are commonly used for serving and eating soups, of which there are many varieties. Rice is a staple of the diet. Typical dishes include *kimchi* (hot pickled cabbage, a particular favorite), *mandu* (meat-filled dumplings), *kuksu* (noodles), and dried fish and other seafoods. Bean curd, made from soybeans, is another basic food, and soy sauce is used for seasoning. American- and European-style restaurants, foods, and eating utensils are increasingly popular, but rice and *kimchi* remain the principal elements of a Korean meal.

Dwellings. The traditional Korean house included a high wall or fence, which created an enclosed courtyard. Windows and doors were fitted with thick, strong paper that allowed some light to enter. The homes of the well-to-do had tile roofs and walls of stone or colored brick. The dwellings of poorer Koreans usually had thatched roofs, woven from rice straw, and mud or stone walls.

Traditionally, the floors of Korean homes were covered with a kind of oiled paper. People ate, sat, and slept on the floors of the main rooms. Heat was provided by the *ondol*, a system of flues under the floor. These were connected to stoves in the kitchen, so that the same fire was used for cooking and heating.

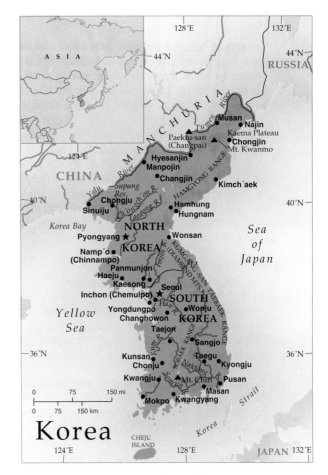

Korea

To keep from soiling the floor covering, shoes were left outside on the ground or on the steps of a narrow wooden porch called a *maru*.

In the South, about 75 percent of the people now reside in cities or other urban areas. Most city dwellers live in brick homes or apartment houses with modern gas or electric heating. Nevertheless, some or all of the rooms will still be kept warm in winter using the traditional *ondol* system of heated floors. In the rural areas of the South, the people have been helped to improve their homes with the aid of government loans.

Sports and Games. Koreans enjoy a great many sports, including soccer, baseball, basketball, volleyball, Ping-Pong, archery, gymnastics, boxing, and wrestling. Of the several kinds of martial arts, the most popular is *tae kwon do*, which has also gained popularity in the United States. Above all, Koreans excel in marathon, or long-distance, running, and they have won prizes in this track event in international competitions, including the Olympics.

Runners in training for marathon races can be seen along many city streets or country roads.

Like children the world over, young Koreans play a variety of games. In one, the object is to swing to great heights on rope swings. Another involves jumping as high as one can from a board balanced on a peg. The Korean top is distinctive because it can be kept spinning for hours. Young Koreans also play a kind of hopscotch, which is especially difficult because the player must kick a pebble from one square to another while hopping on one foot. Young and old alike enjoy flying sturdy Korean kites.

▶ THE LAND

A Mountainous Landscape. Although the country has wide, fertile valleys in the south and west that produce rice and other crops, the traveler finds truth in the old Korean saying that one is never out of sight of mountains. In all, only about one fifth of the land is suitable for cultivation.

The highest of the Korean mountains is Paektu-san (Changpai), an extinct volcano that rises to 9,003 feet (2,744 meters), on the border between North Korea and Manchuria. From this high point the mountains extend southward, close to the eastern coast, to form the backbone of the peninsula. The major

In Korea's rugged terrain, one is never out of the sight of mountains, which cover much of the land. The Sobaek Range (*above*) lies in the southwest.

mountain system is the Taebaek Range and its smaller offshoots, including the Sobaek Range to the southwest. The highest mountain peak in the South is Halla-san, situated in the center of Cheju Island, off the southwestern coast.

Rivers. The Yalu and Tumen rivers mark the northern boundary of Korea. The Yalu flows in a southwesterly direction into the Yellow Sea. The Tumen has a northwesterly flow, into the Sea of Japan, which the Koreans call Tonghae ("eastern sea"). Each of the rivers has swift-flowing tributaries, or branches, that are a source of hydroelectric power. Other important rivers are the Kum, the Han, and the Naktong, which provide water for the rice fields of South Korea.

Climate. In winter, masses of dry, cold air from the interior of Asia bring freezing temperatures to much of the peninsula. In the northern inland areas, winter temperatures remain below freezing for five months of the year. Along the southern coasts, however, warm ocean currents moderate temperatures so that they rarely fall below freezing. The average January temperature for Seoul, in the central part of the peninsula, is about 23°F

($-5°C$). All of Korea has hot summers, with temperatures in the interior usually above 80°F ($27°C$). Rainfall is heaviest along the southern coast, which receives about 60 inches (1,500 millimeters) a year.

Natural Resources. Korea was once covered with forests, but many were cut down for lumber during the Japanese occupation or were burned to clear land for farming. Some native forests still stand in the northern mountains, and a program of reforestation, or planting of new trees, is being carried out in both parts of the country. Such wild animals as leopards and tigers still roam the remote northern forests.

Korea has a wealth of mineral resources—including coal, iron ore, copper, tungsten, zinc, tin, and magnetite, as well as silver and gold—most of which are found in the North. The South has most of the good agricultural land. Both North and South lack petroleum.

▶**THE ECONOMY**

North and South: A Comparison. Before Korea was divided, manufacturing industries were concentrated in the North. In addition to its mineral wealth, the North has extensive hydroelectric resources, based on its rivers, which provided energy for industry. The South, with its more fertile land, produced most of the country's food.

Following the Korean War, both North and South Korea had rapid economic growth, but economic development has been far greater in the South. North Korea, whose economy is controlled by the state, has aimed at becoming self-sufficient in the production of food and other goods. It has little foreign trade, and most of that is with neighboring China. South Korea, by contrast, has concentrated on producing goods for export and is now the world's eleventh largest trading country.

Agriculture and Fishing. In South Korea the number of farmers has been declining, as many of the younger generation move to the cities seeking better-paying work in industry. In spite of a smaller and older farm population, however, the South continues to produce large quantities of food. Rice cultivation, which the government encourages by paying high prices for the crop, provides the largest part of the farmers' income. Improved farming methods have made South Korea's rice production among the highest in the world per

unit of land. The income of farmers, however, still remains lower than that of city dwellers.

In the South, most farms are small and privately owned. In the North, agriculture has been collectivized. The farmers are organized into cooperatives, share farm machinery, and work in teams. Previously, North Korea had to import some of its food. It now claims to be self-sufficient in food production.

In addition to rice and soybeans, basic food crops include barley, corn, potatoes, and sweet potatoes. Cabbages, tomatoes, cucumbers, and a variety of fruits, such as apples, pears, persimmons, and melons, are grown in the South, where bees are also raised for honey and silkworms cultivated for raw silk. Livestock, particularly cattle, pigs, and chickens, are raised in the North and South.

Fishing is especially important, since Koreans generally eat more fish than meat. South Korea has extensive fishing fleets that sail to the far reaches of the Pacific Ocean for their catches. These provide fish for both home consumption and export.

Industry. South Korea's industry has grown remarkably since the 1960's. It now

Most of Korea's fertile agricultural land is found in the South. Here, rice, the chief crop, is being transplanted (*left*). South Korea has also had rapid industrial growth, its major manufactured products including these Hyundai automobiles (*right*).

exports a variety of manufactured goods, including steel, automobiles, ships, chemicals, clothing, television sets, household appliances, and such high-technology products as computers and semiconductors. This industrial expansion has helped raise the average South Korean's income from about $67 a year in 1961 to about $6,500 a year in 1992. Most of South Korea's industry is privately owned and operated, often by large, family-run firms called *chaebol*. But the government plays a strong role in controlling industrial policy.

In North Korea, the government's philosophy of *chuje*, or self-reliance, led to the rapid development of its industry, which includes the manufacture of steel, heavy machinery, trucks, farm equipment, fertilizers, and chemicals, as well as clothing and textiles. Since the economy is state-controlled, the government could stress the growth of heavy industry at the expense of consumer goods. North Korea has since fallen behind the South in industrial production. To be competitive, the North needs foreign technology, which it has not received in a number of years.

▶MAJOR CITIES

Seoul is South Korea's capital and economic and cultural center and the largest city in all of Korea. Situated on the Han River, it lies only some 35 miles (55 kilometers) from the demilitarized zone dividing the country. Much of the city was destroyed during the Korean War, and present-day Seoul consists mainly of modern, high-rise buildings. The city is home to about one quarter of South Korea's population.

Pusan, South Korea's second largest city and chief port, lies on the southeastern tip of the peninsula. Other major South Korean cities are Taegu and Inchon, the port of Seoul. Pyongyang is North Korea's capital and largest city.

See articles on Seoul and Pusan in the appropriate volumes.

▶THE ARTS

Much of what we know about Korea's long history comes from its art. Wall paintings in tombs that date back 2,000 years show scenes of life in the courts of the Korean kings. Ancient pagodas, or temples, Buddhist statues, and paintings used in ancestor worship show the strong influence of Chinese art and of Buddhism and Confucianism on Korean culture.

Metalworking and Pottery. Koreans developed the skills of metalworking at least as early as the 600's B.C. By 668, when most of present-day Korea was unified under the Silla kingdom, court artists were producing exquisite gold and jade jewelry, beautiful golden crowns, and elaborate bronze statues and bells for Buddhist temples. The Silla goldsmiths were among the most skillful in Asia.

Pottery making reached a high point during the time of the Koryo rulers. The famous Korean porcelains known as celadon were produced at this time. In the aristocratic world of

Seoul (*left*) is the capital and largest city of South Korea and one of the world's fastest growing cities. It is home to about one quarter of the South's total population. Pyongyang (*right*) is North Korea's capital and largest city.

the Koryo court, delicate gray-green celadon tiles were used to decorate roofs, walls, and floors. Pitchers shaped like animals and vases formed like flowers show the Korean taste for graceful lines and elegant details.

Painting and Literature. During the long rule of the Yi kings, beginning in the late 1300's. Confucian teachings were stressed, and sculpture and other art forms with close ties to Buddhism declined. Other art forms such as landscape painting and calligraphy, in which writing itself was an art form, became popular in the royal court. One of the most popular painters of the time was Chong Son (1676–1759). He popularized the painting of the Korean landscape by breaking away from lifeless studio painting and traveling around the countryside, painting what he saw.

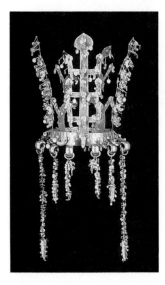

One of Korea's artistic treasures, this gold and jade crown was created by an artisan of the Silla kingdom and dates from the A.D. 400's.

Literature also flourished under the Yi rulers, especially works dealing with Korean history. The Korean alphabet was first developed under the Yi, but most authors continued to write in Chinese.

Love of Nature and Humor. Love of nature can be seen in all forms of Korean art. During village harvest festivals, poems praising nature were often set to music. Buildings were constructed in ways that would make them blend with the surrounding landscape. Folk artists often used more vivid colors than court painters, but their works show the same love for simple, uncluttered lines. Real and imaginary animals, such as tigers, dogs, and dragons, also frequently appear in Korean art.

Korean art often shows a sense of humor. The scholar-painter Kim Hong-do (1760?–1814?) painted realistic and humorous scenes from the everyday life of the working people. The plays performed by masked dancers to rid villages of evil spirits often also poked fun at aristocrats and monks.

The Arts Today. In music and the performing arts, many South Koreans today are experimenting with such originally Western art forms as motion pictures, operas, and the symphony orchestra. Writers have abandoned the traditional Chinese literary forms and are developing a more distinctly Korean body of modern literature. But efforts are also being made to preserve the traditional Korean arts. The study and performance of classical court music, in which pipes, flutes, bells, and an-

The famed Korean porcelains known as celadon were produced during the Koryo period. This vase, which is inlaid with peony and chrysanthemum designs, dates from the mid-1100's.

cient stringed instruments are all used, is encouraged. Court dances that are as old as Korea itself are still popular, as are the livelier folk songs and dances. The exception to this is in the North, where the arts are expected to reflect and glorify the principles of the Communist government and its leaders.

▶HISTORY

Early History to Silla Era.   Korea is an ancient land, whose history dates back some 5,000 years, although much of this is shrouded in legend. In the early struggles over control of the peninsula, several kingdoms rose and fell. The Chinese, who had established the colony of Lolang in northern Korea during the 100's B.C., were driven out in the A.D. 300's, and three small Korean kingdoms emerged. China, however, was to remain a strong influence on Korea throughout much of its history. In A.D. 668 the Silla kingdom defeated its two rivals and united most of the peninsula. Under the Silla dynasty, or ruling family, art and Buddhism both flourished.

Koryo to Yi Periods.   Internal problems led to the decline of the Silla and the rise, in 918, of the Koryo dynasty, which replaced the Silla kings in 935. During the Koryo period, Korea was swept by invasions of Mongols, who became overlords of the country for 100 years.

In 1392, a Korean general, Yi Sung-gi, founded the Yi dynasty. A new capital was established at Seoul, and Confucianism became the official state religion. During this period, the Koreans had to fight off invasions by the Japanese, in 1592 and 1598, and by the Manchus. In 1637, Korea was forced to accept the domination of the Manchus (who soon after became rulers of China), although the Yi kings were to remain on the Korean throne until 1910.

A Hermit Nation.   From 1637 to the 1800's, Korea was a hermit nation, cut off from the outside world except for China. Government

became weak and ineffective, while the scholarly ruling class, or *yangban*, carried on feuds that weakened the country. During the 1800's, U.S., British, and French ships began to visit Korean shores. Competition between Russia and Japan for control over the peninsula led to the Russo-Japanese War (1904–05). After its victory in the war, Japan occupied Korea, which it officially annexed in 1910.

Japanese Rule to Korean War.   The Japanese modernized Korea, developed industries, and built railroads, but the improvements mainly benefited Japan. The Japanese tried to eliminate the Korean language, forcing Koreans to speak Japanese, adopt Japanese names, and become Japanese culturally. After Japan's defeat in World War II in 1945, northern Korea was occupied by armed forces of the Soviet Union and southern Korea by forces of the United States, the two countries having been allies against Japan. The dividing line was 38 degrees north latitude (the 38th parallel).

Efforts to reunite the two parts of the country failed, and in 1948, after elections supervised by the United Nations, the Republic of Korea was established in the South. The Democratic Republic of Korea was created in the North by the Soviet Union that same year. In 1950, North Korean forces, equipped with Soviet arms, suddenly invaded the South in an attempt to forcibly unify Korea under Communist rule. This began the Korean War,

A Dancing Boy was painted by Kim Hong-do (1745–1814?), a scholar-artist who worked at the court of Korea's Yi kings.

A statue of Kim Il Sung (*right*) stands in Pyongyang, capital of North Korea. Kim, who came to power in 1948 and ruled until his death in 1994, was the only leader most North Koreans ever knew. With her children and few belongings, a South Korean refugee (*far right*) flees southward at the outbreak of the Korean War in 1950, barely ahead of invading North Korean forces seeking to reunify the country under Communist rule. The three-year war devastated Korea.

which devastated the country but left it virtually unchanged politically.

See the article on the Korean War following this article.

▶POSTWAR PERIOD AND GOVERNMENT

South Korea: First Decades. Syngman Rhee had been elected South Korea's first president in 1948. Strongly anti-Communist, he was at first popular with the South Korean people, but they became discontented with his increasingly dictatorial rule. Rhee's government was overthrown in 1960, with students leading the rebellion against him. A new popular government, under Chang Myon, was unable to cope with the growing social, economic, and political disorder. In 1961, Chang was deposed in an army coup led by General Park Chung Hee, who established a military government. In 1963, Park was elected president under a new constitution.

During Park's long presidency, South Korea achieved rapid industrial growth and economic prosperity, but his government was marked by authoritarian rule. Park was assassinated in 1979. A government under Choi Kyu Hah briefly held office, but Choi was forced out in December 1979 in a coup by General Chun Doo Hwan, who became president himself.

Revolt and Change. Massive demonstrations against General Chun culminated in a rising against the government in 1980 by the people of Kwangju, which was brutally suppressed by the army. New anti-government protests erupted in 1987. With world attention focused on the 1988 Olympic Games, to be held in Seoul, the government was forced to agree to democratic reforms. These included direct elections for a president who could serve only a single 5-year term. Direct presidential elections, held in late 1987 under a rewritten constitution, were won by Roh Tae Woo, a former associate of Chun. Roh headed the ruling Democratic Justice Party, which was enlarged and renamed the Democratic Liberal Party (DLP) in 1990 and retitled the New Korea Party (NKP) in 1995.

Recent Events. Both North Korea and South Korea were admitted to the United Nations in 1991. Later that year, they signed a landmark treaty of reconciliation and nonaggression. The 1992 presidential elections were won by Kim Young Sam, a former opponent of the military rulers who had joined the DLP two years before. The ruling party kept its legislative majority in the 1992 and 1996 elections for the National Assembly.

Kim Young Sam served as president of South Korea from 1992 to 1998. A leading industrialist, he was the first civilian to hold that office in more than 30 years.

In 1996, Chun and Roh were convicted for their roles in the 1979 coup but were later pardoned. In 1998, in the midst of a nationwide financial crisis, Kim Dae Jung succeeded Kim Young Sam as president.

North Korea: Kim Il Sung and After. For most of its existence, North Korea had only one leader—Kim Il Sung, head of its Communist party, prime minister, and, after 1972, president. Under Kim, the North long remained isolated from most of the world.

Kim Il Sung died on July 8, 1994. His oldest son and designated heir, Kim Jong Il, officially assumed control of the ruling party in October 1997. In September 1998 the legislature named Kim Jong Il head of government but abolished the presidency in tribute to his father.

Tensions over North Korea's nuclear ambitions eased after North Korea and the United States signed an agreement in 1994 designed to eventually dismantle North Korea's nuclear program. Drought and floods contributed to massive grain shortages in the late 1990's, when millions of North Koreans died of starvation. The country's economic problems raised new fears that North Korea might sell its nuclear technology to other countries or launch new attacks on its relatively wealthy southern neighbor.

SHANNON MCCUNE
Author, *Korea: Land of Broken Calm*
EVELYN MCCUNE
Author, *The Arts of Korea*

Revised by DAVID I. STEINBERG
Author, *The Republic of Korea*

KOREAN WAR

Overview. On June 25, 1950, the armed forces of the Democratic People's Republic of Korea (North Korea) crossed the 38th parallel, the line dividing Korea into two parts, and invaded the Republic of Korea (South Korea). The attack, aimed at reuniting the country under Communist rule from the North, touched off the Korean War. Two days later, the United Nations Security Council approved a resolution, introduced by the United States, asking member nations to provide such assistance as necessary to South Korea. The resolution succeeded because the Soviet Union, North Korea's supporter, was absent and unable to veto, or reject, the measure.

Some 16 countries, under the flag of the United Nations, sent military forces to South Korea's defense, most coming from the United States. Many others contributed equipment, supplies, and other support. North Korea's main allies were the Soviet Union, which supplied it with arms, and China, which later poured masses of troops into the conflict. The war raged across the Korean peninsula, causing enormous destruction and loss of life, before an armistice was signed in 1953. Militarily, the war ended with a victory for neither side, but the aggression against South Korea had been repulsed and the right of states to be free from the threat or use of force had been preserved.

For the events leading up to the war and the origins of the division of Korea, see KOREA (History: Japanese Rule to Korean War).

North Korean Offensive. Within the first two days of the war, the well-equipped and well-trained North Korean forces had pushed aside the outnumbered and poorly trained Republic of Korea (ROK) army and captured Seoul, the South Korean capital. Meanwhile, U.S. pres-

General Douglas MacArthur (seated) planned the Inchon landing that proved a brilliant success for United Nations forces in the difficult early months of the war.

Weary U.S. Marines rest briefly during the long retreat from North Korea, after overwhelming numbers of Chinese troops attacked the United Nations lines in November 1950. With China's entry, the Korean War completely changed its course from what was expected to be a quick United Nations victory to a prolonged, bloody conflict.

ident Harry S. Truman had ordered the use of U.S. forces under General Douglas Mac-Arthur, the Far East commander, in support of the South Koreans. On July 5 the first U.S. troops, part of the 24th Infantry Division, sent from Japan, engaged the North Koreans at Osan, south of Seoul. These efforts were intended to delay the North Koreans, who, by August 1950, had overrun all of the peninsula, except for an area around the southeastern port city of Pusan known as the Pusan perimeter. Here the North Korean offensive was stopped, as the U.S. 8th Army and ROK forces regrouped and received reinforcements.

United Nations Counterattack. From Pusan, MacArthur, who had been named to head the United Nations command, planned a daring counterattack. On September 15, an amphibious landing, combining naval, marine, and army forces, was launched against the North Korean-occupied port of Inchon, near Seoul, on South Korea's western coast. Although Inchon's difficult tides and currents made it a hazardous operation, it was a complete success. By late September, Seoul was recaptured. At the same time, the U.S. 8th Army had broken out of the Pusan perimeter and the North Koreans, caught in a two-pronged attack, were in retreat on all fronts. By October, they had fled back across the 38th parallel.

A decision to cross the dividing line into North Korea, to completely destroy its armies and unify the peninsula, was approved by the United Nations General Assembly on October

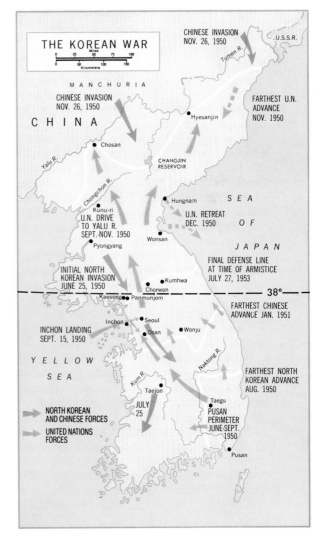

THE KOREAN WAR

CHINESE INVASION NOV. 26, 1950

U.S.S.R.

Tumen R.

MANCHURIA

CHINESE INVASION NOV. 26, 1950

CHINA

Yalu R.

Chosan

Hyesanjin

FARTHEST U.N. ADVANCE NOV. 1950

CHANGJIN RESERVOIR

Chongchon R.

Kunu-ri
U.N. DRIVE TO YALU R. SEPT.-NOV. 1950

Pyongyang

Hungnam

Wonsan

SEA

U.N. RETREAT DEC. 1950

OF

JAPAN

FINAL DEFENSE LINE AT TIME OF ARMISTICE JULY 27, 1953

INITIAL NORTH KOREAN INVASION JUNE 25, 1950

Kumhwa

Chorwon

Kaesong Panmunjom

38°

FARTHEST CHINESE ADVANCE JAN. 1951

Inchon   Seoul

INCHON LANDING SEPT. 15, 1950

Osan

Wonju

YELLOW

SEA

Kum R.

Naktong R.

FARTHEST NORTH KOREAN ADVANCE AUG. 1950

Taejon

JULY 25

NORTH KOREAN AND CHINESE FORCES

UNITED NATIONS FORCES

Taegu

PUSAN PERIMETER JUNE-SEPT. 1950

Pusan

The war developed into a grinding two-year stalemate as North Korean and United Nations peace negotiators debated at Panmunjom. An armistice was finally signed in 1953.

7. Advancing northward swiftly against little opposition, the United Nations forces took Pyongyang, the North Korean capital, on October 19. By November 21 they had reached the Yalu River, part of North Korea's boundary with Manchuria, a region of China. An early end to the war was expected.

China Enters the War. A warning by the Chinese Communist government that it would not allow the destruction of North Korea had been disregarded. Now, claiming that the United Nations advance threatened its borders, China completely changed the nature of the war. On November 25, massive numbers of Chinese troops attacked the United Nations lines. Caught by surprise and overwhelmed, the United Nations forces began a long retreat, which ended, in January 1951, with Seoul once more in Communist hands. From this low point, the United Nations troops slowly but stubbornly pushed northward again, retaking Seoul in March 1951.

MacArthur Dismissed. The Allied aims in the war had now shifted to maintaining South Korea's territorial boundaries and seeking an end to the fighting, avoiding the possibility of the war's expansion beyond Korea. MacArthur, who had urged the bombing of Chinese troop-staging areas inside the Manchurian border, publicly criticized these limited aims. This was in violation of President Truman's directive, and in April 1951, Truman dismissed MacArthur from command. He was replaced by Lieutenant General Matthew Ridgeway, commander of the U.S. 8th Army. See the article on MacArthur in Volume M.

Stalemate and Peace Efforts. Between April and May 1951, some of the heaviest fighting of the war took place between Chinese and United Nations forces. A last Chinese offensive, in May, was repulsed with heavy casualties, and by June, both sides were entrenched along the 38th parallel, where the war had begun. A stalemate had developed, and the war became one of grinding, brutal fighting, as each side fought for a small advantage over the other.

The Soviet Union had proposed negotiations for a cease-fire at the United Nations on June 23, 1951. Representatives of the two sides first met at Kaesong on July 10. The talks, which continued at nearby Panmunjom, went on for two years, an armistice finally being signed on July 27, 1953. Military casualties on both sides exceeded 1.5 million. More than 54,000 Americans had died in action or from injuries and disease. Millions of Koreans had been killed, and many more had been left homeless or become refugees.

CHONG-SIK LEE
University of Pennsylvania
Author, *The Politics of Korean Nationalism*

KOVALEVSKAIA, SOFIA. See MATHEMATICS, HISTORY OF (Profiles).

KREMENTZ, JILL. See CHILDREN'S LITERATURE (Profiles).

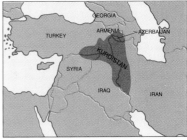

The Kurds are a distinct people of the Middle East, most of whom inhabit a mountainous area called Kurdistan (*see map*). This family lives in Iraq, where Kurds make up about one-fifth of the population.

KURDS

The Kurds are an ancient and distinct people of the Middle East. Most inhabit a mountainous region, long known as Kurdistan ("land of the Kurds"), which includes parts of Turkey, Iran, and Iraq, as well as smaller areas of Syria, Azerbaijan, and Armenia. Although the Kurds have lived in this region for at least several thousand years, they have never possessed an independent country of their own and have had to suffer great oppression at the hands of other peoples. In spite of this, the Kurds have never lost their strong sense of their separate identity. They have their own language and a culture that is both varied and rich.

The People. The total number of Kurds living in the Middle East is estimated at between 12 and 15 million. The largest group, perhaps 7 million, is found in Turkey. In Iraq they make up about one-fifth of the population.

Kurdish belongs to the Indo-European family of languages and is related to Persian. Historically, the Kurds claim descent from the Medes, an ancient people akin to the Persians. In religion, the Kurds are Muslims, most belonging to the Sunni group of Islam.

Land and Economy. Kurdistan is a land of extremely high mountains, including the western ends of the Zagros and Elburz mountain chains. Most settled Kurds are farmers. Some live in towns and cities, while a few maintain a nomadic way of life, seeking pasture for their flocks of sheep and goats. There is export of textiles and handicrafts, particularly the famed Kurdish rugs and carpets.

History. From the 1600's to 1918, much of Kurdistan was ruled by the Ottoman Empire, although Kurdish chieftains exercised some degree of local power. After the empire collapsed in 1918, Kurdistan found itself in its present form.

At the end of the Persian Gulf War of 1991, Kurds in Iraq fled to refugee camps in the north, where they were protected by United Nations peacekeeping forces. In 1992, Iraqi Kurds held their first elections free from Iraqi control. But factional disputes among themselves contine to leave the Kurds vulnerable to the powerful nations surrounding them.

Modern Turkey denies the Kurds existence as a separate people. Iraq recognizes their distinctive identity, but rebellions have been harshly punished. One of the most prominent leaders of Kurdish resistance in modern times is Abdullah Ocalan, head of the Kurdistan Workers' Party (PKK), a guerrilla group leading the Kurdish independence movement in Turkey, Iran, Iraq, and Syria. In 1999, Turkish authorities caught up with Ocalan in Nairobi, Kenya, and brought him back to Turkey to stand trial for the deaths of 30,000 people killed in the PKK's armed struggle. Ocalan's capture sparked protests and rioting by Kurdish supporters in many European cities.

ARTHUR CAMPBELL TURNER
Author, *Ideology and Power in the Middle East*

KUROSAWA, AKIRA. See MOTION PICTURES (Profiles: Directors).

KUSKIN, KARLA. See CHILDREN'S LITERATURE (Profiles).

KUWAIT

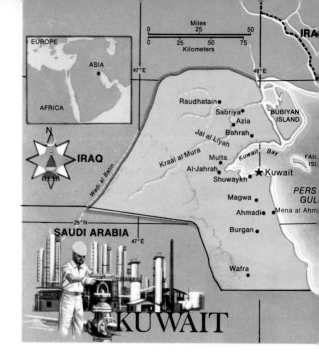

Kuwait is a small nation situated on the Arabian Peninsula in Southwest Asia. Before the discovery of oil in the 1930's made it one of the world's wealthiest countries, Kuwait was a poor, little-known Arab state. Its people had traditionally earned their livelihood from boat building, pearl diving, fishing, and raising livestock. Oil transformed Kuwait, enabling it to finance a broad range of social welfare programs for its citizens. The country's wealth made it a tempting prize to its more powerful neighbor Iraq, which invaded Kuwait in 1990, setting off the 1991 Persian Gulf War.

▶THE PEOPLE

Ethnic Groups, Religion, Language. The Kuwaitis are Muslims. Arabic is the language of the country, although English is widely spoken. Traditionally, less than half the population were Kuwaiti citizens. The rest were immigrant workers and their descendants. Palestinian Arabs long made up the largest group of foreign workers. Others came from various parts of the Middle East. Thousands of Europeans and Americans were also employed by the oil companies. Kuwait has since adopted a policy of relying less on foreigners. Palestinians were hardest hit because of support for Iraq during the war by Palestinian leaders abroad.

Way of Life. Before the oil boom, most of the people lived in the old walled town of Kuwait, in mud and brick houses packed into winding alleyways. The people outside the town were Bedouin nomads, herders of camels, goats, and sheep. This way of life was changed abruptly, in the years following World War II (1939–45), when Kuwait began to export oil in large quantities. Most of the old town of Kuwait was replaced by Kuwait city—a modern capital with wide boulevards, a variety of shops, banks, luxury hotels, and the most up-to-date urban services.

The Welfare State. Kuwait combined certain features of a free enterprise economy with those of a welfare state. Welfare projects in-

Kuwait city is the capital, largest city, and chief port of Kuwait and the commercial and financial heart of the country. Founded in the 1700's, it was originally a small mud-walled town that depended on fishing, pearling, and trade. The city grew rapidly after the development of Kuwait's oil industry in the late 1940's. Kuwait city was occupied by Iraqi troops for some seven months during 1990–91 and much of it was damaged.

clude low-income housing, free medical care and hospitalization, free education, and free lunch and transportation for schoolchildren. The government also constructed retail stores to provide the unemployed with work.

Power stations provided street lighting and electricity for most homes. Water-distillation plants purified seawater so that it could be used for drinking. Until these distillation plants were built, Kuwait had to import most of its water.

In order to oversee the many different services, Kuwait had an exceptionally large proportion of government employees in relation to the population.

Education. Public education is free. One year of kindergarten is followed by twelve years of primary, intermediate, and secondary schooling. Secondary-school graduates can go on to technical institutions and colleges. The University of Kuwait was established in 1966. Some students are sent to colleges and universities abroad at state expense. The system also includes a program of adult education.

▶**THE LAND**

Kuwait is located on the eastern coast of the Arabian Peninsula, at the northwestern tip of the Persian Gulf. Kuwait's neighbors are Iraq and Saudi Arabia. The boundaries with Saudi Arabia were established in 1922. Because the two countries could not agree on which of them should rule the desert area just south of Kuwait on the Saudi Arabian border, they made the region into a neutral zone shared by both. The importance of this territory increased greatly when oil was discovered there. The zone has since been partitioned between Kuwait and Saudi Arabia, but they continue to share the revenue from its oil.

Nearly all of the country is flat, sandy desert, with a few small hills. Here and there a few oases (watered, fertile areas) provide shelter and subsistence for the Bedouin nomads and their flocks and herds. Rainfall is scanty, falling mostly between October and April.

The climate of Kuwait is one of the hottest in the world, often reaching temperatures of 125°F (52°C) in the summer. During the winter months, temperatures are much cooler.

▶**THE ECONOMY**

Agriculture. Kuwait has little agriculture, and most food must be imported. A few farmers earn a livelihood by growing vegetables and cereal grains, such as wheat, in the oases. From their livestock the Bedouin obtain meat, milk, skins, and goat and camel hair for their clothing and tents.

Oil. Since the discovery of oil, Kuwait's economy has been dependent upon that industry. In 1934 the government of Kuwait granted the British-owned Anglo-Iranian Oil Company (British Petroleum Company) and the American-owned Gulf Oil Company the rights to prospect for oil within Kuwait. The two firms formed the Kuwait Oil Company. In 1938 the Burgan oil field, located south of Kuwait city, was discovered. It is considered the richest single oil field in the world. Other fields have since been discovered. The Kuwait Oil Company was nationalized in 1975.

Kuwait's crude oil reserves are among the largest in the world. Oil accounted for nearly 90 percent of its earnings. Revenue from oil increased at such a rapid rate that the per capita (per person) annual income grew from $35 before World II to over $20,000 before the 1990 Iraqi invasion. The country's wealth was so great that other Arab countries depended on Kuwait as a source of funds for their own economic development. The government has also invested much of its oil income abroad.

Industry. Kuwait's industry is based on oil. It includes oil refining, the processing of oil products, and the production of natural gas.

FACTS and figures

STATE OF KUWAIT is the official name of the country.

LOCATION: Southwest Asia.

AREA: 6,880 sq mi (17,818 km²).

POPULATION: 2,000,000 (estimate).

CAPITAL AND LARGEST CITY: Kuwait (including metropolitan area).

MAJOR LANGUAGE: Arabic (official).

MAJOR RELIGIOUS GROUP: Muslim.

GOVERNMENT: Constitutional monarchy. **Head of state**—emir. **Head of government**—prime minister (appointed by the emir). **Legislature**—National Assembly.

CHIEF PRODUCTS: Agricultural—wheat, vegetables, livestock (camels, sheep, goats). **Manufactured**—refined petroleum, petrochemicals, concrete and bricks, prefabricated houses, processed foods. **Mineral**—petroleum, natural gas.

MONETARY UNIT: Kuwaiti dinar (1 dinar = 1,000 fils).

Manufactures include sand-and-lime bricks, concrete, prefabricated houses, and processed foods. Furniture making, fishing, and ship-building are traditional industries.

Kuwait's economy has only recently begun to recover from the effects of the Iraqi invasion and the 1991 Persian Gulf War.

▶CITIES

Kuwait city is the largest city, the capital, and the chief port of Kuwait. It has changed dramatically from its days as a mud-walled fishing village and center of the pearling trade. Graceful sailing ships called dhows once dotted its waters. Today Kuwait city has broad avenues and high-rise buildings. It is the commercial, financial, and industrial heart of the country. Many Kuwaitis fled the city when the country was invaded. Those who remained suffered under the Iraqi occupation.

Other important urban areas include Mena al Ahmadi, an oil port; the port of Shuwaykh; and the new city of Ahmadi, built by the Kuwait Oil Company.

▶GOVERNMENT

Kuwait is a constitutional monarchy. Its ruler is the emir, who belongs to the Sabah family that has ruled Kuwait since 1756. The emir is chosen for life by other members of the family. He exercises power through a prime minister and a council of ministers. Traditionally, the office of prime minister has gone to the crown prince, the intended successor of the emir.

In 1962, Kuwait adopted its first constitution. It provides for an elected legislature, the National Assembly. Its members serve 4-year terms. Only male citizens over the age of 21 who are able to read and write and whose parents have lived in Kuwait since 1920 are allowed to vote and take part in political life. This includes only a small fraction of the total population. But all people living in the country may benefit from the wide range of social services offered by the government.

▶HISTORY

Early History. In the mid-1700's, Arab tribes from the central desert of the Arabian Peninsula migrated to the more hospitable shore of the Persian Gulf. In 1756 they chose the Sabahs to be the ruling family of what is now the nation of Kuwait.

The region was nominally part of the Turkish Ottoman Empire, but the Sabah family was allowed much self-government in local matters. During the 1700's and early 1800's Kuwait was important as a port for all of central Arabia. But attacks on the town of Kuwait by raiding Arab tribes and by Persian Gulf pirates led to its economic decline.

British Influence. Britain became especially interested in Kuwait because the Persian Gulf was a vital waterway on the route to British-controlled India. By the end of the 1800's, Sheikh Mubarak al-Sabah feared that the Ottoman Turks would occupy his country. In 1899 he signed a treaty with Britain, in return for British protection.

In 1914, at the outbreak of World War I, the British recognized Kuwait's independence from Turkey but continued to exercise protection over the country. After the war—under

Kuwait's harsh landscape consists mostly of flat, sandy desert. Beneath the desert sands, however, lie some of the largest oil deposits in the Middle East. Income from the oil has given Kuwaiti citizens, like the young man at right, one of the world's highest standards of living.

Jubilant Kuwaitis welcomed liberating Allied forces in 1991. The country's oil wells, the basis of its economy, were set on fire by retreating Iraqis, but the fires have since been extinguished.

the pro-British rule of Sheikh Ahmad, a nephew of Salem—the country began to flourish. Concessions were signed with the oil companies, and immigrant workers swelled the population. The oil boom and its accompanying prosperity began in 1945, when oil operations, halted during World War II, were resumed.

Independence. When Ahmad died in 1950, Sheikh Abdullah al-Salim al-Sabah came to power. Under Abdullah the country made great economic progress. The increasing oil wealth was used to develop Kuwait as a modern nation and to provide the people with a share of the country's riches.

Kuwait gained full independence from Britain on June 19, 1961.

Abdullah died in 1965 and was succeeded as emir by Sheikh Sabah al-Salim al-Sabah. After his death in 1977, rule in Kuwait passed to Sheikh Jabir al-Ahmad al-Sabah.

To protect Kuwaiti oil shipments during the Iran-Iraq war of 1980–88, the U.S. government, beginning in 1987, reflagged (flew the U.S. flag on) a number of Kuwaiti oil tankers and provided them with a naval escort in the Persian Gulf.

Invasion and War. In spite of its support of Iraq during the war, Kuwait was invaded by its much larger neighbor in 1990. Iraq had claimed Kuwait as part of its territory under Turkish rule. Using the pretext of disputed oil fields and disagreements over oil production quotas, Iraq quickly overran Kuwait, as the emir fled to Saudi Arabia. The aggression was condemned by the United Nations Security Council and by many governments. The United States dispatched military forces to Saudi Arabia and imposed a naval blockade on Iraq. When Iraq refused to withdraw from Kuwait, the United Nations authorized the use of military force by a coalition (alliance) of nations led by the United States. The coalition included troops from several Arab countries. Massive air attacks against Iraq began in January 1991. In February allied armies launched a ground offensive. After some 100 hours of combat, Iraq was driven from Kuwait.

The Aftermath. During its occupation, Iraq had looted hospital equipment, libraries, government records, museums, industrial machinery, private automobiles, and other property from Kuwait. Hundreds of civilians had been killed, tortured, and imprisoned.

Thousands of Kuwaitis had been taken prisoner to Iraq. Others fled to neighboring countries, returning after the fighting ended. Many non-Kuwaiti citizens also fled. The country itself was nearly destroyed during the occupation and the war that followed, and retreating Iraqi troops set fire to most of Kuwait's oil wells. By 1994 oil production had returned to prewar levels, but the costs of the war and rebuilding the economy were substantial.

After the war, Kuwaitis demanded democratic reforms. Elections for the National Assembly, suspended in 1986, resumed in 1992. And a greater number of people were allowed to participate in the 1996 elections, although women were still denied the right to vote.

DON PERETZ
State University of New York at Binghamton
Author, *The Middle East Today*

See also PERSIAN GULF WAR.

KWANZAA. See AFRICAN AMERICANS (Wonder Question).

KYOTO

Kyoto served as the capital of Japan for more than a thousand years (from 794 to 1868) and remains the center of traditional Japanese culture. Situated on the island of Honshu, in the scenic valley of the Kamo River, Kyoto is also an industrial city, with a population of some 1.5 million.

City of Shrines. Kyoto has been called the City of a Thousand Shrines because of the numerous Shinto shrines and Buddhist temples scattered throughout the city and the surrounding hills. Many are as old as Kyoto itself. One of the most famous is the Kinkakuji Temple, also called the Golden Pavilion because of its covering of gold leaf. Another is the Ginkakuji Temple, or Silver Pavilion. Its builder originally intended to cover it with silver leaf but died before he could do so. Nevertheless, over the centuries, the temple's wooden walls have weathered into a soft silver-gray color. Sanjusangendo, the temple known as the Hall of Thirty-Three Bays, contains 1,001 gilded statues of Kannon (or Kuan-yin), who is revered as the Buddhist goddess of mercy.

Other places of especial interest include the Imperial Palace, Nijo Castle, the Katsura Villa, and the Yasaka Shrine. Kyoto also has more than twenty colleges and universities.

History. Kyoto was founded by Emperor Kammu as his capital in A.D. 794, beginning a brilliant age of artistic and cultural achievement, much of it based on Chinese models. Although the emperors continued to reside in Kyoto until the mid-1800's, political power eventually passed to the shoguns, or military rulers of Japan, who often lived elsewhere. During the Ashikaga period (1338–1573), a golden age of arts and letters, the shoguns also made Kyoto their seat of government. Kyoto declined in political importance after the last shoguns, the Tokugawas, moved their capital to Edo in 1603, and in 1868 the emperor, restored to power, transferred the imperial capital to Edo (renamed Tokyo) as well. See also JAPAN (History: Kyoto Shogunate).

Economic Activity. In addition to its historical and cultural attractions, which make tourism one of its chief industries, Kyoto is also important for its manufactured goods. Its famous silk industry, founded in the same year as the city itself, still flourishes. So do such traditional handicrafts as the making of porcelain, dolls, and lacquerware. The city's heavy industry includes copper smelting and the production of machinery and chemicals.

EDWIN BAYRD
Author, *Kyoto*

This view of Kyoto at night shows the ancient Toji Temple (foreground) and the modern Kyoto Tower. Japan's cultural center, Kyoto was also its capital from 794 to 1868.

KYRGYZSTAN

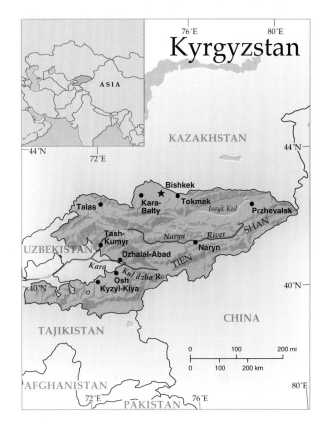

Kyrgyzstan (once known as Kirghizia) is one of the 15 former constituent republics of the Soviet Union. Along with Kazakhstan, Tajikistan, Turkmenistan, and Uzbekistan, it made up the region known as Soviet Central Asia. Kyrgyzstan and the other Central Asian republics proclaimed their independence in 1991, amid the breakup of the Soviet Union.

The People.   The Kyrgyzes make up a little more than 52 percent of the country's population. The largest ethnic minorities are Russians, with about 22 percent of the population, and Uzbeks, from neighboring Uzbekistan, with about 13 percent. Russians are a majority in Bishkek, the capital and largest city, which has about 600,000 inhabitants. (The capital was known as Frunze under the Soviets.)

In religion, the Kyrgyzes, like most of the other peoples of Central Asia, are Muslims. The Russians are Eastern Orthodox Christians. The Kyrgyz language is related to Turkish. In their appearance, the Kyrgyzes are the most Mongol-looking of the Central Asian peoples.

Originally nomadic herders of livestock, the Kyrgyzes have preserved elements from their tribal past, including the extended family. Five to seven families constitute a village community. Several villages form a clan, and several clans a tribe. The tribes are divided into two federations—one located in the north and the other in the south.

The Land and Economy.   The Tien Shan plateau, with its mountain ranges and high valleys, occupies most of the land. The highest peaks are on the border with China in the

A Kyrgyz storyteller has the complete attention of his audience, which is seated in the traditional circular tent, as he relates the history of the Kyrgyz people. Originally nomads, the Kyrgyzes are a mixture of Turkic and Mongol ethnic groups whose language is related to Turkish. Kyrgyzstan was one of the five Soviet Central Asian republics that won independence amid the breakup of the Soviet Union in 1991.

Most of Kyrgyzstan consists of the Tien Shan plateau, with its mountains and high valleys. Now as in the past, animal herding is an important part of the economy.

southeast. The major river is the Naryn, a part of the Syr Darya. Issyk Kul, a large salt lake, lies in the northeast. Kyrgyzstan has important mineral deposits, including coal, mercury, antimony, lead, and uranium.

The climate varies greatly, depending on elevation. Temperatures range from an average of about 35°F (2°C) in winter to about 65°F (18°C) in summer. Rainfall is limited.

Livestock raising remains an important part of the economy. Sheep are grazed on the mountain meadows, and cattle are bred for meat and dairy products. Wheat and other grains, cotton, sugar beets, and tobacco are leading crops. Industry, introduced by the So-

viets, is based on mining, the processing of foods and other agricultural products, and textile manufacturing. The industrial workforce is mainly Russian.

Early History. Kyrgyz history is similar to that of the rest of Central Asia but with more of an impact from China. It was in the struggle against the Chinese, beginning in the 100's B.C., that the Kyrgyzes acquired an identity of their own. Otherwise, the main events of their early history were the Turkic invasions of the A.D. 400's; a short-lived period in the 800's when the Kyrgyzes dominated the region; the introduction of the Muslim religion; and the Mongol conquest of the 1200's.

After breaking away from Uzbek domination in the 1400's, the Kyrgyzes were part of a loose confederation with the Kazakhs (from what is now Kazakhstan), before migrating south to their present homeland.

Russian and Soviet Rule: Independence. The Kyrgyzes were subjects of the ruler of the state of Kokand when they fell under Russian domination in the mid-1800's. After the overthrow of the Russian Empire in 1917, the Kyrgyzes were made part of the Soviet Communist state, becoming a constituent republic of the Soviet Union in 1936. Independence came with the collapse of the Soviet Union in late 1991.

A new constitution was adopted in 1993. It provides for an elected president as head of state, a prime minister to head the government, and an elected 105-member parliament.

MICHAEL RYWKIN
City University of New York, City College
Author, *Moscow's Muslim Challenge:
Soviet Central Asia*

FACTS and figures

REPUBLIC OF KYRGYZSTAN is the official name of the country.

LOCATION: Central Asia.

AREA: 76,641 sq mi (198,500 km²).

POPULATION: 4,500,000 (estimate).

CAPITAL AND LARGEST CITY: Bishkek.

MAJOR LANGUAGE(S): Kyrgyz, Russian.

MAJOR RELIGIOUS GROUP(S): Muslim, Eastern Orthodox Christian.

GOVERNMENT: Republic. **Head of state**—president. **Head of government**—prime minister. **Legislature**—parliament.

CHIEF PRODUCTS: Agricultural—livestock (meat and dairy products), wheat and other grains, cotton, sugar beets, tobacco. **Manufactured**—processed foods and other agricultural products, textiles. **Mineral**—coal, mercury, antimony, lead, uranium.

Index

HOW TO USE THE DICTIONARY INDEX

See the beginning of the blue pages in Volume 1.

houses **A:**368; **H:**171
Japanese family **F:**42
kite festival **K:**266b
marriage rites **W:**101
pearl farm **P:**114
railroad trains **A:**462; **T:**285
rice farming **J:**38
schoolchildren **A:**455; **E:**84
Tokyo **A:**444; **C:**311
traditional hairstyle **H:**7
Japan, Sea of **O:**46
Japan Current (Kuroshio) (Pacific Ocean)
climate of Japan **J:**34
North America, effect on **N:**291
Sea of Japan **O:**46
Japanese Americans **H:**54; **R:**34a
Los Angeles **L:**304
World War II **W:**27
Yasui, Minoru **O:**215
picture(s)
Hawaii **H:**54
Japanese art and architecture **J:**48–51; **O:**227–29
art as a record **A:**438b–438c
decorative arts **D:**71–72
flower arranging **F:**278
furniture **F:**508
houses of paper and wood **H:**171
Japanese prints **G:**303
watercolor painting **W:**59
picture(s)
Japanese prints **G:**305; **O:**228
lacquered box **D:**72
traditional house **H:**171
Japanese beetles **P:**286–87, 290
Japanese bobtail (cat) **C:**138
picture(s) **C:**138
Japanese giant salamander (amphibian) **A:**215
Japanese language **J:**30, 52; **L:**40
Japanese literature **J:**52–53
drama **D:**294
Japanese music **M:**548
lullabies **L:**337
picture(s) **M:**534
Japanese spider crab
picture(s) **C:**591
Japanning (furniture decoration) **F:**511
Japan wax **W:**78
Jarchas (short lyric poems) **S:**386
Jargon (special words used by groups)
teenagers' use **C:**226
Jargon codes **C:**394–95
Jaruzelski, Wojciech (Polish general and political
leader) **P:**362
Jarves, Deming (American glassmaker) **G:**236
Jarvis, Anna (American founder of Mother's Day) **H:**159;
W:138–39 *profile*
picture(s) **W:**138
Jarvis, Gregory (American astronaut) **S:**352
Jarvis Island *see* Howland, Baker, and Jarvis islands
Jasmine (plant)
picture(s)
yellow jessamine is state flower of South
Carolina **S:**297
Jason (hero in Greek mythology) **G:**367–68
Jasper (opaque quartz) **Q:**6; **R:**267
Jasper (Wedgwood pottery) **P:**413
Jasper National Park (Alberta) **J:**54
picture(s) **J:**54
Jasperware (pottery) **A:**316a
Jassy (Romania) **R:**298
Jataka (folk tales and fables from India) **F:**3; **I:**141
Jaundice (disease) **D:**193; **L:**269
Java (British warship) **W:**10

Java (island of Indonesia) **I:**208, 209, 210, 211
Jakarta **J:**13–14
population density **I:**206
prehistoric people **I:**211; **S:**334
soil **A:**452
Java Sea **O:**46
Javelin throw (field event) **T:**252, 257
world records **T:**261
Jawara, Sir Dawda K. (president of The Gambia) **G:**9
Jawfish **F:**197
Jaworski, Leon (American lawyer) **N:**262f
Jaws (framework for holding the teeth)
animals have different kinds **A:**277
fish **F:**184
mammal jaws **M:**65–66
orthodontics **O:**236–37
snakes **S:**216
Jaws (motion picture)
picture(s)
mechanical shark **L:**305
Jawsaq Palace (Samarra, Mesopotamia) **I:**357
Jay, John (American statesman and jurist) **J:**55
The Federalist **F:**78
picture(s) **N:**224
Jayadeva (Indian poet) **I:**141
Jayewardene, Junius Richard (Sri Lankan political
leader) **S:**416
Jayhawkers (free-state men of pre-Civil War days) **C:**335
Jayhawker State (nickname for Kansas) **K:**177, 188
Jay's Treaty (1794) **J:**55; **U:**178; **W:**44
Jazz **J:**56–64; **U:**208 *see also* the names of jazz musicians
and composers
Armstrong, Louis **L:**326
clarinet is a brilliant solo instrument **C:**348
Coltrane, John **N:**320
country music influenced by **C:**563
dance craze in United States **D:**27
dance music influenced by **D:**36
Davis, Miles **I:**74
Goodman, Benny **I:**74
gospel songs **H:**325
guitar **G:**412
Hispanic Americans **H:**135
Memphis (Tennessee) **T:**74
modern music styles combined with **M:**398
music festivals **M:**559, 560
New Orleans **L:**320; **N:**195
percussion instruments **P:**147, 149
rock music, development of **R:**261, 262d
picture(s)
musicians performing on city street **F:**323
New Orleans **N:**195
Preservation Hall Jazz Band **L:**318
Jazz (hand-written book by Henri Matisse)
picture(s) **F:**431
Jazz Age (Roaring 20's) (in the United States)
American literature **A:**210, 211
Chicago **I:**76
Coolidge administration **C:**539–40
Fitzgerald, F. Scott **F:**224
Jazz Singer, The (first talking film, 1927) **M:**491
J-bars (kind of ski lift) **S:**185
Jealousy, feeling of (in psychology) **M:**223–24
Jean (grand duke of Luxembourg) **L:**348
Jean Lafitte National Historical Park and Preserve
(Louisiana) **L:**322
Jeanne d'Arc *see* Joan of Arc
Jeanneret, Charles Édouard *see* Le Corbusier
Jebba (Nigeria)
picture(s) **R:**243
Jebel (Arab word for mountain) *see* the main element of the
name
Jeep (automobile)
picture(s) **A:**544

Jefferson, Martha Wayles Skelton (wife of Thomas Jefferson) J:66
Jefferson, Thomas (3rd president of the United States) **J:65–71**
  agriculture, interest in A:99
  American literature A:199
  archaeology, interest in A:350
  architectural contributions A:380–81; U:128
  author of Declaration of Independence D:60–61
  condemned slave trade in first draft of Declaration of Independence S:194
  currency system of the United States D:257
  friendship with John Adams A:15
  growing up in colonial America C:412
  ideas on education E:82
  introduced ice cream to the United States F:335
  Kentucky and Virginia Resolutions K:227
  Lewis and Clark expedition L:163–64
  Louisiana Purchase L:330
  Michigan, naming of M:258
  Monroe, James, friendship with M:423
  Montesquieu's influence on F:439
  Monticello (Jefferson's home) V:354
  owned slaves A:79e
  political parties P:370–71
  presidential leadership P:448
  quoted B:181; Q:20; W:128
  University of Virginia's founder V:355
  vice presidency V:325 profile
  Washington, D.C., history of W:36
  picture(s) C:2; J:65, 66, 68; P:445
    author of Declaration of Independence D:58
    designed the Rotunda of the University of Virginia A:381; V:350
    political cartoon about Embargo of 1807 J:70
    University of Virginia library U:128
Jefferson Airplane, The (rock music group) R:262d
Jefferson City (capital of Missouri) M:375
  picture(s) M:376
Jefferson Memorial (Washington, D.C.) J:71; W:31
  picture(s) J:71; W:32
Jefferson National Expansion Memorial National Historic Site (Saint Louis, Missouri) M:370; S:16
Jeffreys, Alex (British scientist) G:91
Jeffries, James J. (American boxer) B:353
Jeffries, John (American physician and scientist) B:35
Jejunum (middle part of the small intestine) D:161
Jellaba (costume of Muslim women) M:459
Jelloun, Taher Ben (Moroccan writer) A:342
Jelly and jam
  dictionary definition of jam D:154
  food preservation by means of sugar F:344
Jelly candies C:98
Jellyfish J:72–77
  respond to nearness of prey L:196–97
  special organs catch prey A:280
  picture(s) J:72; O:24
    Portuguese man-of-war A:270
"Jellyfish Stew" (poem by Prelutsky) N:274
Jelly's Last Jam (musical) M:559
Jemez (Indians of North America) I:183
Jemima Puddle-duck, The Tale of (by Beatrix Potter)
  excerpt from P:406
Jemison, Mae C. (American astronaut) A:79c; S:348 profile
  picture(s) G:324
Jena (Germany) G:156
  Schmidt telescope T:59
Jena-Auerstädt, Battle of (1806) N:12
Jenkins, David (American figure skater) O:111
Jenkins, Hayes Alan (American figure skater) O:111
Jenkins' Ear, War of (1739) W:5
Jenner, Bruce (American athlete) O:115
  picture(s) O:115

Jenner, Edward (English doctor) I:98; J:78
  antibodies and antigens A:313
  capturing a killer virus V:370
  medical contributions of the 19th century M:207
  public health P:512
  vaccination and immunization V:260
  picture(s) M:278
Jennet (horse) H:241
Jennings, Thomas L. (American inventor) A:79c
Jennings, Waylon (American singer) C:565
Jenny, spinning see Spinning jenny
Jensen, Johannes V. (Danish author) S:58i
Jenson, Nicolas (French-born Venetian printer) T:369
Jephte (oratorio by Carissimi) B:70
Jephthah (judge of Israel) B:167
Jequitinhonha River (Brazil) D:145
Jerboas (rodents) R:275
Jeremiah (book of the Old Testament) B:158, 159
Jeremiah (Hebrew prophet) J:79, 104–5
  Michelangelo painting B:162
Jeremiah, Letter of (apocryphal book of Bible) B:163
Jerez (Spain) S:374
Jericho (Jordan) J:134
  ancient bricks discovered B:394
  Palestinian self-rule I:376; J:132; P:43
  picture(s) A:353
Jeritza, Maria (Austrian singer)
  picture(s) O:147
Jerky (dried meat)
  colonial American beef dish C:411
Jerome, Saint J:79
  Christianity, history of C:289
  Vulgate (Latin version of Bible) B:157; R:283
Jersey (breed of dairy cattle) C:153
  picture(s) D:4; H:216
Jersey (one of the Channel Islands, Great Britain) I:363
Jersey City (New Jersey) N:174
  picture(s) N:174
Jerusalem J:80–84; P:40c, 41
  Biblical origins of the Jews J:103
  capital city of Israel I:373
  Christianity after fall of Jerusalem C:286, 287
  Crusades C:589, 590
  David conquered D:43
  Israel, history of I:375, 376
  Israel Museum I:374
  Jesus Christ J:86, 87–89
  Latin Kingdom established R:286
  Middle East M:303
  Roman legions conquered J:105
  temple built by Solomon S:251
  map(s) J:81
  picture(s) A:460; C:313; I:369; J:80
    Dome of the Rock I:355; J:83; P:40d
    street market J:84
    Via Dolorosa J:83
    Western Wall A:458; I:374; J:82; P:40d
Jerusalem, Council of (A.D. 50) R:282
Jerusalem artichokes (underground stems) G:41
Jervis Bay (Australia) A:513
Jessamine (plant) see Jasmine
Jessop, William (English civil engineer) R:86–87
Jesters (fools) J:125
  clowns, history of C:386
Jesuits (Society of Jesus) (religious order) R:288
  Canada, missionaries to O:137
  Christianity, history of C:293
  Indians, American I:198
  Loyola, Saint Ignatius L:334
  Martyrs' Shrine (near Midland, Ontario) O:133
  Paraguay P:65–66
Jesus Christ J:85–89 see also Apostles, The; Christianity
  Bible B:156, 163–66
  Boy Jesus (Bible story) B:173–74

Jibing (in sailing) S:11
    boardsailing B:261
Jidda (Saudi Arabia) S:58c
Jiggering (method of forming ceramics) C:177
Jigs (lures for fishing) F:211
Jigsaw puzzles P:553
Jigsaws (tools) T:231
Jihad (Muslim holy war) I:347
"Jim Crow" laws (segregating the races) A:79i; C:347
Jiménez, Juan Ramón (Spanish poet) S:391
Jiménez, Marcos Pérez see Pérez Jiménez, Marcos
Jiménez de Quesada, Gonzalo (Spanish explorer and
        soldier) B:303; C:407–8
Jimmu (mythical first emperor of Japan) J:26, 40
Jimsonweed (plant) P:316; W:106
    picture(s) B:191; W:105
Jinghis see Genghis Khan
"Jingle Bells" (song) C:118
Jinja (Uganda) U:6
Jinnah, Mohammad Ali (founder of Pakistan)
    mausoleum is in Karachi K:193
    Pakistan, history of P:40, 40a
    picture(s) P:40a
Jinns (spirits) see Genies
Jiujitsu see Jujitsu
Jivaro (Indians of South America) I:197, 198
J. J. (robot)
    picture(s) S:476
Joachimsthaler (German silver coin) D:257
Joanna the Mad (queen of Castile and Aragon) S:376
Joan of Arc, Saint (French national heroine) J:112
    Charles VII crowned king of France F:414
    England, history of E:241
    Hundred Years' War H:292
    signature reproduced A:527
Job (book of Bible, Old Testament) B:160
Jobs see Vocations
Job security (in labor-management relations) L:8
Jocho (Japanese sculptor) J:48
    picture(s)
        Buddha Amida J:48
Jockeys (in horse racing) H:232–33
Jodl, Alfred (German soldier)
    picture(s) W:307
Joel (book of the Old Testament) B:159, 160
Joel (Hebrew prophet) B:167
Joe Miller's Jests (early English joke book) J:125
Joey (young kangaroo) K:175
    picture(s) K:174
Joffre, Joseph Jacques Césaire (French army officer)
    World War I W:272
Joffrey, Robert (American choreographer and ballet company
        director) D:34; W:27 profile
Joffrey Ballet B:33
    picture(s) D:33
Jogaila (Lithuanian duke and king of Poland) see Jagiello
Jogging (sport) J:113–14
    aerobic exercise P:225
Johannesburg (South Africa) S:271
    picture(s) S:270
Johansson, Ingemar (Swedish boxer) B:353
John I, II, and III (books of the New Testament) B:166
John (king of Bohemia) L:348
John (king of England) E:239
    kings and lords in the Middle Ages M:291
    Magna Carta M:26
John (antipope) R:290
John XVI (antipope) R:290
John XXIII (antipope) R:291
John II (king of France) K:273–74
John I, Saint (pope) R:290
John II (pope) R:290
John III (pope) R:290
John IV (pope) R:290
John V (pope) R:290

John VI (pope) R:290
John VII (pope) R:290
John VIII (pope) R:290
John IX (pope) R:290
John X (pope) R:290
John XI (pope) R:290
John XII (pope) H:161; R:290
John XIII (pope) R:290
John XIV (pope) R:290
John XV (pope) R:290
John XVII (pope) R:290
John XVIII (pope) R:290
John XIX (pope) R:290
John XXI (pope) R:291
John XXII (pope) R:291
John XXIII (pope) J:114; R:291, 292
John I (king of Portugal) P:394
John IV (king of Portugal) P:395
John VI (king of Portugal) P:395
John, Saint (apostle of Jesus Christ) A:328, 329
    Christianity, history of C:286
    Gospel of B:165
John Asen I and II see Asen
John Brown House (Providence, Rhode Island) R:220
"John Brown's Body" (song) B:411; N:25
John Burroughs Society B:461
John Day Fossil Beds National Monument (Oregon) O:210
    picture(s) O:210
John F. Kennedy Center for the Performing Arts (Washington,
        D.C.) T:159; W:32
John F. Kennedy International Airport (New York City) N:232
    TWA terminal designed by Eero Saarinen A:386; U:136
John F. Kennedy Space Center (Cape Canaveral, Florida) F:260,
        270; S:339
    picture(s) F:270
John Henry (American folk hero) see Henry, John
Johnny Appleseed (American folk hero) see Appleseed, Johnny
John of the Cross, Saint (Spanish mystic and poet) S:18d
    profile, 388
John Paul I (pope) R:291, 293
John Paul II (pope) J:115; P:358; R:291, 293
    Cuban visit (1998) C:600
    picture(s) H:47; P:358
        Cuban visit (1998) C:600
Johns, Jasper (American artist) M:396b; P:31
    picture(s)
        Numbers in Color M:396
Johns Hopkins University (Baltimore, Maryland) M:125; U:220
John III Sobieski (king of Poland) P:361
Johnson, Andrew (17th president of the United
        States) J:116–19
    blocks efforts of Congress for Reconstruction R:118–20
    impeachment I:99
    vice presidency V:327 profile
    picture(s) P:447
        cartoon on purchase of Alaska A:157
Johnson, Ben (Canadian track athlete) O:117–18
Johnson, Bill (American skier) O:117
Johnson, Claudia Alta Taylor see Johnson, Lady Bird
Johnson, Earvin ("Magic") (American basketball player) B:95j
    profile
    picture(s) B:95f, 95j
Johnson, Edward (American writer) A:197
Johnson, Eldridge (American inventor) P:195
Johnson, Eliza McCardle (wife of Andrew Johnson) F:172;
        J:117
Johnson, Harriet Lane (acting first lady in Buchanan's
        administration) B:419; F:170–71
Johnson, Hiram W. (American public official) C:32–33
Johnson, Jack (American boxer) B:353
Johnson, James Weldon (American author and
        educator) A:79b; J:119
Johnson, Jay (American ventriloquist)
    picture(s) V:302

Jordan, Michael (American basketball player) **B:**95j
　　profile; **C:**221 *profile*
　　picture(s) **A:**80; **B:**95f, 95j
Jordan, Vernon Eulion, Jr. (American civil rights leader) **C:**329
　　profile
　　picture(s) **C:**329
Jordan refiner (machine used to prepare pulp for
　　papermaking) **P:**55
Jordan River (Israel–Jordan) **I:**371; **J:**130; **L:**32
Jordan theorem (in topology) **T:**238–39
　　picture(s) **T:**239
Joselito (Spanish bullfighter) **B:**449
Joseph (chief of Nez Percé Indians) **I:**59, 187
　　profile; **M:**428, 440
　　Indian wars **I:**205
　　Nez Perce National Historic Park (Montana) **M:**436
　　picture(s) **I:**187
Joseph (Hebrew patriarch) **J:**133
　　wheat's importance shown in Bible story **W:**158
Joseph, Saint (in the New Testament) **J:**85, 86; **M:**119; **S:**18d
　　profile
Joseph I (Holy Roman emperor) **H:**2
Joseph II (Holy Roman emperor) **A:**524
Joseph Andrews (novel by Henry Fielding) **N:**359
Joséphine, Empress (wife of Napoleon I) **J:**134; **N:**11
Josephus, Flavius (Jewish scholar and historian)
　　Greco-Roman period of Greek literature **G:**359
Joshua (book of the Old Testament) **B:**158
Joshua (military leader in the Old Testament) **J:**134
Joshua trees
　　picture(s) **T:**304
Jospin, Lionel (French premier) **F:**420
Josquin des Prez (Flemish composer) **D:**366; **F:**445; **M:**542
　　choral music, influence on **C:**283
　　Renaissance music **R:**172
Jotunheim (home of giants in Norse mythology) **N:**279
Joule (unit of energy) **H:**89
Joule, James Prescott (English physicist) **H:**89; **P:**234
　　picture(s) **H:**88
Journalism **J:**135–41
　　Bly, Nellie **B:**260
　　cartoons, history of **C:**127–29
　　freedom of the press **F:**163
　　magazines **M:**16–20
　　newspapers **N:**197–205
　　Pulitzer, Joseph, and Pulitzer prizes **P:**533
　　radio news broadcasting **R:**61
　　Schurz, Carl **W:**207
　　science journalists **S:**68
　　Tarbell, Ida **T:**23
　　University of Missouri had first school of **M:**371
　　What are tabloids? **J:**136
　　writing as a career **W:**321
　　Zenger, John Peter **Z:**373
Journals (in bookkeeping) **B:**312
Journals (records of experiences or ideas) **D:**147–48
　　learning to write **W:**319–20
Journals, scientific **S:**67–68
Journeyman plumber **P:**340
Journeymen (of craft guilds) **G:**404, 405
Journeymen (skilled workers who make dies and molds) **D:**156
Jove (Roman god) *see* Zeus (Jupiter)
Joyce, James (Irish writer) **F:**115; **I:**322, 327–28
　　novels **N:**361
　　20th-century English literature **E:**289
Joyner-Kersee, Jackie (American track-and-field star) **O:**117,
　　118; **T:**259 *profile*
　　picture(s) **T:**259
Joystick (computer peripheral) **C:**481
"Joy to the World" (carol) **C:**118
Juana Ines de la Cruz *see* Cruz, Juana Ines de la
Juana la Loca (queen of Castile and Aragon) *see* Joanna the
　　Mad
Juan Carlos I (king of Spain) **S:**379
Juan de Fuca Strait **C:**57

Juan de la Cruz *see* John of the Cross
Juan Fernández Islands (off-shore holdings of Chile) **C:**252;
　　S:281
Juan Manuel, Don (Spanish writer) **S:**387
Juárez, Benito (Mexican statesman) **J:**141; **M:**249–50
　　Indians, American **I:**193–94
　　picture(s) **M:**250
Juba (Sudan) **S:**479
Jubail (Saudi Arabia) **S:**58c
Jubilee Singers (of Fisk University) **H:**325
Judah (fourth son of Jacob and Leah)
　　Judah, Benjamin, and Joseph **J:**133
Judah, kingdom of **I:**374; **J:**103, 104, 132; **P:**40c
Judah Halevi (Hebrew poet) **H:**100
Judah Ha-Nasi (Jewish scholar) **T:**13
Judah (Judas) Maccabee (famous Jewish leader) **H:**28; **J:**105
Judaism **J:**142–49 *see also* Hillel; Jews
　　Abraham was founder of **A:**8
　　Apocrypha **B:**160–61, 163
　　Asian religions **A:**458
　　Bible (Old Testament) **B:**156–63
　　Dead Sea Scrolls **D:**47
　　dietary laws **F:**332
　　divorce **D:**230
　　forms of address for the rabbi **A:**22
　　funeral customs **F:**494
　　Hanukkah **H:**28–29
　　Hasidism **Y:**350
　　Hebrew language and literature **H:**98–101
　　Israel, importance of **I:**375
　　Israel, religions in **I:**370
　　marriage rites **W:**102
　　Middle East, religions of the **M:**299, 304
　　moral codes **C:**287
　　Passover **P:**95–96
　　prayer from the Jewish liturgy **P:**430
　　Purim **P:**549
　　religions of the world **R:**149
　　religious holidays **R:**154
　　saints **S:**18c
　　Talmud **T:**13
　　Ten Commandments **T:**72–73
　　picture(s)
　　　　orthodox Jew at Jerusalem's Western Wall **A:**458
　　　　shofar **M:**299
Judas (Jude, Thaddaeus) (one of the twelve Apostles) **A:**329
Judas Iscariot (one of the Twelve Apostles) **A:**329; **B:**167; **J:**88
Judd, Donald (American sculptor) **M:**396b
Jude (book of the New Testament) **B:**166
Jude, Saint *see* Judas
Judean Plains (Israel) **I:**371
Judeo-Spanish language *see* Ladino
Judges (book of the Old Testament) **B:**158; **J:**103
Judges (in law) **C:**567, 568; **J:**163, 164; **U:**170–71
　　law and law enforcement **L:**86, 90
Judgment (in law) **C:**568
Judgment of Solomon, The (painting by Nicolas Poussin)
　　picture(s) **S:**251
Judicial branch (of the United States government) **U:**164,
　　170–71
Judicial dueling *see* Battle, trial by
Judicial review (power of the Supreme Court to establish
　　fundamental law) **S:**507, 509; **U:**170
　　Marshall establishes **M:**111
Judicial waivers (in juvenile justice) **J:**170
Judiciary *see* Courts
Judiciary Act (United States, 1789) **S:**507, 509
Judith (apocryphal book of Bible) **B:**161
Judo **J:**33, **149–50**
　　Olympic events **O:**107
　　What is the difference between karate and judo? **K:**194
Judson, Edward (American writer) **G:**422
Judy *see* Punch and Judy
Juggling (keeping several objects moving continuously in the
　　air) **J:**151

Juilliard School, The   L:248
Jujitsu (forerunner of modern judo)   J:149
Juju (music)   A:79
Julenissen (Scandinavian Santa Claus)   C:300
Jules and Jim (motion picture, 1961)   M:494
Julia, Raul (Puerto Rican actor)
    picture(s)   H:134
Julian (Roman emperor)
    Christianity, history of   C:289
Julian Alps   A:194b; S:203
Julian calendar   C:15
    religious holidays   R:153
Julianehaab (Greenland)   G:374
Julian the Apostate *see* Julian (Roman emperor)
Juliette Gordon Low Girl Scout National Center (Savannah, Georgia)   G:217
Julius (name of three popes)   R:290, 291
    Julius II and Michelangelo   M:257
Julius Caesar *see* Caesar, Gaius Julius
Julius Caesar (play by Shakespeare)   S:134–35
Jultomten (Swedish Santa Claus)   C:300
July (seventh month of year)   J:152–53
July Fourth *see* Independence Day
Jumanji (book by Chris Van Allsburg)
    picture(s)   C:242
Jumbo (famous circus elephant)   C:310; E:184
Jumeau dolls   D:268
Jumping (field events)   T:256–57
Jumping (in skiing)   S:184c–184d, 184f
Jumping ants   A:319
    picture(s)   A:318
Jumping mice   R:275
Jumping spiders   S:404, 406
Juncos (birds)   H:191
    picture(s)   B:241
June (sixth month of year)   J:154–55
Juneau (capital of Alaska)   A:144, 151, 153
    picture(s)
        state capitol   A:154
Juneau, Joseph (Canadian gold miner)   A:156 *profile*
Juneau, Solomon (pioneer settler in Wisconsin)   M:313
June Bug (early airplane)   A:560
Jung, Carl (Swiss psychologist and psychiatrist)   J:156; P:502; S:75
Jung Badahur Rana (prime minister of Nepal)   N:110
Jungfrau (mountain, Switzerland)   S:543
Jungle, The (novel by Upton Sinclair)   A:208
    led to meat-packing reforms   C:527
Jungle Books (by Rudyard Kipling)   K:260
Jungle Gardens (Avery Island, Louisiana)   L:322
    picture(s)   L:322
Jungles   J:157–58 *see also* Rain forests
Junior colleges   U:220
Junior featherweight (in boxing)   B:352
Junior Girl Scouts   G:215
    picture(s)   G:214
Junior high schools   S:58j
    guidance counseling   G:401
    physical education programs   P:222
Junior lightweight (in boxing)   B:352
Junior Olympic Archery Development   A:366
Junior Red Cross   R:127
Junior rodeos   R:278
Juniper (group of evergreen trees and shrubs)
    picture(s)
        Utah juniper   T:301
Junk (wooden boat)
    picture(s)   S:153
        on the Yangtze River   R:247
Junkers (Prussian landowning class)   B:250
Juno (Roman goddess) *see* Hera
Junto (club organized by Franklin)   F:454
Jupiter (character in Poe's *Gold Bug*)
    picture(s)   F:116

Jupiter (planet)   J:159–62; P:278–80
    asteroids   C:450
    Galileo discovers moons   A:472, 473; G:6
    life on other planets   S:354
    radio astronomy observations   R:74
    space probes   O:9; S:360
    What is the Great Red Spot on Jupiter?   J:160
    picture(s)   P:275; S:353
        with moons   J:159
        ring   J:162
Jupiter (Roman god) *see* Zeus
Juppé, Alain (French premier)   F:420
Jura Mountains   E:344; F:407, 409; S:542
Jurassic Park (motion picture, 1993)   A:291; M:484, 497
    picture(s)
        computer graphics used in making   C:489
Jurassic period (in geology)   E:25, 28
    dinosaurs   D:169, 170–71, 172, 173
    plants   F:387
    prehistoric animals   P:433
    picture(s)
        dinosaurs   D:164–65
    table(s)   F:384
Jurong Industrial Estate (Singapore)   S:180
Jury (in law)   J:163–64
    courts   C:567–68
    how laws are enforced   L:87, 90
    Magna Carta guaranteed jury trials   M:26
    Middle Ages   M:291
Jus sanguinis (law of the blood) (citizenship rule)   C:322, 323
Jus soli (law of the soil) (citizenship rule)   C:322, 323
Justice, administration of
    courts   C:566–68
    crime and criminology   C:575–76
    International Court of Justice (The Hague)   U:73
    jury   J:163–64
    juvenile crime   J:167, 169–70
    law and law enforcement   L:84–92
    municipal government   M:513, 514
    Supreme Court of Canada   S:505–6
    Supreme Court of the United States   S:507–10
Justice, United States Department of   J:164–66
    Attorney General is head of the department and a cabinet member   P:447
    Federal Bureau of Investigation   F:76–77
    Narcotics and Dangerous Drugs, Bureau of   N:17
    Prisons, Bureau of   P:480
Justice of the peace (local official with limited judicial powers)   L:89
Justice Programs, Office of (OJP)   J:165
Justices (of the Supreme Court)   S:507–10
    forms of address   A:22
Justify (to even up lines in printing)   T:370
Justinian I (Byzantine emperor)
    art as a record   A:438a
    Byzantine art   B:487–89
    Greece   G:337
    law and law enforcement   L:84–85
    silk brought out of China   S:174
Justinian and His Court (Byzantine mosaic)
    picture(s)   B:495; L:84; P:16
Just So Stories (by Rudyard Kipling)
    excerpt from   K:261–64
Jute (fiber)   F:109; J:166; P:298
    Bangladesh   B:48–49
    rug weaving   R:354
Jutes (Germanic people)
    invaders of England and the beginnings of the English language   E:236, 265
Jutland, Battle of (1916)   W:277
Jutland Peninsula (Denmark)   D:108, 110; S:58f
Juvenal (Roman satirist)   L:76
Juvenile crime   J:167–70
    mental illness   M:227

University of Kansas **K:**182
Wichita **K:**185
Kansas, University of **K:**181
picture(s) **K:**182
football team **K:**181
Kansas City (Kansas) **K:**185, 189, 190
Kansas City (Missouri) **K:**190; **M:**366, 371, 373, 375, 380
picture(s) **K:**190; **M:**375
Kansas City Star (newspaper) **M:**375
Kansas Cosmosphere and Space Center (Hutchinson, Kansas) **K:**184
Kansas-Nebraska Act (United States, 1854) **K:**191; **U:**184–85
abolition movement **A:**6b
Civil War, events leading to **C:**335
Douglas, Stephen A. **D:**288
Kansas, history of **K:**176, 188
Lincoln leader of movement opposing **L:**243
Missouri Compromise repealed **M:**381
Nebraska, history of **N:**92
Pierce, Franklin **P:**247
Kansas (Kaw) River (Kansas) **K:**179
Kansas State University (Manhattan, Kansas) **K:**181
Kant, Hermann (German writer) **G:**182
Kant, Immanuel (German philosopher) **K:**191; **P:**190
ethics **E:**328
psychology, history of **P:**506
picture(s) **P:**505
Kantrowitz, Mildred (American author) **C:**238
Kanuri (language) **A:**56
Kanzan (Japanese potter) **J:**49
Kao, Charles (English scientist) **F:**107
Kaohsiung (Taiwan) **T:**9
Kaolack (Senegal) **S:**120
Kaolin (china clay) **C:**176; **G:**139; **S:**303
identified by smell **M:**317
Kapital, Das (book by Marx) *see Das Kapital*
Kaplan, Mordecai M. (American rabbi) **J:**145
Kaplan, Viktor (Austrian engineer) **T:**341
Kaplan turbine **T:**341
picture(s) **T:**342
Kapok **K:**192
fibers **F:**109
Karachi (Pakistan) **K:**193
picture(s) **P:**39
Karagie Depression (lowest point in the Soviet Union) **U:**38
Karakoram Mountains (central Asia) **I:**123; **K:**198; **T:**190
Karakul sheep **T:**352
Kara Kum (desert, Turkmenistan) **T:**352
Karamanlis (Caramanlis), Constantine (Greek political leader) **G:**338
Karamzin, Nikolai (Russian historian) **R:**377
Kara Sea **O:**46
Karate **K:**194–95
Japanese art of self-defense **J:**33, 149
What is the difference between karate and judo? **K:**194
Karats (units for measuring purity of gold) **G:**247–48 *see also* Carats
gold jewelry **J:**94
Karelian bear dog **D:**251
Karenga, Maulana (American activist) **A:**80
Kariba, Lake (Zimbabwe–Zambia) **L:**33; **Z:**372, 375
Kariba Dam (Zambezi River, Zimbabwe–Zambia) **Z:**372, 375
picture(s) **D:**17; **Z:**377
Karisimbi, Mount (highest peak in Rwanda) **R:**384
Karlfeldt, Erik Axel (Swedish poet) **S:**58i
Karlovy Vary (Czech Republic) **C:**610
Karlskirche (church, Vienna, Austria)
picture(s) **A:**380
Karma (spiritual law in Hinduism) **H:**129; **R:**146
Karnak (Egypt)
Egyptian temples **A:**371
libraries **L:**171
Temple of Amon-Re **A:**222; **E:**114–15
picture(s)
Temple of Amon-Re **A:**370

Karnataka (state, India) **I:**128
Karnatak music (of India) **I:**143
Karthala, Mount (Comoros) **C:**475
Karting **K:**196
Kärtnerstrasse (shopping street of Vienna) **V:**332j
Kasavubu, Joseph (Congolese politician) **Z:**370
Kasha (cereal made from buckwheat) **G:**284
Kashan (Iran) **I:**359
Kasher *see* Kosher
Kashmir **K:**197–99
India-Pakistan dispute **I:**134; **P:**37, 40a
picture(s)
Himalayas **H:**126
Kashmiri (language) **I:**118
Kashmiris (people of Kashmir) **K:**197
Kaskaskia (Illinois) **I:**74
Kasparov, Garry (Russian chess champion) **C:**492
picture(s) **C:**492
Kasperl (German puppet character) **P:**548
Kassala (Sudan) **S:**479
picture(s) **S:**480
Kassebaum, Nancy Landon (American senator) **K:**189 *profile*
Kassem, Abdul Karim (military ruler of Iraq) **I:**316
Hussein, Saddam **H:**307
Kassites (barbarian conquerors of Babylon) **A:**236
Kastrioti, George (Skanderbeg) (Albanian leader) **A:**162
picture(s)
statue **A:**162
Kat (woody shrub) **Y:**348
Kata (judo training exercises) **J:**150
Katabatic winds **W:**187
Antarctica **A:**292–93
Katahdin, Mount (Maine) **M:**37, 38
picture(s) **M:**37
Katakana (Japanese syllabic alphabet) **J:**30
Katanga (former province of Zaïre) *see* Shaba
Kate Greenaway Medal (book award) **C:**240
Katharevousa (pure form of Greek language) **G:**331
Katherina, Gebel (mountain, Egypt) **E:**106
Katherine (Northern Territory, Australia) **A:**513
Katmai National Park and Preserve (Alaska) **A:**148
Katmandu (capital of Nepal) **N:**109
picture(s) **N:**107
Katydids (insects) **I:**236
picture(s) **E:**55; **I:**230
Katzenjammer Kids, The (comic strip)
picture(s) **C:**128
Kauai (one of the Hawaiian Islands) **H:**50, 52, 60
picture(s)
Waimea Canyon **H:**57
Kaufmann House (Bear Run, Pennsylvania) *see* Fallingwater
Kaunakakai (Hawaii) **H:**50
Kaunas (Lithuania) **L:**263
Kaunda, Kenneth David (president of Zambia) **Z:**372
Kavad I (Persian king) **P:**157
Kavya (style of Sanskrit literature) **I:**140–41
Kawabata Yasunari (Japanese novelist) **J:**53
Kawasaki (Japan) **J:**36
Kaw River *see* Kansas River
Kay *see* Key
Kay (son of Sir Ector, in legends of King Arthur) **A:**441
Kay, John (English inventor) **I:**218
Kayaks (boats) **C:**101; **I:**191
Eskimo **E:**317
picture(s)
Adirondack Mountains (New York) **N:**214
Greenland **G:**374a
Kayangel (island, Palau)
picture(s) **P:**2
Kayapó (Native American language) **I:**197
Kayibanda, Gregoire (Rwandan president) **R:**385
Kazakhs (a people of Asia) **K:**200–201; **U:**34
Mongolia **M:**416
picture(s) **K:**200

Kazakhstan K:200–201
picture(s) K:200
flag F:232
Kazan (capital of Tatar Autonomous Soviet Socialist
Republic) U:43
KDKA (first radio station) C:469; P:135; R:55, 57
Kean, Edmund (English actor) T:160 profile
Kearney, Belle (American writer and politician) M:362–63
profile
Kearny, Stephen (American general) M:239b
Keaton, Buster (American actor) M:489
Keats, Ezra Jack (American author and illustrator of children's
books) C:238
picture(s)
The Snowy Day C:243
wall hanging featuring Peter N:101
Keats, John (English poet) K:202–3
"Endymion," excerpt from K:202
English literature, place in E:282
figures of speech F:122
"I Had a Dove" K:202
"Ode to a Nightingale," excerpt from O:50
romanticism R:303
"When I Have Fears" K:202
Keck, Donald (American scientist) F:107
Keck telescopes T:58–59
picture(s) O:7; T:57
Keel (ridge on the center bottom of a boat) C:99; S:11
delta kite K:266b
Keelung (Taiwan) T:7, 9
Keep (donjon) (of a castle) C:131; F:377
picture(s) C:132
Keep Cool with Coolidge (campaign slogan) C:539
Keflavik (Iceland) I:35
Kegon Waterfall (Japan) W:63
Keijo (Japanese name for Seoul) S:121
Keillor, Garrison (American author and radio
performer) M:339 profile
Keino, Kipchoge (Kenyan runner) O:112
Keita, Modibo (president of Mali) M:62
Kekkonen, Urho K. (president of Finland) F:139
Kellar, Harry (American magician) M:23
Keller, Gottfried (Swiss writer) G:180
Keller, Helen (American author and lecturer) K:203
Ivy Green (Tuscumbia, Alabama) is her birthplace A:138
picture(s) A:142; K:203
Kellogg, Frank B. (American public official) P:106
Kellogg, Steven (American author and illustrator of children's
books) C:231 profile
picture(s)
illustration for Paul Bunyan C:456
Kellogg, W. K. (American cereal manufacturer) M:273 profile
picture(s) M:273
Kellogg-Briand Pact (1928) P:106
Coolidge favored C:540
efforts toward peace between two wars W:284
Stimson Doctrine regarding treaties T:297
Kells, Book of E:257
survival of ancient thought R:284
at Trinity College (Dublin, Ireland) I:322
picture(s) E:256
Kelly, Ellsworth (American painter) P:32
Kelly, Emmett (American clown) C:310
Kelly, Gene (American dancer, singer, actor, and
director) D:34; M:492
Kelly, Grace see Grace, Princess
Kelly, William (American inventor) I:333
Kelmscott Press (founded by English artist, William
Morris) E:263
Kelowna (British Columbia) B:406c
Kelp (seaweeds)
picture(s) A:180; K:258
Kelpfish F:200
Kelsey, Henry (English fur trader) S:51
Kelts see Celts

Kelvin, Lord (William Thomson, 1st Baron of Largs) (British
scientist) G:58; H:87
Kelvin scale (based on absolute zero temperature) G:58;
H:86, 87; T:163
Kemal Atatürk see Atatürk, Mustafa Kemal
Kemble, Fanny (English actress and writer) T:160–61 profile
Kemp, Roger (Australian artist) A:501
Kempen region (of Belgium) B:131
Kempis, Thomas à (German mystic and religious writer)
quotation from Q:20
Kenai Fiords National Park (Alaska) A:148
Kenai Peninsula (Alaska) A:149
Kenana (Sudan) S:478
Kendrick, John B. (American political figure) W:332
Keneally, Thomas (Australian novelist) A:501
Kennedy, Anthony McLeod (American jurist) S:508 profile
picture(s) U:171
Kennedy, Avenue du President (Paris) P:70
Kennedy, Cape (Florida) see Canaveral, Cape
Kennedy, Edward M. (United States senator) K:211
picture(s) K:205
Kennedy, Jacqueline see Onassis, Jacqueline Kennedy
Kennedy, John F. (35th president of the United
States) K:204–10; U:198–99
African American history A:79n
Alliance for Progress G:400
Arlington National Cemetery, buried in N:29
Cold War C:401
consumerism C:527
Cuban missile crisis C:601
Dallas (Texas) museum and memorial D:14; T:132
Peace Corps P:104
President's Commission on the Status of Women W:212b
quotation from Inaugural Address Q:20
Warren Report W:12
White House W:165
Who was Lee Harvey Oswald? K:210
young Bill Clinton met through Boys' Nation C:365–66
picture(s) E:128; M:149; P:452; U:198
debating Nixon N:262c
grave N:29
shaking Nixon's hand K:207
ticker-tape parade K:207
Kennedy, John F., Jr. (son of John F. Kennedy) F:180
Kennedy, John Pendleton (American novelist) A:202
Kennedy, Robert F. (American public official) K:209, 211;
U:201
picture(s) K:205; M:149
Kennedy family (of Massachusetts)
picture(s) K:205
Kennedy International Airport see John F. Kennedy International
Airport
Kennedy Space Center see John F. Kennedy Space Center
Kennel Club, American see American Kennel Club
Kennel clubs (organizations of dog breeders) D:249
Kennesaw Mountain National Battlefield Park (Georgia)
picture(s) G:136
Kennings (phrases in Old English poems) B:144b
Kenny, Elizabeth (Australian-American nurse) M:339 profile
Kenosha (Wisconsin) W:202, 204
Kensington Rune Stone (previously thought to have been left by
Norsemen in Minnesota) M:334
Kent, Rockwell (American artist and author)
picture(s)
illustrations for Moby Dick M:218
Kent, William (English architect) A:380
Kent County (Delaware) D:88, 99
Kent State University (Ohio)
student protest (1970) N:262d; O:75
Kentucky K:212–26
Boone, Daniel, was the first settler B:334
folk dance D:300
Kentucky and Virginia Resolutions K:227
overland trails pioneered by Boone O:271

poverty in Appalachia **P:**419–20
westward movement **W:**142
map(s) **K:**223
picture(s)
    automobile industry **K:**218
    Churchill Downs **K:**220
    coal mining **K:**226
    Cumberland Falls **K:**215
    Cumberland Gap **K:**214
    Fort Knox **K:**220
    Frankfort **K:**224
    horse farms **K:**213, 214
    Lexington **K:**218, 221
    Lincoln's birthplace **K:**220
    Louisville **K:**213
    Paducah festival **K:**216
Kentucky, University of **K:**217
picture(s) **K:**218
Kentucky and Virginia Resolutions **K:**227
Kentucky Derby (horse race) **H:**232–33; **K:**212, **227**
Kentucky rifle
picture(s) **G:**416
Kenya **K:**228–33
conservation programs **C:**521
United States embassy bombing (1998) **T:**117
picture(s)
    cattle grazing **C:**151
    flag **F:**227
    Nairobi **A:**62; **K:**233
Kenya, Mount **K:**230
Kenyatta, Jomo (Kenyan political leader) **K:**233
Keokuk (Native American chief) **I:**179 *profile*
picture(s) **I:**179
Kepi (French police officer's hat) **H:**46
Kepler, Johannes (German astronomer) **K:**234
astronomy, history of **A:**472
Brahe and Kepler **B:**361
physics, history of **P:**233–34
science, milestones in **S:**70
solar system **S:**241–42
telescope **T:**60
picture(s) **P:**234
Kepler's Laws (of planetary motion) **K:**234; **S:**241–42, 244
Keratin (body protein) **B:**273, 292
Kérékou, Mathieu (Benin political leader) **B:**144
Kerensky, Alexander Feodorovich (Russian revolutionary
    leader) **R:**367; **U:**48
Keres (Native American language group) **I:**183
Kerkorian, Kirk (American businessman) **A:**431
Kerkyra (island) *see* Corfu
Kermes (dye extracted from insects' bodies) **D:**369, 371
Kermode's bears **B:**105
Kern, Jerome (American composer) **M:**557, 558; **U:**209
Kernels (inner part of nuts) **N:**431–32
Kerogen (organic matter in oil shale) **P:**175
Kerosene **K:**235; **P:**172
fuels **F:**487
Kerosene heaters **F:**154
Kerosene lamps **L:**233
picture(s) **L:**232
Kerouac, Jack (American novelist)
picture(s) **A:**213
Kestrel (bird)
picture(s) **B:**239
Ketch (sailing vessel) **S:**8
Kettering, Charles Franklin (American inventor and
    businessman) **K:**236
Kettledrum *see* Timpani
Ketubah (Jewish marriage contract) **J:**147
Keuka Lake (New York)
picture(s) **N:**212
Keukenhof Gardens (the Netherlands)
picture(s) **G:**43
Kevlar (plastic fiber) **P:**329
Kew Gardens *see* Royal Botanic Gardens

Key (in music) **M:**538, 540
modern music **M:**397
Key, Francis Scott (American lawyer, author of "The
    Star-Spangled Banner") **M:**120; **N:**20; **W:**11
Keyboard (of a computer) **C:**481, 491
picture(s) **C:**482
Keyboard (of a typewriter) **T:**372, 374
Keyboard instruments **K:236–40**
classical age in music **C:**350
electronic music **E:**155, 156, 157
organ **O:**218–19
piano **P:**240–42
types of musical instruments **M:**552–53, 555
Key deer **F:**264–65
Key grips (for motion pictures) **M:**485
Keyhole saw (tool) **T:**228
Key Largo (Florida)
picture(s) **F:**261
Keynes, John Maynard (British economist) **E:**62 *profile*
picture(s) **E:**62
Keys *see* Locks and keys
Key signatures (in musical notation) **M:**538, 540
Keystone State (nickname for Pennsylvania) **P:**126, 127
Key West (Florida) **F:**264
Key words
headings and entries in indexes **I:**114
how to look up quotations **Q:**19
KGB (organization that directed intelligence activities for the
    Soviet Union) **S:**407
KH-11 (United States spy satellite) **S:**54
Kha (Lao Theung) (Asian people) **L:**41
Khachaturian, Aram Ilich (Armenian composer) **A:**431; **R:**382
Khadijah (first wife of Mohammed) **M:**401
Khafre *see* Chephren
Khalid (king of Saudi Arabia) **S:**58e
Khalifa, al- (ruling family of Bahrain) **B:**19
Khalkha Mongol (language) **M:**416
Khalkhas (a people of Mongolia) *see* Halh
Kham (eastern part of Tibet) **T:**190, 191
Khamenei, Ali Hussein (Iranian spiritual leader) **I:**308, 310
Khamsin (wind)
Jordan **J:**130
Kharg Island (Iran) **I:**307
Kharieh Djami (church, Constantinople) **B:**494
Kharkiv (Kharkov) (Ukraine) **U:**11
Khartoum (capital of Sudan) **S:**479
picture(s) **S:**478
Khasis (early inhabitants of Kashmir) **K:**198
Khatami, Mohammad (Iranian president) **I:**310
Khayr-ad-Din (Ottoman corsair) **O:**262
Khayyám, Omar *see* Omar Khayyám
Khiva (early state in Central Asia) **U:**258
Khmelnytsky, Bohdan (Cossack commander) **U:**11
Khmer (language) **C:**35
Khmer Empire (of Southeast Asia) **C:**35, 37–38
Khmer Republic *see* Cambodia
Khmer Rouge (Cambodian Communist forces) **C:**38; **G:**96;
    S:336
Khoikhoi (Hottentots) (people of southern Africa) **A:**55, 56
Namibia **N:**8
South Africa **S:**269
Khoisan (ancient African people)
languages **A:**56
music **A:**77
Khomeini, Ayatollah Ruhollah (Iranian religious and political
    leader) **I:**307–8, 309, 310
picture(s) **I:**309
Khorsabad (city in ancient Assyria) **A:**240
Khosrow I (Persian king) *see* Chosroes I
Khrushchev, Nikita (Soviet political leader) **B:**389; **K:240–41**;
    R:369; **U:**51
Cold War **C:**401
Cuban missile crisis **C:**601
picture(s) **E:**124

Khrushchev, Nikita (cont.)

re-established national unity **C:**85
picture(s) **C:**77; **P:**459
oil portrait by Orpen **K:**252
King, William Rufus de Vane (vice president, United
States) **V:**326 *profile*
King and I, The (musical by Rodgers and
Hammerstein) **M:**558; **T:**152
King Arthur *see* Arthur, King
Kingbirds **B:**239
King crab *see* Horseshoe crab
Kingdom of God (in Jewish and Christian thought) **J:**89
Kingdoms of living things **K:**253–59; **L:**207–9 *see also*
Taxonomy
animal kingdom **A:**265–67
differences between plant and animal life **A:**264
How many kinds of living things are there? **K:**259
life, food chains in **L:**205
plants **P:**292–321
taxonomy **T:**27, 28
King Edward VIII Falls (Guyana) **W:**63
Kingfish (nickname) *see* Long, Huey Pierce
King George VI Falls (Guyana) **W:**63
King George's War (1744–1748) **F:**463; **I:**203; **U:**175
King James Version (of the Bible) **B:**157–58
Christianity, history of **C:**293
place in English literature **E:**273–74
King John (play by Shakespeare) **S:**135
King Lear (play by Shakespeare) **S:**135
Kingman Reef (Pacific Ocean) **U:**93
Kingo, Thomas Hansen (Danish author) **S:**58h
King penguins **P:**124
picture(s) **B:**231
King Philip's War **I:**177–78, 202; **M:**149; **R:**225; **U:**175
Kings I and II (books of the Old Testament) **B:**158
King's College (Cambridge University, England)
picture(s) **E:**79
Kings Island (amusement park, near Cincinnati, Ohio) **P:**79
Kings Landing Historical Settlement (New Brunswick) **N:**138e
Kingsley, Charles (English writer) **E:**287
poem from *The Water Babies* **P:**351
King's Men (acting company) **S:**132
King-Smith, Dick (British author)
picture(s)
illustration from movie *Babe* **C:**245
Kings Mountain, Battle of (1780) **R:**207; **T:**84
Kings Mountain National Military Park (South Carolina) **S:**304
King snake
picture(s) **S:**209
King Solomon's Mines (book by Haggard) **M:**561
Kings Peak (Utah) **U:**242
Kingsport (Tennessee) **T:**80
Kingston (capital of Jamaica) **J:**16, 17
picture(s) **J:**18
kapok tree **K:**192
Kingston (Ontario)
picture(s)
Old Fort Henry **O:**132
Kingston, Maxine Hong (American writer) **A:**214a
Kingstown (capital of Saint Vincent and the Grenadines) **S:**19
King William's War (1690–1697) **F:**462–63; **I:**203; **U:**175
Kinkajous (animals related to raccoons) **R:**27
Kinkakuji Temple (Kyoto, Japan) **K:**310
Kinneret, Lake *see* Galilee, Sea of
Kino, Eusebio Francisco (Italian missionary)
Arizona, history of **A:**412
Kinsale, Battle of (1601) **I:**323
Kinshasa (capital of Democratic Republic of Congo) **Z:**367
Kinship (in the family) **F:**37–38
Kinyarwanda (language) **R:**384
Kinyeti, Mount (Sudan) **S:**477
Kiowa (Indians of North America) **I:**180
Kiphuth, Robert J. H. (American swimmer) **S:**536
Kipling, Rudyard (English writer and poet) **K:**260–64
"The Elephant's Child" (story) **K:**261–64

English literature, place in **E:**287
quoted on San Francisco **S:**31
Kipphardt, Heinar (German playwright) **D:**302
Kiprenski, Orest (Russian painter) **R:**373
Kiptanui, Moses (Kenyan athlete) **T:**263
Kirantis (a people of Nepal) **N:**107
Kirchhoff, Gustav Robert (German physicist) **C:**210
Kirchner, Ernst (German painter) **M:**391
picture(s)
Self-Portrait with Model (painting) **G:**172
Kirghiz (a people of Central Asia) *see* Kyrgyzes
Kirghizia *see* Kyrgyzstan
Kiribati (island nation in the southwestern Pacific) **K:**265–66
Christmas Island **P:**8
picture(s)
flag **F:**241
Kiritimati *see* Christmas Island
Kirkland, Lane (American labor leader) **L:**16 *profile*
picture(s) **L:**17
Kirkland Lake (Ontario) **O:**133
Kirkpatrick, Jeane (United States representative to the United
Nations) **K:**266a
Kirkwood gaps (in asteroid belt) **C:**450
Kirstein, Lincoln (American ballet director) **B:**33
Kiruna (Sweden) **S:**527
Kirundi (language) **B:**462
Kisatchie National Forest (Louisiana) **L:**322
picture(s) **L:**316
Kishinev (capital of Moldova) *see* Chisinau
Kiska Island (Alaska) **A:**158
Kismayu (Somalia) **S:**254
Kiss, The (painting by Klimt)
picture(s) **K:**271
Kissinger, Henry (American statesman) **K:**266a
Kissing gourami (fish) **F:**204
Kiss Me, Kate (musical by Porter) **M:**558
Kisumu (Kenya) **K:**232
Kitakyushu (Japan) **J:**36
Kitasato, Shibasaburo (Japanese bacteriologist) **B:**127a
Kitchen
cooking-related fires **F:**146, 149, 154
Hindu kitchen considered sacred **I:**121
safety in the home **S:**4–5
picture(s)
colonial life **C:**410, 421
interior decorating **I:**259
Kitchen (vegetable) gardens **G:**26, 49, 51; **V:**288–94
picture(s) **G:**28
Kitchen Table (painting by Cézanne)
picture(s) **P:**28
Kites **K:**266b–270
early attempts to fly **A:**557
Franklin's experiment with electricity **F:**455
How does a kite fly? **K:**267
picture(s) **K:**267, 268, 269
Franklin's experiment with electricity **F:**454
Italian kite festivals **K:**270
Japanese festival **K:**266b
Kithara *see* Cithara
Kitikmeot (administrative region of Nunavut) **N:**413
Kittatinny Mountains (New Jersey) **N:**166
Kitti's hog-nosed bat (smallest mammal) **M:**66
Kitt Peak National Observatory (Arizona) **A:**410; **O:**7; **T:**329
picture(s) **A:**408; **O:**8; **S:**488, 489
Kitty Hawk (balloon) **B:**36
Kitty Hawk (North Carolina) **N:**320
aviation history **A:**560
Wright brothers **W:**318
Kivalliq (administrative region of Nunavut) **N:**413
Kivu, Lake (Rwanda) **L:**33; **R:**384
Kiwanda, Cape (Oregon)
picture(s) **O:**203
Kiwis (birds) **B:**220; **N:**238; **O:**247
picture(s) **B:**230; **O:**246

Kizhi (Russia)
  picture(s)
    Church of the Transfiguration   **R:**371
Klaipéda (Lithuania)   **L:**263
Klamath (Indians of North America)   **I:**187
Klamath Mountains (California–Oregon)   **C:**20, 21; **O:**202, 204
Klamath weed (plant) *see* Saint-John's-wort
Klammer, Franz (Austrian athlete)   **O:**115
  picture(s)   **O:**114
Klaproth, Martin (German chemist)   **U:**230
Klee, Paul (Swiss artist)   **K:**271; **M:**392
  Blue Rider group   **G:**172
  watercolor painting   **W:**61
  picture(s)
    Twittering Machine (painting)   **M:**392
Klein, Felix (German mathematician)   **M:**169
Kleist, Heinrich von (German writer)   **G:**179
Klestil, Thomas (Austrian president)   **A:**525
Klič, Karl (Czech artist)   **P:**477
Klimt, Gustav (Austrian painter)   **A:**522; **K:**271
  picture(s)
    Kiss, The   **K:**271
Kline, Franz (American artist)   **M:**396b
  picture(s)
    Black Reflections (painting)   **M:**396a
Klondike gold rush   **G:**252; **M:**324; **Y:**364–65
Klondike Gold Rush National Historical Park
    (Alaska/Washington)   **A:**148; **W:**22
Klondike Highway (Yukon Territory)   **Y:**362
Klopstock, Friedrich (German poet)   **G:**177
Klotz family (Bavarian violin makers)   **V:**344
Kluane National Park (Yukon Territory)   **Y:**363
Kneading (working dough into a uniform texture)   **B:**387, 388
Kneecap *see* Patella
Knesset (Israeli parliament)   **I:**374; **J:**82
Knickerbocker, The (early literary magazine)   **M:**19–20
Knife *see* Knives
Knifefish   **F:**192, 193
Knife River Indian Villages National Historic Site
    picture(s)   **N:**331
Knight, Death, and the Devil (engraving by Dürer)   **G:**303
Knight Commander of the Order of the British Empire (British
    award)
    picture(s)   **D:**67
Knights and knighthood   **K:**272–77
  armor   **A:**433–34
  Arthur, King   **A:**440–43
  castles   **C:**131–32
  decorations and medals   **D:**65
  duels and dueling   **D:**345
  fighting men supplied to a feudal lord   **F:**100
  heraldry   **H:**110–12
  Japanese samurai   **J:**41–42
Knights Hospitalers (Knights of Malta) (crusading order)   **M:**64
Knights of Labor   **L:**13–14; **U:**188
Knights of Malta *see* Knights Hospitalers
Knights of the Round Table (of King Arthur)   **A:**440, 442
Knitting   **K:**278–82; **T:**142
  skill in colonial America   **C:**412
Knitting needles   **N:**102
Knives   **K:**283–85
  Bowie knife   **B:**347
  penknife   **P:**142
  stone knives used by prehistoric surgeons   **S:**512
  picture(s)
    Inca ceremonial knife   **I:**173
Knobs (area of Kentucky)   **K:**214
Knocking (in an engine)   **G:**62
Knocking on wood (superstition)   **S:**503
Knossos (city of ancient Crete)   **A:**228–29, 372
  picture(s)
    ruins of Minos' palace   **A:**355
    wall painting   **A:**228

Knots   **K:**286–88
  macramé   **M:**6–7b
  rugs and carpets   **R:**353
  textile-making   **T:**142
Knots (measurement of speed)   **K:**286; **N:**77
Knott's Berry Farm (amusement park, California)   **P:**79
Knowlton's Rangers (in Revolutionary War)   **H:**12
Know-Nothing Party   **F:**128; **P:**371
Know thyself (Socrates' motto)   **P:**189
Knox, Henry (American general)
  Revolutionary War, campaigns of   **R:**201
  picture(s)
    Washington's first Cabinet meeting   **C:**2
Knox, John (Scottish reformer)   **K:**289; **R:**132
  Protestantism   **P:**490
  picture(s)   **R:**131
Knoxville (Tennessee)   **T:**79, 81, 83, 86
  International Energy Exposition   **F:**17
Knuckle coupler (for railroad cars)   **R:**89
KO (knockout, in boxing)   **B:**352
Koalas (marsupials)   **K:**290; **M:**113, 114, 115, 116
  Australian wildlife   **A:**506
  picture(s)   **A:**507; **M:**74; **S:**30
Kobe (Japan)   **J:**36
Koch, Marita (German runner)   **T:**259 *profile*
  picture(s)   **T:**259
Koch, Robert (German doctor and pioneer
    bacteriologist)   **K:**291
  contributions to medicine   **M:**208
  microbe cultures   **M:**277–78
  picture(s)   **M:**279
Kocharyan, Robert (Armenian president)   **A:**432
Kodachrome film   **P:**216
Kodak cameras   **E:**48
Kodály, Zoltán (Hungarian composer)
  folk music, use of   **H:**294
Kodiak bear   **B:**104, 107
Kodiak Island (Alaska)
  picture(s)
    Russian Orthodox church   **A:**145
Koestler, Arthur (Hungarian-born writer)   **H:**294
Kofa Mountains (Arizona)
  picture(s)   **G:**98
Koferlein, Anna (German dollhouse exhibitor)   **D:**261
Kohala Mountains (Hawaii)   **H:**51
Kohinoor (diamond)   **D:**144
  picture(s)   **D:**146
Kohl, Helmut (West German political leader)   **G:**165, 166;
    S:59
Kohli, M. S. (Indian mountain climber)   **E:**371
Kohn, Misch (American artist)
  picture(s)
    The General (aquatint and collage)   **G:**306
Kokand (early state in Central Asia)   **K:**312; **U:**258
Kokee Park (Hawaii)   **H:**52
Kokeshi (Japanese wooden dolls)   **D:**272
Kokoschka, Oskar (Austrian expressionist painter and writer)
  picture(s)   **A:**522
Koldewey, Robert (German archaeologist)   **W:**218
Kolehmainen, Hannes (Finnish runner)   **O:**109
Kolingba, André (Central African Republic president)   **C:**171
Kolinskies (yellow mink)   **O:**259
Kollwitz, Käthe Schmidt (German artist)   **G:**172
Komarov, Vladimir Mikhailovitch (Soviet cosmonaut)   **S:**352
Komen, Daniel (Kenyan athlete)   **T:**263
Komenský, Jan Amos (Czech educator and theologian) *see*
    Comenius, John Amos
Komodo monitors (Komodo dragons) (lizards)   **A:**452; **I:**361;
    L:275
  picture(s)   **A:**271, 452
Komondor (dog)   **D:**245
  picture(s)   **D:**249
Kompong Som (Cambodia)   **C:**37
Konan-Bédié, Henri (president of the Ivory Coast)   **I:**420
Konaré, Alpha Oumar (president of Mali)   **M:**62

Konbaung kingdom (of Burma) B:457
Kondratieva, Marina (Soviet ballet dancer)
  picture(s) B:30
Kong, Kingdom of (African state) I:420
Kongo peoples (of Africa)
  sculpture A:72
Königsberg, seven bridges of (topological problem) *see* Seven
    bridges of Konigsberg
Konigsburg, E. L. (American author of children's books) C:231
  profile
Kookaburra (Australian bird) A:506
Koonwarra plant (extinct flowering plant) F:280
Kootenay River (British Columbia)
  picture(s)
    dam C:61
Kopavogur (Iceland) I:35
Kopet Dag (mountains, Turkmenistan–Iran) T:352
Köppen, Wladimir (German climatologist) C:362
Kora (African musical instrument) A:78
Korab, Mount (Albania) A:161
Koran (holy book of Islam) A:344; K:292–93
  Arabic literature A:341
  Islamic illumination I:355, 357
  Islamic prayer P:431
  Mohammed M:401
  Sura of the Cow summarizes Mohammed's resentment of
    the Jews J:106
  teachings of Islam I:351
  picture(s) A:54, 345
    Islamic illumination A:342; I:358
Korbut, Olga (Soviet gymnast) O:113
Korda, Sir Alexander (Hungarian-born English motion picture
    director) H:294
Kore (figure in Greek sculpture) S:95
Korea K:294–302
  New Year N:208
  printing, history of P:478
  picture(s)
    Sobaek Range K:296
    students playing the kaya-ko O:230
Korea, Democratic People's Republic of (North
    Korea) K:294–302
  Korean War K:302–4
  picture(s)
    flag F:232
    Pyongyang K:299
Korea, Republic of (South Korea) K:294–302
  Korean War K:302–4
  Pusan P:552
  Seoul S:121
  picture(s)
    automobile industry A:461
    flag F:232
    Korean War refugees K:301
    Pusan P:552
    Seoul K:299
Korean Americans
  Los Angeles L:304
  picture(s) L:305
Korean art K:298–99
  picture(s)
    gold and jade crown K:299
Korean language K:294; L:40
Korean literature K:299
Korean music K:299–300
Korean Service Medal (United Nations award)
  picture(s) D:67
Korean War (1950–1953) K:302–4
  Eisenhower, Dwight D. E:125
  jet aircraft J:92
  MacArthur, Douglas M:2
  Pusan P:552
  refugees R:137–38
  Seoul S:121

Truman, Harry S. T:327
  United States, history of the U:197, 198
  Unknown Soldier U:227
  picture(s)
    United States Air Force uniform U:114
    United States Army uniform U:111
    United States Marine Corps uniform U:123
Korin (Japanese painter) J:49
Koroma, Johnny Paul (Sierra Leone political figure) S:172
Koror (capital of Palau) P:40b
Koryo dynasty (Korea) K:300
  pottery making K:298–99
Korzeniowski, Teodor Jósef Konrad *see* Conrad, Joseph
Kos (island in the Aegean Sea) I:364
Kosciusko, Mount (Australia) A:504, 511; M:506
Kościuszko, Thaddeus (Polish general) P:361; R:203
Kosher (food acceptable under Jewish law) J:148
  food in Israel F:336
Košice (Slovakia) S:201
Kosovo (autonomous province of Yugoslavia) N:305; S:125;
    Y:354, 355, 356, 359
  picture(s)
    refugees Y:359
Kosovo, Battle of (1389) S:125; Y:357
Kosrae (Pacific island) M:280; P:9
Koss, Johann Olav (Norwegian speed skater) O:119
Kossuth, Lajos (Hungarian patriot) H:298
  picture(s) H:298
Kota (people of Gabon)
  sculpted guardian figures A:72
  picture(s)
    sculpture A:438e
Kota Kinabalu (capital of Sabah, Malaysia) M:58
Kotka (Finland) F:137
Kotor (Yugoslavia) Y:356
  picture(s) M:442
Koufax, Sandy (American baseball player) B:89 *profile*
  picture(s) B:89, 94
Kountché, Seyni (Niger president) N:252
Kouros (figure in Greek sculpture) S:95
Kourou (French Guiana) F:466
Kouyate, Mamoudou (Mali storyteller)
  picture(s) A:76c
Kovalevskaia, Sofia (Russian mathematician) M:167 *profile*,
    169
  picture(s) M:167
Koven, Reginald de *see* De Koven, Reginald
Kowloon peninsula (Hong Kong) H:203, 204
Koxinga (Chinese pirate general) *see* Cheng Ch'eng-kung
Koyaki (a people of Siberia) A:386d
Koyokon (Indians of North America) I:188
kPa *see* Kilopascal
Kraals (South African villages) S:269
Krakatau (Krakatoa) (volcanic island, Indonesia) I:208
Kramer, Gustav (German scientist) H:193
Kramer, Ingrid (German diver) D:229
Kramer, Jack (American tennis player) T:97 *profile*
  picture(s) T:97
Kramskoi, Ivan (Russian painter) R:374
Kranach *see* Cranach, Lucas
Krasner, Lee (American artist) P:378
Krause, Barbara (German swimmer) O:116
Kravchuk, Leonid (Ukrainian president)
  picture(s) C:459; U:12
Krementz, Jill (American photographer, author, and illustrator of
    children's books) C:234 *profile*, 238
  picture(s)
    photograph from *A Very Young Rider* C:236
Kremlin (Moscow, Russia) M:465–66, 468
  public museum M:526
  picture(s) C:313; R:363; U:42
    Cathedral of the Dormition R:372
Kremlin (fortress) (in Russian towns) R:371
Krenek, Ernst (Austrian-American composer) C:285; G:189

Kress, Rush H. (American businessman and art collector) **N:**39
Kress, Samuel Henry (American business executive and art collector)
    National Gallery of Art **N:**39
Kress Collection (of art) **N:**39
Kreutzer, Rodolphe (French violinist) **V:**345
Krewes (carnival organizations, New Orleans) **C:**116
Krieghoff, Cornelius (Canadian painter) **C:**72
    picture(s)
        The Habitant Farm (painting) **N:**41
Krill (marine crustaceans) **C:**591; **P:**284
    Antarctica's marine ecosystem **A:**293
    food of penguins **P:**121
Krimml Falls (Austria) **W:**62, 63
Krio (language of Sierra Leone) **S:**171
Kristallnacht (November 9, 1938) **H:**159c
Kristensen, Tom (Danish author) **S:**58i
Kristiansand (Norway) **N:**347
Kritis (songs in Indian music) **I:**143
Kroetsch, Robert (Canadian writer) **C:**87
Kronach *see* Cranach, Lucas
Kronborg Castle (Elsinore of *Hamlet*)
    picture(s) **D:**108
Kruger, Paul (South African statesman) **S:**273
Kruger National Park (South Africa) **A:**53
Krung Thep (Thai dialect) **T:**148
Krung Thep (Thailand) *see* Bangkok
Krutt (cheese made from camel's milk) **C:**195
Krylov, Ivan Andreevich (Russian fabulist) **F:**4
Krypton (element) **E:**174; **N:**105, 106
    gases in industry **G:**61
    meter, standard measure of the **W:**110
K'san Historic Indian Village (British Columbia) **B:**406b
Kshatriyas (Hindu caste) **H:**128
Kuala Lumpur (capital of Malaysia) **M:**58; **S:**334
    picture(s)
        Petronas Towers **S:**334
Kuba (African people) **A:**73, 74
    picture(s)
        mask **A:**73
Kubelsky, Benjamin (American comedian) *see* Benny, Jack
Kubitschek de Oliveira, Juscelino (president of Brazil) **B:**384
Kublai Khan (Mongol ruler of China) **M:**418
    Beijing **B:**127d
    China, history of **C:**269
    grandson of Genghis Khan **G:**94
    Japanese conquest averted **J:**42
    Lamaism adopted as state religion **T:**191
    Marco Polo **E:**403–4; **P:**380
Kuching (capital of Sarawak, Malaysia) **M:**58
Kudu (antelope)
    picture(s) **A:**298
Kufic (Arabic script) **A:**344
Kühne, Wilhelm (German physiologist) **F:**91
Kuiper Airborne Observatory **O:**8–9
Kukenaam Falls (Guyana–Venezuela) **W:**63
Kukla and Ollie (puppets) **P:**548
Ku Klux Klan (organization in the United States that advocates white supremacy) **A:**79h, 79j; **R:**34a
    Birth of a Nation (motion picture) **M:**488
    Reconstruction period **R:**120
Kukui (tree) *see* Candlenut tree
Kulbak, Moishe (Yiddish poet) **Y:**351
Kumaratunga, Chandrika Bandaranaike (Sri Lankan president) **S:**416
Kumasi (Ghana) **G:**197, 198
Kumayaay (Indians of North America) **I:**187
Kumquat (citrus fruit) **O:**189
    picture(s) **O:**186
Kun, Béla (Hungarian Communist leader) **H:**298
Kuna Indians (of Panama) **I:**195; **P:**44
    picture(s) **C:**172; **N:**294; **P:**45
Kundera, Milan (Czech novelist) **C:**612; **N:**363
K'ung Fu-tzu *see* Confucius

Kunigunde, Saint
    picture(s)
        statue of **G:**168
Kunin, Madeleine May (American political figure) **V:**318
    profile
    picture(s) **V:**318
Kunlun (mountains in Tibet) **T:**190
Kuo Hsi (Chinese artist) **C:**274
    picture(s)
        Clearing Autumn Sky over Mountains and Valleys (painting) **C:**275
Kuomintang (nationalist party of China)
    Chiang Kai-shek **C:**217
    China, history of **C:**271
    Mao Zedong **M:**90
    Sun Yat-sen **S:**497
Kuparuk (Alaska) **A:**152
Kupffer cells (in the liver) **L:**268, 269
    picture(s) **L:**269
Kura River (republic of Georgia) **G:**148
Kurdish language **K:**305; **M:**299
Kurdistan (region in the Middle East) **K:**305
Kurds (a people of the Middle East) **I:**311; **K:**305
    genocide **G:**96
    Iraq **H:**307; **I:**316
    Jordan **J:**129
    Syria **S:**549
    Turkey **T:**344
    picture(s) **K:**305
        handmade rug **R:**355
        Iraq **I:**311, 315
Kure Island (Hawaii) **H:**50
Kurfürstendamm (street in Berlin, Germany) **B:**146
Kuril (Kurile) Islands (north of Japan) **I:**365
Kurosawa, Akira (Japanese film director) **M:**494, 495 *profile*
Kuroshio *see* Japan Current
Kurzeme (province, Latvia) **L:**80
Kush, Land of (Africa) **A:**65; **S:**479
Kushan dynasty (India) **I:**136
    Persia, ancient **P:**156
Kushites *see* Cushites
Kuskin, Karla (American author and illustrator of books for children) **C:**234 *profile*
Kutchin (Indians of North America) **I:**188
Kutenai (Indians of North America) **I:**188
Kuts, Vladimir (Soviet runner) **O:**110
Kuwait **K:**306–9
    invasion by Iraq *see* Persian Gulf War
    Organization of Petroleum Exporting Countries **O:**221
    per capita income **A:**347
    Persian Gulf War **P:**158
    picture(s)
        Arabs **K:**308
        flag **F:**232
        oil-well fires **K:**309
Kuwait (capital of Kuwait) **K:**306, 308
Kuznetsk Basin (Russia) **S:**170
Kwa (language) **A:**56
Kwajalein (atoll, Marshall Islands) **M:**112, 113
Kwakiutl Indians (of North America) **I:**188
Kwan, Michelle (American figure skater) **I:**45 *profile*
Kwangchow (China) *see* Canton
Kwangju (South Korea) **K:**301
Kwanzaa (festival observed by African Americans) **A:**80
Kwashiorkor (protein-deficiency disease) **N:**429
Kwasniewski, Aleksander (Polish president) **P:**362
Kwoleck, Stephanie (American scientist) **P:**329
Ky, Nguyen Cao (Vietnamese military and political leader) **V:**337, 338
Kyaks *see* Kayaks
Kyanite (mineral)
    picture(s) **M:**316
Kyd, Thomas (English dramatist) **D:**298; **E:**273
Kyoto (Japan) **J:**41, 42; **K:**310; **T:**216
    picture(s) **O:**229

PHOTO CREDITS

The following list credits the sources of photos used in THE NEW BOOK OF KNOWLEDGE. Credits are listed, by page, photo by photo—left to right, top to bottom. Wherever appropriate, the name of the photographer has been listed with the source, the two being separated by a dash. When two or more photos by different photographers appear on one page, their credits are separated by semicolons.

J-K

2 © Elissa Spiro
3 The Granger Collection; The Granger Collection; Corbis-Bettmann; Corbis-Bettmann.
4 The Granger Collection; The Hermitage: Home of President Andrew Jackson, Nashville, TN.
5 Historic New Orleans
6 The Bettmann Archive
7 © Bruce Mathews—Midwestock
8 © Larry Downing—Corbis-Sygma
9 National Archives
10 © Vernon T. O'Brien—Aero-Pic
11 Sotheby's—Art Resource
14 © Hamilton Wright
15 © Elizabeth Marshall—Liaison Agency
16 © Michael George—Bruce Coleman Inc.
17 © Eric Carle—Bruce Coleman Inc.
18 © Jules Bucher—Photo Researchers
19 Scala/Art Resource
20 National Portrait Gallery
22 The Granger Collection
23 The Granger Collection
26 © Cameramann International Ltd.
27 © Cameramann International Ltd. (all photos on page).
28 © Helen Marcus—Photo Researchers; © Cameramann International Ltd.; © Cameramann International Ltd.
29 © Cameramann International Ltd. (all photos on page).
30 © Cameramann International Ltd.
31 © Cameramann International Ltd. (all photos on page).
32 © George Obremski—The Image Bank
33 © Jean-Marc Barey—Photo Researchers; © Joan Lebold Cohen—Photo Researchers.
34 © Michael Yamashita—Woodfin Camp & Associates
35 © Cameramann International Ltd. (all photos on page).
36 Japan Suisan Koku Company
38 © Cameramann International Ltd.; © Ethan Hoffman—Archive Pictures.
39 Japanese Consulate General; © Cameramann International Ltd.
41 © Shashinka Photo Library
42 The Granger Collection; Shashinka Photo Library.
43 © Cameramann International Ltd.
44 © Cameramann International Ltd.
45 © Shashinka Photo Library; © Laurie Platt Winfrey Inc.
47 Imperial Household Agency/AP/Wide World Photos
48 © Shashinka Photo Library
49 Museum of Fine Arts, Boston, Fenollosa-Weld Collection
50 Metropolitan Museum of Art. Purchase, Gift of Mrs. Russell Sage, by exchange, 1980; Metropolitan Museum of Art. The Harry G.C. Packard Collection of Asian Art, Gift of Harry G.C. Packard and Purchase, Fletcher, Rogers, Harris Brisbane Dick and Louis V. Bell Funds, Joseph Pulitzer Request and The Annenberg Fund, Inc. Gift, 1975; Metropolitan Museum of Art. Purchase, Rogers Fund, 1936.
51 The Metropolitan Museum of Art, The Arts of Japan in the Sackler Galleries for Asian Art. Photograph by Sheldan Collins.
53 Reproduced by courtesy of the Trustees of the British Museum; © Cameramann International Ltd.
54 © George Hunter—Tony Stone Images
55 © National Portrait Gallery/Smithsonian Institution/Art Resource

56 © David Redfern—Retna Ltd. (all photos on page).
58 Frank Driggs Collection—Archive Photos; Frank Driggs Collection—Archive Photos.
59 NBC-Globe Photos; The Granger Collection.
60 Michael Ochs Archives; UPI/Corbis-Bettmann.
61 Frank Driggs Collection—Archive Photos; UPI/Corbis-Bettmann.
62 UPI/Corbis-Bettmann; © David Redfern—Retna Ltd.
63 Frank Driggs Collection—Archive Photos; David Redfern—Retna; © Jak Kilby—Retna, Ltd.
64 © David Redfern—Retna, Ltd.; UPI/Corbis-Bettmann.
65 Copyrighted by the © White House Historical Association; Photograph(s) by the National Geographic Society; The Granger Collection; The Granger Collection.
66 The Granger Collection (all photos on page).
67 © Claudia Parks—The Stock Market
68 Francis Mayer—Independence National Historical Park
69 © Thomas Jefferson Memorial Foundation
70 The Granger Collection (all photos on page).
71 © Henryk Kaiser—Leo de Wys
72 © Ron & Valerie Taylor—Bruce Coleman Inc.
73 © Dave B. Fleetham—Tom Stack & Associates; © E. R. Degginger—Photo Researchers.
74 © Kim Taylor—Bruce Coleman Inc.; © D. P. Wilson—Science Source—Photo Researchers; © D. P. Wilson—Science Source—Photo Researchers.
75 © William J. Hebert—Tony Stone Images; © Peter Parks/Mo Yung Productions/Norbert Wu.
76 © Stuart Westmorland—Tony Stone Images; © Ron Sefton—Bruce Coleman Inc.; © Robert Yin—Liaison Agency.
77 © Ben Cropp/Mo Yung Productions/Norbert Wu
78 Parke, Davis & Company, Detroit
80 © Dave Bartruff
82 © Richard Steedman—The Image Bank
83 © Louis Goldman—Photo Researchers; © G. Rossi—The Image Bank.
84 © Paul Conklin
85 Scala/Art Resource
87 Scala/Art Resource
88 Scala/Art Resource
89 Scala/Art Resource
90 © Chuck Keeler—Tony Stone Images
93 NOAA Photo Library—NESDIS
97 R. Guillemot, *Connaissance des Arts*—Collection Bulgari; Ben Feder; R. Guillemot, *Connaissance des Arts*—Louvre, Paris; *Connaissance des Arts*—Ancienne Collection of Maurice Sandoz.
98 Courtesy of Van Cleef and Arpels; Courtesy of Cartier; Courtesy of Van Cleef and Arpels.
102 Scala/Art Resource
103 Scala/Art Resource
104 Scala/Art Resource
105 © Richard Nowitz—The Image Bank
107 New York Public Library, Picture Collection, Astor, Lenox and Tilden Foundations
110 © V. Phillips—Leo de Wys
113 "Run for Life,"—Connecticut Mutual Life Insurance Co.—Authenticated New International
116 Copyrighted by the © White House Historical Association; Photograph(s) by the National Geographic Society; The Granger Collection; The Bettmann Archive; The Bettmann Archive.
117 The Granger Collection; Tennessee State Library Archives.
118 The Granger Collection (all photos on page).
120 Copyrighted by the © White House Historical Association; Photograph(s) by the National

Geographic Society; © Fred Ward—Black Star; UPI/Bettmann Newsphotos; AP/Wide World Photos.
121 UPI/Corbis-Bettmann; AP/Wide World Photos.
122 AP/Wide World Photos
123 UPI/Bettmann Newsphotos; © Burt Glinn—Magnum Photos; UPI/Bettmann Newsphotos.
124 AP/Wide World Photos
128 Independence National Historical Park
129 © F. Sautereau—Rapho/Photo Researchers
131 © Bruno Barbey—Magnum Photos; © Rene Burri—Magnum Photos.
132 © Armando Curcio Editore SPA
135 © James Drake—Capital Cities/ABC, Inc.
136 © Richard Dunoff—The Stock Market
137 © Frances M. Roberts—Richard Levine
138 © Craig Blakenhorn; The Bettmann Archive; Time Inc. Reprinted by permission.
139 © Eddie Adams—Corbis-Sygma; UPI/Bettmann Newsphotos; © Frank Trapper—Corbis-Sygma.
140 © 1923 Time Inc. Reprinted by permission.
142 © Gilles Rousseau
144 © Catherine Ursillo—Photo Researchers
145 © Ted Spiegel—Black Star
146 © John Bryson—The Image Bank
146a © Geoffrey Hiller—Black Star
146b © Ted Spiegel—Black Star (all photos on page).
147 Japan Tourist Association
156 UPI/Bettmann Newsphotos
157 © Clark Hall—Photo Trends
158 © Harrison Forman
159 Jet Propulsion Laboratory
160 Jet Propulsion Laboratory
161 Jet Propulsion Laboratory (all photos on page).
162 Jet Propulsion Laboratory
163 © William Hubbell—Woodfin Camp & Associates
164 Courtesy of the Department of Justice
167 © Craig Strong—Liaison Agency
168 © Michael Newman—PhotoEdit/PNI; © Alon Reininger/Woodfin Camp & Associates.
169 © John Eastcott/Yva Momatiuk/Photo Researchers; © John Eastcott/Yva Momatiuk/Woodfin Camp & Associates.
170 © A. Ramey—Woodfin Camp & Associates
173 The Granger Collection; Galerie Maeght.
174 © Greg Vaughn—Tom Stack & Associates; © Dave Watts—Tom Stack & Associates.
175 © Dave Watts—Tom Stack & Associates
176 © Aneal Vohra—Unicorn Stock Photos; © Jeff Morgan—Midwestock.
177 © Don Smetzer—Tony Stone Images; © Sheila Beougher—Liaison Agency; © Jeff Morgan—Midwestock.
178 © Aneal Vohra—Unicorn Stock Photos (all photos on page).
180 © Daniel Dancer
181 © Cotton Coulson—Woodfin Camp & Associates
182 © Aneal Vohra—Unicorn Stock Photos
183 © Cotton Coulson—Woodfin Camp & Associates; © Aneal Vohra—Unicorn Stock Photos; © Cotton Coulson—Woodfin Camp & Associates.
184 © Herbert L. Stormont—Unicorn Stock Photos; © Bob Thomason—Tony Stone Images; © Rod Furgason—Unicorn Stock Photos; © Tom Dietrich—Tony Stone Images.
185 © David Fitzgerald—Tony Stone Images
186 © Bob Thomason—Tony Stone Images
188 Kansas State Historical Society; UPI/Corbis-Bettmann.
189 UPI/Bettmann; © Mike Roemer—Liaison Agency.
190 © Kevin Sink—Midwestock